GENERAL ARMORY
TWO

ALFRED MORANT'S Additions and Corrections to
BURKE'S GENERAL ARMORY

GENERAL ARMORY
TWO

ALFRED MORANT'S Additions and Corrections to
BURKE'S GENERAL ARMORY

Edited and Augmented by

CECIL R. HUMPHERY-SMITH
B.Sc., F.S.G., F.H.S.

GENEALOGICAL PUBLISHING CO., INC.
BALTIMORE   1974

American Publisher
GENEALOGICAL PUBLISHING CO., INC.
Baltimore, Maryland
1974

Published in conjunction with
TABARD PRESS LTD.
10 Snow Hill,
London EC1.

Library of Congress Catalogue Card Number 73-13238
International Standard Book Number 0-8063-0583-5

Printed in England by The White Rose Press, Mexborough, Yorkshire

INTRODUCTION

————

Listings of names with descriptions of the coats of arms associated with them have been made since the earliest heraldic times. Many of the early ones were fully illustrated with painted shields and date from the thirteenth century. These are the Rolls of Arms described by Sir Anthony Wagner in *Heralds and Heraldry* (1947) and in *A Catalogue of English Mediaeval Rolls of Arms* (1950). In their introductions to Papworth's *Ordinary*, (Tabard 1961), G. D. Squibb and A. R. Wagner describe these early sources in relevant detail.

The written descriptions of arms made by the early Heralds gave way in due time to the compilations of the antiquaries of the sixteenth and seventeenth centuries and their alphabetical collections or armories. These writers merely put down in terms of blazonry what they saw being used in association with names (see *Family History*, Vol. 1, No. 1 (1962), page 2 etc. and *Summer Exhibition Catalogue*, English Family History, Canterbury (1963), items 36, 64, 93). Many such listings have survived, particularly from the Tudor and Stuart periods. They contain often tens of thousands of names and their associated coats of arms. All that their compilers claim, however, is that at some time or other someone of the name listed has used the coat of arms described—or something like it, for the compilations are full of errors—and it is not often that entries in these works are accompanied by any indication whether the coat of arms is borne with authority or not. Some of the arms described may have been adopted genuinely before the days when there was a legal granting authority and most have probably been granted by such an authority to a person of the name. Some have been merely invented or misappropriated. In the pages of Burke's *General Armory* can be found arms for the name Harokins; someone inexpert in palaeography had misread a 'w' and thus Harokins obtained the arms of Hawkins, perhaps to the delight of the heraldic stationer or engraver!

A glance at any armory or list of coats of arms will show that persons of the same surname may have quite different arms and indeed there may be different origins for their common name. There is as much error in believing that persons of the same surname are necessarily related by blood as that every name has a coat of arms. Nothing could be further from the truth. Then there is the question of the use of arms. Although for decorative purposes any coat of arms may be employed, to claim a proprietory right to personal identifying insignia entitlement must be established by proving an undoubted male lineal descent from the original grantee or bearer on record with the appropriate Office of Arms. It must not be forgotten that there are in England, Scotland and Ireland authorities vested with the power of control over the use of armorial bearings for personal identification, and that their jurisdiction covers the British Isles and the dominions of the British Sovereign. The Kings of Arms of the English Court, the College of Arms in London, and the Lord Lyon King of Arms of the Scottish Court, have full jurisdiction over heraldic matters in their provinces. The Chief Herald of the Genealogical Office at Dublin Castle controls heraldic matters in Ireland. The Offices of Arms also have records which, for historical reasons, may not be complete for all arms authoritatively borne in former times, but nevertheless contain all coats of arms which may be borne with proper authority. In the matter of the bearing of arms it is to these authorities that the would-be user should turn to establish his right, and if he believes that such a right exists he may employ a competent genealogist to obtain the evidence. Considerable assistance is afforded by the reference sources given in the present collection.

The first "General Armory" was included in the four-volume *Encyclopaedia Heraldica* of the herald William Berry in 1828. This was followed by *The British Herald or Cabinet of Armorial Bearings* by Thomas Robson in 1830, and then in 1842, appeared the first *General Armory* by John and John Bernard Burke. This went through several editions until J. Bernard Burke, then Ulster King of Arms, produced the last edition in 1884; in this more than 60,000 coats of arms were listed. This was founded on the Heralds' Visitations, county histories, the writings of Dugdale, Camden, Guillim, Edmundson, Berry, Nicholas and others, and was truly a monumental compilation. It has been twice reprinted by photo-lithography, but never updated.

Almost contemporarily with Burke, John Woody Papworth was compiling his *Ordinary*. This appeared in 1874 and contained most of what is in Burke's *General Armory*. His friend Alfred Morant completed the work for publication and added a great deal of material that was not in Burke.

It will be found that the only difference between the 1878 edition of Burke's *General Armory* and the 1884 edition is the addition of two supplements. Morant's own copy of the 1878 edition of Burke's *General Armory* was fully interleaved in two volumes and contained the supplements from the 1884 edition. To nearly every page Morant added a great deal of extra material and corrections from some sixty additional sources (see *Family History*, Vol. 2, No. 11, page 137). The two volumes were acquired by the late Father Wallace Clare and lent to the present Editor whose father, Frederick Humphery-Smith M.B.E., made a complete typescript copy, which he carefully checked against Morant's original manuscript additions and corrections. Sincere thanks are due to him for his painstaking work and generous collaboration. The attempt to serialise the copy in *Family History* was abandoned in favour of this publication by Tabard. The original volumes are now in the library of the Irish Genealogical Research Society.

To this present collection the editor has added an appendix of names appearing with associated coats of arms in a further selection of sources, mostly printed heraldic books which have been published since Burke and Morant made their collections. This is far from complete and reference should be made to many other sources. The *Index of Pedigrees and Arms Contained in the Manuscripts of the British Museum*, compiled by R. Sims (1849), reprinted by the Genealogical Publishing Company, Baltimore (1970) is most useful. This has a slight disadvantage in being indexed under counties rather than under a simple index but is of considerable value and importance. More coats of arms will be found in references given by J. B. Whitmore in *A Genealogical Guide* (1953) and G. W. Marshall in *The Genealogist's Guide* (1903); in Harleian Society volumes LXVI, LXVII, LXVIII, LXXVI and LXXVII; in *Family History;* in the many editions of Burke's *Peerage* and *Landed Gentry;* in the seven editions of Fox-Davies's *Armorial Families;* thirty editions of *Knights Bachelor;* Gayre's *Armorial Who is Who* (1961 *et seq.*); *The Coat of Arms; The Genealogist; Miscellania Genealogica et Heraldica;* and in Howard and Crisp *Visitations of England and Wales, etc.* (1887 *et seq.*) and in numerous recent publications.

It is possible that published works contain between them blazons of all coats of arms officially recorded up to about 1900 and a small proportion of those granted in the present century but it must be emphasised that recourse to the College of Arms or the Lyon Court is very important for anyone concerned with authentic records of arms and for information on many thousands of new blazons added by grants of the present century.

In what follows, inconsistencies in blazoning and spelling have been retained where it appears clear that Morant's original source was in the form given. This may be of interest to students of archaisms and the etymology of blazonry.

Cecil R. Humphery-Smith,
The Institute of Heraldic and Genealogical Studies,
Canterbury, 1973.

Morant annotated many arms he records with their difference marks and also makes small line drawings of some difficult or unusual blazons. For obvious reasons of economy and typography, the editor has extracted these onto one page and wherever a symbol appeared in Morant's text an asterisk has been inserted referring to that page.

Cudderley

Errington
Feilden
Fitch
Forterie
Foster
Gold
Goldding
Gore
Green
Harrison
Hide
Hodson
Honywood
Huntley
Hynd
Lambert
Marshall
Pendreth
Pudsey
Rookwood
Savile
Sherard
Wentworth
White
Wickins
Wiseman
Wither
Wyvell

Deard
Delme
Dundas
Eckersall
Elliott
Fairclough
Gibbs
Gray
Hall
Herne
Hill
Holme
Hopman
Hyde
Keck
Law
Leverland
Lloyd
London
McKie
Maclatchy
Mehmet
Merrill
Neilson
Palmer
Pearce
Perkins
Richardson
Robinson
Rooch
Rous
Sandiland
Scawen
Shippen
Shrigley
Smith
Smith
Smith
Spicker
Stewart
Stuart
Thorold
Vans
Vigor
Webster
Wedderburn
Wescombe
Whitworth
Woolley
Young
Young

Garth

Grice

Camden

Fetheir

Hodgetts

Folliott

Londons

Lorke

Grimsby

Hart

Horwood

Lake

Lambert

Heron
Musgrave
Tempest
Tempest
Tyldesley

Mounteney

Mounteney

Shakestaffe

Rylands

Raby
Whitlebury

Mekton
Naunton
Scremby
Sheperwast
Skipton
Sleghtes
Somervile
Stallingburgh
Thirkwald
Wystowe

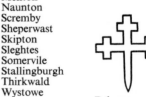

Thomason

Pakeman

Tippingwell

Winterfall

Heron

GENERAL ARMORY TWO

A

ABANK. Arg. a china colar tree rest. *Berry.*

A'Barrow. Same as Abarough but without bordure.

Abbes or Abbs. Arg. a lady Abbess, a crozier on her left arm in bend, hands conjoined and elevated upon her breast ppr. *Berry.*

Abbot (Robert, Archbishop of Canterbury, 1611–33). Same as Abbot, Lord Mayor of London, 1638.

Abbot (Guildford). Same arms as Lord Mayor of London, 1638.

Abbot (Salop). Arg. 3 escutcheons quarterly sable and . . . *Robson.*

Abbott (Byles juxta Howden). Arg. a chev. betw. 3 wolves heads erased gu.

Abbott. Arg. a chev. betw. 3 griffins heads erased gu. *Robson.*

Abbs. Gu. on a fesse betw. 3 escallops or, 5 fusils in fess, sa.

Abdene. Erm. on a cross az., 5 bezants. *Robson.*

Abdy (Kent). Same arms as of Yorkshire, London, Felix Hall, co. Essex and Chobham Place, Surrey, Bart; but has Az. instead of Or.

Abdy (Essex). Or a chev. betw. 2 couple closes and 3 trefoils sa. *Robson.*

Abdy (Essex). Or a chev. cotised sa. betw. 3 trefoils slipped vert. *Robson.* Crest: an eagle's head erased ppr.

Abeladame. Vert a deer—goat's head arg. *Berry.*

Abell (Kent). Arg. a chev. betw. 3 bears heads gu. *Cady.*

Abell. Sa. 2 bars or in chief 3 plates. *John Abell.*

Abelyon. Gules on a cross patonce arg. 5 escallops arg. *Robson.*

Aberbrothock (town of), Scotland. Arg. a portcullis gu. chains az. *Berry.*

Aberdeen (Bishopric of). Az. a temple arg. St. Nicholas stands in the porch mitred and vested ppr. his dexter hand elevated to heaven praying over 3 children in a boiling cauldron of the first in his sinister a crozier or. *Berry.*

Abery. Gules 6 escallops 3, 2, 1, arg.

Alford. Gules fretty erm.

Abine or St. Abine. Erm. on a cross gules 5 annulets or. *Robson.*

Abingdon Monastery (Berks). Arg. a cross patonce sa. betw. 4 martlets of the last.

Abington (Philip de). *A.* Sir Robert Abington co. Cambridge temp Edw. I (same as of Abingdon, co: Cambridge).

Abney (Lord). Arm. on a cross engr. sa. 5 bezants. Crest: a demi-lion or, holding an ogress (a pellet).

Abney. Gules a fesse engr. arg. over all a bend az.

Abrahall (Urchingfield co. Hereford). Az. a chev. betw. 3 hedgehogs or. *Dingley.*

Abrahall (London, 1633). Az. 3 boars statant or. *Harl. MS. 1358 fo: 18b.*

Abraham (Lancs). Sa. a cross patonce or. *Shaw.*

Abram. Sa. a cross moline or.

Abris. Az. a chev. betw. 3 mullets arg. *Cady.*

Abtot (Earl of Worcester) temp Wm. II. Party per pale or and gules 3 roundles counterchanged. *Guillim.*

Abtot (Hereford). Per pale or and gules 3 roundles counterchanged, *Syl. Morgan.*

Abtot. Or 2 lions pass. guard. gu. Gefrai d'Abtot or Abetot *E.F.*

Abure (Cornwall). Erm. on a saltire gules 5 annulets or.

Aburton. Or a fesse gules betw. 3 mullets pierced sable. (+ vide Aberton).

Aburton. Or, on a fesse gules 3 crosses patee fitchee arg.

Acaster (Nr. York, 1379). . . . on a chev. . . . three covered cups . . . .

Acard. Vairy, arg. and gules a label of 3 arg.

Acard. Gules 6 escallops arg. 3, 2 and 1.

Acheche. Or 2 bars az.

Accles. Or 4 pales az.

Acche (Co. Devon). Gu. 2 demi-lions pass guard. in pale couped or. *V.*

Acester (Gloucester). Arg. a chev. az. with a label of 3 in chief gules. Arg. an eagle displayed with 2 heads sa. on a chief vert. 3 mullets of the first. Crest: a Sand Glass ppr. (also crest: a cock gules).

Achingham. Az. fretty arg. a bordure engr. or. *Robson.*

Ackelom. Arg. an escut betw. 8 torteaux gu. Crest: a sagittarius.

Aclaham (Acclome). 41 Edw. III. Gu. semy of 5-foils and a maunch arg.

Acleward or Aylward. Sa. a chev. betw. 3 garbs or. *V.*

A Court (East Carleton, co. Norf. and London). Paly of 6 erminois and az. on a chief or an eagle displayed sa. charged on the breast with 2 chevrons arg. *Dashwood.*

Acoustant. Or a fess az. Crest: a sceptre and pilgrims staff in X.

Acre (Jamaica). Az. 3 escallops arg.

Acre (Westmorland). Az. on a cross arg. 5 escallops gules.

Acquell. Paly of 6 arg. and az. on a chief of the second a lion pass. or.

Acton. Per bend indented arg. and az. *Cady.*

Acton. Per fess indented arg. and gu. on a chev. az. 3 crosses crosslet fitchy or. *Cady.*

Acton. Barry of 6 az. and or on a canton gules, a cross patty arg.

Acton. Gyronny of 8 or and gules.

Acton (Wolverton, co. Worcs.). Gu. a fess and a bordure engrailed, erm. Crest: a hand holding a sword. *Nash.*

Acton. Vert. a chev. betw. 3 mullets or. *Robson.*

Acton. Gu. a fess arg. a bordure engr. erm.

1

Acton (London). Quarterly, arg. and gules: per fess indented on a bend of the second 3 crosses or on a chief of the second an annulet betw. 2 palets of the first. *Robson.*

Acton. Quarterly arg. and gu. on a bend az, 3 crosses patty fitchy or on a chief an annulet counterchanged.

Acton. Quarterly, per fesse indented arg. and gu. on a bend az. three crosses formee fitchee or. and with an annulet in chief counterchanged. Hugh Acton, London.

Acton (London, Baronetcy 1629, Extinct., Sir William Acton, Lord Mayor of London, 1641). Gu. crusily of crosses crosslet fitchee or two lions pass. arg.

Acton (Aldenham, co. Salop). Baronetcy 1643.

Acton (Alderley and Chester). Vert. a chev. betw. 3 mullets or. *Randle Holme.*

Acworth (Suff.). Arg. a griffin segreant az.

Adam (Co. Devon). Arg. on a bend az. three trefoils slipped or. *V.*

Adam (Loudon and Spowston, co. Norf.). Erm 3 cats, a mountain in pale az. Crest: Or. A boar's head arg. couped gules.

Adams. Erm. 3 cats pass. in pale their tails turned up between their hind legs az. Sir William Adams, Baronet of Sprowston, Norf. *Cady.*

Adams (East Hardwick, co. Yorks. 1665). Gules a lion ramp. betw. 3 escallops or., a chief arg. as many palets engr. of the first. Crest: A demi-griffin segreant erminois winged and beaked az. holding an escallop arg. *Dugdale, p. 17.*

Adams (Scansby, co. Yorks. 1665). Gu. a lion ramp. betw. 3 escallops or, on a chief as many palets engr. sa. Crest: a demi-griffin segreant ermine beaked and winged az. holding an escallop or. *Dugdale p. 176.*

Adams (Camblesforth, co. York 1665). Same arms.

Adams (Owston, co. York 1612). Same arms.

Adams. (Granted to William Adams of the Middle Temple, counsellor at law, by Borough Garter 1639). Gu. on a bend or betw. 2 bezants 3 martlets sa. *Guillim.*

Adams (London). Erm. a chev. chequy or and sa. betw. 3 roses az. *Vis. of Lon.* 1633. Crest: A tiger's head erased erm. charged with a chevron as in the arms.

Adams. Gu. a chev. betw. 3 leopard faces arg.

Adams. Arg. a chief dancetty sa.

Adderley (Blackhaugh, Sheriff of Staffs. temp Eliz.). Arg. on a chevron sa. 3 mullets of the first. *Fuller.*

Adderstone. 3 martlets within a bordure engr. arg. *V.*

Addington (London). Per pale erm. and ermines on a chev. betw. 3 fleurs-de-lis, 4 lozenges counterchanged sa. and arg. Thomas Addington, *V.*

Addis (Co. Hertford and London). Arg. a chev. not touching the sides of the shield betw. 3 crosses patty gu. *Vis. Lon. 1633.* Crest: a cock erm.

Addison (Offerton, co. Durham and Ovingham, co. Northumberland). Sa. a chev. arg. betw. 3 eagles displayed or. *Surtees* and *Robson.*

Addison. Erm. a galley sa. flags gu. on a bend of the last 3 annulets or. On a chief az. 3 leopards faces arg. Crest: A unicorn's head transpierced with an arrow. Motto—"Let the Deed Show".

Aderonne (Co. Surrey). Arg. a chev. or. *Cady*

Adelin. Arg. 3 chess rooks sa. *Robson.*

Adelly (Somerset). Gu. on a fess arg. three crosses sa.

Aderton. Or 2 bendlets within a bordure sa. *Cady.*

Adgare (Wedderlie, Scotland). Sa. a lion ramp. arg.

Adey (Duddington, co. Kent). Gu. on a bend arg. 3 leopard faces vert.

Adelaide (Bishopric). Arg. on a cross per fess and per pale gu. betw. four mullets of six points arg. pierced of the field a bishop's crozier in pale surmounted by a bishop's mitre.

Affeton (Co. Devon). Arg. a chev. betw. 3 fleurs-de-lis sa. *Lysons.*

Agborough. Az. a chev. engr. betw. 3 escallops erm. Granted by Walker, Garter in 1633 to Sir Robert Agborough alias Townsend. *Guillim.*

Agenal (Co. York, temp. Edw. II). Gu. a lion pass. guard. betw. 10 crosses crosslet or. *F. Y.*

Agmondesham (Co. Buckingham). Arg. on a canton sa. a fleur-de-lis or. *V.*

Agmondesham. Erm. on a canton sa. a fleur-de-lis or. *V.*

Agmondesham. Arg. on a chev. az. betw. 3 boars heads couped sa. as many crosses crosslet or.

Ainsworth (Plessington, co. Lancs.). Gu. three battle axes or. *V.L.*

Airey. Gu. on a chev. arg. 3 cinquefoils of the field. *Robson.*

Aishe (Co. York). Arg. 2 chevrons sa. Thomas Aishe. *Eliz. Roll.*

Aitkin (Edinburgh). Arg. on a chev. az. betw. 2 cocks in chief and a buckle in base gu. 3 anchors of the field. *Robson.*

Akland. . . . on a bend . . . betw. 2 lions ramp. . . . 3 oak leaves . . .

Akroyd (Halifax, co. York). Az. a chev. arg. in base a stag's head erased ppr. charged with a lozenge arg. on a chief of the last two stags' heads erased ppr. each charged with a lozenge of the second.

Alanby. Arg. a chev. engr. within a bordure engr. az. quartered by Medleton 1875.

Albany (Co. Worcester). Az. a chev. erm. betw. 3 fleurs-de-lis arg. *Nash.*

Alberton. Arg. a chev. betw. 3 wolves' heads erased sa.

Albon. Vert. a bend arg. charged in chief with a cross patty fitchy gu. *V.*

Alcock (London). Arg. on a fess gu. betw. 3 scythes sa. an escallop or. *Vis. Lon. 1633.*

Alcock. Arg. a chev. engr. betw. 3 moor cocks sa. *Cady.*

Aldam. Sa. a chev. engr. or betw. 3 owls arg. on a chief of the second 3 roses gu. beaked or. *Cady.*

Aldawne. Bendy wavy of eight or and az.

Aldburgh (Of Aldburgh, co. York). Arg. a fess dancetty betw. 3 cross crosslets az. *Bargrave.*

Alder (Alnwick, Northumberland) 1675. Az., on a bend arg. 3 billets of the field.

Aldersey (Or Adersey, Cheshire). Az. 3 annulets or.

Aldersey (Co. Stafford). Arg. a bend sa. betw. in chief a rose and in base a fleur-de-lis gu.

Aldred. Barry paly indented arg. and gu.

Aldred. Gu. a chev. engr. betw. 3 griffins' heads erased or. *Cady.*

Aldrington. Sa. 3 beavers or. *Cady.*

Aldwen (Co. York). Gu. on 2 bars within a bordure arg. 4 martlets in pale sa. *V.*

Aldwen (Co. York). Arg. 3 bars humetty gu. betw. 4 martlets in pale sa. *V.*

Alexander (Co. Chester 1535). Same arms as of Dover, co. Kent. *V.*

Alexander. Gu. a lion ramp. sejant in a chair and holding a battle axe arg.

Alexander. Same arms with a label of 3 points or. *Leland Collec. II. 688*, Thomas Alexander of Gray's Inn. 1658.

Alexander (Sir William Alexander, Knt., Lord Chief Baron of Exchequer, 1827). Same arms as of Alexander of Boghall, co. Edinburgh.

Alexander (Manchline, co. Ayr). Same arms. *Debrett.*

Aleyn. Per bend sinister fracted arg. and sa. 6 martlets counterchanged. John Allyn, Suffolk. *V.*

Aleyn (London). Or on a fess . . . 3 lions ramp. quartering erm. on a chev. sa. 3 bezants. *Vis. Lon. 1633.*

Aleyn (Essex). Gu. on a chev. engr. or betw. 3 plates each charged with a talbot pass. sa. 3 crescents az. *Cady.*

Alford (London). Same arms as of Alford of Holt, co. Denbigh, but a crescent for difference, the pears are erect. *Vis. Lon. 1633.*

Aliff (London). . . . on a chev. engr. . . . betw. 3 stag's heads embossed . . . as many estoiles . . .

Allington. Sa. a bend betw. 12 billets arg. William Allington. *Dug. O. J.*

Alington (Lord Alington, *Z.540,* Sir Giles Alington, *V.*). Same arms as Alington of Wymondley, co. Herts.

Alington. Bendy of eight or and arg. a lion ramp. az. in chief 2 chaplets vert. roses gu.

Alisander. Barry of six or and az. a bordure gu. *F.*

Allcott. Arg. on a bend sa. betw. 2 ogresses a demi-lion of the first.

Allanby. Arg. a chev. az. within a bordure engr. of the same. Thomas Allanby.

Allen (Blundeston, Suff. Baronetcy 1672). Same arms as Allen of Cheshire and Wilts. and Suffolk.

Allen (Brindley, co. Cheshire). Granted by Sir Richard St. George, 1613. Per bend sinister or and sa. six martlets counterchanged. *Ormerod.*

Allen (Chester and Bowsworth). Per bend sinister sa. and arg. 6 martlets counterchanged. *Randle Holme.*

Allen (Great Withingham, Norf.). Arg. a chev . . . betw. 3 magpies ppr. *Cady.*

Allen. . . . sa. a chev. rompu erm. betw. 3 griffins heads erased arg. *Robson.*

Allen (London, 1568). Same arms, quartering sa. a chev. erm. betw. three unicorns' heads erased arg. for Hedd. *C.L.*

Allen (London). Per pale arg. and sa. on a chev. engr. betw. three talbots sejant collared two cloves counterchanged. *W.*

Allen or Aleyn (London). Sa. a cross potent or a crescent for difference. Crest: a demi-lion ramp. az. holding a rudder or. *Vis. Lon. 1633.*

Allen (Rosall). Arg. a chev. engr. betw. 3 griffins heads az. on a chief of the last an anchor betw. 2 bezants.

Allen (Founder of Ushaw College, Durham). Arg. 3 conies sejant in pale sable.

Aller or Aure (Co. Devon). Arg. 3 popinjays vert. *Lysons.*

Allestowe. Paly of 6 arg. and sa. on a chev. gu. a cross crosslet or. *V.*

Alleyn (Rayley, Essex). Az. on a chev. engr. or betw. 3 plates each charged with a greyhound courant sa. collared as the second as many crescents of the first. *V.V.*

Alleyn (Essex). Same arms. *W.*

Alleyne. Per bend sinister double dancetty arg. and sa. six martlets counterchanged. *V.*

Allington (Alderford, Norfolk). Sa. billetty arg. on a bend engr. . . . a leopard's head or. *Cady.*

Allington. Sa. a bend engr. arg. betw. 6 billets or. *Robson.*

Allowy.

Alloway (Queen's County, Ireland). Gu. a lion salient betw. 2 crescents in chief and 2 swords in base arg.

Allsopp (Co. Derby). Sa. three plovers rising arg. legged and beaked gu. quartering arg. three bears passant ppr.

Allwood (Co. Devon). Az. a chev. betw. 3 bucks heads erased arg. *Robson.*

Allyn (Bampton, co. Devon). Same arms as Allen of Dale Castle, co. Pembroke but with annulet sa. in the dexter chief for difference. *V.D. 1620.*

Alport (Cannock, co. Stafford). Quartered by Fletcher of Dudley. Barry wavy of eight arg. and az. on a bend gu. three mullets or. Crest: a demi-lion ramp. erminois collared with a mural crown gu. *V. Vis. Lon. 1633.*

Aispathe. Arg. a bend sa. cotised gu. within a bordure of the third. *Cady.*

Alston (Edwardston, Suffolk and Chelsea, Middlesex, descended from a second son of the Alstons of Saxham Hall. Sir Joseph Alston, of Chelsea, younger brother of Sir Edward Alston, Knt. M.D., President of the College of Physicians, was created a baronet in 1681). Same arms as Altson of Odell. A martlet for difference. *Vis. Lon. 1633.*

Almonbury (Co. York, King James' School). . . . 3 lions pass. guard 2 and 1 on a chief . . . 3 fleurs-de-lis.

Alneto (Maidford, co. Northampton). Arg. a lion ramp. gu. charged on the shoulder with an escutcheon or 3 martlets az. *Baker.*

Alpe (Fransham, co. Norfolk 1758). Arg. a chev. sa. betw. 3 stags heads . . . *Dashwood.*

Alsop (Winslip Hill co. Worcester). Quartering or 3 boars pass. . . . *Debrett.*

Alsop. Sa. a chev. betw. 3 birds or. *V.N. p. 43.*

Alsop (Alsop, Co. Derby and Leicester 1619). Sa. a chev. betw. 3 doves or a mullet for difference. *Lysons and C.C.*

Alured (Hull, co. York). Gu. a chev. engr. betw. 3 griffins' heads erased arg. *F.Y.*

Alvensleben. Or on 2 bars az. 3 roses arg.

Alvestry (Alvaston). Arg. a chief gu. over all on a bend az. 3 escutcheons per pale or and gu.

Alwyn Alias Halywell. Or on a bend sa. 3 goats bendwise statant arg. armed of the first. *V.*

Amedas (London). Az. a chev. erm. betw. 3 oak branches each with 3 acorns and 4 leaves slipped or tied with a wreath within a bordure engr. of the last. Robert Amedas. *V.*

Amades. *Cady and Guillim.*

Amand. Amane, or Amarme, *V.*

Amanri. Barry wavy of 6 arg. and gu. a label of 5 points az. Robert de Amanri. *F.*

Ambersam. Arg. on a chev. az. betw. 3 boars heads couped sa. five cinquefoils or. *V.*

Ambres. Gu. a chev. betw. 3 rowels arg. *Cady,*

Ambrose. Gu. 3 books closed 2 and 1 arg.

Amcotes (Astrop, co. Lincoln, granted 1548). *W.*

Amervill. Sir Thos. Amervill, Norfolk *V.*

Ames (Linden, Long Horsley, co. Northumberland). Granted 1874. Arg. on a bend betw. 2 cotises and as many annulets sa. a quatrefoil betw. 2 roses of the field.

Ammory (Oxfordshire). (sometimes gu.). correction 'armed'. *V.*

Amorie. Amory (Co. Devon. M.P. for Tiverton 1868). *Debrett.*

Amias (Norfolk). Erm. on a chev. sa. 3 acorns slipped arg. *Robson.*

Amory or Hamory. Barry wavy of 6 gu. and arg. Sir Richard Hamory. *L.*

Amory. Arg. 2 bars wavy and a baton gu. Sir Roger d'Amory. *L.*

Amory. Barry wavy arg. and gu. Sir Richard Amory. *N.Y.*

Amory. Barry of 5 arg. and gu. a baston of the last. Sir Roger d'Amory. *L.*

Amory. Barry nebuly of 6 arg. and sa. a bend or. *V.O. p. 175.*

Amundeville. . . . 3 chevs. . . . *Cotton MS. Julius F.8. fo.59*

Amyes (Hoddesdon, co. Salop.). Arg. on a bend sa. 3 roses of the first.

Ancketill. Anketill (London). Same arms and crest. *Vis. Lon. 1633.*

Andbly. Arg. 3 chevs. over all a fess gu. *V.*

Anderson. Sir Edmund Anderson, Chief Justice of the Common Pleas. Arg. a chev. betw. 3 crosses crosslet sa. quartering sa. 3 fetterlocks or. *Dug. O.J.*

Anderson (St. Ives co. Hunts.—Bart. 1628). Same arms with the crosses flory and quartering sa. 5 estoiles in saltire arg. *Guillim.*

Anderson (Haswell Grange). Gu. 3 annulets interlaced arg. betw. 3 oak branches arg. acorned or. *Eliz. Roll XIX.*

Anderson. Per chev. nebuly az. and vert. 3 stags lodge 2 and 1 . . . in the fess point a bugle horn stringed. Crest: A stag lodged . . . Motto "Nil Desperandum auspice Deo".

Anderson (Alnwick and Newcastle-on-Tyne) Vert. 3 bucks lodged arg. attired or. *Visitation 1615.*

Anderton (Euxton and Ince, co. Lancs. descended from Anderton of Anderton). Sa. a chev. betw. 3 shackle bolts arg. quartering Ince. *Harl. MS. 1468 fo. 96.*

Anderton (Claiton, co. Lancs.). Sa. 12 annulets divided into three chains of 4 each, palewise arg. two and one. *Harl. MS.*

Anderton (Euxton and Ince, co. Lancs. descended from Anderton of Anderton). Sa. a chev. betw. 3 shackle bolts arg. quartering Ince. *Harl. MS. 1468 fo. 96).*

Anderton (Claiton, co. Lancs.). Sa. 12 annulets divided into three chains of 4 each, palewise arg. two and one. *Harl. MS. 1468 fo. 96.*

Andrews (Lathbury, co. Buckingham)—insert Baronetcy 1611.

Andrews (Risborow, co. Norfolk). Same Arms. *Cady.*

Andrews (London). Same arms and Crest, but a martlet for difference . *Vis. Lon. 1633.*

Andrewes (Co. Hants). Arg. on a chev. engr. gu. betw. three quatrefoils vert. as many mullets or.

Andrewes (Co. Hants.). The same arms within a bordure compony gu. and arg. *V.*

Andrews (Suffolk). *V.*

Andrews (Co. Worcester). *V.*

Andrews. Arg. on a chev. engr. gu. betw. 3 mullets sa. as many quatrefoils or. *V.*

De Andrews. Same arms but quatrefoils or pierced az. *W.*

Androwey, or Andwey. Amendment . . . insert 8 or *V.*

Anell. Or a parrot gu. within a bordure arg. charged with a fleur-de-lis az.

Anes. Insert 'a' lion. . . .

Angell. Amend four fusils. *Vis. Lon. 1633.* But another coat shews 3.

Anlaby. Arg. a chev. betw. 3 chess rooks sa. a chief of the last. *Cady.*

Anhelet. *V.*

Anke, or Ankey. *V.* Gregory de Anke. *Y.*

Anleby, or Anselby. *V.*

Anlett. Gironny of 8 az. and arg. 4 annulets or. *Harl. MS. 1458*

Anlett (Suffolk). Az. 3 annulets arg. *Dingley.*

Anlett (Temp. Edwd. IV). Per saltire gu. and az. four annulets in cross or. *V.*

Anabelles. Or 2 bars invected above but engr. below gu. *V.*

Anne (Exeter). Arg. on a bend sa. 3 martlets of the first in chief a crescent on the second. *V.*

Anne (Frickley, co. York 1666). Arg. on a bend sa. 3 martlets of the field. Crest: A women's head couped at the breast hair dishevelled. *Dugdale p. 284.*

Anne. Gu. on a bend arg. betw. 2 cotises or 3 popinjays vert. William de Anne *V.*

Annering. Amend Arg. 'or' *Cady.*

Annesley (Cornwall, co. Oxford). *V.O.*

Annesley Thomas. *V.*

Annesley John de. *S.*

Annesley (Eynsham, co. Oxford). *V.O. p. 217.*

Ansam. Erm. on a canton sa. a fleur-de-lis or. *V.*

Ansell. Paly of 6 arg. and az. a bend gu. *Cady.*

Ansell. *V.*

Anson (Shugborough, co. Stafford). Arg. 3 bendlets engr. gu. quartering Carrier. *Erdeswick.*

Anstaboth. *V.*

Anstaboth or Anstalboth. *V.*

Anston. *V.*

Anstum. *V.*

Antingham. Gu. a bend arg. *Harl. MS. 1414.*

Antingham (Norfolk). Sa. a bend engr. betw. two cotises or. *Cady.*

Antingham. *V.*

Antrobus. *Vis. Lon. 1633.*

Anveby. . . . on a chev. az. 3 bezants. *Cady.*

Anvers (Cheshire). *V.*

Anvers. Sir Thomas de *N.* (The mullets pierced).

Anvers. Gu. a chev. betw. 3 chess rooks or. *Cady.*

Anvers or Anvery. Sir Thomas Anvers, co. Chester. *V.*

Ap Bran. Quartered by Eyton. Arg. a chev. betw. 3 crows sa. each bearing in its beak an ermine spot.

Ap Dulfyn. Gu. a bend betw. 3 spears heads arg. *V.*

Apiliard, Appleyard or Appulyard. *Cady.*

Apledorfield. Henry de Apelderfild *A.A. Harl. MS. 6137.*

Ap-Madock, or Ap-Madoke. *V.*

Appleby (Linton, co. York 1665). Same arms. *Dugdale p. 209.* Sir Henry de Appleby *E.F.L.N.* Sir Henry Appleby co. Stafford, temp. Edw. I. Sir Edmond Appleby. *S.*

Appleby (Leicestershire). *C.C.*

Appleby (John Appleby, temp. Rich. II) Add. in orle. *O.*

Applegarth (Copley, co. Surrey, confirmed by Dethick 1569). Az. a chev. or betw. 3 owls arg. in chief a fleur-de-lis erm. *Guillim.*

Appleyard. A chev. o owls.

Appleyard. A chev. or betw. 3 owls arg. *V.*

Appleyard (Bartswick Garth, Holderness Co. York).

Appleyard (Bartswick Garth, Holderness, co. York). Az. on a chev. or betw. 3 owls arg. a mullet for difference. *F. Y. Cady.*

Appryand. *V.*

Appuley or Apuley or Apleby. Az. 3 bucks lodge or. *V.V.*

Appuley or Appurley. Add. stalked vert. *V.V. Cady.*

Ap Raen. Sa. a chev. arg. betw. 3 lures of the second stringed or. Thomas ap Madoc ap Raen. *V.*

Apris. Add. Howel ap Res. *E.*

Apsland (Haydon). Arg. a chev. betw. 3 escallops sa. *Coll. Tops. viij. 279.*

Apsley or Apesley. Add. Sir John Aspelee. *V.*

Ap Vaughan (Kynvillem ap Dulfyn ap Vaughan). Gu. a bend betw. 3 spear's heads arg. *V.*

Ap Walter (Roxwell co. Essex). Gu. 2 lions pass. or a mullet for difference. *V.E.1612.*

Arbalester. Erm. a cross bow bent in pale gu. *V.*

Arcalon. Arg. 3 bars gemel sa. Sire William Arcalon. *O.*

Archard (Yorkshire). Insert temp. Edw. II. *F.Y.*

Archard. *V.*

Archard (Richard Archard). Az. three arrows or. *Harl. MS. 1548.*

Archat. Add. Sire Richard Archat. *M.*

Aechbold (Litchfield, co. Stafford). 1670.

Archdeacon Ede Lercadekne *A. Harl. MS. 6137.* Sir Thomas le Ercadekne. *N.* Sir Adam de Arcedeacon *A.* Sir   de Archdeacon Wigmore, co. Devon. *V.* Sir Geffrai le Ercedekene *E.F.* with a label of 3 points az.

Archdeacon. Arg. on 3 chev. sa. 13 bezants 5, 5 and 3. Thomas le Archdeacon or Archdekin. *E.*

Archer (Welland). Vert. 3 arrows arg. *Nash.*

Archer (Kilkenny). . . . . a chev. erm. betw. 3 pheons. *Notes and Queries.*

Archer. Gu. a chev. arg. betw. 3 fleurs-de-lis or. *Cady.*

Archer (Netherthorpe, co. Oxford). Az. 3 arrows erect or. *V.O.*

Arches (Devonshire). Add: *Cotton MS. Julius F. viij.*

Arches. Gu. 3 pairs of arches 2 and 1 arg. Sir William Arches. *T. Harl. MS. 6137.* But Gu. 3 arches conjoined in fess arg. caps and bases or. *T. Ashmole MS. 1120 fo. 175.*

Architects (Institute of British Architects, Incorporated in 1837) . . . on a stone platform . . . 2 lions ramp. guard. supporting a Norman column ornamented with chevron mouldings . . Motto: "Usui Civium decori urbium". **Seal.**

Ardeburo. Arg. a chev. engr. betw. 3 escallops gu. *V.*

Arden. Arg. a bend betw. 3 martlets sa. *Cady.*

Ardene. Arg. a lion ramp. az. Le Sire de Ardene. *A.*

Arderbouche. Quartered by Peniston of Bampton. Arg. a chev. engr. betw. 3 escallops sa. *V.O. p. 153.*

d'Arderne. Or a lion ramp. vair. Monsire Wakehide d'Arderne. *Y.*

Arderne. Insert: "in pale" or William Arderne. *E.F.*

Arderne. Add: Boudulf Arderne. *E.F.*

Arderne. Or a lion ramp. betw. 7 crosses crosslet sa. (or within an orle of crosslets).

Arderne of Hawnes, co. Bed. Gu. three crosses crosslet and on a chief or a martlet azure.

Ardes. *V.*

Ardonff. *V.*

Ardys. *V.*

Argan. *V.*

Armarle. Az. 2 bars and a bordure arg. all goutty de sang. *V.*

Armarle. Arg. goutty de sang 3 bars humetty az. *V.*

Armenters. Chequy or and az. a lion ramp. gu. Mon. John de Armenters. *D.*

Armeston. *Add: C.C. 1619.*

Armiger or Armeier (North Creek).—Insert: and Cley.

Armistead (Easingwold, co. York). Or a chev. embattled sa. betw. 3 pheons gu. within a bordure of the second. *Debrett.*

Armitage. Doncaster, co. York and London. (Granted by Segar, Garter). Arg. 3 crosses bottony gu. Crest: A demi-lion ramp. arg. holding a crosslet bottony gu. *Vis. Lon. 1633.*

Armitt (Fife, Scotland). Arg. a chev. betw. in chief 2 mullets and in base a crescent gu. *Cady.*

Armorer (Belford, co. Northumberland). Gu. a chev. betw. 3 sinister arms fesswise bent the hands open gauntletted the back part outward armed arg. the elbow pieces or. *V.*

Armorer (Sir Nicholas . . . Ireland), Add: *V.*

Armourers Company of: read also . . . The Arms granted to the Company of Armourers by Thomas Hawley, Clarenceux 15 Oct. 1556. are: Arg. on a chev. sa. a gauntlet betw. 4 swords in saltire silver purfled, pomelled and hilted on chief sa. a plate charged with a plain cross gu. and placed betw. 2 helmets silver garnished gold. The Crest was granted at the same time. **Original Grant.**

Arneford or Arnford. Add: *V.* Sometimes, Barry of 12 az. and or a bordure erm. *V.*

Arnham (Rector of Postwick, co. Norfolk, ob. 1787).... on a chev.... 3 boars heads erased ... His **tomb.**

Arnold (Leesthorpe, co. Leicester). Granted by Byshe 1653. Same Arms as Arnold (Gloucestershire). *Guillim.* Add:

Arnold. Insert: Co. Gloucester, granted 1653. Add: *Harl. MS. 1041 fol. 54.*

Arnold (London). Gu. 3 pheons arg. a chief barry nebuly arg. and az. (query vair). *Vis. Lon. 1633.*

Arnold (Kyneham, co. Gloucester) Sa. a chev. or betw. 3 lures arg. *Dingley.*

Arnold. Amend: "Ermine" insert: Sir Nicholas Arnold, co. Gloucester. *V.*

Arras. After sa. insert: *V.*

Arsacke or Arsake. *V.*

Arsick. Quarterly or and gu. on a bordure sa. ten bulls heads couped arg. Manarsch Arsick. *Cotton MS. Julius C.7 fo. 119.*

Arthur. Insert: Co. Berks. Bart . . .

Arthur (Wiggenhall, co. Norfolk). Heiress mar. in 1656 John Colby of Banham. Per bend sinister gu. and az. a lion ramp. arg.

Arthur (Springfield, co. Essex). Insert: Granted Segar, Garter . . . Sir Thomas Arthur. *T.* William Arthur, co. Somerset. *V.* and with a crescent for diff. *Harl. MS. 1386 fo. 94.*

Arthur (Wales). *V.*

Arthur. . . . and a chief arg. Add: *V.* (another . . .). Add: *V.*

Artoure. Gu. a chev. betw. 3 sharp toes shoes turned upwards arg. *Cady.*

Artore. Gu. a chev. betw. 3 Irish brogues or. *Harl. MS. 1603.*

Arundel. . . . of Trerice insert: *V.* delete 1773 and read 1768 following "and one arg." Insert: 2 and 3 sa. 3 chevs. arg.

Arundel. Sa. 6 martlets 2, 2 and 2 arg. Catherine Arundel 1526. **Seal.**

Arundel. Erm. on a canton . . . a cross lozengy . . . John Arundel *Harl. MS. 380 fo. 123b.*

Arundel. Gu. a lion ramp. or. Le Conte d'Arundell. *B.E.G.V.N.P.* Richard, Earl of Arundel K.G.

Arundell. Arg. 6 swallows sa. Sir John Arundell. Trerese, co. Devon. *V.*

Arundel. Gwarnick, Cornwall 1613. Sa. 3 chev. arg. In church. St. Mary, Lambeth.

Arward or Arwood. *Cady.*

Arwood. Arg. 3 leopards courant az. *Cady.*

Arwood. Arg. 3 hares courant in pale az. *V.*

Ascheton. Barry of 5 arg. and sa. a bend gu. Robert Ascheton. **Seal** 1341.

Asdale. Add: Thomas Asdale. *X.*

Ashaw. Insert: (Lancashire) and add: *V.*

Ashbee. *V.*

Ashborne. Arg. on a bend gu. 3 escallops of the first. *Harl. MS. 1603.*

Ashby (Robert de Ashby, temp. Edw. I). Arg. a lion ramp. sa. fretty of the first. *V.*

Ashby. Gu. a chev. betw. 3 eagles with 2 heads arg. *Cady.*

Ashby. Insert: Hanfield, Middlesex.

Ashby. Insert: co. Leicester and add: *1619 C.C.*

Ashcomb (Lynford. co. Berks.). Baronetcy 1696, same arms. *Guillim.*

Ashcomb (Co. Oxford). Same arms. *V.O. p. 332.*

Ashe or Eshe. *V.*

Ashe (Richmond). Arg. 2 chevs. and in the dexter chief a crescent sa. *Cady.*

Ashe (Freshford). . . . &c.

Ashe (London). Same arms and Crest: a martlet or for diff. *Vis. Lon. 1633.*

Ashe (Quartered by Bowyer-Smith). Arg. on a chev. sa. another erm.

Ashe. Insert: of the North Add: *V.*

Ashert. Gu. a chev. or in chief a fleur-de-lis of the second. *Cady.*

Ashethroser. Arg. a chev. betw. 3 crows ppr. *Cady.*

Asheton (Crofton, co. Lancaster). *Cotton MS. Tiberius D. 10.*

Ashton (Co. Lancaster). *W.*

Ashfield (Harfield, Middlesex). Bart. 1621. Ext. Az. a chev. betw. 3 eagles displayed with 2 heads or.

Ashford (Cheshire). Per chev. arg. and sa. *Cady.*

Ashley. Insert co. Chester and add: *V.*

Ashley of Ashley. Quarterly arg. and sa. on a bend gu. 3 mullets of the first. *Ormerod.*

Ashow. Insert: Lancashire, and add: *V.*

Ashridge Monastery (Bucks). Add: *Tanner.*

Ashton. Arg. 2 bars sa. a bendlet gu. Sire Robert de Ascheton 15th Edw. iij. **Seal.** Sir Robert Ashton. Constable of Dover Castle. *V.*

Ashton. Arg. a chev. betw. 3 garlands az. *Cady*

Ashton. Add. *V.V.*

Ashton. Quartered by Beconsall. *Harl. MS. 1519. fo. 35.* and by Preston of Arton in Craven, co. York. *Harl. MS. 1487. fo. 140.*

Ashwell (Tallenhow co. Bedford and London). Az. a chev. or betw. 3 greyhounds heads couped arg. a mullet for diff. Crest: A swan sa. *Vis. Lon. 1633.*

Askam (Dyghton). Az. a chev. betw. 3 fleurs-de-lis and a bordure sa. *Constable's Roll xvj.*

Aske. Robert Aske, Leader of Pilgrimage of Grace 1536. Aske (Richmond, co. Yorks.) same Arms. *F.Y.*

Askeby (Cheshire). *V.V.*

Askeby. Sir Robert de Askeby. *Y.* Roger de Askeby. *Y.* Sir Robert de Asscheby *N.*

Aslack, Aslake or Asloke. *V.*

Aslacke. Sa. a chev. betw. 3 roses arg. *Cady.*

Aslyn. Or a chevron embattled on the top gu. *Harl. MS. 1386 fo. 34 b.*

Aslin or Asslam. Or, a chev. embattled betw. three roses gu. stalked and leaved vert. *V.*

Aslyn. Arg. on a chev. sa. 3 lozenges of the first each charged with a cross crosslet sa. *V.*

Aslyn. Arg. on a chev. gu. three lozenges of the first each charged with a cross crosslet sa. *V.*

Asmant. Gu. 2 bars dancetty arg. William Asmant. *V.*

Aspall (Suffolk). . . . add: Sir Robert Aspall. *N.* Sir   de Aspall Suffolk temp. Edw. j. *V.* Another, . . . after, bracket. insert *Cady.*

Aspall (Suffolk). Crest: insert **Seal** of Thomas de Aspall.

Aspland. See Apsland.

Aspthorpe. Arg. a chev. betw. 3 martlets sa. *V.*

Assent. *V.*

Assethorpe. *V.*

Astley. Arg. a lion ramp. gu. charged on the shoulder with a cinquefoil erm. Sir Thomas Astelee. *Y.*

Asterby (Co. Lincoln). Sa. a bend betw. six estoiles or.

Asteley. Gu. on a chev. betw. 3 fleurs-de-lis arg. as many martlets sa. *Cady.*

Astley. Gu. a lion pass. guard. arg. betw. 3 crosses crosslet or.

Astley (Rudgeley, co. Stafford). . . . . a chev. . . . . betw. 3 quatrefoils. . . .

Astley. Az. a lion pass. guard. arg. Sir Guy de Astley. *V.*

Astley. Az. a lion pass. guard. arg. betw. 7 crosses crosslet or. *V.*

Astley. Az. semy of crosses crosslet or a lion pass. guard. arg. Robert Asteley. *Y.*

Aston (Tixall, co. Stafford and London). Same Arms and Crest, a mullet on a crescent for diff. *Vis. Lon. 1633.*

Aston (Co. Chester). Per chev. sa. fretty or and erm. *Harl. MS. 1553. fo. 7.*

Aston. Arg. a chev. betw. 3 fleurs-de-lis sa. *Cady.*

Aston. Or a chev. betw. 3 lozenges gu. *Cady.*

Aston. Per chev. sa and arg. on a canton or a rose and thistle conjoined ppr. *V.L. p. 154.*

Aston (Cheshire). *V.*

Aston (Enfield, co. Middlesex). Add: *V.* Sir Richard de Astone *N.*

Aston. Az. crusily or a bend betw. 2 cotises arg. Sir Richard de Astone *N.V.*

Aston (Manor of, co. Warwick). Az 2 bars or quartering 2nd gu. 3 towers arg. 3rd quarterly az. and gu. in the 1st and 4th a cross crosslet in the 2nd and 3rd a canton arg. 4th or on a saltire az. 4 billets. **Seal.**

Astwicke or Astwyke. Insert: Pontefract, co. York. 1665.

Athael (Sherborne).

Atclyffe. *V.*

Athallyate. Shrewsbury. Same arms. *Cady.*

Atherton (Atherton, co. Lancaster . . .). Add: *Harl. MS. 1549 fo. 151.* Sir William Adyrton, co. Lancaster *V.*

Atherton. (Lancashire). *V.* Sir William de Asherton *S.*

Athill. Arg. on a chev. sa. three gouttes or *V.* William Athill. *V.*

Athowe (Brysley—insert, and Lynn).

Athull. Arg. 2 bars engr. az. *V.*

Athie. Gu. on a chev. engr. betw. 3 martlets arg. as many pierced cinquefoils az. *Eliz. Roll xxxv.*

Athyll. Sa. on a chev. or betw. 3 garbs arg. banded gu. an annulet . . . *V.* The garbs or. *V.*

Atkins (Staffordshire). After Clarenceux insert 1600 . . . and in Crest: after pelican, insert sa. ppr. *Vis. Lon. 1633.*

Atkinson (Co. Nottingham, 1614). Arg. an eagle displ. gu. armed az. on a chief of the last 3 bezants. *W.*

Atkinson (Morland, co. Westmorland, and Lee, Kent). *V.*

Atkinson (London) same arms and crest. *Vis. Lon. 1633.*

Atkyns. After Pitt insert: Granted by Camden in 1600 to . . . Atkyns, Dr. of Physic.

Atkyns (Yelverton, co. Norfolk).

Atkins (Norwich and Lord Mayor of London). Same arms.

Atlath. . . . 3 bars . . . over all a lion ramp . . . **Seal** of Thomas Atte Lathe of Willinghall, Norfolk. 27 Edw. iij.

Atmore (Bray). Or a chev. gu. betw. 3 martlets sa. *V.O. p. 189.*

Aton De. See also Etton. *V.*

Atsea. Or on 2 bars wavy gu. as many shrimps of the first. *V.*

Atsea. Or on 2 bars wavy gu. three shrimps of the first, 2 and 1. *V.*

Atsea. Gu. on 3 bars wavy or as many shrimps of the first. *V.*

Atoste. Arg. a chev. betw. 3 crosses patty gu. *V.*

Atte Chambre (Norfolk). Arg. 3 chevs. sa.

Atte Chaumbre. Shree.

Atte Chaumbre. Sheriff of Northamptonshire temp. Ric. ij. *Fuller.*

Atterton (Slingsby, co. York). Gu. 3 martlets arg. *Eliz. Roll xxiv.*

Atthawes (London 1777). Arg. on a chev. erm. betw. 3 carpenters squares sa. a padlock of the last. *Robson.*

Atton. Or a bat volant gu.

Atton. Or a bat displayed vert. *N.*

Attowne (Kent). Arg. on a chev. sa. 3 crosses crosslet of the first. *V.*

Atwater. Vert. a lion ramp. guard. with 2 bodies ramp. counter rampant or within a bordure engr. arg. *V.V.*

Atwater. Add: *V.V.*

Attwater (Bishop of Lincoln granted by Wriothesley 1500). Barry wavy of 6 erm. and gu. on a chev. betw. 3 prawns or a rose of the second barbed vert. seeded gold enclosed by two lilies in chev. as the rose slipped vert. *V.*

Atwater (Wm. Atwater, Bishop of Lincoln 1514–21). Barry wavy of 8 erm. and gu. on a chev. betw. 3 dolphins naiant embowed or a rose sa. enclosed by two gillyflowers vert.

Atwell (Mamhead, co. Devon).

Atwill (Co. York and co. Devon). Same arms. *Harl. MS. 1465.*

Atwell. Sa. a chev. arg. and a pile counterchanged. *V.*

Atwell. Arg. a chev. engr. az. betw. 3 birds vert. beaked and legged gu. *V.N. p. 105.*

Atwill (Exeter). Arg. 2 chevs. and over all a pile voided sa. *Harl. MS. 1538 fo. 1.*

Atwood (Suffolk). Insert: (or 8) acorns . . . *V.*

Atwyne. *V.*

Aty or Attye (Newington, co. Middlesex).

Atye (Kilburn, co. Middlesex and London). Same arms, a crescent for diff. Crest: an ermine pass. ppr. on a cap of maintenance. *Vis. Lon. 1633.*

Aubemarle. Insert: Co. Dorset. *V.*

Aubemarle. Add: Sir Geffrey de Aubemarle. *N.*

Aubenerell. Gu. crusilly or a bend masculy erm. *Cady.*

Aubrey. Erm. 4 bends gu.

Audby or Eudeby. Delete (another, arg.) and add: *V.*

Audeley. Or 3 ravens in pale sa.

Audenard. Barry of 6 arg. and gu. a bend az. Sire de Audenard. *A. Harl. MS. 6137.*

Audeley. Arg. 3 chevs. over all a fess gu. *Harl. MS. 1404 fo. 4.*

Audeley. Gu. fretty or on a bordure arg. 8 fleurs-de-lis sa. *V.*

Audley. Hewgh Audley, Earl of Gloucester. *Q. Harl. MS. 6595 Y.* John de Audley. *Y.*

Audley (Co. Lincoln 1640). Quarterly 1 and 4, erm a chev. gu. 2 and 3, a fret or all within a bordure gobony arg. and az. *Yorke.*

Aulderton (of that Ilk). Vert. on a bend arg. three crescents sa. in the sinister chief a mullet of the second. *Guillim.*

Aunsell. *X.*

Ausham. Arg. on a canton sa. a fleur-de-lis or. *V.*

Aureichier or Aurticher. *V.V.*

Austen. Derhams, Middlesex. Baronetcy 1714. Az. on a chev. betw. 3 doves or as many quatrefoils vert. *Guillim.*

Austen (London). Az. on a chev. or betw. 3 doves of the second as many quatrefoils vert. Crest: A dove arg. holding in its beak a branch of trefoils stalked and leaved vert. *Vis. Lon. 1633.*

Austen (Bexley, co. Kent). Baronetcy 1660. Same arms as Austen (Grovehurst and Broadford, co. Kent) &c. But *bears* paws. *Guillim.*

Austen. Arg. a lion pass. reguard. gu. collared or on a chief az. a bezant betw. 2 estoiles arg.

Austin. Az. on a chev. betw. 3 lapwings or as many quatrefoils vert. Thomas Austin 1634. In old church at Shoreditch.

Austyn. *V.*

Auntesheye. Per pale or and arg. . . . bars wavy gu. Sire Richard de Auntesheye. *N.*

Avene. Gu. three chevs. arg. Sire Leysen de Avene. *N.*

Avenebury. Gu. 3 lions ramp. tails forked arg. Osborn de Avenebury. *F.*

Averam. Arg. a canton sa. *Harl. MS. 1078 fo. 24.*

Averinges. Quarterly arg. and gu. a bordure sa. *Cady.*

Avery (Mells, co. Somerset). Gu. a chev. betw. 3 annulets or: Quartering, Az. a rams head arg. horned or. *V.S.*

Avery (Co. Gloucester). Gu. 3 chevs. arg. *V.*

Avery. Gu. 3 chevs. or. *Cady.*

Avesnes. *V.*

Awbry (Braknock, confirmed by Cook 1652). Az. on a chev. betw. 3 hawks heads erased or a martlet gu. *Guillim.*

Awdyer. Gu. on a bend or 3 eagles heads erased vert.

Awys. *V.*

Axtell. Az. a chev. betw. 3 talbots pass. arg. **Book Plate.**

Ayer or Ayre. Add: *Harl. MS. 1392. V.N. p. 188.*

Ayliffe. Sa. a lion ramp. or cotised gu. betw. 3 crosses paty of the second. *V.*

Ayloffe (Braxted Magna, Essex). Insert baronetcy 1612. Sa. a lion ramp.—insert: or . . . Sir Wm. Ayloffe of Braxted Magna, Baronetcy 1612. Ext. 1781.

Ayloffe (Co. Wilts. and Dorset). Quarterly gu. and sa. a lion ramp. or collared arg. within a bordure of the last charged with torteaux and ogresses alternately. *V.*

Ayloffe (Co. Kent). Quarterly gu. and sa. a lion ramp. or collared az. betw. 3 crosses formy fitchy or within a bordure arg. charged with 16 torteaux and ogresses alternately. Thomas Ayloffe. *W.*

Aylway (Co. Oxford). Az. a lion ramp. arg. betw. 3 crosses fitchy or.

Aylworth (Essex). Gu. a lion dormant or. *Syl. Morgan. p. 77*

Ayncotts. *V.*

Aynsworth. Arg. on a bend sa. 3 crescents of the field. *V.*

Ayre (Wotton, Devonshire). *V.D.*

Aysshe (Co. Devon). Arg. 2 chevs. sa. *V.D.*

Ayshford (Co. Devon 1688). Arg. on a chev. voided sa. 3 bunches of ashen keys vert.

B

BAA, or BAO (Bedfordshire). *V.*

Babalake. *V.*

Babeham or Babehaw (London). . . . betw. three—insert—dexter.

Babeham (Cobham, co. Berks). Same Arms. *V.*

Babepull. Add: *Cotton MS. Tiberius D.10.*

Babington (East Brigford, co. Nottingham &c.). Babington (London) *Vis. Lon. 1633.*

Babington (but really Abington). Arg. on a bend gu. 3 eagles disply. or. *V.*

Babthorp (Co. York). *V.*

Babthorp (Co. York). *V.*

Babwell or Babbwell (co. Middlesex). Sir John Babbwell. Middlesex temp. Edw. j with the bendlet gu. *V.*

Bache (Stanton, co. Derby). After bordure—insert—az. . . . *Visitation 1663.*

Bacheler. After az. insert—*V.*

Bacheler. Arg. a chev. betw. 3 wings . . . *Cady.*

Backomb (co. Devon). Arg. a chev. betw. 3 bats displ. gu. *V.*

Bacon (Redgrave, co. Suffolk). Bacon (Shrubland Hall, co. Suffolk). Same Arms and Crest and quartering, Barry of 6 or and az. a bend gu. over all a fleur-de-lis on a mullet for diff. *Vis. Lon. 1633.*

Bacon. Az. 3 boars in pale arg. *V.V.*

Bacon (Middlesex). Gu. a boar statant or *Cady*

Bacon. Gu. 3 boars pass. or 2 and 1. *Cady.*

Badd (Cayne, co. Hants.). Gu. a chev. arg. betw. two couple closes or.

Badewe. Arg. on a bend double cotised sa. 3 eagles displ. in pale of the bend. or. Sir Hugh Badew. *V.*

Badisford. Az. on a bend betw. 2 cotises arg. 3 eagles displ. gu. *V.V.*

Badisford. *V*.*

Badley. Per chev. gu. and sa. a greyhound arg. within a bordure. *Cady.*

Badwell. Sa. a chev. engr. or betw. 3 mullets arg. *Cady.*

Badwell. Of Baxsted. Sa. a chev. or betw. 3 mullets arg. *Cady.*

Baeshe (Stanstead, co. Hertford). Add: Granted by Cook, Clarencieux 1571. *Guillim.*

Bagehott (Cos. Cambridge, Gloucester and Leicester). Same arms. *C.C. 1619.* See also Bagot.

Bagnall (Staffordshire and Wales).

Bagnall (London). Same arms and crest, a fleur-de-lis or. *Vis. Lon. 1633.*

Bagot or Bacot. Add: Sir William Bagott. *L.N.* Sire John Bagot. *Y.*

Bagot. Erm. on a bend sa. 3 eagles displ. arg. Sir William Baghott, co. Cambridge. *V.*

Bagot (Blithfield, co. Stafford. Baronetcy 1627). Erm. 3 chevrons az. *Guillim.*

Bagot (William Bagot, Sheriff of Warwick &c.). Add: *E.*

Bagot (From glass in Worcester Cathedral). After co. Stafford insert: ? 1566. Sir John Bagot. *S.* Sir Loys Bagot. *V.* Sir Wm. Bagot 1407. **Brass** in Baginton Church, co. Warwick.

Bagot (of Blithfield, co. Stafford). *Guillim.*

Bagsham. Gu. 3 quarrels arg. *V.*

Bagster. Arg. on a bend az. 3 stars of the first. *V.*

Bagworth. *V.V.*

Baikie. Add: or Backie. *A.A.*

Bailey (Bart., of Glanusk Park, co. Brecon). Insert: Baronetcy 1852.

Bailey (Stoneyhurst, co. Lancaster). Quartered by Sherborne. Vert. an eagle displ. arg. armed or. *Harl. MS. 1549. fo. 12.*

Baillol (Bywell). Az. a lion ramp. arg. crowned or within a bordure per bordure gu. and of the second. Hugh Baillol. *P.*

Bainbridge (Bishop of Durham 1507, Archbishop of York 1508 and a Cardinal). Az. 2 battle axes in fess arg. on a chief or as many pierced mullets gu.

Bainbrigge (Granted to Sir Wm. Bainbridge of Derby 1582). Arg. a chev. ermines betw. 3 battle axes sa. *Lysons.*

Bainbrigg or Bambridge (Leicestershire). Add: *C.C. 1619.*

Bainbry (Co. York). Az. 2 pole axes or headed arg. on a chief of the second 2 mullets of the first pierced gu.

Baines. Baynes (Granted to Captain Adam Baynes of Knosthrop, co. York in 1650 by Wm. Ryley. Norroy.). Same arms with a bezant in the dexter chief. *Northern Grants ljv.*

Baird. Or a boar pass sa. on a canton az. a sword erect. Sir William Baird.

Bakepuce. Gu. 2 bars arg. and in chief 3 horse shoes or. Sire Johan de Bakepuce. *N.*

Bakepuz. Az. crusily and a chev. or. Sir Rauf de Bakepuz. *E.*

Bakepull. Same arms. *V.*

Baker. Arg. 2 bars sa. on a chief of the last 3 swans.

Baker. Barry of 10 arg. and az. over all a bend gu: quartering or a lion ramp.

Baker (Originally of Battel, co. Sussex). Correction: *sa! az!* *W.*

Baker. Arg. a tower betw. 3 keys erect az. *V.* *

Baker (London, confirmed by Cook), after London. Insert: Surgeon to Queen Elizabeth. Add: *W. Vis. Lon. 1633.*

Balas. Or 2 chevs. gu. on a canton arg. 3 bends of the second *V.* * But the canton or quarter gu. charged with 3 bendlets arg. Sir George Balas. *V.*

Balcaskie (Scotland). Add: *Cady.*

Balch (Co. Somerset). Highham and Horton, co. Somerset and Tavistock, co. Devon. *V.S.* Balch of Virginia and Philadelphia, America descended from the above. Same arms. *Harl. MS. 1455 fo. 168.*

Balderston (Co. Lancaster). Richard de Balderstone. *Y.*

Baldington. Add: *V.*

Bales (Wilby, co. Suffolk). Or a lion pass betw. 3 crosses formy sa.

Bales or Bayles (co. Essex). Same arms.

Baldry. Add: Sir Thomas Baldry, London. *V.*

Bale (Carleton-Curlew &c. bart.). Insert: 1643. Add: *C.C. 1619.*

Bale (Carleton Curlew, co. Leicester, Baronetcy 1643. Ext. 1563 confirmed by Segar). Per pale az. and gu. an eagle displ. arg. The field per pale vert. and gu. *C.C. 1619.*

Balfour (Mountquhanny co. Fife &c.)...*Crawfurd.*

Balister (Co. Devon. 14th cent.). Az. 3 cross bows bent or. *Lysons.*

Ball. . . . a chev. . . . betw. 3 fleurs-de-lis . . . on a chief 3 lozenges.

Ball (Lincoln's Inn, London). Add: *Vis. Lon. 1633.*

Ball (Northamptonshire, granted 1613). Insert: by Segar.

Ball (London). Arg. a lion pass. sa. on a chief of the second three 4-foils of the first. Crest: A demi-lion ramp. sa. semy of 4-foils arg. and holding a 4-foil arg. stalked and leaved vert. *Vis. Lon. 1633.*

Ballard (Swepston, co. Leicester and London). Sa. a griffin segreant erm. in dexter chief a fleur-de-lis or Crest: a demi-griffin erm. *Vis. Lon. 1633.*

Ball (Recorder of Exeter. 1632). Arg. a chev. gu. betw. 3 fire-balls sa. fired gu. *Colby.*

Ball. Sa. a chev. betw. 3 bombs. erect or.

Ballengor. Arg. a chev. gu. betw. 3 dragons heads erased ppr.

Ballett (London . . . Essex). Add: *V.E. 1634.*

Balliawle. Add: *V.*

Ballowe. Arg. on a chev. sa. 3 escallops of the first. *Collinson, Somerset iij. 176.*

Balumy. Or 3 bars dancetty vert. *Randle Holme.*

Balun. Barry dancetty of 6 arg. and gu. Walter de Balun. *E.*

Balun. Barry dancetty of 6 gu. and or. Thomas Baloun. *Y.*

Bambell. Or a pelican vulning sa. *Randle Holme.*

Bamfield. Add: *W.*

Bamfield (Co. Devon). Same arms. *V.D.*

Bamfield. Paly of 6 arg. and vert. on a bend gu. three mullets of the first. *V. V.O. p. 138.*

Banastre. Arg. 3 chev. gu. Sir Robert Banastre, Lord of Newton in Makerfield and Walton-le-dale, co. Lancaster. The heiress mar. Langton. Sir William Banastre. *J.*

Banckys (London). Sa. on a cross betw. four fleur-de-lis or a torteau. *Vis. Lon. 1633.*

Banester (Westminster). Add: Sir William Banastre. *N.*

Banaster (Darwyn, co. Lancaster). Arg. a water bouget betw. 4 fleurs-de-lis 2 and 2 sa. *Harl. MS. 6159. fo. 17.*

Banester (of Darwen, co. Lancaster, 1567). &c. delete on a and read 'in' chief, delete: gu. *Harl. MS. 1468. fo. 28.*

Banester (Preston, co. Lancaster) &c. Add: *V.L.*

Bangor (1451). Add: John Bangor, granted 1457. *W.*

Banister (London). Arg. a cross flory sa. Crest: a peacock ppr. *Vis. Lon. 1633.*

Bank. Arg. a chev. betw. 3 falcons heads erased sa. *V.*

Bankes (Wimbledon, Surrey). Sa. a chev. engr. betw. 3 fleurs-de-lis arg. *Robson.*

Banks. Or an eagle displ. sa. looking to the sinister: impaling az. a fess bendy of 6 per fess counter changed or and sa. in chief an estoile or. Sir Jacob Banks, a Swede, London 1698. *L.N.*

Banks (London). Sa. on a cross betw. 4 fleurs-de-lis or 5 pheons az. Crest: A dragons head couped sa. semy of fleurs-de-lis or. *Vis. Lon. 1633.*

Bapthorpe. Gu. fretty arg. on a canton barry of 6 arg. and az. martlets in orle of the first. *V. V.* *

Bapthorpe (Sussex). Arg. fretty gu. on a canton barry of 8 arg. and az. a cross patty gold. *V.*

Barantine. Add: Sire Dru de Barantin. *N.*

Barantine (Co. Buckingham). Same arms. *V.*

Barbary Merchants (Company of). Arg. an elephant ppr. a canton quarterly of France and England.

Barber (London, *Camdens grants*). Add: *W.*

Barbers Company of (London). Insert: confirmed to the Company of Barber Surgeons by Dethick and Others 2 June 1569. *Grant.*

Barbie. Or a lion ramp. gu. crowned az. oppressed by a fess. *Cady.*

Barcas (Newcastle). Az. a chev. betw. 3 crescents or *Robson.*

Barchaile. Arg. a bend betw. 3 figures wavy sa. Sir Robert de Barchaile alias Dobenhale. *R.*

Barclay (Garthie, Scotland). Gu. on a chev. betw. 3 crosses patty arg. as many hearts of the field. *Robson.*

Barclay (Collernie, co. Fife). *Robson.*

Bardolphe. Arg. a chev. ermines betw. 3 crosses crosslet fitchy sa. *Cady.*

Barclay (Johnston, Insert: Scotland . . .), *Lyon Register.*

Barclay (Balmakewan, Insert: Scotland . . .) *Robson.*

Barclay (Kippo). Az. a chev. betw. in chief 2 crosses patty arg. and in base a mullet or.

Barclay (Towie, co. Aberdeen . . .). *Robson.*

Barcroft (Barcroft, co. Lancaster 1664). Add: *V.C. 1664.*

Bard (Staines, Middlesex. Baronetcy 1644).

Bardfield. *V. V.* *

Bardney (Benedictine Abbey, co. Lincoln). Sa. an annulet environing a crozier the foot enwrapped by a snake, in chief 2 coronets arg.

Bardolfe. Insert: co. Hereford. Add: *V.*

Bardolph (co. Stafford). Arg. a chev. debruised betw. 3 crosses bottony fitchy sa. *Harl. MS. 1386. fo. 36.*

Bardolph (London). Az. a mascle—insert: arg. Crest: delete gu. to read: or at end—delete or and substitute arg. Add: *Vis. Lon. 1633.*

Bardsey (Bardsey-in-Furness). A canton insert: 'of the last'. *Vis. Lon. 1633.*

Bardwell (Norfolk). Add: Mons William Bardwell *T.*

Bardwell. Gu. 3 bars gemel and a canton erm. Robert Bardewell. *V.*

Bardwill. Gu. 3 bars gemel or a canton erm. *V.*

Barett. Add: on the bend. *V* *.

Barkele. see Berkeley.

Barington or Berington (Moresborough, co. Chester). Sa. a bordure arg. *Harl. MS. 1535. fo. 8.* But query, 3 greyhounds omitted.

Berkeley (London). Gu. a chev. betw. 10 crosses patty arg. quartering Knight and Felton a for diff. Crest: a mitre charged as the first coat for diff. *Vis. Lon. 1633.*

Barker (Allowed by the Deputies of Camden . . .).

Barker (London). Same arms, a mullet for diff. *Vis. Lon. 1633.*

Barker (Kent, Middlesex and Surrey). Insert: also of Great Yarmouth.

Barker. Barry of 8 or and az. a bend or Capt. John Barker, Engineer, quartering gu. a lion ramp. arg.

Barker (Co. Essex). Per chev. nebuly or and sa. a lion ramp. counterchanged. *V.E. 1612.*

Barker (Robert Barker, Sheriff of Newcastle 1572). Sa. a bat displ. arg. a mullet for diff. on a chief gu. 3 cinquefoils or. *Carr MS.*

Barker. Az. on a bend arg. betw. 2 estoiles or a naked boy front faced ppr. the toungue of a bear statant sa. estoiled or on a chief arg. 3 roses radiated or Richard Barker, Bishop of Carlisle 1570, confirmed 23 April 1571. *Harl. MS. 5847. fo. 26.*

Barker. Barry of 10 or and sa. a bend gu. *V.E. 1634.*

Barker (London). Or on a fess dancetty vert. 3 fleurs-de-lis arg. in chief an annulet for diff. Crest: a dove holding in its beak an olive branch. *Harl. MS. 1358.*

Barker (London). Gu. a fess chequy or and az. betw. 6 annulets arg. quartering az. 2 bars arg. on a canton az. a chev. betw. 3 pheons arg. charged with an eagles head sa. betw. 2 mullet gu. over the whole a crescent on a mullet for diff. Crest: a falcon rising or. *Vis. Lon. 1633.*

Barker (Suffolk).

Barker (London). Same arms. Crest: an heraldic antelope sejant or. *Vis. Lon. 1633.*

Barkerolles. Insert: co. Gloucester. *V.* Sire William de Berkerolles. *N.*

Barkesworth. Chequy arg. and gu. on a bend az. *V. V.* * Sir Robert de Barkesworth. *N.*

Barkham (Southam, Norfolk). Bart. Same arms and crest as Barkham (London). *Vis. Lon. 1633.*

9

Barkepuis (Leicester temp. Edw. ij.). Gu. 2 bars betw. 3 horseshoes or. *Robson.*

Barcley. Gu. a chev. betw. 8 roses arg. Sir Thomas Barcley. *L.N.*

Barkly (Co. Rutland). C.R.

Barkston (Co. York). Arg. a bend sa. cotised gu. betw. 3 fleurs-de-lis az. *Fairfax's Book of Arms.*

Barley (Dronfeild-Woodhouse, co. Derby). Barry wavy of 6 arg. and sa. a chief per pale erm. and gu. charged with a fleur-de-lis or. *Lysons.*

Barley. Henry Barley (Abberly Hall, co. Herts). *V.*

Barley (Co. Derby). Arg. 3 bars wavy sa. a chief gu.

Barlingham. Gu. 3 bears arg. Sir Richard de Barlingham. *N.*

Barlow (Slebetch, co. Pembroke bart extinct). Add: John Barlowe, Granted temp. Hen. vj. *V.*

Barlow (Co. Derby). Barry wavy of 6 arg. and sa. a chief gu. and canton erm. *V.*

Barlow. Sa. an eagle displ. with 2 heads arg. standing on a piece of tree raguly of the second Sir . . . de Barlough. *V.*

Barmoyt. Or 2 chevs. without a bordure gu. *Cotton MS. Tiberius D.10.*

Barnake. Insert: *V** (another . . .).

Barnard. Archibald Barnard, a Gascoine, born in England Lord of Halnaby co. Lincoln. Granted 24 Nov. 1580. *Harl. MS. 6169. fo. 1.*

Barnard (Pirton, co. Oxford). Add: a mullet within an annulet for diff. *V.O.*

Barnard (Lincolnshire 1640). Arg. a bear ramp. sa. a bordure engr. of the last. *Yorke.*

Barnard (Co. York, Norfolk and of Pirton, co. Oxon.). Arg. on a bend az. 3 escallops of the first in the sinister chief a mullet enclosed by an annulet.

Barnard. Arg. a chev. sa. on a chief gu. 3 mullets or Sir Philip Barnard. *V.*

Barnard. Sa. an annulet betw. 2 greyhounds ramp. endorsed reguard. or collared gu. *Cady.*

Barnard (Co. Hants.). Sa. 2 greyhounds ramp. reguard addorsed arg. in chief betw. them a fawn's head cabossed or. *V.*

Barneby (Barnby Hall in Cawthorne, co. York). Or a lion ramp. sa. armed and langued gu. powdered with escallops arg. *Hunter ij 233.*

Barnby (Co. York). Or on a lion ramp. sa. within an orle of 5 mullets az. 6 escallops arg. *Fairfax's Book of Arms.*

Barne (London). Arms and Crest Insert: Sir . . de Barne, Normerston, co. Bucks. *V.*

Barnes (London 1614). Insert: confirmed by Camden.

Barnes (Lord Mayor of London 1552). Az. on a chev. engr. az. betw. 3 shovellers sa. as many 3-foils or.

Barnes (Bishop of London 1504). Az. a lion ramp. or over all on a fess sa. 3 crosses crosslet fitchy gu.

Barnes (London). 1552. Arg. on a chev. wavy az. betw. 3 ducks sa. as many trefoils slipped or.

Barnfeild or Barnfield (Edgmont, co. Salop confirmed by Camden 1604). Or on a bend gu. 3 mullets pierced arg. an annulet gu. for diff. *Guillim.*

Barnesdale. (1604). Add: Granted by Camden to Dr. Barnesdale.

Barneyes. Insert: or Barneis. *V.*

Barnw.

Barnewell (London). 1446. Per pale arg. and gu. 3 otters pass. counterchanged.

Barningham. Arg. a bear statant (or passant) sa. muzzled or within a bordure engr. gu. *Constable's Roll XV.*

Barningham (Co. York, temp Edw. ij). Same arms. *F.Y.*

Barnsley. Borough of co. Yorks., **Book Plate** Insertion. . . . Motto: Spectemur Ageo.

Barnsley (London). Sa. a cross betw. 4 roses arg. Crest: a man's head affronti ppr. *Vis. Lon. 1633.*

Baron (Bradwell . . . Essex). Add: *V.E. 1634.*

Baron (exemplified by Camden . . .). Add: *Vis. Lon. 1633.*

Baron. Gu. 2 chevs. compony az. and arg. betw. 3 garbs or *V**

Baron. Sa. a martlet betw. 3 estoiles arg. within a bordure engr. or. *W.*

Baron (Saffron Walden, Essex and London). Az. 2 lions pass. guard. in pale arg. *C.C.* and *Harl. MS. 1359. fo. 38.*

Baron. Gu. a chev. compony arg. and az. betw. 3 garbs or *V**.

Baron (Mayor of Exeter, 1706). Gu. a chev. compony sa. and or betw. 3 garbs . . . *Colby.*

Baron (temp. Hen. vj). Gu. on a chev. arg. betw. 3 garbs or 5 palets and another chev. az. *V.*

Baronby. *V.**

Baronby or Baroughby. *V.V.**

Barr. Gu. 3 bars compony arg. and az. Monsire Thomas Barr quartering Barry of 6 or and az. a bend gu. *S.*

Barrantine. Add: Sir William Barrantine. *E.R.* Dru Bartin G. and with an annulet for diff. Sir Drew Barentine, Lord Mayor of London 1398. *W.*

Barre. Az. 2 lions pass. guard. within a bordure engr. or. Monsire William Barre. *S.*

Barre. Arg. on a bend betw. 2 cotises az. and as many martlets sa. 3 escallops or. Francois de a Barre. *V.*

Barre or Barrey. Insert: co. Norfolk.

Barre or Barrey. . . . of Marlingford, Norfolk. *Cady.*

Barre. Arg. 2 pales sa. over all as many palets gu. *Randle Holme.*

Barre. Barry embattled and counter embattled arg. and gu. *Randle Holme.*

Barrett (Granted to Leonard Barrett of Defonden by Cooke, Clarencieux 1575) Arg. a chev. engr. gu. betw. 3 bears pass. sa. muzzled or.

Barrett (Exeter). Chequy arg. and sa. *Colby.*

Barrett. Insert: Westhall, Suffolk. *V. V**.

Barrett. Arg. semy of crosses crosslet a lion ramp. gu. crowned or. Sire Steven Barret. *O.*

Barrette. Insert: co. Dorset. Sa. a. chev. arg. *V.*

Barrette (London). Erminois 3 bars gu. on a canton arg. a female bust couped at the shoulders ppr. *Robson.*

Barriff. Insert: London. Az. on a chev. engr. . . . Same crest as above. *Vis. Lon. 1633.*

Barrington (Barrington Hall, co. Essex, ext. bart) insert: 1611. Add: Sir Nicholas de Barington, Essex, temp. Edw. j. *V.N.*

Barrington. Arg. 3 chevs. gu. a label erm. *Cady.*

Barrington. Sir . . . de Barington co. Leicester. *V.* Addition to Barrington, Somerset.

Barrington. Add: Sir Phillip Barington *L.N.V.*

Barron. *V.**

Barron (Temp. Edw. iv.). Gu. a chev. counter compony arg. and az. betw. 3 garbs. or. *V.*

Barron. Arg. on a bend engr. gu. 3 leopards faces or Nicholas Barron. M.D. London.

Barron (Gurre). Or 3 ravens ppr. *V.*

Barron (West Hereham, Norfolk). Sa. a chev. chequy arg. and sa. betw. 3 garbs.

Barron. Read of Hitchin.

Barroughby. Az. a chev. betw. 3 boars heads couped arg.

Barrow. . . . a demi-boar ramp. arg. 3 billets betw. 2 cotises in bend. *Cady.*

Barrow-in-Furness (Town of co. Lancs.). **Book Plate.** Borough of Barrow-in-Furness. Gu. on a bend or betw. in chief a serpent nowed arg. and in base a stag trippant or a bee and an arrow on a chief arg. a steamship with 2 masts sails spread and 2 funnels. Motto: Semper sursum.

Barry (Wynscott, co. Devon). Arg. 2 bars gu. a crescent for diff. *Guillim.*

Barry (High Beckington, co. Devon). 1624, Barry of 6 arg. and gu. a crescent for diff. *V.D.*

Barry. . . . Oxford. Add: Sir Robert de Barre. *E.F.N.* Sir . . . de Barry co. Oxford. *V.*

Barry (Vincent Barry . . . Barry (Eynesham, co. Oxford). Same arms. *V.O.*

Barry. Gu. 2 bars gemell arg. John Barry. *Y.*

Barry. . . . Embattled gu. Add: Sir John Barry. *V.*

Bartholomew. Insert: of Exeter.

Bartlet. Sa. on a chev. . . . as many trefoils slipped ppr. Add: *Harl. MS. 1404. fo. 142.*

Bartlytt (London). Sa. on a chev. betw. 3 birds arg. as many pierced 5-foils vert. *Harl. MS. 1404. fo. 142.*

Barwen. Arg. a chev. betw. 3 hearts sa. *V.*

Barwiss. Arg. a bend az. cotised gu. Add: Thomas Barwiss. *V.*

Basevile. Add: Godfrey de Basevile. *A. Harl. MS. 6137.*

Basford (Roger Basford, Sheriff of London, temp. Henry viij.). Sa. 3 dancing bears or. *Fuller.*

Bashe. . . . triple towered . . . *V.V.**

Bashett. Insert: or Bachet. *V.V.**

Basill. Arg. 3 annulets sa. *W.*

Basinge. . . . 2 mullets pierced of the field insert: *V.*

Baskervile. Gloucestershire, Herefordshire, Hertfordshire. Add: Walter de Baskervile. *B.* Sir John de Baskervile. *E.F.*

Baskervile (Herefordshire and Warwickshire). Add: Sire Richard de Bascrevile *N.* Baskerville. *I.* Sire Walter de Baskervil. *F.*

Baskervile. Arg. on a chev. gu. betw. 3 hurtes as many crosses crosslet or Sir Richard Baskervile. *V.* Sir Walter de Bascrevile. *N.*

Baskervile. . . . as many mullets or Add: Sir Walter de Baskervile. *L.*

Baskervile. . . . as many fleurs-de-lis. Add: or John Baskervil. *Y.*

Baskerville. . . . Same as Baskerville of Erdisley. Add: *Vis. Lon. 1633.*

Basnett. *V.**

Baspoole. . . . Three lions ramp. sa. substitute gu. *V.**

Basquer (Matthew Basquer, Hythe, Isle of Wight) Per bend or and arg. a lion ramp. az. on a chief of the last a cross patty fitchy of the second betw. 2 mullets of the first. *V.*

Bass (Burton-upon-Trent). . . . A chev. sa. betw. 3 ogresses. *Debrett.*

Bassano (London, Essex &c.). Add: *Vis. Lon. 1633.*

Basset. Insert: of Yetton . . . Erm. on a canton gu. a. mullet. *V.*

Basset. Arg. 2 bars az. in chief 3 chaplets of roses gu. Sir William Basset. *N.V.*

Bassett (Uly, co. Gloucester). Erm on a canton gu. a mullet arg. *Atkyns.*

Bassett (Cornwall). Add: Thomas Bassett, Cornwall. *Y.*

Bassett (North Luffenham, co. Rutland). Same arms. *C.R. 1618.*

Bassett. Paly of 6 or and gu. a canton erm. Sire Raffe Basset. *A.H.*

Basset. Paly or and gu. on a canton arg. a cross patty sa. Sir Rafe Bassett. *C.*

Basset. Sir William Bassett of Claverton co. Somerset. Knighted by Charles ij. a mullet or on the canton for diff.

Bassett. Arg. 3 bars az. in chief as many hurts. *V.*

Bassett. Barry nebulee of six &c. . . . Add: Phillip Bassett *D.E.F.V.*

Bassett (Beaupre, co. Glamorgan) &c. (another . . . Add: *V*.*

Bassett. Arg. 3 bars nebuly or wavy sa. Sir Rauf Bassett. *J.*

Bassett (Umberly, co. Devon 1620). Or 3 bars wavy gu. *V.D.*

Bassett. Barry nebuly of 6 arg. and sa. a label of 5 points gu. Rauf Bassett. *E.*

Bassingbourne. Gyronny of 6 arg. and gu. a baston az. Sir Giles Bassingbourne.

Bastard (Cornwall). Or on a chev. az. a martlet of the first. *V.C. p. 303.*

Bastard. (Kitley and Buckland Court, both co. Devon.) Add: *V.D.*

Batch (Fersfield, Norfolk). Arg. on a bend gu. 3 bucks heads cabossed or.

Batchelor (Easingwold, co. York). Add: *V.*

Batchelor (Horstead, co. Norfolk). Add: *Blomfield iv. 14.*

Batchworth. Add: *V.*

Bateman (Sheriff of Essex. temp. Ric. ij.). Sa. 3 lions dormant arg. *Fuller.*

Bateman (Essex). . . . Couchant—insert: or dormant and add: *V.V.**

Bateman (Middleton by Youlgrave, co. Derby &c.). . . . Add: *Vis. Lon. 1633.*

Bateman. Arg. on a bend sa. three—delete: hurts, substitute plates. *V.*

Batescombe (Co. Dorset). Arg. a chev. sa. betw. 3 bats displ. gu.

Bath (Granted to Henry James Bath &c.). . . . Add: *Nicholas.*

Bathurst (London). Same arms as (Hampshire, Kent and London) a martlet on a crescent for diff. *Vis. Lon. 1633.*

Batley (Town of co. York). Per chev. az. and arg. on a chev. gu. betw. in chief a fleece pendent and a garb . . . and in base a cross flory pierced sa, three estoiles arg.

Battie (Wadworth &c. co. York). Insert: *1665.* Add: *Dugdale. p. 167?*

Battine. Per pale sa. and or a chev. betw. 3 bugle horns stringed counter changed. **Book Plate.**

Baudwin. Sa. a bend betw. 6 billets arg. *V.**

Bause (Sire William Bause). Gu. 2 bars betw. 3 escallops arg. *O.*

Baunfeld. Insert: Cornwall *V.* delete: (another az.).

Baunfield. Add: Sir Thomas Baunfeld, co. Devon. *V.*

Baunfeld (Co. Cornwall). Az. on a bend or 3 pierced mullets gu. *V.*

Baulnfield. Or on a bend gu. 3 pierced mullets arg. *Cady.*

Bavant. Erm. two bars gu. charged . . . Add: Walter Bavant. *Y.*

Bavent. Arg. a chev. gu. within a bordure sa. bezanty. Sire John de Bavent. *O.*

Bavent. *V.*

Bevent. Add: Sir Robert Bavent. *V.*

Bawcombe (Co. Devon). Arg. 3 bats displ. sa. *Lysons.*

Baud. Bawreth, Essex. temp. Hen. 4th *V.* Sir William Baude. *S.*

Bawde (Lincolnshire). Add: *V.*

Bawden. Insert: Cornwall. *V.C. p. 303.*

Bawdesay. Arg. 2 bars. . . . on a canton gu. a maunch arg. *Cady.*

Bawdewyn or Bawdwen. Add: *V.**

Badrip. *V.*V.*

Bawle. Add: Sir Henry Bawle. *V.*

Baxby (Co. York). Erm. 2 bars gu. *F. Y.*

Baxter (Sharphill, co. York 1585). Arg. on a bend az. 3 stars of the first. *F. Y.*

Baxter (Yorkshire). . . . (another, or Add: *V.*).

Baxter (Co. Nottingham). Erm. on a chev. gu. 3 bezants. *V.*

Baxters, Company of (Edinburgh). Add: *Berry.*

Bayley. Gu. a chev. engr. erm. betw. 3 martlets arg.

Bayley (Middle Temple). Add: an annulet for diff. *W.*

Bayliff or Bayliffe. Arg. on a chev. gu. three martlets or between as many human hearts of the second, three martlets or. *V.*

Baylis (Co. Gloucester; granted 1755). Add: *Robson.*

Bayly (Woodford, Essex). Or on a chev. gu. betw. 3 martlets sa. as many plates *V.E. 1634.*

Baynard (Norfolk). Sa. a chev. or. *V.*

Baynard. Gu. 3 chevrons erm. *V.*

Baynard. Sa. a chev. or a chief per fess of the first and second. Add: Sir Roger Baynard. *V.*

Bainbridg. Arg. on a chev. betw. 3 martlets sa. as many bucks heads cabossed of the field. *Eliz. Roll. xx.*

Baynes (Ewele, Surrey). Per chev. az. and arg. in chief two doves volant respecting or in base a peacock in pride ppr. *Robson.*

Baynes or Bayn (Cheshire). Az. on a chev. insert: 'counter' Embattled &c. *V.*

Baynham (Kent and Gloucestershire). Add: *V.*

Baynton. Sa. a bend fusilly arg. Sir Robert Baynton *R.* Sir John Beynton. *V.* Sir William de Braddone. *G.*

Bayntun-Rolt. Insert: 1762-1816.

Bayon (Co. Hunts.). Arg. 3 water bougets ppr. *Syl. Morgan. p. 31?*

Bayons (Lincolnshire and Essex). Add: Sire Robert de Bayouse. *N.*

Bayons. Gu. 2 bars and in chief 3 escallops arg. Sir Walter Bayons co. Lincoln. *V.* Sir William Bayons *L.V.Y.*

Bayouse (Lincolnshire). Add: Sir William de Bayouse. *N.*

Beacatt. Arg. a chev. engr. betw. 3 cats faces erased gu. *Harl. MS. 1404. fo. 130.*

Beach (In Netherton Church, co. Wilts.). Vairy arg. and gu. on a canton or a harp az.

Bealblinger. Arg. 2 talbots pass. respectant betw. as many chevronels sa. within a bordure engr. gu. *V.*

Beale (Essex). Az. a chev. betw. 3 ducal coronets or. *Morant's Essex. ij. 137.*

Beale (London). Add: *Vis. Lon. 1633.*

Beale (Woodhouse, co. York). Sa. on a chev. betw. 3 griffins heads erased or as many mullets of the field a crescent for diff. Crest: A unicorn's head erased or crined sa. *Dugdale. 1665. p. 189.*

Beale (Maidstone Court &c. . . .). Insert: 1660.

Bealieu Add: ("Roll of Northern Arms" &c. . . .).

Beamont. Barry of 6 gu. and erm. Le Sire de Beamont co. Devon. *Y.*

Beamont.

Bearcroft. Sa. on a chev. betw. 3 wolves heads erased arg. a mullet betw. 2 crescents gu. *Nash.*

Beard (North Kells, co. Lincoln). Add: *Harl. MS. 1550. fo. 51.*

Beare (Quarterly Borlase, Cornwall). Arg. a chev. betw. 3 bears pass. sa muzzled or *Lysons.*

Beare (Killigarth, and Bryn co. Cornwall). Add: *V.*

Beston (Beeston, co. Chester). 34th Edw. iij. in a bend . . . over all a label of 3 . . . . Henry de Beston Seal.

Beaubras. Barry of 14 az. and or *V.** Sir Robert Beaubras. *V.*

Beauchamp (Fifield, co. Essex). Add: *V.* Sir Johan de Beuchamp. *N.*

Beauchamp (Cumberland). Insert: extinct temp. Hen. vij. *Lysons.* William Beauchamp. *X.*

Beauchamp. Arg. on a bend gu. 3 annulets or. *V.*

Beauchamp. Sa. a chev. betw. 3 lions heads erased arg. crowned or. *V.*

Beauchamp. Sa. a chev. or betw. three lions' heads erased arg. Add: Bewcham. *V.*

Beauchamp (London and Northamptonshire). Sa. a chev. arg. betw. 3 lions heads erased of the second crowned or for diff. *Vis. Lon. 1633.*

Beauchamp. Gu. a bend vair in the sinister chief an annulet arg. for diff. *V.*

Beauchamp. Sa. an eagle displ. arg. armed or Sir John de Beauchamp. *B.*

Beauchamp. Quarterly or and gu. on a bend of the last. William Beauchamp. *B.* de Bedford. *P.* Walter Beauchamp. *C.* Beauchamp, Baron of Bedford. *V.E.* a bendlet or baston.

Beauford. Per Pale &c. . . . label of three points az. and delete: bezantee and read: charged with a fleurs-de-lis or.

Beaufort. Sire John Beaufort. *S.* i.e. John de Beaufort, Earl of Somerset, eldest natural son of John of Gaunt. He used these arms before his legitimation. His brother Henry used a crescent for diff. and his brother Thomas a mullet. *Z. 322.*

Beaufort. Az. a tower arg. masoned sa. issuing therefrom a demi-naked woman ppr. **Book Plate.**

Beaufoy. Quartered by Wilder, Er. on a bend az. 3 cinquefoils arg.

Beaufoy. Arg. a chev. betw. 3 eagles displ. gu. John and William Beaufoy. *V.*

Beaufoy (Co. Warwick). 1619. *W.* Beaufoy, Emscott, co. Warwick. 1676, *L.N.*

Beaufoy. *V.*

Beauley (Of the South). Per Bend embattled— delete: 'and enhanced' gu. and arg. and read: John Beauly del South. De gu. et d'argent embeleif battaillee. *X.*

Beaumont (Co. Leicester). Az. a lion ramp. betw. 5 fleurs-de-lis or.

Beaumont. Az. semy of fleurs-de-lis and a lion ramp. or Le Sire de Beaumont. *S. Y.* Lewis de Beaumont, Bishop of Durham 1318. Francis Beaumont, Judge of the Common Pleas. 1593.

Beaumont. Az. semy of fleurs-de-lis and a lion ramp. or over all a bend compony arg. and gu. Sir Henry Beaumont. *I.M.V.O.N.*

Beaumont. Az. a lion ramp. within an orle of 10 crosses crosslet or a bendlet compony arg. and gu. Sir Henry Beaumont. *V.* The bendlet charged with 3 mullets sa. Beaumont. *V.* The bendlet compony erm. and gu.

Beaumont (Gracedieu, co. Leicester &c . . . arms &c. same as Beaumont of Coleorton). Add: also Beaumont of Giteham, co. Devon. *V.D. 1624.*

Beaumont (Fangfoss, co. York 1612). Gu. a lion ramp. within an orle of 7 crescents arg. and charged on the breast with a mullet for diff. *F. Y.*

Beaumont (Barrow-upon-Trent, co. Derby). arms and motto same as Beaumont of Coleorton, insert, a crescent' for diff. &c. . . . *Lysons.*

Beaumont (Whitley, co. York created 1628 &c. . . .). Insert Sir Thomas Beaumont. Q. and with a label of 3 points or Sir Thomas Beaumont, the younger. Q..

Beaumont (Stoughton Grange, co. Leicester &c. . . .). Add: Beaumont of Hackney. Same arms.

Beaumont (Buckland, co. Surrey). Add: Beaumont, to read: arms &c. same as the preceding Beaumont.

Beaumont (Co. York). Erm. 2 bars gu. a chief or. *Fairfax's Book of Arms.*

Beaumont (Co. Devon). Barry of 6 gu. and erm. *Y.*

Beaupel. Gu. a bend vair—delete—(another, cotised) . . . Add: Sire Robert Beaupel. *N.* of co. Cornwall. *V.*

Beaupeyl. Gu. a bend vair. Sire Robert Beaupel. *O.*

Beaupere. Add. *V.*

Beauple. Add: Sir . . . de Beauple. *V.*

Beaupre (Wells). Insert: co. Norfolk . . . *Cady.*

Beaupre. Or a lion ramp. vair a dexter baston gu. Monsire Raufe de Beaupre. *Y.*

Beaupre. *V.*

Beauvoyre. Or 2 chevs. within a bordure gu. *V.*

Beaver. Erm. a bend az. *V.**

Beawley (Query Boyle). Per bend embattled arg. and gu. Monsire John de Beawley. *Harl. MS. 1368. fo. 34.*

Beawpell. Add: John Beaupell. *Y.* Monsire Bewpell (co. Devon and Cornwall). *Y.*

Bechampe. *V.*

Beche (Berkshire). Add: Sir Johan de Beche. *N.* and with a label of 5 points az. Sir William Beche. *V.* arg. on a bend gu. 3 stag's heads couped or a martlet in chief sa. Sir John de la Beche. *L.*

Beche. *V.*

Beche. Vairy arg. and gu. in the dexter chief a martlet sa. Monsire Nichol de Beche. *Y.*

Beche. Vairy arg. and gu. on a canton of the second a garb of the first. Sir John Beche. *V.*

Becher (Kent). *V**.*

Beck (London). Quarterly or and sa. in the first quarter a blackbird sa. in the second and third a mullet or and in the fourth a pike fish in bend ppr. Crest: a blackbird ppr. *Vis. Lon. 1633.*

Beck (Upton, co. Chester). Or a raven ppr.

Beckering (Tuxford, co. Nottingham). Add: Sir Christopher Bekering. *R.*

Beckering. Chequy arg. and gu. a bend az. Sir Thomas de Bekerynge. *M.N.Y.*

Beckering. Chequy arg. and gu. a bendlet sa. William Bekering. *Blunt. V.*

Beckering. Chequy arg. and gu. on a chev. sa. three escallops or *W.* Add: Sir Thomas Bekeringe. *S.* The   arg.

Beckett (Norfolk). Arg. on a chev. gu. 3 roses of the first barbed vert. *Berry.*

Beckett. Or on a chev. betw. 3 lions heads erased gu. a fleur-de-lis of the first. *V.*

Beckett (Wiltshire). Add: *C.L.*

Beckingham (Kent). Arg. a chev. betw. 3 bucks heads cabossed gu. attired or. *V.* and *Cady.*

Beckingham. . . . 2 chevs. . . . betw. 3 stags heads cabossed . . . Seal of John de Beckingham 1385.

Beckingham. Barry of eight gu. and arg. on a canton &c. . . . Add: *V**.* The canton arg. *V.*

Beckley or Bistley. Add: *V.*

Beckley (Northcott, co. Devon). Arg. a chev. engr. betw. 3 ravens sa. *V. V**.*

Beckley (Norfolk). Arg. a chev. embattled betw. 3 griffins heads erased sa. each charged with a plate. *Blomfield.*

Beckmore. *V.**

Beckton. *V.V.**

Beckwith (Aldborough &c., York &c.). Add: Beckwith (Clint, co. York). *F.Y.* Roger Beckwith (co. York.) *Eliz. Roll xxxij.* Beckwith (Arkton, co. York). Arg. a chev. betw. 3 hinds heads erased gu. a crescent for diff.

Beckwith (Yorkshire). Arg. a chev. gu. fretty 'or' —substitute, arg. . . . (—delete 'both' engr.). Add: *Eliz. Roll xxj.*

Beckwith (Co. York). Arg. a chev. gu. fretty or betw. 3 hinds heads erased of the second. *Fairfax's Book of Arms.*

Beckwith (Handale Abbey, co. York). *Dugdale 383.*

Beckworth. Alias Smith (Collis). Sa. on a chev. arg. betw. 3 griffins heads erased or a boars head fesswise couped enclosed by 2 pheons gu. *V.*

Bedell (London). Gu. a chev. engr. betw. 3 escallops arg. a bordure of the last, a fleur-de-lis for diff. Crest: A stag's head erased ducally gorged or. *Vis. Lon. 1633.*

Bedewynd. . . . a chev. . . . Seal of Richard Bedewynd of Reading 1397.

Bedford. Paly of 6 arg. and gu. a bend az. *Syl. Morgan.*

Bedingfeld (Oxburgh, co. Norfolk, bart). Add: Sir Thomas Bedingfield, Norfolk. *V.* Sir Robert Bedingfield, Alderman of London 1703.

Bedingfield. Add: Bedingfield, London, descended from Bedingfield of Oxburgh. Same arms and crest. A mullet in an annulet for diff. *Vis. Lon. 1633.*

Bedle or Bedell (London). Gu. on a chev.—insert: 'engr.' betw. . . . *Vis. Lon. 1633.*

Bedle (London and Suffolk). Sa. on a fess arg. betw. 3 saltires couped or as many mullets gu. Crest: An arm couped at the elbow and erect in armour ppr. the hand grasping a cutlass by the blade all ppr. *Vis. Lon. 1633.*

Bedolfe (Co. Stafford). Arg. a chev. debruised betw. 3 crosses crosslet fitchy sa. *Harl. MS. 1404. fo. 114.*

Bedwell (Scotland). Az. on a chev. betw. three 3-foils slipped or a crescent gu. *Cady.*

Beecher. Insert: Shorne, Kent (granted 6 Oct. 1574) &c.

Beecher (London, *Vis. Lon. 1568*) &c. Add: Henry Beecher, Alderman of London. *V.* Sir William Beecher of Howbury, co. Beds. 1660? *L.N.*

Beekenshall (Lancashire). This really the coat of Ashton quartered by Beconshall. *Harl. MS. 1549. fo. 35; 1535. fo. 48b.*

Beere (Co. Kent). 1586. Arg. a bear ramp. sa. and a canton gu. *W.*

Beer. Az. a bend betw. 2 cotises arg. and 6 martlets or Sir Reynard de la Beer. *S.*

Beeston (Beeston, co. York). Sa. a chev. betw. 6 crosslets fitchy or *F.Y.*

Beeston. Sa. a bend betw. 6 bees volant en arriere arg. a crescent for diff. William Beestone. 1639. *V**.* Tomb in St. Mary's Church, Lambeth, Surrey. Add. *MS. 6409.*

Beices. Or a lion ramp. gu. crowned az. a bordure sa. bezanty. Hameris Beices. *A.*

Beighton (Wirksworth, co. Derby). Insert: Granted 1675.

Beiston. *V.*

Beke (Abbey White Knights, co. Berks.). Or 2 bars dancetty sa. on a chief az. 3 annulets arg. *V.*

Bekemore. Arg. on a bend sa. 3 pheons pointing to the dexter chief or. *V.*

Bekenore. Per fess az. and or in chief 3 lions ramp. in fess arg. crowned or. Jon de Bekenore. *A. Harl. MS. 6137.*

Bekering. See Beckering.

Bekins. Add: Walter Bekins. *Y.*

Belasyse (Earls of Fauconberg and Barons Belasyse of Worlaby, co. Lincoln). (see Bellasyse). Add: Belasyse (Newborough, co. York. Baronetcy 1611).

Bele. Insert: Canterbury. *V.*

Belesby (of Belesby, Sheriff of Lincolnshire, temp. Ric. ij.). Arg. a chev betw. 3 steel gads sa. *Fuller.*

Belesme. Az. a lion ramp. within a bordure or Roger de Belesme, Earl of Arundel and Shrewsbury. *V.*

Beley. Sa. on a chev. engr. betw. 3 eagles heads erased arg. as many hurts. Henry Beley, Abbot of Tewkesbury. *U.* Elected 1509. But *U. Ashmole. MS.* adds a chief or charged with a cross patty fitchy enclosed by 2 annulets gu.

Belford (Co. Kent). Arg. a chev. sa. in base a rose gu.

Belgrave. (North Kilworth and Belgrave, Leicestershire). Add: *C.C. 1619.*

Belgrave (Leicestershire). *V.*

Belhouse. Arg. 3 lions ramp. gu. within a bordure indented sa. Sir William de Bellehouse. *N.*

Belhouse or Belhus. Or on a bend gu. five lozenges vair. *V.*

Belhouse. Insert: Reigate, co. Surrey. Az. on a chev. or betw. three-insert: 'church' bells.

Belhouse. Or a saltire gu. Add: William Belhouse. *V.*

Belkemore. Gu. a bend within a bordure engr. arg. John Belkemore. *Y.*

Bell (Boston, co. Lincoln). . . . 3 church bells . . . **Seal.**

Bell (Lynn, Norfolk). Sa. a chev. betw. 3 church bells arg. *V. Cady.*

Bell (Gloucestershire). Insert: Sir Thomas Bell, Gloucester. *V.* He was thrice Mayor of Gloucester.

Bell. Gu. 4 bars arg. in chief a martlet **Monument** in Hartlepool Church co. Durham. *Surtees.*

Bell. Sa. a chev. betw. 3 bells and as many estoiles arg. in chief a crescent. *Robson.*

Bell (Kirkconnel, co. Dumfries). Az. three bells or. Add: Bell (Crawford, Middlesex). Same arms.

Bell (London). Az. an eagle displ. arg. in chief 3 fleurs-de-lis or. *Vis. Lon. 1633.*

Bellamy (London). Az. on a bend or cotised arg. 3 crescents az. This is in substitution for the printed reference: Sa. on a fess, which is deleted for the above. Crest: as here described. *Vis. Lon.1633.*

Bellas. Add: *Robson.*

Bellases (Loodworth). Same Arms Bellasyse or Belasyse &c. a crescent for diff. Richard Ballasis. *Eliz. Roll xix.*

Bellchamber or Bellschamber. *V.*

Bellenx. *V.*

Bellenden. Az. 9 martlets 3.3.2 and 1 arg. Sir John de Belleden. *N. Harl. MS. 4033.* But 14 martlets 3.3.2.3.2 and 1. *N. Harl. MS. 6137.*

Bellers. Add: *S.*

Bellers (Stoke). Per pale indented gu. and az. a lion ramp. arg. *V.*

Bellers. Insert: Keytilby.

Bellew. *V.*

Bellhouse. Arg. 3 lions ramp. gu. Sir John de Bellhous *L.N. Harl. MS. 6137.* Sir John de Belhouse, Essex temp. Edw. j. *V.*

Belliald (Thorpe, co. Northampton). Per chev. arg. and gu. billety counterchanged *V.**

Bellingham. Gu. 3 bendlets arg. on a canton of the first a lion ramp. arg. *V.**V.*

Bellingham. Arg. fretty gu. on a canton of the second a lion ramp. of the first. *V.**

Bellingham. Barry of 6 arg. and gu. on a canton of the second a lion pass. of the first. *V.*

Bellingham. Gu. fretty arg. on a canton of the first a lion ramp. of the second. *V.*

Bellingham (Newstead, co. Lincoln). Sa. fretty or on a chev. az. 3 lions heads erased of the second.

Belliston. *V.*

Belson (Aston Rowant, co. Oxford). Gu. on a chev. engr. betw. 3 greyhounds heads erased arg. collared or as many hurts. *V.O.*

Belsted (Norfolk). Barry of 6 arg. and sa. a canton quarterly or and of the first. *V.*

Belsted. Barry of six—Insert: or of 10 ar. and sa. &c. . . . *V.*

Belston (Co. Devon). Or on a bend gu. 3 crosses patty arg. t. Henry iij. *Lysons.*

Belt (Bossall Hall, co. York) &c. . . . Add: Belt (Overton, co. York 1665). Same arms. *Dugdale. p. 152.*

Beltoft. *V.*

Belton. *V.**

Belvale. Add: John Belvalle. *V.*

Belwood. Insert: Leathley, co. York 1665. Add: *Dugdale p. 213. V.*

Benbow (Newport, co. Salop) &c. . . . Add: Benbow of London. Clerk of the court 1623.

Bendall (Middlesex, granted 1629). Insert: by Sir George Clarencieux.

Bendesley. Per pale or and gu. a chev. betw. 3 escallops counterchanged. *V.*

Bendish (Stowmarket, Suffolk). Az. a chev. betw. 3 rams heads erased arg. attired or.

Bendish (Steeple Bumstead, co. Essex) &c. . . . amend 'rams' to read 'goats'. *Cady.*

Bendish (Topesfield Hall, co. Suffolk). Insert: and Southtown, Suffolk. Add: Sir Thomas Bendish. Ambassador from Charles j to the Grand Seigneur. *Cady.*

Bendish (Essex). Amend to read: Or on a chev. sa. betw. 3 goats heads erased az. as many escallops of the first. *V.*

Bewdley (Town of, in co. Worcester). Arg. an anchor az. the ring or the anchor surmounted by a fetter lock of the second within it a sword erect ppr. and a rose. gu.

Bendlowes (Essex). Add: William Bendlowes, Serjeant at Law. Same arms. *Dug. O. J.*

Bendlowes. Quarterly per fess indented or and gu. on a bend az. a 5 foil betw. 2 martlets of the first. *V.E. 1634.*

Bene. Arg. a chev. gu. within a bordure sa. bezanty. *Cady.*

Benefeld. Sa. a chev. betw. 3 martlets arg. Richard Benefeld.

Benger. Quarterly az. and arg. a bend vert. *Harl. MS. 1465. fo. 15.*

Benhall (Robert Benhall, temp. Richard II). Add:

Benington. Sa. a chev. betw. 3 lions heads erased or *V.V.**

Bennet (Cornwall). Gu. 3 demi-lions ramp. arg. *Lysons.*

Bennet (London). Add: John Bennett, Vintner, London. Granted by Cooke. *W.*

Bennett. Sa. a chev. erm. betw. 3 teazles or leaved vert. *Harl. MS. 1603.*

Bennet. Erm. an inescutcheon gu. over all a bend sa. William Bennet. *V.*

Bennet (Essex). Vert. on a chev. betw. 3 demi-lions ramp. or as many 5 foils az. *V.E. 1634.*

Bennett (Sir Thomas Bennett, Lord Mayor of London, *Camdens Grants*). Add: *Harl. MS. 1349.*

Bennett (Faringdon, co. Berks.). Add: Bennett (London). Same arms and crest, a crescent for diff. *Vis. Lon. 1633.*

Bennett. Arg. a chev. gu. betw. three torteaux. Add: Bennett (Lord Sherard, i.e. Bennett Sherard, Stapleton, co. Leicester). *Guillim.*

Bennett. Arg. three church bells &c. . . . Add: *V.V.**

Bennitt (Stourton Hall, co. Worcester). . . . Motto . . . Add: *X.A.*

Benolt. Insert: Calais. *V.*

Benson (London). Arg. on a chev. betw. 3 goats heads erased sa. as many escallops arg. Crest: A goats head erased per fess sa. and gu. charged with an escallop arg. *Vis. Lon. 1633.*

Benson. Arg. on a bend cotised gu. three 3-foils slipped vert. *Hoare.*

Benson (Charwelton, co. Northants 1670). Arg. on a chev. sa. betw. 3 antelopes heads erased of the second as many escallops of the first.

Benteley. *V.*

Bentham. Add: Bentham (co. Gloucester). *V.* Thomas Bentham, Bishop of Lichfield &c. 1460. Same arms.

Bentley. Arg. 2 bars and a canton sa. *V.V.**

Bentley. Arg. on a bend az. 3 annulets or. *V.*

Bentley. Or a bend vair betw. 2 cotises engr. sa.

Benyon (Esmondum, co. Sussex). Insert: and London. *Vis. Lon. 1633.*

Beram. Per pale sa. and arg. 3 bears statant counterchanged muzzled gu. *V.**

Beram (Kent). Or 3 bears statant in pale sa. *V.*

Beraston (Aldenham, co. Hertford). Granted, insert 'by Camden'.

Berden. Arg. an eagle displ. az. membered gu. Add: Wm. Berdene. *Y.*

Berdewell. Arg. a goat salient gu. armed or.

Bere. Per pale . . . muzzled gu. *V.*

Bereham. *V.**

Bereland or Beerland. *V.V.**

Berens (Kevington, co. Kent). Add: Berens (Chiselhurst, Kent). Granted in 1586. Same arms.

Beresford (Beresford, co. Stafford &c. &c.). Add: Beresford, London, Granted to Geo. Beresford by Wm. Hervy. 1563. Same arms and crest, and quartering, per chev. arg. and or 3 pheons sa. *Vis. Lon. 1633.*

Berew. Purp. a chev. arg. . . . Add: *V.* W.*

Berford. Erm. on a canton sa. a 5-foil or. *V.**

Berford. Arg. a chev. betw. 3 bears heads erased sa. muzzled arg. *Harl. MS. 1603.*

Bergami. . . . Arg. a chev. sa. betw. 2 cocks combatant in chief and a lion ramp. in base gu. *Robson.*

Berghope. Arg. a chev. az. *V.*

Bergis. Sa. 2 lions pass. guard. arg. crowned or. *Cady.*

Berhalgh. Arg. 3 bears pass. sa. muzzled or. Richard Berhalgh. *X.*

Berham (Lancashire). *V.**

Beriffe (Essex). *V.E. 1634.*

Berindon or Beringdon. Insert: *V.* before (another, or).

Beringham. Gu. 3 owls arg. Sir Ric. Beringham. *L.*

Beringham. Arg. on a bend gu. cotised sa. three escallops or Add: Sir Walter Beringham. *L.*

Beringham. Sa. a pile arg. over all a chev. counterchanged. Add: *V.*

Berington (Bradwell, co. Chester). Az. simply. *Harl. MS. 1535. fo. 8.*

Berington. Sa. 3 greyhounds courant arg. collared gu.

Berington (Winslow, co. Hereford). Sa. 3 greyhounds pass. in pale arg. *Dingley.*

Berington (Bradwell and Sandbach, co. Chester). Sa. 3 greyhounds courant in pale arg. collared gu. a bordure of the second.

Berkedon. *V.*

Berklay. Quarterly or and az. a bendlet purp. Giles de Berklaie. *F.*

Berkeley. Gu. a chev. erm. Roger Berkeley. *V.*

Berkeley (Lord Berkeley of Stratton &c. . . . .). Insert: Sire Moris de Berkeley. *S.*

Berkeley. Gu. a chev. arg. Moris de Berkele. *A. Harl. MS. 6137. B.D.* Thomas de Berkele. *E.F.*

Berkeley. Gu. crusilly and a chev. arg. Sir Thomas de Berkeley *G.H.Y.L.* and with a label az. Sir Thomas Berkeley the Son. *H.*

Berkeley. Gu. crusilly patty and a chev. arg. Sir Thomas de Berkeley. *L.* Sir Morice de Berkeley. *K.J.N.Y.* and with a label az. Morice de Berkeley. *K.*

Berkele. Gu. crusilly patty arg. on a chev. of the last a crescent az. Sir James Berkele. *S.*

Berkeley. Gu. crusilly patty arg. on a chev. of the last 3 fleurs-de-lis sa. *V.*

Berkeley. Az. 2 lions pass. or. *V.V.**

Berkeley (Beverstone, co. Gloucester). Add: *Harl. MS. 1603.*

Berkeley (Gilbert Berkeley, Bishop of Bath &c. . . .). Add: *Cotton MS. Cleopatra C. iij. fo. 36b.*

Berkeley. Gu. a chev. betw. ten roses—insert: 'or 5 foils' arg. Add: Berkeley of Wymondham, co. Leicester. Baronetcy 1611. *C.C. Harl. MS. 6183. fo. 5.*

Berkeley. Gu. a chev. betw. ten roses—insert: 'or 5 foils' arg. Add: Berkeley of Wymondham, co. Leicester. Baronetcy 1611. *C.C. Harl. MS. 6183. fo. 5.* Sir John Barkeley. *Q.S.*

Berkeley. Routland, co. Lincoln. Same arms. *V.*

Berkeley. Gu. a chev. arg. betw. 3 crosses patty or. Sire Johan de Berkeley. *N.*

Berkerolls. Az. a chev. or betw. three crescents arg. *V.** Add: Sir William Berkerolles, Lord of Coytie. temp. Edw. j. *V.* But the crescents or. *N.*

Berlingham (co. Essex). Barry of 6 gu. and arg. Sir John Berlingham. *V.*

Bermingham. Per pale indented or and gu.

Bermingham (Lord of Thremore). Add: Foulke Bermingham. *V.*

Bermondsey. Cluniac Abbey, co. Surrey. Per pale az. and gu. a bordure arg. *Tanner.*

Bernake. Erm. a bend gu. Add: Sir Richard Bernake. *V.*

Bernard (Earl of Bandon). Insert: Sir Henry Bernard (London) 1677. *L.N.*

Bernard (Abington, co. Northants.). Add: Robert Bernard, Serjeant at Law.

Berne. Arg. on a chev. betw. 3 dexter hands apaumy couped at the wrist sa. a cross crosslet or. *V.*

Berne. Sa. a chev. betw. 3 hands erect couped at the wrist arg. *Cady.*

Berners (Soham, co. Cambridge). Or 2 bars embattled counter-embattled gu. in chief 3 torteaux. *Robson.*

Bernham. Sa. three lions ramp. arg. Add: *V.*

Berningham (Norfolk). Add: Sir Waute de Beryngham. *N.V.Y.*

Berningham. Bendy of 10 gu. and or. *Harl. MS. 1603.*

Beronden. Gu. on a bend arg. three roses sa. Add: *V.* W.* Sire Gilbert de Borondone. *N.*

Berondon. Sa. on a bend arg. three 5-foils of the first. Sir John Berondon. *V.*

Berry (Cotton, co. Devon). Erm. on a bend az. 3 fleurs-de-lis or. *V.V.**

Berry (Burly, co. Devon). Add: *V.D. 1620.*

Berry (Ludlow, co. Salop). Erm. on a bend az. 3 fleurs-de-lis or a crescent for diff.

Berry (Penzance, co. Cornwall). Add: *V.**

Berry (Essex). Erm. on a bend engr. gu. 3 fleurs-de-lis or. *V.* co. Leicester 1619. *C.C.*

Berry. Quarterly erm. and az. . . . Add: Sir Adam de Barry. *V.*

Berryman (Devonshire). Add: *V.D.*

Berryman (Exeter). Arg. a chev. betw. 3 talbots sa. *Colby.*

Bertingham. Arg. on a bend betw. 2 cotises az. 3 escallops or. *Cady.*

Berton. Or 3 chevs. sa. *V.**

Bertant. Paly or and gu. on a canton az. a rowel arg. Sir Gauter Bertand. *C.*

Borwell. Az. on a bend or 3 mullet of the first. *V.*

Berwis. *V.V.**

Besill or Besills. V.

Benny. Quarterly, per fess indented gu. and or in the first quarter a lion pass. guard. ar. Add: Besney or Besyn. Same arms. *V.*

Best (Donnington, co. Berks). Arg. on 2 bars gu. 6 plates.

Best (John Best, Bishop of Carlisle 1561–70, granted by Dalton). Arg. on a chev. sa. betw. in chief 2 birds russet beaked and legged gu. and in base a book or in a black cover three pheons of the first. *Harl. MS. 1359. fo. 49.*

Besney (Hertfordshire). Add: and with a crescent on the shoulder for diff. Edward Bestney. Some. Co. Cambridge. *V.*

Bestley.

Beston (Buxton, co. Chester, 34th Edw. iij). . . . a bend . . . a label of 3 . . . **Seal** of Henry de Beston.

Beston. Vert. a lion ramp. arg. crowned gu. Add: Sire de Beston. *Y.V.*

Besville. *V.V.**

Betham. *W.*

Bethel. Arg. on a chev. betw. 3 boars heads truncked sa. a martlet of the field. *Drakes. York. 252.*

Bethome (Adwell, co. Oxford). Add: *V.O.*

Bethum. *V.** Add: Sir Richard de Bethum, co. Lancaster. *V.*

Betsworth (Tyning, co. Sussex). Az. a lion ramp. per fess. or and arg. on a canton gu. 2 lances in saltire of the third. Crest: A demi-lion supporting a broken lance or headed arg. *Visitation 1634.*

Bettenson (Seven Oaks, co. Kent). . . . All within a bordure engr. amend 'erm.' for 'az.'. Crest: . . . Collared—insert: *Vis. Lon. 1633.*

Bettesworth (Chidden in Hambledon, co. Hants. 1665). Az. a lion ramp. per fess or and arg. on a canton of the last a sword pomelled gold surmounted of a spear of the last.

Betts (Ermingbend, Norfolk). Sa. on a bend arg. betw. 2 cotises or. three 4-foils pierced gu. *Cady.*

Bettyston. *V.**

Betune. Or a lion ramp. sa. Monsire Robert de Betune. *D.*

Beumund. Sa. 9 martlets in orle arg. Sir Godfrey de Beumund. *F.*

Beurley. Or a chief gu. betw. 3 torteaux. *V.V.**

Beury or Bewry. Add: John Beuyr. *V.*

Bevan (Granted 1695—insert—by Sir George Clarencieux—to William Bevan &c. . . .).

Beveley. Insert: (Cornwall). . . . *V.V.**

Beveridge (Kent, Chichester and Normandy). Add: Thomas Beveridge, co. Chester 1595, granted by Lee. *W.*

Beverley. Arg. a chev. sa. betw. three ogresses. Add: *V.*

Beverley. Insert: 'Great Smeton', Yorkshire. Arg. a chev. sa. &c. . . . Add: *Dugdale. 1665.*

Beverley (Yorkshire—insert: 'and co. Chester'). Add: *V.*

Beverley. Insert: co. Derby. Arg. a chev. sa. betw. three—delete: Pales, substitute 'pellets'. Add: *V.*

Beverly. Insert: co. Derby. Arg. a chev. gu. betw. three hurts.

Bevile. *V.*

Bevot. Or Beavot (Leeds, co. York. 1665). Sa. a chev. engr. erm. betw. 3 wolves heads erased arg. *Dugdale. p. 26.*

Bewchamp. Bendy gu. and erm. *Cady.*

Bewellez (Suffolk). Or a lion ramp. gu. *Cady.*

Bewick. Per bend or and gu. a billet arg. betw. three boars heads couped sa. *Harl. MS. 1404. fo. 132.*

Bewley (Kent). Add: *V.*

Bewley (London). Erm. on a canton arg. an orle gu. *Vis. Lon. 1633.*

Bewley. Arg. a chev. betw. 3 herons heads erased sa. *V.** and beaked gu. *V.*

Bewris or Bewrys. Add: *V.*

Bexwell. Arg. six annulets sa. &c. . . . Add: *Harl. MS. 1458.*

Beyfeard. Add: *V.*

Beykle. *V.**

Biancourt. Gu. a bend engr. arg. *Syl. Morgan.*

Biblesworth. Az. 3 eagles displ. or *Y.* Walter de Biblesworth *E.Y.* Sir Walter Biblesworth temp. Edw. j. *V.* Sire Hugh de Biblesworth. *N.*

Bickerdyke. Add: Crest: on a wreath or and gu. an eagle displ. vert.

Bickerton (Bickerton, co. Chester 1330). Add: *V.*

Bickerton (Roden, co. Salop). Sa. on a chev. arg. 3 pheons of the field.

Bickerton (Essex and Beby, co. Leicester). Add: *C.C. 1619.*

Bickerton (Essex and Beby, co. Leicester). Add: *C.C. 1619.*

Bickerton (Upwood, co. Huntingdon, bart—insert: 1778 . . . Sa. on a chev. or—substitute 'erminois' (*Berry*) three pheons of the first—substitute 'az.'.

Bickerton (That Ilk, and Lufness, Scotland). Add: *Guillim.*

Bickham (Leicester, 1781). . . . a chev. gu. betw. 3 leopards faces az. on a chief per fess arg. and gu. in the upper part a greyhound sa.

Bickley (Bickleigh, co. Devon and Sussex &c. . . .). Add: *Vis. Lon. 1633.*

Bickleigh (Co. Devon). Arg. a bend engr. betw. 3 crows sa. *Lysons.*

Bicklonde. Gu. 2 lions ramp. arg. a quarter sa. fretty or. John Bicklonde. *Y.*

Bicknor. Az. 6 lions ramp. or a dexter baston gu. *W.V.**

Biddulph (Elmhurst, co. Stafford &c. . . . co. Warwick bart.). Insert: 1664.

Bigbury (Bigbury, co. Devon). Add: *V.*

Bigod (Settrington, co. York). Per pale or and vert. a lion ramp. gu. quartering or on a cross engr. gu. 5 escallops arg. and or a bend sa. *F.Y.*

Bigod. Le Conte Mareschal. *P.V.** Roger Bigod Counte Mareschal. *H.* But Conte de Norfolk. *Y.X.*

Bigot. Gu. a lion pass. or. Hugh le Bigot *B.C.*

Bigot.

Billesby. Insert: co. Lincoln. Arg. a chev. betw. three stone bills insert: 'picks for querns' sa. Add: *Visitation 1562. Cady.*

Billesdon. Az. 4 bendlets gemelled and in the sinister chief an eagles head erased or. Sir Robert Bilisden. *Harl. MS. 1349.* Sir Nicholas Bilsdon temp. Edw. iv. *Harl. MS. 6137. fo. 44.*

Billeston. *V.** Add: Sir Robert Billesdon, Haberdasher, Lord Mayor of London. ? *V.*

Billing or Billinge. Insert: co. Cornwall.

Billingsley (London). Add: *Vis. Lon. 1633.*

Billington. Per pale or and az. on a chev. betw. 3 fleurs-de-lis two bars gemelle all counter changed. *L.N. p. 226.*

Bilney (Norfolk). Add: Monsire de Bilney. *Y.* Sir Roger de Bilney *N.L.V.* William Bylney. *Y.*

Bindlosse (Borwick, co. Lancaster). Insert: Bart., 1641. &c. . . .). Add: *V.L.*

Bingham (Binghams—Melcombe, co. Dorset &c. . . .) insert: Robert Byngham, co. Dorset. *V.*

Bingham (Kent). Visit. co. Notts. 1614. &c. . . .). Add: *Vis. Lon. 1633.*

Bingham. Per pale arg. and sa. a lion ramp. or armed gu. (another, the lion crowned or). Add: *V.*

Bingley. (Blyth, Nottinghamshire. Visit 1614). Add: Bingley (London). Same Arms and crest, except that the canton sa. is charged with a cross patty arg. surmounted by an annulet gu. *Vis. Lon. 1633.*

Binning (London). Gu. 3 boars heads erased in pale arg. *Vis. Lon. 1633.*

Birch. Arg. on a bend gu. 3 bucks heads cabossed or a label of 5 arg. *V.**

Birch (Birch Hall). . . . Amend crenelle 'or' to read arg. *Vis. Lon. 1633.* Add: Sir John Birch Baron of the Exchequer. *Dug. O.J.*

Birch (Garnstone, co. Hereford, descended from Birch of Birch Hall). Same arms—Add: 'but the chief or'.

Birche. Add: Birche (Essex). Same arms. *V.*

Bird (Over and Nether Lockoe, co. Derby). Sa. a chev. embattled and counter embattled arg. *Lysons.*

Bird (1606). Add: *V.* Add: Granted to Sir William Bird, Doctor of Laws, by Camden, March 1606. He was Dean of the Arches in 1619.

Birmingham Borough of. **Book Plate.**

Birmingham. Az. a bend engr. or Sir William Birmingham *I.N.O.J.E.F.* Sir Thomas Berming-ham. *L.* and with a label gu. Sir Thomas de Bermyngham. *N.* the label of 5 points. Sir Thos. Bermingham, co. Worcester. *V.*

Birom. (Hulland and Ashbourne-green.) Insert: co. Derby. . . .

Biron. Gu. three bends arg. (another adds a label az.). Add: *A.* Add: Sir James Birun. *A. and Harl. MS. 6137.*

Birton. . . . gutte d'eau. Add: *V.*

Birtwesil. Add: *V.L.*

Bisburg. Arg. 2 bars each cotised sa. *V.*

Bishbury. Arg. 2 bars sa. each closetted of the same. Henry Bisbery. *V.*

Bishop (Dorsetshire and Somersetshire). Insert: Granted by Segar 1627. Add: *Vis. Lon. 1633.* Add: Bishop of Hollway, co. Dorset. *Guillim.* Bishop (Parham, Sussex. Baronetcy 1620). Same arms.

Bishop (Norfolk). Same arms. Add: Granted by Segar 1628.

Bishop (Sedlescombe, co. Sussex). Quarterly sa. and or in the second and third quarters a lion ramp. of the first over all on a bend or 3 escutcheons sa. *Topographer and Genealogist iij. 368.*

Bishop. Arg. on a bend cotised gu. 3 bezants. *Cady.*

Bishop (Norfolk). Same arms. *W.*

Bishop (Co. Salop). Erm. on a bend gu. betw. 2 cotises . . . 3 bezants. *W.*

Bishop (Co. Lincoln). Arg. on a bend betw. 2 cotises gu. 3 plates 1640. *Yorke.*

Bishoppe (Bristol, co. Somerset). Add: *V.**

Bishopsdale. Bendy of 8 or and gu. *Randle Holme.*

Bishopsdon. Or 4 bendlets az. a canton erm. *V.** Sir John Bishopsdon. *V.Y.* But bendy or and az. a canton erm. *N.*

Bishopton (Warwickshire). *V.*

Bishopton. Bendy of ten or and sa. Add: Sir William de Bisshopesdonne *F.* but Bissopestor *E.*

Biskell. Arg. 2 lions ramp. gu. on a canton sa. a fret or. *Robson.*

Biskell. Quarterly or and sa. a bend gu. Sire . . . de Biskelle. *V.*

Bissett (Co. York). Gu. on a bend arg. 3 escallops sa. *V.V.**

Bissett. Gu. on a bend arg. 3 escallops sa. a label of 3 points per pale az. and or Sir William Bissett. *V.*

Bisset. Az. on a bend or three escallops gu. Add: *V **

Bistley or Bestley. Arg. a chev. engr. sa. betw. three cornish choughs ppr. *V.*

Biston (Belton, co. Lincoln, *Vis. Lon. 1568*). Add: . . . fleur-de-lis of the second 'for diff.' *C.L.*

Biston. Sa. a bend betw. 6 crosses crosslet bottony or. *Constable's Roll. xij.*

Biston, Byston or Beiston (Beeston, co. Yorks). Sa. a bend or betw. 6 crosses crosslet bottony arg. Ralph Beiston. *Eliz. Roll. xxiv.*

Bix. Gu. a chev. or within a bordure vair. *Add. MS. 5507. fo. 387.*

Blabey or Blabley (Co. Leicester). Add: *V.**

Blackborn (Sussex). Add: *Syl. Morgan.*

Blackborne. Arg. on a bend sa. a lozenge of the first charged with a saltire gu. *Cady. Constable's Roll. xiij.*

Blackborne (Co. York. temp. Edw. ij.). Arg. on a bend sa. 3 lozenges of the first each charged with a saltire gu. *F.Y.*

Blackbourne. Gu. a lion ramp. erm. fretty sa. *V.V.**

Blackenham or Blakenham (Suffolk). Add: Sire Thomas de Blakenham. *N.*

Blackett. Az. a bend betw. 2 cotises and 6 crosses crosslet fitchy or.

Blackett (Woodcroft). Az. a chev. betw. 3 mullets sa. *Eliz. Roll. xviij.*

Blackett (Wylam, co. Northumberland). Add: Blackett (Newcastle-on-Tyne, Baronetcy 1684). Same arms.

Blackham. (London, Baronetcy 1696). Arg. 2 bars betw. 9 crosses crosslet . . . or? arg. *Robson.*

Blackleech (London). Barry of 6 sa. and or. Crest: A hawk ppr. billed or. *Vis. Lon. 1633.*

Blackman (London and East Indies). Erm. amend to read: 'Ermines'.

Blacknell (Warwickshire and Berkshire). Add: Sir John de Blacknall amend, co. Warwick. *V.*

Blacksmiths. Company of (London). Add: Granted 12. ap. 1490.

Blackstone (Castle Priory, Wallingford, co. Berks.). Add: Blackstone (Newcastle-upon-Tyne). Same arms. *V.* Blackstone (Gibside, Baronetcy 1642). *Guillim.*

Blackwall (Blackwall, in the Peak, co. Derby &c.). Add: Blackwall (London). *Vis. Lon. 1633.*

Blackwell (Sprouston Hall, co. Norfolk). Add: *Vis. Lon. 1633.*

Blackwell. Per pale arg. and az. on a chief gu. a lion pass. guard. or all within a bordure erm. *L.N. p. 459.*

Bladlow. Per chev. arg. and sa. in chief. . . . with 8 fleurs-de-lis Add: *V.*

Bladwell (Suffolk). Add: *Vis. Lon. 1633.*

Blage. Arg. a chev. betw. 3 garbs sa. *V.**

Blagge. Arg. 2 bendlets engr. gu. Robert Blagge, Baron of the Exchequer. 1512. *V.*

Blair. Hunter . . . bart, insert: 1786.

Blake (Suffolk). Gu. a pale sa. on a bend or three martlets of the second. *V.*

Blake (Wiltshire). . . . Crest: . . . Add: *Vis. Lon. 1633. W.* Add: Sir Richard Blake, London 1675 "ye King's tayler," *L.N.* Robert Blake, Generall at Sea, buried in Henry vij chapel, 4 Sept. 1687. *V.S.*

Blake or Rich. Arg. a chev. az. betw. 3 garbs . . . bound or. *Collinson Somerset j. 260.*

Blake. Per chev. az. and arg. . . . in base a bat displ. . . . *V.*

Blakeden (Cuthbert Blakeden. Sergeant of the Confectionery to Henry viij). Erm. 3 lions ramp. gu. within a bordure engr. *In Thames Ditton Church, Surrey.*

Blaket. Gu. a chev. vair. Sir John Blaket co. Buckingham. *V.*

Blaket. Gu. a chev. vert. Sire Johan Blaked. *N.*

Blakeney. . . . Motto . . . ab alto. Add: *V.*

Blakeney. Az. a chev. arg. betw. 3 leopards heads or. *V.*

Blaker (°Salisbury). 1613. Add: By Segar Garter.

Blaket (Gloucestershire). delete: (another six). Add: Sir Edmund Blaket. *V.*

Blaket (Cos. Gloucester, Notts. and Hereford &c.). Add: Sir John Blaket. *V.*

Blaket. Or on a chev. betw. three mullets . . . Add: *V.*

Blakingham (Suffolk). *V.*

Blakiston (Blakiston, co. Durham &c. . . .). Add: Sir Matthew Blakiston, Lord Mayor of London. 1760. Baronetcy 1763.

Blakiston (London, bart). Add: Blakiston (Seaton, co. Durham). *Surtees.*

Blakwell. Insert: co. Derby. Add: *V.*

Blamore. Arg. a lion ramp. gu. within an orle of the second on a canton az. a pierced mullet or. Crest: An heraldic tiger sejant la. ducally gorged and lined or. Motto: "superna tunc terrena."

Blanchard (Wiltshire and Somersetshire). Add: *Collinson Somerset. j. 139.*

Blanshard (Redcar, co. York). Same arms.

Bland (Kippaz Park, co. York). Add: *Dugdale p. 350.*

Bland (Co. York). Arg. on a bend sa. three pheons or. *Eliz. Roll. xxviij.*

Bland. Gu. 2 bars or an orle of martlets of the last. John Blande. *Y.*

Bland (Blandsfort, Queen's co.). Add: Bland (London). *Vis. Lon. 1633.*

Blanson. Per saltire az. and gu. 3 annulets or on a chief arg. a fret sa. Add: *V.**

Blandson. Per saltire az. and gu. over all 3 annulets or a chief of the last fretty vert. *Harl. MS. 1458.*

Blanson. Per saltire gu. and az. in the first 3 annulets or on a chief arg. a fret sa. (of fretty sa.). *Harl. MS. 1465.*

Blanton. *V.V.**

Blashford (London). Barry wavy of 6 or and gu. on a chief az. 3 pheons of the first for diff. Crest: A swan's head and neck arg. *Vis. Lon. 1633.*

Blaumester. *V.**

Blaxton (Hetton on the hill). Arg. 2 bars and in chief 3 cocks gu. on the upper bar a mullet of the field for diff. *Eliz. Roll. xx.*

Blayds (Oulton House). Insert: and Leeds. Add: *Whitaker's Leeds.*

Blencowe (Marston St. Lawrence, co. Northampton). Insert: temp. Hen. vi. Add: *W.*

Blenkinsop (Holbeche). Gu. 6 annulets or within a bordure engr. arg.

Blenkinsop (Cumberland). Same arms.

Blennerhassett (Ballyseed, co. Kerry &c. . . .).

Bleverhassett (Suffolk). Same arms. *V.*

Bleton. Az. on a bend arg. 3 crosses moline gu. John de Bleton. *V.*

Blewet (Hampshire). Add. Sir John Blewett, co. Hants. temp. Edw. j. *V.*

Blewett. Or a chev. betw. 3 eagles displ. vert. Sir. Walter Blewet, co. Gloucester temp. Edw. j. *V.* or Bluet. *N.*

Blewett. Insert: cos. Devon and Cornwall. Or a chev. betw. 6 eagles displ. vert. Add: V.

Blighe (Tapsham, co. Devon). Arg. 3 martlets betw. 2 bendlets gu. and as many red roses stalked and leaved vert.

Bliss (Brandon Park, Suffolk). Per bend sa. and gu. a bend lozengy arg. and az. betw. 4 fleurs-de-lis or.

Bliss or Blisse (Market Harborough, co. Leicester). &c. Add: *V.*

Blisworth. Co. York. temp. Edw. ij. Arg. 2 bars gu. in chief 3 torteaux. *F. Y.*

Blithe (Lincolnshire). Add: *Visitation. 1562.*

Blois (William de Blois, Earl of Montaigne &c.). . . . on a chief—insert: or . . . of the first. Add: Membered az.

Blodlow. Arg. a chev. sa. betw. 3 griffins heads erased gu.

Blofeld (Lynn, Norfolk 1672). Arg. a chev. gu. betw. 3 trefoils slipped vert.

Blome (Seven Oaks, co. Kent). Add: *Vis. Lon. 1633.* Add: The arms of Richard Blome "the undertaker of Guillim's 'Display of Heraldry'". *Guillim.*

Blomefield. Sa. . . . three-insert: 'broom' . . . Add. The Rev. Francis Blomefield the historian of Norfolk.

Blonfyld. Or 3 pales gu. a canton erm. *Robson.*

Blount (Soddington, co. Worcester, bart). Add: William Blount. *Y.E.T.*

Blount (Tittenhanger, co. Herts.). Same arms. *Guillim.*

Blount (Co. Salop and London). Barry nebuly of 6 or and sa. quartering arg. a lion ramp. gu. crowned or a bordure engr. sa. bezanty. a mullet over all for diff. *C.L.*

Blount or Blunt (Essex). Insert: Sir Thomas Blount. *S.* Sir William Blount, Essex. *V.* Sire Hugh Blount temp. Edw. j. *V.* Sire Huge le Blount. *N.E.*

Blount (Gloucester). Add: *V.* Crest: a lion sejant erm. crowned or. *Vis. Lon. 1633.*

Blount. Quarterly arg. and gu. on a bend sa. three crosses crosslet fitchy or. Thomas Blount. *X.*

Blount. Chequy arg. and gu. a bendlet sa. William Blount. *Y.*

Blower (West Ham, co. Essex, granted in 1570). Or a chev. vert. betw. 3 pomeis. *V.E. 1634.*

Bloy. Arg. on a chev. az. 3 griffins gu. Sire Adam de Bloy. *O.*

Bloys (Ipswich, co. Suffolk). Add: confirmed by Segar.

Bloys (Grandisborough, Suffolk). Baronetcy 1686. Same arms.

Bludworth (Co. Norfolk). Chequy arg. and sa. on a bend of the first 3 eagles displ. of the second. **Brass** in Tasebury church, Norfolk. The field or and sa. and a bend or *Cady.*

Bluet (Holcombe-Regis, co. Devon). Add: *Collinson Somerset iij. 29.*

Bluett (Broadclist, co. Devon). Same arms. *V.D. 1620.*

Bluett. Or an eagle displ. gu. Sir John Bluett G.L.N. Sir John Blewett, co. Hants. *V.*

Blundell (Ince Blundell, co. Lancaster &c.). Add: Robert Blundell. *E.F.*

Blundell. Per pale erm. and sa. a chev. counterchanged. Add: *V.*

Blundell (Harlington, co. Bedford). Add: *V.*

Blundell (Crosby, co. Lancaster). Sa. ten billets arg.—insert—4.3.3. and 1. and at end. *V.L.*

Blundell (Preston, co. Lancaster). Add: *V.L.*

Blunt (Ewe, Salop). Or 2 bars nebuly sa.

Blunt (Sheriff of Newcastle 1548). Sa. 3 bars nebuly or. *Carr MS.*

Blyford (Norfolk). Quarterly arg. and gu. on a bend sa. three mullets of the first. *Cady.*

Blygfeld. Arg. on a bend sa. 3 plates. Sire Thomas Blygfeld. *S.*

Blyth (Granted to Benjamin Blyth of Magdalen College, Oxford, 1859). Per fess az. and gu. a lion pass. and in chief two stags trippant or.

Blythe. Erm. 3 stags at gaze gu. John Blythe (Bishop of Salisbury 1493).

Blyth. Thomas Blyth, (Quarreby and Barnby, co. York 1566). *W.*

Blythe. Arg. a chev. gu. betw. 3 lions ramp. sa. Dr. Sam Blythe, Master of Clare Hall, Cambridge, 1713.

Blythe (London). Erm. on a fess gu. 3 lions ramp. or. Crest: a lion sejant gu. *Vis. Lon. 1633.*

Blythe (Yorkshire). Erm. three bucks gu. attired &c....

Blythe (Barnby and Rotherham, co. York). 1585. Same arms, quartering Stapleton, Sir Philibert, Aldeburgh. Goddard and Rampston. *F.J.*

Boade (Essex). Sa. 2 chevs. betw. 12 escallops, 6.3. and 3. arg. *V.E. 1558.*

Board (Co. Worcester). Quarterly gu. and sa. three martlets arg. *Nash.*

Boardman. Arg. a chev. vert. bordered gu. Crest: &c. Add: *Randle Holme.*

Bockerell (Andrew Bockerell, Lord Mayor of London). Sa. 2 bucks courant arg. within an orle of bezants. *V.*

Boking (Suffolk). *V.*

Bockmonster. see Buckmaster.

Bodelly. .... thereon three square buckles ... Add: The buckles round. *V.*

Bodelsgate (Cornwall). Gu. delete within the bracket another az. Add: *V.*

Bodkin (Recorder of Dover 1834). Arg. a bend gu. betw. 3 crosses crosslet sa. within a bordure of the second. *Debrett.*

Bodleigh. Add: *V.**

Bodleigh (Co. Devon). Sa. a goat salient arg. attired or. *W.*

Bodley or Bodlegh. Add: *V.*

Bodmin Monastery (Cornwall). Add: *Tanner.*

Bodrigan or Bodrugan. .... about 1331 insert. *Y.* &c....

Boevey. Or on a chev. sa. 5 plates.

Boffrey. *V.*

Bogge (Scotland). Add: *Guillim.*

Bogle. Or on a chev. gu. betw. 2 roses in chief and a demi-lion in base a crescent therefrom issuing a cross crosslet fitchy ... betw. two plates.

Bohun or Boun. Az. a bend arg. betw. 6 lions ramp. or Sire Edmond de Boun. *O.*

Bohun (Earls of Hereford, Essex &c....) Add: *Z.143.* Sir Henry de Boun *B.H.* with a label gu. Humphrey de Bohun *V.H.B.D.E.J.L.N.P.K.C. G.*

Bohun or Boone (Lincoln). Add: Philibert Bohun. *V.* Sire Gilbert de Boun *N.E.*

Bohun (Tressingfield, co. Suffolk). Add: *V.*

Bohun. Az. a bend arg. cotised or. Add: Humphrey Bohun. *K.*

Bohun. Az. a bend erm. betw. 2 cotises arg. and 6 lions ramp. or. Sir Humphrey de Bohun. *N. Harl. MS. 6137.* Sire Omfrey de Boun. *N.*

Bohun. Az. a bend betw. 2 cotises arg. and 6 lions ramp. or. Joan de Boun. *E.* Sire Henri de Boun. *N.*

Bohun. Bohun, az. on a bend arg. cotised or betw. six lions ramp. of the third, three mullets gu. delete— (another sa.). Add: William Bohun, Earl of Worcester. *Q.V.*

Bohun (Essex). Arg. a bend betw. 2 cotises and 6 lions ramp. sa. *V.*

Bohun. Az. a bend per bend indented arg. and gu. between two cotises of the second and 6 lions ramp. or. Sir Edmond de Bohun. *N.*

Bokeland. An eagles head ... Crest ... Add. *V.**

Bokeland. Insert (Scotland). Arg. an eagle displ. reguard ... and Add: *V.*

Bokynham (Suffolk). Or a lion ramp. gu. over all on a bendlet az. 3 bezants. *V.*

Bolbeck. Add: Sire Hugh de Bolbecke. *B.Y.*

Bold. Arg. two chev. gu. on a canton of the second a cross patonce or. Add: *V.** The cross patty. *V.** Sir John de Bold, co. Lancaster. *V.*

Boldington. Add: *V.*

Boleche, Boloch and Boleigh. Add: *V.V.**

Boleigh. Arg. on a chev. gu. betw. 3 torteaux as many bezants. *Cady.*

Bolehouse. Arg. 3 lions ramp. gu. *Cady.*

Bolein. (Salle co. Norfolk). Arg. a chev. gu. betw. 3 bulls heads couped *Cady.*

Boleyn. Arg. a lion pass. sa. .... Add: *V.V.**

Bolhall or Bolhalth. Sa. a chev. arg. a canton erm. Add: *V.*

Bolhalth. Sa. a chev. arg. and canton or. *Cady.*

Bolhalth. Arg. a chev. sa. and canton erm. *V.**

Boliers. Sa. billetty and a bend arg. Bandwyn Boliers. *A. Harl. MS. 6137. A.* Bandwin de Boulers. *F.*

Bolingbroke. .... on a chev. ... betw. 3 mullets ... another mullet. Seal. *Harl. MS. 1497. fo. 306.*

Bolitho (Exeter). .... a chev. ... betw. 3 fleurs-de-lis. *Colby.*

Boldworth. Or a lion ramp. purp. collared arg. Sir William Bolkworthy. *L.*

Bolle. Alias Bolles (Worthin, co. Suffolk) granted 1528, insert— by Benolt, Clarencieux ... Add: *Guillim.*

Bolle or Bolls. Arg. 3 annulets gu. a chief indented vert. *Cady.*

Bolle or Bolles (Wortham, co. Stafford). Arg. a chev. gu. betw. 3 mullets sa. on a chief of the third a lions head erased enclosed by 2 lozenges or. *V.*

Bolles (Co. Cambridge, temp. Edw. vj.). Arg. on a chev. betw. 3 boars heads couped sa. as many escallops or a bordure vert. bezanty. *Fuller.*

Boller. Arg. a chev. gu. betw. three bull's heads cabossed sa. Add: *V.*

Bolletis. Gu. a bend fusily or. *V.*V.*

Bolliers. Sa. billetty and a bend arg. Bandwin Bollers. *A. Harl. MS. 6137. A.* Bandwin de Boulers. *V.* but with a bendlet. Bandwin de Boulers. *E.*

Bolling (Rev. Edward James. ....). Add: *Vis. Lon. 1633.*

Bollingbroke. Insert-co. Lincoln. Sa. a chev. betw. three pillars or.

Bolney (Bolney, Sussex 1541). Add: Crest granted in 1541.

Bolron. .... With a savage's head. Add: *V.*

Bolron. Insert—co. Chester. Arg. a bend lozengy betw. six hammers ... Crest: ... Add: *V.*

Bolron. Arg. a bend betw.—insert—5 or—6 lozenges ... *V.V.**

Bolter (South Creake, co. Norfolk). insert— *Visitation 1613.*

Bolter. Arg. on a chev. gu. .... Add: *Randle Holme.*

Bolton (Co. York). Arg. on a chev. gu. 3 lions pass. guard. of the first. *V.*

Bolton or Boulton. Arg. on a chev. gu. 3 lions pass. guard. or Robert de Boulton. *Y.*

Bolton (Woodbridge, co. Suffolk). Granted 26. Aug. 1615—insert—by *Camden.*

Bolton (Bolton, co. Lancaster). Sa. a hawk arg. insert—billed arg. *X.*

Bolton, Borough of, co. Lancaster. **Book Plate.** q.v.

Bolton (Offord Cluny, co. Hunts). Sa. a hawk arg. billed or *V.H.*

Bolton (Lord Mayor of London 1667). Same arms, *X.* A mullet for diff. *Vis. Lon. 1633.*

Boltune. Arg. on a bend sa. 3 eagles displ. or. John de Boltune. *G.*

Bomvilers. Sa. a bend betw. 9 billets arg. 4 and 5. V. Bandwyn de Bonvylers. *V.*

Bonam. Gu. a chev. vair betw. 3 crosslets fitchy arg. *Cady.*

Bomuster. Arg. on a bend betw. 2 crosses patty fitchy gu. 3 bezants. *Cady.*

Bonaventor. Per pale az. and or a chev. vair betw. 3 lions ramp. counterchanged. *Cady.*

Bond (Brookland, Mosbury, co. Devon). Arg. on a chev. sa. 3 bezants. *V.*

Bond (Sir George Bond, Lord Mayor of London 1587). Add: *Vis. Lon. 1633.*

Bond (Thorpe, co. Surrey). Add: William Bond. *V.* Bonde, Clerk of the Green Cloth. *V.* John Bond ob. 1578. The crosslet patonce sa. Anthony Bond 1576.

Bonde (Coventry, co. Warwick). . . . Add: *V.*

Bone. Gu. billetty or. 3 lions ramp. arg. Joan de Bone. *E.*

Bonefeld. Arg. a chev. betw. 3 quinces . . . Add: *V.**

Bonefield or Bonefeld. Az. a chev. betw. 3 pears pendent or sa. for diff. *Cotton MS. Tiberius D.10.*

Bonham (bart—insert—1852).

Bonham (Essex). Gu. a chev. wavy betw. 3 crosses patty fitchy arg. *V. Harl. MS. 1542.*

Bonham. Gu. on a chev. betw. 3 crosses patty fitchy arg. a chev. wavy sable. *V.*

Bonham (Orsett House, co. Essex). . . . Add: *V.E. 1634.*

Boningham. Sa. a chev. or betw. 3 fleurs-de-lis arg. *V.** Sir . . . de Boningham. *V.*

Bonney. Arg. a chev. betw. 3 goats heads erased sa. *Eliz. Roll. xxi.*

Bonton. Add: *V.*

Bonvill. Sa. 6 mullets arg. pierced gu. a beacon az. *V.*

Bonvile (Bonvile). Or on a bend sa. 3 mullets arg. pierced or Sir John Bonville. *Y.*

Bonvile (Devonshire). Or on a bend sa. three mullets arg.—delete—(another or). Add: Sire Nicholas Boneville. *O.V.*

Bonvillers. Arg. a bend betw. 8 billets sa. *V.*

Bonytham. Arg. a chev. betw. 3 fleurs-de-lis sa. Add: *V.*

Boodam (Co. Lincoln 1660). Per pale gu. and erm. an eagle displ. or.

Boode (Essex). Add: *V.E. 1558.*

Booker (Vilindra, co. Glamorgan). Per pale or and vert. an eagle displ. within a bordure charged with 4 roundles and as many fleurs-de-lis all counterchanged. *Nicholas.*

Booker or Boocher (London). The same. But with eight fleurs-de-lis, Add: and the eagle crowned not gorged. *Vis. Lon. 1633.*

Bookey. Gu. on a bend arg. . . . Add: In Thanet Church, Kent. *Robson.*

Boone. Az. on a bend arg. cotised or. betw. six lions ramp. of the last 3 escallops gu. Gilbert Boone. Serjeant at Law. *Dug. O.J.*

Boord. *Harl. MS. 5844* and *MS. of heraldic miscellanies c. 1600* gives trick of arms of "Boordle Doctor".

Boorne (Essex). or 3 squirrels sejant ppr. on a chief gu. 3 crosses patty of the field. *V.E. 1634.*

Boothby (Broadlow Ash, co. Derby, bart.). Add:

Boothby. Boothby (Chingford, co. Essex. Baronetcy 1660). Same arms.

Boothby (London). Arg. on a canton sa. a lions gamb. erased in bend or. *Vis. Lon. 1633.* Crest: A lions gamb erased and erect per fess indented or and sa.

Bootle-cum-Linacre (Borough of, co. Lancaster, granted 4th Nov. 1869). Arg. on a chev. betw. 3 fleurs-de-lis az. as many stags heads cabossed or on a chief sa. 3 mural crowns of the field. Crest: Upon a rock a lighthouse ppr. Motto: Respice Aspice Prospice.

Booth. Vairy arg. and gu. a bendlet of the second. Sir William Booth. *R.*

Bordrouch. Vert. a bordure arg. *Randle Holme.*

Borefeild. Add: *Y.*

Boreston or Borreston. Add: Granted by Camden 1606 to Philip Boreston.

Borgillon. Quarterly or and gu. over all a bend sa. betw. 6 annulets, 3 in each of the second and third quarters 2 and 1 arg. Sire Robert Borgyloun. *N.*

Borgilon. Quarterly or and gu. over all a bend sa. betw. 2 annulets one in each of the second and third quarters arg. Sir Robert Bourgillon. *N. Harl. MS. 6137.* The annulets or. *V.*

Borington. Quarterly or and gu. on a bend sa. two mullets arg. *Cady.*

Borlase (Cornwall, originally of Borlase in the parish of St. Wenn). . . . *V.** Add: Borlase (St. Newlyne, Cornwall). Same arms. *V.*

Borman (Devonshire and Somersetshire). Insert: *V.S.*

Borne. Erm. on a bend az. 3 lions ramp. or. Sir John de Borne. *A. Harl. MS. 6137.*

Borne (London). Arg. on a chev. betw. 3 lions ramp. sa. a crescent for diff. a chief ermines. Crest: a demi-dragon gu. holding a marigold slipped and leafed or. *Vis. Lon. 1633.*

Borne. Erm. a bend az. Add: John de Borne. *A.*

Borough (Middlesex). Erm. 2 chevs. sa. betw. 3 chaplets gu. *V.*

Borowe. Add: *Cady*

Borrett (Kent). Barry of 4 arg. and gu.

Borwash. see Burghers.

Boscawen (Cornwall). Vert. a bull argent attired and unguled or. on a chief erm. a rose gu. *Lysons.*

Boshall. Sa. a chev. arg. and canton erm. *V.*

Boslingthorp or Boselingthorp (Lincolnshire). . . . *V.** Add: Sire Richard de Boslingthorpe. *N.V.*

Bosom. Arg. 3 besoms gu. *Cady.*

Bossard. Arg. 2 bars a bordure and in chief 3 mullets sa. Sir Hugh Bossard. *O.*

Bossard. Sa. 3 bars humetty arg. on the uppermost as many mullets of the first. Sir Hugh Bossard. *O.*

Bostock (London). Sa. a fess humetty arg. Crest: An heraldic antelope statant arg. arg. maned and horned or. *Vis. Lon. 1633.*

Bosuile or Bosville. Add: Simon Bosvile. *V.*

Boteller (Gillinge   ). Ermines a chev. betw. 3 covered cups. *V.*

Boteller (Co. York). Gu. a chev. betw. 3 covered cups or. *V.*

Boteller. Arg. a chev. engr. betw. 3 wine piercers or the handles sa. banded gold. *Harl. MS. 1404. fo. 105.*

Boteler. Gu. on a bend arg. 3 covered cups sa. *V.*

Boteler. Arg. 2 bendlets az. Raf. le Botiler. *F.* But the bendlets gu. Sire Rauf. le Botiller. *O.*

Boteler. Or 2 bendlets gu. a chief sa. Sir Henry le Botler. *J.*

Boteler. . . . 2 bendlets . . . on a chief . . . 3 mullets. Henry le Boteler. *Seal. Cott. MS. Tiberius D.10. fo. 771.*

Boteler. Arg. a bend betw. 6 covered cups. sa. *V.* Boteler, Wildeche. *V.*

Boteler. Az. a bend arg. betw. 6 covered cups or. Monsire John Boteler. *S.*

Boteler. Az. a bend betw. 6 cups or. Sire William le Boteler, Wimme. *N.*

Boteler (Of Borde Warrington, co. Lancaster). Az a bend betw. 6 covered cups or. *V.* William le Boteller, Baron of Warrington. *Nobility Roll 25 Edw. j.*

Boteler. Insert—Bedminton, co. Gloucester. Gu. two bars erm.

Botelet. Az. on a bend arg. three martlets gu. Add: *V.*

Boteler. Az. a chev. betw. three cups covered or. Add: Sir John Boteler. *S.*

Boteler or Botteller (Kirland, co. Lancaster). Same arms. *V.*

Boteler (Bardfield, Essex). Arg. on a bend gu. 3 chevrons erm. *V.*

Boteler. Gu. 2 bendlets erm. Boteller of Bedmanton. *V.*

Boteler. Arg. three boars . . . Add: *V.*

Botell (Essex) Gu. a chev. betw. 3 combs arg. Botell, Prior of St. John of Jerusalem in England. *V.*

Boterel. Gu. seven bezants . . . Add: Thos. Boterel. *F.*

Boterells (Devonshire). Add: Sire William de Boterells. *N.*

Botetourt. Or 3 bendlets az. a canton arg. *V.*

Bothell. Arg. a chev. gu. betw. three—delete—(another, two)—three combs arg. . . . *V.*V.*

Bothell. Arg. a chev. betw. 3 blue bottles az. slipped vert. *Cady.*

Bothell. Arg. a chev. gu. betw. 3 gilly flowers of the second cupped vert. *V.*

Bothingham (Cornwall). *V.*

Botoner. Arg. on a chev. betw. 3 lions heads erased gu. crowned or as many bezants.

Botreaux or Botreux (Devonshire). Add: Sir Reginald Botreux. *V. E. Harl. MS. 6137. F.* Sire Renard de Boterels. *N.*

Bottreaux (Co. Cornwall). Chequy or and gu. on a bend az. 3 horse shoes arg. Quarterly Hastings.

Botrells (Shropshire). Add: *V.*

Botreux. Chequy or and gu. a bend vert. *Cady.*

Botreux. Chequy or and gu. a bend vair. Le Sire Botreaux. *V.Y.*

Botringham. Arg. a bendlet gu. Add: *V.**

Botringham (Devonshire). Arg. three bendlets gu. Add: *V.* Sire Henry de Botringham. *N.* Sire Otes de Botringham. *O.* Sir de Botringham. Cornwall. *V.*

Botringham. Insert: (Essex). Arg. an eagle . . . and Add: also collared or.

Bottlesham. Gu. 3 bird bolts arg. Sir Thomas B. co. Northampton. *V.N.*

Bottlesham (Norfolk). Gu. 3 bird bolts in a fess arg. *Blomfield.*

Bottlesham (Bishop of Llandaff and then of Rochester 1373–89. az. 3 bird bolts 2 and 1 points in base arg. *Bedford.*

Bottrell. (Essex). Chequy or and gu. a chev. az. Add: *V.*

Bouchier (Little Stainbridge, co. Essex). . . . Add: Sir James Bourchier of Essex, Oct. 1610. Granted by Camden. The leopards are sometimes called ounces. *Harl. MS. 6095. fo. 15b.*

Boues. Or 3 water bougets az. Hughe de Boues. *A.*

Boughton (Co. Warwick). Arg. on a chev. betw. 3 crosses bottony fitchy sa. as many bucks heads cabossed or a chief gu. charged with a goat courant arg. *V.*

Boughton. Arg. a chev. couped—delete—(another indented). Add: *Cotton MS. Tiberius D. 10.*

Boughton. Sa. three owls arg. . . . Add: *V.*

Boulter. Sa. a chev. betw. 3 human skulls arg.

Boulton (Co. York). Gu. a chev. betw. 3 mullets pierced arg. in chief 2 bird bolts feathered or.

Boulton. Sa. a falcon ppr. on a canton or a sea crab gu.

Bouly (Sellers, co. Kent). Arg. a chev. betw. 3 griffins heads erased sa. *Robson.*

Boume. Insert: London. Sa. a chev. per pale arg. . . .

Bounteyn Arg. an eagle displ. parted per pale issuing from the sinister . . . quartering sa. a salient arg. over all on an escu. . . . a rose. . . . *V.*

Bourchier (Granted to Sir James Bourchier of Little Stambridge, co. Essex). in 1610. Sa. 3 lions pass. or. *V.E. 1634.* But 3 ounces statant in pale or spotted sa. *Harl. MS. 6095. fo. 15b.*

Bourdillon. Arg. a chev. gu. betw. 3 ink molines sa. **Book Plate.**

Bourghope. Arg. on a chev. az. 3 fleurs-de-lis or Add: *V.**

Bourne. Arg. a chev. gu. betw. 3 lions ramp. sa. Richard Bourne. *V.Y.*

Bourne (Wavertree, near Liverpool). 1865. Arg. a chev. ermines betw. 3 lions ramp. gu. in chief an escallop of the last. *Debrett.*

Bourne (Bobbingworth, co. Essex). Arg. a chev. betw. 4 couple closes gu. and 3 lions ramp. sa. *Morants Essex. p. 149.*

Bourken. . . . On a chev. engr. . . . betw. 3 boars heads. a cross. . . .

Bourne (Essex). Per pale arg. and az. a chev. counter changed betw. 4 shacklebolts gu. bolted or a martlet for diff. *V.E. 1552.*

Bourne (London). 1570. Add: *L.L.*

Bourne (Chesterton, co. Oxford). Add: *V.O.*

Bourne (Wells, co. Somerset). Add: *V.S.* Add: John Bourne (c. Worcester). *W.*

Bourne (Testwood House, Hants.). Add: *Q* Sir Thomas Borne. *Q. Ashmole MS. 1120.*

Bourne (Hackinsall, co. Lancaster). Add: *A.A.*

Bourne (Kent). Arg. on a bend az. 3 lions ramp. Or. *V.*

Bourne (Sir Christopher de Bourne). Gu. a lion ramp. arg. within a bordure engr. or. *R.*

Bourne. Arg. a chev. gu. betw. three lions pass. sa. *V.**

Bourne. Erm. a bend az. *V.**V.*

Bourninge. Per pale az. and sa. 3 chevs. or. *Harl. MS. 1385. fo. 53.*

Bousfield. Insert: Coniston, co. Cumberland, Gu. three chevs. interlaced. . . .

Bouverie. Des Add: London. 1684. Baronetcy 1713.

Bovey (London). Erm. on a bend gu. betw. 2 martlets sa. 3 gouttes or.

Bovile. Quarterly or and sa. in the first quarter a martlet gu. Sir John Bovile. *L.N.*

Bovy (Warwickshire). Add: Bovy (Hill Fields, co. Warwick). Baronetcy 1660. Ext.

Bowater (Coventry and London). Exemplified by Cooke, Clarencieux and afterwards by Sir Wm. Segar, Garter. Arg. an escu. sa. charged with a crescent of the field all within an orle of martlets of the second. *Vis. Lon. 1633.*

Bowcher (East Harptree, co. Somerset). Gu. a chev. or betw. 3 lamps arg. fired ppr. *V.S.*

Bowden (Bowden, co. Chester). Add: *V.*

Bowden (Co. Devon). Sa. a chev. betw. seven griffins heads erect couped arg. langued and each devouring a cross or . . . *W.*

Bowden (Edinburgh). Sa. a lion pass. guard. betw. 2 crescents in pale erminois.

Bowell (Berry Court, co. Hants.). Granted—insert—by Bysche.

Bowen (Llewenny, co. Denbigh and London). Sa. 3 roses . . . *Vis. Lon. 1633.*

Bowen (Quartered by Edwardes of Gileston Manor). Gu. a chev. betw. 3 Bowens knots arg.

Bower. Or on a chev. betw. 3 eagles heads erased sa. as many mullets of the field.

Bower (London). Sa. a 5-foil erm. in chief 3 talbots heads couped arg. a mullet for diff. Crest: A Talbots head couped sa. *Vis. Lon. 1633.*

Bower (London). Sa. a cross patty arg. in the dexter chief an escallop . . . Crest: A Boar pass. arg. *Vis. Lon. 1633.*

Bowerman or Bowreman (Devonshire and Wiltshire). Add: Bowerman (Hemoke, co. Devon). Same arms. *W.* Also: insert following description of the first. Crest . . . sa. . . . *Vis. Lon. 1633.* and after second Crest. *V.**

Bowes (Much Bromley, co. Essex 1634). Erm. 3 bows bent in pale gu. on a chief az. as many lions pass. or. *V.E.*

Bowes (Thornton, co. Durham). Erm. 3 bows strung in pale gu. in chief 3 torteaux. *Surtees.*

Bowes (Durham and Yorkshire). Add: Sir William Bowes. *V.* Sir William Bowes of Strettlam. *Eliz. Roll.*

Bowes (Lord Mayor of London 1545). Add: *V.*

Bowes (London). Erm. 3 bows bent in pale gu. in chief a fleur-de-lis sa., for diff. *C.L.*

Bowes. Erm. 3 bows in pale gu. stringed sa. betw. the two dexter bows a crescent in chief of the first. Ralph Bowes of Barns. *Eliz. Roll. xx.*

Bowland. Sa. an eagle displ. . . Crest: . . . beaked or. Add: Humphry Bowland Kinfare, co. Stafford. *V.*

Bowle. Arg. a chev. betw. 3 lapwings heads erased sa. Richard Bowle. *V.*

Bowles (Walington, co. Hertford). Arg. on a chev. sa. betw. 3 boars heads fesswise couped gu. armed or as many escallops of the fourth a bordure engr. vert. bezanty. *V.*

Bowman (Hethleton, co. Dorset). Add: Bowman (Salisbury, co. Wilts. and Kyrkswald co. Cumberland). Granted by Sir Edw. Bysche Clarencieux 1696. Same arms. *Guillim.*

Bowman. Arg. two bows gu. strung or one within the other in saltire. *V.**

Bowring (Claremont, Exeter). Add: *Cady: Debrett.*

Bowring (Co. Devon temp. Edw. iv.). Gu. a chev. betw. 3 lions ramp. or. *Lysons.*

Bowtheby. Add: *Guillim.*

Bowyer (Denham Court, Bucks. . . . Bart.). Insert—1660.

Bowyer (Leighthorn, Sussex). Baronetcy 1627. Or a bend vair cotised sa.

Bowyer (London, descended from Bowyer of Knightersley, co. Stafford). Or a bend vair cotised sa. for diff. Crest: A falcon rising arg. billed or. *Vis. Lon. 1633.*

Bowyer (Camberwell, co. Surrey)—Delete—(another gu.).

Bowyer (Charlwood, co. Surrey and London). The same arms. Add: *V.*

Bowyer (Knipersley, co. Stafford). bart.—insert —1660.

Bowyer (Co. Hants.). . . . . a chev. flory counter flory . . . betw. 3 goats heads erased . . . *Robson.*

Bowyers. Company of (London). Sa. on a chev. betw. three floats or—substitute—arg. Add: *Cotton MS. Tiberius. D. 10.*

Bowyers (Company of, London). Arg. on a chev. betw. 3 floats sa. as many mullets gu. *Guillim.*

Box (London). Sa. a lion pass. arg. betw. 3 griffins heads erased of the second beaked or. Crest: A dove rising arg. holding in its beak a cross patty fitchy gu. *Vis. Lon. 1633.*

Box (Sussex). Add: Sir Henry Box, Essex. temp. Edw. j. *V.*

Boxe (London). *Vis. Lon, 1568.* Add: William Box, Alderman of London. *V.*

Boxhull or Boxmell (Sussex). Add: Sir Allan de Boxhull, Surrey. temp. Edw. j. *V.N.O.*

Boxley-Abbey (Kent). Add: *Tanner.*

Boxsted. Quarterly arg. and gu. on a bend sa. five bezants. Add: Sir Rauf de Boxstede. *N.* (The bezants un-numbered.).

Boxton. Sa. 3 round wells arg. William Boxton. *V.*

Boxworth (Cambridgeshire). Gu. a lion ramp. . . . Add: Sir William Boxworth temp. Edw. j. *V.*

Boxworth. Or a lion ramp. gu. collared arg. Sir William de Boxworth. *N.*

Boyce or Boyse. Add: *V.*

Bowland (London). Az. on a saltire engr. or an escallop sa. *Vis. Lon. 1633.*

Boyes. Arg. a chev. sa. betw. three acorns . . . Add: *V.**

Boyland. Sa. an eagle displ. arg. armed gu. Add: Sir Richard Boyland. *Syl. Morgan. p. 60. V.*

Boyle (Viscount Shannon). Add: a az. for diff. *Harl. MS. 4040. fo. 272.*

Boyle (Viscount Dungarvon). Same arms. A mullet sa. for diff. *Harl. MS. 4040. fo. 296.*

Boyle (Viscount Blessington). . . . . a sa. for diff. *Harl. MS. 4040. fo. 312.*

Boyley (Kentish Town, Middlesex). Granted by Dethick, Garter 24. Jan. 1569. Per bend embattled gu. and arg.

Boyley. Per bend sinister embattled gu. and arg. *V.V.**

Boynam or Boynham (Essex). Gu. a chev. wavy betw. 3 crosses patty fitchy arg. *Cotton MS. Tiberius. D. 10.*

Boynton (Rowcliff, co. York). Az. a chev. betw. 3 crescents arg.

Boys (Co. Devon). Arg. a chev. gu. betw. 3 cockatrices sa. *Lysons.*

Boys (Lincoln). Add: Ernaldus de Bois *E.F.B.G.P.* John de Boys. *A.D.* Sir Robert Boys, co. Lincoln. *V.*

Boys (Hoston, co. Norfolk). Add: Sire Johan du Boys. *N.* and Add—

Boys (London). Same arms. *Vis. Lon. 1633.*

Boys. Arg. 2 bars and a canton sa. James de Bois. *E.*

Boys (Cornwall). Arg. a chev. sa. betw. 3 slipped acorns or cupped vert. *V.*

Boys (Walberton, co. Devon). Temp. Edw. ij. arg. a chev. gu. betw. 3 oak trees ppr.

Boys. Arg. on a chev. sa. 3 bezants. John de Boys. *Y.*

Boys. Arg. on a chev. sa. 5 bezants. Sir Nicholas de Boys. *V.N.*

Boys. Insert—co. Bucks. Arg. on a chev. sa. three bezants a bordure of the second bezantee. *V.* The Bordure az. *V.**

Boyse or Boyes. Arg. on a bend sa. 12 bezants 4.4. and 4. in cross of the bend. *V.*

Boyvill. Or 3 bendlets sa. *V.*

Boyvill (Suffolk). Quarterly or and sa. in the first quarter a lion pass. gu. William de Boyvil. *C.*

Boyville. Gu. four bendlets arg. Add: *V.*

Bozoun (Wissonset, Norfolk). Arg. 3 bird bolts gu. headed or. *Cady.*

Brabazon (Spropton, co. Leicester). Add: Brabazon, co. Stafford. *Fuller. co. Leicester. 1619. C.C.*

Brabazon (Earl of Meath). Add: Sir Roger Brabazon *N.V.*

Brabazon. Gu. on a bend arg. 3 martlets sa. Sir Roger de Brabazon *Nobility Roll 25. Edw. j.*

Brabon or Brabourne (London and Devonshire, 2 May 1629). . . . Add: *Vis. Lon. 1633.*

Bracebridge or Brasbridge (Lincolnshire).

Bracebridge. Or 3 chevrons fretted in base sa. *Randle Holme.*

Braceworth. Arg. 3 bendlets gu. Sir John de Braceworth. *O.*

Brackenbury (Sellaby, co. Durham). Add: *V.*

Brackstone (London 1751). Erm. on a canton sa. a horses head couped arg. bit and reins gu. **Book Plate.**

Bradbourne (Bradbourne, co. Derby). Arg. on a bend gu. 3 pierced mullets or. *Lysons.* Monsire de Bradbourne. *Y.* But the mullets or pierced vert. John de Bradburne. *Y.*

Bradborne. Arg. on a bend gu. three mullets or. Add: *V.* Sir Humphry Bradborne, The Hogh, co. Derby. *V.* quartered by Holte.

Bradbourne (London). Arg. on a bend gu. 3 mullets or a mullet for diff. Crest: a tree erased ppr. fructed with pineapples or. *Vis. Lon. 1633.*

Bradbury (Essex and Suffolk). . . . Add: *V.E. 1612.* Sir Thomas Bradbury, Lord Mayor of London. *V.*

Braddene, Braden and Bradens (Rutland and Northumberland). Add: Sire Geffrey de Braddene. *N.* Sir Geffrey Braddern, co. Northampton. *V.* William Braddene. *X.* But shown as fusilly William de Braddone. *G.*

Bradeston. Arg. a bend lozengy (another five fusils) in bend gu. Add: *V.*

Bradestone. Arg. a chev. betw. three boars heads couped sa. *V.*V.*

Bradestone. Sa. a chev. betw. 3 boars heads couped arg. *V.**

Bradford. Az. on a bend arg. 3 martlets or.

Bradford (Town of, co. York). Per pale gu. and az. on a chev. engr. betw. 3 bugle horns stringed or a well sable.

Bradley (Co. Lincoln). 1640. Or a chev. gu. betw. 3 crosses patty fitchy sa. *Yorke.*

Bradley or Bradeley. Gu. a chev. arg. . . . Crest: A boar sa. . . . garland vert. Add: *V.V.**

Bradley. Gu. a chev. betw. three boars heads erect and couped or. Add: Bradley of Coventry. Same arms. *Cady.*

Bradley (London). Gu. on a chev. arg. betw. 3 boars heads couped or a cross crosslet sa. *Vis. Lon. 1633.*

Bradley. Insert—of Navenby. *F.Y.* Arg. a chev. sa.

Bradligh. Per chev. or and az. *Cady.*

Bradoke (Adbaston, co. Stafford). Arg. a greyhound salient within a bordure engr. sa. *Erdeswick.*

Bradshaigh or Bradshaw (Co. Limerick &c.). . . . Add: *A.*

Bradshaw (Belper, &c.). . . . Add: *V.* Add: Bradshaw (London). Same arms. *Harl. MS. 1476. fo. 103.*

Bradshaw (Moorham, co. Leicester &c.) . . . . Add: *C.C.*

Bradshaw. Arg. 2 bendlets sa. Sir William Bradshaw. *S.* Thomas Bradshawe. *X.*

Bradshaw. Arg. 2 bendlets sa. an annulet for diff. Henry Bradshaw. Chief Baron of the Exchequer. 1552. *Dug. O.J.*

Bradshaw (Darcy-Lever, co. Lancaster). Add: *V.* Add: Bradshaw (Pendleton, co. Lancaster). Same arms, but a 5 foil gu. in the fess point. *V.L. 1619.*

Bradshaw (Prisale, co. Lancaster). Arg. three annulets betw. two bendlets sa. *V.L.*

Bradshe. Sa. 2 bendlets betw. 3 hawk bells arg. *Cady.*

Bradston or Bradeston. Add: Sir Thomas Bradstone. *Q.V.*

Bradston (Norfolk). Arg. on a canton az. a rose or. *Guillim.*

Bradstone. Arg. on a canton gu. an owl arg. *L.N. p. 226.*

Bradstone. Arg. on a canton gu. a cross or. Thomas Bradstone. Norfolk. *V.*

Bradwarden. Barry of 6 erm. and ermines. *V.* Thos. Bradwarden, Archbishop of Canterbury 1349.

Bragdon or Bragden. (*Vis. London 1568*). Add: *C.L.*

Brage (Essex and London). Add: Bragge (Hatfield Peverell, co. Essex). Same arms. *Collinson. Somerset. ij. 77.*

Bragg (Somersetshire). Add: *Collinson. Somerset' ij. 562.*

Braham (Bucks.). Add: *V.*

Braham. Error for Abraham—(Swarthmoor Hall, co. Lancaster). Sa. a chev. betw. 3 estoiles of 8 rays arg. *F.L.*

Brainthwyt (Ringwood, co. Hants.). Or two bends engr. sa. Add:

Braithwaite (London). 1588. **Seal.** Braithwaite, co. Devon and Norfolk.

Brakeley. Chequy erm. and gu. . . . Add: *V.*

Brakeley or Brakley. Sa. two bars vaire . . . Add: *V.*

Brakenbury. Az. 3 chevs. fretted in base or.

Brampton. Az. three round buckles or. *V.*

Brampton or Brompton. Or 2 lions pass. gu. Sir Brian de Brampton. *E.F.V.Y.*

Brampton. Arg. a bend dancettee az. Add: *V.*

Bramston. Quarterly gu. and vert. . . . Add: *V.*

Bramtot. Add: *V.*

Branch. Insert—Brothby, Scotland. Arg. a chev. sa. . . . Add: *Guillim.*

Branche (Lord Mayor of London). Arg. a lion ramp. gu. over all a bend sa. quartering gu. a fess vair in chief a unicorn pass. betw. 2 mullets or for Wilkinson. *C.L.*

Branche (Norfolk). Arg. a lion ramp. gu. over all a bendlet sa. John Branche. *V.*

Branche. Arg. a lion ramp. gu. over all on a bend sa. three pierced 5-foils arg. Sir Philip Branche. Norfolk. *V.*

Branche. Arg. a lion ramp. gu. armed az. oppressed . . . field—insert—*V.** Crest: . . .

Branchester (Co. Wilts.). Arg. on a bend gu. 3 martlets or.

Branchescombe. . . . a chev. vair betw. 3 martlets . . . Seal of Ric. de Branchescombe 5th Edw. iij.

Brand (Baron Dacre). Delete the whole. See—Trevor.

Brand (Mousley, co. Surrey). Insert—'granted' . . . Add: *W.*

Brandeston. Add: Sir Hugh de Braundeston.

Brandt (London, originally of Hamburgh). Arg. the stump of a tree eradicated ppr. flaming at the top also ppr. Crest: a similar stump. *Vis. Lon. 1633.*

Brans. Per pale or and az. 4 bars counterchanged. *V.*

Bransby (Shottisham, co. Norfolk). Insert—Sheriff of Norfolk 1680.

Branshath, Bramspath, Branspeth or Branspauche. Arg. three bars and a canton sa. Add: Branspeth, co. Westmorland. Same arms. *V.*

Brassy. Quarterly per fess indented sa. and arg. in the first quarter a duck of the second beaked and legged gu. *Harl. MS. 1465. V.*

Bray. Or 3 bars vert. *V.*

Bray. Quarterly arg. and azure a bend gu. *V.**

Bray. Vair 3 bendlets gu. Sir Robert Braye, co. Northampton. *V.* Sir Robert Bray. *N.*

Bray (Oxfordshire). Add: *V.V.** Monsire de Bray. *V.*

Bray (*Vis., co. Notts. 1614*). Add: *V.*

Bray. Gu. on a chev. or betw. three—insert—'saracens' heads . . . Add: *V.*

Bray. Arg. a chev. sa betw. three ogresses . . . Add: *V.*

Bray (London). Arg. a chev. vair betw. 3 eagles legs erased a la cuisse sa. *Vis. Lon. 1633.*

Bray. Arg. a chev. betw. three parrots (or popinjays) . . . Add: *V.*V.*

Braybec. Gu. a bend fusilly or a label of 3 or 5 points arg. *V.V.** John de Braybec. *E.*

Brayford. Arg. 2 bars sa. on a canton of the last a cock or. *Cady.*

Brayle. Or two barnacles extended ppr. *V.**

Brayle. Or 3 barnacles expanded in pale sa. *V.*

Braylesford. Arg. on a bend sa. three cinquefoils or. Add:*V.*

Braylford. Arg. two bends az. . . . Add: *V.*

Braylford. Arg. two bars sa. on a canton . . . Add: *V.*

Braytoft (Lincolnshire). Add: *V.* at end, after crusily arg.

Brecknock or Brecknoy. Add: Sir David Brecknock. *V.*

Breison. Or a lion ramp. az. Sir Piers de Breison. *L.*

Bremer (London). Arg. a lion ramp. az. on a chief of the last 3 mullets or. Crest: A demi-lion ramp. az. holding a mullet or. *Vis. Lon. 1633.*

Bren. Arg. a chev. betw. three *dexter* hands couped at the wrist sa. Add: *V.** and Add: sinister. *V.*

Brendesley. Insert—One of the co-heiresses married Lowis of Silston. *V.N. 140. V.*

Brenne. Add: *V.**

Brentisle, Brentisley or Brentsley. Add: *V.* Sir John de Brentisley. *Y.*

Breon. Or 3 chevs. sa. Richard de Breon. *V.*

Breouse. Renald de Breouse. Az. 2 bars vairy erm. and gu. *A.*

Breouse. Or crusilly and a lion ramp. tail forked and renowed sa. Sir Peres de Breouse *N.*

Brerehaugh. Arg. a bend raguly sa. betw. 6 ogresses.

Breres (Preston). co. Lancaster and Amerton, co. York. Confirmed by Sir George, Norroy 12 Sep. 1613. Erm. on a canton gu. a falcon volant or. *Whitakers Leeds ij. 68.*

Brereton (Brereton, co.—delete—Chester, substitute, co. York).

Brerehays or Brerehaghs (Allerton near Leeds, co. York). Vairy arg. and sa. on a canton gu. a rose or. *Whitakers Leeds ij. 124.*

Brerton. Sa. two bars arg. Sir John Brerton. *F.*

Brescy. Arg. a bend engr. az. fimbriated or. Add: *V.V.**

Bretaigne. Insert—Earl of Richmond, co. York. *N.*

Breston (Norfolk). Quarterly arg. and sa. bendlet gu. *V.*

Bretby. Chequy arg. and az. Add: Sir . . . de Bretty. *V.*

Breton. Insert—Leyrbreton—Essex. Az. two chevs. or Add: *V.*

Breton (Halstead, co. Essex). Same arms with in chief as many mullets of the second. *V.* Add: also 3 mullets. *V.*

Breton. (Leicestershire,London). Insert—co. Lincoln, &c. Add: Sire Robert Breton. *O.Y.S.* Sir John Breton. *Y.* Sire William Bretoun. *N.V.*

Breton (Barwell, co. Leicester 1619). Az. a bend betw. 6 mullets pierced or a mullet for diff. *C.L.*

Breton (Essex and Suffolk). Quarterly or and gu. a bordure az. Add: Sir John Breton. *A. D.N.V.*

Breton. Quarterly or and gu. a bordure engr. az. Add: *E.*

Breton. Az. a bend arg. fretty gu. . . . Add: *V.*

Breton. Arg. a chev. betw. three escallops gu. Add: Roger Breton. *Y.* Breton (Walton, co. Derby. heiress married Loudham (Londham). Same arms.

Brett (Devonshire and Kent). Add: *V.**

Brett. Arg. on a lion ramp. betw. 8 crosses crosslet fitchy gu. an estoile at the shoulder or. *V.*

Brett (Ireland). Add: *V.**

Brett (Sir William). . . . . Add: *V.*

Brett (Somersetshire). delete—(another nine). Add: Sir W.B. Brett. Justice of the Common Pleas 1868. Same arms.

Brette. Arg. on a bend gu. 6 billets palewise as the first. *V.*

Brett (South Maperton—insert—co. Dorset). . . . *Syl. Morgan.*

Brett. Gu. in chief a lion pass. guard. or Sir Amyas Brett, the son. *Q.*

Bretton. Az. a bend betw. 6 pierced mullets or. Sir William Bretton, co. Lincoln. temp. Edw. j. *V.*

Bretton. Az. on a bend arg. betw. 6 mullets or frets gu. Richard Bretton. *V.*

Brewas or Brewase. Or—delete—two, substitute three chevs.—delete—(another three). Add: *V.W.* Add: Sir Johan de Brewase *E.F.C.*

Brewase. Az. a lion ramp. within an orle of crosses crosslet or. William de Brewase. *E.* The lion crowned. gu. De Brewes. *V**

Brewer (Co. Devon). Gu. 2 bars wavy or. *V.*

Brewer (London and Somersetshire). Add: Brewer (London). Same arms and crest, but a martlet for diff. *Vis. Lon. 1633.*

Brewers. Company of (London). Insert—granted 1460—and Exeter—also Newcastle on Tyne.

Brewes. Az. semy of crosslets and a lion ramp. or William de Breouse, Brewes or Brus. *A.D.E.B.* Thomas le Brewes. Sir John de Brewes, co. Bucks. temp. Edw. j. *V.*

Brewes. Arg. a lion ramp. tail forked and nowed betw. 7 crosses crosslets gu. Sir Giles Brews. temp. Edw. iij. *V.*

Brewes. Az. a lion ramp. betw. seven crosslets fitchee arg. Add: ? or. Brewes of Gower, Wales. *V.*

Brewes. Barry of 6 three az. and three vairy gu. and erm. *Harl. MS. 6589.* Bignold Brewes. *Y.*

Brewes. Barry of 6 three vairy erm. and gu. and 3 az. Giles de Brewse, Bishop of Hereford 1200. William de Brewes. *E.F.* Sir William Brewes, Brecon. *V.*

Brews (Sir Piers brews co. Gloucester, temp. Edw. iij. Or a lion ramp. tail forked and nowed betw. 8 crosses crosslet sa. *V.*

Brewton. Az. a lion ramp. arg. crowned and armed gu. *Cady.*

Brickley. Arg. a chev. engr. betw. 3 martlets sa. *Cady.*

Bridge (Bosbury, co. Hereford and Essex). Add: *V.V.**

Brideshall or Bridleshall (Lincoln and Lancashire). Arg. 2 bars gemel az. in chief 3 mullets gu. Sire Gilbert de Briddelshale. *W.* Sire Gilbert de Bridelshall, co. Lincoln temp. Edw. j. *V.*

Bridport (Mayor of Exeter 1349). Or a bend az. betw. 6 double roses gu. *Colby.*

Brige. Insert—(Norfolk) Arg. three owls . . . Add: *V.*

Brigford. Add: *V.*

Brigg (Greenhead Hall, Huddersfield, co. York). Gu. a bend vair betw. 2 cinquefoils all within a bordure az. charged with roundlets. . . .

Briggs (Halifax and Birstwith Hall, co. York). Add: Briggs (Blackburn, co. Lancaster 1876). Same arms.

Briggs (Norfolk). Barry or and gu. a canton sa. *Cady.*

Brigham (Cannon End, co. Oxford). Add: *V.V.**

Bright (London, *Vis. Lon. 1568*). Add: *C.L. p. 84*

Bright (Carbrook and Badsworth, co. York). Add: Bright. Wharlow co. York. Same arms and Crest. *Foster.*

Bright. Per pale az. and gu. a bend betw. 2 mullets in pale arg. Granted by Borough in 1641 to Bright of Carbrook, co. York. *Guillim.* Bright, Badsworth, co. York Baronetcy 1660 *Guillim.* Bright, Claybroke, co. Northumberland. Same arms.

Brightwalton. Sa. on a bend arg. 3 crosses crosslet of the first in the sinister chief a pierced mullet of the second. *V.*

Brightwen (Great Yarmouth, Norfolk). Az. a chev. betw. 3 lions ramp. arg.

Brightwell (London). Arg. on a cross sa. 5 cinquefoils of the field. *Vis. Lon. 1633.*

Briket or Buket. Add: *V.**

Brindesley. Per pale or and sa. . . . Add: *V.*

Brine ( ). Gu. a lion pass. guard. between 3 crosses crosslet or. *V.*

Brinton (William Brinton, Esq., Brook Street, Grosvenor Square, London). Brinton (Kidderminster). Same arms.

Brinton. Gu. a lion ramp. tail forked erm. Adam de Brinton. *F.E.*

Brinton. Gu. a lion ramp. arg. tail forked. Add: *V.*

Brisbon or Brisbone. Add: *V.V.**

Brisco. (Crofton Hall, Cumberland, bart.). Add: Brisco, Yarwell, co. Northampton, Adam Brisco. *W.* Same arms and with a martlet in chief for diff. Brisco. co. Hereford. *W.*

Briscoe. Arg. 3 greyhounds courant 2 and 1 sa. collared gu. John Briscoe. *Dug. O.J.*

Brisingham (Co. Norfolk). Or a chev. gu. and a chief az. *Blomfield.*

Bristowe (M.P. for Newark 1870). Erm. on a bend cotised sa. 3 crescents or. (Query).

Britiffe (Recorder of Norwich). Arg. a chev. engr. betw. 3 escallops sa. *Blomfield.*

Britchebury. Arg. 2 bars az. on a canton of the second a mullet or. M. Avery Britchebury. *S.*

Britley. Sa. two lions pass. guard. or . . . Add: *V.*

Brito (Sheriff of Norfolk). 1278. Quarterly arg. gu. a bordure az.

Brittridge (London). Sa. on a bend or betw. 2 cinquefoils arg. 3 bears heads erased sa. muzzled arg. *Vis. Lon. 1633.*

Brius. Gu. in chief a lion pass. guard. arg. billetty sa. Robert Brius. *E.*

Broad. Arg. a pale sa. . . . Add: *V.**

Broad (Chiswick, co. Middlesex, granted by Bysche, Clarencieux 1627). Gu. a chev. or betw. 3 leopards faces arg. ducally crowned of the second.

Broadgate (London). Arg. 5 mascles conjoined in bend betw. 2 lions pass. guard. gu. Crest: An arm embowed vested or tied round the elbow vert., hand holding a broken halbert. *Vis. Lon. 1633.*

Broadhead (Bretton, co. York). Erm. a lion ramp. . . . in chief 3 eagles displayed gu. *Hunter ij. 397.*

Brocas (Beaurepayre, co. Hants.). Insert—Heiress married Pixhall temp. Hen. viij. Add: Sir Barnard Brokas. *V.S.* Sir John Brockas. *Q.Y.*

Brocas. Sa. a lion ramp. quard. or and a label of 3 points gu. Sir Bernard Brocas. *S.*

Brokas. Sa. a leopard ramp. arg. *Cady.*

Brocket. Insert—London. Or a cross patonce sa. . . . Add: *Vis. Lon. 1633.*

Brockhole (Lancashire). Add: *V.L. V.*

Brockhole. Arg. three—read—bears pass. sa. *V.**

Brockhole. Arg. 3 brocks statant sa. *V.*

Brocklehurst (Hurdsfield co. Chester). Arg. a chev sa. betw. three brocks—insert—pass. ppr.

Brocklehurst (Butley Hall near Macclesfield). Same arms.

Brockman. Insert: Essex. Per fesse indented or and az. . . . Add: *V.E. 1612.*

Brocton. Insert—co. Stafford. Gu. a chev. betw. three bears pass. or (Another within a bordure arg.). Add: *W.V.**

Brocton (Co. Stafford). Gu. a chev. betw. 3 brocks statant arg. *W.*

Brodway. Insert—by Bysche.

Brograve (Hamels, co. Hertford, Lancashire and London).—Insert—Baronetcy 1662. ext. 1707.

Brogynyne. Arg. a lion ramp. sa. over all a bendlet sinister gu.

Brograve, Burgrave or Boroughgrave (Norfolk &c. . . .). Add: *V.*

Broke (Madeley Court, co. Salop). Add: Sir Robert Broke, Chief Justice of the Common Pleas 1554, quartering arg. a cross flory. *Dug. O.J.*

Broke (Sergeant at arms to King Hen. viij.). Or a bull pass. gu. over all a pale erm.

Brokehole or Holbrok. Or crusilly and a chev. gu. Thomas de Brokehole. *E.*

Brokeholes. Arg. a chev. betw. 3 badgers heads erased sa. Sir Geffry Brokeholes. *S.*

Brokeman (Essex). Quarterly per fess indented or and az. 3 martlets counterchanged. *Robson.*

Brokesby (Melton Mowbray, co. Leicester) Add: *C.C. 1619.* On the canton a mullet or, Sir John Brokesby. *V.*

Brome (Clifton near Banbury, co. Oxford, ob. 1667). Sa. on a chev. arg. 5 slips of broom ppr. flowered or. *Guillim.*

Brome (Calveton, co. Notts). *Visitation 1569* and *1614.* Add: *V.N. 1614.*

Brome (Halton, co. Oxford). Same arms. Add: *V.O.* Brome (Clifton, co. Oxford). Same arms. *V.O.*

Brome. Az. on a bend betw. 2 cotises arg. 3 water bougets of the first a mullet in chief of the bend for diff. Sir William Brome. *V.* or Broun.

Bromeall. Add: *V.*

Bromehall. Add: *Cady. V.*

Bromfield (Kent—insert—and London). . . . On a canton or a spear's head az. embrued gu. *Vis. Lon. 1633.*

Bromfield (Staffordshire, *Her. Coll. London*). Add: *Vis. Lon. 1633.* Add: Bromfield (Southwark, Surrey, Baronetcy 1661). Same arms.

Bromfleete. Add: Nicholas Bromflete. *V.*

Bromflete (Baron of Vesey). Add: Sir Henry Bromflete. *V.*

Bromle. Add: *V.*

Bromley. Arg. on a chev. az. 3 bezants a bordure of the second. *Cady.*

Brompton. Or. a chev. betw. three griffins segreant vert. Add: *V.* Add: Brumpton or Brympton. *V.*

Bromton. Add: Brian de Bromtone. *E.* But the escallops or Baudwin de Brunton. *F.*

Bromton. Or 2 lions pass. gu. over all a bendlet sa. John de Bromton or Brunton. *F.*

Bromwich. Or a lion ramp. sa. guttee d'or &c. . . . Add: *V.*

Brond or Brounde (London 1204 &c. . . .). Crest: A demi-griffin—insert—segreant. Add: *Vis. Lon. 1633.*

Brone. Az. a chev. betw. 3 escallops arg. within a bordure engr. gu. Sir John Brone temp. Edw. iv. *Harl. MS. 6137. fo. 44.*

Brooke (Horringer, co. Suffolk). Add: Brooke (London). Gu. on a chev. arg. a lion ramp. sa. crowned or. *Vis. Lon. 1633.* David Brooke. Chief Baron of the Exchequer 1553. for diff. *Dug. O.J.*

Brooke (London). Arg. on a bend sa. a hawk's lure or. Add: *V.* Add: Brooke (Huddersfield, co. York). Same arms.

Brooke (Lord Cobham, Sir Edward Brooke &c. &c. . . .). Add: Sir Thomas Brooke co. Somerset. *V.*

Brooke (Lord Cobham). Gu. on a chev. or 3 lions ramp. sa. Thomas Brooke, Lord Cobham. *V.* Le Sir de Cobham. *S.* Le Sir de Cobham quartering arg. a tower sa. *T.* Sir John de Cobham. *Nobility Roll 25. Edw. j.*

Brooke (Staffordshire). Add: Brooke (Oxford). Same arms. *Cady.*

Brooke (Ash Kent). Per bend arg. and sa. two eagles displ. counterchanged.

Broome (Clifton, near Banbury, co. Oxford 1667). Sa. on a chev. arg. five slips of broom ppr. flowered or. *Guillim.*

Brougheppe. Arg. on a chev. az. 3 fleurs-de-lis or *V.*

Brougham, Broughan, Bronhan or Brouchan. Add: *V.*

Broughton (Broughton, co. Stafford bart.). Add: Sir John de Broghton. *X.* Broughton (London). Same arms and crest with a crescent for diff. *Vis. Lon. 1633.*

Broughton (Essex). Add: Sir Robert Broughton temp. Edw. iv. *Harl. MS. 6137. fo. 44.*

Broughton (Co. Somerset). Az. a chev. erm. betw. 3 bucks heads cabossed arg.

Broughton (Somerset). Insert—Granted in 1591. Sa. a chev. . . . Add: *V.S.*

Broughton (Co. Stafford). Gu. a chevron betw. 3 brocks statant arg. *W.*

Broughton (Broughton, co. Stafford). Same arms. *Erdeswick.*

Broughton (Co. Stafford). Arg. a chev. sa. betw. 3 boars pass. gu. *Robson.*

Broughton. Arg. a cock gu. beaked and legged or Add: *V.**

Broughton. Insert—Kent. Arg. on a bend sa. three martlets or. Add: *V.*

Broun. Gu. a bend erm. on a chief az. three torteaux. Add: *V.**

Brow. Insert—co. Devon. Arg. on a chev. gu. three roses of the first. Add: *V.*

Brow or Browe (Herts.). Add: Sir Hugh de Browe. *S.*

Browker (London and Southwark). Add: *W.*

Brown (Richmond Hill, co. Lancaster, bart.—insert—1873). Add: Brown (Beilby Grange, co. York). Same arms.

Brown (Coulstone . . . Gu. a chev. betw. 3 roses arg. *Guillim.*

Brown (London. Vis. Lon. 1568). Add: Sir John Brown, Lord Mayor of London. *V.*

Brown (Co. Bucks and London). Arg. a chev. betw. 3 cranes sa. Quartering, sa. demy of crosses patty fitchy a lion ramp. or. *C.L.*

Browne. Az. a chev. betw. 3 escallops or within a bordure gu. *Harl. MS. 1404. fo. 26.*

Brown of Stockinghal Arg. 2 bendlets sa. in the fess point a roundlet.

Brown of Westhal. Az. an eagle displ. double headed arg. *Syl. Morgan. 59.*

Brown. Alias Weare. Per chev. gu. and sa. 3 hinds or. *V.**

Brown or Broune (Essex). Sa. a bend erm. on a chief. arg. 3 torteaux. *V.*

Browne (Viscount Montagu: Add: Brown (Arncliff Hall, near Northallerton). Same arms and with a mullet for diff. Browne of Kiddington, co. Oxford. Baronetcy. 1659.

Browne (London). Or on a bend betw. 2 dolphins embowed az. three 3-foils slipped of the field. *C.L. p. 50.*

Browne (Co. Bedford). Arg. 2 bendlets sa. separated by an ogress in the dexter chief point. *W.*

Browne (Great Yarmouth, Norfolk). Gu. a chev. arg. betw. 3 lions gambs erased in bend ppr.

Browne. St. Ives, co. Hunts. and London. Arg. on a. chev embattled counter embattled sa. 3 escallops of the field. on a canton quarterly gu. and az. a leopards head or. Crest: On a wreath a swans head and neck betw. 2 wings az. charged with 3 escallops or. one on the neck and one on each wing, in the beak an acorn slipped and leaved ppr. *Vis. Lon. 1633.*

Browne (Norfolk). Arg. a bend sa. *Cady.*

Browne. Granted 1659. Or on a bend gu. cotised sa. 3 martlets of the first. *Robson.*

Browne. Per pale gu. and sa. on a chev. engr. arg. 3 escallops az. *Harl. MS. 1404. fo. 26.*

Browne (Midlewich, co. Chester). Or on a bend betw. 2 cotises az. 3 water bougets arg. *W.*

Browne (Marsh Hall, co. Derby). Insert—confirmed Flower, Norroy.

Browne (Writtle, co. Essex). Add: *V.E. 1612.*

Browne. Az. a lion ramp. arg. semy of crosses crosslet fitchy gu. *W.*

Browne. Sa. a lion ramp. arg. pelletty. *W.*

Browne. Sa. 3 lions pass. in bend betw. 2 cotises dancetty arg. *Cady.*

Browne (Devonshire). Gu. a chev. betw. three lions gambs. erect . . . Add: *V.**

Browne (London 1633). Sa. 3 lions pass. betw. 2 bendlets arg. a 5 foil in chief for diff. *Harl. MS. 1358. fo. 61b.*

Browne (Sir Mathew Brown, Beckworth, Surrey). Sa. 3 lions pass. in bend betw. 2 bendlets engr. arg. *V.*

Browne. . . . On a bend . . . betw. 2 cotises . . . and three 3-foils slipped . . . as many lions pass . . .

Browne (Weald Hall, co. Essex). Add: Browne (Northampton and Norfolk). Same arms.

Browne. Gu. a chev. or betw. 3 lions gambs erect and erased within a bordure arg. on a chief of the last an eagle displ. sa. Sir Humphrey Browne *Harl. MS. 1404. fo. 120.* The eagle crowned or. Sir Wiston Browne. Essex. *V.*

Browne (Essex). Gu. a chev. betw. three lions gambs erect and erased arg. a chief and bordure of the second. Add: *Harl. MS. 1404. fo. 120.*

Browne (Co. Hereford). Per pale or and arg. a chev. betw. 3 escallops gu.

Browne (Harwood, co. Hereford.) . . . . Crest: . . . Add: *V.*

Browne (Islington). Add: Browne (Bury St. Edmunds, Suffolk). Same arms. *V.L.*

Browne (London). Arg. on a chev. betw. 3 griffins heads erased gu. 3 bowers arg. Crest: A greyhound's head erased per fess arg. and or. around its neck a wreath of laurel vert. *Vis. Lon. 1633.*

Browne (London, granted 23 Feb. 1615). Gu. on a chev. betw. 3 leopards arg. as many escallops az. *W.*

Browne (Co. Chester). sa. a lion ramp. arg. depressed by a baton compony or and gu. within a bordure of the second. *W.*

Browne. Per bend arg. and sa. a bend of lozenges counterchanged. *Harl. MS. 1404.*

Browne. Or an eagle displ. sa bezanty armed gu. *Harl. MS. 1603.*

Browne (Lord Mayor of London). 1661. Add: Browne alias Moses. Baronetcy. 1660.

Browne (London). Sa. a chev. embattled betw. three swans arg. Add: *Harl. MS. 1404. fo. 153.*

Browne (London). Arg. 2 bendlets betw. 2 ogresses. *Vis. Lon. 1633.*

Browne (London). Sa. 3 lions pass. betw. 2 bendlets arg. in chief a 3-foil slipped erm. Crest: A griffin's head erased sa. collared arg. and charged with a 3-foil slipped erm. *Vis. Lon. 1633.*

Browne (London). Az. a chev. betw. 3 escallops or a bordure engr. gu. Crest: A stork az. beaked and legged gu. ducally gorged or. *Vis. Lon. 1633.*

Browne (London). Az. a chev. betw. three escallops or. Add: *Vis. Lon. 1633.*

Brown (Walcot, co. Northants.). Baronetcy 1621. Az. a chev. betw. 3 escallops and a bordure or.

Browne (Lord Mayor of London). Az. on a chev. betw. 3 escallops or a crescent gu. a bordure engr. of the last. *C.L.*

Browne (Norwich, confirmed by Cook, Clarencieux 1581). Sa. 3 cranes arg.

Brown (Sir Thomas Brown, Doctor of Physic, Norwich, 1671). Arg. 2 bendlets sa. betw. 2 ogresses. *L.N.*

Browne. Arg. a chev. betw. 3 pierced mullets sa. *V.*

Browne. Or a chev. engr. betw. 3 stocks of trees eradicated sa. *Cady.*

Browne (Sheriff of Newcastle 1435). Gu. a chev. betw. 3 lions gambs erect and erased arg. a bordure of the same over all on a chief arg. an eagle displ. sa. *Carr MS.*

Browne (Newark, co. Notts). Per pale gu. and sa. on a chev. engr. arg. betw. 3 leopards heads or as many escallops az. *V.* and *V.N. 189.*

Browne (   ). Per pale gu. and sa. on a chev. engr. arg. betw. 3 leopards heads or as many hurts. *Cady.*

Browne (Norfolk). Granted by Bysche, Clarencieux 1668. Gu. a bar gemelle betw. 3 spear heads arg.

Browne. Arg. 3 martlets in pale betw. 2 flaunches sa.

Browne. Insert—Oxford. 1678. Arg. on a bend az. three escallops or.

Browne. Insert—(London). Arg. a chev. sa. fretty or betw. three roses gu. slipped vert. *W.*

Browne. Sa. a chev. erm. betw. three leopards heads within a bordure or. *V.**

Browne. Insert—London. Arg. a chev. sa. betw. three roses gu. seeded az. stalked and leaved vert. *Vis. Lon. 1633.*

Browne. Arg. a chev. sa. betw. 3 roses gu. seeded az. *V.**

Browneshin. Arg. a chev. betw. three bulls heads cabossed sa. Add: But couped sa. *V.V.**

Brownrig or Brownrigg. Add: Brownrigg (Bishop of Exeter). **Tomb** in Temple Church. Same arms.

Brownsword (Symonds Inn, London). Arg. a chev. betw. 3 boars pass. sa.

Browte. Add: Robert Browte. *V.*

Broxborne. Add: *V.*

Broxholme (Co. Lincoln 1640). Arg. a chev. betw. 3 brocks heads erased az. *Yorke.*

Bruant. Add: Sir Walter Bruant. *V.*

Brudenall or Brudenell. Add: Lord Brudnell. *W.*

Brudenell (Stanton Wyvile, co. Leicester and Northamptonshire). Add: Brudenell (co. Bucks and London). Same arms and 1st Crest. *Vis. Lon. 1633.*

Brudenell. Arg. a chev. gu. betw. three chaplets az. Query—chapeaux.

Brudenell. Arg. on a chev. gu. betw. three steel caps az. an escallop or. Add: Baron Brudenall. *V.*

Brudenell or Bruddenell. Add: *V.V.**

Bruen (Stapleford, co. Chester). Add: *V.*

Bruer (Co. Devon t. Hen. iij.). Arg. 4 bars gemelles az. overall a chev. engr. gu. *Lysons.*

Brugg. Quarterly az. and or. over all a bend gu. *Harl. MS. 1465. fo. 15b.*

Bruggford. Add: *Ashmole MS. 833. fo. 47.*

Brughall. Paly of 6 arg. and sa. on a bend gu. 3 escallops or. *Cady.*

Bruley. Erm. on a bend gu. 3 chevs. arg. *V.O. 154.*

Bruley, Brulye or Bruly. Add: Herti (or Roger) de Bruili. E. William Bruley, Waterstoke. co. Oxford. *V.*

Brune. Az. a lion ramp. arg. Monsire de Brune. *Y.*

Brun. Az. a lion ramp. arg. goutty de sang Sire Richard le Brun. *N.* Thomas Brune. *Y.*

Brunham. Insert—or Burnham. Add: *V.*

Bruning, Bruen or Bruining. Add: *W.*

Brunskell (Barnard Castle, co. Durham). Arg. a chev. sa. on a canton of the second an escallop. or. *Surtees.*

Brunskill (Bowes, co. York 1664). Same arms. Crest: A cubit arm erect hand holding an escallop. *Dugdale.*

Brunton. Or 2 lions pass. gu. over all a bendlet sa. John de Brunton. *F.*

Brus. Erm. a lion ramp. tail nowed and forked gu. Sir Richard Brus, Norfolk, temp. Edw. iij. *V.*

Bruse (Kent). Add: Piers de Brus. *B.P.* Piers de Brus de Skelton. *Y.*

Bruse. Az. a lion ramp. or crowned and armed gu. within an orle of crosses crosslet of the second. Sir John Bruse. *Q. Harl. MS. 6595.*

Brusly. Erm. on a bend sa. 3 chevrons arg. *Nash.*

Brute or Bruit. Add: Richard le Brut. *E.*

Bruton. Quarterly gu. and or. a bordure engr. az. *V.*

Bruyin or Bruyn. Add: Sir . . . de Bruyin, Cumberland. *V.*

Bruyne. Arg. an eagle displ. sa. armed and langued gu. *Harl. MS. 1603.*

Bryan. Az. on a chev. arg. three crescents gu. in chief . . . *V.*

Bryan. Az. on a chev. or three crescents of the first . . . *V.*

Bryan. Quarterly or and az. . . . . *V.**

Bryan. Gu. 3 lions pass. 2 and 1 or, quartering gu. a saltire or. Bryan, co. Kilkenny. M.P. for Kilkenny 1865. *Debrett.*

Bryane. Add: Sir William de Bryane. *H.*

Bryers (Walton, co. Lancaster). Arg. 3 swans sa. quartering az. 3 swans arg. for Walton. *V.L. 1664.*

Bryger. Add: *V.*

Brykes or Bryckes. Add: *V.*

Brympton or Brumpton. Add: V.

Buche. Sa. a chev. betw. 3 boars statant arg. armed gu. *V.*

Bucher. Quarterly or and gu. a canton erm. and bordure sa. bezantee. Add: Sire Captan de Bucher. *H.*

Buck (Hamby Grange, co. Lincoln, bart.). Insert: 1660.

Buck. Quarterly gu. and vert., a buck betw. three pheons arg. . . . Add: *V.*

Buck (Co. Lincoln). Barry pily of 10 or and az. a canton erm. *Yorke.*

Buck (Sir John Buck of Hanby, Sheriff of Lincolnshire, temp. James j.). Barry bendy or and az. a canton erm. *Fuller.*

Buck (Flotmanby, co. York). Lozengy or and az. a canton erm. *Dugdale.*

Buck (Rotheram, co. York). Fusilly or and az. a canton erm. (*Hunter ij. 178.*

Bucke (Cambridgeshire). Add: *V.**

Buckenham (Norfolk). Arg. a lion ramp. gu. armed or over all on a bend az. 3 bezants. *Cady.*

Buckenham (Mayor of Exeter 1541). Arg. a lion ramp. within a bordure engr. gu. a mullet of the last. *Colby.*

Buckett (London). Arg. a cross humetty gu. in the dexter a leopards face az. *Vis. Lon. 1633.*

Buckingham (Lord Mayor of London 1705). Insert: *Le Neve in his Pedigree of Knights*, gives the field argent.

Buckingham (James Silk Buckingham). Az. a lion ramp. arg. quartering 2nd arg. on a chev. az. betw. 3 crosses crosslet sa. 3 swords erect., 3rd Erm. on a chev. az. betw. in chief 2 anchors and in base a medal suspended by a blue ribbon. **Book Plate.**

Buckland (West Harptree, co. Somerset 1623). . . . a stag . . . couchant . . . *V.S.*

Buckland. Arg. three lions ramp. gu. a quarter sa. fretty or. Add: Sir . . . de Buckland. *V.*

Buckle (New Hall, co. Haddington &c. . . .). Add: Arms of Sir Cuthbert Buckle, Knt. Lord Mayor of London, ob. 1594. Granted by Cooke *W.*

Buckley (Bart—insert—1868, of Dinas Mawddwy &c. . . .).

Buckminster (Peterborough). Add: Sir William de Buckminster *N.V.*

Buckminster. Arg. semy of crosslets and a lion ramp. sa. Sir William Buckminster. *O.*

Bucknell. Arg. 2 chevs. gu. betw. 3 bucks heads cabossed sa. Sir Wm. Bucknell, Oxey, co. Herts. 1670. *L.N.*

Buckside. Sa. two bucks courant arg. *V.** attired or. *V.*

Buckton of Helmswell. Quartered by St. Quintin . . . 3 chevs. braced . . . betw. 3 bucks heads erased . . . *F.Y. p. 127.*

Buckton (John de Buckton, temp. Richard ii.). Add: *V.*

Buckton. Arg. 3 bars gemel and a canton sa. Robert Buckton. *V.*

Buckton. Arg. on a bend sa. 3 martlets or quartering gu. a pile arg. temp. Edw. ij. *F.Y.*

Bucy. Or 3 water bougets az. Sir Hugh de Bucy. Fiefeld. *V.*

Buffar (Greenwich, Kent). Arg. 2 chevs. betw. 3 mullets gu. in chief 2 bars sable. *Robson.*

Buffken. Or a chev. betw. 3 esquires helmets az.

Bugg (Co. Essex). Az. 3 water bougets or within a bordure arg. *V.E. 1612. V.*

Bulkeley (Bulckeley, co. Chester). Add: *V.*

Bulkeley. Sa. a chev. betw. 3 bulls heads or. *Cady.*

Bulkeley (Spapenhall, co. Derby, descended from the Bulkeleys' of Leek, co. Stafford). Sa. 2 chevs. betw. 3 bulls heads cabossed arg. a canton or. *Lysons, Derby. ccvij.*

Bulkworthy (Co. Devon). Sa. a bend vair. (*Lysons.*)

Bull (London). Gu. on a chev. arg. betw. three bull's heads couped of the second . . . Add: Granted by Segar to Randal Bull of London, Clockmaker to Queen Elizabeth and Jas. j. *Gullim.*

Bukeshull. Arg. crusilly and a lion ramp. gu. Walter Bukershull. *Y.*

Bull. Arg. a chev. sa. betw. 3 roses gu. *Cady.*

Bullen (Brecon). Add: Bullen, Alderman of London. *V.*

Bulman (Sussex). Sa. 2 bars wavy arg. in chief a bull pass. or. *Berry.*

Bullin. Erm. a chev. wreathed gu. and sa. betw. 3 bulls heads couped sa. collared or. *A.A.*

Bullingham. Az. an eagle displ. arg. on a chief or 3 crosses crosslet gu. *Harl. MS. 6829. fo. 60.*

Bullmore. Az. 3 canary birds or.

Bullock (Aborfield, co. Berks.). Add: *W.*

Bullock or Bulloke (Essex). Add: *V.*

Bullock (Totham, co. Essex). Gu. a chev. erm. betw. 3 bulls heads cabossed or. *V.E. 1612.*

Bullock (Hampshire). Gu. a chev. . . . cabossed arg. Add: *V.**

Bullock (Essex, confirmed 9 Feb. 1602). Gu. a chev. erm. betw. 3 bulls heads cabossed or. *W.*

Bulman or Bullman. Add: John Bulman. *V.*

Bulmer or Bullmer. (Essex and Yorkshire). Add: Bulmer of Marrick, co. York. Sir Rauf. de Bulmer. *M.N.S.V.* John Bulmer. *V.*

Bulmer of Leven. Gu. billety and a lion ramp. or on the shoulder a crescent gu. for diff. *Eliz. Roll. xxxi.*

Bulmer (Wilton and Pinchinthorpe, co. York). Gu. billetty and a lion ramp. or quartering Grey of Barton. Or a lion ramp. az. debruised by a bend company arg. and gu.

Bulmer or Bullmer. Add: Sir Roger de Bolmere. *N.*

Bulmer. Gu. a lion ramp. or billettee sa. Add: Sir Wm. Bulmer temp. Hen. viij.

Bulteel (London). Az. a chev. or betw. in chief 2 swans arg. beaked and legged gu. and in base a pair of shears of the third. Crest: A swan as in the shield betw. 2 wings arg. *Vis. Lon. 1633.*

Bumsted (Suffolk). Add: *V.*

Bunbury (Stanney Hall, co. Chester, bart). Insert: 1681. Add: *Guillim.* Add: Bunbury (London). Same arms and crest, a crescent for diff. *Vis. Lon. 1633.*

Bunce (Kent and London). Add: *Vis. Lon. 1633.*

Bungey (Kent, Dorking, Surrey &c. . . .). Add: Granted by Cooke to John Bungay of Mistold, Kent. *W.*

Bunhope. Arg. on a chev. az. 3 fleurs-de-lis. *Cady.*

Bunn (Of the Morfe, co. Salop). Arg. a chev. betw. 3 mullets sa.

Bunney, Bunney (Yorkshire and co. Durham). Add: *Dugdale. p. 279. V.W.*

Bunting. Abbot of Bury St. Edmonds Abbey, 1511. Arg. a chev. gu. betw. 3 buntings az.

Burbage (London). Arg. on a chev. engr. vert. betw. 3 boars heads couped sa. 5 gouts or. Crest: a boars head erased arg. betw. 2 sprigs of acorns or. *Vis. Lon. 1633.*

Burchurst. temp. Edw. iij. Gu. a lion ramp. tail forked or. *Erdeswick.*

Burdens (Co. Wilts). Arg. on a bend sa. three bezants. *V.*

Burdet or Bordet. Az. 2 bars or on the upper bar 3 martlets gu. Sir Robert Bordet. *N.V.*

Burdett. Paly of 6 arg. and az. on a bend gu. 3 martlets or. *V.*

Burdett (London). Same arms. *Vis. Lon. 1633.*

Burdett (Burthwaite, co. York). since of Acomb, near York—insert—Bart. 1665.—bart.—insert —1765. Add: Monr. John Burdet. *S.* Roger Burdet. *Y.*

Burdet. Az. 2 bars or an orle of martlets gu. Monsire Roger Burdet. *Y.*

Burdett. Az. 2 bars or. Sire William Burdett. *N.* Monsire Richard Burdett. *Y.* Sir William Burdett, co. Leicester. *V.*

Burdett. Paly of 6 arg. and gu. on a bend or 3 martlets gu. *Robson.*

Burdett (Confirmed by Francis Burdett of Burthwaite, co. York 1599). Paly of 6 arg. and sa. on a bend gu. 3 martlets of the first. *North Country Grants. 44.*

Burdeux. Arg. 2 bars sa. in chief 3 annulets of the second. *V.*

Bure. Erm. on a mount vert. issuing from park palings with gate ppr. a lion ramp. or holding in the dexter paw a scimitar all ppr. on a chief indented sa. 2 lions ramp. arg.

Burell (Saltash, co. Cornwall). Arg. on a bend sa. 3 stags heads cabossed or. *V.C.*

Bures. Arg. on a bend sa. 3 barbel naiant or. *Moule. 76.*

Burfield. Paly of 6 arg. and sa. a bend gu. *Cady.*

Burghill or Burghull (Ireland). Paly of 6 arg. and sa. on a bend gu. 3 escallops or but the escallops arg. *Harl. MS. 1603.*

Burgg. Quarterly az. and or over all a bend (or bendlet). gu. *V.V.**

Burgeys (Kent). Arg. on a chev. gu. 3 talbots passant or.

Burgh (Hugo Burgh, Sheriff of Shropshire, temp. Hen. vj.). Az. a chev. betw. 3 fleurs-de-lis erm. *Fuller.*

Burgh. Gu. on a bend arg. 3 leopards heads sa. *W.*

Burgh (Bermingham, co. Norfolk). Gu. on a bend or 3 leopards heads sa.

Burgh or Borne (Middlesex). Arg. a chev. erm. betw. 2 couple closes sa. and 3 chaplets gu. *V.*

Burghepp or Burghopp. Add: *W.*

Burghersh (Devonshire and Norfolk). Add: Sir Berth de Borways. *O.* Bartholomew Burwashe. *Q.* or Bourgheyche and Borwache. *S.N.* Burhesse. *Y.* John Bourghershe. *Y.* Sir Stephen Biorwash. *L.*

Burgherse. Gu. a lion ramp. or a label of five points az. Herbert de Burgheise. *A.* Berthe Burgherse. *Harl. MS. 6137.*

Burghill (Brecon, and Bungay, co. Suffolk). Add: Roger de Burghhulle. *E.*

Burghope. Arg. on a chev. az. 3 fleurs-de-lis. or *V.**

Burgoine (Addlethorpe, co. York). Az. a talbot pass. arg. *Dugdale. p. 27.*

Burgoyne. Az. a talbot statant arg. collared gu. lined or at the end of the line a knot. *V.*

Burgoyne. Gu. a wolf pass. or on a chief crenelle arg. three martlets az. Add: John Burgoyn, Sutton, co. Beds. Auditor. *V.*

Burgoyne. Az. a chev. betw. three estoiles or on a chief embattled arg. as many fleurs-de-lis of the first. *V.*

Burgoyne (Sutton Park, co. Bedford). . . . . bart.— insert—1856. Add: *V.*

Burkley. Sa. a chev. betw. 3 bulls heads arg. *Nash.*

Burles. Vert. a chev. or betw. three spear heads arg. *Robson.*

Burley. Arg. a lion ramp. sa. debruised with a fess chequy or and az. Add: Sheriff of Shropshire temp. Hen. iv. *Fuller.*

Burley (Branscroft Castle, co. Salop). Arg. a lion ramp. sa. armed and langued gu. over all a fess countercompony az. and or. *Erdeswick.*

Burley. Gu. two bars gobonated arg. and az. *V.*

Burley. Barry of 6 gu. and erm. a bordure compony sa. and or. *Harl. MS. 1603.*

Burlimachi (London). Arg. a cross az. *Vis. Lon. 1633.*

Burly (Granted to Thomas Burly, of Deepden, co. Suffolk, 4 April 1597).

Burlz (Suffolk). The same. Add: *W.*

Burman (Newington, Kent). Or 2 talbots pass. sa. langued gu. betw. 3 flaunches of the second. *Robson.*

Burman. Arg. on a chev. gu. betw. 3 pelicans heads erased gu. as many stars or in chief a crown betw. 2 "paunsiers" ppr. *Cady.*

Burnam. Or a bend betw. 2 crosses crosslet sa. *V.*

Burnand (Essex). Arg. on a bend az. 3 escallops of the first. *V.*

Burnell (Ireland and Essex). Arg. a lion ramp. sa. overall a baton gu. Add: Hue Burnell. *E.* Phillip Burnell. *D.* But the lion over the bendlet. *F.*

Burnell (Holgate, co. Salop). Arg. a lion ramp. sa. crowned or within a bordure az. Add: Le Sire le Burnel. *S.* Burnell, quartered by Ratcliff, Lord Fitzwalter. *U.* Sir Edwd. Burnell. *V.* Robert Burnell, Bishop of Bath and Wells 1275.

Burnell. Arg. a lion ramp. sa. crowned or. Add: Sir Edward Burnell. *I.N.V.* Sir Nicholas Burnell. *V.* Philip Burnel. *G.*

Burnell (Philip Burnell. *E.F.*). Arg. a lion ramp. sa. on a bendlet gu. 3 martlets of the field. *F.*

Burnell (William Burnell, Auditor to King Henry viij. 1571). Arg. a lion ramp. sa. within a bordure gu. bezanty. His **tomb** in Wykburn Church. *V.N. p. 99.*

Burnell (London). Az. on a bend arg. 3 escallops sa. Crest: On a cap of maintenance gu. a greyhound sejant arg. Granted by Cooke, 1570. *Vis. Lon. 1633.*

Burnell (Crok-Burnell, co. Devon). Arg. a chev. ermines betw. 3 barnacles sa.

Burnell, Burnhill or Byrnell. Add: Sir de Byrnell, Hold. co. Oxford. *V.* Add: *V.*

Burney. Arg. 2 bars embattled counter embattled erm.

Burnham. Gu. a chev. or betw. 3 lions heads erased arg. *V.*

Burnham. Gu. a chev. arg. fretty sa. betw. 3 lions heads erased of the second. *V.*

Burr. Or a cross aiguise voided az. &c. . . . Add: Burre (London). Same arms, a crescent for diff. *Vis. Lon. 1633.*

Burrage. Arg. a chev. engr. vert. goutty. betw. 3 boars heads couped sa. *Cady.*

Burrard (Walhampton, Hants, bart). Insert—1769.

Burrell (Milfield and Brome Park, co. Northumberland). **Note:** Field arg., chief sa. *Vis. Lon. 1633.*

Burrell. Az. 6 barrulets arg. on a chief gu. 3 leopards heads or. Henry Burrell. *V.*

Burridge. Or a chev. betw. 3 lions ramp. gu. *Robson.*

Burroughs (Great Yarmouth). Az. a chev. erm. betw. 3 fleurs-de-lis. arg.

Burroughs (Norfolk). Az. a chev. betw. 3 horseshoes arg. *Blomfield.*

Burrowes (Kent). Vert. a bend wavy betw. 2 fleurs-de-lis arg. *Robson.*

Burrowes (Norham, co. Devon). Az. a bend wavy betw. 2 fleurs-de-lis erm. Burrowes, Kent. *W.*

Burrowes. Az. a bend wavy betw. three fleurs-de-lis erm. Crest: . . . Add: *V.**

Burston. Gu. a chev. arg. betw. three camel's heads . . . Add: *V.*V.*

Burston (Kent). Quarterly arg. and sa. on a bend gu. 3 lions heads erased of the first. *Harl. MS. 4108. fo. 66. Vis. Lon. 1633.*

Burstowe. Insert—Surrey. Gu. three falcons arg. Add: *W.*

Burt. Arg. on a chev. gu. betw. three bugle horns sa. . . . Add: Dr. Burt Warden of Winchester College, Oxford, ob. 1679. *Guillim.*

Burte (Co. Bucks. &c. . . .). Add: *V.O. p. 151.*

Burton. Or on a chev. gu. betw. three torteaux as many crescents or. *Cady.*

Burton (Tibenham, co. Norfolk). Arg. a lion ramp. sa. tail elevated and turned over the head. *Guillim.*

Burton (Tolethorp, co. Rutland &c. . . .). Add: *Visitation Lon. 1633. C.C. 1619.* Add: Sir Thomas Burton. *S.X.* Sir Thomas Burton, Kensley, co. York. *V.*

Burton (Derbyshire). Add: *V.V.**

Burton (Stapleforth, co. Notts. &c.). Add: *W. C.L.*

Burton or Bourton (Ireland). Add: But a chevron. *W. Harl. MS. 1404. fo. 27.*

Burton. Arg. a bend wavy sa. Sir John de Burton. *S.* Sir Thomas Burton of Kynesley, co. York. *V.*

Burton (Wemby   ). Paly of 6 vert. and erm. on a bend gu. 3 escallops erm. *W.*

Burton (Co. Rutland). Arg. on a bend betw. 2 cotises sa. 3 lions heads erased or. *In Bristol Cathedral.*

Burton (London). Quarterly 1 and 4 arg. a bend wavy sa. 2 and 3 . . . a fleur-de-lis . . . Crest: An arm embowed hand holding a spear. *Vis. Lon. 1633.*

Burton (Co. Notts.). Arg. a chev. gu. betw. 3 bugle horns sa. garnished or. *Cady.*

Burton (London). Sa. a chev. engr. betw. 3 owls arg. *Vis. Lon. 1633.*

Burton. Insert—co. Devon. Sa. a goat ramp. arg. Add: *W.*

Burton. Barry of six arg. and erm. on a bend gu. three escallops or. Add: *V*.

Burton. Arg. a chev. betw. three boars heads couped sa. Add: Sir William Burton. *Cady.*

Burton. Paly of six or and gu. on a bend sa. three trefoils arg. Add: *V*.

Burton. Paly of 6 or and gu. on a bend sa. three bulls heads arg. *Cady.*

Burton-upon-Trent. Town of. . . . **Book Plate.** Motto: Honor alit artes.

Burton-Lazer-Hospital (Leicestershire). Add: *Tanner.*

Burwashe. Or a lion ramp. gu. tail forked. Add: Henry Burwash, Bishop of Lincoln. 1320. Sir Barthelomewe Burwash. *Q.*

Burwash (London). Arg. a chief gu. over all a lion ramp. double-tailed or. Crest: out of a square tower per pale arg. and gu. a demi-lion or. *Vis. Lon. 1633.*

Burwell (Woodbridge, co. Suffolk). Add: Burwell, Sir Jeffry Burwell of Woodbridge, Suffolk, and Lord of the Manor of Rougham. *Cady.*

Burwell. Paly of six arg. and sa. on a bend or a teal's—insert—(or Swan's) head erased az. Add: beaked gu. in chief of the bend. *V.*

Bury. Borough of, co. Lancaster. **Book Plate.** Motto: Vincit omnia industria.

Bury. Arg. on a bend az. three leopards faces or. Add: *W.*

Bury. Sa. a chev. insert—arg. betw. . . . Add: (or wreaths twisted arg. and az.). *V.*

Bury. Sa. a chev. arg. betw. three hatbands wreathed of the second and az. Add: *V.*

Burye (Bedford 1566). Add: *Vis. Lon. 1633.*

Burys or Buris. Add: Sir John Burys. *V.*

Busby (Addington)—insert—co. Bucks. 1661. *L.N.*

Busham (Baroby co Lincoln). . . . Add: Busham (Cornwall). *Harl. MS. 1458.*

Bushell (Myerscough Cottage, co. Lancaster). Add: Bushell (Whitby, co. York 1665). *Dugdale. p. 82.*

Busiard (Suffolk). Add: Busserarde (Norfolk) Same arms. *V.*

Buskin. Or a chev. betw. three helmets az. Add: *V.*

Buskin (Goore Court, Ottham, Kent). Granted by Cooke. *W.*

Bussell (Co. Warwick). Sa. a chev. betw. 3 water bougets arg. *V.**

Bussell or Bushell. Add: Bussell (Bradley, co. Devon). Same arms. *Lysons.*

Bussey (Lincoln and Cambridgeshire). Add: Sir Miles Bussey. *V.*

Bussey. Arg. three bars sa. Add: Le Sire de Bussy. *Y.* John Bussey *S.Y.* Sire Hugh de Bussy. *N.*

Buswell. Alias Pelsant (Chepston, Northants, Baronetcy 1713). Gu. a bend counterembattled betw. 2 crosses crosslet arg. quartering sa. a fess betw. 3 pelicans arg. *Guillim.*

Buther (Staplehurst—insert—Kent). Sa. a chev. erm. betw. three terriers arg. Query . . . leopards. *Cady.*

Butler (Dr. William Butler ob. 1617). Sa. a fess lozengy betw. 3 covered cups or. **Tomb** in St. Marys Church, Cambridge.

Butler. Lord Dunboyne. Or a chief indented az. on a bend of the second 3 escallops of the first. *Harl. MS. 4040. fo. 410.* The bend gu. and escallops arg. *W.* and *Harl. MS. 1603.*

Butler (Kirkland, co. Lancaster 1567). Add: *V.*

Butler (Rawcliffe, co. Lancaster 1664). Add: *V.L.*

Butler (Wardington, co. Oxford). Az. a chev. betw. 3 covered cups or a mullet for diff. *V.O.*

Butler. Arg. a chief indented az. over all on a bend gu. 3 escallops of the second. *V.**

Butler (Sussex). Arg. a chev. betw. three gimlets az. handles or. Add: William Butteller. *Harl. MS. 1386. fo. 94.*

Butler (Bewsey &c...). Add: William de Botteler, Baron of Warrington. *Nobility Roll. 25. Edw. j.*

Butler. Az a bend betw. 3 covered cups or. *Harl. MS. 6137. fo. 44.*

Butler. Arg. a bend betw. 6 covered cups sa. *V.**

Butler. Arg. 2 bendlets betw. six covered cups sa. quartering . . . a cross ? moline . . . and a bordure engr. Sir Andrew Butler. *T. Ashmole MS. 1120.*

Butler. Arg. a chev. az. betw. three wine piercers . . . Add: *V.*

Butler. Gu. a chev. arg. betw. three tigers . . . Add: *V.**

Butnor. Insert—co. Warwick.

Butteler. Arg. three boars in pale sa. Add: *V.*

Butteller (Calais). Gu. a chev. betw. 3 tigers couchant regard. arg. Oruel Butteller. *V.*

Butteler (Sussex). Arg. a bend betw. 2 cotises gu. and 3 covered cups sa. *Cady.*

Buttell. Gu. a chev. betw. 3 conies courant arg.

Butterwike. Add: *V.**

Butterworth (Belfield, co. Lancaster 1664). Add: *V.L.*

Buttery (Northamptonshire). Add: Foulk Buttery, Marston. *W.* given to Cressant Buttery alias Mutany of Lawrence Marston, co. Northampton, by Cooke. *W.*

Button of Dyffryn. Az. 3 bats or. *Nicholas.*

Butts (Sir William Butts of Thornap, co. Norfolk, Chief Physician to King Henry viij). Az. on a chev. betw. 3 estoiles or as many lozenges gu. Crest: A bay horse's head couped. *Blomfield. ix. 386.*

Butts (Norfolk). Same arms. *W.* Robert Butts, Bishop of Norwich 1738. Same arms.

Buxton (Shadwell Court, co. Norfolk). Add: *Vis. Lon. 1633.*

Bydall. Arg. in chief dexter a crescent and sinister an annulet sa. *Harl. MS. 2021.*

Bydesdon. Az. 4 bendlets or. *V.*V.*

Byest (Shropshire). Add: Granted in 1586.

Byest. Gu. 3 bundles of as many arrows arg. feathered and banded or. *V.**

Byfield. Sa. on a bend or betw. 5 bezants 3 and 2 three fleurs-de-lis of the field, a chief or *Cady.*

Bykeley. Arg. a chev. engr. betw. three cronels sa. Add: *V.*

Byles (Sir John B. Byles, Justice of the Common Pleas 1858). Per bend sinister embattled arg. and gu.

Bynde (Sussex). Or on two bars gu. 6 martlets arg. three and three. *V.*

Byrche. Or a chev. wavy betw. three eagles displ. az. Add: Baron of the Exchequer. *Dug. O.J.*

Byrde (Sheriff of Newcastle. 1450). Arg. 3 demi-birds az. rising from wreaths or and gu. a crescent for diff. *Carr. MS.*

Byrkle. Arg. a chev. engr. betw. 3 ravens sa. *V.*V.*

Byrnande (Yorkshire). Insert—of Knaresborough temp. Edw. ij. *F.Y.*

Byrom (Salford, co. Lancaster). Arg. a chev. betw. 3 hedgehogs sa. a canton gu. for diff. *V.L.*

Byrom (Manchester 1664). Arg. a chev. betw. 3 hedgehogs sa. a canton az. *V.L.*

Byon. Arg. 3 bendlets gu. Sire John Byron, co. Nottingham. *V.* Sire James Byron. *N.* Sir Richard Byron. *S.M.* and with a label az. Sir John Byron le fils. *P.* Sir Jame de Byrune. *F.* But the label sa. and of 5 points Sir James de Biroune. *E. Harl. MS. 6137.* The bendlets enhanced. *E.*

Byron (Newstead, co. Nottingham). Same arms and quartering with addition of Colwick. *V.N. 1614.*

Byrton. Paly of 6 arg. and gu. on a bend sa. 3 water bougets of the second. Sir . . . de Byrton. *V.*

Byrton. Paly of 6 or and gu. on a bend sa. 3 water bougets arg. Sire John de Byrton. *S.Y.* Monsire de Birton. *Y.*

Byrton. Quartered by Thornhill of Fixby, Arg. a chev. betw. 3 crosses crosslet fitchy gu.

Byshe. Or a chev. betw. three roses gu. and c.

Byshe (Surrey and Sussex). Same arms. *W.* Edward Bysh *Dug. O.J.*

Byrtwysell (Amcote Hall, co. Lancaster). Add: *V.L.*

Byselly. Gu. a chev. arg. betw. 3 battle axes of the second staves or. *V.**

Byssett. Az. on a bend cotised or three escallops . . . Add: *W.*

Bystley. Add: *V.**

Bythemore. Alias De La More, Barruly . . . and . . . on a chev. . . . . 3 mullets . . . *Collinson. Somerset. j. 185.*

C

CABORNE, or CABOURNE. Add: *V,* Cabron, Quartered by Slingsby, in chapel at Single-thorpe, co. York, the lozenges each charged with an erm. spot. *V.*

Cabourne, or Cabron (Thrasthrop, co. Lincoln). Add:.

Cabourne, Sa. a chev. arg. voided gu. betw. 3 lozenges of the second in chief a chough . . . *Cady.*

Cadiman (Norfolk and London: granted 1633). Insert—granted to Thomas Cadiman, Doctor of Physic to the Queen. *Guillim.*

Cairns (Baron Cairns of Garmoyle—created 1878). Gu. 3 martlets ppr. within a bordure or. Crest: a martlet ppr. Supporters—2 hawks ppr. Motto—"Effloresce".

Calane, or O'Calane (Ireland). Or on a bend gu. within a bordure az. 3 martlets arg.

Calcote, or Caldecott (Morant's, Essex). Insert—ij. 560 . . .

Calcott (Co. Rutland). Arg. 3 bendlets sa. *C.R.*

Calcroft. Erm. 3 lions pass. guard. in pale gu. Ric. and Thos. Calcroft, Chesterfield, co. Derby, temp. Hen. vj.

Caldecot. Arg. 3 calves gu. *Cady.*

Caldicott (Co. Dorset). Az. 3 arrows in pale or.

Caldwall (Essex). Arg. a bend betw. 2 crosslets gu. *Morant's, Essex, j. 219.*

Calfe. Arg. 3 calves pass. gu. Add: *V.*

Callander (that Ilk, co. Stirling . . .).

Callander (Westertown, co. Stirling). Baronetcy 1798. Sa. a bend chequy or and gu. betw. 6 billets of the second. *Robson.*

Callander, of Craigforth. Same Arms.

Callis. Quarterly arg. and gu. a bend purp. Lincoln, 1640. *Yorke.* Robert Callis, Serjeant at Law. *Dug. O.J.*

Callis. Sa. a chev. betw. 3 towers or a demi-lion issuing from each arg. *Cady.*

Callow. Arg. on a chev. betw. 3 leopards faces sa. . . . Crest . . . Add: *V.*

Calthorp. Az. a lion ramp. or depressed by a bend sa. with a silver ermine spot in the upper part of it. Sir John Calthorpe. *V.*

Calthorpe. Arg. a bend az. *Guillim.*

Calvering. Quarterly arg. and gu. on a bend sa. 3 mullets of the first. Sir Alayn Calveringe. *Q. Harl. MS. 6595.*

Calvert (Lord Baltimore, extinct 1771). Add: *Z. 651.* Add:

Calvert (Danby Wisk, co. York). quartering arg. and gu. a cross flory counterchanged for Crossland. *F.Y.*

Calvort (Little Hadham, co. Hereford). *Harl. MS. 4040. fo. 462.*

Calvert (Warwickoe and Lord of Zeveresi in Flanders). Or 3 martlets sa. *Harl. MS. 4040.*

Calybut. Add: *V.*

Cam. Arg. 6 eagles displ. 3.2. and 1. sa. Sir Richard Cam. *A. Harl. MS. 6137.*

Cambird. Add: *W.*

Cambria. 3rd son of Bruti. Arg. 2 lions pass. reguard. gu. *Cady.*

Camden. Insert—London. Or a fesse engr. betw. six crosses fitchy sa. Crest . . . . Add: *Vis. Lon. 1633.* Add: †

Camells. Or camels sa. *V.V.**

Camerey or Camery. Add: *V.*

Campbell (Aberuchill). Gyronny of 8 or and sa. a bordure embattled vert. *Guillim.*

Campe (London). Sa. a chev. betw. three griffins heads erased or. Add: *V.** (Another arg.). Add: *V.*

Campe (London). granted in 1604. Sa. a chev. betw. 3 griffins heads erased or. *V.*

Campion (Witham, co. Essex and London). Add: *Vis. Lon. 1633.*

Camvile or Camville (Co. Warwick . . .). Insert: Geffray de Camville. *F.V.I.V.*N.* Thomas de Camville. *E.* Robert de Camvile. *A.* William de Camvile. *G.* Hugh Camville. *Y.* And with a label of 5 points gu. William de Camville. *E.*

Camvile. Vert. an eagle displ. . . . Add: *V.V.**

Canbroke or Canbrook. Add: *V.*

Cancefield (Cancefield and Aldingham, co. Lancaster).

Candishe. Sa. three crosses crosslet or . . . . Add: *V.*

Canley. Arg. on a chev. sa. 3 leopards heads jessant fleurs-de-lis of the first. *V.*

Cannon (Co. Pembroke; granted). Insert—by Camden, February 1614.

Canon. Add: *V.**

Cantelow or Cantelupe (Co. Salop). Delete—(another, or). Add: *V.*

Cantelow or Cantelupe. Insert—London. Add: *V.*

Canthen. Gu. a chev. (another, erm. —insert—*V.*)

Cantlow (Prior of Bath Abbey 1489–99). Arg. an eagle rising . . .

Canton (Co. Kent). Add: *V.*

Canton. Gu. 2 Bars and in chief as many mullets arg. Sir Johan de Canntone. *N.* Sir John Cantone, co. Leicester, temp. Edw. j. *V.*

Cantwell (Ireland). Gu. 5 annulets or 2. 2. and 1 a canton erm. *V.*

Canvill. Az. an eagle regardant to the sinister rising wings overt and inverted or beaked gu. Richard Canvill. *V.*

Capel (Lord Mayor of London 1503). Insert—*V.E. 1612.* Add: *V.*

Capel (Earl of Essex). Insert—1661.

Capell (Co. Hereford). Arg. a chev. gu. betw. three torteaux. Add: Sir Richard de Capele. *N. Harl. MS. 6137. L.N.V.*

Capell. Sa. on a bend double cotised or three ogresses. *Cady.*

Capenhurst. Arg. three capons sa. Add: *Guillim.*

Caps (Cornwall). Sa. on a bend betw. 2 cotises or 3 ogresses. *V.*

Caps (Kent). The same as preceding Capps, without the escallop Add: Roger Cappus. *V.*

Capps or Capys (Co. Gloucester). Same arms. *V.*

Cappus (Kent). Add: *V.*

Cappus (Kent). Arg. on a chev. betw. 3 trefoils sa. as many escallops of the first. *V.*

Caradoc. Baron Howden. Arg. on a chev. az. betw. in chief a griffin pass. gu. wings erminois and in base a boar's head erased ppr. 3 garbs or. *Debrett.*

Carbill. Arg. on a chev. betw. 3 fowls sa. as many estoiles or. *Cady.*

Card (Dublin). Az. a chev. or betw. 3 mullets of 6 points arg.

Cardelyon or Cardelon. Add: *V.*

Cardegan. Arg. a chev. betw. 3 boars heads couped within a bordure sa. *V.V.**

Cardeton. Add: or Cardelon.

Cardigan, or Cardican (Wales). Add: *V.V.**

Cardoyll. Gu. 6 annulets in pale arg. *Harl. MS. 1458.*

Cardwell. Insert—co. Lancaster . . . a battle-axe of the first. Add: *F.L.*

Carell. Serjeant at Law. Barry of 6 arg. and sa. in chief 3 martlets of the last. *Dug. O.J.*

Caresville. Arg. three bars gemels sa. Add: John Caresville. *X.* William Caresvill. *V.*

Carew (Carew Castle, co. Pembroke &c.,). Add: Sir Nicholas Carew, co. Devon. temp. Edwd. j. *V.K.N.* Sir John Carew. *Q.*

Carew (Bickley, co. Devon 1620). Same Arms. *V.D.*

Carew. Or 3 lions pass. sa. a label gu. Sire Johan de Carew. *N.* Sir John de Carew the younger. *Q.*

Carew (Antony, Cornwall; bart.). Insert—1641 . . .

Carew. Arg. 3 bars gemel sa. Mons Pers de Carew. *S.*

Carewell. Sa. three chev. arg. Add: *V.*

Carey (Gothele). Az. 3 swans arg. *Collinson. Somerset. j. 356.*

Carey (Guernsey &c. . . .). Add: Sir Oswald Carey *V.* Carey (Chilton Foliot). *Z. 334.* Carey (Adenham, co. Hertford). *Z. 399.*

Cariges. Add: *V.*V.*

Cariges. Arg. a bend gu. betw. 3 birds . . . *Cady.*

Carill. Arg. on 3 bars sa. as many martlets of the first, 2 and 1. *V.*

Carington. Sa. a bend masculy arg. *Cady.*

Carkike (London, granted). Insert—by Cooke . . .

Carle. Gu. a chev. betw. three ducks rising arg. Add. *V.**

Carleton (Brightwell and Holcombe, co. Oxford) . . . Add: *V.* Add: Carleton (London). Same arms and crest, a mullet for diff. *Vis. Lon. 1633.*

Carlile (Carlile   ). Arg. on a chev. sa. betw. 3 cornish choughs ppr. as many estoiles or. *V.*

Carlyon (Co. Cornwall). . . . Add: *Lysons.*

Carmarthen or Camarden (Chislehurst, co. Kent and London). Add: *Vis. Lon. 1633.*

Carminow (Carminow, co. Cornwall). . . . Az. a bend or. Insert—*V.*

Carminow (Polmagan, co. Cornwall. 1620). Az. a bend or and a label gu. *V.C.* Thomas Carminhow. *Y.*

Carminow, Carmynow or Carminaw (Cornwall). Add: *V.V.**

Carnaby. Add: William Carnaby. *X.*

Carnaby. Arg. 2 bars az. and in chief 3 hurts on a canton vert. 3 bars and a chief or charged with a demi-lion issuant az. Sir Reynold Carnaby. *Constable's Roll xij.*

Carnegy (London, Granted 1826). Arg. an eagle displ. az. charged with a star of 8 points within a bordure engr. gu. charged with 8 bezants.

Carnsew. Add: *V.C. 303.*

Carpenter. Paly of 6 az. and gu. on a chev. arg. 3 crosses crosslet of the second in chief a mitre or. **Monument** at Westbury. John Carpenter, Bishop of Worcester 1440. Dr. Carpenter, *Lansdowne MS. 255. fo. 7.*

Carpenter (London, Herefordshire, Gloucestershire and Kent). Az. underlined, margin; sa. and deleted, *Vis. Lon. 1633.*

Carpenter (Cobham, co. Surrey and Sussex). Granted 4 March 1663. Insert—by Bysche, Clarencieux.

Carpenters. Company of (London). Insert—Granted by Clarencieux 1466. Add: Carpenters (Company of, London). Same arms. But on the chev. a joiners square or and a golden reel with line arg. *Cotton MS. Tiberius. D. 10.*

Carr (Sleaford, co. Lincoln). Insert—Baronetcy 1611, and Lancs. Gu. on a chev. or underlined, margin; arg.

Carr (St. Helens, Auckland 1730). Author of the list of Arms of Mayors and Sheriffs of Newcastle on Tyne, quoted in this work as *Carr MS.* Gu. on a chev. arg. 3 mullets sa.

Carr (Cocker   ). Same arms. *Eliz. Roll. xx.*

Carr. Gu. on a chev. arg. 3 estoiles sa. in chief a crescent for diff. Sir John Care. *V.*

Carr (City of Cork). Gu. a chev. betw. 3 demi-lions couped arg. as many mullets of the field quartering, vert. on a chev. between 3 unicorns heads erased as many mullets sa. *Burke.*

Carre (Middlesex). Gu. on a chev. arg. 3 estoiles sa. a canton erm. *C.L. p. 83.*

Carell or Carril. Insert: Warnham (Sussex and Kent). Arg. on a —insert— 'plain' bend . . . Add: *V.*V.*

Carell (Chiddington, Kent. 1575). Arg. on a bend az. 3 griffins heads or a bordure of the second. **Tomb** in Chiddington Church.

Carrick or Carrack (Co. Gloucester). Add: *Vis. Lon. 1633.*

Carrick (Quartered by Cornwallis). Or a lion ramp. gu. on a chief of the last a swan wings expanded arg. betw. 2 annulets or.

Carrington. Arg. on a bend sa. 3 mascles of the first. Sir William Carington. *V.*

Carrington (Carrington, co. Chester &c. . .). Add: *V.*

Carrington (Ogbourne St. George, co. Wilts). Same arms. Sir John Caryngton. *V.*

Carrington (Spannton, co. York). 1612. Sa. on a bend arg. 3 lozenges of the field a crescent for diff. *F.Y.*

Carington. Sa. on a bend arg. 3 mascles of the field. *Syl. Morgan.*

Carron. Gu. a chev. betw. three escallops arg. Add: Sir Noel Carron *W.* Noel de Caron Ambassador from Holland 1589. *Aubrey Surrey. j. 9.*

Carrowe. Carrowe (London 1568). Or 3 lions pass. in pale sa. within a bordure company or and sa. *C.L.*

Carsett (Co. Cornwall). Gu. a bend arg. betw. 6 bezants. *V.*

Carstairs (Warboys, co. Huntingdon). Az. on a chev. arg. betw. 3 green roses slipped ppr. as many buckles of the field.

Carston. Add: *V.*

Carswell (London). Arg. 3 bars gemelles sa. Crest: An arm embowed in mail ppr. hand holding a cross crosslet fitchy or. *Vis. Lon. 1633.*

Carter (St. Columb, co. Cornwall . . .). Add: Carter, Author of the 'Analysis of Honour'. Same arms. *Guillim and Randle Holme.*

Carter (of Petersfield, co. Hants., M.P. for Winchester 1847). Same arms, quartering 2nd gu. a chev. betw. 3 crosses crosslet fitchy arg. for Bonham. 3rd sa. 3 pitchforks palewise 2 and 1 arg. for Pyke. *Debrett.*

Carter (Nicholas Carter M.D. Willesborow, Kent and London). Sa. 2 lions ramp. combatant or. *Guillim.*

Carter (granted by Segar, Garter in 1612 to Carter of London). Arg. a chev. sa. betw. 3 catherine wheels vert. *Guillim.*

Carter (London; granted 1612). Add: *Vis. Lon. 1633.*

Carter (correct to Setrington, co. York . . .) *Dugdale.*

Carter (Kinmel, co. Denbigh). Az. a talbot pass. betw. 3 oval buckles or. *V.L. 1660.*

Carter. Gu. a chev. betw. 3 lozenge buckles or. *Cady.*

Carter. Arg. on a chev. betw. three catherine wheels sa. as many cinquefoils of the first Add: *V.**

Carthorp (Quartered by Bulkeley). . . . Add: *V.V.**

Carthuze. Add: *W.*

Cartier (Guernsey). . . . insert az. A chev.—insert —or betw. three quatrefoils pierced—add— arg. . . .

Cartwright (South Wheatley, co. Nottingham). Add: Cartwright (Newland, co. York 1612). Same arms. *F.Y.*

Cartwright (Derby). Insert—confirmed by Flower 1574.

Cartwright (London). Add: *Vis. Lon. 1633.*

Carvell. Arg. three bendlets sa. . . . Add: *V.V.**

Carus (Thomas Carus Justice of the King's Bench 1556). Az. a chev. betw. 10 cinquefoils arg. *Dug. O.J.*

Carvaile. Arg. 3 chevs. sa. on a canton of the second a tower of the first. *Harl. MS. 1407. fo. 74. b.*

Carver (Canterbury, Granted by Segar 29 June 10 James j.). Az. a pelican arg. vulning herself gu. betw. 8 fleurs-de-lis of the second.

Carver (Norfolk). Sa. a chev. erm. betw. 3 crosses crosslet arg.

Carvile (Berwick-upon-Tweed). Add: Carvill New Mankton, co. York 1614). Same arms. *F.Y.*

Carwardine (Sons of the late Rev. Thomas Carwardine). Add: *Berry.*

Cary. Gu. a chev. betw. 3 swans wings elevated arg. *W.*

Caryll (London). Arg. 3 bars sa. in chief as many martlets of the last. Crest: On a mount vert. a stag lodged or. *Vis. Lon. 1633.*

Case (Ince; and Red Hazels &c.) . . . Add: Case (Hayton, co. Lancaster 1664). Same arms. *V.L.*

Caselton. Arg. a castle gu. bezanty on a chief sa. a "mitter" betw. a 5-foil and an annulet or. *Cady.*

Caselyn. Or 6 billets az. a label of 5 points gu. *V.**

Caselyn. Or 6 billets 3. 2. and 1. az. a label of 3 points gu. Edmund Caselyn. *V.* the label of 4 points. Edmond Caselyn *Cotton MS. Tiberius. D. 10.*

Casey (Ireland). Add: *V.*

Cashe or Cushe. Arg. on a chev. sa. 3 fountains ppr. *Syl. Morgan.*

Cassey (Deerhurst, co. Gloucester). Add: *V.*

Casshe. Add: *V.*

Cassy. Arg. on a bend gu. three round buckles or. . . . . Crest: An eagle displ. . . . Add: Thomas Cassy. *V.*

Castleford. Arg. a chev. betw. 3 towers tripple towered gu. *V.V.**

Castleford. Per fess sa. and barry wavy arg. and az. overall a square castle towered at each corner of the second. Roger Castleford, Whisperdale, co. York 1585. *W.*

Castell (Berkshire). Add: Sir William Castell, co. Warwick. *V.*

Castell (Thomas Castell, Sheriff of Newcastle 1439). Per fess indented sa. and or in chief a castle or in the dexter a chief crescent gu. *Carr MS.*

Castell. Gu. 3 towers or. Sir Nicholas Castell. *V.*

Castell (Raveningham, Norfolk). 1614. Arg. 3 towers gu.

Castell. Gu. three bars vair. Add: Le Sire de Castel. *Y.*

De Castells (Bishop of Bath and Wells also Hereford in 1501). Arg. 3 bendlets counterembattled gu. He was a Cardinal. *Ciaconius.*

Castelliott. Az. on a chev. betw. 3 lozenges or 2 mullets gu. pierced or. *Cady.*

Castelyn (Vis. London 1568). Add: *C.L.*

Caster (Norfolk). Sa. an eagle displ. barry of six arg. and gu. Add: Sir John Caster, Norfolk, temp. Edw. j. *V.* Sire Johan de Castre. *N.*

Caster. Gu. a chev. arg. betw., 3 lozenges *V.* round buckles or. *Cotton MS. Tiberius. D. 10.*

Castillon (Blenham Valence . . . co. Berks.). Insert 1565. . . . in the dexter point arg. Insert—? or.

Castinworth, Chastelyn, or Chestline. Add: *Nash.*

Castleford (Wypershall, co. York). Add: 1585. *W.*

Castleford. Sa. a castle in perspective . . . Add: *V.**

Castle Hodingham (Benedictine Priory of Essex). Arg. 2 billets one in bend dexter (aliter in pale). az. surmounted by another sinister (aliter in fess) gu.

Castleton (Suffolk, Surrey and Lincolnshire). Add: *V.** Add: Castleton (Bury St. Edmunds, Suffolk, Bart. 1641). Same arms.

Castleton. Az. on a bend or 3 (? eels) coiled palewise of the first. *V.*

Castlyn. Az. on a bend or three castles sa. Crest: . . . Add: *V.*

Caston. Gu. a chev. nebuly erm. betw. 3 crosses crosslet or. *Harl. MS. 1386. fo. 36.*

Caston (Norfolk). Add: *V.*

Castor. Sa. an eagle displ. barry of ten arg. and gu. Add: *N.*

Castre (Norfolk). Same arms. Add: Sire Johan de Castre. *N.*

Castre. Arg. an eagle displ. barry arg. and gu. Add: Thomas de Castre. *Y.*

Castre. Az. an eagle displ. barry of 8 arg. and gu. Sir John Castre or de Castre. *L.*

Catcher. Per fesse sa. . . . . Add: *Vis. Lon. 1633.* Add: John Catcher (Sheriff of London 1587, Granted by Cooke). *W.*

Catcher (London 1652). Per fess gu. and sa. an eagle displ. erm.

Cater (Kempston, co. Bedford). Sa. a chev. erm. betw. 3 salmons hauriant arg. *L.N. 1660.*

Catesby (Whiston, Althorpe—Hinton and Ashby —Ligers, co. Northants). Arg. 2 lions pass. guard sa. crowned or. *C.R.* Sir William Catesby *V.*

Catesby (Co. Warwick). Same arms. *C.W.*

Cateshall or Cateshull. . . . . as many mullets— insert—'pierced' gu. Add: *V.*

Cateshull. Az. on a chev. arg. betw. 3 lozenges or as many mullets gu. *V.*

Catharne (Co. Pembroke). Per fess az. and vert. in chief a cat couchant coward tail reflexed over the back in base a pierced 5-foil arg. *V.*

Catherton (Kent) . . . a chev. . . . . betw. 3 annulets. . . .

Catlyn. Per chev. az. and or 3 lions pass. guard. in pale counterchanged. William Callyn Leybourn, Kent. Granted 1470. *Harl. MS. 1359. fo. 5.*

Catlyn (Robert Catlyn, Raunds, co. Northants). Per chev. az. and or 3 lions pass. guard. in pale counterchanged within a bordure arg. *W.*

Catlin (Lord Chief Justice, temp. Elizabeth). Add: Catlyn (Kirby Cane, co. Norfolk 1662). Same arms. *L.N.*

Catlyn (Hatford Hall, co. Norfolk, certified 1 Dec. 1555). Per chev. az. and or 3 lions pass. guard. in pale counterchanged on a chief arg. as many adders nowed erect sa. *Harl. MS. 1359. fo. 62b.*

Catricke. Add: *V V.**

Catts. Az. 3 cats pass. guard. in pale arg. *Cady.*

Catterick. Chequy arg. and sa. a bordure of the first. (Antient arms.)

Cattey. Sa. 3 cats pass. guard. in pale arg. *Harl. MS. 1404. fo. 130.*

Catty. Or a lion ramp. guard. gu. holding a sword ppr. betw. 3 estoiles of the second over all a chevron sa. *Robson.*

Catton. Gu. two cats pass. guard. arg.—margin; (? or). *V.*

Catton. Sa. a bend . . . Crest: . . . owl arg. Add: *V.**

Cauley (Cowley). Add: *V.**

Caunton (Quartered by Markham, of Markham). . . . Add: *V.N. 23.*

Causton (Causton, co. Essex). Add: *V.W.*

Causton. Arg. on a bend sa. three crosses crosslet fitchee of the field. Add: Robert Causton. *Y.*

Causton. Arg. a bend betw. six crosses crosslet sa. *V.** Add: Causton. Arg. on a bend az. 3 crosses crosslet fitchy of the field. Robert Causton. *X.* Sir Richard Kawston. *V.*

Cauthorpe. Arg. a chev. betw. 3 escallops gu. *V.N. p. 16.*

Cavell (Cornwall). Arg. a calf pass. sa. *Lysons.*

Caver (Quartered by Flower of Langer, co. Notts.). Add: *V.N. 121.*

Cawsse. Insert—Norfolk. Sa. a chev. . . . Add: *V.*

Cawston. Bendy of six arg. and sa. *V.** But sa. and arg. *V.*

Cawston. Sa. three bends arg. Add: *V.*

Cawton (Thirsk, co. York 1612). Gu. 2 bars and in chief 3 mullets arg. all within a bordure engr. sa. *F.Y.*

Cayley (Crompton, co. York bart.). Insert—1661. Also after 'according to Dugdale' to end of sentence. Add: But *Guillim* gives sa. a bend betw. 6 Crosses patty fitchy arg. and at end. Add: Sir John Cayle. *V.*

Cayley. Chequy or and gu. a bend erm. *V.* Sire Adam de Cayli. *N.*

Cecill. Sa. three bends arg. Add: *V.*

Cecill or Cecyll. Sa. two chevs. arg. Add: Thomas Cecyll. *V.*

Ceely (St. Ives, co. Cornwall). . . . Crest: . . . Add: Ceely (Plymouth). *Lysons.*

Celvy (Warley). Sa. a bend or. *V.*

Cely. Arg. on a chev. gu. betw. 3 eagles displ. sa. as many bezants each charged with a plate. Sir Benet Celey. *V.*

Cerne. Per fess arg. and gu. a lion ramp. within a bordure counterchanged. Philip de Cerne. *A.E.*

Cesyr. Arg. on a bend—delete purp.—and amend to gu. *V.V.**

Chachemayd. Add: *V.*

Chadworth (London). Add: *V.** Add: Sir John Chadworth or Shadworth, Lord Mayor of London 1401. *Harl. MS. 1349.*

Chaffin (Chettle, co. Dorset). Gu. a talbot pass. or a chief of the second. *Cady.*

Chagford (Co. Devon, temp. Edw. j.). Sa. crusilly fitchy 3 lions ramp. arg. *Lysons.*

Chalenor. Gu. a chief or a baston compony az. and arg. *Y.*

Chalk (Yatton, co. Somerset 1624). Gu. 3 bars wavy arg. *V.S.*

Challener. Az. a chev. betw. in chief 3 estoiles and in base a cross arg. *Robson.*

Challennor (Chitlington, Sussex). Az. a chev. betw. 3 mascles or. *Berry.*

Chalon. Gu. a bend or. *Z.606.*

Chaloner (Guisborough, co. York, bart.). Insert—1620, extinct —insert—1640. Add: *Dugdale. p. 201.* Add: Sir Thos. Challoner, Knt. Sometime Governor to Henry, Prince of Wales. *Guillim.*

Chaloner (Co. Stafford). Arg. 2 bars vert. over all a lion ramp. gu. *W.*

Chaloner (Duffield, co. Derby). Az. a chev. betw. 3 cherubs heads arg. *Lysons.*

Chaloner (Co. York). Az. on a chev. betw. 3 mascles or as many mullets sa. *Fairfax's Book of Arms.*

Chaloner. Insert—co. Stafford. Arg. two bars vert. overall a lion ramp. gu. Add: *W.*

Chalons (Devonshire). Gu. two bars betw. six (another eight) martlets 3. 2. and 1. Add: Sir John Chalons. *V.*

Chalons. Gu. 2 bars vert. (?) betw. 9 martlets arg. *V.**

Chalun. Add: *V.*

Chamber (Visit. Notts., borne by John Chamber, Sheriff of Newcastle in 1437). . . . Add: *V.* Add: Chamber (Mayor of Newcastle 1440). Gu. a chev. betw. 3 cinquefoils pierced or a crescent for diff. *Carr MS.*

Chamber (Dagenham, Essex). Same arms. *V.E. 1634.*

Chamber (Gaddesby, co. Leicester). Add: *Harl. MS. 1431. fo. 24.*

Chamber. Quarterly arg. and az. (another, or and az.) a chev. counterchanged. Add: *V.*

Chamber. Quarterly arg. and az. a chev. engr. counter engr. counterchanged. *V.*

Chamber. Sa. three goats courant arg. . . . Add: *V.*

Chamberlayn (London). Gu. an escutcheon arg. within an orle of cinquefoils or. Crest: . . . Add: *Vis. Lon. 1633.*

Chamberlayne. Arg. a chev. betw. 3 fylfots gu. *Harl. MS. 2116. fo. 76b.*

Chamberlayne. Arg. a chev. gu. betw. 3 leopards heads az. *V.*

Chamberlayn. Or on a bend gu. three lozenges vair. Add: *V.*

Chamberlayne (Astley, co. Warwick). . . . Add: Chamberlain London). Same arms and crest. *Vis. Lon. 1633.*

Chamberlayne (Newton Harcourt, co. Leicester). . . . Add: *C.C.* Add: Chamberlayn (Sherborne, co. Oxford). granted in 1585. Same arms. Chamberlayne, Tankerville. *V.* Sire Richard Chaumberlein. *N.S.*

Chamberlayn (Sheriff of Oxfordshire, temp. Eliz.). Gu. a chev. arg. betw. 3 escallops or. *Fuller.*

Chamberlain. Arg. on a bend sa. 5 bezants Quartered by Bowyer-Smith.

Chamberlin (Norfolk). Gu. a chev. arg. betw. 3 escallops or. *Cady.*

Chamberlyn (Gedding, Suffolk). Arg. 3 chevs. braced sa. on a chief of the last as many bezants. Sir Rauf Chamberlyn. *V.*

Chamberlyn. Arg. a chev. betw. 3 leopards heads gu. Add: *V.*

Chambernoun. Az. a chev. or. Sir John de Chambernoun. *A.* But gu. a chev. or in *A. Harl. MS. 6137.*

Chambers. Arg. a chev. . . . voided erm. betw. 3 gun chambers vomiting fire ppr. on a chief az. a pelican or betw. 2 fleurs-de-lis gu. *Cady.*

Chambers (London and Barkway, co. Herts). Add: *Vis. Lon. 1633.*

Chambers (Selling, Kent). Sa. a chev. betw. three cinquefoils or. *Hasted iij. 25.*

Chambers (Co. York). Arg. a chev. sa. betw. 3 chevrons sejant (*sic*) gu. *Eliz. Roll xxiij.*

Chambers (Kilmainham). . . . read—Ermines for Er. an eagle . . . in the third line.

Chambir. Add: *V.V.**

Chamblayn. Add: Chamblyn alias Spicer in Notts. *W.*

Chamblin. Arg. an eagle displ. gu. armed or. Sire . . . de Chamblin. *V.*

Chamborn or Chamburn. Az. 3 bars arg. Sir Rauf de Chamburne. *V.*

Chambre (Spratton, Northamptonshire). Add: *Baker.*

Chamond or Chaumond. Add: *V.*

Chamoun. Add: *V.*

Champayne. Arg. three bars nebulee gu. (another, barry nebulee of six arg. and gu.). Add: Robert de Champayne. *F.*

Champion. Arg. two bars nebulee gu. Add: John Champion, Kent. *V.*

Champney. Sa. a chev. arg. betw. 3 crosses erm. *W.*

Champneys (Orchardley, co. Somerset). bart.— insert—1767. Per pale or underlined and margin—? arg.

Champneys (Orchardley, co. Somerset). Per pale embattled sa. and arg. a lion ramp. *Harl. MS. 1445. fo. 57.*

Champneys (Hall Place and Osthanger, co. Kent). Add: *V.*

Chanceaux or De Cancellis (Co. Devon). Arg. a chev. az. betw. 3 mullets sa. *Lysons.*

Chandos (Sir John . . . one of the Kts. of the Garter. 11th plate on the Sovereign's side. Delete—arg. margin, correction—substitute, or.

Chandoys or Chandoz (Cheshire). Add: John Chandos. *Y.* Sir Roger de Chandos, temp. Edw. iij. *V.*

Changer. Barry of 6 or and az. per pale indented counterchanged. *Randle Holme.*

Channesley. Add: John de Channesley. *V.*

Channon (John Channon, Colthoop). Gu. a lion ramp. arg. within a bordure compony or and az. *Y.*

Chanse. Barry of 22 sa. and arg. a lion ramp. gu. Thomas de Chansi. *G.*

Chanseill. Sa. six eagles displ. or. *V.*

Chanserire. Add: *Y.V.*

Chanseul. Add: *V.*

Chantrell (Quartered by Docton). . . . Add: Chantrell (Wm. Chantrell, Brampton, co. Devon). *V.* Same arms.

Chansens. Gu. 3 eagles displ. arg. Thomas de Chansens E. John de Chansens. *F.*

Chansens. Sa. 3 eagles displ. or. Emeri de Chansens. *E.F.*

Chapell or Chappell (Cambridgeshire). Second line chaplet underlined margin—query 'chapel'.

Chapell or Chappell (Co. Cambridge and Gamlingay, co. Huntingdon). For fess arg. and vert. a chapel of the first roofed gu. betw. 4 escallop shells counterchanged. *Cotton MS. Julius F. viij.*

Chapman. Or on a bend az. cotised gu. 3 bezants. *Cady.*

Chapman (Highbury Park, co. Middlesex). Add: *Vis. Lon. 1633.*

Chapoin. Add: *V.*

Chappell (London). Add: *Vis. Lon. 1633.* Margin —insert—Crest: a lion ramp. gu. holding an anchor az. *Vis. Lon. 1633.*

Chard. Quarterly or and gu. over all a label of five points az. Add: *Vis. Lon. 1633.*

Chardelowe or Shardelowe. Add: *V.*

Chareter. . . . in chief 2 birds . . . in base a fleur-de-lis. . . . *Seal.*

Charilton. Add: *V.*

Charington. Add: *Harl. MS. 1404.*

Chark (London). . . . a Greek upsilon gu. Add: Crest, On a plate a Greek upsilon gu. outside the plate a circular scroll inscribed DIA THE ETENHE. *Vis. Lon. 1633.*

Charles (Ireland). . . . an eagle displ. arg.-underlined and ? or. Add: John Charles, Recorder of Exeter 1558. *Colby.*

Charles or Chareles. Add: *V.*

Charleston. Arg. on a chev. vert. three eagles displ. or. Add: Sir John de Charlestone. *N.* Sir John de Charleston, Essex. *V.*

Charleston or Charlton. Add: Sir John Charleston.

Charleton. Az. three swans—insert—close, arg. *V.** Sir John Charleton. *V.*

Charleton. Arg. a chev. engr. betw. three griffin's heads erased sa. *V.**

Charleton. Az. a chev. or betw. three swans arg. *V.V.**

Charleton (Hesleyside, co. Northumberland). Add: Le Sire de Charleton. *S.T.* Sir John Charlton. *V.* Thomas Charleton, Bishop of Hereford 1327–44.

Charlton (London). Or a lion ramp. gu. Crest: a lions face gu. *Harl. MS. 1476.*

Charley. Az. a chev. betw. 3 hawks lures or. *Cady.*

Charlston (Essex). . . . delete—(Another sa). Add: *V.*

Charnells (Leicestershire). Add: Sir Thomas de Charnelles. *E.*

Charnfield or Sharnfield. Add: *V.** Sir . . . de Charnefelde. *V.*

Charnocke (Charnocke, co. Lancaster). Add: *V.*

Charnocke (Leyland, co. Lancaster). Add: *Harl. MS. 1437 fo. 272.*

Charnock (Cheshire). Add: *V.*

Charon or Charrone. Add: *V.** Add: Sire Richard Charrone *N.V.P.Y.*

Charron (Durham). Sa. 3 water bougets arg. *Surtees.*

Charteray. Arg. a chev. betw. three cinquefoils gu. Add: Charteray. Arg. a chev. betw. 3 septfoils gu. Sir John Charteray. *Y.*

Chartsey (Kent). . . . three hawks heads erased arg. Add: beaked or *V.V.**

Chartley. Chartley Arg. a chev. betw. 3 perukes sa.

Charqhayes. Arg. on a bend gu. 3 hawks of the first. *Cady.*

Chastel (Sir Will del Chastel). Gu. 2 bars arg. on a canton of the second a castle sa. *N.*

Chasteleyne or Le Chesteleyne. Add: *V.*

Chastelon. Sa. a lion pass . . . Add: Sir Makelon Chatelon. *V.*

Chastelyn or Castlyn. Gu. on a bend or 3 towers sa. each with another on the top. *V.*

Chaston. Gu. 3 bars vair. Thomas Chaston. *Y.*

Chaucer (Geoffrey Chaucer, of Woodstock). . . . Add: Sir Thomas Chaucer. *V.*

Chaumond. See Chamond.

Chaumont (Colton, co. York 1665). Arg. a chev. counter embattled betw. 3 birds heads erased sa. *Dugdale. p. 30.*

Chaunceur (Upton, Northamptonshire). Arg. a chev. betw. 3 annulets gu. *Baker.*

Chauncy. Az. three wolves pass. in pale betw. two flaunches or each charged with an anchor sa.—margin—? az. Add: *Harl. MS. 1358. fo. 60b.* Add: Crest: a demi-lion ramp. az. goutty d'or holding an anchor of the last. *Vis. Lon. 1633.*

Chauncy. Insert—co. Lincoln Arg. a chev. gu. . . . Add: Sir Philip de Chauncy. *N.V.*

Chauncy. Or two chev. gu. . . . bezantee. Add: *V.**

Chauncy. Arg. a chev. betw. 3 annulets gu. Sir Philip de Chaunsey. *N.*

Chaundler (London). Per chev. az. and gu. 3 cherubs heads winged or. Crest: Out of clouds ppr. a cherub's head winged or. *Vis. Lon. 1633.*

Chaures. Add: Paterick de Chaures. *E. Harl. MS. 6137.*

Chaures. Arg. 6 barrulets gu. over all 8 martlets in orle vert. Piers or Patrick de Chaures. *F.*

Chaurs. Gu. crusilly and a bendlet or. Hereni de Chaurs. *F.*

Chawney or Chaury (London). . . .

Chaworth (Alfreton, co. Derby). Add: Sir Thomas de Chaworth *A.I.J.X.N.* Sir Christopher Chaworth. *R.* Sir William Chaworth. *S.* and with a label gu. Sir William de Chaworth. *I.*

Chaworth. Barry arg. and gu. a bend sa. Henri de Chaworth. *X.Y.*

Chaworth (Annesley, co. Nottingham). Add: Sir Patrick Chaworth. *D.* But barry of 10 *Z. 109. N.Y.*

Chaworth (Co. Oxford). 1645. Barry of 8 arg. and gu. so many martlets in orle sa. *Guillim.*

Chaworth (Wiverton, co. Notts). Barry of ten arg. and gu. an orle of martlets sa. *V.N.1614*

Chaworth (Harthill, co. York 1612). Same arms, a mullet for diff.

Chawrey. Or on a chev. sa. betw. three birds . . . a covered cup or Add: *V.* Sir Richard Chawrey, Lord Mayor of London 1494. The annulet arg. *V.*

margin
Adds:

Chaury or Chawrey. Arg. two bars gu. . . . Add: *V.*

Chawser. Margin—Chaucer.

Chedder. Add: *Collinson Somerset ij. 156. V.**

Chedleworth. Add: *V*

Chedwarden. Or 2 leopards pass. reguard. *Cady.*

Chedworth. Or on a chev. gu. 3 martlets arg. *V.*

Cheke (Bludhall, Suffolk). Arg. a cock gu. *W.*

Cheke (Debenham, Suffolk). Or a cock gu. armed crested and jelloped sa. *W.V.**

Chein (Straloth.   ). Az. a bend arg. betw. 6 crosses patty fitchy or. *Guillim.*

Chellery. Arg. a whirlpool gu. Add: *V.*

Chellery. Arg. a bend voided betw. 2 cotises gu. quartering arg. 3 roundlets. *Cady.*

Chelley. Arg. a bend voided betw. 2 cotises gu. *Cady.*

Chellory. Arg. a bend wavy gu. betw. two bendlets of the last. Add: Chellory, called Kingston. *V.V.**

Chelmick (Raydon, co. Salop). Granted by Cooke. Vert. 3 lions ramp. guard. or *W.* confirmed 1 June 1582. *Harl. MS. 1359. fo. 123b.*

Chelton or Chilton. Arg. a chev. gu. Add: *V.*

Chemington. Arg. a chev. betw. 3 rams heads erased sa. *Cady.*

Chenduit. Arg. on a bend az. 3 coronels reversed or *V.** Sir John Chenduyt. *V.*

Chendut. Add: *V.**

Chenew or Cheynow. Add: *V.*

Cheney (Sherland, in the Isle of Sheppey) . . . Add: Sir Thomas Cheney, Shepey, Kent. *V.* and quartering arg. a chief per pale indented or and gu. charged on the dexter with a rose of the last for Shotesbroke. Sir John Cheney, K.G., and Sir Thomas Cheney K.G.

Cheney (Lord Cheney) . . . of Toddington—insert —Bedford. Add: Cheney (Sussex) *V.* Same arms. Henry Lord Cheney of Toddington ob. 1587. quartering Shurland, Shottesbrooke, and Broughton.

Cheney. Quarterly arg. and sa. a bend lozengy gu. *V.* Add: Cheney, co. Cambridge. *V.* Cheney (Thorngumbald, co. York). *F.Y.*

Chenire. Gu. 3 buck goats arg. *Cady.*

Chepstow. Arg. a lion ramp. gu. . . . Add: *V.*

Chequer. Add: Sir Laurence de la Chequer *I. V.*

Cherbron. Add: Sir Henry Cherbron. *V.*

Cherington (Co. Essex). Add: *Morant's Essex. j. 210.*

Cheriston. Alias Haleighwell. Or on a bend gu. 3 goats bendwise statant arg. armed or. *V.*

Cheritson. Insert—or Chiverston . . . and Add: *V.**

Cherley. Insert—or Chorley.

Chernoke (Chester). Add: *V.*

Cheryton. Arg. a chev. betw. 3 goats heads erased gu. attired or. *V.*

Cheselden or Chesselden. Add: *V.*

Chesehunt or Chesnut. Gu. 3 bendlets erm. Sir Richard Chesehunt. *Q.* Sir Rignald Chesehunt. *Q.*

Cheseedon. (Uppingham, co. Rutland). Granted by Dalton, Norroy 1560. Arg. a chev. betw. 3 crosses ancry. gu. *C.R. 1. 50.*

Cheselten. Sa. a chev. betw. 3 chisels arg. *Harl. MS. 1404. fo. 105.*

Chesham. Chequy arg. and vert. on a canton gu. a chess rook of the field . . . Add: *V.* and another the chess rook or. *V.*

Cheshull. Vaire arg. and gu. on a bend sa. three escallops or. Add: *V.*

Cheshull. Vairy arg. and gu. on a bend sa. 3 escallops of the first (of co. Essex). *W.*

Chesseldon. Add: *V.*

Chessendon. Insert—co. Dorset. Add: *V.*

Chester (Sir William Chester, Lord Mayor of London 1560). . . . Add: Chester (Lillington, co. Bedford). Same arms. Add: *V.*

Chester. Gu. 3 lions pass. guard. in pale or within a bordure az. Contee de Chestre. *Y.*

Chester (Chicheley, Bucks). . . . Add: *V.*

Chester. Gu. a chev. arg. betw. three buckles lozengy or. Add: William Chester or Chestree. *Y.*

Chester (Amesbury, co. Gloucester). . . . Add: Chester (London). Same arms. But hawks lures or. Crest: a lions gamb erased per fess gu. and erm. *Vis. Lon. 1633.*

Chesterton. Add: *V.*

Chestlet. Add: *V.**

Chestlet. Per fess arg. and az. a tower gu. betw. 4 escallops 2 and 2 counterchanged. *V.*

Chetilton. Arg. on a chev. gu. 5 bezants a bordure gu. a label of 5 az. Sir Matthew de Chetilton. *V.*

Chetwood. Arg. a lion ramp. gu. Add: *V.*

Chetwynd (Viscount Chetwynd). . . . Add: Sire John Chedewynt. *O.* William Chetwynde. *S.* Sir Philip Chetwyn, co. Stafford (the mullets pierced).*V.*

Chevening (Chevening, Kent). Add: *V.*

Chevergott. Sa. on a bend or 3 goats gu. *Cady.*

Cheverell (Wiltshire). Arg. three lions pass. in pale sa. Add: Sir Thomas Cheverell. *V.*

Cheverell or Cheverall (Wiltshire). Add: Sir Alexander Cheverell. *V.L.N.*

Cheveron or Cheverton. Gu. two chev. erm. *V.V.**

Chevereston. Or on a bend gu. 3 goats arg. John de Chevereston. *Y.*

Cheverston (Co. Devon). Or on a bend gu. 3 goats pass. arg. *Lysons.*

Cheymew. Add: *V.V.**

Cheyndrett. Az. a chain in pale or a label of 3 gu. Rauf. Cheyndrett. *Harl. MS. 4033.*

Cheyndute. Gu. a lion—delete—salient, substitute ramp. reguard. . . . Add: *V.*

Cheyne (Sheppey, co. Kent). Az. on a canton arg. a crescent gu. Add: *MS. 14307. fo. 116.*

Cheyney or De Castinets. Add: *V.*

Cheyney. Arg. on 2 chevs. az. 4 chevs. couched dexter and sinister. or.

Chibborne. (Essex). Arg. on a chev. betw. 3 dexter gauntlets gu. as many 5-foils of the first. *V.E. 1634.*

Chich. Add: *V.V.**

Chiche. Az. 3 lions ramp. arg. *V.*

Chicheley (Cambridgeshire). Add: *V.*

Chicheley. Arg. a chev. betw. 3 goats heads erased az. collared and attired or. *Cady.*

Chichester (Devonshire). 2nd line after 'field'. Add: *V.** (another . . .).

Chichester. Erm. on a canton sa. a covered cup arg. John Chichester, Lord Mayor of London 1369. *W.*

Chichley (London temp. Ric. ij.). Or a chev. engr. betw. 3 cinquefoils gu. *Fuller.*

Chichley. Or a chev. betw. 3 cinquefoils gu. Sir . . . de Chichley. *V.*

Chiderlegh (Cornwall and Devonshire). Add: Cady.

Chidiock (Dorset). Add: John Chideok. *Y.*

Chieftain. Sa. a chief arg. a bend of the last. *Randle Holme.*

Chiesly (Kersewell, Scotland). Add: *Guillim.*

Child (Newfield and Stallington Hall, co. Stafford, bart. Insert—1868

Child (London). Gu. a chev. engr. erm. betw. 3 doves arg. Crest: On a mount vert. a dove rising arg. *Vis. Lon. 1633.*

Child (London and Worcestershire). Granted 28 Jan. 1700—Insert—to Sir Francis Child, Lord Mayor of London . . .

Chilmick. Insert—Granted by Cooke. Add: *W.*

Chilmington (Chillington, Kent). Arg. 3 chevs. az. betw. 9 crosses crosslet sa. *Robson.*

Chipman. Sa. two lions pass. and counterpass. betw. as many chevs. arg. Add: *V.* Also Chipenham. *V.*

Chipenham or Chipnam. Sa. 2 lions pass. respectant the first or the second arg. betw. two chevrons as the last. *V.**

Chipenham. Gu. a chev. engr. betw. 3 dolphins embowed arg. *V.N. p. 129.*

Chipleigh. Az. a chev. betw. 3 stags heads cabossed or. *Collinson Somerset iij. 260.*

Chipmanden. Add: *V.*

Chirchingham. Arg. 3 bars gu. in chief as many torteaux over all a bendlet sa. Sir Walter de Chirchingham. *R.*

Chittercrofte or Chitecroft. Add: *V.*

Chittoke (Suffolk). Add: *W.*

Chiverton (Trehinsey in Quithlock). Insert—co. Cornwall. Add: *V.C. Vis. Lon. 1633.*

Chobington. Arg. a chev. gu. betw. 3 squirrels sejant sa. cracking nuts or. *V.*

Choke. Gu. three bars wavy within a bordure arg. Add: *V.*

Cholmly. Insert—London. . . Crest: a demi-griffin segreant—insert—sa. holding a helmet—add—arg. *Vis. Lon. 1633.*

Cholwell or Cholwill. . . . line three—delete—towards the chief substitute—downwards. Crest: . . . Add: *W. V.D.*

Cholwill (Co. Devon granted by Camden 1613). Arg. on a bend sa. 3 broad arrows or feathered and headed arg. *Syl. Morgan.*

Chooke or Coot. Insert—Norfolk . . . two lions combatant—delete—ppr. Add: az. armed gu. Add: *V.*

Chooke (Middlesex). *V.*

Chopin. Insert—London. Add: *W.*

Chopinge. Add: Same arms, with a chief gu. charged with 3 apples slipped and leaved or. Chopinge (London).

Chopman (Northumberland). Per chev. arg. and gu. a chev. counterchanged. *Eliz. Roll xxxiv.*

Choppin. Vert. a goat pass. arg. collared gu.

Chorley. Arg. a chev. betw. 3 blue-bottles az. slipped vert. *Cotton MS. Tiberius D. 10.*

Chorley (Chorley, co. Lancaster) and Leek, Stafford. Add: *V.V.**

Chorley (Chorley, co. Lancaster). Arg. on a chev. gu. betw. 3 blue bottles ppr. as many mullets of the field. *V.L.* Quartering sa. 3 swans arg.

Chracheth. Gu. a bend fusilly or a label of 5 points arg. *F.*

Christie (Glyndebourne, co. Sussex). M.P. for Lewes 1874. Az. a holy lamb arg. on a chief or a castle with 3 towers betw. 2 baskets.

Christison (Sir Robert Christison). Insert—Edinburgh, Bart. Insert—1871. . . .

Christmas (London). Raguly arg. margin—or. Add: *Vis. Lon. 1633.*

Christmas (East Sutton, Kent). . . . on a bend sa. 3 bowles or. *Robson.*

Christopher. Arg. a chev. gu. betw. 3 bunches of grapes ppr. *Cady.*

Christophers. Arg. a chev. sa. betw. 3 pine cones slipped erect gu. each with 2 leaves vert. *V.*

Christopher (Aylford, co. Lincoln 1661). Same arms with a chief sa. Sir Robt. Christopher *L.N.*

Chudleigh (Ashton, co. Devon bart.). . . . Insert—Sir . . . de Chudley, co. Devon. *V.*

Church. Arg. 2 bars sa. in chief 2 ogresses. *Cady.*

Church. Az. a lion ramp. arg. over all a bend gu. *Cady.*

Church. Az. a lion ramp. to the sinister arg. *Blomfield.*

Churchill (Churchill, co. Dorset). . . . Add: *L.N.*

Churchyard. Arg. a chev. sa. betw. 3 nags heads erased gu. bridled or. *Cady.*

Chyner. Add: *V.*

Chymerston. Or on a bend gu. 3 water bougets arg. Sir John Chymerston. *V.*

Circester (Warwickshire). Add: Sir Thos. de Circester. *N.*

Cirencester Abbey (Gloucestershire). Second line . . . attired or—insert—*Tanner.*

Clamvill. Or six martlets az. 3. 2. 1. *Randle Holme.*

Clapeham. Add: Sir Robert de Clapeham. *X.*

Clapham (London and Northampton). Add: Granted by Segar. 1599.

Clapham (Warwickshire and Yorkshire). Add: Clapham (Bearnsley, co. York, 1665). Quartering Thornton, Sutton, Otterburn, Malevere and Moon. *Dugdale. p. 43.*

Clapham (Barnstaple, co. Devon). Visitation 1620—insert—and London. Add: *V. Vis. Lon. 1633.*

Clapham. Arg. a chev. gu. a wine broach (or piercer) of the first. *V.*

Clare (Earls of . . .). Add: *V.* Gilbert de Clare, Conte de Gloucestre. *P.* Contee de Glocestre *D.E.F.G.J.L.N.B.Z. 101, 140, 379, 441.* And with a label az. Sir William de Clare. *B.* Sir Richard de Clare *L.N.* Sir Thomas de Clare *C.D.E.F.* Sire Gilbert de Clare. *J.*

Clare. Or 3 chevs. gu. within a bordure engr. sa. Sir Nicholas de Clare. *L.N.*

Clare. Erm. on a chev. sa. betw. 3 leopards heads . . . Add: Gilbert de Clare Suffolk. *W.*

Clare. Arg. a canton gu. *V.*

Clare (Robert Clare of Dublin). . . . Add: Clare (co. Salop 1562). Same arms.

Clarell (Tickhill). . . . Add: Sir John Clarell. *V.*

Clarence (John de Clarence). Add: Planche. Sir Bartholomew Clarence. *V.* John de Clarence. *Z. 311.*

Clarendon. Add: *V.* Sir Roger de Clarendon nat. son of Black Prince.

Clarendon. Gu. a bend or. Sir Roger de Clarendon *S.*

Clarges (St. Martin's-in-the-Fields, co. Middlesex, bart). Insert—1674. Add: *Guillim.*

Clark. Add: Clarke (co. York). A mullet arg. for diff. *V.* and on the mullet a crescent. Clarke of Iteringham, co. York. *V.*

Clarke (Baron of the Exchequer). Or a bend az. a plate for diff. *W.*

Clarke (Waste Court, Abingdon, co. Berks.). Granted to John Cremer Clarke by Woods, Garter 8 Jan. 1876. Vert. on a bend erm. betw. 2 cotises or and 3 crosses patty arg. as many swans of the third.

Clarke (Northamptonshire). Add: Henry Clerke, Serjeant at Law. *Dug. O. J.*

Clarke. Per chev. az. and or in base an eagle displ. in chief 3 leopards heads all counterchanged. Edmund Clarke, *Dug. O.J.*

Clarke (Snailwell, co. Cambridge). . . . Add: Clarke (Norfolk). Same arms. Sir . . . de Clarke, co. York. *V.* and on the mullet a crescent sa.

Clake (Itringham, co. York). *V.*

Clarke (Co. Hereford, *Her. Coll.*). Add: *Dingley.*

Clarke (Hampshire). Az. a chev. betw. three sea mews arg. *Cady.*

Clarke. Arg. a chev. betw. three columbines pendent and slipped vert. *W.*

Clarke (London and Norfolk). Gu. a saltire betw. 4 horses heads couped arg. *Vis. Lon. 1633.*

Clarke (London). Az. 3 escallops in pale or betw. 2 flaunches erm. on a chief 3 lions ramp. . . . Crest: Out of a ducal coronet or a demi-bull ramp. erm. horned or. *Vis. Lon. 1633.*

Clarke (London and Essex). Or on a bend engr. az. 3 lozenges of the field. Crest: A Talbots head or on the neck a collar engr. az. charged with 3 lozenges or. *Vis. Lon. 1633.*

Clarke (Oxfordshire). Augmentation granted—insert—to Sir John Clark of North Western. Add: The canton sinister az. 3 fluers-de-lis or a bendlet arg. *V.O. p. 23.* Add: Clarke of Tuarendon. *V.*

Clark (Long Sutton, co. Somerset 1628. Granted by Cook 1576). Gu. 2 bars arg. in chief three 5-foils erm. *V.S.*

Clarke (Baron of the Exchequer). Or on a bend engr. az. a plate in chief. *W.*

Clarke (Mayor of Newcastle 1439). Arg. on a bend betw. 2 swans gu. 3 plates a mullet for diff. *Carr. MS.*

Clarke (Land Abbey, co. Leicester). Baronetcy 1661. Arg. on a bend sa. betw. 3 ogresses as many swans ppr. on a canton sinister az. a demi-ram mounting arg. armed or. betw. 3 fleurs-de-lis of the last over all in the canton a baton sinister gu.

Clarke (Berks: granted). Insert—by Woods, Garter, 8 Jan. 1876 to John Cremer. Clarke of Waste Court. . . .

Clarkson (Kenton, co. Nottingham. Visit. Notts). . . . three annulets or—underlined and ? arg. *V.N.*

Claryll. Arg. 6 martlets 3. 2. and 1. gu. *V.*

Clavering (Baron Clavering). Add: Monsire Robert Clavering. *S.* Robert Fitz Roger, Lord of Clavering. *V.*

Clavering. Quarterly or and arg. a bend sa. a label vert. John Clavering, son of Robert le Fitz Roger. *K.N.*

Clavering. Quarterly or and gu. on a bend sa. three mullets arg. Sir Alexander de Clavering Essex. temp. Edw. j. *V.N.* But the mullets or Sir Alayn Claveringe. *O.*

Clavering (Axwell Park, co. Durham, bart). Insert—1661.

Clavesley (Co. Somerset). Add Clavesley. Same arms. *Collinson Somerset. iiij. 73.*

Claville (Co. Dorset 1623). Arg. on a chev. sa. 3 caps of maintenance or.

Claxton (Cheshire). Add: *V.*

Claxton (Suffolk, London). arg. a fess betw. 3 boars sa. *Vis. Lon. 1633.*

Claxton. Gu. a chev. betw. 3 hedgehogs arg. on a quarter barry of 5 arg. and az. a canton of the first charged with 3 martlets or. *V.*

Clay (London). Add: *Vis. Lon. 1633.*

Clay (Piercefield, co. Monmouth). Add: Clay (Reigate, Surrey). Granted by Camden 1613. Same arms.

Claydon (Ashdown, co. Essex and London). Add: *Vis. Lon. 1633.*

Cleaver. Bishop of Bangor and afterwards of St. Asaph 1806–15. Sa. 2 bars betw. 3 castles or. *Bedford.*

Cleaver. Az. 2 bars company or and sa. betw. 3 castles arg. masoned sa.

Clayton (Little Harwood, co. Lancaster 1664). Arg. on a bend sa. 3 roses or. *V.L.*

Clayton. Gu. on a bend arg. 3 roses of the first in chief a crescent of the second. *V.*

Clayton (Little Harwood and Lentworth, co. Lancaster). Add: *V.L. 1664.*

Clayton. Gu. on a bend arg. 3 roses of the first in chief, a crescent of the second. *V.*

Clayton (Co. Stafford). . . . fitchy— delete— sa. substitute az. *V.N. p. 9.*

Clayton (Thomas Clayton M.D.). Add: *Guillim.*

Clayton. Chequy gu. and or two chev. sa. Add: *V.*

Clealand. Az. a hare salient arg. betw. a hunting horn in sinister chief and a rose in dexter base both of the second.

Cleasby (Sir Anthony Cleasby, Baron of the Exchequer 1868). Erm. a lion pass. az. betw. 2 bendlets gu. on a chief of the second 3 lozenges or.

Cleasby. Arg. 3 bendlets gu. a canton erm. John Cleasbye. *Eliz. Roll. xxvij.*

Cleather (Cornwall). Vert. a chev. betw. 3 swords points downwards or. *Lysons.*

Cleaver (Bygrave, co. Herts. 1660). Or 3 bars gu. on a canton arg. a fess and 3 mascles in chief sa. *L.N.*

Cleborne (Kellerby, co. York). Add: *F.Y.*

Cleborne (Kilbarem, Ireland). Arg. 3 chevs. braced in base a chief and bordure all sa.

Clederow. Sa. on a chev. or betw. 3 eagles displ. double headed arg. 5 annulets gu. *V.*

Clement (Kent). Add: Quartered by Castlemain. *Cady.*

Clement. Arg. two bends wavy sa. . . . Add: Sir Richard Clement 1528. **Tomb** in Ightham Church, Kent.

Clement (Mole, Kent). . . . a bend nebuly . . . in chief 3 fleurs-de-lis . . . a bordure nebuly . . . *Robson.*

Clement (Plymouth, co. Devon 1620). Arg. 2 bends wavy sa. on a chief gu. 3 estoiles or. *V.D.*

Clement. Gu. a chev. erm. betw. 3 portcullises or. *V.*

Clement. Insert.–Kent: Arg. three bars nebulee and a bend sa. on a chief gu. as many leopards faces or Add: *V.* W.*

Clemsby (Leicestershire). Add: *N.* Sir John Clemsby temp. Edw. j. *V.*

Clenehond. Add: *V.*

Clenkard or Clynkard (Granted by Sir Edward Walker 1664). Arg. on a bend cotised sa. 3 eagles heads erased of the field beaked or. *Guillim.*

Clenkard (Sutton Place, Kent). Same arms.

Clepole (Narborough, co. Notts). Add: Clepole (Granted by Cooke to James Clepole of Norbourne, co. Northampton 1583). *W.*

Clerke (London and co. Bedford). Per chev. az. and or in chief 3 leopards faces of the second and in base an eagle displ. of the first. Crest: A goat ramp. arg. horned or against an oak tree fructed ppr. *Vis. Lon. 1633.*

Clerke. Or two bars az. . . . . Crest: In clouds ppr. . . . Add: *W.*

Clerke. Az. a bar or on a chief of the last 3 escallops gu. *W.*

Clesby (Co. York). Add: *V.*

Clevedon (Essex). Add: Sir John de Clevedon. *N.*

Clevehound. Add: *V.*

Cleveland. Insert—(Birkenhead, co. Chester): Per chev. sa. and erm. . . .

Cliderow (Goldstanton). Arg. on a chev. gu. betw. 3 eagles displ. sa. 5 annulets or. *Fuller.*

Cliffe (Cos. York, Devon and Essex). Arg. three popinjays . . . Add: John Clyffe of the Wold. *X.*

Cliffe (Co. York). Arg. a chev. betw. 3 popinjays vert. membered gu. *C.R. p. 37.*

Cliffe (Co. Essex). Same arms. *V.E. 1612.*

Clifford (Frampton co. Gloucester). Add: *V.*

Clifford. Chequy or and az. a bend gu. Walter de Clifford *F.B.P.* Reinand de Clifford. *E.* Sir Johan de Clifford. *N.* Roger de Clifford. *P.*

Clifford. Chequy or and az. on a bend gu. 3 lions ramp. arg. John de Clifford. *E.*

Clifford (Co. Somerset). Chequy or and az. on a bend gu. 3 leopards faces arg. *W.*

Clifford. Or—delete—(another, arg.) . . . Add: *V.*

Clifton (Clifton and Lytham Hall, co. Lancaster). Margin—Sa. on a bend arg. 3 mullets gu.

Clifton (Gervase Clifton, Treasurer of Calais. 36 Hen. vj). Sa. semy of 5-foils and a lion ramp. arg. *Seal. Harl. MS. 6829. fo. 25.*

Clifton (Clifton Hall, co. Nottingham, bart.). . . . Add: Sir Gervas Clifton. *V.*

Clifton (Clifton Hall, co. Notts.). Exemplified to Robert Henry Markham . . . on assuming name of Clifton. . . . Add: *V.N.*

Clifton (Norfolk). Chequy az. and or a bend erm. *V.** Sir Adam Clifton.

Clifton (Norfolk). Chequy or and gu. a bend erm. Sir Adam Clifton. *V.X.Y.*

Clifton (Bokenham—insert—and Fakenham).

Clifton (Kent). Sa. on a bend arg. three mullets gu. Add: Robert de Clifton. *S. V.* John Clyfton. *Y.*

Clifton (London, cos. Herts and Middlesex). Add: *Guillim.*

Clifton (Co. York). Add: Clifton Arg. a lion ramp. within an orle of 5-foils sa. Sire John de Clifton. *S.*

Clifton. Sa. on a bend arg. 3 crescents gu. in the sinister chief a crescent of the second Sir Nichol de Clyfton. *S.*

Clifton. . . . 2 bendlets . . . in the sinister chief a crescent . . . Nicholas de Clifton. *Seal.* 1466. *Harl. MS. 6829. fo. 25.*

Clifton (Sheriff of Norfolk). Add: *Fuller.*

Clifton. Arg. a chev. sa. betw. three roses gu. Add: Roger de Clifton. *F.E. Y.*

Clifton. Or a chev. sa. betw. 3 cinquefoils gu. *V.** Geoffry de Clyftone. *V.*

Clifton. Sa. on a bend arg. 3 crescents of the field. *Constable's Roll xvj.*

Clifton. Sa. on a bend arg. 3 crescents gu. in the sinister chief a crescent arg. for diff. Sir Nycol de Clyfton. *S.*

Clings. Sa. six lions ramp. arg. 3. 2. and 1. Add: Sir William de Clinge. *A.*

Clint (London). Add: *Robson.*

Clinton. Paly of 6 or and az. a canton erm. Sire Johan de Clinton. *E.*

Clynton (Ireland). Arg. a lion ramp. gu. armed and langued az. debruised by a fess of the last charged with 3 mullets arg. *Robson.*

Clippesbye (Clippesby, co. Norfolk 1594). Quarterly arg. and sa. on a bend gu. 3 mullets arg. quartering: 3 martlets within a bordure: an eagle displ. and over all a bendlet: a chevron betw. 3 herons: a fish haurient: crusilly and a saltire: on a chief 3 roundlets: a lion ramp. a chev. betw. 3 lions ramp. and barry of 8. **Brass** in Clippesby Church.

Cliste (Visit, Gerard. Devon, temp. Hen. iij). Sa. a chev. betw. 3 mullets or.

Clivedon Or a lion ramp. sa. crowned gu. Renard de Clivedon. *E.V.* Sir John Clifton. *L.*

Clobbs (Quartered by Holte . . .). Add: *V.O. 173.*

Clobery (Bradston, co. Devon . . .). Add: *V.D.*

Clobery (Co. Devon and London). Arg. a bend engr. betw. 2 cotises plain sa. Crest: a goats head erased arg. attired or. *Vis. Lon. 1633.*

Clodshall (Saltley, temp. Edw. iij). Per pale indented . . . and . . . half an orle of martlets on the dexter side . . .

Clonvyle. Arg. 2 chevs sa. in chief five horseshoe nails . . . *Cady.*

Cloos. Add: Bensley, *Experpta. p. 364.*

Clopton (Lyston, co. Essex). Sa. a bend arg. betw. 2 cotises dancetty or. *V.E. 1612.*

Clopton (Co. Somerset). Add: Clopton of Clopton, co. Bucks. *V.*

Clopton (Slegwidge). Sa. a bend dancetty erm. betw. 2 cotises or. *Eliz. Roll.*

Clopton (Sledwick, co. Durham 1615). Paly of 6 or and az. overall a lion ramp. sa. quartering, per pale or and gu. a cross patty fitchy counter-changed. *Robson.*

Clopton. Sa. a bend arg. betw. 2 cotises or. Mons Walter Clopton. *T. Harl. MS. 6137.*

Clopton (Kentwell, Suffolk). Sa. a bend arg. betw. 2 cotises indented or and with an annulet on the bend for diff. Mons Walter Clopton. *T.*

Clopton (Lord Mayor of London 1491). Add: *V.* Quartering per pale or and az. a cross patty fitchy at the foot, counterchanged.

Clopton or Clotton. Arg. two bars gu. fretty or. Add: both quartered by Davies of Kent.

Clopton. Gu. a fesse betw. six pears or.

Close (Drumbanagher). Insert—Newry . . . *Debrett.*

Clough (Thorp Stapleton, co. York). . . . . *Vis. Lon. 1633.*

Clovile, Clovell, Clovyle or Clonvyle. Add: of Cloville Hall, co. Essex. *V.E. 1612.*

Clowes. Add: Clowes (confirmed by W. Dethick, Garter 27 Nov. 1595 to Wm. Clowes of London). Same arms and crest. *Vis. Lon. 1633.*

Clowes (Broughton Hall, co. Lancaster). Az. on a chev. engr. betw. 3 unicorns heads erased or as many torteaux. *F.L.*

Clun (Town of, co. Salop). . . . a chev. erm. betw. 3 chessrooks—Quartering . . . on a cross patty pometty—5 crosslets . . .

Clusines (Ireland). Arg. a lion ramp. vert. *Robson.*

Clutton (Co. Salop 1670). Arg. on a chev. gu. betw. three annulets of the second another chev. erm. *Guillim.*

Clybury. Add: *W.*

Clyburne. Arg. 3 chevs. braced in base sa. a chief gu.

Clyderow. Gu. on a bend arg. 3 mullets az. in the sinister chief a martlet or. *V.V.**

Clyndut. Az. a chev. or and a label gu. Sir Rauf. Clyndut. *V.*

Clynke or Cluyke. Add: *V.*

Clynton (Co. Down). Add: *Cady.*

Clynton. Paly of 6 or and az. a chev. erm.

Clyston (Norfolk). Gu. a bend erm. *Guillim.*

Coachmakers of London. Arg. 3 sedan chairs without staves sa. *Randle Holme.*

Coakes (Norwich). Or a chev. gu. betw. 3 lions pass. guard. of the same.

Cobb (Adderbury, co. Oxford).... Add: The fishes haurient. *V.O. 1634.*

Cobb (Yarmouth). Add: Cobb (Ottringham, co. York 1666). Same arms and crest, a crescent for diff. *Dugdale. p. 332.*

Cobb or Cobbis (Norfolk). Add: Cobb: (Beverley co. York 1660). Same arms. *L.N.*

Cobb (Wisbeach). Insert—co. Cambridge ... 2 ducks respectant—insert—or ...

Cobbile. Add: Cobyle. *V.*

Cobeham. Add: *V.*

Cobham. Arg. a lion ramp. chequy or and sa. Sire Rauf de Cobham. *O.*

Cobham (Lord Cobham of Kent). ... Add: Baron Cobham *Z. 316.* Sir Reginald Cobham of Sterburgh, Surrey. *V. Q. Harl. MS. 6599.* And with a label of 3 points or Sir John Cobham. *Q.*

Cobham. Gu. on a chev. betw. 3 fleurs-de-lis arg. as many mullets az. Sir Stephen Cobham. *W.*

Cobham. Gu. on a chev. betw. 3 fleurs-de-lis arg. as many mullets az. a bordure of the last.

Cobham. ... a chev. ... betw. in chief a mullet and a fleur-de-lis ... and in base a cross crosslet. **Seal** of Thomas de Cobham, 9th Edw. iij.

Cobham of Chafford. Gu. a chev. or betw. in chief 2 mullets piereced and in base a cross each point terminating in a spear head arg.

Cobham (Cowling, Kent). Gu. on a chev. or 3 fleurs-de-lis az. *W.* Sire Henri de Cobham. *N.* Thomas de Cobham, Bishop of Worcester 1317–28.

Cobham. Gu. on a chev. or betw. 3 fleurs-de-lis ... as many estoiles sa. Sire John de Cobham. *Y.*

Cobham. Gu. on a chev. or three mullets az. Add: Sire Renand de Cobham. *V.*

Cobham. Gu. on a chev. or 3 cinquefoils pierced az. Add: *V.*

Cobham (Cobham, Kent, Ralph Cobham 1402). ... 3 crosses crosslet. In the dexter chief an estoile.

Cobham. Gu. on a chev. or 3 martlets sa. Add: Sir John Cobham. *Q.*

Cobham. Insert—Hoo and Beluncle, co. Kent. Add: *V.*

Coblegh. Add: *Lysons.*

Cobleigh. Add: *V.**

Cobley (borne by the late Major-General Thomas Cobley). ... Add: *V.*

Coche or Cochey. Gu. an eagle displ. barry of six—insert—8 or 10. Add: *V.*V.*

Cock. Az. 3 cocks arg. crested and jelloped gu. armed sa. in the fess point a plate. Ralph Cock, Sheriff of Newcastle 1626. *Carr. MS.*

Cock. Arg. 3 bars sa. in chief as many annulets gu. *Syl. Morgan.*

Cock (London and Norwich). Sable 3 bends arg. on a chief or 3 cocks gu. Crest: on a mount vert. a lion sejeant guard. ppr. over its head a scroll inscribed "Non vi sed voce". *Vis. Lon. 1633.*

Cocke (Co. Cornwall). Arg. a chev. engr. gu. betw. 3 eagles heads erased sa. on a canton az. an anchor or.

Cocke (Co. Devon). Same arms. *V.C. 303.*

Cockayne or Cokayne. Add: Cockayne (Ashbourne, co. Derby). Same arms. *V.* Cockayne (London). Same arms. *Vis. Lon. 1633.*

Cockayne or Cokeyne (Dorsetshire). Add: Sir Renaud de Coykin. *N.*

Cockburn or Cockborne (Cockburn, Scotland). Add: *V.** Sir Robert Cockborne, (Scotland). *V.*

Cocke (Lancaster Herald 1559). . . . a chev. invected . . . betw. 3 parrots heads erased sa.

Cocke. Insert—co. Kent: Sa. on a chev. or 3 cinquefoils . . . Add: *W.*

Cocket. Or a chev. betw. three cocks sa. . . . *V.**

Cockfield (Cos. Essex and Warwick). *V.V.**

Cockfield. Arg. three cocks gu. Add: Thomas de Cokfelde. *X.*

Cockington (Devonshire). Add: John de Cokerington. *Y.*

Cockington. Gu. 9 cocks 3. 3. 2. and 1 or Sir Henry de Cockington. *A.*

Cockington. Or a chev. az. betw. 3 cocks gu. Add: *V.*

Cockram (Newton). Insert—and co. Dorset.

Cockroft or Mayroid. Sa. an elephant pass. arg. on a chief sa. 3 mullets pierced or.

Cocks (Dumbleton, co. Gloucester, bart.). Insert —1662...

Cocks (Cos. Gloucester and Suffolk). Add: Cocks (Betshanger, Kent). Same arms.

Cocks (London). Arg. a chev. betw. 3 stags heads cabossed sa. *Vis. Lon. 1633.*

Cocksey. Insert—(Evesham, co. Worcester): Arg. on a bend sa. . . . Add: *V.W.*

Cocksedge (Norfolk). Arg. a cock gu.

Cockson (Yorkshire). . . . Crest: a demi-lion ramp. or -underlined, margin—? vert.

Cockson (London). Same arms and crest. But the lion in crest vert. *Vis. Lon. 1633.*

Codd, Coad, Coode, or Codde (Cornwall). Add: *V.C. 1620.*

Codford. Arg. on a chev. az. . . . Add: *V.*

Codford or Codeford. Arg. on a chev. az. betw. three—insert—'sinister wings', —insert—'elevated' gu. five plates. Add: *V.*

Codham. Add: Sir Nicholas Codham. *V.*

Codon or Codun (Suffolk). Arg. a chev. gu. in base a crescent of 'the last'—underlined— Add: *V.* The crescent of the second. *V.*

Coe. Arg. 2 bars az. over all a pale gu. a bordure indented vert. *Randle Holme.*

Coetmore (Nantconwy, co. Cardigan). Az. a chev. betw. 3 spear heads arg.

Coderugge. Gu. 3 lions ramp. or a label arg. Baudewin de Coderugge. *E. Y.*

Coffin. Gu. 2 bars embattled on the top arg. Sir Thomas Coffin. *V.*

Coffin (Portland, co. Dorset). Add: *V.*

Cogan (Oxford . . .). Add: Cogan (London). Gu. 3 laurel leaves arg. Crest: a lions head erased gu. semy of estoiles arg. exemplified by Segar, Garter 13 Nov. 1632. *Vis. Lon. 1632.*

Coghill (Coghill, co. York and Bletchington, co. Oxford). Add: *V.O.*

Coghill (Coghill, co. York and Glan Barranhane, co. Cork). Add: Coghill (Knaresborough, co. York), 1612. Same arms. *F. Y.*

Coghlan. Per pale or and gu. 3 lions pass. guard. in pale counterchanged.

Cokain, Cokayne or Cockayne (Ashbourne, co. Derby . . .). Add: Sir John Cokayn. *S.*

Cokeham. Arg. a lion ramp. double queued az. fretty or. Add: *V.*

Coker (Mapowder, co. Dorset). . . . three leopards faces or—delete—(continue a bordure engr. sa.). Add: *W.*

Coker. Arg. on a bend gu. 3 leopards heads or Coker, co. Oxon. William Coker. *V.* Coker as quartered by Jane Seymour 3rd wife of Henry viij. *Z. 488.*

Cokerham (Derbyshire). . . . three leopards faces of the first. Add: *V.* (another, the faces or) Add: *V.V.* Add: Sir John Cokerham. *V.*

Cokerham (Collumpton, co. Devon 1620). *V.D.*

Cokerington. Arg. a chev. gu. betw. 3 cocks of the last combed and armed az. John de Cokerington. *X.Y.*

Cokesay. Add: Sire Wauter Cokeseye. *S.* Sir John Cokesay. *V.*

Cokesford (Launton, co. Oxford). Confirmed Feb. 1611—insert—by Camden.

Coket. Arg. a chev. betw. 3 cocks. sa. armed gu. within a bordure compony of the second and first. *V.*

Cokeworth (Cornwall).

Cokeworthy (Co. Devon). Same arms. *Lysons.*

Cokyll. Add: Sir Thomas Cokyll. *V.*

Colborne (Norwich and Great Yarmouth). Arg. a chev. betw. 3 bugle horns sa. garnished or.

Colborne (Bruton, co. Somerset). . . . Add: *V.S.*

Colbroke. Arg. a lion ramp. gu. depressed by a fesse or . . . Add: *V.*

Colby (Kensington, co. Middlesex). Insert—Baronetcy 1720. . .

Colby. Az. a chev. engr. betw. 3 escallops within a bordure engr. or. *V.*

Colby. Az. a chev. engr. betw. 3 escallops or. *Dug. O.J.*

Colby (Middleham, co. York). Az. a chev. or betw. 3 escallops arg. a bordure engr. of the second. *V.*

Colby (Exeter and Heavitres). Az. 2 chevs betw. in chief 2 escallops and in base as many palmers staves saltirewise or.

Colchester (London, Somersetshire). . . . Add: *V.* *

Colclough (Ireland . . .). Add: *W.* Add: Coleclogh (London 1568). Same arms, quartering sa. a fess betw. 3 martlets arg. for Lockwood. *C.L.*

Coldale. Add: *V.V.* *

Cole (Farnham, co. Essex). Erm. a bull pass. sa. within a bordure engr. of the second bezanty. *V.E. 1634.*

Cole (Depeden, Suffolk 1665). Or a bull pass. sa. a bordure of the second bezanty. *L.N.*

Colebine. Arg. a chev. betw. 6 mullets az. *C.W.*

Cole (Slade, co. Devon. . .). Add: *V.D. 1620.* Add: Cole (London). Same arms. Crest: a demi-dragon vert. issuing from a ducal coronet or and holding an arrow or headed and feathered arg. Certified by Segar, Garter. *Vis. Lon. 1633.*

Cole. Arg. a bull pass. sa. . . . on a canton sinister az. a harp of Ireland . . . Crest: . . . Add: Cole of Enniskillen. 1630.

Cole (Nailsea, co. Somerset 1623). Per pale or and gu. a bull . . . pass. counterchanged armed arg. an annulet for diff. *V.S.*

Cole (Treworge, Cornwall). Per pale or and gu. a bull pass. sa. armed &c. or a bordure of the last bezanty.

Cole (Shenley, co. Herts. 1640). Add: Granted to Richard Cole. High Sheriff of Herts. by Sir John Borough. Garter.

Cole (Holyborne, co. Hants.). Add: *Guillim.*

Cole (Newcastle-upon-Tyne). Add: Cole, Sheriff of Newcastle 1622. *Carr MS.*

Cole. Arg. a chev. gu. betw. three scorpions . . . Add: *V. V.E. 1634.*

Colebrooke (Gatton, co. Surrey, bart.). Insert—1759.

Colebrooke (Southgate, Middlesex). Gu. a lion ramp. arg. crowned or on a chief of the last 3 martlets sa. a mullet for diff. **Book Plate.**

Colepeper or Culpeper (Kent . . .). Add: Colepeper (Wakehurst, co. Sussex. Baronetcy 1628). Same arms with a crescent for diff. *Guillim.*

Colepepper. Arg. a chev. sa. betw.—insert—9 or . . . Add: *V.*

Colepepper. Arg. a chev. sa. betw. 3 martlets gu. *V.* *

Colepeper. Arg. a chev. sa. betw. 5 martlets. 3 and 2 gu. Sir Thos. Colpeper. *S.* Quartering arg. a bend engr. gu.

Coleridge (Baron Coleridge). Insert—1874. . . . an otter—insert—pass. . . . Add: Dr. William Hart Coleridge Bishop of Barbadoes. Same arms.

Coles (Hampton-in-Arden, co. Warwick). Gu. on a chev. arg. pelletty betw. 3 lions heads erased or 4 bars sa. *C.W.*

Colke. Or 3 bendlets sa. Thomas Colke. *Y.*

Colle (Suckley, co. Worcester). Arg. on a chev. gu. betw. 3 lions heads erased sa. bars and plates of the first.

Collens. Arg. on a chev. betw. 3 rooks sa. as many mullets of the first. *Cady.*

Collett (Lockers House, Hemel Hempstead, Herts). Sa. on a chev.—insert—'arg.' . . . voided . . .

Colliar or Collyar (Darlston, co. Stafford). Add: Sir R. P. Collier, Solicitor General 1863.

Collimore (London). Add: *Vis. Lon. 1633.*

Collingwood (Branton, Northumberland, M.P. for Berwick on Tweed). Arg. a chev. betw. 3 stags heads erased gu. *Guillim.*

Collingwood (Northumberland). Arg. a chev. az. betw. 3 stags heads erased sa. in the mouths a leaf vert.

Collingwood. Arg. a chev. betw. 3 stags heads erased sa. each having in the mouth a leaf. Sir Cuthbert Collingwood. *Eliz. Roll. xxxiij.*

Collis (Insert—co. Kerry, Ireland). Arg. a chev. betw. 3 lions heads erased gu. Crest: a dexter arm throwing an arrow ppr.

Collumbers. Arg. a chev. betw. 3 martlets sa.

Collyer. Gu. on a chev. engr. betw. 3 boars heads erased or as many palets sa. each charged with an oak leaf of the second. *A.A.*

Collyn (Cornwall). Arg. a chev. betw. 3 crows sa. *V.*

Colman (London). Quarterly sa. and arg. a cross flory betw. 4 mullets all counterchanged. *Vis. Lon. 1633.*

Colnett. Insert—co. Hants. Or on a chev. gu. betw. 3 columbines arg. as many flower pots of the field. Add: *V.*

Colshill or Colsell. Add: *V.* *

Coltman (Hagnaby Priory, co. Lincoln). Insert—and London. Az. a cross patonce—insert—quarterly—pierced or betw. four mullets—insert—pierced arg. Add: *Vis. Lon. 1633.*

Colton (Colton, Kent). . . . a chev. betw. 3 griffins heads. *Robson.*

Columbell (Darley, co. Derby). Sa. 3 doves arg. *V.*

Columbers. Gu. a bend or. John de Columbers. *V.*

Columbers. Bendy az. and arg. a chev. or betw. 3 bezants. *Collinson Somerset iij. 264.*

Colvile (Cambridge and Lincolnshire). Add: Sir Geffry Colville, co. Leicester temp. Edw. j. *V.* Colvile (London). Same arms and crest. *Vis. Lon. 1633.*

Colvile (Isle of Ely). Add: John Colville of Marshland. *Y.*

Colvile. Gu. billetty or. William de Colevile. *V.*

Colvile. Or six billets gu. 3. 2. and 1. Add: *V.V.**

Colvile Or 10 billets gu. 4. 3. 2. 1. Sir William de Colvill. 6. Edw. j. *V.E.*

Colvile. Arg. 3 lions pass. in pale az. Geffrey de Colville. *A.*

Colway (Inner Temple). Arg. on 3 chevs. sa. fifteen annulets or. *Cady.*

Colwell (Cos. York, Kent and Worcester). *Harl. MS. 1566.* Add: *V.*

Colwell. Arg. 3 lions pass. in pale sa. bezanty. *V.*

Colwyke. Arg. on a bend az. 3 bezants in the sinister chief a cross crosslet fitchy of the second. *V.*

Colyra. Arg. 3 bats displ. sa. *V.*

Combe. Erm. 3 lions pass. guard. in pale gu. Richard de Combe. *Y.*

Combe (Cobham Park, co. Surrey and Oaklands, co. Sussex). Add: Combe (Stratford upon Avon) Same arms. *Harl. MS. 1359. fo. 110b.* Sir Richard Combes. Hemel Hempstead. Herts. *1660. L.N.*

Combe (Somersetshire). Add: *V.S.*

Combe. Erm. on a bend gu. 3 combs bendwise or. *V.*

Combe. Arg. on a chev. gu. three garbs or. Add: *V.*

Combemartin. Add: *Baker.*

Comberton (Co. Lincoln). Or a chev. betw. 3 martlets sa. Sir Thomas Comberton. *V.*

Combmakers Company of, (London). Insert—Incorporated 13th Charles j.

Compere (London). . . . on a chev. . . . betw. . . . 3 roundles . . . as many cinquefoils . . .

Compion. Or a maunch (another, a water bouget) within a bordure engr. sa. Add: *V.*

Compton (Carham Hall, co. Northumberland). . . betw. 3 helmets—delete—az. substitute 'arg.'. Add: Sir Henry Compton, Lord Compton. *V.* Sir William Compton. *V.*

Compton (Cheshire). Add: *Harl. MS. 1535 fo. 11b.*

Compton. Insert—co. Warwick. Or on a bend sa. 3 mullets of the field. Add: *V.*

Compton. Insert—(Catton). Sa. 3 cats pass. guard. arg. collared and belled or. Add: *V.V.**

Comyn (Whitby, co. York). 1665. Arg. a chev. betw. 3 garbs sa. *Dugdale. p. 72.*

Conesby. Gu. 3 conies—insert—sejant arg. within . . . Crest: . . . Add: Sir Humphry Conesby, co. Hereford. *V.*

Coney (Lynn, co. Norfolk 1479). Sa. 3 conies sejant arg.

Coney or Coyney. Insert—co. Stafford. Add: *V.*

Congrill. Add: *V.V.**

Coningsby. Arg. a chev. betw. 3 conies courant palewise sa. *V.*

Coningston or Coningeston. Or 3 conies sa. *V.V.**

Conran. Vert. a chev. or betw. 3 wolves heads erased arg. *Harl. MS. 1441.*

Constable (Halsham and Burton Constable, Holderness, co. York). Add: *V.*

Constable. Barry of 6 or and az. Le Constable de Holderness. *Y.*

Constable (Constable Burton, co. York). Barry of 6 or and az. on a canton arg. a teazle ppr. *Foster.*

Constable (Flamburgh and Everingham, co. York). Add: *Dugdale. p. 119.*

Constable. Quarterly gu. and vair a baston arg. Monsire le Constable, Seigneur de Hamburg. *Y.*

Constable (Manor House, Otley, co. York). . . . vair . . . Add: *V.* Sir John de Constable. *I. Harl. MS. 6589.* Sir Richard Constable. *S.* Robert Constable. *Y.* and with a crescent for diff. Constable of Cliff. co. York 1666. *Dugdale p. 339.* Also Constable of Kexby, co. York 1612 with a crescent on a crescent. *F.Y.* Constable Quarterly vair and gu. a bend or Sir John de Constable. *I.* Constable Quarterly vair and gu. a bendlet engr. or. Sir Robert de Constable. *M.N.*

Constable (Dromonby, Cleveland). . . . Or an annulet—add—'for diff.' *F.Y.*

Constable. Gu. a bend or. *Cady.*

Conway (Buckinghamshire, Gloucestershire and Warwickshire). Add: Sir John Conway temp. Queen Elizabeth. Conway (Bobringham, co. Flint., Baronetcy 1660. Ext. 1721.

Conway. Arg. a chev. couped betw. 3 crosses patty fitchy sa. *Harl. MS. 1386. fo. 36.*

Conway or Conwey. Add: Sir Hugh Conway, co. Warwick. *V.*

Conway. Az. a lion pass. guard. paly of 6 . . . within a bordure engr. of the last. Add: *V.V.**

Conway. Sa. on a bend arg. cotised erm. three roses gu. Add: Sir Hugh Conway co. Worcester *V.*

Conway. Az. a lion pass. arg. goutty . . . betw. 3 dexter gauntlets the back parts outwards arg. *W.*

Cony. Arg. a rabbit sejant sa. *Randle Holme.*

Cony (Bassingthorp, co. Cumberland—insert—Granted by Segar—1612).

Conycliff. Add: *V.*

Conyers (London and Danby Wiske, co. York). Az. a maunch or. Crest: A sinister wing gu. *Vis. Lon. 1633.*

Coodd (Ireland). Arg. a chev. sa. betw. 5 ogresses. *Lansdowne MS. 255. fo. 27.*

Coodd (Ireland). Or a chev. sa. betw. 5 ogresses 2. 1. and 2.

Cook (London). *Her. Off. Int. MS. Vincent No. 154.* Add: Granted by Segar.

Cooke (Norfolk). Arg. a chev. engr. gu. betw. 3 tigers heads erased of the second collared or. *V.* W.*

Cook. Az. a plain bend within a bordure invected both per pale or and gu. counterchanged. *Randle Holme.*

Cook. Arg. 12 martlets . . . separated by 3 piles from the chief in point sa. *Harl. MS. 1113. fo. 24.*

Cook. Az. on a chev. engr. arg. betw. two couple closes or and 3 pierced cinquefoils erm. two lions combatant purp. *C.L. p. 42.*

Cooke (Wheatley, co. York, bart.). Insert—1661.

Cooke (Co. Devon and Trerice, co. Cornwall). Add: *V.D. 1620. V.C. p. 304.*

Cooke (Co. Devon). Arg. a chev. betw. three raven's heads . . . Add: *V.*

Cook (Thorne, co. Devon). Erm. on a bend betw. 2 cotises gu. 3 lions pass. guard. or. *Guillim.*

Cook. Arg. 3 bends sa. a crescent for diff. John Cooke, Sheriff of Newcastle 1469. *Carr MS.* and with a mullet for diff. John Cooke, Sheriff of Newcastle 1614. *Carr. MS.*

Cooke (Fulwell-Hache, co. Essex). Add: *V.*

Cooke or Cook (Little Stalybridge, co. Essex). Add: Cook, Mayor of Exeter 1692. *Colby.* Same arms.

Cooke (Clifton, near Bristol). Insert—and London. Add: *Vis. Lon. 1633.*

Cooke (Giddea Hall, Essex). Add: *Harl. MS. 1542.*

Cooke (Liversale Park, co. York). Or a chev. gu. betw. 3 lions pass. guard sa.

Cooke Sir Philip Cooke, temp. Edw.. iv Or a chev. chequy az. and gu. betw. 3 cinquefoils of the second. *Harl. MS. 6137. fo. 44.*

Cooke (Giddy Hall, Essex). Or a chev. counter-compony gu. and purp. betw. 3 cinquefoils az. Sir Anthony Cooke. *V.*

Cooke (Lord Mayor of London 1462). Add: *V.*V.E. 1634.*

Cooke Vairy or and vert. a bend erm. *V.*

Cooke (Linstead, co. Suffolk). Add: Cooke (Broome or Bromhill, co. Norfolk). Same arms: *Cady.* Baronetcy *1663.*

Cooke. Az. a bendlet arg. betw. 6 fleurs-de-lis or. *W.*

Cooke (Burstow, co. Surrey, Granted). Insert—by Bysshe. . . .

Cooke (London and Dunmow, Essex). Gu. 3 crescents or on a canton of the last a martlet sa. *Vis. Lon. 1633.*

Cooke (London). Or a fess chequy arg. and gu. betw. 3 cinquefoils az. Crest: A unicorn's head couped collared chequy arg. and gu. *Vis. Lon. 1633.*

Cook (Blackheath, co. Kent). Gu. on a fess voided of the field betw. 3 woolpacks arg. as many crescents or.

Cooke. Arg. 3 bars az. in chief as many hurts.

Cooke. Insert—of Dublin. Gu. a chev. or betw. 3 crescents arg. a canton of the last within a bordure erm.

Cooksey (Ireland). Gu. on a bend arg. 3 roses of the field seeded az. barbed vert. *Robson.*

Coolene. Co. Staffs. Arg. a chevron sa. betw. 3 cornish choughs ppr.

Cooling. Gu. on a chev. betw. 3 bezants a trefoil slipped of the field. Crest: a dragon's head erased vert. gorged with a bolt collar or. marked "Sir . . . Cooling Bart.". (I find no Baronetcy of Cooling; this entry therefore should be received with caution).

Coolyn (Co. Devon). Sa. a chev. betw. 3 talbots heads erased arg.

Coolin or Cowlin. Arg. a chev. sa. betw. 3 coots ppr. (Obviously the same coat as Coolene.) *The above form an insert page marked 'from the Somerset Herald'.*

Coope (Co. Northampton). Arg. on a chev. az. betw. 3 roses gu. stalked and leaved vert. as many fleurs-de-lis per fess or and of the first. *V.*

Cooper (Brockburn, co. Hants.). Baronetcy 1622. Gu. a bend engr. betw. 6 lions ramp. or.

Cooper (Walcot, Somerset, bart.). Insert—1828.

Cooper (Woohara, New South Wales, bart.). . . . Add: *V.L.*

Cooper. Gu. a bend erm. betw. 6 lions ramp. or. *Visitation of Durham. 1615.*

Cooper (Colne-Green, co. Hereford). . . . Add: Cooper (London 1578). Same arms. *C.L.*

Cooper (Carneford, co. Lancaster 1664). Add: *V.L.*

Cooper (Failford, co. Ayr). Arg. on a bend engr. betw. 2 lions ramp. gu. 3 crescents of the field all within a bordure chequy arg. and az. *A.A.*

Cooper (Icklesham, co. Sussex). Arg. on a chev. engr. az. betw. in chief 2 stags heads cabossed and in base 3 doves gu. as many annulets or. *Bury.*

Cooper (Thurgarton, co. Notts). Add: *V.N. V.*

Cooper (Granted to Robert Chester Cooper, Esq. Lewes, Sussex). Insert—1811.

Coopers. Company of, (London)—marginal note: These arms were granted by Clarenceaux in 1509 and confirmed in 1530, but in the grant the chevron is described as being charged with a "Royne betwixt 2 brode axes". Add: *Guillim.*

Coopers. Company of, (Glasgow). Gyronny of 8 gu. and sa. a chev. betw. 2 annulets and an Imperial crown in chief or a crosslet and in base a hammer and compasses betw. 2 adzes az. on a chief of the last 3 lilies slipped arg. the . . . . within a double bordure inner or outer gu. **Stained glass** in Glasgow Cathedral.

Coote (Cos. Lincoln and Suffolk). Arg. three coots ppr. Add: or sa. *V.*

Cope (Brewern, co. Oxford bart.) Insert—1713. . . .

Cope. Insert—(Co. Northampton). Arg. on a chev. az. betw. three roses gu. stalked and leaved vert. as many fleurs-de-lis per fess or and arg. Add: *V.**

Copeland (London and Bootle, co. Cumberland). Add: Copeland (London Bridge. temp. Edw. ij). *F. Y.*

Copildyke or Copildike or Copledyke (Co. Kent). . . . No remarks. Add: Copuldike (West Wickham, Kent). Same arms. Sir John Copuldick. *S.*

Copildyke, Copuldike or Copledyke (Co. London). Add: *V.*

Copinger. Gu. 3 bendlets or on a fess vert. 3 plates. *V.V.**

Copinger (London). Bendy of 6 or and gu. on a fess az. 3 plates a bordure ppr. *Vis. Lon. 1633.*

Copland or Coupland. Arg. 2 bars and a canton gu. over all a bend az. Sir John Coupland. *V.*

Copland. Arg. two bars and a canton gu. (another az.). Add: Sir John Coupland. *V.*

Copleston (Copleston, Warleigh &c. in the co. Devon). Add: *V.*

Copleston (Shipton George and Nash). Add: *Cady.*

Coplestone (Eggsford, co. Devon). Arg. a chev. gu. betw. 3 leopards heads az. *V.D. 1620.*

Coplestone (Bondon, co. Devon). Same arms with a mullett for diff. *V.D. 1629.*

Coplestone (Co. Devon). Arg. a chev. betw. 3 3 griffins heads erased sa. *V.*

Copley (Co. Worcester and London). Arg. a cross patonce sa. Crest: A griffin sejant or collared and lined gu. *Vis. Lon. 1633.*

Copoldyke (Harrington, co. Lincoln). Add: and quartering, lozengy . . . and erm. **Seal** of John Copuldyke. 15th cent.

Corance or Corane. Sa. a bordure arg. a label of 5 points gu. *A. Harl. MS. 6137.*

Corbet (Moreton Corbet, co. Salop bart. . . .). Add: Sire Peres Corbet. *N.* Sir Piers Corbet of Walesborough, co. Gloucester temp. Edw. iij. *V.* Corbet (Kingston-upon-Hull). co. York. 1666. *Dugdale. p. 359.*

Corbet (Sprowstown, co. Norfolk). . . . Add: 5 foil for diff.

Corbet (Chadesley Corbet). Add: Nash.

Corbet (London). Add: Corbet (Clipsham co. Rutland). 1618. Same arms. *C.R.*

Corbet. Or a raven within a bordure engr. sa. *V.*

Corbett. Or 3 ravens sa. Sir William Corbett. *F.* Sir Roger Corbett *E.G.V.* Sir Thos. Corbett. *L.N.*X. Sir Thomas Corbett, co. Gloucester. temp. Edw. ij. *V.*

Corbet. Or 2 crows in pale sa. *K.*

Corbet. Or 2 ravens sa. Thomas Corbet. *B.*

Corbet. Or 2 ravens in pale sa. Robert Corbet. *A.* Sir Piers Corbet *V.D.E.G.P.H.N.* Sire Thomas Corbet. *J.* of Caux *P.X.*

Corbet. Or 2 ravens in pale sa. within a bordure engr. gu. Roger Corbet, Lye. *V.* But the bordure engr. gu. bezanty. Sir Peter Corbet, Hope. *V.*

Corbet (London). Or 3 ravens sa. a mullet for diff. *Vis. Lon. 1633.*

Corbett. Or 5 ravens 2. 2. and 1 sa. *V.*

Corbet. Or six ravens . . . 2 lions pass. guard.—insert—in pale arg. Add: Thomas Corbett *E.F.* Thomas Corbet, Albrighton, co. Salop. temp. Edw. j. married the heiress to Strange of Knocking. *V.*

Corbet (Hadley, co. Salop.). a branch of Corbet of Moreton . . . Add: *V.*

Corbet. Arg. 2 bars and a canton gu. *V.* Robert Corbet. *S.* and with a label. *Sir* John Corbet *O.*

Corbet. Arg. 2 bars and a canton gu. a label of 3 points. M. Robert Corbet, the Son. *S.*

Corbett (Houghton). Gu. on a chev. or 3 ravens sa. *V.*

Cordall. Gu. a chev. erm. betw. 3 griffins heads heads erased arg. *V.**

Cordall (Huntingdon). Same arms. *Cady.*

Cordell (Enfield, co. Middlesex). Insert—Granted by Camden 1612 and, following Crest : . . . Add: *Vis. Lon. 1633.*

Cordwainers, or Shoemakers, Company of, (London). Insert—Granted by Cooke 1579.

Coringe. Erm. on a chev. sa. three 5-foils or. *V.** Robert Corynge. *V.*

Coringes. Erm. a chev. betw. 3 cinquefoils or. *Harl. MS. 1404. fo. 93.*

Corken or Corkin (London). Arg. five fusils conjoined in fess gu. in chief 3 martlets sa.

Cormailes. Per chev. gu. and az. a chev. betw. 3 roses or. *A.A.*

Cornall or Cronall. Arg. a bend betw. three cronels sa. *V.** Another betw. six cronells sa. *V.*

Corne. Add: *V.**

Cornay. Sa. a chev. arg. Thomas Cornay. *V.*

Cornell. Arg. 5 towers 2. 2. and 1. gu. *V.*

Cornell. Or 5 towers in cross sa. *V.*

Cornell or Cornull. Add: *V.*

Cornewall (Moccas Court, co. Hereford, bart.). Insert—1764.

Corney. Arg. a chev. engr. betw. 3 bugle horns sa. *V.*V.*

Cornforth. Az. on a chev. or 3 escallops . . . in chief a lion pass. of the second.

Cormock. Az. on a bend or 3 escallops gu . .

Cornell (Co. Warwick). Or a chev. vert. *Guillim.*

Cornish (Essex and Kent). Add: *V.* Add: Cornish (London). Same arms and crest, a martlet on a crescent for diff. *Vis. Lon. 1633.*

Cornish (Exeter). Per pale az. and sa. a chev. embattled betw. 2 roses in chief and in base a cross potent or. *Colby.*

Cornwall. Arg. on a bend az. 3 bezants. Sir Richard Cornwall. *R.*

Cornwall. Arg. on a bend sa. 3 plates. Sir Ric. Cornwall. *R.*

Cornish. Sa. a chev. betw. 3 roses arg. *Collinson Somerset iij. 401.*

Cornwall (Crockham, co. Berks). . . . . a bend lozengy—insert—or fusilly . . . Add: *V.V.** Sir John Cornwall. *V.*

Cornwall (Court in St. Stephen, Brannell, co. Cornwall). Add: *L.* Conte de Cornwall. *B.N.P.C.Y.G.J.D.E.F.L.V.Z.*

Cornwall. Geoffrey de Cornwall, Baron of Burford. Arg. a lion ramp. gu. crowned or within a bordure engr. sa. bezanty. *Z.* 99.

Cornwall. Or a lion ramp. gu. crowned gold over all on a bend sa. 3 bezants : quartering Pourcell. *Harl. MS. 1449. fo. 102.*

Cornwall (Co. Oxford). Delete—(Another engr.). Add: Sire Edmond de Cornwall. *V.N.* Symon de Cornwale. *Y.*

Cornwall. Arg. a lion ramp. gu. crowned or on a dexter baston sa. 3 mullets of the third. Sir Geoffrey Cornwall. *O.Y.* But the mullett on a bend sa. *V.*

Cornwall. Erm. a lion ramp. gu. crowned or within a bordure engr. sa. bezanty. Sir Bryan Cornwalle. *S.* Sir John Cornwayle. *T.* Sir Geoffrey de Cornwall, Baron of Burford *Z.* 99. Sir John Cornwall, Baron of Fanhope and Millbrook. ob. 1443. *Z.* 258.

Cornwall (Co. Warwick). Add: *V.*

Cornewall. Or 5 castles in saltire gu. *Cady.*

Cornwallis. Arg. a lion ramp. gu. a dexter baton sa. bezanty. Sir Edmond Cornwallis. *L.*

Corona (Adlington, co. Chester). Add: Thomas de Corona. *V.*

Corona. Az. a chev. arg. betw. 3 crowns or. *V.**

Corrance (Rendlesham . . . co. Suffolk). Insert—descended from Urren alias Currance, London.

Corrigan. Sir Dominic John Corrigan, Bart. Insert—1866 . . . .

Corser. Arg. on a chev. sa. three horses heads couped of the first. Add: *V.*

Corson (Norfolk). Erm. a bend compony arg. and sa. *Fuller.*

Corzon. Add: *V.**

Cosen (Kenninghall, Norfolk, Granted by Cooke). Az. a chev. wavy arg. betw. 3 eagles displ. or. *W.*

Cosh (Devonshire). Add: *V.*

Cosine. Insert—(Kent). Add: *W.*

Cosin. Gu. a chev. betw. 3 keys erect wards upwards arg. *Cady.*

Cosine (Co. Dorset). Az. a lion ramp. tail forked and renowed or goutty de sang crowned arg. Robert Cosine. *V.*

Cossen. Alias Madern (Penzance). . . . Add: *V.C. p. 304.*

Costes. Add: *V.*

Cosworth (Cosworth, co. Cornwall). . . . . Add: Cosworth (London). Same arms. *V.*

Cosworth. Arg. on a chev. az. betw. 3 sinister wings elevated sa. 5 bezants. *V.*

Cosyn (London). Erm. a chev. per pale or and sa. *V.**

Cosyn (London and Newcastle-on-Tyne, Granted by Ryley, Norroy 12 May 1647). Erm. a chev. engr. per pale or and sa.

Cotell (Terling, co. Essex). Or on a bend gu. 10 cronels arg. *V.E. 1634.*

Cotel. Or a bend gu. Sire Elys Cotel. *N.* Thomas Cotel. *Y.* Cotel, co. Somerset. *V.*

Coteel (Devonshire). Add: Crest: a demigreyhound arg. winged or. *Vis. Lon. 1633.*

Cotes (Bishop of Chester 1554–5). Az. Moses' ark with staves and cherubim ppr. in chief the sun in glory issuing from clouds arg.

Cotham or Cotton. Add: *V.**

Cotone. Barry of 6 arg. and az. 3 buckles in chief gu. Ralf de Cotone. *Y.V.*

Cotterell (South Repps, co. Norfolk). Add: *V. L.N. p. 409.* Add: Sir Clement Cotterill, Groom Porter to James I, Cotterell (Hadley, Middlesex). Same arms.

Cottesmore (Brightwell Baldwin, co. Oxford). Add: *V. Dug. O.J.*

Cottingham (Co. Chester). Sa. 2 hinds counterpass. the one facing to the sinister surmounting the other in fess arg. *V.*

Cottingham. York, (John de Cottingham, temp. Richard II). Sa. a chev. engr. betw. three plumes arg. Add: ? cinq pierced.

Cotton (Connington, co. Huntingdon, bart.). Insert—1611.

Cotton (Alkington, co. Salop). Az. a chev. erm. betw. 3 hanks of cotton erect arg. *W.*

Cotton (The Priory, Leatherhead, co. Surrey). Add: Cotton (Totnes, co. Devon). Same arms.

Cotton (Kent). Arg. on a chev. betw. 3 griffins heads erased sa. a mullet of the first. *V.*

Cotton. Az. on a chev. betw. 3 hanks of cotton arg. a fleur-de-lis *V.E. 1634.*

Cotton (Etwall Hall, co. Durham). Add: Cotton (Lord Mayor of London). Same arms. quartering; or an eagles leg erased gu. on a chief indented az. a plate betw. 6 mullets arg. *Vis. Lon. 1633.*

Cotton (Cumbermere, Cheshire). Baronetcy 1677. Same arms.

Cotton. Arg. a chev. betw. 3 griffins heads erased sa. *Cady.*

Cotton (Landware, co. Cambridge). Sa. a chev. betw. 3 griffins heads erased arg. Sir John Cotton. *V.*

Cotton (Starston, co. Norfolk). Same arms.

Cotton. Arg. 3 bars sa. over all as many cotton hanks or. *W.*

Cotton. Vert. a leopard ramp. reguard. az. Add: Sir William Cotton. *V.*

Cotton (Ridware, co. Stafford). . . . arg. armed gu.—insert—*V.*

Cotton (M.P. for London 1874). Az. a chev. arg. betw. 3 eagles displ. . . . *Debrett.*

Coucy. Barry of 6 vair and gu. a bend or. Thomas de Coucy. *C.* and *Harl. MS. 6589.*

Couderay. Gu. 6 billets or. William Couderay. *X.*

Couderors. Add: *V.**

Couderow. Arg. a chev. betw. 3 talbots statant sa. *V.*

Coullce or Colle. Per pale indented gu. and arg. a bull courant counterchanged within a bordure sa. bezanty. *V.V.**

Coulter or Coulthard. Arg. on a chev. az. 3 wheels
          or   or
          az.   arg.
of the field. *Robson.*

Couradus (London, originally of Lubeck). Sa. a chev. betw. 3 unicorns heads erased or. Crest: A unicorns head erased or. gorged with a collar sa. charged with 3 bezants. *Vis. Lon. 1633.*

Courteene (Aldington, or Aunton, co. Worcester). . . . Add: *Vis. Lon. 1633.*

Cove (Co. Hereford). Add: Sir John Coue. *L.N.Y.*

Covell (London). . . . *Vis. Lon. 1633.* . . . at end: confirmed by Segar 1629.

Covell. Az. a lion ramp. arg. goutty de prie armed and langued gu. over all a bend gu. *Cady.*

Coventre, or Coventreye, Coventry. Add: Coventry (London, Lord Mayor 1425). Same arms. *V.*

Cow (Kent and Norfolk). Add: *V.*

Cow. Gu. a bend arg. cotised or. Sir Joan de Coue. *N.L.Y.*

Coward. Arg.—underlined—Add: *Collinson Somerset. iij. 468.* Add: Coward (Wells, co. Somerset). Same arms. *V.S.*

Cowdrey (Co. Berks.). Add: Cowdrey. Gu. 6 billets or. Monsire Cowdrey. *Y.* Sir Peres de Couderai. *E.F.* Sir Thomas Cowdray. *V.L.N.O.* Sir John Coudray. *L. Harl. MS. 6589.*

Coventry. Town in (Warwick). **Book Plate.** Add: Motto: Camera Principe.

Cowell. Az. a lion ramp. guard. or on a chief dovetailed of the last 3 plates gu. each charged with as many bezants. *A.A.*

Cowfold. Barry of—insert—12 or . . . . Add: *V.*

Cowght. Cought. *V.* Gu. a bend erm. betw. 6 bezants. Sir Armony Cowgthe. *V.*

Cowley (London). Insert—Granted by Camden, 1604. *Vis. Lon. 1633.*

Cowley. Arg. on a chev. sa. three leopards heads or. Add: *V.**

Cowper (Earl Cowper). Add: Cowper (London). Same arms. *Vis. Lon. 1633.*

Cowper (Norfolk 1644). . . . on a bend engr. . . . . betw. 2 lions ramp. . . . 3 billets . . .

Cowper (Carleton Hall and Unthank, Cumberland). Add: *A.A.*

Cowper. Arg. on a bend betw. 2 lions ramp. sa. 3 plates. John Cowper, Serjeant at Law. *Dug. O.J.*

Cowper (Sir Richard Cowper, Knt. of Temple Elfont, co. Surrey, nephew of John Cowper, Serjeant at Law . . .). Add: Cowper (London 1568). Same arms. *C.L.* Cowper (co. Leicester 1619). Same arms. *C.C.*

Cowper or Cogar. Arg. on a chev. gu. betw. 3 laurel leaves slipped vert another chev. erm. *Guillim.*

Cowper. Az. on a chev. engr. arg. betw. three cinquefoils erm. 2 lions combatant sa. Add: *V.**

Cox alias Cokks (London). Add: Edmund Cox alias Cokks. London. Granted 25 Jan. 1554. *Harl. MS. 6169. fo. 26b.*

Cox. Sa. a chev. betw. 3 bucks scalps arg. . . . and with a mullet for diff. Add: Thomas Cox of Tilmanstone, Kent. *V.*

Coxwell. Arg. a bend wavy sa. betw. six cocks gu. quartered by Rogers. Exemplification by Young, Garter 1850.

Coyking or Coykin. Add: *L.*

Coyking. Gu. 3 bendlets erm. Sir Roland Koykyng. *V.*

Coyking. Bendy of 6 gu. and erm. Sir Renaud de Coykin. *N.* Bendy of 6 erm. and gu. Sir Roland Coykin. *L.*

Coyne (Co. Stafford). Or on a bend sa. three 3-foils slipped arg. Coney or Coyney. *V.**

Coyney (Weston Coyney, co. Stafford). . , Add: *V.*

Coyshe (Quartered by Rolls). Gu. an eagle displ. barry of 6 erminois and az. *Burke.*

Cozans. See Cusance.

Crabb. Insert—(Exeter). Az. a chev. betw. 2 fleurs-de-lis in chief and a crab in base or.

Crade or Crode. Erm. on a chev. engr. sa. betw. three estoiles. Add: *V.*

Cradock (Hartforth, co. York). Add: (London.) Same arms and crest. *Vis. Lon. 1633.*

Cradock (Richmond co. York). Same arms 1665. *Dugdale. p. 106.* Sir Richard Cradock. *S.* Sir David Cradock. *V.*

Cradock (Craswell Castle, co. Stafford). Arg. on a bend az. 3 garbs or. *Cady.*

Cradock or Cradoke. Add: *V.*

Craford (Cos. Essex and Kent). . . . Or on a chev. vert.—delete—(another sa.). Add: Sir Wm. Craford. *V.*

Craford (   ). Or on a chev. sa. three hawks heads erased arg.

Craggs (Carlton, Kent). Sa. on a bend or betw. 3 mullets erm. as many crosses crosslet of the first.

Crakenthorpe (Westmorland). Or a chev. betw. 3 pierced mullets az.

Crakenthorp. Add: *V.*

Crakey (Granted to Wm. Crakey or Crokey alias Johnssone, co. York. 4 June 1496 by Carlyle, Norroy). Per pale arg. and sa. on a chev. 3 escallops counterchanged *Harl. MS. 6169. fo. 1.*

Cramlington (Co. Westmorland). Insert—co. York) . . . Add: *Syl. Morgan.*

Cramond (Auldbar, Scotland). . . . . Az. a bend or. betw. three—underlined—'2'. *Guillim.*

Cramp (Dudinghurst, co. Essex). Add: *V.E. 1634.*

Cranber or Craneburne. Add: *V.*

Crane (Norwich). Or on a chev. betw. 3 cranes rising az. as many 5-foils of the field. *Blomfield.*

Cranesley. Add: Cranley. Same arms. *V.*

Cranmer (Sutterton and Aslerton, co. Notts.). Add: Sir Caesar Cranmer (Whitehall 1677). *L.N.*

Cranmer (Aslerton, co. Notts). 1564. Same arms, quartering; Arg. a fess fusilly gu. on each fusil an escallop or. *V.N.*

Cranmore. margin—and Cranmer—insert—London, confirmed by St. George, Clarenceux. Add: *Vis. Lon. 1633.*

Cransley. Arg. a chev. betw. 3 cranes az. *Cady.*

Crathorne (Salaby, co. Lincoln and Crathorne, co. York). Add: Crathorne (London). Same arms and crest: a fleur-de-lis for diff. *Vis. Lon. 1633.*

Crawcester. Add: John Crawcestre. *X.*

Crask (Co. Cambridge). Sa. a chev. betw. 3 fleurs-de-lis arg. on a chief gu. as many lozenges or. *Cole.*

Crawhall. Arg. a chev.—insert—sa. . . . Add: *Robson.*

Crawnford. Arg. 2 lions pass. in pale sa. crowned or. Sir . . . de Crawnford. *V.*

Craycroft. Per pale vert. . . . three crows—insert—*V.** (another . . .).

Craycroft (Lincolnshire 1640). Per pale vert. and gu. on a bend indented or 3 martlets sa. *Yorke.*

Craycroft (Co. Lincoln). Per bend gu. and vert. on a bend dancetty arg. 3 ravens sa. *V.*

Crean. Arg. a wolf salient ppr. betw. 3 hearts gu.

Crehington. Erm—delete—and Add: *V.*

Crekhampton. Arg. on a bend gu. 3 cinquefoils or. *V.*

Crepin. Arg. 3 bars gu. William Crepin. *C.*

Crepyn. Arg. 3 bars engr. gu. *C.*

Creppinge. Gu. billetty or a lion ramp. arg. Sire Johan de Creppinge. *N.V.*

Cresacre (Barnborough, co. York). Add: *V.*

Creseby. Gu. a bend and a half arg. a quarter erm. John de Creseby. Mirst. *X.* Also gu. 2 bends arg. a quarter erm. *X.*

Creseley. Arg. three chevs. sa. Add: *V.*

Cresignes. Az. 3 bars gemel and a chief arg. Robert de Cresignes. *C.*

Cressenor, Cresnor or Cresnall. . . . Add: *V.*

Cresson. Paly of 6 arg. and sa. on a chev. gu. a cross crosslet or. *V.*

Cressy. Arg. a lion ramp. tail forked sa. a label of 3 points gu. Sir Roger de Cressy, co. York. *N.V.*

Cresset. Arg. a lion pass. in bend sa. depressed by a bend gu. Add: Arg. a lion ramp. tail forked. sa. Sir William de Cresci. *I.E.N.V.* Monsire de Crissie. Seigneur de Hodesake. *V.*

Cressey or Cressie. Add: Henry Cresset. *V.*

Cressy (Birkin, co. York). Same arms, quartering 2. Gu. a lion ramp. vair; 3 or a fess az. in chief a label of 3. gu. *Dugdale 1666.*

Cressy (Freuse, co. Norfolk). Sa. 3 beacons arg. *Blomfield.*

Cressy (Lincolnshire 1640). Arg. a lion ramp. sa. in the dexter chief point a 5-foil gu. thereon a mullet or. *Yorke.*

Cressy. Arg. on a bend betw. 2 cotises sa. 3 crescents or. *V.*

Creswell or Creswyll—amend—em—to read—cabossed.

Cresswell (of Cresswell, Northumberland). Arg. on a bend sa. 3 bulls heads cabossed of the field. *Eliz. Roll. xxxiv.*

Creting (Lord Creting). John de Creting. *Y.*, was summoned . . . Add: Sir Adam de Creting. *A.E.G.* Sir John de Cretinge. *V.*

Cretinge (Suffolk). Add: Sir Adam de Cretinge. *D.I.* Sir John Creting. *V.F.*

Cretowne or Cretownes. Add: V.

Crewe (Urkington, co. Chester). Az. a lion ramp. arg. quartering; az. 2 bars arg. over all on a bend gu. 3 arrows arg. for Done.

Crewe of Trafford. Az. a lion ramp. arg. a label of 3 points of the same.

Crewell. Add: *V.*

Crewz (Ireland). Az. a bend betw. 6 escallops arg. *Cady.*

Creye. Gu. a bordure arg. over all a baston sa. Sir Robert Crey or de la Crey. *I.*

Criol (Aldbury, co. Hertford). Add: *V.**

Cripps (Cirencester). Add: Horseshoes or.

Crispe (Queeks and Clive Court, in Thanet, co. Kent). Add: *V.*

Crispe (Hammersmith, co. Middlesex, bart.). Insert—1665 . . . Add: *W.*

Crispe (London). Same arms and crest. Add: *Vis. Lon. 1633.*

Crispin. Barry indented of 4 pieces the one within the other arg. and gu.

Cristy. Add: *V.V.** quartered by Tyndale.

Croak. Arg. a chev. gu. in base a lion couchant . . . on a chief . . . 3 fleurs-de-lis . . . *Robson.*

Croft (Croft Castle, co. Hereford, bart.). Add: Croft (Felmingham, co. Norfolk and London). Same arms. *Vis. Lon. 1633.*

Croft. Quarterly per fess indented arg. and az. in the first quarter a lion pass. gu. Sir Hugh Crofte. *V.* Herbert Croft, Bishop of Hereford 1662.

Croft (Castle Croft, co. Hereford). Quarterly per fess indented az. and arg. in the first quarter a lion pass. guard. or Sir Hugh Croft. *L.*

Crofton. Out of place.

Croke (Chilton and Chequers, co. Bucks). Add: *Vis. Lon. 1633.*

Croker. Temp. Ric. ij. arg. a chev. engr. gu. betw. 3 ravens ppr. *V.*

Croker (Hooknorton . . .—margin—read also Crokker. Add: *V.O.*

Crokker (Lineham, co. Devon). Arg. a chev. engr. gu. betw. 3 martlets sa. *V.D. 1620.*

Crombe. Arg. a chev. engr. gu. on a chief of the last 3 escallops as the first. Sire Simon de Crombe. *E.*

Cromer. Arg. a chev. gu. betw. 3 boars heads erased . . . tusked or. *Cady.*

Cromer. Insert—(Yarmouth, Norfolk). Or a chev. vair. betw. 3 crows sa. Crest. A crow as in the arms. Add: *V.*

Cromer. Az. a chev. betw. 3 saltires couped arg. *V.*

Crompe. Sa. a chev. betw. 3 quatrefoils or. *V.**

Cromwell (Lord Cromwell). Arg. a chief gu. over all a bend az. *Lysons. V.*

Cromwell. Az. a lion ramp. tail forked arg. crowned or. John de Cromwell. *K.*

Cromwell. (Putney, Surrey). Quarterly per fess indented az. and or 4 lions pass. counterchanged. Cromwell, Lord of Okeham. Same arms. *V.*

Cromwell. Sir Roger Cromwell, Or 6 annulets gu. 3.2.1. *V.*

Cromwell. Gu. 6 annulets or 3. 2. and 1. Sir John de Cromwell. *I.M.Y.N.*

Cromwell (Cormbridge). Same arms.

Cromwell. Gu. 6 annulets or 3. 2. and 1. within a bordure engr. compony arg. and az. *V.*

Cromwell (Co. Huntingdon). Add: *V.*

Cromwell. Arg. a chief az. over all a bend gu. Sire Rauf de Cromwell. *J.* Simon de Cromwell. *E.*

Cromwell. Arg. a chief gu. and a bend az. *V.* But a baston az. Raufe de Cromwelle. *G.* Thomas Cromwell, Lamelay. *V.*

Cromwell. Arg. a chief gu. and bend gobonated or and az. Add: Arg. a chief gu. a baston company or and az. Sire Richard de Cromwell. *O.* John Cromwell. *Y.*

Cromy or Crony. Add: *V.**

Crook. Gu. on a bend erm. 3 cinquefoils az. *Robson.*

Croone (*London, Her. Off.*). Add: Confirmed by Wm. Segar, Garter. *Vis. Lon. 1633.*

Cropall or Cropell. Az. a chev. betw. 3 pheons arg. *V.*V.*

Cropley (St. James, Clerkenwell, co. Middlesex). Add: Cropley (London). Confirmed by Sir Ric. St. George, Clarenceux, 26 Apr. 1634. *Vis. Lon 1633.*

Crosby. Sa. a chev. betw. 3 rams arg. *V.**

Cross or Crosse. Gu. a chev. paly of six arg. and or. betw. 3 crosses . . . Add: *V.V.**

Cross or Crosse. Gu. a chev. betw. 3 crosses crosslet arg. *V.V.**

Crosse. Temp. Edw. ij. Arg. on a bend sa. a cross patty or.

Crosse. Arg. on a bend sa. a cross crosslet betw. 2 crabs . . . *Cady.*

Crosse. Gu. on a chev. arg. three 5-foils az. *Cady.*

Crossing (Hugh Crossing, Alderman of Exeter 1629). . . . Add: *V.D.*—marginal reference—Crossing (Exeter 1620).

Crossley. Insert—Halifax, co. York, Bart. Insert —1863. Gu. a chev. indented erm. . . .

Crouchard. Add: *V.V.**

Crouch (London). Arg. on a pale sa. a martlet betw. 2 crosses patty or all within a bordure engr. of the second. *Vis. Lon. 1633.*

Crouchman. Arg. two chevs. sa. Add: *V.**

Croun. Arg. a fess gu. in chief 2 millrinds in base an annulet of the second. *Banks. j. 62.*

Crowan. Az. 3 wolves pass. arg. (another collared or). Add: *V.*

Crowcher. Or a bend potenty vert. *Randle Holme.*

Crowke. Add: *V.V.**

Crowley. Arg. a chev. gu. betw. 3 herons az. *V.**

Crowmer (Sir Wm. Cromer, Lord Mayor of London 1413). Arg. a chev. engr. betw. 3 crows sa. *V.**

Crowmer (Kent). Same arms. *V.*

Cromer. Arg. a chev. betw. 3 rooks volant sa. *V.**

Crowther (London and co. Salop). Add: *Vis. Lon. 1633.*

Crowton. Arg. on a chev. gu. betw. 3 martlets . . . Add: *V.*

Croxford. Arg. a chev. betw. 3 round buckles points to the sinister sa. *V.*

Croy. Or a bend az. Sir William Croy. *L. Harl. MS. 6589.*

Crugg or Crugge. Insert—temp. Henry iii. Add: *V.*

Cruger (Olveston, co. Gloucester). Arg. on a bend engr. az. betw. 2 greyhounds courant sa. three martlets of the field.

Crulle or Curle. Add: *V.*

Crumwell. Arg. a chev. gu. over all a bendlet az. *V.*

Cruse or Croise. Insert—Ireland. Add: *Harl. MS. 1603. V.*

Cruso (Norwich and London). *Visitation London.*—insert—*1633.*

Crymes (Buckland Mona chorum, co. Devon). Or 3 bars gu. each charged with as many martlets arg. on a chief of the last 2 bars nebuly az. *V.D. 1620.*

Cryon. Arg. a chev. betw. 3 martlets sa. Sire William Cryon. *Y.*

Cudderley. Margin—† Add: *V.*

Cuddon (Shanfield, Norfolk). Arg. a chev. gu. on a chief az. 3 bezants. *Cady.*

Cuddon (Shadingfield Lodge, Great Yarmouth 1862). Same arms.

Cuddon (Norwich 1678). Same arms.

Cudner. Arg. a chev. betw. 3 storks heads erased sa. *Vis. Lon. 1633.*

Cufande (Great Yarmouth, Norfolk). Barry of 10 arg. and gu. a canton of the same.

Cuffe (Granted by Barker 1544). *V.S.* John Cuff of Ilcester. *V.*

Cuily. Add: *Y.*

Culcheth (Culcheth, co. Lancaster). . . . eagles wings elevated. Add: *V.* swaddled gu. banded or. Add: *V.**

Culcheth (Culcheth, co. Lancaster 1664). Arg. a raven sa. standing on a child in a cradle. gu. *V.L.*

Culchech. Add: *V.**

Culey. Add: *Harl. MS. 1404. fo. 78b.*

Culey or Cuiley (Co. Notts). Add: *V.N. 188.*

Cullum (Hawsted and Hardwick House, co. Suffolk). Bart extinct . . . Add: Cullum, London and co. Suffolk). Same arms and crest. *Vis. Lon. 1633.*

Culnet. Gu. a bend wavy arg. *Cady.*

Culpepper (Suffolk). Gu. a chev. engr. betw. 3 martlets arg. *Blomfield. iv. 31.*

Culy (Sir Hugh Culy, co. Derby, temp. Edw. j.). Arg. a chev. betw. 3 pierced mullets sa. *V.* Sire Hugh de Culy. *N.*

Cure (London). Add: Granted in 1588. *W.*

Curle (Soberton, co. Hants). Insert—Bart. 1678 . . . Add: *V.*

Curle. Vert on a chev. arg. three 5-foils gu. *V.**

Currance (London, Granted to Allan Urin alias Currance by Sir Wm. Segar, Garter 27 Feb. 1619). Arg. on a chev. betw. 3 crows sa. as many leopards faces or. Crest: A crow wings elevated sa. holding an escu. sa. charged with a leopards face or. *Vis. Lon. 1633.*

Currer (Skipton, co. York 1665). Erm. 3 bars sa. each charged with a closet arg. on a chief az. a lion pass. of the second. a canton or. *Dugdale. p. 231.*

Currie. Arg. 2 bendlets sa. betw. 5 ogresses in saltire, in chief a rose.

Curson (Kedleston, co. Derby). Add: Sir Robert Curson. *V.*

Curson. (Water Perry, co. Oxford, bart.). Insert —1661 . . .

Curson. Arg. on a bend sa. 3 popinjays or collared and membered gu. in the sinister chief a crescent gu. for diff. Sir Roger Curson. *S.*

Curson (Norfolk). Gu. on a bend or 3 escallops sa.

Curson (Norfolk). Arg. a bend gu. bezantee. Add: Sir Johan Cursoun. *N.*

Curson. alias Markham. Arg. on a bend gu. four bezants. *V.*

Curson (Litheringset, Norfolk). Erm. a bend counter compony arg. and sa. Monsire John Curson *T.* and with a martlet in chief gu. for diff. Monsire Curso. *T.*

Curson. Vairy gu. and or on a bordure sa. 8 martlets arg.

Curson. Erm. a bend chequy arg. and sa. Add: *V.*V.*

Curson. Gu. billettee on a bend or 3 escallops sa. Add: Robert Curson. *T. V.*

Curson. Paly of six arg. and sa. on a chev. gu. a crosslet or. Add: *V.*

Curtain. See Mc Curtin.

Curteis. Or a chev. betw. 3 pierced mullets gu.

Cutteis. Gu. a chev. vair betw. 3 bull's heads . . . Add: *V.** Robert Curtys, Auditor. *V.*

Curteis (Somerleis and Dronfield, co. Derby). Per—insert—saltire, delete sa. . . . Add: *Lyson's Derby clviij.*

Curtis. Gu. a chev. vair betw. 3 bucks heads cabossed arg. *Cady.*

Curwen (Workington, co. Cumberland). . . . Add: Curwen (London). Same arms and crest. *Vis. Lon. 1633.*

Curzon. of Breadsall, heiress mar. Dethick. Gu. on a bend arg. 3 horseshoes azure. *Lysons.*

Curzon (Co. Derby). Same arms. Curzon.

Curzon. Erm. a bend chequy sa. and arg. *V.*

Curzon (Kedleston). Vairy or and gu. on a bend sa. 3 popinjays or. *Edmondson.*

Curzon (Loking, co. Berks). Add: Richard Curzon Esquire of the Body to Hen. vj.

Curzon (Falde, co. Stafford). Add: John Curzon—margin extension—1350.

Curzon. Arg. a bend compony or and az. . . . in pale of the second . . . Add: John Curzon (Bellingford, Norfolk). *V.*

Cusance. Arg. a bend engr. sa. an escallop . . . "en la sou'rein piece" William Cusance. *Y.*

Cusance or Cozans. Arg. a bend fusilly sa. a label of 5 points gu. Sir William Cozans. *R.*

Cusanor or Cusavor. Add: *V.*V.*

Cushe or Cush. Add: *V.*

Cust (Belton, co. Lincoln). Add: Cust (Leasowe Castle, co. Chester). Bart. 1876. Same arms.

Cust (Stamford, co. Lincoln). Insert—Baronet 1677. Granted 31 May 1663—insert—by Sir Edw. Bysche.

Cuthbert or Cuthburst. Add: *V.*

Cutler (Ipswich, co. Suffolk). *Grant of Arms.*

Cutts. Erm. on a bend engr. sa. 3 plates *Harl. MS. 1476. fo. 100.*

Cutts (Co. Cambridge). Same arms. *Cady.*

Cyfrewast. Arg. 3 bars gemelle az. Sir John Cyfrewast. *V.*

D

DABERNON or D'Abernoun (Stoke D'aberon, co. Surrey). Add: Sir John Dabernon. *E. Harl. MS. 6137.* and with a label arg. Sir John Dabernoun, the son. *N.O.*

Dabgreene or Dabgreyne. Add: *V.V.**

Dabigni. Or 2 chevs. engr. within a bordure engr. of the last. *V.**

Dabitot (Hindlip, co. Worcester). Add: Geoffrey d'Abitot. *F.*

D'Abrichecourt. Add: Sir John Dapscourt. *T.* Sansett Dabrichcourt. *S.* Nichol Dabrichcourt. *S.*

Dabrichcourt. Gu. 2 bars and a bordure erm. Mon. Nichol Dabrichcourt. *S.* Sansett Dabrichcourt. *S.* Sir John Dapscourt. *T.*

Dabrichcourt. Erm. on 3 bars humetty gu. 9 escallops or 3. 3. and 3. Monsire John de Dabrichcourt. *S.*

Dabridgecourt. Add: *V.*

Dackcombe (Stepleton, co. Dorset). Add: *V.* Towers with spires. *V.*

Dacres. Arg. a chev. gu. betw. 3 pellets . . . Add: *V.**

Dacres (Malfeld, co. Stafford and London). Arg. a chev. sa. betw. 3 torteaux each charged with an escallop of the first. Henry Dacres. *V.*

Dad. Az. a bend or and bordure erm. *Robson.*

Dagworth. Erm. on a chev. gu. 3 bezants. *V.* Sir Thomas Dagworth. *X.Y.*

Dakeham. Gu. 3 church spires arg. on each a ball and cross crosslet fitchy or. *V.*

Dakyns (Linton, co. York). Add: Dakins (Hackness, co. York). Same arms. Dakins (Rowton, co. York). Same arms. A crescent upon the lion for diff. *Eliz. Roll. xxvij.*

Dakeyn (Stubbing, co. Derby, confirmed by St. George, Norroy 1611). Gu. a lion pass. guard. betw. 2 mullets in pale or betw. 2 flaunches arg. each charged with a griffin segreant sa. *Guillim.*

Dalby. Arg. a chev. sa. a bend engr. and a canton of the last. *Harl. MS. 1404. fo. 104.*

Dalby. Arg. a bend engr. and a canton sa. *V.*

Dalby (Co. York). Gu. a chev. erm. betw. 3 ink molines or. *Fairfax's Book of Arms.*

Dalby. Gu. a chev. erm. betw. three round buckles or. Add: *V.* Add: Dalby (Overton, co. York). Same arms, a mullet for diff. Crest: a mules heads erased arg. a mullet for diff. *Vis. Lon. 1633.*

Dalby. Insert—Chester. Arg. two chevs. engr. and a canton sa. *V.*V.*

Dalderby. Add: *V.*

Dale (Brentwood, co. Essex). Add: *V.E. 1612.*

Dale (London 1568). Sa. on a chev. or betw. 3 cranes rising arg. 7 torteaux. *C.L.*

Dale (Winkell, co. Chester). Gu. on a base vert. a swan arg. collared sa. *Harl. MS. 1535. fo. 123.*

Dale. Gu. a swan close arg. membered sa. Sir Thomas Dale. *S.*

Dale (Flagg, co. Derby). Paly of 6 gu. and arg. a bend erm. on a chief az. 3 garbs or.

Dale. Arg. on a bend sa. three talbots (another wolves) . . . Add: Valentine Dale. *Dug. O.J.*

Dale. Arg. on a bend sa. 3 wolves pass. of the field. Dr. John Dale. *V.*

Dalling (Burwood Park, co. Surrey, bart.). Extinct . . . Add: *V.*V.*

Dalston (Dalston Hall, co. Cumberland, bart.). Extinct 1765 . . . Add: John de Dalston. *X.*

Dalton (Thurnham, originally of Bispham, co. Lancaster). . . . Add: quartering, Barry of 6 arg. and az. in chief 3 lozenges gu. *V.L. 1664.*

Dalton. Sir Richard Dalton, co. Lancaster. *V.*

Dalton. Az. crusily or a lion pass. guard. arg. Sir Robert de Dalton. *O.*

Dalton (York and London). Az. semy of crosses crosslet a lion ramp. reguard. arg. charged on the breast with a mullet gu. *C.L.*

Dalton (Shank's House, co. Somerset). Az. a lion ramp. betw. 9 crosses crosslet arg. a canton erm. *A.A.*

Dalton (Co. Derby). Az. a lion ramp. within an orle of crosses crosslet arg. *Dugdale Derby. 1662.*

Dalway (Carrigfergus, co. Antrim. M.P. for Carrigfergus 1868). Arg. 3 lions pass. guard. gu. 2 and 1. *Debrett.*

Dameck or Dameke. Add: Sir . . . Dameke. *V.*

Damend or Damenor. Add: Sir Gerard Damener. *V.*

Damerville. Or a bend engr. betw. 5 torteaux in saltire.

Damme (Sydistroud, Norfolk). 1461. Sa. a chev. erm. betw. 3 dolphins of the last.

Damme. Sa. a chev. arg. betw. 3 dolphins or. *Cady.*

Damorie. Add: *V.**

Damvers. Add: *V.*

Danby (Danby, co. York). Add: Danby (Thorp Perrow, co. York). Same arms, quartering, Gu. 3 lozenges arg; and arg. on a saltire sa. an escallop betw. 6 billets of the first. *F.Y.*

Danby. Erm. on a chev. gu. 3 fleurs-de-lis or. *W.*

Danby (Yafford, co. York). Arg. 3 chevs. braced sa. in chief a fillet and as many mullets of the second. *V.*

Danby. Arg. 3 chevs. braced sa. in chief as many mullets of the last. *Harl. MS. 1407. fo. 74b.*

Dancaster. Or on a bend az. (? 3) castles arg. Robert Dancastre. *Y.*

Dancell or Dansell. Add: *V.*

Dancy. William Dancy, Alderman of London. Per pale arg. and or two bars nebuly gu. *V.*

Dancys. Add: *V.*

Dandeleigh. Arg. two bars gu. each charged with three crosses crosslet or. Add: Philip Dandelegh. legh. *V.* Daundeleghe. *Y.* D'Andelegh. *X.*

Dandeley. Arg. on 3 bars gu. 6 crosses crosslet or. Sir Richard Dandeley. *V.*

Dandeleigh. Az. a canton or a bordure gu. bezantee. Add: *V.*

Dandelion or Dent de Lion (Margate, Isle of Thanet, temp. Edw. j.). Sa. 3 lions ramp. and 2 bars dancetty arg. The heiress married Petyt.

Dane (Stortford, co. Hereford). Add: *C.L.*

Danell. Add: Sir Richard de Danell. *V.*

Daniel (Auburn, co. Westmeath). Add: quartered in the second quarter by Tyssen Amherst. of Didlington, co. Norfolk.

Daniell (Co. Gloucester). Insert—and co. Norfolk . . . Paly of 6 . . .

Daniell (Tideswell, co. Derby). Add: *V.V.*

Daniel. Az. a bendlet betw. 6 escallops or. Sir John Daniel. *E.*

Daniell. Arg. on a bend sa. 3 escallops of the first. *V.*

Danis. Add: *V.*

Dannay. Arg. on a bend az. betw. 2 cotises . . . 3 cinquefoils . . . John Dannay. *Y.*

Dannett or Dannet (London). Add: also Dannett, co. Leicester, 1619. *C.C.*

Dannett. Sa. goutty a canton arg. Sir John Dannett. *V.*

Dansert. Add: Le Sire Dansert. *W.*

Dandesey. Per pale or and arg. 3 bars nebuly gu. Monsire John Dandesey. *S.*

Dansey (Rev. Wm. Dansey, Rector of Donhead, St. Andrew, Wilts.). . . . Add: Dansie (London). Same arms and crest. *Vis. Lon. 1633.*

Dantrey or Dantree (Norfolk). Add: Sir Laurence Dantrey. *Syl. Morgan.*

D'Anvers (Culworth, co. Northampton). . . . Add: Sir Thomas Danvers. *V.*

Danvers (Rothley, co. Leicester 1619). Arg. on a bend gu. 3 martlets or in the sinister chief a 3-foil slipped. *C.C.*

Danvers (Dantsey, co. Wilts). Same arms. *Z. 345.* Sir Thos. de Anvers. *N.*

Danvers (London). Erm. on a bend . . . 3 martlets. Crest: A wyvern sejant. *Vis. Lon. 1633.*

Danyell (Daniell). Az. 2 bars arg. a chief gu. Hugh Danyell. *Y.*

Danwikes or Danwykes. Add: Roger Danwikes. *V.*

Darby (Colebrookdale, co. Salop). Add: *Burke's Illustrations.*

Darby (Benington, co. Lincoln). Add: *V.* Sir Wm. Darby. *W.*

Darcy. Arg. an inescutcheon sa. within an orle of 3 (? 8) cinquefoils gu. Sir John Darcy. *L.O.R.*

Darell (Pagham, co. Sussex). Az. a lion ramp. or crowned arg. within a bordure of the last. *V.N.p. 90.*

Darell (Co. Wilts.). Az. on a lion ramp. or crowned arg. a cross crosslet at the shoulder. *V.*

Darell (Calehill, Kent). Add: *V.* Darell (co. Notts.). Same arms. *V.N.*

Darling (London). Arg. a chev. ermines betw. 3 ewers sa. *Vis. Lon. 1633.*

Darmin, Darmine or Darmyne. Add: Sir Gu ' Darmine. *V.*

Darnell (Heylings, co. Lincoln, bart.).—insert— 1621 . . .

Darrell. Arg. three bars sa. on the first as many roses of the field. Add: Paul Dayrell. *V.*

Darsett. Add: *V.*

Darward. Add: *V.*

Dassett (Ricel, co. York). Add: Dassett (Hilmorton, co. York). Same arms. *F.Y.*

Daston. Gu. a chev. engr. betw. 3 eagles displ. arg. Add: *V.*

Daubeney. Gu. two chev. within a bordure or. Add: William Daubeny, Beauvoir. *B.P.*

Daumis. Sa. a chev. betw. 3 boars heads couped arg. *Cady.*

Dauncester. Az. a bend cotises dancetty arg. *Randle Holme.*

Dauncy. Arg. on a bend az. betw. 2 cotises gu. 3 cinquefoils or. *V.*

Dauncourt. Add: Sir Thomas de Daunecourt. *V.*

Daungate or Denewgate. Add: *V.*

Daunt (Ireland). Sa. 3 beacons with ladders fired ppr. Thomas Daunt. *V.*

Dauntsey. Az. a lion ramp. combatant with a dragon both arg. John Dauntesey. Sheriff of Wiltshire. temp. Hen. iv. *Fuller.*

Dauntesey. Per pale arg. and or two bars nebuly gu. John de Dauntesey. **Seal.** Walter Daundsey. *V.*

Dauntre. Gu. a bend arg. betw. two cotises indented or. Add: (or dancetty). *V.*

Davell. Arg. a chev. betw. 3 martlets sa. *Cady.*

Davell (Sheriff of Newcastle 1497). Or 2 bars sa. *Carr MS.*

Davenport (Davenport, co. Chester). Add: Sir Humphrey Davenport, Chief Baron of the Exchequer. *Dug. O.J.*

Davenport (Salford, co. Lancaster 1664). Same arms, a canton—insert—'gu' for diff. *V.L.*

Davent or Davenett. Add: Sir Vincent Davent. *V.*

Daverston or Deverston (Co. Suffolk). Arg. 3 battle axes gu. quartering arg. on a chev. sa. a cross crosslet or. *V.*

Daveye. Arg. on a chev. sa. betw. 3 pierced mullets gu. a crescent of the first. Sir Philip Daveye. *S.*

Davie (Ferguson Davie, Creedy, co. Devon, bart.) Insert—1846. . . . .

Davies (London and Shropshire). Add: *Vis. Lon. 1633.*

Davies (London). Gu. a chev. engr. betw. three boars heads erased arg. Crest: On a cap of maintenance a boar pass. arg. *Vis. Lon. 1633.*

Davies. Insert—(London). Arg. on a bend sa. three mullets of the field. *Vis. Lon. 1633.*

Daville (Roger Daville, co. York). Or 2 bars betw. 6 fleurs-de-lis sa. 2. 2. and 2. *Eliz. Roll. xxiij.*

Davis (Hollywood, co. Gloucester, bart.). Insert —1845 . . .

Davis. Gu. a chev. engr. betw. three boars heads erased arg. *V.*

Davis (Middleton, co. Salop). Same arms. *W.*

Davis (Westbury, near Bristol, Baronetcy 1845). Arg. a chev. nebuly betw. 3 mullets pierced sa.

Davy (Norfolk). Sa. a chev. erm. betw. 3 annulets arg. Gregory Davy of Gunthorp.

Davy (Ingoldsthorpe . . . Norfolk). Add: Davy (London). Same arms, a crescent for diff. *Vis. Lon. 1633.*

Davy. Arg. a chev. sa. betw. three mullets pierced gu. Add: *W.*

Davye (Creedy, co. Devon). Baronetcy 1641. Arg. a chev. sa. betw. 3 pierced mullets gu.

Dawes (Stapleton, co. Leicester—insert—1619). C.C. Add: Dawes (Putney, Middlesex, Baronetcy 1663, extinct 1741). Same arms. John Dawes, Alderman of London. V. Sir William Dawes, Bart., Bishop of Chester 1707. Archbishop of York 1714–24.

Dawes. Or 3 eagles displ. gu. armed az. W.

Dawes (Westbroke, Bolton). Or on a bend engr. betw. 6 battle axes. Crest: Az. 3 swans with wings elevated arg. beaked and membered sa.

Dawkin (Kilrough   ). Gu. a chev. arg. betw. 3 lions ramp. or. Nicholas.

Dawnay (Cowick, co. York). Insert—Baronetcy 1642— . . . Add: Dugdale. p. 264.

Dawnay. Arg. on a bend betw. 2 cotises sa. 3 annulets or. William Dawney. V.

Dawney (Sesay, co. York) . . , delete (another martlets) Add:Eliz. Roll. xxiij.

Dawney (Selby, co. York). 1683 Sa. 3 annulets betw. cotises arg. Drake's York. 341.

Dawney (London). Arg. on a bend vert. three roses or Add: V.W.

Dawney. Arg. on a bend cotised az. three wolves pass. or. Add: V.

Dawney. Arg. on a bend betw. 2 cotises sa. 3-foils or. Sir Hugh Dawney, co. York. V.

Dawney. Arg. on a bend vert. betw. 2 cotises az. three 5-foils or. Sir Nicholas Dauny. V.

Dawson (Groton House, Suffolk). . . . of the last three martlets — and ? 'daws' . . . Add: (Coverham, co. York. confirmed 21 Dec. 1858). quartered by Duffield. The daws beaked and membered gu.

Dawson (Azerley, co. York—insert—Visitation). Add: W.

Dawson (Moyola, formerly Castle Dawson, Londonderry). Add: Dawson (Newcastle-on-Tyne). Same arms. Robson.

Dawson (Newcastle). Az. on a bend engr. arg· three daws (another ravens). ppr. Crest: A daw ppr. V.*

Dawtree. Insert—(Norfolk). Gu. a bend arg. cotised or. Add: V.

Dawtrey. Gu. on a bend arg. betw. 2 cotises or 3 escallops sa. Sir James Dawtre. V.

Dawtrey. Gu. a bend arg. betw. 2 cotises engr. or. Add: Lyon Dautry. Y.

Dayes. Sa. a chev. betw. 3 crosses crosslet arg. Quartered by Southworth. Harl. MS. 1445. fo. 107. Collinson Somerset. j. 219.

Daywill. Add: Sir John Daywill, temp. Edw. j. V.

Deach Add: V.*

Deacon (London). Or a chev. gu. fretty or betw. 3 roses gu. stalked and leaved vert. Crest: a demi-eagle wings elevated or. Vis. Lon. 1633.

Deakin (Col. Henry James Deakin, of Werrington Park). Insert—near Launceston, Cornwall. . . .

De Aldburgh (Sir William de Aldburgh, Lord of Harewood Castle, co. York 1365). Gu. on a lion ramp. arg. a fleur-de-lis az. at the shoulder. Add: V.

Deal (Town of   ). Per pale gu. and or. 3 demi-lions pass. guard. in pale of the second conjoined with as many demi-hulls of ships . . .

Deale. Arg. on a bend sa. 3 wolves pass., of the first. V.

Dean or Den (Norton petrach, co. Devon). Arg. a lion ramp. ppr. W. Sir John de Dene. N.V.

Deanclough. Or 2 bars in chief a canton dexter and in base a canton sinister all gu. Randle Holme.

Deane (Cobsale, co. Notts.). Or a lion ramp. ppr. W.

Deane (London). Arg. a lion pass. guard. tail coward gu. on a chief of the last 3 crescents or. Robson.

Deane (London). 1568. Gu. a lion sejant guard. or on a chief arg. 3 crescents of the field. C.L.

Deane or Deene (Co. Lincoln). Delete (another three). Add: V.

Deane. Arg. on a chev. gu. betw. 3 birds sa. as many crosses patty of the first. V.*

Deane (General Richard Deane, one of the Generals under the Commonwealth). Arg. on a chev. gu. betw. 3 ravens ppr. as many crosses crosslet or.

Deane of Halling, quartered by Lambard. Arg. on a chev. betw. 3 birds sa. as many 5-foils or all within a bordure az. bezanty.

Deane. Insert—co. Devon. Arg. a chev. erm. betw. three butterflies volant gu. Add: W. and Harl. MS. 1404.

Deane. Bishop of Bangor. Arg. a chev. gu. betw. 3 cornish choughs ppr. Made Archbishop of Canterbury in 1501 when he added on the chev. 3 pastoral staves or.

Deane (Berkeley, co. Wexford). Add: A.A.

Deaphole, Deypholl or Deypole. . . . Add: The lion pass. V.

Deard. Arg. a bend az. betw. 6 mullets gu. †

Death, D'aeth or Dick (Dartford, co. Kent). Add: Vis. Lon. 1633.

De Bad. Gu. a chev. betw. 3 mullets arg. Sire Walter de Bad, co. Bedford. Temp. Edw. j. V. The mullets pierced. N.

De Beauboir (London). Arg. a chev. betw. 3 quatrefoils gu. C.C. Eliz.

De Beauvoir (Jersey and Guernsey). Add: This is the coat of Cartier. Wm. de Beauvoir mar. Jenette de Cartier, the heiress, early in 16th cent.

Debenham or Dabenam (Suffolk). (—delete—another az.) and at end—(another arg.). Add: V

Debenham. Sa. a bend betw. two crescents arg. V.*

De Bykele. Arg. ? a chev. betw. 3 birds sa. Collinson Somerset iij. 15.

Deckling or Dreckling. . . . —delete—of the first, read sa. Add: V.

Decons (Wasperton, co. Warwick). . . . betw. three roses—insert—gu. . . . Add: Granted to Robert Decons of Wasperton 1619. W.

De Crespigny (Champion de Crespigny, Champion Lodge, Camberwell, Surrey). Bart.— insert—1805. . . .

De Cryoll alias Deicrow (London and Enfield, Middlesex 1634). Add: The key on the canton was granted to De Crioll, Lieutenant of Dover Castle.

De Den. Arg. on 2 bars az. 4 crosses patty or 2. and 2. Sir John de Den. V.

Dedham. Az. a chev. engr. and canton or. Add: V.

Dedham. Az. a plain chev. and a canton engr. or Harl. MS. 1386. fo. 34.

Dedham. Az. a chev. engr. and a canton indented at the bottom or. V.

Deen. Insert—Kent. Gu. a chev. arg. betw. 10 bezants. Add: V.

De Ewil (Egmarton, co. Notts). Arg. on a chev. sa. 3 fleurs-de-lis. or. Robson.

Deffe or Deyff. Add: V.

DeFoix. Add: DeFoix (Earl of Kendal 1446). Arg. 2 cows pass in pale gu. armed and unguled and with bells around their necks or. quartering: or. 3 palets gu. overall a label of 3 points sa. charged with 15 escallops arg. Wright's Heylyn and Cady.

Degge (Co. Derby and Callow Hill, co. Stafford). Add: Granted by Dugdale 1662. Sir Simon Degge 1669. L.N.

DeGore. Arg. 3 lions ramp. az. on a chief gu. a demi-lion ramp. issuant or. V.*

Degrey (Merton Hall, Thetford, Norfolk). Barry of 6 arg. and az. in chief three annulets gu. *Debrett.*

Deincourt. Az. a fess indented betw. 10 billets or. (Banks ij. 149).

Dekkes. Add: Sir Robert Dekkes. *V.*

De la Barre. Arg. on a bend cotised az.—re-read —betw. two martlets three escallops or. Add: Francois de la Barre. *V.*

Delaber. Add: Simon de la Bere. *E.*

De la Bere. Az. a bend or cotised arg. betw. 6 martlets of the second. Sir Kinnard de la Bere. *V.*

Delabourne (Ireland). Per pale az. and gu. 3 lions pass guard. in pale or.

De la Chambre. . . . . fessways of the second— insert—fired ppr. Add: *Berry.*

De la Fountain (Belchamp St. Paul, Essex). Granted by Camden 22 Feb. 1619. Gu. a bend and in the sinister chief a 5-foil arg.

De la Forde. Arg. a greyhound springing sa. Add: *V.**

Delahay. Arg. a bend betw. 2 cotises sa. and three escallops gu. *Robson.*

Delahay (Spaldington   ). Arg. on a bend sa. betw 2 cotises vert. 3 escallops or. *V.*

De la Launde. Per pale gu. and az. 3 lions pass. guard. in pale or. Henri de la Launde. *G.*

De la Leie. Az. 3 chevs arg. Sir Thomas de la Leie. *E.*

De la Lond. Add: *V.*

Delamarche. Barry of twelve arg. and az. overall a lion ramp. gu. Add: Sir Payne Delamarche. *V.*

De la Mare. Arg. on a bend az. 3 eagles displ. or. Sire Johan de la Mare. *N.* Sir Thomas de la Mare, Essex. *V.* Sir Hugh de la Mare, temp. Edw. iij. *V.* Thomas de la Mare, Abbot of St. Albans ob. 1396. His **Brass.**

De la Mare. Gu. 2 lions pass. guard. arg. Sir John de la Mare. *S.* Sir Robert de la Mare. *Y.* Sir Robert de la Mare, co. Hants. temp. Edw. iij. *V.* Pers de la Mare. *E.F.*

De la Mare. Barry dancetty of 6 or and gu. Mon. Piers de la Mare. *S.*

De la More. Arg. 7 barrulets az. over all a chev. gu. Bartholomew de la More. *F.* Bartholomew de la More. *E.*

De la More. *alias* By the more. Barruly . . . and . . . on a chev. . . . 3 mullets . . . *Collinson Somerset. j. 185.*

Delamore. Gu. a bendlet arg. betw. 6 fleurs-de-lis or. *Robson.*

Delamore. Gu. a water bouget arg. *V.*

Delaours. Vairy or and az. a bend gu. and a label arg. Sir William Delaours. *Y.*

Delapine (Co. Kent). Add: *W.*

Delaplanch (Co. Buckingham). Arg. billettee a lion ramp. sa. crowned or. Add: Sir James de la Planche temp. Edw. iij. *V.*

De la Reur (Co. Kent). Add: *V.**V.*

Delariver (Co. Berks.). Arg. a fret sa. and canton gu. *V.*

Delariver (Co. York). Add: *Tonge p. 18.*

De la Roche. Sa. 2 lions pass. guard. in pale arg.

De la Roche. Az. 3 bendlets or a bordure gu. Gwy de la Roce. *A.*

De la Roce. Or 3 bendlets az. a bordure gu. cantory of fleurs-de-lis arg. Guy de la Roce. *A. Harl. MS. 6137.*

De la Tour. Add: Gilbert de la Tour, Bavarke, co. Dorset. *V.*

De la Tombe (London). Arg. a chev. betw. 3 human skulls sa. *Harl. MS. 1486. fo. 4b.*

De la Tun. Gu. 6 bendlets 3 sinister and as many dexter vair Robert de la Tun. *E. Harl. MS. 6137.*

De la Val. Erm. 3 bars vert. over all a bend gu.

De la Vand. Arg. on a mount and in front of a tree ppr. a lion pass. gu. on a chief az. 3 mullets or. **Book Plate.**

De la Ware. Gu. crusilly and a lion ramp. arg. Sire Joan de la Ware. *E.L.N.Y.I.* Roger de la Ware. *K.A.* And with a label az. Sire John de la Warre. *L.*

Delawne (London). Az. a cross lozengy or on a chief gu. a lion pass. guard. or semy of pellets and holding a fleur-de-lis or. Crest: A winged bull sejant or holding a book gu. *Vis. Lon. 1633.* Confirmed by Segar. *1612.*

Delfe. Arg. a chev. gu. fretty arg. betw. 3 delves sa.

Del Ile. Or a lion ramp. az. Le Conte del Ile. *B.D.E.G.*

Delme (Sir Pet Delme, Alderman of London). Gu. an anchor in pale arg. betw. 2 lions pass. or. †

Delves (Delves Hall, co. Stafford). Add: *V.*

Delves (Dodington, co. Chester, bart.). Insert— 1621 . . . Add: *V.*

Delves (Co. Lancaster). Add: *V.*

Delwood. Arg. an eagle displ. double headed sa. standing on a piece of a tree raguly vert. *V.** And with a crescent for diff. Henry Delwood. *V.*

De Lyle. Gu. a chev. betw. 3 (probably gletver) leaves or. Sir John de Lyle, Lord of Leyburn. *P.*

De Maigne. Per pale sa. and arg. 3 chevs. betw. as many 5-foils all counterchanged. *Berry.*

Demel. Gu. a chev. arg. betw. 3 garbs or on a canton arg. a fleur-de-lis. or.

Den (Co. Huntingdon). Add: Sire John de Deen. *O.* Sire . . . de Den. *N.*

Denardeston (Co. Suffolk). Az. 2 bars arg. on a chief gu. a lion pass. guard. or. Sir Pere de Dennardestone. *N.*

Dene (Co. Huntingdon). Arg. on 2 bars sa. 6 crosses patty or 3. and 3. *V.*

Dene. Barry of six gu. and arg. on a canton of the last a tower triple-towered of the first. John Dene. *Y.*

Denham. Arg. on a bend sa. 3 mullets of the first. Sir John Denam. *V.*

Denham. Or 3 martlets in bend sa. quartering, gu. 3 martlets in bend arg. *V.*

Denham. Quarterly or and sa. in each quarter three martlets counterchanged. *V.*

Dennis or Dennes (Co. Devon). Erm. 3 poleaxes within a bordure engr. gu. *Harl. MS. 1458.*

Denston. Arg. a chev. betw. two couple closes engr.—insert—'on the outer edge'—sa. Add: *Harl. MS. 1386. fo. 34b.*

Denston.—insert—(Co. Suffolk). Az. two lions pass. guard. or. Add: *V.*

Dent (London). Sa. a fesse dancettee arg. . . . Add: *Vis. Lon. 1633.*

Dent (Wandsworth Common, co. Surrey). Insert —and Northumberland. Add: *Eliz. Roll xxxiv.*

Denton (Denton Hall, co. Cumberland). Add: Denton (London). Same arms. *Vis. Lon. 1633.*

Denton (Nawton, co. York). Or 2 bars gu. in chief 3 martlets of the second a canton az. *Dugdale. p. 63.*

Denton. Arg. a chev. engr. voided of another sa. *Randle Holme.*

Denton. Gu. a chev. betw. three crescents arg. Add: Richard Denton. *Y.*

Denys. Arg. a chev. sa. betw. 3 pierced mullets gu. Chesterton, co. Hunts. 1352. John Denys and with a bordure . . . his brother Thomas; But with a bordure engr. their brother Philip. . . . *Cotton. MS. Julius. F. viij. fo. 36.*

Denys. Arg. a chev. sa. betw. three mullets gu. Add: *V.*

DeOrbaston. Arg. 2 chevs. gu. on a canton of the second a lion ramp. of the second. *V.**

Depden. Arg. a bend gu. *V.*

De Pentheney (De Pentheney). Sa. a chev. erm. betw. 3 pheons arg. all within a bordure engr. of the last charged with 13 hurts, quartered by O'Kelly.

De Pin. Gu. a chev. betw. 3 (probably pine) leaves or. Sir Thomas de Pin. *F.*

De Quester (London). Az. a chev. or in chief 2 mullets in base a dove arg. Crest: A six pointed mullet or. *Vis. Lon. 1633.*

Dering (London). Or a saltire and chief sa. Crest: A stag's head az. *Vis. Lon. 1633.*

Derly (Co. Chester). temp. Hen. vj. Arg. a chev. engr. sa. betw. 3 garbs.

Dernested or Dernestode. Add: *V.*

Dernford. Sa. an eagle displ. arg. Crest: ... Add: William de Dernford. *F.E.V.*

Dervill. Gu. a lion ramp. and a fleur-de-lis arg.

Derwentwater. Arg. 2 bars gu. on a quarter a canton of the last a cushion of the first. Le Sire de Derwentwater. *Y.* John Derwentwater. *Y.*

Derwentwater. Arg. 2 bars gu. on a canton of the second a lozenge. arg. *V.*

Derwentwater (Derwentwater, co. Cumberland). Add: M. John Derwentwater. *S.X.*

Desanges. Az. a greyhound courant towards the sinister arg. on a chief gu. 2 cherubs heads or. *Robson.*

Desap. Baron of Okehampton. Chequy or and az. 2 bars arg. *Lyson's Devon.*

Deschamps. Sa. on a chev. betw. 3 garbs or. another chev. arg. bordered sa. **Book Plate.**

Desmaistris (London). Az. a chev. betw. 3 mullets of 6 points or. Crest: A mullet of 6 points or. *Vis. Lon. 1633.*

Desnay (Co. Lincoln). Arg. 3 lions pass. in pale gu. *V.V.**

Despencer. Quarterly arg. with gu. fretty or. overall a bend sa. in the first quarter a martlet of the last. Sire Hugh le Spencer. *S.*

Despencer (Earl of Winchester). Add: Le Despenser (Steward to Hen. j. 1105). *Z. 332.* Sir Hugh le Spencer, Lord of Glamorgan. *P.Q. Harl. MS. 6589.* Sir Hugh le de Spencer. *V.* Le Sire de Spencer. *T.S.* Hugh de Despencer. *Z. 140. A.E.J.G.D.H.* and with a label az. Sir Hugh le de Spencer 1318. *N.* Philip Spencer. *O.*

Despencer. Barry of 6 or and az. Mons Phil le Despencer. *Syl. Morgan. 11.*

Despencer (Earl of Gloucester). Add: *Q.*

De Stafford. Or on a chev. gu. 3 swans ppr.

Dethick (Lord of Brysdale). Or on a bend az. 3 horseshoes arg. *Nash.*

Detling. Or—delete—(another arg.). Six lions ramp. az. 3. 2. and 1. Add: *D.A. Harl. MS. 6137.* Sir John Detling.

Deton. Sa. on a chev. betw. 3 crescents arg. ... as many martlets vert. Add: *V.W.*

Deton. Same arms. Add: *V.*

Deton. Sa. a chev. betw. 3 crescents arg. each charged with another crescent gu. *V.**

Devall. Sa. on a plain bend betw. 2 cotises indented arg. a cross crosslet fitchy in the dexter chief gu. Richard Devall. *V.*

Devenish (Cos. Sussex and Dorset). Add: Devenish, London. *Vis. Lon. 1633.*

Dever. Add: *V.*

Devere. Arg. on a bend az. 3 crescents or in chief a label of 3. gu.

De Vic (Geurnsey, bart.). Insert—1649, extinct, —insert—confirmed by Camden 1612. ...

De Vismes. Count (France). Insert—cos. Devon and Gloucester.

Devis (Calcutta). Gu. a chev. erm. betw. 3 boars heads erased. ...

Devischer (London). Az. 3 mermaids ppr. Crest: A dolphin erect ppr. *Vis. Lon. 1633.*

Dew. Gu. on a chev. arg. betw. three 5-foils or. 5 mullets az. *V.V.**

Dewin (Gwiner, co. Cornwall). ... Gu. on a chev. arg. three cinquefoils sa. Add: *V.C. 304.* 5-foils. *V.*

Dewsbury Borough of. Chequy ... surmounted by by a fleece and imposed thereon a cross fitchy. ... Motto: Deus Noster Refucium et virtue. **Book Plate.**

Dewrant. Az. 4 bendlets potent counterpotent arg. *Randle Holme.*

Dexwell. Arg. a chev. betw. 3 fleurs-de-lis. sa. *V.*

Deyer (Co. Huntingdon). Sa. 3 goats statant arg.

Deynes (Norfolk) Or 2 bars gu.

Deyville. Gu. demy of fleurs-de-lis a lion ramp. arg. Sire Johan Deyville. *N.*

Dickens (Leaton and Bobbington, co. Stafford). Add: *Vis. Lon. 1633.*

Dickens (London). Granted 16 June 1625—insert—by Segar; Add: *Vis. Lon. 1633.*

Dickins. Bendy of six erm. and gu. *V.** Add Sir Reginald Dickings, co. Devon. *V.*

Dickenson (London). Az. a chev. betw. 3 crosses formy or. *Vis. Lon. 1633.*

Dickinson. Or a bend engr. betw. 2 lions ramp. gu. ... Add: Dickinson (co. Oxford).

Dickwand or Dickward. Sa. 3 annulets arg. each charged with 7 torteaux. *V.V.**

Dierwell. Arg. a chev. gu. betw. 3 fleurs-de-lis sa. *V.*

Dideston. Add: *Guillim.*

Dighton (Howstow, co. Lincoln, London, Worcester). Add: Dighton (co. York) Same arms. *Eliz. Roll xxiv.*

Dighton. Per pale gu. and arg. an antelope counterchanged. ... Add: Robert Dighton, Stourton, co. Lancaster. *V.*

Dikens. Arg. a chev. sa. fretty or betw. 3 violets purp. ... Add: *V.**

Dildarne. Add: *V.*

Dillon (Ireland). Arg. a lion ramp. betw. 7 mullets gu. over all a fess az. in chief 2 crescents sa. *Cady.*

Dinant (Joxeus de Dinant). Arg. 3 lions ... az. crowned or. *Dugdale's Baronage. j. 143.*

Dinnorby. Arg. a bend az. in chief 3 gauntlets ... *Cady.*

Dirwell or Dierwell. Arg. a chev. gu. betw. 3 fleurs-de-lis sa. *V.*

Dirton. Insert—co. York ... Add: *V.*

Dishington. Arg. on a bend sa. 3 escallops of the first. *Guillim.*

Dismoes or Dismos. Add: Dysmars. Same arms. *Harl. MS. 1404. fo. 99.*

Disney (Lincolnshire). Add: Monsire William Disney. *S.* Monsire de Disny. *Y.*

Dister. Gu. a chev. or betw. three eagles displ.—insert—'with 2 heads' arg. Add: *W. Cady.*

Dive. Sa. on a bend sinister arg. 3 birds of the first. *V.**

Dixon (Knells, co. Cumberland). Insert—and Houghton, co. Westmorland.

Dixon (Hillsborough Hall, co. York). Add: Granted 21 July 1846. *Foster.*

Dixton. Add: *Syl. Morgan.*

Dixwell (Coton Hall, co. Warwick, bart.). Insert—1716 ...

Dixwell (of Cotton). Vert. on a chev. betw. 3 fleurs-de-lis arg. as many fleurs-de-lis. *C.W.*

Dixwell (Barham, co. Kent). Insert—Bart. 1660. Ext. 1716.

Dixy (Sir William Dixy, Lord Mayor of London 1585). Az. a lion ramp. and a chief or. *C.L.*

Dixy (Bosworth, co. Leicester. Baronetcy 1660). Same arms.

Dobbins. Add: Dobbins (London). Same arms. Crest: An acorn slipped and leaved ppr. *Vis. Lon. 1633.*

Doberich. . . . . on a bend . . . 3 fleurs-de-lis . . . quartering; az. an estoile arg.

Dockeley or Dockesey. Add: Sir Edward Docksey, co. Salop temp. Edw. iij. *V.* Sir Richard de Dockseye. *N.M.*

Dockwra (Lord Dockwra) . . . . Add: Dockwra, Puttridge, co. Hertford. Same arms.

Dockwra (London). Add: Thomas Docwra, Prior of St. John of Jerusalem in London. 1504. *U.*

Doctor's Commons or College of the Professors Of Civil and Canon Law. Add: The arms of Dr. Henry Harvey the Founder.

Dodbrook. Add: *V.**

Dodd. Arg. a chev. gu. betw. 3 haydoodes (or bluebottles). az. slipped vert. *Harl. MS. 2151. fo. 110.*

Dodmer (Lord Mayor of London 1529). Add: *V·*

Dodmer or Dodmore. Add: *V.**

Dodson (Hey, co. Cornwall). . . . . Add: *V.C. p. 304.*

Dodsworth (Cos. Salop and York). Add: Dodsworth (Badswoth, co. York). 1666. Same arms. *Dugdale. p. 287.* Dodsworth (Thornton Watlass, co. York). Same arms. *F.Y.*

Dodsworth (Co.—insert—Thornton Watlass). Add: confirmed in 1610. *Northern Grants xlvj.*

Dodsworth (Barton, co. York). 1666. Arg. on a chev. sa. betw. 3 bugle horns stringed of the second, as many bezants. *Dugdale. p. 313.*

Dodsworth (Newland Park, co. York. bart.). Insert—1784.

Dodsworth (Stranton, Durham). Arg. a chev. betw. 3 bugle horns stringed sa. a canton gu.

Dodworth. Arg. on a bend engr. sa. 3 roundles . . . each charged with a roundle erm. *Constable's Roll. xvj.*

Doe (Sir Charles Doe, London 1665). Az. a doe trippant or betw. 3 bazants. *L.N.*

Dogate. Add: *V*

Dogget. Erm. on a bend sa. 3 talbots heads erased arg. *V.V.**

Dolesley or Dolseley. Add: *V.V.**

Dolliffe (London). Add: Sir James Dolliffe 1714. *L.N.*

Dolling (co. Dorset). Barry dancetty of 4 arg. and sa.

Dolseley. Gu. a chev. arg. Add: *V.*

Dolsey. Add: *V.*

Dombrain. Gu. a chev. betw. 3 fleurs-de-lis arg.

Donagh (Newtown, co. Louth 1721). . . . . a chev. betw. in chief . . . ramp. . . . and in base a boar pass. . . .

Done (Utkinton, co. Chester . . .). Add: Sir John Done. *W.*

Donhead. Arg. a lion . . . of the last and az.—insert—*V.*

Donne (granted 1605). Add: granted by Camden to Sir Daniel Donne, Doctor of Laws.

Donne. Az. on a bend or an annulet gu. *C.R.*

Donsell. Insert—co. Devon . . . Gu. a bend arg. betw. 3 (another 4) crosiers or. Add: *V.*

Doobel. . . . granted—insert—by Camden. . . .

Doolan (Ireland). Gyronny of 8 sa. and arg. an annulet counterchanged.

Doon. Az. a wolf ramp. arg. John Doon. *V.*

Dorchester. Or six lions ramp. sa. 3. 2. and 1. Add: Sir Oliver Dorchester. *V.*

Dormer (Baron Dormer). Add: Sir Robert Dormer, Eythorpe, co. Oxford. *V.* Michell Dormore, Thumly. *W.*

Dormer (Lee Grange, co. Bucks, bart). Insert—1661 . . .

Dormer (Wing, co. Rutland). Insert—Baronetcy 1615 . . . three martlets of the first. Add: (or sa.) *V.***V.*

Dorrant. Sa. a chev. indented and in chief 3 fleurs-de-lis arg. *V.S. p. 120.*

Dorrington (London). Sa. 3 bugle horns stringed arg. Crest: On a mount vert. a stag. lodged arg. in its mouth an acorn slipped ppr. *Vis. Lon. 1633.*

Dorstell. Add: *V.V.**

Dossie (Sheffield, originally of France). Sa. 3 eagles rising or.

Dorulle (Ireland). Sa. a chev. engr. arg. betw. 3 plates each charged with a pile gu.

Dove (Camberwell, co. Surrey, granted). Insert—by Cook, Clarencieux . . .

Dover (Richard de Dover). Gu. 2 lions pass. guard. or. B. Richard Fitz le Rey. *A. Harl. MS. 6137. fo. 89b.*

Dovers (Tatington, Suffolk). Arg. a chev. betw. 3 pierced mullets sa. *Cady.*

Dowdall or Dowdal (London). Add: *V.**

Dowes (Co. Essex). Add: *V;* the lions sa.

Downe or Downes. Add: *V.** Francis Downe or Downes, Little Hyde, co. Hereford. *W.*

Downes (Ireland). Arg. 5 doves in saltire gu.

Downes. Insert—co. Chester. Sa. a buck springing arg. attired or. Add: *V.*

Downham (Bishop of Chester 1561. Granted 6 May 1561). Az. on a chev. or betw. in chief 2 doves arg. beaked and legged gu. and in base a dragon's head erased of the third a red rose enclosed by a pair of closed books or in black covers. *Harl. MS. 1359. fo. 50.*

Downfrist. Gu. on a bend betw. 2 cotises arg. 3 eagles displ. vert. Sir John Downfrist. *V.*

Downhall. Or a bend indented sa. in chief a pierced mullet gu. *V.*

Downing (Skibbereen, co. Cork. M.P. for Cork 1868). Gu. a lion ramp. erm. collared or. *Debrett.*

Dowriche. Add: *V.D. 1620.*

Dowrish. Arg. on a plain bend within a bordure engr. sa. another bend of the first. *W.*

Dowrish. Arg. 2 plain bendlets and a bordure engr. sa. a label of 3 points az. *W.*

D'Oyly (Anciently DeOiglii, DeOilly and DeOyly). Add: *V.*

D'Oyly (Greenland and Marlow, co. Bucks. . . . . afterwards . . . co. Oxford). Insert—Baronetcy 1666 . . .

Draiesfield. Gu. a chev. raguly of two bastons couped at the top arg. Christopher Draiesfield. *Harl. MS.. 1386.*

Drake (London). Arg. a dragon—delete, substitute, wivern gu. betw. two flanches of the second. Crest: On a tower or a wivern sejant gu. *Vis. Lon. 1633.*

Drake. Insert—co. Devon. Arg. a chev. purp. betw. 3 battle axes . . . Add: *V.*

Drakeley. Arg. a chev. sa. betw. three drakes heads erased az. *V.** Add: Swans heads. *V.*

Drakelow or Dracelow (Co. Essex). Add: Sir Thomas Drakelowe. *V.*

Drakelow. Gu. a chev. erm. betw. 3 griffins heads erased arg. *V.**

Drakelow. Arg. on a chev. gu. betw. 3 eagles heads erased sa. as many crescents or. *V.*

Dralesfeild. Gu. a chev. raguly of two bastons couped at the top arg.

Dransfield (Co. Essex). Add: *V.*

Dransfeld. Paly of 6 sa. and arg. on a bend of the first 3 mullets or. Christopher Dransfeld. *V.*

Draper (Major General Sir William Draper. . .). Add: *Vis. Lon. 1633.*

Draper (London). Granted—insert—by Camden. Feb.

Draper (   ). Gu. 3 bendlets or on a chief per fess erm. and arg. in the upper part as many mullets sa. *Collinson Somerset ij. 333.*

Draper (Sheriff of Newcastle 1610). Az. a chev. betw. 3 mullets of 6 points arg. *Carr MS.*

Draper (Newcastle). Add: *Eliz. Roll. xxxv.*

Draper. Gu. 2 bends or on each 3 fleurs-de-lis vert. Add: *V.**

Draycote (Draycote, co. Stafford). Insert—1566. Add: Richard Draycott. *V.*

Dracote (Co. Stafford). Or fretty gu. on a canton ? az. a fess dancetty betw.   billets gold. Sir John Dracote. temp. Edw. iij. *Erdeswick.*

Draycott or Dracot (Cos. Derby and Stafford). Add: *V.**

Draycott (Co. Stafford). Or fretty gu. on a canton az. a cross patonce arg. Add: Sir Philip Dracote. temp. Richard. I.

Draydon (Canons Ashby). Az. a lion ramp. in chief a globe betw. 2 stars or. *Fuller.*

Drayton (Robt. Drayton of Norfolk). Per pale indented az. and gu. a lion ramp. or. *V.*

Drayton (Co. Norfolk). Gu. on a chev. arg. 3 crosses az. *Cady.*

Drayton. Gu. on a bend arg. 5 trefoils slipped vert. Add: *V.*

Drayton. Az. a bend betw. 6 crosses crosslet fitchy or. Sir John Drayton. *V.*

Dreffeld. . . . . on a chev. . . . . betw. 3 lions heads erased . . . as many buckles . . . Seal of Thomelin Dreffeld.

Dreux. Chequy or and az. a bordure gu. Robert of France, Earl of Dreux. *Z. 93.* John de Dreux, Earl of Richmond. *Z. 93.*

Drew (Cos. Cornwall and York). Erm.—delete—(another or.). Add: *Harl. MS. 1404. fo. 143.*

Drew or Drewe (Cliff and Higham alias Norton). . . . Add: Drew (Youghal, co. Cork). Same arms. *A.A.*

Drew. Or a chev. sa. betw 2 couple closes gu. and 3 heathcocks of the second. *V.V.**

Drew or Dew. Gu. on a chev. arg. betw. three cinquefoils or five mullets az.

Drewe (East Grinstead, Sussex). Erm. a lion pass. gu. betw. 3 fleurs-de-lis az.

Driffield. Arg. a chev. betw. 3 lions heads erased sa. Add: William Driffield de la Walde. *X.*

Driffield (Easingwold, co. York 1665). Erm. on a bend sa. 3 boars heads erased arg. *Dugdale. p. 384.*

Drift. Az. 3 geese arg. a crescent for diff.

Drokensford. Quarterly az. and or 4 caps like doge's caps counterchanged. *V.*

Drownsfield. Gu. 2 bastons couped inguine of a chevron or. Christopher **Drownsfield.** *X.*

Druell (co. Devon). Sa. a chev. betw. 3 bunches of daisies arg. *Colby.*

Drummond (Earl of Melfort 1686). Arg. 3 bars wavy gu. quartering or. a lion ramp. gu. armed and langued az. within a double tressure flory counter flory of the second. *Crawfurd.*

Dryden (Canons Ashby, co. Northampton). . . . . . . in chief a—insert—'celestial'.

Dryton. Arg. on a bend az. 3 water bougets or a crescent of the second. *V.V.**

Drywood (Shipton, co. Essex) Insert—*V.E. 1634.* . . . .

Du Boys. Arg. 2 bars gu. a canton of the last overall a bend sa. Sir Johan Du Boys. *N.* Sir Roger le Boys. *S.*

Duckenfield. Sa. a chev. betw. 3 crescents or. Crest: . . . Add: *V.*

Duckenfield. Same arms. The chev. charged with three crosses crosslet of the field. *V.*

Duckett (London). Sa. a saltire betw. 4 crosses patty arg. Crest: a plume of ostrich feathers sa. *Vis. Lon. 1633.*

Duckett (Co. Devon). Sa. 10 martlets or. *Cady.*

Duckhome. Gu. a bordure invected gobony arg. and az. *Randle Holme.*

Duckworth. Arg. on a chev. az. betw. 3 ducks gu. 3 crosses patty or *Randle Holme.*

Dudenan. Barry of 6 or and gu. a bend az. Sire . . . de Dudenan. *A.*

Dudley (Clapton, co. Northampton, bart.). Insert—1660 . . .

Dudley (Granted by Cooke to John Dudley. Sergeant of the Pastry to Queen Elizabeth). Or 2 lions pass. within a bordure engr. az.

Dudley. Az. a chev. engr. or. Add: *V.*

Duff (Muirtown, near Inverness). Or. 2 lions ramp. gu. Duff, quartering; per fess vert. and gu. a fess dancetty erm. in chief a buck's head cabossed betw. the attires a pheon inter 2 escallops or and in the base a pheon of the last. *Robson.*

Duffield (Madmonham, co. Bucks. &c.) . . . Add: *Ashmole MS. 763. V.*

Dugdale (Co. Leicester and Shustock, co. Warwick). Add: (London) confirmed by Dethick, 10th Aug. 2. Eliz.). Same arms. Crest: A mullet on a crescent for diff. *Vis. Lon. 1633.*

Duke (Benhall Lodge and Brompton, co. Suffolk, bart). Insert—1661. Add: *Cady.*

Dukenfeld. Az. on a chev. betw. 3 crescents or as many crosses crosslet of the first.

Duly. Insert—(co. Bucks.). Add: *Harl. MS. 1386 fo. 34.*

Dun (1606). Add: Sir Daniel Dun. *W.*

Dunbar (Earl of March). Add: *H.P.Y.* Add: Le Conte Patrick de Dunbarre. *P.D.V.* Patrick Conte de Dunbarre. *Y.* Le Conte Patrick. *H.J.*

Duncalf (Otringham, co. York). Add: a mullet for diff. *F. Y.*

Dunch. Sa. a chev. or betw. in chief two towers and in base a fleur-de-lis arg.

Dunclent. . . . . on a bend . . . betw. 2 cotises . . . 3 escallops . . . *Nash.*

Dundas (Arniston, co. Edinburgh). Add: Robert Dundas, Solicitor General for Scotland. †

Dundas (Viscount Melville). Add: Dundas Papdale, Orkney. M.P. for Orkney and Zetland 1852). Same arms. *Debrett.*

Dune. Sa. an eagle displ. with two heads arg. . . . . Add: *V.*

Dune. Gu. on a bend arg. 3 popinjays vert. Monsire de Dune. *Y.*

Dungan (Earl of Limerick). Gu. 3 lions pass. or each holding in the dexter paw a close helmet arg. garnished or. *Harl. MS. 4040. fo. 135.*

Dunkeswell (Cistercian Abbey of co. Devon). Gu. 2 bendlets wavy one arg. the other or.

Dunscombe (Confirmed to Nicholas Dunscombe . . .). 3 talbots heads—insert—'erased'.

Dunscombe (Mount Desert). Co. Cork. Same arms.

Dunstable. Arg. a chev. erm. betw. 3 door staples . . . Add: *V.*

Dunstable. Arg. a chev. betw. 3 escallops sa. Add: *V.*

Dunstanvil (Earl of Cornwall . . .). Add: *Z. 50.*

Dunstavile or Dunstavill. Arg. a fret gu. on a canton of the second a lion ramp. guard. . . . . Add: *Vis. Lon. 1633.* Add: Sir Walter de Dunstanville. *A.* Sir Walter Dunstanvill, Baron of Castlecombe and Lord of Colerne and Heytesbury. *V.*

Dunstanville (Castlecomb). Arg. fretty gu. a bordure engr. sa. over all on a canton of the second a lion pass. or. *V.*

Duntze (Exeter). Sa. a holy lamb pass. arg. *Colby.*

Durants. Arg. a chev. sa. betw. 3 bugle horns of the last lip and mouthpiece or. stringed az. *V.*

Durants. Arg. a chev. engr. sa. betw. 3 bugle horns of the last . . . Add: *V.**

Durward (Co. Essex and Cloughton, co. York). Erm. on a chev. sa.—delete—(another az.). Add: *V.*

Durward (Co. Norfolk). Insert—and co. Essex. Add: *V.*

Durward. Erm. on a chev. sa. 2 annulets or. Crest: . . . Add: *V.*

Dusherd. Barry of 6 arg. and gu. *Robson.*

Dyer (Aldebury, co. Hertford. &c.). Add: *V.** Sir James Dyer. *V.*

Dwight (John Dwight 1728). Sa. a chev. erm. betw. 3 leopards heads arg.

Dwnn. Az. a wolf ramp. arg.

Dychant. Erm. 2 bars gemel and a chief gu. John Dychant. *X.* Robert Dychant. *Y.*

Dyckons (Co. Bedford). Arg. a chev. sa. fretty or betw. 3 violets az. stalked and leaved vert. *V.*

Dyke (Horeham, co. Sussex, bart.). Add: Dyke (London). Same arms and crest: *Vis. Lon. 1633.*

Dylderne. Add: *V.**

Dymocke (Erdington, co. Warwick). Add: *Harl. MS. 1404. fo. 131.*

Dymoke (Scrivelsby, co. Lincoln). Add: Sir John Dymoke. *S. Y.* Sir Robert Dymoke. *V.*

Dynge. Arg. a chev. betw. 3 eagles displayed sa. Sir John Dynge. *V.*

Dyntees and Dyntrey. Add: Sire . . . de Dyntrees. *V.*

Dyseley. Gu. a chev. arg. betw. 3 battle axes of the second handled or. *V.*

Dyson. Arg. a lion ramp. gu. in chief 2 crescents betw. as many mullets pierced sa. in base of the same gu. Add: *V.**

Dyson (Ireland). Arg. a lion ramp. gu. betw. in chief 2 crescents sa. enclosed by as many mullets of 6 points pierced in base 3 of the last as the second over a fess az. *Harl. MS. 1392. fo. 146.*

E

EAME (Sir Henry Eame, KG.,). Or a demi-lion ramp. gu. issuing out of a fess sa. *Guillim.*

Earning (London). Granted—insert—by Bysche . . .

Easby (St. Agatha's Abbey at co. York). Sa. a bend or over all a crosier in bend sinister staff arg. crook or.

East (Hall Place, co. Berks., bart.). Insert—1764 . . . Add: *Vis. Lon. 1633.*

Easthorpe.

Eastland. Az. a bend or cotised az. betw. 6 wicker baskets of the second. *V. V.**

Ebblewhite see Heblethwayte.

Ecclesfield. Arg. 2 bars nebuly sa. *V.O. p. 248.*

Eccleshall (Co. Worcester). Add: Sir Robert Eckleshall temp. Edw. j. *V.N.*

Eccleston (Eccleston, co Lancaster). . . . Add: *Vis. Lon. 1633.*

Echingham. Az. fretty arg. a bordure engr. or. Monsire de Echingham. *Y.* Sir Robert Echingham. *V.* Echingham, Kent. temp. Edw. j. *Harl. MS. 5803.*

Eckersall (West Drayton, Middlesex). Arg. a bend betw. 6 martlets gu. †

Ecligges or Eclinges, Sa. 6 lions ramp. arg. Sir William de Ecligge. *E.*

Eden (West Auckland, co. Durham and Maryland, N. America, bart.). Insert—1776.

Eden, Edon or Iden. (Sandwich, co. Kent &c.). Add: *W.*

Edenham (Swaldale). Add: Robert Edenham. *X.*

Edendon or Edington (Bishop of Winchester 1346–66). . . . 3 bars wavy . . . *Brit. Mus.* Add: *MS. 12443.*

Ederstone. Arg. on a chev. gu. 5 bezants—insert—*V.* (Another, 5 lozenges or). Add: *V.*

Edeyn (Sussex). Az. a chev. betw. 3 esquires helmets or. Alexander Edeyn. *V.*

Edgcombe (Co. Devon). Gu. on a bend erminois betw. 2 cotises arg. 3 boars heads couped of the third langued gu. *Harl. MS. 1404. fo. 134.*

Edgcombe (Co. Devon). Gu. on a bend sa. betw. 2 cotises or 3 boars heads fesswise couped arg. Sir Piers Egcombe. *V.*

Edge (London and co. Stafford). Add: *W.*

Edington or Erdington. Az. 2 lions pass. or within a bordure arg. William Edington, Bishop of Winchester. 1346–66. *Harl. MS. 6100.*

Edington. Az. 2 lions pass. or within a bordure gu. Sire Henri de Erdingtone. *N.*

Edmands (Sutton, co. Surrey &c. . . .). Add: *A.A.*

Edmonds (Winslow, co. Buckingham). . . . Add: *V.C. p. 304.*

Edmonds (Quartered by Sneyd). Az. a chev. betw. 3 carpenters squares arg.

Edmonds (Granted to Sir Clement Edmonds . . .). Add: *Syl. Morgan.*

Edmonds (London and co. Suffolk). . . . 3 martlets . . .

Edmonds (London). Same arms. Crest: A wing erect per pale arg. and or. Add: *Vis. Lon. 1633:* confirmed by Sir John Borough.

Edmons (London, granted 12 June 1640). Insert—by Sir John Borough.

Edolphe (Hinxell, co. Kent). Add: *V.*

Edwards (Roby Hall, co. Lancaster). Arg. a lion ramp. guard. sa. armed and langued gu. on a chief dancetty of the second 2 eagles displ. of the field.

Edwards (Pyenest, co. York, bart.). Insert—1866.

Edwards (York and Walton on Thames). Erm. a lion ramp. guard az. on a canton arg. a spread eagle sa. *Robson.*

Edwards (Bermondsey). Sa. a lion ramp. or goutty sa. a canton of the second. *W.*

Edwards (Southampton). Erm. a lion ramp. gu. (**Monument** in Steyning Church, Sussex).

Edwards (Co. Flint). Add: Edwards (created Sheriff of Shropshire temp. James I.) Same arms. *Fuller.*

Edwards (Shrewsbury, co. Salop). Add: *W.*

Edwards (Tyrington, co. Norfolk and London). Add: Edwards (York, Baronetcy 1691). Same arms. Edwards (Shrewsbury, Baronetcy 1678). Same arms.

Edwards (London). Az. a fess betw. 2 martlets arg. on a canton of the second a martlet of the first. Crest: A stag's head arg. collared az. charged with 3 martlets arg. *Vis. Lon. 1633.*

Edwards (London). Arg. a fess ermines betw. 3 martlets sa. Crest: a ducal coronet a tiger statant or. *Vis. Lon. 1633.*

Edwards (London). Arg. a bull pass. sa. horned or. *Vis. Lon. 1633.*

Edwards (London). Arg. 3 dragons heads erased vert. Crest: A dragon's head as in the arms devouring a human hand ppr. Confirmed by Segar 22 Sept. 2. Charles. *Vis. Lon. 1633.*

Edwell. Sa. a chev. betw. 3 suns in splendour arg. a crescent for diff. *C.R. p. 16.*

Edyngham. Erm. a bend engr. . . . goutty gu. on a chief sa. a bucks head or.

Egbaston (Co. Leicester). Arg. on a lion ramp. gu. a 5-foil of the first over all a bendlet az. Sir Richard de Echebastone. *N.V.*

Egerton (Shaw, co. Lancaster, 1664). Add: *V.L. 1644.*

Egerton. Sa. a chev. betw. 3 pheons arg. Crest: A buck's head . . . Add: *V.V.**

Egerton (London). Sa. a chev. betw. 3 pheons arg. quartering: Erm. a fess gu. fretty or: Arg. a chev. betw. 3 water bougets sa: and vert. a chev. betw. 3 talbots pass. arg. *C.L.*

Eglesden (Essex). Gu. a chev. vair betw. 3 roundlets . . . on a chief dancetty or a grey-hound courant sa. *Harl. MS. 1404. fo. 110.*

Egles (Copwood, Sussex). Sa. 6 lions ramp. or 3. 2. and 1. *Robson.*

Eglesfield (Arms in the hall of Queens Coll. Oxon). . . . Add: Eglesfield (Ambrogg, Cumberland). Same arms. *V.* Eglesfield (Leckonfield, co. York). Same arms. Eglesfield (Stapleton in Holderness, co. York). Same arms, a crescent for diff. *F.Y.*

Eglescliffe. Bishop of Llandaff 1323 . . . a stork close . . . Seal *Dallaway.*

Egleston. Per pale gu. and vert. an eagle displ. arg. armed or. Add: *V.**

Egremond. Or a lion ramp. az. charged with a fleur-de-lis of the field. Crest: A lions head gu . . . Add: *V.*

Egrenhall or Egrewall. Add: *V.*

Egrevale or Egrewall. Add: Sir Robert Egrivale. *V.*

Ekeleshall. Gu. a bend betw. 6 martlets or. Sir Robert de Ekeleshall. *N. Harl. MS. 6137.*

Ekeney. Az. 2 lions pass. guard. or a label of 3 points arg. Sir . . . de Ekeney. *V.*

Ekins (Weston Favill, co. Notts). Add: Eykin of Windsor.

Eland or Elane. Delete (another or). Add: Eland (Hull, co. York). *Tonge p. 69.*

Eland. Gu. 2 bars betw. 8 martlets arg. 3. 2. and 3. Sir Thomas Elande. *S.*

Eland. Arg. on a bend az. 3 escallops of the field. Sir Hugh Eland, Essex. temp. Edw. j. *V.*

Eland (Carleton Juxta, Snaith, co. York). Gu. 2 bars betw. 9 martlets arg. 3.3.3. *F.Y.*

Eland (Co. York). Arg. on a bend gu. 3 escallops or. Sir Hugh de Elaunde. *N.*

Eld (Seighford Hall, co. Stafford). Arg. a chev. sa. betw. . . . Add: *Erdeswick* gives the chev. gu.

Elders. Per chev. arg. and az. a bordure engr. gu. *Harl. MS. 1535. fo. 13b.*

Elders. Per chev. sa. and arg. a bordure engr. gu. *Robson.*

Elderton or Ilderton. Insert—(Northumberland). Add: *V.*

Eldred (Cos. Norfolk, Suffolk and London; granted). Insert—by Dethick . . . Add: Eldred (London). Same arms, a mullet for diff. Crest: a demi-lion holding a baton raguly . . . *Vis. Lon. 1633.*

Eldred or Eldridge. Add: **Brass** of John Eldred 1632, Great Saxham, Suffolk, also his **Seal.** ix. James i. *Gages Hengrave.* Eldred (Oxford 1645). Or a bend raguly sa. in base a martlet gu. *Guillim.*

Eldres or Eleris. Add: *V.*

Elsden. Gu. a chev. or betw. 3 crosses flory arg.

Eleys or Elley. Barry of 10 arg. and sa. over all a bend gu.

Elford (Co. Cornwall). Add: *V.C. p. 304.*

Elicott. Add: *V.*W.*

Eliot (Port Eliot and St. Germans, co. Cornwall). . . . Add: Eliot (London). Same arms, on the fess a martlet for diff. *Vis. Lon. 1633.*

Eliott (Sir John Eliott, bart. MD. 1778). Insert— of Peebles, Scotland.

Elioth. Add: *F.Y.*

Eliston, Elliston or Elaston. Per pale gu. and vert. an eagle displ. arg. *V.E. 1634.* Elaston, co. Chester. *Harl. MS. 1535. fo. 13b.*

Elkington (Shawell, co. Leicester). . . . Gu. 6 crosses crosslet, three in chief—insert—2 and 1 and three in base—insert 1 and 2.

Elkington (Co. Lincoln). Gu. crusilly and three swans arg. *V.*

Elkington. Gu. three ducks betw. nine crosses crosslet arg. Add: *V.**

Ellacombe (Patent 5 Oct. 1849). Arg. on a chev. engr. sa. betw. 3 stags courant ppr. as many crosses patty of the first.

Elland. Add: Sir John Eland, co. York. *V.*)

Elland (of Elland, co. York). Barry of 6 arg. and gu. 6 martlets or. *F.Y.*

Ellerker. Az. fretty arg. a chief and bend of the last over all *Harl. MS. 1404. fo. 108.*

Ellerton. Arg. a chev. betw. 3 bucks heads sa. Add: Roger de Ellerton (Swaldale). *X.*

Ellesdon. Add: *Hutchins.*

Ellesfield. Barry wavy of 6 arg. and sa. Add: *Y.*

Ellesfield. Barry nebulee of 6 arg. and sa. Add: *V.**

Ellesfield. Quarterly arg. with gu. fretty or overall on a bendlet sa. three mullets of 6 points of the third Alayn de Ellesfeld. *G.*

Ellesfield. Barry nebuly (or wavy) of 6 arg. and sa. Sir Gilbert de Ellesfeld. *V.O.Y.* Sir John de Ellesfeld. *N.*

Ellesfield. Barry wavy arg. and sa. a label gu. Gilbert de Elscheffeld. *N.*

Elletson. Add: *F.L.*

Elliott (Eskelton, Scotland). Gu. on a bend engr. (or indented) or a flute of the first.

Elliott of Stobbs, co. Roxburgh. Gu. on a bend or a baton az. a sinister canton of the Badge of Baronet of Nova Scotia. Supporters: A Ram and a Goat. Motto: "Soyez Sage". †

Ellis or Elys (Kiddall Hall, co. York). . . . Add: Ellis (London). Same arms and crest: *Vis. Lon. 1633.*

Ellis (Kent, Granted by Cooke). Erm. a lion pass. gu. *W.*

Ellisden or Elesden (Co. Essex). Add: crosses crosslet.

Ellisdon or Elysden. . . . Add: But crosses crosslet. *V. V.**

Ellison (Thorne, co. York). Gu. a chev. betw. 3 eagles heads erased or. *Hunter j. 179.*

Ellison (Sheriff of Newcastle 1544). Gu. a chev. arg. betw. 3 griffins heads erased or. *Carr. MS.*

Ellison (Co. Tyrone). Gu. on a chev. betw. 3 eagles heads erased gu. a 3-foil vert. *A.A.*

Ellnor. Add: *Vis. Lon. 1633.*

Elman. Add: Sir Richard Elman. *V.*

Elmbrige. Chequy arg. and sa. Roger Elmbrige. *V.*

Elmeden or Elmedon. Add: *V.* William Elmedon. *X.*

Elmer. Per bend embattled arg. and gu. 6 martlets counterchanged. Add: co. Northants.

Elmested. Add: John Elmsted. *V.*

Elmhirst (Houndhill, co. York). Barry wavy of 6 arg. and sa. a canton of the second. *Dugdale. 1665.*

Elphinstone (Lord Balmerinock). Insert—1604. Add: *Crawfurd.*

D'Elstone. Gu. crusilly arg. a lion ramp. or. John D'Elstone or D'Estone. *E.*

Elston (Brockholes   ). Arg. 3 plates sa. on a bend of the last 3 mullets or.

Elston (Brockholes, co. Lancaster). Add: *V.* quartered by Pilkington.

Elswike or Elswyke (Insert—Ribchester). . . . Add: *V.*

Ellham (Kent). . . . a bend vair cotised sa.

Eltoft (Co. Lincoln). Add: *V.*

Eltoft or Eltofts (delete—Farnley; substitute, Fernhill in Craven). . . . Add: *F. Y.*

Eltoft (Yorkshire). Sa. 3 chessrooks arg. *F. Y.*

Elton (Elton, co. Chester). Add: *Ormerod.*

Elton. Barry of 6 gu. and or on a bend sa. 3 mullets of the second. *Robson.*

Elton (Co. Berks and London. *Her. Off. London*). Insert—confirmed by Segar. Add: *Vis. Lon. 1633.*

Elwarch (Lord of Penrak, co. Glamorgan). Vert. a chev. betw. 3 wolves heads erased or.

Elvinde.

Elwes (Habelsthorpe, co. Notts.). . . . Add:

Elwes (London). Same arms, a martlet for diff. *Vis. Lon. 1633.*

Elwick (Seaton, co. York). Arg. 3 boars pass. az.

Elwike. Arg. 3 boars az. *V.*V.*

Elwin (Tottington, co. Norfolk . . .). Add: *Dashwood.*

Ely (Robt. Ely, London 1330). . . . a chev. . . . betw. in chief 2 leopards heads . . . and in base a garb . . . on a chief . . . a fish naiant . . .

Eman (Windsor, co. Berks.). Add: *Vis. Lon. 1633.* The lion not crowned.

Embleton (Newcastle on Tyne). Arg. on a bend sa. 3 crescents of the field. *Robson.*

Emerick. Barry of 6 or and sa. a baston erm. Sir John Emerike. *Y.*

Emeryke. Add: *V.*

Emesley, Ernele or Evell. Add: *V.*

Emlam. Gu. semy of martlets or. *K.*

Emperor (Brook, Norfolk 1750). Per pale or and . . . an eagle displ. with 2 heads pean beaked and armed gu. **Monument** in St. Johns Maddermarket Church, Norwich.

Emson. Add: *V.*

Emsone. Vert a chev. betw. three phials in the shape of lacrymatories or. *V. fo. 236.*

Enby or Eneby. Add: *V.*

Enderby. Arg. 3 chevs. sa. *V.*

Enderby (Co. Bedford). Arg. 3 chevrons sa. over all a pale erm. *Harl. MS. 1404. fo. 103.*

Enefele. Gu. an inescutcheon arg. within an orle of 8 martlets or. Sir Henry de Enefele. *Y.*

Enfield. Gu. an inescutcheon within an orle of martlets or. Hugh de Enfield. *Y.*

Enfield. Arg. on a canton gu. bezanty a mullet or. Sire Bartelmeu Enefeld. *N.*

Enfield. Arg. on a canton sa. a mullet or pierced gu. Add: *V.* Add: Sire Bartholomew Enfield. *L. Harl. MS. 6137.*

Engborne. Or 3 hawks bells gu. *V.*

Engham. Barry of 6 or and sa. per pile counterchanged. William Engham. *V.*

Engham. Insert—Great Chard, co. Kent. Add: *V.*

Engledue. Or a chev. embattled betw. three mullets gu. *V.**

Englis or Englys. Add: Sir Thomas Englis. Tarone. *V.*

English (Co. Lincoln). Add: *V.V.**

English (Cos. Kent, Lancaster, Stafford and Essex). Add: *Vis. Lon. 1633.*

Engleys. Sa. 3 lions ramp. arg. Sir Johan de Engleys. *N.* Sir John Englys (Northumberland and Cumberland). temp. Edw. j. *V.*

English (Buckland, Maidstone, Kent). Sa. 3 lions pass. arg.

English (Ovington Manor and Bocking, co. Essex). Add: *V.* Add: William English . *Y.*

Englowise. Add: *Collinson Somerset iij. 159.*

Englysvill.

Engs. Add: *V.*

Ensake. Paly of 6 az. and or on a bend sa. 3 mullets pierced . . .

Ensam. Erm. on a canton sa. a fleur-de-lis or. *V.**

Enswell. Add: *V.L.*

Ent. Add: Sir George Ent of East Laughton, co. Lincoln, President of the College of Physicians. *Guillim.*

Entwisle. Add: *V.*

Enyon. Add: or Enyan. Add: *Guillim.*

Enyon (Flore, co. Northants, Bart. 1642). Arg. a chev. engr. betw. 3 ravens sa.

Ercedekne (Co. Devon). Arg. 2 chevs. sa. *Lysons.*

Erderne. Chequy az. and or a chev. gu. Sir . . . de Erderne. *F.*

Erdeswick. Add: *C.L.*

Erdington (Barrow, co. Leicester). Add: Sir Thomas Erdington. *V.S.* Henry de Herdington. *F.*

Erdington. Arg. a lion ramp. gu. charged on the shoulder with a cinquefoil of the first . . . Crest: . . . Add: *Cady.*

Ereby. Gu. 2 lions pass. arg. a label or. Sire Johan de Ereby. *N.*

Ereby. Arg. fretty sa. On a canton gu. a 5-foil or. Sire Thomas de Ereby. *N.*

Ereford or Eresford. Add: Sir Thomas Ereford. *V.*

Eresby (Co. Lincoln 1640). Or on a chev. betw. 3 annulets gu. as many crescents of the first. *Yorke.*

Erisey (Erisey, co. Cornwall). . . . Add: *V.C. p. 304.*

Ermynd. Insert—Cornwall.

Erneley. Insert—(Cos. Wilts. and Sussex). *V.*W.*

Ernelle (Co. Kent). Add: *V. W.*

Ernell. Arg. on a bend sa. 3 eagles displ. with 2 heads or. *W.*

Ernies (Espeak, co Lancaster). Arg. a raven rising sa. on a mount vert.

Ernley (John Ernley). Sheriff of Wilts. . . . Add: Ernley (New Sarum co. Wilts., Baronetcy 1660. Same arms. Sir John Ernley. Chief Justice of the Common Pleas. 1509. *Dug. O. J.*

Erpingham or Eppingham (Co. Norfolk).

Erpingham or Eppingham (Co. Norfolk). Add: Sir John de Erpingham. *O.* Sir Thos. Erpingham. *T.* Walter de Herpingham. *Y.*

Erpingham . . . Erpingham. Az. an inescutcheon within an orle of 8 martlets or. Sir Thos. Erpingham. *S.* Erpingham. Vert. an inescutcheon arg. within an orle of 10 martlets or. *Harl. MS. 6829. fo. 6.*

Errington (Errington and Beaufront, co. Northumberland). Add: Errington (London). Same arms. Crest: a unicorn's head erased quarterly arg. and az. † for diff. *Vis. Lon. 1633.*

Erskine. (Earl of Mar). Add: *Crawfurd.*

Eryssy (Ob. 1522). Arg. a chev. sa. betw. 3 escus. gu. each charged with a griffin segreant or. **Brass** in Church at Grade, Cornwall.

Eagston. Add: *V.*

Esingold. Or on a bend az. 3 dexter hands clenched and couped at the wrist arg. *V.*

Eskeney. Add: *V.*

Eslinge. Add: *V*.* The heads fesswise and coupled arg. Rafe Eslings. *V*.

Eslinge. Az. a bend betw. 2 cotises and six boars heads couped or. Raffe de Eslynge. *A*. The heads bendwise. *A*. *Harl. MS. 6137*.

Eslinge. Az. 3 bendlets betw. 6 boars heads fess wise 3 and 3 or *V*.

Esmonde (Lord Esmonde, Baron of Limerick, co. Wexford . . .). Supporters: reads—Two small, small is underlined and marginal? male.

Espayne or Espaine. . . . a bend—insert— substitute—(or bendlet) Add: *V*.

Esse (The parent stock &c. . . .). Add: *V*.

Esse (Bucknell, co. Oxford). Arg. 2 chevs sa. *V.O.*

Esse (Quartered by Yeo). Same arms. *Harl. MS. 3288. fo. 56*.

Esse or Ashe. Co. Devon confirmed by Camden 1613. Arg. 2 chevs. sa. on each a trefoil or. *Syl. Morgan*.

Esserington. Arg. on 2 bars az. 3 mullets or. John de Esserington. *Y*.

Essex (London). . . . three eagles displ. arg. —underlined—? or. *V*.*

Essex (London, Granted by Cooke). Az. a chevron embattled on the top erm. with 3 eagles displ. arg. *W*.

Essex (Bewcot, co. Berks, Baronetcy 1612). Barry a chev. erm. betw. 3 eagles displ. arg.

Essex. Az. on a chev. engr. betw. 3 eagles displ. or a plain chev. erm. Sir William Essex. *V*.

Essex (Co. Middlesex). Add: Sir William Essex. *V*.

Essington (Cowley, co. Gloucester). Add: *Vis. Lon. 1633*.

Essington. Arg. 2 bars and in chief three 5-foils az. *V.N. p. 153*.

Estafford. Or a chev. gu. Le Baron de Estafforde. *J.N.*

Estatford. Or a chev. gu. betw. 3 martlets sa. *V*.

Estafford. Or. on a chev. gu. 3 bezants. Sir Robt. de Estafford. *B*.

Estatford. Or on a chev. betw. three martlets gu. as many bezants. Add: *V*.

Estauntone. Vairy arg. and sa. a canton gu. Sire William de Estauntone. *N*.

Estbery or Isbury. Add: *V*.

Estbury. Bendy wavy of six arg. and sa. Add: *V*.

Estcourt (Shippenmayne, co. Gloucester). Add: *Vis. Lon. 1633*.

Esteby. Co. Lincoln. Sa. a bend betw. 6 estoiles or. *V*.

Esteley (Co. Leicester). Add: see Asteley.

Esteley or Estley. Add: Sir Giles de Estley, co. Leicester. *V*.

Esterley. Arg. a lion ramp. gu. charged on the shoulder with a 5-foil of the field. Sir Andrew de Esteley. *H*. Sir Nicholas Estleigh. *I.N.*

Esteney. Add: Sir Richard Esteney. *V*.

Estengrave. Add: Sire John de Estengreve. *E.J.Y.*

Esterling. Add: John de Esterling. *G*.

Esterling. Paly of 6 az. and arg. on a bend gu. 3 cinquefoils or. *V*.

Estfield (Lord Mayor of London 1530). . . . Add: *V*.

Estgaston. Arg. on a bend gu. 3 annulets of the first in the sinister chief a cross patty per pale az. and gu. *Harl. MS. 1404. fo. 108*.

Estmerton or Esmerton. . . . of the field—delete— (another, the mullets or). Add: Sir . . . de Estmerton. *V*.

Estokes. Bendy of 10 or and az. a canton gu. Henry de Estokes. *F*.

Eston. Az. a chev. betw. three mullets or. Add: John Eston. *V*.

Estone. Az. crusilly arg. a bend gu. fimbriated or. Sir Richard de Estone. *E.F.*

Estotevile, Estotteville, or Estotvile. Add: Sir Robert Estotvile, Essex temp. Edw. j. *V.A.B.N.O.*

Estotville. Barry of 12 arg. and gu. 3 lions ramp. sa. Sir Nicholas Estoteville, temp. Edw. iij. *V.N.* Walter de Stotville. *C*.

Estotville or Stutville. Barruly arg. and gu. 3 cocks sa. Sir William de Estotville de la Mazche. *B.V.*

Estourges. Add: *V*.*

Estrume. Gu. a chev. betw. 3 mullets of 6 points. Sir John le Estrume. *E*.

Etclun. Arg. a chev. gu. betw. five torteaux. Add: 3 torteaux. *V*.

Ethelston. Or an eagle displ. gu. armed az. Sir . . . de Ethelston, co. Chester. *V*.

Etherington (Great Driffing and Ferriby, co. York). Add: Etherington (Ebberstone, co. York 1612). Same arms. *F.Y.*

Etherington (Kingston-upon-Hull, co. York, bart). Insert—1775 . . .

Eton (Co. Warwick). Add: Sir Nicholas Eton, temp. Edw. j. *V*.

Eton or Etton (Gilling, co. York). Barry of ten— delete—(another six). Add: Barry of 12. *S*. Barry of 14. *V*. temp. Edw. ij. *F.Y.*

Eton. Insert—(Co. Essex). Or on a chev. az. three leopards faces . . . Add: *V.E. 1612*.

Eton (John Eton). Arg. 2 annulets conjunct sa. within an orle of 3-foils slipped vert. *V*.

Eton. Arg. a chev. engr. betw. 3 boars heads couped sa. Add: *V. V.*

Etton. Insert—Fresbe, Sa. a chev. erm. betw. 3 leopards faces or. Add: *V*.

Etton. Insert—Fresby, Sa. on a bend betw. 3 leopards faces or as many elm leaves vert. on a canton arg. a cross moline—insert—or patty) gu. *V*.

Etton. Barry of 8 or and az. on a canton sa. a cross patonce of the first. Add: Sir John de Etton. 1425. *V*.

Etton. Arg. 3 bars gemelles gu. on a canton sa. a cross patonce or. Add: Sir John Etton. 3rd Hen. vj. *V*.

Etton. Gu. a bend wavy betw. 2 bendlets arg. *V*.

Ettrick (High Barns, co. Durham). Add: Ettrick (Wimborne Minster, co. Dorset). Same arms.

Eure (Co. Buckingham, temp. Henry III). . . . —delete—(another cinquefoils). Add: Eure (co. York), quartering Ayton, Vesey, and Tyson. Same arms. *F.Y.*

Eure. Quarterly or and gu. on a bend sa. three escallops arg. Sir Rauf de Eure. *S.V.* (Co. York). Sir John de Eure. *M.N.* Henry de Eure. *E*.

Eure. Quarterly . . . and . . . over all a bend . . . Hugh de Ever. 14th cent. **Seal.**

Eustace. Az. a bend arg. betw. 10 crosses crosslet fitchee or. Add: (But 6 crosslets only). *V*.

Evans (   ). Arg. 2 bars sa. on a canton . . . a pheon or. *Dingley*.

Evans-Browne (Kirkby-Bedon, co. Norfolk). 1796. Arg. a chev. betw. 3 boars heads couped sa. quartering arg. a chev. betw. 3 mullets sa. pierced. *Dashwood*.

Evans (London). Arg. a chev. sa. betw. 3 martlets of the second each holding in its beak an ermine spot. Crest: a demi-lion ramp. or holding in its paws 3 branches of palm vert. *Vis. Lon. 1633*.

Evanson. Arg. a chev. sa. betw. three magpies ppr. *Randle Holme*.

Eveby. Add: Robert de Eveby. *A*.

Ever. Quarterly . . . and . . . a bend . . . **Seal of** Hugh de Ever. 14th cent.

Everard (Co. Leicester). Arg. on a chev. betw. 3 estoiles gu. as many mullets sa. *Shaw.*

Everard or Evard. Add: *V.*

Everdon. Erm. a chev. betw. 3 mascles gu. Add: *V.*

Everingham (Baron Everingham . . .). Add: Sir Adam Everingham. *F.I.M.N.X.Y.* Reynold de Everingham, quartering, sa. a bend betw. 6 crosslets arg. *S.*

Everingham. Gu. a lion ramp. vair a dexter baston or. Sire Thomas de Everingham. *Y.*

Everingham. Quarterly arg. and gu. a bendlet of the second, charged with a pierced mullet of. *V.**

Everingham (Rokkle). Quarterly arg. and sa. a bendlet gu. charged with a pierced mullet or. *V.*

Everingham (Roklay or Rokeley). Quarterly arg. and sa. a baston gu. John Everingham. *Y.*

Everingham. Quarterly arg. and sa. a bendlet of the last. Monsire Laurence Evingham. *S.*

Everingham of Flamborough. Quarterly gu. and sa. a bend or. *Constable's Roll. xiij.*

Everley. Or on a bend az. 3 escallops of the first Wat de Everleie. *E.F.*

Evers or Eure (cos. Lincoln—insert—1640, and York)—delete—(another escallops).

Evers. Quarterly or and gu. a bendlet sa. Henry de Evers. *F.*

Evers (Bolton   ). Quarterly arg. and gu. over all on a bend sa. 3 escallops arg.

Eves (William Eves . . .). Add: *C.L.*

Evington. (Spalding, co. Lincoln). . . Add: *W.*

Evington. Az. 3 bars arg. in chief as many plates. Add: *V.*

Ewen (Co. Essex). Add: *V.*

Exeter. Arg. a chev. gu. betw. 3 billets (another, delves). sa. Add: *V.V.**

Exilby. Insert—co. York. . . . Add: *Eliz. Roll. xxviij.*

Exmew. Arg. a chev. compony . . . Crest: . . . laurel ppr. Add: *V.**

Eyland (Co. York). Arg. on 3 bars gu. 6 martlets of the field in chief a crescent for diff. John Eiland. *Eliz. Roll. xxxij.*

Eylston. Per pale gu. and vert. an eagle displ. arg. armed or. *V.*

Eynell. Az. a chev. arg. overall on a canton of the last a holy lamb. gu. *Harl. MS. 1404. fo. 108*

Eyre (Bradway, co. Derby). Arg. on a chev. sa. three 4-foils of the first.

Eyre (Ketton, co. York, 1585). Same arms— Eyre (Bromham . . . quartering or 3 pincers sa. for Padley: and sa. a cross engr. betw. 3 pomegranates slipped or for Whittington. *F.Y.*

Eyre (Ryton, co. Notts.). Add: *V.N.*

Eyre (Normanton upon—Sore, co. Notts.). Add: *V.N.*

Eyre (Co. Buckingham). Eyre (Belton, co. Leicester 1619).

Eyre (Co. Buckingham). Add: Thomas Eyre, co. Bucks. granted 1476. *V.*

Eyre (Belton, co. Leicester). Arg. on a bend sa. three 4-foils slipped of the first. *C.C.*

Eyre (Lord Mayor of London 1445). Add: *Harl. MS. 1347.*

Eyre (London). Gu. on a chev. or betw. 3 leopards heads . . . Add: Granted to Henry Eyre, of London in 1589. *W.*

Eyre (Co. Suffolk). Add: *Cady.*

Eyre. Gu. a boar saliant arg. collared and chained or. Add: *V.**

Eyres (London). Arg. on a chev. sa. 3 quatrefoil or a bordure az. Crest: On a mount vert. leg in armour couped at the thigh, quarterly arg. and az. *Vis. Lon. 1633.*

Eyre (Rowter, co. Derby). Or on a chev. gu. 3 quatrefoils arg. *Visitation. 1683.*

Eyre (Stratton, co. Derby). Same arms within a bordure gu. *Visitation. 1683.*

Eyseldon or Eysseldon (Co. Devon). Add: *V.*

Eyton (Duddlestone, co. Salop). Arg. a lion ramp. sa. *Syl Morgan. p. 78.*

Eyves (Fishwick, co. Lancaster . . .). Add: *V.L.*

F

FACHELL. Az. 3 bendlets erm. *V.*

Fachell or Vachell. Bendy of 6 az. and erm. *V.*

Faconbridge. Arg. a lion ramp. within a bordure invecked arg. . . . Add: Faconbridge (Otterington, co. York 1612). Same arms. *F.Y.*

Fagge (Wiston, co. Sussex . . .). Add: *V.*

Fagger alias Silver Locke (Sussex and Essex). Sa. a chev. engr. betw. 3 padlocks arg. *Harl. MS. 1432. fo. 9.*

Fair (Scotland). See also Fere.

Faire, Phaire or Ferre (Colonel Robert Faire 1649, Grange, co. Cork). Gu. a fer-du-moulin arg. over all a bendlet az.

Fairbairn (Sir Peter Fairbairn, Knt. 1839). Insert —Leeds, co. York.

Fairborne (Newark, co. Notts.). Add: Sir Palmer Fairborne 1670. *L.N.*

Fairclough (Cos. Hertford, Lancaster, Lincoln and London). Add: *Vis. Lon. 1633.* (†).

Fairfax (Stedman and Dunsley, co. York). Dugdale—insert—'visit'. Add: the Dunsley branch bore the canton sa. *Dugdale. p. 230.*

Fairford. Arg. guttee de sang three lions pass. reguard. az. crowned or. *V.V.**

Fairford. Arg. goutty-de-sang 3 lions pass. in pale gu. bezanty crowned or. *V.V.**

Fairsted. Arg. a chev. erm. betw. 3 greyhounds courant ppr.

Falage. . . . 3 pails . . . *V.*

Falcon. Erm. 2 chevs engr. paly az. and sa. betw. 3 falcons ppr. billed or and holding in the beak a lure of the last.

Falconer or Fawconer (Norfolk). Arg. two falcons gu. within a bordure sa. *Cady.*

Falconer (Lord Mayor of London 1414). . . . trefoils slipped or—underlined—Add: *Harl. MS. 1349.* arg.

Fallesle, Fallvesle or Fawsley (Co. Northampton). Gu. 2 chevs. or.

Fallesley (Co. Bucks). Sir John de Fallesle. *S.V.*

Fallowfield. Or 3 greyhounds courant in pale . . . **Book Plate.**

Fallon. Az. 2 greyhounds ramp. respecting arg. supporting betw. them a sword erect ppr. in the centre chief point a castle of the second.

Fallowbrome. Arg. 5 jays ppr. *Randle Holme.*

Falls (Dublin). Add: *V.*

Falstofe. Quarterly az. and or on a bend gu. three escallops arg. . . . Add: Sir John Falstoffe. *V.S.* Thomas Falstoffe, Bishop of St. Davids. 1543.

Fancourt. Az. billetty or on a canton arg. 5 billets in saltire sa. Sir Gerard de Fanecourt. *Y.*

Fanecourt. Az. 9 billets 3.3.2 and 1 or a canton erm. Gerard de Fanecourt. *E.*

Fanhope (Co. Cornwall). Add: i.e. Cornwall, Baron of Fanhope.

Fannell or Faunell (Co. Northampton).—delete— (another arg.). Add: Sir William Fannel. *V.V.**

Fannell (Co. Northampton). Add: Sir William Fannell, co. Northampton. *V.*

Fannell. Arg. a bend gu. within a bordure sa. bezanty. Roger Fannell. *Y.*

Fanshaw (Fanshawgate, co. Derby). Add: *Vis. Lon. 1633.*

Fanshawe (Dengey Hall, co. Essex). Add: *V.E. 1612.*

Fanshaw (Dronfield, co. Derby). Or two chev. erm.—read—'ermines'.

Fanshawe (Augmentation granted to Thomas Fanshawe . . .). Add: Sir Richard Fanshaw, Knt. and Bart. Secretary of the Latin tongue to King Charles ij. Ambassador to Spain and Portugal. ob. 1666.

Fareway. Add: *V.*

Farwell or Farewell (Hill Bishop, co. Somerset). Add: *Harl. MS. 1559. fo. 126b.* Add:

Farwell. Sa. on a chev. betw. 3 escallops arg. a mullet pi. for diff. a branch of Farewell of Hill Bishop, co. Somerset. *Harl. MS. 1445. fo. 198.*

Farindon (Wierden, co. Lancaster). Arg. a chev. gu. betw. 3 leopards heads sa. *Harl. MS. 1468. fo. 94.*

Farington or Worden, co. Lancaster. Add:

Farington (Little Farington and Lingard, co. Lancaster). Same arms, a crescent az. for diff. *Harl. MS. 1549.*

Farington (Ribbleton, co. Lancaster). Same arms, a mullet az. for diff. *Harl. MS. 1549 : 6159.*

Farington (London). Same arms. *Guillim.*

Farington (London 1568). Arg. a chev. gu. betw. 3 leopards heads purp. *C.L.*

Farmbrough. Gu. on a bend engr. betw. 2 garbs another bend invected of the first charged with 3 crosses crosslet.

Farmer (Co. Leicester: granted 1663). Insert—by Walker, Garter.

Farnaby (Keppington, Kent. Granted by St. George. Clarenceux, 1703). Arg. 3 bars gemelle gu. on a bend or a lion pass. of the second. *Guillim.*

Farnaby (Canterbury, Kent). Granted to John Farnabey, by Walker, Garter. 3 May 1664). Gu. 2 bars gemelles arg. on a bend or a lion pass. of the field armed and langued az.

Farnan. Per chev. or and az. in chief two horses heads erased holding teazles in their mouth az. in base a golden fleece. Crest: A horse's head as in the arms. Motto: 'Perseverance'.

Farden (Sedlescomb, co. Sussex). Add: *Guillim.*

Farnehill. Add: John Farnehill. *X.*

Farraway (Penhallam, Cornwall). Quartered by Stowell. Arg. a chev. betw. 3 escallops sa. *Harl. MS. 1445. fo. 193.*

Farrer (Brayfield, co. Bucks.). Add: *Vis. Lon. 1633.*

Farrer (Bentlo, co. York). Add: Farrer (Hull, co. York), Wareham, co. Dorset, co. Hertford and London). Same arms. Farrer (Ewoot, co. York). Granted by Camden 1609). Same arms.

Farrington (John Farrington, citizen of London). . . . Add: *Vis. Lon. 1633.*

Farrington (Chichester, co. Sussex, bart.). Insert —1697. . . .

Farrington (Chichester). Arg. on a chev. gu. betw. 3 leopards faces sa. a mullet of the first. *Harl. MS. 6164.*

Farwey. Arg. a chev. betw. 3 escallops sa. *Harl. MS. 1141. fo. 8.*

Fasakyr. Barry nebuly of 6 erm. and vert. *V.**

Fascet (Norfolk). Arg. on a bend az. 3 dolphins haurient or.

Faslake. Add: *V.*

Fastolfe. Quarterly or and az. on a bend gu. 3 crosses crosslet of the first. Sir John Fastolfe KG., *V.*

Fauconberg. Arg. a lion ramp. az. Sir Walter de Fauconberg. temp. Edw. j. in a co-heiress of Piers Brus, Lord of Skelton. *V. I.N.S.*

Fauconberg. Arg. 2 bars fusilly az. William de Fauconberge. *F.*

Fauconberg. Arg 2. bars fusilly sa. Henry de Fauconberge. *Y.N.*

Fauconberg. Arg. a lion ramp. az. a dexter baton compony or and gu. Sir Walter Fauconberge. *M.N.Y.*

Fauconberg (Quartered by Peniston). Arg. a lion ramp. az. within a bordure sa. *V.O. p. 153.*

Fauconberg (Sire Roger Fauconberg). Arg. on a lion ramp. az. a fleur-de-lis or at the shoulder. *S.*

Fauconbridge. Arg. a lion ramp. az depressed by a bend or. Sir Walter Fauconbridge, Essex temp. Edw. iij. *V.*

Fauconer. Add: *V.N. p. 188.*

Faugen. Add: *V.*

Faugeane. Or 3 bendlets countercompony or and gu. *Harl. MS. 1441.*

Faukenor. Insert—Co. Lancaster. Add: Sir John Faukenor, co Derby temp. Edw. j. *V.*

Faukes of Linley. Sa. a falcon in the sinister chief a mascle arg.

Fauconer (Hurst, co. Kent). Quarterly arg. and az. a falcon volant or. *Robson.*

Faulconer or Fawconer. Paly of 6 arg. and az. on a bend gu. three 3-foils slipped or. *V.V.**

Fauconer. Arg. 3 falcons close gu. Sire Johan le Fauconer. *N.*

Faulkener (Uppingham, co. Rutland 1659). Paly of 8 arg. and az. over all on a bend of the second three 3-foils or.

Faunt. Add: *C.C.*

Favell. Arg. a bend gu. within a bordure sa. bezanty. Sire William Favel. *N.* Monsire Favel. *Y.*

Favell (Kirby Hall, Catterick, co. York). Add: Favell (Craven, co. York). *V.* the escallops arg.

Favill (Fazeley Hall, co. York). Sa. a chev. betw. 3 eagles displ. arg. *Robson.*

Fawconbridge. Arg. three lions pass.—insert— 'in pale'. Add: *V.*W.*

Fawconbridge. Sir William Fawconbrig. Arg. 3 lions pass. guard. in pale gu. *V.*

Fawggan (Ireland). Or 3 bendlets compony gu. and arg. *V.*

Fawkoner (Cos. Bucks and Hants). Add: *V.V.**

Fawsley (Northants.). Gu. 2 chevs. or. *Cady.*

Fayreweather or Fawether (Brissett, co. Suffolk). Insert—Granted by Segar. Garter.

Fazakerley (Kirby, co. Lancaster 1664). Erm. three bars vert., a canton gu. Add: *V.L.*

Featherstonhaugh (Hopton, co. Worcester). Add: *A.A.*

Feilden (Didsbury, near Manchester). Add: Feilding (London). Same arms and crest without the quartering † for diff. *Vis. Lon. 1633.*

Felbrigge (Simon Felbrigge.). . . . Add: Sir Roger Felbrige. *R.* Mons. Simon Felbrige. *S.* Mounsire Felbrige. *T.* Sir Robert Felbridge. *J.* And with a pierced mullet arg. on the shoulder. Sir George Felbrige. *S.*

Felde. Sa. a chev. betw. three garbs arg. Add: *V.*

Felde. Arg. a chev. vert. betw. three pomies. Henry Felde. *V.*

Felmyngham. Sa. a chev. erm. betw. 3 covered cups or. *W.*

Felter. Add: *V.*

Feltgrave. Add: John Feltgrave. *X.* ? error for Fitz Rafe.

Felton (Litcham, co. Norfolk). Add: Sir Johan de Felton. *L.* Sir William Felton. *Q.* And with a mullet for diff. Nicholas Felton, Bishop of Bristol 1617. Ely, 1619–28.

Felton (Playford, co. Suffolk, bart.). Insert— 1620 . . .

Felton (Co. Gloucester). Gu. two lions pass. in pale arg. (another within a—delete—substi- tute 'tressure' flory . . . Add: *X.Y.*

Felton. Gu. 2 lions pass. erm. *T.* Sir Robert de Feltone, co. Gloucester, temp. Edw. iij. *V.N.* William Felton. *Y.* And with a mullet in chief or for diff. Sir Roger de Feltone. *O.*

Feltone. Gu. 2 lions pass. arg. over all a baton compony or and az. Sire William de Feltone. *N.*

Felton (Suffolk). Or on a bend az. cotises gu. 3 plates. *V.*

Feltone. . . . on a chev. . . . betw. 3 pierced mullets . . . 5 saltires couped . . . **Seal** of Simon de Feltone.

Fen. Vert. on a lion ramp. or a fess gu. Richard de Fen. *Y.*

Fencotes. . . . a chev. engr. . . . **Seal** of John de Fencotes. 1365.

Fenes. Add: Sire Johan de Fenes. *N.A.*

Fenn (East Dereham, co. Norfolk). Add: *Vis. Lon. 1633.*

Fenner. Erm. two chev. sa. Add: Sir Richard Fenner (Suffolk). *V.*

Fennor (Suffolk). Erm. 2 chevs gu. a label of 3 az. *Cady.*

Fennor (Co. Sussex). Granted 10 Nov. 4 Philip and Mary—insert—1557 by Sir Thos. Hankey, Clarenceux. Add: *Guillim.*

Fenroder. Gu. on a chev. or three—insert— Insert—'saracens'. . . . Query error for Bray. Dame Juliana Bray impaled by Fenrother. *V.*

Fenrother (London). Gu. on a chev. betw. 6 shackles in pairs or. 3 heathcocks az. a bordure engr. of the second ogressy. *V.*

Fenrother. Gu. on a chev. arg. betw. 3 buckles or. as many storks az. a canton of the second charged with a man in red breeches on the top of a tower sa. holding a Dutch banner, a bordure engr. of the . . . pelletty. In Chobham Church, Surrey, 1573.

Fenton (Sheffield c. 1500). Az. semy of hearts and 3 lions pas. 2 and 1. arg. *Harl. MS. 506.*

Fenwick (Fenwick, co. Northumberland). . . . Add: Fenwick (London). Same arms and crest, a fleur-de-lis for diff. *Vis. Lon. 1633.*

Fenwyke. Arg. three martlets gu. on a chief of the last as many martlets of the field. Add: *V.* John de Fenwyk. *Y.* Add: Fenwick (Walling- ton, Northumberland). *Eliz. Roll. xxxiij.*

Fere. Insert—(Scotland). Az. an anchor or. Add: *W.*

Fereby. Arg. a chev. engr. betw. three lions heads erased sa. Add: *V.*

Fereby. Sa. a chev. betw. 3 lions heads erased arg. *Berry.*

Feringes. Add: Lucas de Feringes. *A.* Richard Feringes. *A.*

Ferington (Ferington, co. Lancaster). Arg. a chev. gu. betw. 3 leopards heads sa. *V.*

Ferley. Arg. 3 chevs. per chev. sa. and gu. Sir Theobald Ferley. *V.*

Fermor (Welches, co. Sussex). Add: Fermor (Tuxford, co. Notts. 1614). Same arms. Baronetcy 1802. *V.N.*

Fermour. Add: *V.*

Fermor. Gu. 3 bendlets or on a chief per fess erm. and arg. 3 fleurs-de-lis in the upper part sa. Thomas Fermor. *Dug. O.J.*

Ferne (London). Per bend dancetty or and gu. a mullet for diff. Crest: A garb betw. two wings or. *Vis. Lon. 1633.*

Fernefold or Fernwold (Sussex). Sa. a chev. engr. betw. 3 bucks heads erased arg. *V.**

Fernley (Visit. London 1568). . . . Add: *V.** Fernley (co. Lancaster). Same arms. *V.*

Feronnes. Gu. a chev. or betw. 3 horseshoes arg. *V.*

Ferrers. Vairy or and gu. a baston (or bendlet) az. Sire Thomas de Ferrers. *N.*

Ferrers (Bere Ferrers, co. Devon). . . . Add: Ferrers, co. Cornwall. *V.C. p. 304.*

Ferrers (Buswithgy and Trelowarren, co. Corn- wall. Heiress married Vyvyan). Or on a bend sa. 3 horseshoes arg. William Ferrers. *V.Y.*

Ferrers (Churston, co. Devon). Same arms.

Ferrers (London). Or on a bend gu. betw. two cotises az. 3 horseshoes or. Crest: An ostrich arg. in its beak a horseshoe. *Vis. Lon. 1633.*

Ferrers (Newton Park, co. Cornwall). . . . as many horseshoes—delete—'of the field' (an- other, . . . or). Add: *V.*

Ferrers (Skellingthorpe, co. Lincoln, bart.). Insert—1628 . . .

Ferrers or Ferreis (Co. Hertford). Add: William de Ferrers. *F.*

Ferrers (Co. Lincoln). 1640. Arg. on a bend gu. betw. 2 cotises az. 3 horseshoes ar. *Yorke.*

Ferrers (London 1568). Same arms. *C.L.*

Ferrers. Vairy or and gu. on a canton az. a bend arg. betw. 2 cotises and 6 lions ramp. of the first. Sir Thomas de Ferrers. *L.*

Ferrie (Glasgow). Az. an anchor arg. in chief a mullet of 6 points betw. 2 crescents or.

Ferrier (Boughton, near Liverpool). Add: Ferrier (Great Yarmouth, co. Norfolk). Same arms.

Fersax. Purp. a chev. betw. 3 garbs arg. *W.*

Fetheir (temp. Richard II). Add: William Fetheir.†

Fetherstonhaugh (Kirk Oswald, co. Cumberland) Add: Fetherstonhaugh (of Stanhope). Same arms. *Eliz. Roll.*

Fetherston (Blacksware, co. Hertford). . . . Add: Fetherston (London). Same arms. *Vis. Lon. 1633.*

Fettiplace (Chilfrey and Fernham, co. Berks., bart.). Insert—1661 . . . Add: *V.O.*

Feyce. Arg. 4 bars az. William Feyce. *V.*

Fichcocke. Insert—'or Fychcocke. Add: *V.V.**

Field (Stanstedbury, co. Hertford). . . . three garbs—delete—arg. substitute 'or' Add: *Guillim.*

Fiennes. . . . Baron Saye and Sele . . . Add: Fiennes. Az. 3 lions ramp. or Roger Fenes. *Y.* Sir James Fenys, Essex. *V.* And with a label gu. Sir Giles de Fenz. *N.*

Fife. Insert—Wedacre, co. Lancaster 1664. Or a lion ramp. gu. armed . . . on a chief of the 2nd . . . two stars of the first. Add: *V.L.*

Fiffe (Scotland). Arg. a lion ramp. betw. 4 roses in saltire gu. *Guillim.*

Filbert or Filbutt. Add: *V.V.** and *Cotton MS. Tiberius. D. 10.*

Fillingham (Fillingham, Suffolk). Sa. a chev. erm. betw. 3 covered cups or.

Filioll (Woodlands, co. Dorset and Owldhall, co. Essex). Add: Sir John Filiol or Filol or Fyllioll. *N.F.E.* Sir William Filliol. *V.* And with a mullet or on a canton for diff. Sir John Filliol. *L.* Sir John Filliol, the son. *L.*

Fillioll (Essex). Or 3 chevs. gu. over all a fess gu. charged with 3 griffins segreant arg. Sir Thomas Fillioll. temp. Edw. j. *V.*

Filmer (East Sutton, co. Kent . . .). Crest: A Falcon—delete—volant, substitute, 'rising'. Add: Filmer (London). Sa. 3 bars or in chief as many 5-foils of the last. Same Crest: *Vis. Lon. 1633.*

Filtelton or Filtilton. Add: Sir John Fillilton. *V.*

Finch (Earl of Aylesford). Add: Finch (Eastwell, co. Kent). Baronetcy 1611.

Finch (Kent). Arg. a chev. engr. betw. three griffins pass. sa. *V.*

Finch (Tenterden, Kent). Same arms a 5-foil for diff. *Robson.*

Finch. Arg. 2 chevs and in chief 3 griffins heads az. *A.A.*

Fincham. Barry of 6 arg. and sa. a bend arm. *V.*

Fincham (Norfolk). Arg. 3 bars sa. a bend erm. *V.* Simeon de Fincham. temp. Hen. V. *Seal.*

Fincham (Of Fincham, co. Norfolk). . . . 3 birds . . . 2 and 1. **Seal** of John Fincham 20th Ric. ij.

Finchinfield. Add: *V.W.*

Finderne. Arg. a chev. couped betw. 3 crosses bottony fitchy sa. *Cotton MS. Tiberius. D. 10.*

Finderne. Arg. a chev. betw. 3 crosses patty fitchy sa. *V.** Sire . . . de Fynderne. *V.*

Findon. Arg. a chev. the top ending with a cross patty. *Harl. MS. 1386. fo. 34.*

Fineaux (Langham, co. Kent). . . . —delete— (another, arg.)— . . . Add: *V.*

Fineux. Per chev. vert. and . . . 3 eagles displ. John Fineux Chief Justice of the Kings Bench. 1495. *Dug. O.J.*

Finzel (Frankfort Hall, co. Somerset). Add: *A.A.*

Fiott (Jersey). Add: *Robson.*

Firebrass or Firebrace. . . . bart.—insert—1698 . . .

Fish (London). Erm. on a saltire engr. gu. 5 lions heads erased or. *Vis. Lon. 1633.*

Fish (Coventry. *Her. Visit.*). . . . Add: Walter Fish, Stowmarket, Suffolk. *W.*

Fishacre (Fun. Ent. Ulster's Office). Add: Fishacre, co. Devon. *Lysons.*

Fishcock. Gu. a chev. erm. betw. 3 portcullises or. Clement Fishcocke. *Harl. MS. 1386. fo. 94.*

Fishead. Or 3 water bougets az. William Fisheade. *Y.*

Fisher (Justice of Common Pleas 1502). . . . Add: *Vis. Lon. 1633.*

Fisher (Cos. Gloucester, Hertford and Stafford). Add: Sir Edward Fisher. London 1533. *Harl. MS. 1358.* Fisher (London). Same arms. Crest: A demi-lion ramp. guard. or holding a shield gu. *Vis. Lon. 1633.*

Fisher (London, Cos. Herts and Stafford). Granted—insert—'by Camden, July' . . . Add: *Harl. MS. 6095. fo. 32.* Sir Thomas Fisher. London. *W.*

Fisher (   ). Gu. 3 demi-lions ramp. or on a chief indented of the second a cross moline erm.

Fisher (Packington Magna, co. Warwick, bart.). Insert—1622 . . .

Fisher (Hartwell Park, co. Northampton). Arg. a chev. vair betw. 3 demi-lions ramp. erased gu. *W.*

Fisher (Great Yarmouth, Norfolk). Same arms.

Fisher (Co. Bedford). Arg. on a chev. betw. three demi-lions ramp. gu. as many bezants. Sir Michael Fisher. *V.*

Fisher (Cottesford, co. Hertford and London). Same arms.

Fisher. Insert—(Lotsford, Herts.). Arg. on a chev. betw. three demi-lions ramp. gu. as many escutcheons of the first. Add: *W.*

Fisher (Co. Northampton) Arg. 3 demi-lions ramp. couped gu. within a bordure of the last charged with 8 bezants. *W.*

Fisher (Llwyn Derw. Glamorgan). Arg. on a chev. engr. betw. two couple closes . . . and 3 demi-lions ramp. guard. gu. each supporting betw. the paws a dexter gauntlet ppr. 3 bezants. *Nicholas.*

Fishide. Per fess sa. and gu. an eagle displ. arg. Add: *V.**

Fishide. Erm. on a bend engr. az. three 5-foils or. *V.*

Fishide. Or an ealge displ. az. Sir Walter Fishide. *V.*

Fishpoole (Essex). Or a bend wavy between 2 plain cotises az. *Suckling Papers.*

Fitch (Canfield, Essex. 1578). Same arms. † for diff.

Fitton. Arg. on a bend az. 3 garbs or in chief a crescent of the second for diff. Sir Richard Fytton. *S.*

Fitton. Arg. 2 chevs. and a canton gu. *V.**

Fitton. Arg. on a bend az. three chev. or. Add: Sir Ric. Fytton. *V.*

Fitz Elys (Newton). Arg. a bar dancetty in chief az. *X.*

Fitz-Alan. Gu. a lion ramp. or. John le Fitz Allen. *A.B.* Sir Richard Fitz Alain Counte de Arundell. *H.*

Fitz-Allen. Barry of 6 or and gu. Sir Bryan le Fitz Allyn. *J.A. Harl. MS. 6137. H.K.*

Fitz-Allen. Baron of Bedale. Barry of 10 or and gu. *Nobility Roll. 28 Edw. j.*

Fitz-Alleyne. Add: Sir Bryan Fitz-Allen. *N.*

Fitz-Alured. Insert—(Ireland). Add: *W.*

Fitz-Andrew. Add: *V.*

Fitz-Barnard (Holcomb Burnell, co. Devon). . . . Vert.—underlined, and marginal—query, 'Vair'.

Fitz-Bery (Ireland). Arg. a chev. betw. 3 lions ramp. gu. *Cady.*

Fitz-Clarence (Earl of Munster). . . . marginal note: The baton was originally az. charged with 3 anchors or.

Fitz-Elys (Waterpirie, co. Oxford). Add: *V.*

Fitz-Eustace (Co. Leicester). Add: Sire Thomas FitzEustace. *N.*

Fitz-Eustace (Co. Lincoln). Add: Sir Thomas Fitz Eustace, co. Lincoln. *V.*

Fitz-Geffrey Co. (Bedford and Rusildon, co. Northampton). Add: *V.**

Fitz-Geffrey (Co. Bedford). Add: Sir John le Fitz-Geffrey. *A.B.C.J.P.V.*

Fitz-Geffrey (Co. Bedford). Sa. a bull statant arg. his tail betw. his legs. *V.*

Fitz-Gernagon. Barruly or and az. an eagle displ. gu. armed of the second. Gernagon Fitz Gernagon of Tanfield. *Y.*

Fitz-Gerald. Add: Warin le Fitz Gerald. *B.*

Fitz-Hamon or Fitz-Hamond (Lord of Gloucester). Add: *Sandford.*

Fitz-Hamon (Glamorgan). Sa. a lion ramp. guard. or incensed gu. *Nicholas.*

Fitz-Harding. Quarterly gu. and or a baston arg. Nicholas Fitz Harding temp. Hen. ij. *Cotton MS. Julius C. vij. v. 113.*

Fitz-Harry (Ireland). Gu. 2 lions ramp. or attired and langued az. a chief of the second. *Robson.*

Fitz-Henry (Co. Essex). Add: Sir Richard Fitz Henry. *Y.*

Fitz-Henry (Ireland). Arg. a lion ramp. az. crowned or. *Cady.*

Fitz-Herbert. Arg. a chief vairy or and gu. over all a bend sa. *V.** Fitzherbert, Norbury, co. Derby. *V.*

Fitz-Herbert (Baron de Teissier. France and England). Or on a mount a boar pass. sa. on a chief gu. a crescent betw. 2 estoiles arg. *Burke.*

Fitz-Herbert (Tissington, co. Derby. bart.). Add: Sir Piers Fitz-Herbert, Lord of Blancavenny in Wales. *V.*

Fitz-Herbert. Arg. a chief vairy or and gu. a bend sa. *V.O.* Beybrook, co. Oxon.

Fitz-Herbert (Mayne, co. Dorset). Gu. 3 lions ramp. within a bordure engr. or. *Hutchins ij. 540.*

Fitz-Herbert. Arg. a bend cotised engr. betw. six martlets sa. Add: Thomas Fitz Herbert. *X.*

Fitz-Hervei (Sheriff of Norfolk 1187). Gu. on a bend arg. 3 trefoils slipped vert. *Dashwood.*

Fitz-Hugh. Or 3 bars az. over all an eagle displ. gu. beaked and armed or. Jernigan Fitz-Hugh. Tanfield. *P.*

Fitz-Hugh. Gu. 3 lions ramp. or within a bordure engr. arg. *S.* Sir Edmon Fitz-Hugh. *S.*

Fitz-Hugh (Cos. Oxford and York. temp. Edw. III). Add: Sir Henry Fitz-Hugh. *S.* Fitz Hugh quartered by Catherine Parr 6th wife of Hen. viij. *Z. 490.* And with a label of 3 points gu. Sir Henry Fitz-Hewgh. *L. Harl. MS. 6137.*

Fitz-Hugh (Lord Fitz-Hugh, summoned to Parliament 1273) . . . Add: *V.*

Fitz-Ives. Gu. a bend betw. 6 lozenges or. *V.*

Fitz-John (Co. Lincoln). Sa. 2 bars arg. in chief 3 plates. Sir Adam le Fitz-John *N.V.Y.*

Fitz-John. Quarterly or and gu. a bordure indented arg. and az. John le Fitz-John. *C.*

Fitz-John. Quarterly or and gu. a bordure vair. Add: John Fitz-Hugh. *F.* Richard le Fitz-John. *D.E.N.*

Fitz-John. Chequy or and gu. Sir Robert le fitz John. *I.*

Fitz-Jues. Add: *V.**

Fitz-Kerif (Ireland). Arg. a lion ramp. az. crowned or. *V.*

Fitz-Lewis (Thornden, Essex). Sa. a chev. betw. 3 trefoils arg. *Fuller.*

Fitz-Martyn. Add: M. Nicole le Fitz-Martin. *B.X.Y.*

Fitz-Mores, Fitz-Moris, or Fitz-Moores. Arg. six moorcocks gu. (another, sa.). Insert—*V.* . . .

Fitz-Nicoll or Fitz-Nicold. Add: Fitz Nicoll. *V.** Fitz Nicolas. *V.D. iij. 91.*

Fitz-Nicoll. Quarterly gu. and or a bend sa. *Harl. MS. 1465.*

Fitz Mahewe. Per pale az. and gu. 3 lions ramp. or. Herbert le Fitz. Mahewe. *B.*

Fitz Mahew. Per pale az. and gu. 3 lions ramp. erm. Philip le Maheu. *E.* Le Fitz Mahew. *F.*

Fitz-Osborne. Gu. 2 bars and a quarter arg. *Cady.*

Fitz-Osborne. Paly of 6 arg. and gu. a canton of the second. *Cady.*

Fitz-Otes (Fitshall, co. Norfolk). Add: *V.** But 3 bendlets. *V.* Add: Sir Hue le Fitz Othes. *D.E.*

Fitz-Otho. Bendy of 7 az. and or a canton erm.

Fitz-Payne (Baron Fitz-Payne, Summoned to Parliament 1299). . . . Add: Robert le Fitz Payne. *K. Harl. MS. 6137. V.* Isabel Fitz Payne. 1347. **Seal.** Maud Fitz Payne. 1356. **Seal.** *Dallaway.*

Fitz-Payne. Arg. a chev. vair betw. 3 lions ramp. az.

Fitz-Piers. Gu. 3 chevs. compony arg. and gu. *V.** But counter—compony. *V.*

Fitz-Piers. Gu. 3 lions ramp. or (another, a bordure engr. arg.). Add: *V. V.** Reginald Fitz Piers. *V.* Reynald Fitz-Piers. *Y.B.E.*

Fitz Piers. Sa. 3 lions ramp. or. Reynand le Fitz Piers. *D.*

Fitz-Ralph (Co. Berks). Add: *V.*

Fitz-Ralph. Barry of six arg. and gu. in chief three buckles of the second. Crest: . . . Add: William le Fitz Rafe. *F.* Robert Fitz Rafe. *L.* Descended from Ralph de Cotone.

Fitz-Raulf (Co. Suffolk). Add: Sire William Fitz-Rafe. *N.* Sir William Fitz-Raufe, Pebmarsh, Suffolk. With 11 fleurs-de-lis on the chevs. 5. 3. and 3. *V.*

Fitz-Renald. Gu. 3 lions ramp. or within a bordure indented arg. Sir Reynald le Fitz Renald. *O.*

Fitz Reinald. Gu. 3 lions ramp. arg. Sir Johan le Fitz Reinald. *J.* Fitz-Reinauld. Gu. 3 lions ramp. or Sir John de Fitz Reinauld. *J.N.*

Fitz-Richard. Gu. a chev. betw. 3 unicorns arg. Sire Hamond le Fitz-Richard. *O.*

Fitz-Robert (Co. Northumberland). Add: Sir Walter Fitz-Robert. Arg. 2 chevs. gu. *Syl. Morgan.* Add: Fitz-Robert. Sire Walter le Fitz Robert. *N.V.*

Fitz-Roger (Co. Lincoln). Insert—Sire Robert Fitz Roger. *N.* Robert Fitz Roger, Clavering. Add: *V.* *P.Y.E.F.*

Fitz Roger. Quarterly or and gu. a bendlet sa. Sir Robert Fitz Roger. *E.F.D.H.*

Fitz Roger. Quarterly or and arg. a bend sa. Robert le Fitz Roger. *K.*

Fitz-Roger. Arg. a lion ramp. purp. Sir Roger Fitz:Roger. *V.* Sir Robert de Fitz. Roger. *J.Y.*

Fitz-Roger (Whitington). Vert. 3 boars or on a bordure arg. fleurs-de-lis az.

Fitz-Rogon (Co. Devon). Az. a chev. arg. betw. 3 chessrooks or. *Lysons.*

Fitz-Ronard. Or 2 chev. gu. on a canton . . . Add: *N.*

Fitzroy (Reginald Fitzroy or de Dunstanville, son of Henry I. Earl of Cornwall. ob. 1176). Gu. 2 lions pass. guard or over all a baton. az. *Z. 50.*

Fitz-Simon. Az. a lion ramp. erm. Sir Rauf Fitz-Simon. *N.*

Fitz-Simon. Az. 3 eagles displ. or a canton erm. *V.** Sir John Fitz-Simon. *N.* Fitz-Simon, co. Hertford. temp. Edw. j. *V.*

Fitz-Symon. Arg. three eagles displ. vert. Add: Sir . . . de Fitz Symon, Essex. *V.*

Fitz-Symon. Az. 6 eagles displ. or a canton erm. John Fitz-Symon. *N. Harl. MS. 6589.*

Fitz Symon. Gu. 3 chessrooks erm. Symon le Fitz-Symon. *E.*

Fitz-Urse. Insert—(Co. Somerset). Or on a bend sa. 3 bears heads . . . Add: *V.*

Fitz-Vrian. Same arms.—insert—?.

Fitz-Vrian (Llangadock, co. Carmarthen). Add: Fitz-Vrian (Llangadock). Arg. on a chev. sa. betw. 3 crows ppr. and a bordure engr. gu. bezanty a crescent of the first. Thomas Fitz-Vrian. *V.* Thomas ap John Fitz-Urian of Llangadock, co. Carmarthen. Gentleman Mace Bearer or Sergeant at Arms to Henry viij. Granted by Wriothesley. Garter. 1526. *Guillim.*

Fitz-Walter (Berney, co. Bucks). Quarterly or and gu. on a bend az. 3 fleurs-de-lis in pale arg. *V.*

Fitz-Walter. Gu. on a bend arg. 3 fleurs-de-lis. Add: *V.*

Fitz-Warren. Quarterly per fess indented arg. and gu. in the first quarter a martlet (sometimes a mullet sa. Sir Fowk Fitzwarren). *L.*

Fitz-Water (Co. Cumberland). Arg. a chev. sa. betw. three—insert—'round', buckles gu. *V.* and *Cotton MS. Tiberius. D.10.*

Fitz-Water (Milo Fitz-Water . . .). Add: *Guillim.*

Fitz-Water. Quarterly or and gu. on a bend az. three fleurs-de-lis. arg. Add: *V.**

Fitz-Williams (Baron of Lisford). Gu. on a bend betw. two cotises arg. 3 martlets vert. *Harl. MS. 4040. fo. 454.*

Fitz-William (Mablethorpe, co. Lincoln). Arg. a chevron betw. 3 crosses crosslet and a bordure sa. bezanty. *V.*

Fitz-William. Arg. on a bend sa. three estoiles of the field. Add: *V.*

Fitz-William. Barry of eight—insert—or 10 . . . Add: Rauf Fitz William. *G.*

Fitzwilliams (Co. Cornwall). Add: *V.*

Flambert (Cos. Cambridge and Essex). Add: *V*, after three dolphins vert. (another az.). Add: *Cady.*

Flambard. Bishop of Durham 1099–1128. Gu. on a chev. engr. arg. 3 dolphins naiant embowed vert.

Flandringham or Flandringe. Add: *V.V.**

Flatesbury (Ireland, *Ulster's Office*). . . . Add: *V.*

Flatman (London 1682). . . . arg. a chev. . . . betw. 3 garbs . . . quartering paly of 6 . . . and . . . . with . . . a chev. . . .

Flatterbury, Flattesbery or Flatebury. . . .. Add: *V.V.**

Flaxal. Insert—of Waxhall . . . Add: *V.*

Fleet (London). Add: confirmed by Dethick 1573. *Vis. Lon. 1633.*

Fleete (London; granted 13 May 1691). Insert—Sir John Fleet. Lord Mayor.

Fleete. Arg. a lion ramp. gu. over all on a bend sa. 3 mullets or. *V.** Sir Laurence de Fleete, co. Lincoln. *V.*

Fleetwood (Calwick, co. Stafford). . . . Add: William Fleetwood, Recorder of London. *Dug. O.J.*

Fleetwood (Rossall, co. Lancaster). . . . Add: *V.L. 1664.*

Fleetwood (London). Add: *Vis. Lon. 1633.*

Fleggh. Per pale . . . (another engr.)—insert—*Y.* . . . per pale sa. and arg. . . . Add: *V.*

Fleming (Cos. Essex, Hants, Kent and Salop). Add: Fleming (Southampton). Same arms. *V.*

Fleming (Aldringham, co. Lancaster). Arg. 3 bars az. in chief as many maunches gu.

Fleming (Cornwall). Chequy or and gu. *V.C. 304.*

Fleming (Boghall, Renfrewshire). Gu. a chev. embattled within a double tressure flory counterflory arg. quartering az. three 5-foils arg. for Fraser. *Robson.*

Fleming (Sir Francis Fleming. Lieut of the Ordnance. Granted 1550). Per saltire or and gu. a chev. betw. 3 owls arg. beaked and legged of the first in chief a culverin lying bendwise az. fired ppr. on the mouth a ball. sa. *V.*

Fleming. Or a chev. az. betw. 3 bulls sa. goutty or. *V.** Sir Thos. Fleminge. *V.*

Fleming of Wathe. Barry of 6 arg. and az. in chief 3 lozenges gu. *Constable's Roll. xj.*

Flemyngham. Add: *V.**

Fleshers Company, of Edinburgh. Arg. 2 pole axes in saltire endorsed ppr. betw. 3 bull's heads couped sa. on a chief az. a boars head couped betw. 2 block brushes or. *Berry.*

Fletcher (Swinford, co. Leicester and Coventry, co. Warwick). Add: Fletcher (London). Same Arms. Crest: A demi talbot ramp. az. eared or and ducally gorged of the last. *Vis. Lon. 1633.*

Fletcher. Arg. a chev. betw. 3 mullets sa. Crest: Out of a ducal coronet or a plume of 3 ostrich feathers az. banded gold. Add: *W.* Fletcher (Towton, co. York 1665). Same arms, a crescent for diff. *Dugdale. p. 19.*

Fletchers, Company of (London).—delete— 'az.', substitute 'sa' . . . Add: granted in 1467.

Flete. Add: *V.*

Flete. Chequy or and gu. a sinister canton arg. *V.*

Fletwick (Co. Bedford). Add: Sir David Fletwick, Co. Bedford. temp. Edw. iij. *V.*

Flint (Norwich). Sa. on a chev. engr. arg. betw. 3 crescents erm. 2 lions combatant gu. *Cady.*

Flood (London). Vert. a chev. erm. betw. 3 wolves heads erased arg. *Vis. Lon. 1633.*

Flote or Floelte. Add: *V.*

Flower (Viscount Ashbrook). . . . each holding in the beak an—written in—'erm.' spot sa.

Flower. Erm. on a canton gu. an owl arg. with a ducal coronet about the neck or. *Nash.*

Flower (Chilton, co. Wilts). Add: *Vis. Lon. 1633.*

Flowerdew. Per chev. arg. and sa. 3 bears pass. counterchanged. Edward Flowerdew, Chief Baron of the Exchequer. 1585. *Dug. O.J.*

Flowerdew. Per chev. engr. arg. and sa. 3 bears pass. 2. and 1. counterchanged langued gu. *Cady.*

Floyer (Floyer Hayes, co. Devon). Add: *V.*

Fludd or Flood (Millgate, Kent). Add: *Guillim.*

Flyar or Flyer (London). Sa. a chev. erm. betw. 3 arrows points downwards arg. Crest: A stag's head erased or holding in its mouth an arrow arg. *Vis. Lon. 1633.*

Flye or Flyght. Add: *V.* Flight of Caister, Norfolk, quartered by Harrison.

Fockingham (Leeds, co. York). Arg. a chev. betw. 3 pierced cinquefoils sa. *Eliz. Roll xxiv.*

Fogelston, Foghelston or Foulstone. Insert—co. Kent. Add: *V.*

Fogg or Fogge (Richbury, co. Kent). Arg.— delete—(another, or). Add: Sir John Fogge Kt. Comptroller of the Household and a Privy Councillor to Edw. iv.

Fokeram or Fokerham (Co. Berks.). Add: The bend engr. Sire Richard Fokeram. *N.* but fusilly Richard Fokeram. *E.* Thomas Fawkerham. *Y.*

Fokeram. Arg. a bend engr. az. Sir Richard Fokeram. *V.*

Folborne (Co. Cambridge). Add: But wiverns not dragons. Sir John Folbourne, co. Cambridge, temp. Edw. j. *V.*

Folcard or Folkard. Sa. a chev. betw. 3 covered cups arg. John de Folcard, Alderman of Norwich 1449.

Folcher. Insert—co. Derby. Erm. on a bend gu. three bezants. delete (another, plates). Add: *V.*

Folebarne. Add: *V.*

Foleborne. Or a chev. betw. 2 wiverns sa. Sire Johan de Foleborne. *N. Harl. MS. 4033.* But 3 wiverns. *N. Nicholas. p. 155.*

Folgnardby. Arg. 3 swans rising sa. *V.*

Foliott. Arg. 2 lions pass. guard gu. Sampson Foliot. *V.* Sansnin Foliott. *E.*

Foljambe (Steeton Hall, co. York 1665). Sa. a bend betw. 6 escallops or. Crest: A leg in armour couped at the thigh quarterly or and sa. Dugdale says: "This family has for many years used their arms with supporters", viz. An antelope quarterly sa. and or and a tiger arg. *Dugdale. p. 53.*

Foljambe (Walton, co. Derby, bart.). . . . Add: Thomas Folegambe. *E.* Sir Godfrey Foljambe, Walton, co. Derby. *V.* Arms of the family confirmed by Flower 1587.

Foljambe (Wakefield, co. York). Add: Monsire Godfrey Foljambe. *S.*

Foljambe (Oldwick Hall, co. York). Sa. on a bend betw. 6 escallops or an escu. arg. charged with a lion ramp. az. *Foster.*

Folkes (Cambridge). . . . a chev. erm. betw. 3 fleurs-de-lis. . . . on a chief . . . 3 roundels . . . *Cole.*

Folkingham (Barton, co. York). Insert—1584. Add: *V.**

Follyott (Sir John Follyott, Kent). Az. 6 annulets 3.2. and 1. or. *V.*

Folliot (Pyrton, co. Worcester). Add: Hugh Folliot, Bishop of Hereford 1219–34. Same Arms.

Folliott (Lord Foliot, of Ballyshannon. . .). Add: *Harl. MS. 4040. fo. 438.*

Folliott. Gu. a bend betw. 6 crescents arg. Sir Edmond Folliott. *M.*

Folliott. Gu. a bend betw. 6 crescents pendent or † Esmond Folliott. *Y.* and *Harl. MS. 1386. fo. 34.*

Folyott. Barry nebuly of 6 erm. and gu. Sir Geoffry Folyott. *V.*

Folliott. Gu. a bend arg. *Y.F.* Sir John Folyott, Norfolk. *V.* Sire Richard Foliot. *E.J.N.L.B.M.- Y.* And with a label or Sir Edmond Foliot. *N.*

Folman. Arg. a chev. erm. betw. 3 ducal coronets sa. *V.*

Folton. Gu. 2 lions pass. arg. crowned or. Le Sire de Folton. *T. Harl. MS. 6137.*

Folvile (Kersby, co. Durham). Add: **Seal** in *V.H.*

Foote (London, Lord Mayor of London 1651). Insert—Baronetcy 1660.

Foote (Veryan, Lambesso in St. Clements and Truro, co. Cornwall). Add: Foote (Telogorick, Cornwall). Same arms. *Lysons.*

Forcer. Sa. on a chev. engr. or betw. 3 leopards faces arg. as many annulets of the first. *Surtees.*

Ford (Ember Court, co. Surrey, bart.). Insert— 1793 . . .

Ford (Islington, cos. Derby, Surrey, Sussex and Wilts). Add: Sir Richard Ford. *I. Harl. MS. 6589.* Sir Richard de la Forde. *I.*

Ford. Az. 3 lions ramp. or crowned. Sir Adam Ford or de la Forde. *K. Harl. MS. 6137* and *6589. N.* Sir Adam Ford, co. Wilts. *V.*

Ford (Chagford, Ashburton, Bagtor and Nutwell, co. Devon). Add: Ford, Mayor of Exeter 1656. *Colby.* Forde 1524. Same arms. *W.* John Ford of Ashberton, co. Devon. *V.*

Forde. Az. 3 lions ramp. or quartering, per fess or and erm. a lion ramp. per fess az. fretty arg. and gu. *Dug. O.J.*

Ford (Frating, co. Essex). Add: *V.E. 1558.*

Ford (London, Richard Ford, Lord Mayor of London 1671). . . . Add: *Guillim.*

Forder. Per fess erm. and arg. a lion ramp. az. and gu. fretty of the second. *V.**

Fordham. Or 2 bars wavy gu. on a chief az. 2 towers of the first. *Nash.*

Forlong (Co. Lanark). Arg. on a mount vert a tree ppr. in front of it a boar pass.

Forman (London). Az. 3 greyhounds heads erased arg. collared gu. studded or. *Vis. Lon. 1633.*

Forman or Freman. Add: Sir William Forman, Alderman of London. *V.* . . . Add: *V.**

Formby. Insert—(Lancashire). Add: *F.L.*

Formi. Quarterly gu. and or a sinister baton sa. and a label of 5 points arg. *J.*

Forneaulx. Sa. (another gu.—insert—*Harl. MS. 1404. fo. 114.*). . . . Add: *V.*

Fornivall. Add: *V.*

Forset or Forsett (Co. Middlesex 1611). Add: *V.* See also Faussett.

Forster (Angmering, Sussex). Az. a lion ramp. arg. goutty de sang. *Berry.*

Forster. Sa. a chev. engr. arg. betw. 3 arrows or feathered and headed of the second. *V.*

Forster (Co. Cumberland and London). *Her. Off London c. 24.* Add: *Vis. Lon. 1633.*

Forster (Stokesley, co. York, Baronetcy 1649). Arg. a chev. vert. betw. 3 bugle horns sa. *Dug. p. 71.*

Foster (Smawes, co. York). Same arms, a martlet for diff. *F.Y.*

Foster (Sir Thomas Foster, Justice of the Common Pleas). Same arms. quartering; arg. on a bend sa. 3 birds or. *Dug. O.J.*

Forster (Rothwell, co. York). Arg. a chev. engr. vert. betw. 3 bugle horns sa. stringed of the second *Dugdale. 1665. p. 204.*

Forster (Durham). Arg. a chev. vert. betw. 3 bugle horns sa. stringed or a canton gu.

Forster (Lysways Hall, co. Stafford, bart.). Insert—1874 . . .

Forster (London). Quarterly per fess indented arg. and sa. on the first and fourth quarters a bugle horn stringed sa. *Vis. Lon. 1633.* Crest: A talbot pass. arg. collared and lined or. *Idem. p. 286.*

Forster (Thomas Forster). Sa. a hart trippant arg. betw. 3 bezants on each a pheon of the first within a bordure compony or and gu. *V.*

Forster. Sa. on a chev. betw. 3 bugle horns or as many pheons az.

Forster. Sa. a chev. engr. betw. 3 arrows or feathered arg. Add: *V.**

Forster. Erm. on a canton sa. an owl arg. *V.**

Forstesburi. . . . 3 lions ramp. . . . a canton erm. Henry Forstesburi.

Forterie (London). Arg. 3 boars heads erased sa. † for diff. Crest: A pair of wings arg. *Vis. Lon. 1633.*

Fortescue. Az. a bend engr. arg. plain cotised or a mullet on the bend for diff. Sir John Fortescue *V.*

Fortescue (Winston, co. Devon). . . . Az. a bend engr. arg.—insert—'plain' . . . Add: Lewis Fortescue, Baron of the Exchequer 1542. Fortescue, Fallowpit, co. Devon. Baronetcy 1664.

Fortescue (Parkinson-Fortescue, Lord Carlingford). Insert— 28 Feb. 1874.

Fortescue (Wood, co. Devon, bart). Insert— 1666 . . .

Fortescue (Stapleford Abbots, co. Essex). Add: *V.E. 1634.*

Fortescue. Az. a bend engr. arg. betw. 2 cotises or in chief a mullet sa. Sir John Fortiscue. *V.*

Fortior. Or a chev. betw. 2 couple closes gu. *Randle Holme.*

Fortry (London). Arg. 3 boars heads erased sa. Crest: A boar's head erased sa. langued or. *Vis. Lon. 1633.*

Fossard (Doncaster, co. York . . .). Add: Robert Fossard. *P.X.*

Foster (Hornby Castle). Per chev. az. and erm. a chev. paly of 8 arg. and gu. betw. 3 bugle horns stringed . . . ; in chief betw. the horns a sun ppr. Crest: A stag's head.

Foster (Co. Northampton). Arg. a chev. gu. betw. 3 bugle horns vert. stringed or. *V.*

Foster ( ). Arg. on a chev. engr. sa. betw. 3 bugle horns of the second as many escallops of the field. *A.A.*

Foster (The Bogue Estate, Jamaica . . .). Add: *A.A.*

Foster (Co. Northumberland). Az. a chev. or in chief two leopards faces and in base a bugle horn of the last. Add: *V. Harl. MS. 1392.*

Foster (Co. Nothumberland). Arg. on a chev. vert. three leopards faces or. Add: *W.*

Foster. Az. a chev. or in chief a bugle horn betw. two leopards heads arg. *W.*

Foster. Az. a chev. or in chief 3 leopards faces gold, a bordure compony or and gu. *W.*

Foster. Arg. on a bend sa. three bucks heads cabossed or. Crest: . . . Add: *V.**

Foster (Essex). Az. a lion ramp. arg. goutty purp. *V.*

Foster (Iden, Sussex). . . . Add: *W.*

Foster (Co. Huntingdon). Add: John Foster. *V.*

Foster (Cos. Lincoln and—insert—'Stokesley').

• • •

Foster (Tadcaster, co. York). Sa. a chev. erm. betw. 3 arrows or feathered arg. in chief † for diff. *Eliz. Roll xxxij.*

Foster. Vert. a chev. betw. 3 butterflies volant arg. Robert Foster. *V.*

Foster. Sa. a buck trippant arg. betw. three bezants, each charged with a pheon of the field. Add: *V.**

Foston. Arg. on a chev. sa. 3 crescents of the first. *V.*

Fotherby. Gu. two chevs. arg. on the first three fleurs-de-lis of the field. Add: John Fotherby. *V.*

Fotheringhay. Arg. 2 lions pass. reguard. sa. *Y.*

Foudras. Az. 3 bars arg. in chief a saltire or. George Foudras. *V.*

Foullelode (Co. Salop). Arg. in chief a lion pass. guard. gu. in base 3 leopards heads sa. 2. and 1. *V.*

Foulkton (Co. York). Sa. a chev. betw. 3 bucks heads cabossed arg. *Dugdale. 135.*

Founder or Foundaure. Add: *V.V.**

Founders, Company of (London; granted by Cooke, Clarenceux). Add: Granted by Cooke, 8 Oct. 1590.

Fowbery (Newbold, co. York). Vert. a stag at speed arg. attired or. *Eliz. Roll. xxij.*

Fowell (Fowell's Combe, co. Devon). . . . Add: *V. Collinson Somerset iij. 256.*

Fowke (Cos. Dorset, Stafford and London). Add: *Vis. Lon. 1633.*

Fowke (Elmsthorpe, co. Leicester). Add: Granted by Camden. *W.*

Fowle (River Hall, co. Sussex). Add: Fowle (Sir Thomas Fowle, London 1686). Gu. a lion pass. betw. 3 roses or. *C.N.*

Fowler (Ricott, co. Bedford). Add: *V.*

Fowler (Gnoll, co. Glamorgan). Az. on a chev. arg. betw. 3 lions pass. guard. or as many crosses formy sa. quartering . . . a cross flory . . . betw. three crescents. *Nicholas.*

Fowler (Harnage Grange, co. Salop bart.). Insert —1704 . . . Add: Az. on a bend arg. betw. 3 lions pass. guard. or as many crosses moline sa. *Guillim.*

Fowler (Islington, co. Middlesex, bart.). Insert— 1626 . . .

Fowler. Az. a chev. betw. 3 herons or storks or. *V.*

Fowler (Co. Stafford). Erm. on a canton gu. an owl arg. *Erdeswick.*

Fowler (St. Thomas, co. Stafford). Erm. on a canton gu. an owl or. *Guillim.*

Fowler. Erm. on a canton gu. a boars head erased . . . *Robson.*

Fowler (Windlesham House, Bagshot, co. Surrey) Add: Sir Richard Fowler, Ricott. Same arms. *V.*

Fownes or Fones (Plymouth, co. Cornwall). Add: *W.*

Fownes (Co. Stafford). Az. 2 spread eagles in chief and a mullet in base or. *Shaw.*

Fox (Lord Holland). . . . Add: Sir Stephen Fox, Knt. London. 1665. *L.N.*

Fox (Little Eppleton, co. Durham). Add: Fox (Ireland). Arg. a lion ramp. and in chief 2 dexter hands appaumy all ppr. *Robson.*

Fox (Cos. Hereford and Leicester). &c. Add: *V.*

Fox (Ratcliff and Bosworth, co. Leicester). . . . Add: *C.C. 1619.*

Fox (London). Add: Granted to John Fox, London. 1586. *W.*

Fox (Bromfield, co. Salop). Or a chev. betw. three foxes heads erased gu. *Harl. M.S. 6110 fo. 14b.*

Fox. Gu. a chev. erminois betw. three lions heads erased or on a chief barry nebuly of 4 arg. and purp. on a pale az. a pelican all within a bordure of the third. *V.O. p. 157.* John Fox, Ropesley. *V.* But also given as. Gu. on a chev. erm. betw. 3 lions heads erased or a pale az. charged with a pelican vulning herself gold a bordure of the third charged with hurts. *V.*

Fox (Edward Fox, Bishop of Bath and Wells). . . . Add: within a bordure of the second. *U.*

Fox (Co. Cornwall, Brislington House, Bristol &c.). . . . bend engr. erm.—insert—'plain' . . .

Fox (Granted to Stephen Fox, Clerk of the Kitchen to King Charles ij. by Sir Edwin Walker 1658). Same arms. *Guillim.* Sir Charles Fox, Contractor for the Building for the Great Exhibition of 1851. Same arms. **Seal.**

Foxall (London). Insert—granted 1579 . . . Add: *W.* following description of Crest.

Foxcott. Add: *V.*

Foxcroft (Weetwood, co. York 1665). Az. a chev. or betw. 3 foxes heads erased ppr. *Dugdale. p. 48.*

Foxley (Co. Berks). Add: M. John de Foxlee. *S.* Sire Johan Foxlee. *N.*

Foxton (Dodworth). Arg. a chev. gu. betw. 3 bugle horns sa. *V.*

Framlingham. (Granted by Cooke). Gu. on a chev. betw. 3 esquires helmets plumed or three feathers one or with 2 arg. mullet charged with a crown for diff. *W.*

Framlingham or Fremlin (Hartlip, co. Kent). Add: *V.**

Frampton (Bishop of Gloucester 1681). Gu. 3 bars and in chief as many crescents or.

Franceis (Lord Mayor of London 1400). Add: *V.W.*

Franceis. Per bend sinister sa. and or. *Randle Holme.*

Frances. Arg. a chev. betw. 3 eagles displ. gu. Crest: . . . Add: Franceis (Fornworke, co. Derby). Same arms. *V.* Sire Robert Fraunceys. *S.*

Franceis. Arg. a chev. engr. sa. betw. three pierced mullets gu. *V.**

Francis (Co. Derby; granted 4 May 1577). Add: Adam Fraunces. *Y.W.*

Francis (Co. Derby; *Har. MS. 1400*). Add: *V.**

Francis. Per bend sa. and or a lion ramp. *C.C.* Sir Adam Francis. *V.* Sir Edward Francis, co. Derby. *W.*

Francis (Co. Derby). Per bend az. and arg. a lion ramp. counter changed. Add: *W.*

Francis (co. Derby). Erm. on a canton sa. a harp arg. *W.*

Frances or Fraunces. Erm. on a canton sa. a harp arg. stringed or. *Guillim.*

Franke (Essex). Arg. a bend engr. sa. betw. two cornish choughs ppr. *V.E. 1612.*

Frankland (Thirkleby, co. York, Baronetcy 1660). Az. a bend betw. 2 dolphins or. *Guillim.*

Franklin (Rainham, co. Norfolk). Add: *V.** Add: Franklyn (co. Devon). Same arms except that the dolphin is or. *V.*

Franklyn (Moore, co. Hertford, and—insert— 'Willesden', also Granted by Camden 1599). Add: *Vis. Lon. 1633.*

Franklyn (Kent). Arg. on a bend betw. two dolphins embowed bendwise gu. 3 lions heads erased bendwise or. *W.*

Franklyn (Gonalston, co. Notts.). Arg. on a bend betw. 2 lions heads erased gu. a dolphin embowed enclosed by 2 martlets or.

Franklyn (Buckmaster, co. Devon). Az. a bend betw. 2 dolphins embowed bendwise or. *W.*

Franklyn (Co. York). . . . a dolphin betw. 2 birds or . . . Crest: . . . two sprigs vert. . . . Add: *Vis. Lon. 1633.*

Fransham. Per pale indented or and az. six martlets 2. 2. and 2. counterchanged.

Fraunces. Arg. 2 chevs. betw. 3 mullets sa. *V.*

Fraunces. Arg. a chev. engr. sa. betw. 3 pierced mullets gu. *V.*

Frauncis. Arg. on a bend betw. 2 cotises gu. three owls or. Sir John Frauncis. *V.*

Fraxines. Add: *V.*

Frear (London, granted Feb. 1602). Insert—by Camden. Thomas Frear, M.D. . . . three dolphins—insert—naiant embowed . . . Add: *W.*

Frebody (East Grinstead, Sussex). Add: *Vis. Lon. 1633. V.*

Freby. Add: *Harl. MS. 1404. fo. 142.*

Freche. Arg. two chev. gu. on a canton az. a fleur-de-lis or. Add: *V.** and canton—underlined—'quarter'. *V.*

Freeman (London). Az. 3 lozenges arg. Crest: a demi-lion ramp. gu. charged on the shoulder with a 5-foil or. *Vis. Lon. 1633.*

Freeman (London). Az. 3 lozenges conjoined in fess arg. *Vis. Lon. 1633.*

Freeman (London and Northampton). Az. 3 lozenges arg. 2. and 1. Crest: a demi-lion ramp. gu. charged on the breast with a lozenge arg. *Vis. Lon. 1633.*

Freeman (Norfolk). Or a chev. betw. 3 fleurs-de-lis per pale arg. and gu. *W.*

Freeman. Barry nebuly of 6 arg. and az. on a chev. sa. 3 martlets or a chief gu. charged with a lion pass. guard betw. 2 anchors erect gold. *V.*

Freeman (Co. York). Az. three lozenges in fess or—delete—(another, arg.). Crest: a demi-fox arg. . . .

Freeman. Same arms, a bordure arg.—insert—the lozenges 2. and 1. Add: *Vis. Lon. 1633.*

Freeman. Or on a chev. per pale arg. and gu. three fleurs-de-lis counterchanged. Add: *V.**

Freford or Freeford. Add: *V.*

Freford. Gu. a bend betw. six mascles arg. John de Freford. *Y.*

Frekylton. . . . a chev. . . . betw. 3 fleurs-de-lis . . . a bordure engr. . . . **Seal.** temp. Edw. iij.

Freme. Land Steward of the Berkeley estates while in the hands of Hen. viij . . . 2 chevs. . . . betw. 3 coronets. On **Brass** formerly in Berkeley Church, co. Gloucester.

Fremling (Maidstone, Kent). Gu. a chev. betw. 3 visored helmets plumed arg. *Philpot 1619.*

Fremond. Per chev. ermines and gu. a chev. betw. 3 fleurs-de-lis or. *V.*

Fremoult (Norfolk). . . . a chev. . . . betw. 3 inkmolines. *Blomfield.*

French (Co. Devon). Add: *V.V.**

French (Stream, co. Sussex). Add: Sometimes with a label of 3 points az. French.

French. Insert—Kent. Sa. a bend arg. betw. 2 dolphins naiant or. Crest: . . . Add: *W.*

French (Sussex). Gu. a bend betw. 2 dolphins embowed bendwise arg. *W.*

French. Sa. bendlet betw. 3 fishes haurient arg. *W.*

French. Per pale sa. and az. a wolf pass. arg. Add: *W.*

Frend. Gu. a chev. betw. 3 bucks heads cabossed erm. Add: *V.* Add: Frend. Same arms. But stags heads erm. attired or. *V.*

Frend (Little Chart, Kent). Gu. a chev. erm. betw. three bucks heads cabossed arg. attired or. *Cady.*

Frende. Or a chev. sa. betw. 3 bulls heads cabossed gu. armed arg. Add: *V.V.**

Frene. Gu. 2 bars per fess indented—insert—point in point . . .

Frene. Gu. 2 bars vair. Hugh de Fren. *V.*

Frenes. Gu. a bend az. fimbriated indented or. Sir Walter de Frenes. *N.* But the fimbriation arg. Sir Hugh de Frenes. *N.*

Frenes. Bendy of 6 az. and or. Hereford. *V.*

Frenes. Bendy of 6 or and gu. Sir Walter Frenes, co. Hereford. *V.*

Frennes. Per bend az. and arg. two bends engr. counterchanged. Sir Hugh de Frenes. *V.*

Frere (Co. Leicester). Sa. a chev. betw. 3 dolphins embowed arg.

Frescheville. Add: Monsire de Frechevile. *Y.* John Frechvile. *Y.* Frechevile, Staveley, co. Derby. *V.* And with a pierced mullet gu. on the bend for diff. Sir Rauf Frescheville. *S.*

Frese. Erm. on a chev. sa. 3 withered branches arg. Add: *V.*

Frese (London). Arg. an eagle displ. sa. quartering gu. a fleur-de-lis or. Crest: an eagle displ. sa. in its beak a mullet or. *Vis. Lon. 1633.*

Fresche. Per pale sa. and az. a wolf salient arg. *W.*

Freshford. Add: *V.***V.*

Freschevill. Az. on a bend betw. 6 escallops arg. a pierced mullet gu. in chief of the bend. Monsire Rauf Freschevill. *S.*

Frew (Scotland). Gu. on a chev. arg. 3 mullets az. *Robson.*

Frewod. Arg. on a chev. sa. an escallop of the first. Add: *V.*

Freyne. Gu. 2 bars indented az. and or. Rauf Freyn. *Y.*

Freyne. Gu. 2 bars indented arg. and az. Monsire de Freyn. *Y.* Hugh Freneyes. *Y.E.V.*

Freyne. Erm. 4 bars and in chief a demi-lion issuant gu. *V.*

Frier (of the Mountains of Dublin).

Frier. Per pale or and sa. 3 chevs. counterchanged in the dexter chief a lion ramp. of the second *Harl. MS. 1441.*

Froghall or Frognall (co. Kent). Add: *V.*

Fromantrill. Add: *V.V.**

Fromonds (Cheyhamco, Surrey and Hadlow, co. Kent). Add: *W.*

Fromont (Sparsholt, Hants.). Az. a chev. or. betw. 3 fleurs-de-lis arg.

Frost (Co. York). Arg. a chev.—delete—(another, a fess) . . . Add: *V.*

Frost (Norwich) . . . 2 chevs . . . overall a pelican vulning.

Frost (Norfolk). Erm. on a chev. voided az. betw. three 3-foils of the same 3 pelicans. . . . vulning gu.

Frost (Meadows Frost, Esq. J.P.). &c. . . . Add: Frost (Suffolk and Norwich). Same arms.

Froston (Suffolk). Arg. on a chev. sa. five 5-foils of the first. *V.*

Frothingham (South Frothingham, co. York). Insert—1584. Add: *F.Y.* Add: Frothingham (Holderness, co. York). *V.*

Frowicke (Wyley, co. Herts and North Mims, co. Middlesex).—delete—(another arg.). Add: Frowicke (   ). Same arms. *V.**

Frowicke (Lord Mayor of London 1435 and 1444). Add: Frowicke (Justiciarius Angliae). Same arms, the mullet sa. *V.*

Fry. Arg. 3 bars vert. *V.*

Fryer (Clan—amend to read 'Clare', co. Essex & c.). Add: *V.E.1612.*

Fryth (Thornes, Shenstone, co. Stafford). . . . Sa. on a chev.—insert—'counter'.

Fulford (Littleham, co. Devon). Gu. a chev. arg. Sir John Fulford. *Syl. Morgan.*

Fulford (Co. Devon and Pollard, co. Dorset). Add: Sir Humphry Fulford. *V.*

Fulferd or Fulford. Arg. a chev. betw. 3 inkmolines sa. *V.V.**

Fuller (Hyde House and Germans, co. Bucks). Add: Fuller, Inner Temple. Baronetcy 1687. Sir John Fuller, Kt. Chamberhouse, Berks. *L.N.* Fuller, co. Essex. 1634. *V.E.*

Fullerton. Marginal pencil reference 'says' blazon all wrong. †

Fulthorp. Sa. semee of annulets or a lion ramp. arg. Add: Sir Roger Fulthorp. *V.*

Furneauix (Paignton and Buckfastleigh, co. Devon). Add: Sir Simon de Forneax. *V.*

Furner (Brighton, co. Sussex). Az. a chev. vairy arg. and gu. betw. 3 lions ramp. or. *Debrett.*

Furness Abbey. Sa. a bend chequy arg. and az. *Tonge Tanner* gives the bend counter compony.

Furneux. Add: Mahen de Furneux. *G.*

Furnival (Baron Furnival . . . 1295). . . . Arg. a bend betw. six mascles—underlined—for ? martlets. Add: Sire Thomas de Forneval or Furneval. *N.K.H.J.V.B.* Gerard de Furnivall. *E.* Walter de Furnivalle. *C.* Sir Thomas de Furnival Baron of Sheffield. *Nobility Roll 25. Edw. j.* And with a label az. Sir William Furnival. *B.* And Furnivall, co. Hertford, temp. Hen. iij.

Furnivall (Worksop, co. Lincoln 1279). Arg. a bend betw. 6 martlets gu. a bordure of the last.

Furnivall. Arg. a bend gu. betw. 6 martlets sa. *V.*

Furnivall. Or a bend betw. 6 martlets gu. George Furnivall. *B.* Thomas Furnivall. *E.* Gerard Furnivall, Munden, his heiress married John Ufflete. *V.*

Futter (Thompson, co. Norfolk). Sa. a swan arg. betw. 2 flaunces or. *Blomfield.*

Fylingley. Add: *V.*

Fynch (Quartered by Tamworth). Sa. 3 bars arg. on the centre bar 3 martlets az. on a canton gu. a saltire of the second. *Harl. MS. 1436.*

Fysher (Lydhamwicke, co. Wilts.). Granted . . . —insert—by Camden.

Fytton. Erm. three annulets conjoined gu. Add: Sir John Fytton. *V.*

Fytton. Arg. on a bend az. 3 garbs. or. *V.*

G

GABOM. Arg. on a bend gu. 3 eagles displ. in pale of the shield or. William de Gabom. *F.*

Gabriel or Gabryell. Add: *V.*

Gabriell. Or 6 billets sa. Monsire Bartholomew Gabriel. *Y.*

Gaceline. Or 6 billets 3.2. and 1. az. a label of 5 points gu. Sire Symon Gaceline. *J.*

Gaddes. Arg. 3 billets sa. Richard Gaddes. *V.*

Gageworth or Gagworth. . . . marginal Query—Dagworth.

Gainsford. Add: *V.O.* Sir John Gainsford, Surrey, the greyhound coloured or. *V.*

Gaits (Scamer, co. York). Per pale az. and gu. 3 lions ramp. guard. arg. *Eliz. Roll. xxiv.*

Gall (Edinburgh). Arg. a bear sejant gu. in chief 2 crescents of the last in base an arm in armour fessways couped holding a dagger in pale ppr.

Gallane (Ireland). Arg. a chev. betw. 3 cocks gu.

Gallard or Galiard (*Her. Office, London*). Insert—confirmed by Segar. Az. a bend arg.—underlined—margin—'or' Add: *Vis. Lon. 1633.*

Gamage (Coyte and Roylade, co. Hertford). Add: Gamage (London). Same arms, quartering gu. fretty vair for Horne.

Gamage. Arg. a chief az. over all a bend gu. *Y.*

Gamage. Arg. a chief az. over all a bend fusilly gu. a label of 5 points arg. Adam de Gammage. *F.* Nichol de Gamage. *E.* the label or.

Gamage or Gammage. Arg. a chief az. over all a bend fusilly gu. Pain de Gamage. *F.* Rauf Gamage. *V.*

Gamage (Wales). Add: *V.V.** Sir William Gamage (Coyte). *V.*

Gamage. Arg. a bend lozengy gu. a chief az. Add: *V.** Add: Rauf Gamage. *V.*

Game. Insert—or Gam. (Newton in Brecknock). *Cady.* Add: Gamme. Sir Davy Gamme. Same arms. *V.*

Games. Or a lion pass. gu. Add: a pierced mullet on the shoulder. *V.*

Gamoll or Gamull (Co. Chester). *Coll. of Arms. London.* Add: Gamull (London). Same arms. Crest: a cubit arm erect vested gu. cuffed arg. hand ppr. holding three 3-foils slipped or. *Vis. Lon. 1633.*

Gams. Insert—or Gam (Newton, co. Brecknock). Add: *Cady.*

Ganford or Granford. Add: *V.**

Gant (Earl of Lincoln, Baron Gant). Add: *Nobility Roll. 25. Edw.j.*

Gantlet (Netherampton, co. Wilts.). Granted . . . —insert—by Walker, Garter.

Garband. Az. a tilting spear and battle axe . . . Add: *V.*

Garband (Jamaica, granted 28 Oct. 1768). Or a battle axe in bend sinister surmounted of a lance in bend dexter and in chief a dart barways pheon headed and feathered all ppr.

Gardell. Az. a chev. or betw. 3 fleurs-de-lis. arg. *V.*

Garden (Co. Cambridge). Add: Sir Thomas Gardyn. *N.V.*

Gardener (Himbleton, co. Worcester). Add: *W.*

Gardener. Per fess az. and arg. a camel tripping to the sinister gu. *Randle Holme.*

Gardener (Calais). Add: Gardener, co. Lincoln. *W.* Gardener, Northall, co. Lincoln, the lions pass. guard. *V.*

Gardener. Sa. a chev. betw. three half spades arg. Add: *V.*

Gardiner (London). Az. 6 griffins heads erased or. *Vis. Lon. 1633.*

Gardener (London). Sa. a chev. betw. three bugle horns arg. garnished or. *Z. 293.*

Gardener (Prior of Tynemouth). Same arms. *Tonge. p. 36.*

Gardiner (London). Per pale or and gu. a fess betw. 3 hinds trippant . . . Crest: . . . Add: *Vis. Lon. 1633.*

Gardiner (London and Beccles, co. Norfolk). Add: Gardner (Chardacre, Surrey). Same arms. *W.* Gardner (Lord Chief Justice of Ireland.) ob. 1619. *W.*

Gardiner (Richard Gardiner, D.D.). . . . Add: *Guillim.*

Gardiner (Letherhead, co. Surrey). . . . with eight *pellets*—underlined—and margin 'torteaux'. *V.* Add: Gardner of the Collar. *Harl. MS. 1404. fo. 129.*

Gardiner. Or a chev. gu. betw. 3 griffins heads erased az. *V.E. 1634.*

Gardner (London). Az. on a chev. embattled arg. betw. 3 griffins heads erased arg as many martlets sa Crest: A griffins head erased az. gorged with a mural crown or. *Vis. Lon. 1633.*

Gardner (Lancashire). Az. on a chev. betw. 3 griffins heads erased arg. as many martlets sa. on a chief or 3 crosses patty gu. *Robson.*

Gardner or Gardener (Wallingham and Bishops Norton, co. Lincoln). Add: Gardner (London). Same arms. Crest: a griffins head erased arg. *Vis. Lon. 1633.*

Gardner. Erm. on a chev. gu. 2 lions pass. respective arg. *Robson*

Gardners. Insert—(London). Add: *V.* Gardiner, Lord Mayor of London 1478.

Gardner (London). Pur. on a chev. arg. 3 escallops az. a chief of the third a cross patty or betw. 2 griffins heads erased of the second. *Harl. MS. 1404. fo. 108b.*

Gardon or Gavdon (Ireland). Arg. a chev. betw. 3 pierced cinquefoils gu.

Gare (Co. Kent). Add: Sir Simon At-Gare. *V.*

Garenne. Insert—i.e. Warren.

Garfoote (Hyde, co. Essex). Insert—*V.E. 1634* ...

Garford. Sa. 3 goats salient arg. Also Gatesford and Gayteford. *V.*

Garginton or Garwinton. Add: *V.*

Gargrave (Nostel, co. York). Add: Sir William Gardegrave. *V.*

Gargrave. . . . . Gargrave (Sir Thomas Gargrave, Sheriff of Yorkshire. temp. Elizabeth). Lozengy arg. and sa. on a bend of the first 3 crescents of the second. *Fuller. Hunter ij. 214.*

Garland (London). Or 3 pales gu. a chief per pale az. and gu. in the dexter chief a chaplet or in the sinister a demi-lion ramp. of the last. *Vis. Lon. 1633.*

Garnett. Gu. a lion ramp. arg. crowned or. within a bordure engr. of the last. *V.*

Garneys (Morningthorpe, Norfolk). Arg. a chev. engr. az. betw. 3 escallops sa. *Cady.*

Garnish. Arg. on a chev. az. betw. 3 escallops sa. a crescent or. Sir Christopher Garnish. Suffolk. *V.*

Garrard (London: granted 18 Dec. 1632). Add: Granted by St. George, Clarenceux in 1632 to John Garrad, one of the Grooms of the Privy Chamber to King Charles i. *Guillim.*

Garrard (London). Az. two lions—insert—ramp. guard. . . . . Crest: A wivern—insert—couchant . . . Add: *Vis. Lon. 1633.*

Garrett (London). Arg. a lion pass. betw. 2 flaunches sa. Crest: A lion pass. ermines holding a fleur-de-lis or. *Vis. Lon. 1633.*

Garry. Or 3 chevrons and a pile counter changed. **Book Plate.**

Garshall or Garshale (Cos. Warwick and Leicester . . .). Delete—(another gu.). Add: Sire Thomas de Garshalle. *N.*

Garth (Morden, co. Surrey and Headham, co. Durham). Add: *Vis. Lon. 1633.*

Garth or M'Grath (Galloway, Scotland). Quarterly per pale and chev. arg. and gu. †

Garter (Co. Norfolk). Or on a cross quarterly pierced . . .

Garter (London). Granted by Segar 1612. Similar arms and crest; But query, cross not pierced and 5 caltraps. *Vis. Lon. 1633.*

Gartside. Add: *V.L.*

Garway. Arg. a pile surmounted by a—delete—bend, substitute 'fesse' . . . Add: Garway (London, Lord Mayor 1640). Same arms. Crest: On a rock ppr. a cornish chough sa. beaked and legged gu. *Vis. Lon. 1633.*

Garwinton. Sa. a chev. betw. 3 pomegranates pendent arg. Add: *V.**

Garwinton, see Garginton.

Garwynton. Or on a chev. betw. 3 woodbine leaves gu. . . . Add: *V.*

Gaskarth (Hilltop, Cumberland). Or a chev. betw. 3 arrows ppr. points downwards. *Lysons.*

Gason. Az. a bend erm. cotised arg. betw. 3 goats heads . . . Add: *V.**

Gasselyn or Gasselyne. Add: Sir Edmund de Gascelyn, co. Hants. *V.N.* Gascelin. Or billetty sa. Sire Edmond Gaselyn. *O.* and with a label gu. Geffry Gascelyn. *B.* Gasceline. Or billety az. a label gu. Sir Walter Gasselyn Gasselyn or Gastelyn Or billety az. a bend gu. *L.N.* Sire Johan Gascelyne. *N.* Sire John Gasselyn de la Commune. *L.* Gacelin. Or billetty sa. a label of 5 gu. Edmond Gacelin. *E.* The label gu. fretty sa. Edmund Gasselin. *F.*

Gastelyne (Essex). Az. 4 hawks bells or conjoined in saltire by a double and wreathed cord alternately arg. and sa. *Cady.*

Gateford (Co. Salop). Add: *V.* John Gateford, Co. York. *Eliz. Roll. xxvj.*

Gatford. Sa. 3 goats ramp. arg. *V.**

Gategang (Durham). . . . a chev. . . . betw. . . . 3 goats heads couped. *Surtees.*

Gatentrye (Co. York). Arg. a chev. gu. betw. 3 mullets az. *Eliz. Roll. xxviij.*

Gates (Co. Essex and Semer, co. York). Add: *F.Y. p. 639.* Add: Gates (Thorne Park, co. York). 1665. Same arms, quartering Baldington, Capdow and Fleming. *Dugdale. p. 76.*

Gathpath or Gatpath. Vert. a chev. betw. 3 goats heads erased arg. armed or. *V.V.**

Gather (Scotland). Arg. a lion ramp. gu. quartering az. 3 goats or. *Cady.*

Gattiscombe. Add: *V.**

Gatton. Chequy arg. and az. Hamon de Gatton. *A.D.V.*

Gatton (Throwly, Kent). Same arms. Add: *MS. 14307. fo. 21.*

Gaudine. Add: *Cady.*

Gaunt, de. Add: Giles Gaunt. *V.*

Gaunt. Barry of 6 or and az. a bend gu. Gilbert de Gaunt, Swaledale. *X.N.P.* Geffry de Gaunt. *C.*

Gaunt. Az. an inescutcheon arg. Le Chastelon de Gaunt. *Y.*

Gaure. Or a lion ramp. crowned gu. a bordure indented sa. Sir John de Gaure. *D.*

Gausil. Add: Thomas Gausill. *X.*

Gaveston (Earl of Cornwall). . . . . Add: *V. Z. 141.*

Gawseworth. Insert—Chester. . . .

Gay (Elmsted and Peckham, co. Kent). Add: *V.*

Gaye. Gu. 3 lions ramp. arg. betw. 9 crosses crosslet or. *V.**

Gayer (London). Erm. a fleur-de-lis sa. on a chief of the last a mullet or. Crest: a lion ramp. sa. holding a tilting spear erect or. *Vis. Lon. 1633.*

Gaynsford (Idbury, co. Oxford). Add: and with an annulet for diff. Nicholas Gaynesford. temp. Hen. vij. In Church at Carshalton, co. Surrey.

Gays. Az. on a bend arg. 3 mullets gu. *V.*

Gaythold. Or a bend sa. . . . Add: *V.*

Geale. Arg. 2 bars sa. in chief three lions heads erased of the same langued gu.

Gearing (Winterton, co. Lincoln). . . . on a canton—delete—arg. substitute 'or'. Add: Crest: a leopards head winged or collared gu. charged with 3 mascles or. *Vis. Lon. 1633.*

Gebbe. Gu. a chev. erm. betw. 3 pine cones slip pendent or. *V.*

Gedding (Co. Norfolk). Add: Sir Robert Gedding, Leeford. *V.*

Gedding. Gu. a chev. or. betw. 3 griffin's heads erased arg. William Gedding temp. Henry IV. *V.* Sir John Geddinge.

Gedding. Gu. a chev. or betw. 3 griffins heads erased arg. on a chief of the second a lion pass. of the first. betw. 2 torteaux. *V.**

Gedney (Co. Suffolk). Add: *V.*

Geere (London). Gu. 2 bars arg. charged with 3 mascles of the field on a canton or a leopards head sa. Crest: An arm in armour, embowed and holding a broken falchin. *Vis. Lon. 1633.*

Geering (South Denchworth, co. Berks). Or on 2 bars az. 6 mascles of the field on a canton sa. a leopards head of the first.

Geffy. Erm. on a canton sa. a saltire engr. arg. *V.*

Geffrey. Arg. a chev. az. betw. 3 martlets gu. *Cady.*

Geffry (Co. Cornwall). Add: Geffrey . . . 5 billets in saltire . . . in chief a label of 3 points . . . Seal of Sir Robert Geffrey of London. 1658. Geffrey. Or 5 billets 3 and 2 sa. a label of 3 gu. *V.* The billets *in saltire* Geffrey, co. Cornwall. *V.V.**

Geffrays (London). Sa. a griffin segreant or a bordure engr. of the last. *Vis. Lon. 1633.*

Gegge. Arg. on a chev. betw. in chief 2 crescents and in base a cross bottony fitchy sa. a mullet of the first. *Harl. MS. 6829. fo. 52.*

Gelbe. Gu. a chev. erm. betw. 3 pine cones pendent or. *V.**

Geldart (Dr Geldart, co. Cambridge). Add: Geldard (Wiggenthorpe, co. York). Same arms. *Dugdale. 1665. p. 213.* See also Gildart.

Gelliat or Gellyot (co. York). . . . three boars heads (another, wiverns—insert—'*V.*', another fishes . . .

Geloner. Sa. a bend betw. 3 peacocks heads and necks erased arg. *V.*

Gelour. Arg. a bend gu. betw. 3 eagles heads erased sa. *V.*

Genevill (Baron Genevill:). . . . Add: Geffry de Genneville. *B.C.D.E.J.*

Le Genn. Arg. 3 lions ramp. sa. William le Genne. *A.*

Gennett or Jennett (Nargreave, co. Worcester). Arg. 2 chevs. betw. 2 martlets gu. quartering Jennets and Denham.

Gent (Essex). Erm. a chev. and a chief indented sa. *Morant's Essex ij. 354.*

Genton (Essex). Per bend sa. and arg. a bend raguly counterchanged. *V.*

Gerard (Sir Gilbert Gerard, Master of the Rolls 1581). Az. a lion ramp. erm. crowned or quartering arg. 3 torteaux betw. 2 bendlets sa. *Dug. O.J.*

Gerard (Creewood, co. Chester). Az. a lion ramp. erm. ducally crowned or. *Ormerod.*

Gerard (Co. Lancaster). Az. a lion ramp. erm. Add: *V.*

Gerdelley. Az. on a chev. engr. or betw. three fleurs-de-lis arg. a hurt. *V.*

Gergan, Gergand or Geerewood. Add: *V.**

Gergond (Cornwall). Per pale gu. and arg. 3 triangular castles counterchanged. *V.*

Gernald. Add: *V.*

Gernegan (Tanfield, Richmond). Add: shire. *V.*

Gernon. Or on a bend az. three escallops of the field. Add: Sir Nicholas Gernon. *V.*

Gernon. Arg. a chev. betw. three bucks heads couped sa. (another, bucks head gu.). Add: *V.*

Gernon. Or on a bend az. an escallop or. Add: *V.*

Gernon. Arg. a chev. sa. betw. 3 bucks heads cabossed gu. *V.**

Gernon. Arg. a chev. sa. betw. 3 bucks heads cabossed of the second attired or. *V.*

Gerton. Gu. 12 billets . . . Add: Sir Thomas Gerton or Gorton. *V.*

Gervays. Az. 3 beacons with ladders or. . . . Add: *V.*

Gerveis (Granted to Wm. Gerveis of Great Pitley, co. Lancaster by Camden, May 1614). Sa. a chev. erm. betw. 3 birds arg. *Syl. Morgan.*

Gerwoys. Gu. 3 greyhounds courant in pale arg *V*

Gerveys (Bonathlac, co Cornwall). . . . Add: *V.C. p. 304.*

Gerveys. Arg. a chev. az. betw. 3 escallops sa. Robert Gerveys. *X.*

Gethyn. Arg. a chev. engr. az. betw. three birds rising sa. . . . Add: *V.* *V.*

Gevill (Quartered by Cave . . . Rutland). . . . Add: *C.R. p. 37.*

Gey. Arg. a lion ramp. sa. over all on a bend gu. 3 round buckles or. Wat de Gey. *E.F.*

Gibault or Gibaut (Jersey). Az. a tower or masoned sa.

Gidden. Arg. 2 bars az. betw. in chief a cross gu. and in base a chev. of the last. *Randle Holme.*

Gibbes. Arg. 3 battle axes in fess sa. co. Devon. *Harl. MS. 1458.* Sir Henry Gibbs, co. Warwick. 1619. *W.*

Gibbes. Or on a chev. sa. two cats . . . Add: *V.**

Gefforth. Az. a chev. or betw. 3 goats heads erased arg. *V.*

Gibbins. Arg. a lion ramp. gu. over all on a bend of the first 3 crosses patty fitchy sa. *W.*

Gibbons (Glamorganshire). Or a lion ramp. sa. armed gu. over all on a bend of the last 3 crosses patty fitchy arg.

Gibbon or Gubyon (Norfolk). Or a lion ramp. sa. over all on a bendlet gu. 3 escallops arg. *W.*

Gibbon. Sheriff of Norfolk 1513. *Dashwood.* Same arms.

Giddon. Sir Francis Gibbon (Thursford, Norfolk). Same arms. 1682. *L.N.*

Gibbon (Rolvendon, co. Kent). Granted—insert —by Segar . . .

Gibbon or Guybon (Sheriff of Norfolk 1513). Add: Crest: a demi-lion ramp. sa. charged with 3 escallops.

Gibbon. Arg. a lion pass. sa. over all two bills or battle axes in saltire the staves gu. headed of the first. *V.*

Gibbon (London). Az. a lion ramp. guard. betw. 3 escallops arg. Crest: A demi-wolf ramp. reguard. arg. murally gorged gu. *Vis. Lon. 1633.*

Gibbons (Sittingbourne, co. Kent. bart). Insert— 1872 . . .

Gibbons (Oxford). Sa. a lion ramp. guard. or over all two bars gu.

Gibbs (Mr. Harrington Gibbs, Merchant of Bristol). Gu. 3 battle axes arg. 2 and 1: quartering 2nd. a fret gu. 3rd. Or on a bend az. 3 cinquefoils arg. †

Gibbs (Co. Hertford). Add: Gibbs (London). Same arms, within a bordure or. Same Crest: *Vis. Lon. 1633.*

Gibbs or Gybbes. Paly bendy sinister arg. and gu. on a bend arg. two fleurs-de-lis. or. *V.*

Gibon. Arg. a chev. sa. betw. three lions heads erased gu. . . . Add: *V.**

Gibon. Or a chev. gu. betw. three lions heads erased sa. Add: *V.**

Gibons or Gibus. Add: *V.** Thomas Gibons. *V.*

Gibon. Or a chev. gu. betw. 3 lions heads erased az. *V.*

Gibson (Hatton Garden, London 1716). Gu. an anchor arg. on a chief or 3 roses of the first.

Gibson (Staveley, co. York). Add: *Guillim.*

Gibson. (Teede, co. Lancaster.) Granted 5 June 1557–8. Gu. 3 lions pass. in pale and 2 bars humetty arg. *Harl. MS. 1359. fo. 80.*

Gibthorp, Gythorpe or Gilthorpe. Add: *V.*

Gibwyn (Wales). Arg. on a bend az. 3 lions ramp. of the field. *Robson.*

Giffard. Erm. 2 bars gu. on a chief of the last a lion pass. guard. or. Osborne Giffard. *E.Y.*

Giffard (Lord Giffard of Brimsfield). . . . Add: Sir John Giffard *D.E.F.G.C.N.* Sir John Giffard. Brymmesfled, co. Gloucester. *V.* William Giffard. *Y.* And with a label of 5 az. Giffard le Bef. *A.* John Giffard de Bef. *E.* And with a label of 3 sa. Sir Simon Giffard, co. Gloucester. *V.* Sir Esmond Giffard. *N.*

Giffard. Arg. crusilly a lion ramp. gu. William Giffard. *E. Y.*

Giffard (Robert Giffard). Or 5 annulets one within the other vert. embracing and depressed by a cross engr. gu. *A.*

Giffard. Gu. 3 lions pass. in pale arg. within a bordure or. Elys Giffard. *A.*

Gifford (Robert Gifford). Arg. 5 annulets one within the other az. alternatively oppressing a cross engr. sa. *Harl. MS. 6137.*

Gifford (Scotton, co. York 1612). Gu. 3 lions pass. in pale arg. in dexter chief a pierced mullet for diff. *F. Y.*

Gifford (London). Arg. a lion statant guard. gu. on a chief az. 3 stirrups or. Crest: a demi-lion ramp. az. holding a stirrup or. *Vis. Lon. 1633.*

Gigon. Add: *V.**

Gilbard (Co. Sussex). . . . Add: *C.L. p. 37.*

Gilbard or Gilbert. Arg. on a chev. gu. three roses of the field a bordure sa. *Cady.*

Gilberd (Quartered by Richard Wilkynson). . . . Add: *C.L. p. 57.*

Gilbert (Co. Devon). Erm. on a chev. sa. 3 roses arg. *V.*

Gilbert (Compton, co. Devon). Arg. on a chev. sa. 3 roses of the first. *V.D. 1620.*

Gilbert. Erm. on a chev. engr. sable 3 roses arg. *C.C. p. 57.*

Gilbert (Exeter 1539). Or on a chev. sa. 3 roses of the field. *Colby.*

Gilbert (Colchester, co. Essex). Arg. on a chev. betw. 3 leopards faces az. as many roses of the field. *V.E. 1634.*

Gilbert (Somerson, co. Suffolk and London). Add: *C.L.*

Gilborne (Co. Kent). Add: *V.**

Gilderch. Sa. a chev. arg. betw. three martlets or. *V.V.**

Giles or Gille. Insert—(Norfolk). Per fesse gu. and az. . . . Add: *V.*

Gill (Co. Hertford). Add: *Vis. Lon. 1633.*

Gill (Hertfordshire 1634). Lozengy or and vert. a lion ramp. guard. gu.

Gill (Co. Hertford). Sa. a bend or on a chev. arg. 3 mullets of the first, a canton of the second charged with a lion ramp. gu. *Harl. MS. 1404. fo. 109.*

Gill (Dartford, Kent). Sa. on a chev. arg. 3 pierced mullets of the first, a canton or charged with a lion pass. guard. gu.

Gill (Bokeland, co. Hertford). Sa. on 2 chevs. arg. betw. in chief a canton or charged with a lion pass. guard. gu. and in base a pierced 5-foil of the second. 3 pierced mullets in the lower chev. as the field. *W.*

Gill (Bickham Park, co. Devon). Add: *A.A.*

Gilles. Per fesse gu. and—delete—'or' . . . read 'or' *V.**

Gillesland (Co. Lincoln). Chequy or and gu. Sir . . . de Gillesland. *V.*

Gilliott. Per bend indented sa. and arg. "D'argent a une chief de sable endentes embeleif": ill port bend indente de sable et d'argent. Nicholas Gilliott, Merkington. *X.*

Gilliott. Erm. on a bend sa. 3 fishes heads erased arg. *V.N. 166.*

Gilman (London). Arg. a man's leg couped at the thigh in pale sa. gartered below the knee or in the dexter chief an annulet of the second. Crest: An arm embowed sa. holding a javelin or lined or. *Vis. Lon. 1633.*

Gilpin (Hockliffe Grange, co. Bedford. bart). Insert—1876 . . .

Gilpin (Scaleby, co. Cumberland). Add: Gilpin (Leighton Buzzard. M.P. for Bedfordshire 1851). Same arms. *Debrett.*

Gipp or Gypses. Add: *Vis. Lon. 1633.*

Girley (Co. York). Erm. 3 martlets gu. *Eliz. Roll. xxxj.*

Girlington or Gerlington. . . . Co. Lancaster. Insert—*V.L. 1664.* . . . volant sa.—insert—*V.** . . .

Girlington (Co. York). Arg. a chev. betw. three gadflies sa. *Eliz. Roll. xxix.*

Girlington (Co. Lincoln 1640). Add: Girlington (Hackford, co. York). Same arms, quartering Montfort and Aclom. *F. Y.*

Gise. Lozengy gu. and vair a canton or. Sir Anncell de Gise. *E.A.* and with a mullet sa. on the canton for diff. *F.*

Gissing or Gissinge. Add: *V.* Sir Thomas Gissing. *S.*

Gistelle. Gu. a chev. erm. Gaultier de Gistelle. *C.*

Glagg. Delete—(another, or). . . . Add: *V.*

Glagge. Gu. on a bend or three 5-foils of the field.

Glanfield. Az. a lion ramp. arg. a label of 3 points gu. *V.*

Glanton. Az. on a chev. betw. 3 crosses patonce arg. an annulet sa. for diff. *V.*

Glasbrook. Add: Glazebrook of Glazebrook, Co. Lancaster. Same arms. *F.L.*

Glascock (Much Dunmow . . . co. Essex). Add: *Vis. Lon. 1633.*

Glasscock (Briseth and High Easter, Essex). Erm. on a chief sa. betw. 3 cocks az. legged and combed or a bezant. *V.E. 1634.*

Glastenbury (Co. Dorset). Arg. a bend lozengy sa. Add: Glastonbury. Arg. a bend engr. sa. Sir Henry Glastonbury. *L.N.* John Glastonbury. *Y.* But shewn or described as a bend fusilly sa. Sir Henry Glastonbury. *R.V.*

Glastenbury. Or a bend engr. sa. Add: Sir Henry Glastonbury (Co. Somerset). *V. Y.*

Gleg (Dr. Thomas Gleg, Edinburgh 1672). . . . Add: Glegg of Gayton. Same arms. *Randle Holme.*

Glegg. Sa. two lions pass. guard. arg. depressed by as many palets gu. Add: Glegg (Wyrall, co. Chester). *V.*

Glenham, Gleman or Glemham. Add: *V.* Henry Glemham, Bishop of St. Asaph. 1667-70.

Glenton or Glynton. Add: Henry Glenton, Founder of Kenilworth Priory. *V.*

Glesquine. Arg. an eagle displ. . . . a baston gu. *Cady.*

Glisson (Rampisham, co. Dorset). Add: Francis Glisson, M.D. Add: Dr. Glisson, Professor of Physic to Cambridge University. *Cady.*

Glisson or Cliston (Co. Somerset) . Add: *V.S.*

Gloucester (Co. Gloucester). Arg. three lions —insert—ramp. . . . Add: Monsire de Gloucestre. *Y.* Sir Walter de Gloucestre. *N.O.*

Gloucester (John de Gloucester, Sheriff of London 1345). Gu. a chev. arg. betw. in chief 2 leopards faces or and in base a fish haurient of the second. *Harl. MS. 1349. fo. 63.*

Glover (Co. Norfolk). 1611 . . . Add: Glover (London). Same arms and in centre chief an estoile or. *Vis. Lon. 1633.*

Glover (London). Az. a fess embattled erm. betw. 3 crescents arg. Crest: An eagle displ. ermines. *Vis. Lon. 1633.*

Glover (Thomas Glover, Esquire of). . . . Add: *Guillim.*

Glyd (Sussex and London). Arg. on a bend az. betw. 3 annulets sa. 6 fleurs-de-lis 2.2. and 2. betw. 2 crosses crosslet or. Crest: A demi-griffin sa. winged collared and lined gu. *Vis. Lon. 1633.*

Glyd (Sussex). Arg. on a bend betw. 3 annulets sa. 6 lucies 2.2. and 2.

Glyn (Cornwall). Arg. an eagle displ. double headed sa., a bordure of the last bezanty. *V.*

Glyn (Baron Wolverton). Insert—1869. . . .

Goadefroy. Gu. an anchor—insert—in pale. . .

Goband. Sa. a bend betw. 6 martlets arg. Sir John Goband. *V.*

Goband, Gobond or Gobaud. Gu. 2 bars or in chief 3 bezants. Sir Johan Goband. *N.* Sir John Goband, co. Lincoln. *V.* Monsire de Goband. *Y.*

Gobion. Bendy of six or and az. a lion pass. guard. arg. . . . Add: Sir Hugh Gobyon. *V.*

Gobion (Sir Hugh Gobion temp. Edw. ij.). Barry of 12 arg. and gu. a label of 3 points az. *E. F. Y.*

Gobion. Paly of 8 arg. and gu. on a bend sa. three escallops of the first. *V.* But the escallops or. Sir Hugh Gobyon. *V.*

Gobion. Barry of eight arg. and gu. on a bend sa. three escallops or. *V.*

Godard (Walpole, co. Norfolk). Gu. an eagle displ. or . . . Add: *V.*

Godbold (Hatfield, co. Essex). . . . Add: *V.E. 1634.*

Godbow. Add: *V.*

Goddard. Gu. an eagle displ. or Guybon Goddard, Serjeant at Law. *Dug. O. J.*

Goddard (Cliffe Pypard &c., co. Wilts.). Add: Goddard (co. Norfolk). Same arms. *W.*

Goddin (Co. Kent). Add: *W.*

Goddinge. Add: *V.*

Goderich. Arg. 2 lions pass. guard. sa. Sir William Goderiche. *S.*

Godfrey (Great Yarmouth, co. Norfolk). Sa. a chev. betw. 3 pelicans arg. vulning gu.

Godfrey (Kent). Sa. a chev. betw. 3 pelicans heads and necks erased or vulned gu. *W.* Sir Edmondsbury Godfrey 1666. Same arms. A crescent for diff. *L.N.*

Godhand. Arg. a chev. countercompony or and az. betw. 3 sinister hands apaumy couped sa. *V.*

Godmanston or Goodmanston. Add: *V.*

Godmanston. Gu. an eagle displ. arg. Joan de Godemonestone. *E.*

Godolphin (Baron and Earl of Godolphin . . . co. Cornwall). . . . Insert—*V.*

Godolphin (Cornwall). Gu. a double headed eagle displ. arg. betw. 3 fleurs-de-lis or. *V.C. p. 304.*

Godschalk (London). Per bend wavy az. and arg. a bend wavy counterchanged. Crest: A wing arg. charged with a bend as in the field. *Vis. Lon. 1633.*

Godwin (Co. Devon). Or 2 lions pass. az. *Colby.*

Godwin. Or 3 lions ramp. sa. . . . Add: *V.* Thomas Godwyn, Bishop of Bath and Wells, 1584–90. *Harl. MS. 1359. fo. 119.*

Gokin or Gookeine. Add: Gokin or Gookin (Bekisborne and Ripple Court, Kent, quartering Durant 1575). Same arms. *Hasler's Kent iv. 132.*

Golafre of Blakesley. Barry nebuly of 6 arg. and gu. on a bend sa. 3 bezants. *Baker.*

Golafre. Barry wavy gu. and arg. on a bend sa. 3 bezants. John Golafre. *X.*

Golafre (Fyfield, co. Berks.). Add: Sire John Golafre. *S.* (Barry wavy).

Golafre. Arg. 4 bars wavy gu. on a bend sa. 3 bezants Sir John Golafre ob. 1442. **Tomb** in Fyfield Church, Berks.

Golafre. Vairy gu. and arg. on a bend sa. 3 bezants, Thomas Golafre. *Y.*

Golbore. Add: *V.*

Golborne. Arg. on a bend sa. 3 crosses patonce or. Add: Sir Thomas Golborne. *V.*

Gold (London). Or on a chev. betw. 3 roses az. as many bunches of grapes of the field. Crest: A hawk rising holding in its beak a bunch of grapes † for diff. *Vis. Lon. 1633.*

Goldesburg. Per pale or and az. on a chev. betw. 3 bulls heads erased as many fleurs-de-lis all counterchanged. *Nash.*

Golding (Halstead, cos. Essex and Suffolk). Add: *V.* † for diff. *V.E. 1558.*

Golding. Vert. 3 goldfinches or. *Randle Holme.*

Golding (Colson Bassett, co. Notts.). Insert—Baronetcy 1642 . . . Add: *V.N. 1614.*

Goldingham (Barnham, co. Norfolk). . . . Add: *V.*

Goldingham (Norfolk). Arg. 2 bars wavy gu. *V.*

Goldingham. Barry nebuly of 6 erm. and gu. Mon. Alexander Goldingham. *S.*

Goldingham. Barry wavy arg. and gu. a label az. Sire Aleyn de Goldingham. *N.*

Goldington (Co. Bedford). Add: Sir Rauf de G. *N.*

Goldington. Gu. a bend flory counterflory or. *V.*

Goldington. Or 2 lions pass. gu. crowned arg. *V.* Sir Robert Goldington, co. Beds. temp. Edw. j.

Goldington. Or 2 lions pass. guard. sa. Sir John de Goldington. *R.* and with a label gu. Sire John de Goldington. *O.*

Goldington. Or on a bend az. five fleurs-de-lis of the first palewise. Add: *V.*

Goldoury (1528). Add: *V.* Add: Reginald Goldourg. *Cotton MS. Tiberius. D. 10.*

Goldoury. Sa. a chev. or betw. 3 wolves heads erased arg. *V.*

Goldsmith. Sa. on a chev. betw. 3 wolves heads erased arg. a crescent . . . error for Goldourg.

Goldsmith (London and Kent). Gu. a chev. arg. between 3 goldfinches arg. beaked and legged or. on a chief of the third a lion pass. of the first. *Vis. Lon. 1633.*

Goldwell. Az. a chief or. over all a baton arg. . . . Add: *V.*

Goldwell. Az. a chief or over all a lion ramp. arg. billettee. Add: sa. Add: Goldwell (Wisbeach, co. Cambridge and Bury St. Edmonds, co. Suffolk). Same arms. Geoffrey Goldwell (Great Chard, Kent). Same arms. *V.*

Golover. Arg. 3 bars nebuly gu. on a bend sa. as many bezants. *V.*

Golston. Barry nebuly of 6 arg. and gu. on a bend sa. 3 bezants. *V.*

Gomersall (London). . . . Add: *C.L.*

Gonneys or Gouneys. Gu. a chev. erm. *X.*

Gonton. Gu. 3 round buckles or. points to the sinister. Add: *V.*

Gonway or Goneway. Add: *Harl. MS. 1404. fo. 115.*

Gooch (Clewer Park, co. Berks. bart.). Insert—1866 . . .

Gooch (Benacre Hall, Suffolk). Baronetcy 1746. Per pale arg. and sa. a chev. betw. 3 talbots statant counterchanged on a chief gu. as many leopards heads or. John Gooch (London). *V.*

Gooch. Paly of 6 arg. and sa. a chev. betw. 3 talbots pass. of the first the talbots spotted sa. a crescent gu. for diff. Dr. Gooch. *Cady.*

Gooddaye. . . . Crest: . . . sejant erm.—read 'ermines'. Add: *Vis. Lon. 1633.*

Goode. Add: *V.C. 304.*

Goodden (Bower Hinton . . . co. Somerset). Add: *Collinson Somerset. iij. ii.*

Goodladd (Essex). Arg. on a chev. az. a sun betw. two crescents. *Cady.*

Goodman. Per pale ermines and erm. an eagle displ. with two heads per pale arg. and sa. Add: *V.*

Goodman (*Ulster's Office*). Add: *V.*

Goodmanston. Az. an eagle displ. or. *V.*

Goodneston (Co. Kent). Add: *V.*

Goodricke (Ribstone Hall, co. York.). . . . Add: Sir Henry Goodrich. Bart. of Ribstone Park. Envoy Extraordinary to the King of Spain in 1682. bore for supporters two naked boys ppr and for Motto: "Fortior leone justus." *Blomfield.*

Goodwin or Goodwyn. Add: Per pale gu. and or. a lion ramp. &c., *Vis. Lon. 1633.* Add: Granted to Goodwin (East Grinstead, co. Sussex).

Goodwin (Rawmarsh, co. York). *Dugdale—* amend to *1666* and Add: Granted by Camden 24 May 1665.

Goodwin (Torrington, co. Devon). . . . Add: Goodwin (London). Same arms and crest, but a crescent instead of an annulet. *Vis. Lon. 1633.*

Goodwynston (Kent temp. Hen. iij). Sa. 3 martlets betw. 7 crosses crosslet arg. *Robson.*

Googe. Insert—Wales and London. Per pale sa. and arg. . . . Add: *V.*

Googh or Googe. Add: *V.** John Gough. *V.*

Goold (Sir Henry Goold Serjeant at Law 1693/4). Az. a lion ramp. or betw. 3 rolls arg. *L.N.*

Gore (London). Gu. a fess betw., three crosses crosslet fitchy or † for diff. Crest: On a mount vert. and heraldic tiger salient arg. *Vis. Lon. 1633.*

Gore. Az. 3 lions ramp. arg. on a chief gu. a demi-lion ramp. couped or. George de Gore. *V.*

Gorges (Wraxall, Langford &c., . . .). Add: John le Gorge. *X.* Sir Theobald Gorges. *V.*

Gorges. Arg. 5 annulets one within the other az. *V.*

Gorges. Rauf de Gorges. Az. 5 annulets one within the other arg. *V.*

Gorges (Lord Dundalk). . . . Add: *Harl. MS. 4040. fo. 446.*

Goring (Highden, co. Sussex, bart.). Add: *V.* Add: Goring (Burton, Sussex, Baronetcy 1622). Same arms. *Guillim.*

Gorney. Sa. a chev. betw. 3 bulls heads cabossed or. Armed gu. Sir John Gorney. *V.*

Gorney. Arg. a bend engr. az. Sir William Gorney, Normandy. *Q. Harl. MS. 6595.*

Gorney (Co. Essex). Az. on a bend cotised arg. three leopards faces gu. crowned or. Add: *V.*

Gorsuch (London). Coat granted by Cook in 1574 to Robert Hillson of London and continued to the descendents of Gorsuch to bear as their paternal coat). Sa. 2 bars engr. arg. betw. 3 fleurs-de-lis or. Crest: Out of a ducal coronet per pale arg. and gu. a demi-lion ramp. guard arg. *Vis. Lon. 1633.*

Gorton (Gorton and other places, co. Lancaster). Add: Sir Thomas Gorton. *V.*

Gosewyn or Goswyn. Add: *Harl. MS. 1404. fo. 59.*

Gosheche or Gostresche. Arg. a bend lozengy of the first and gu. *V.**

Gosholmh. Add: *V.*

Gosselyn. Gu. a chev. or betw. 3 crescents erm. *V.*

Gostile (Northamptonshire). Gu. an annulet or. *Syl. Morgan.*

Gostwick (Willington, co. Bedford. bart.). Insert —1612 . . .

Gostwick (Co. Bedford. Master of the Horse to Hen. VIII). Add: Sir John Gostwyke co. Bedford. *V.*

Gostwick (Co. Cornwall). Arg. a bend gu. betw. 2 cotises and 6 ravens sa. on a chief or 3 mullets vert. *V.*

Gotesley or Gotysby. Add: *V.*

Gotham. Or—delete—(another, arg.). . . . Add: *V.*

Gotham. Erm. on a bend gu. three barrulets wavy or. Add: *V.*

Gotham. Gu. 3 goats pass. arg. *V.**

Gotham (Richard Gotham). Gu. 3 goats statant arg. *V.*

Gotham (Lees in Norton, co. Derby). Per fess embattled or and sa. 3 goats trippant counterchanged. *Lysons.*

Gough (Co. Lincoln). 1640 and Wales. Add: Matthew Goughe. *V.*

Gould (Exeter . .). . . . Crest: . . . demi-lion ramp.—insert—az. . . . Add: Gould (London). *W. Vis. Lon. 1633.*

Goulston (Co. Hertford). Arg. 3 bars nebuly vert. on a bend of the first 3 torteaux.

Gournay. Or a lion ramp. sa. within a bordure gu. Robert de Gourney. *B.* Sir William de Gournay. temp. Edw. j. *V.*

Gousall (Kent. temp. Edw. iij.). az. simply.

Goushill (Co. Essex). Add: *V.*

Goushill (Co. Derby). Add: the heiress mar. Wingfield 16th cent. Sir Nicoll Goushill. *S.* and with a label of 3 points az. Monsire Nicoll his Son. *S. Lysons.*

Goushill (Norfolk). Barry of 6 arg. and gu. a canton erm. *V.*

Gousley. Add: *Y.*

Goverley. Insert—Kent, Add: *V.*

Govis or Gouvis of Crichal. Vair a bend eng. gu. Brian de Gouvis. *E.*

Gowby. Add: *V.*

Gowe. Add: David Gowe. *V.*

Gower. Az. a chev. betw. 3 griffins heads erased or. *V.O. 216.*

Gower (Durham). Add: *C.*

Gower (Stainsby, co. York). Gu. a chev. arg. betw. 3 gowers or wolves pass. of the second: quartering arg. on a saltire gu. 3 crosses crosslet or for Crathorne. *F. Y.*

Gowrla (of that Ilk). Arg. 3 falcons close gu. *Guillim.*

Gowtheton. Add: *V.*

Goylin. Az. on a bend betw. 2 eagles displ. arg. . . . Add: *V.*

Goylin. Per pale gu. and az. add: *V.V.**

Goylin. Per pale gu. and az. on a bend arg. 3 garbs vert. in the sinister chief an eagle displ. of the third. *Harl. MS. 1404. fo. 109.*

Grace (Barons of Courtstown). . . . Add: Grace (Beconsfield, co. Bucks and London). Same arms and crest: a mullet for diff. *Vis. Lon. 1633.*

Grace. Per chev. gu. and or 3 gem rings counterchanged. *V.*

Grace (Ellington, co. Hunts.). Add: *V.H. 1613.*

Grace of Newland. Gu. a lion ramp. or head and mane arg. *Randle Holme.*

Grace. As quartered by Gascoigne of Barnbow, co. York. *Dugdale. p. 289.*

Grace. Gu. a lion ramp. the head arg. divided by a line of erasure from the body within an orle of 7 cinquefoils or. *V.*

Grafton. Gyronny of eight erm. and sa. a lion ramp. or. Granted by Camden Feb. 1605. *Syl. Morgan.*

Grafton (Grafton Flyford, co. Worcester and co. Stafford). . . . Add: Grafton (London). *V.*

Gramary. Gu. billettee or a lion ramp. arg. Add: William Gramary. *Y.*

Gramary. Henry. Gu. crusilly bottony or a lion ramp. arg. *Y.*

Grandison or Grandson (Co. Lancaster). Add: *V.** Add: Sir William Grandison temp. Edw. j. *V.* Sir William Grauntson. *I.Q. Harl. MS. 6595. H.I.K.N.* Sir Peers de Graunson. *V.*

Grandison. Paly of 6 arg. and az. on a bend gu. 3 round buckles or. Sir Otheo de Graundison. *R.* Sir William Grandeson. *V. Y.*

Grandison. Paly of 6 arg. and az. on a bend gu. three escallops or. Sire de Granson. *F.* Otes de Grantson. *A. Harl. MS. 6137. D.E.* But paly az and arg. *J.X.*

Grandon (Co. Leicester). . . . —insert—*Cady.* Crest: . . .

Grandon. Vairy arg. and sa. on a bend gu. 3 eagles displ. of the first. Sir John Grandon. Co. Warwick. t. Edw. j. *V.*

Grandone. Vairy arg. and sa. a bendlet or. Sir John de Grandon. *L.N.*

Granetz (Wales). Or a lion ramp. sa. goutty d'eau. *V.*

Grange (Sir Henry Grange alias Garnett). Gu. a lion ramp. arg. crowned or within a bordure engr. of the last. *V.*

Grange (Wolsingham. co. Chester &c.). Insert —1568 . . . Add: *C.L.*

Granson. Az. on a bend arg. 3 escallops gu. Monsire de Granson. *Y.*

Grant (Ingoldesthorpe Hall, co. Norfolk). Gu. a lion pass. guard. arg. imperially crowned ppr. betw. 3 antique crowns or. *A.A.*

Grant (Crundall, co. Hants. 1716). Arg. 3 lions ramp. and a chief az.

Grant. Canon of Exeter. Same arms. *Colby.*

Gant. Misspelt, correct to read Grant (Aberlour, co. Banff. 1810 . . .).

Grassell. Sa. two bars engr. or. Henry Grarscle. *V.*

Graunford. Arg. 2 lion pass. in pale sa. crowned or. *V.*

Graunte. Erm. on a chev. gu. 5 plates. *V.*

Grave or Grane. Per bend gu. and vert.—insert— *V.* (another, vert. and gu. an eagle displ. or). Add: *V.*

Graver.

Gravenor. See Grosvenor.

Graves (Granted in 1592 to Graves, co. Northampton). James Grayve, co. York and John Grave, London. *W.*

Graves. Gu. an eagle displ. crowned arg. Richard Graves. *Dug. O.J.*

Graves or Grove (Hull, co. York). Or on a chev. gu. an escallop of the field. *F.Y.*

Gravesend (Kent). Or 3 eagles displ. sa. a canton erm. *V.* Sir Stephen de Gravesend. *N. Harl. MS. 6589.*

Gravesend. Erm. on a bend sa. 3 martlets arg. *V.V.**

Gravette (London). Az. a fess embattled erm. betw. 3 wolves heads erased arg. Crest: A wolf statant per pale erm. and arg. *Vis. Lon. 1633.*

Graville. Az. 3 round buckles, tongues to the dexter or. *V.*

Gray. Gu. a lion ramp. arg. holding in its dexter paw a thistle all within a bordure engr. of the second. †

Gray (Baron Gray) . . . Add: Sir Thomas Gray. *S.Y.* and with a baton az. Sir Thomas Gray. *M.*

Gray (M.P. for Bolton 1868). Az. a lion ramp. within an orle of annulets arg. a bordure indented erm. *Debrett.*

Gray (Crompton Fold, Lancashire). Same arms. *F.L.*

Gray (Bishopwearmouth, co. Durham). Add: Gray of Heton. Same arms. *X.Y.*

Gray (Ralph Gray, Sheriff of Newcastle 1628). Barry of 6 arg. and az. on a bend gu. a bezant in chief 6 martlets for diff. *Carr. MS.*

Gray (Thomas Gray, Barton, co. York). Barry of 6 arg. and az. a bend gu. in chief a crescent for diff. *Eliz. Roll. xxx.*

Gray or Grey (Granted in July 1612 by Camden to Sir Richard Grey Secretary in Ireland). Arg. 3 bars az. in chief as many annulets gu.

Graydon (Hemisland, Kent). Az. 3 otters each holding in its mouth a fish arg. *Robson.*

Greathed (Lincoln 1745). . . . 4 bars betw. 10 martlets 3.2.2.2. and 1. **Tomb** in Lincoln Cathedral.

Greathed (Co. Dorset). Arg. 2 bars plain betw. 2 others engr. per pale az. and sa. an orle of martlets gu.

Green (John Green, Judge of the Sheriff Court, London. 1633–4) Az. 3 stags statant or a slipped 3-foil in chief for diff. *Harl. MS. 1358. fo. 43.*

Green. Vert. 3 bucks statant at gaze or. *Z. 490.*

Green (Poulton Hall, co. Chester). Az. three bucks trippant erminois—insert—sometimes or. . . . .

Green or Greene (Ireland). Az. an anchor betw. 3 escallops arg.

Green (Great Milton, co. Oxford). Az. a chev. erm. betw. 3 bucks statant or. *V.O.*

Green (London). Az. 3 bucks trippant or. Crest: A buck's head couped or. *Vis. Lon. 1633.*

Green (Essex). Per fess gu. and arg. a lion ramp. arg. and sa. crowned or. *V.*

Green (Witham, co. Essex). Gu. a lion ramp. arg. *V.E. 1612.*

Green. Az. 3 bucks statant or. Sire Thomas Green. *S.*

Green (Stretly, co Essex. 1634). Az. 3 bucks trippant or in the middle chief a 3-foil slipped charged with a †.

Green correction: (I. Wilby; 2. co. Norfolk). Add: *W.*

Green (Co. Northampton). Az. three bucks pass. or—delete—(another, ppr.). Add: Sir Thomas Green. *V.* And with a mullet in chief or for diff. Sir William Green, co. Oxford, confirmed by Camden Feb. 1605. *Harl. MS. 6095. fo. 22.*

Green (Newby, co. York). Add: *V.W.*

Greene. Arg. on a chev. gu. 3 fleurs-de-lis sa. an escallop of the field. *Constable's Roll. xv.*

Green. Arg. fretty sa. on a canton of the second a buck pass. or. Add: The canton az. and buck courant or. *V.V.**

Green. Chequy—delete—or and arg. (another, . . .). Add: John Greene. *X.*

Green (Sheffield). Green (Bancke, co. York 1666). Same arms. Add: *Dugdale. p. 306.*

Greenacre. Sa. 3 covered cups arg. an annulet for diff. Robert Greeacre.

Greenaker. Vert.—delete—(another, sa.). . . . . Add: *V.V.**

Greenall (Dalton Hall, Warrington. M.P. 1874). Or on a bend gu. 3 bugle horns stringed. . . .

Greenall (Walton Hall, co. Lancaster, bart.). Insert—1826.

Greenaway. See Greenway.

Greene (Chester). Gu. on a lion ramp. per fess arg. and sa. crowned or a trefoil slipped vert. *Harl. MS. 1535. fo. 15b.*

Greene (Mitcham, co. Surrey granted). Insert— by Bysche. . . .

Greene (Alderman of Chester, 1602). Insert—*V.*

Greenford. Per fess vert. and or a lion ramp. counterchanged. Add: *V.*

Greenford (Levanton, co. Kent). Add: *V.*V.*

Greenhow. Arg. on a bend engr. sa. 3 bugle horns of the first.

Greensted. Gu. a chev. erm. betw. 3 squirrels or. *V.**

Greenstreet (Sittingbourne, co. Kent, 1451). Add: *Hasted.*

Greenstreet. Gu. 3 bars vair. Sir Andrew de Graunstride. *N.* Sir Andrew Grensted, co. Somerset. *V.*

Greenstreet (Ospringe, co. Kent, confirmed). Insert—by Sir John Borough, Garter . . .

Greenaway (Quartered by Salway). Arg. a chev. rompu. betw. 3 trefoils slipped sa.

Greenway. Arg. a chev. betw. 3 crosses bottony fitchy sa. This coat was sometimes borne as the paternal coat by Biddulph (Bart. 1664) they having married the heiress of that family. It is now quartered. *Guillim.*

Greenway or Grenway. Insert—co. Stafford. Add: *Dingley. V.* Greenway (London). *V.*

Greenwood (Stapleton, co. York. 1666) Sa. a chev. erm. betw. 3 saltires or a mullet for diff. *Dugdale. p. 311.*

Greenwell (Greenwell Ford, co. Durham).Add: *V.*

Greenwood. Delete 'arg.' ? sa. a chev. erm. betw. 3 saltires arg. *Harl. MS. 1404. fo. 125.*

Grefylde. Arg. on a bend gu. 4 lozenges of the first. *V.*

Gregory (Pliston, co. Devon). Or on a chev. az. betw. 3 mullets of the last as many decrescent . . . *Robson.*

Gregory (Lord Mayor of London, 1451). Add: *Harl. MS. 1349.*

Grenould. Arg. on a chev. sa. 3 stags of the first. *V.N. 189.*

Greley. Gu. 3 bendlets arg. John Creley. *Y.*

Greley or Greyley. Gu. 3 bendlets or. Sir Robt. de Grelei. *E.* Sir Thomas de Greley. *N.* Sir Thomas de Greyley. *I.J.*

Grelley. Gu. 3 bendlets "embelief" or. Wm. Greiley. *B.*

Grelley. Gu. 3 bendlets enhanced or. Johan de Grelli. *G.* Sir . . . de Greyley, Lord of Manchester, co. Lancaster. *V.*

Grendon (Grendon, co. Warwick . . .). Add: Sire Rauf de Grandene. *I.* de Grandone. *N.* Grendon. *H.* Sir Robert de Grendone. *E.F.*

Grendon (Co. Leicester). Arg. 2 chevs. gu. a label az.

Grendon. Arg. 2 chevs. gu. a label vair. Sir Robert de Grandone. *N.*

Grenely. Vert a chev. betw. 3 martlets arg. *V.*

Grenfeld. Arg. on a bend gu. 4 lozenges of the first. *V.**

Gresham (Granted to Sir Richard Gresham, Lord Mayor of London, by Barker, Garter in 1537). Arg. a chev. ermines betw. 3 pierced mullets sa. on a chief gu. a pelican enclosed betw. 2 lions legs erased or armed az. *V.*

Gresham (John, Sheriff of London). . . . Add: Guillim says "that the chief was an augmentation to Sir John Gresham".

Gresley. Az. on a bend betw. 2 lions ramp. arg. 3 martlets of the field. *Constable's Roll. xvij.*

Cressall. Quarterly arg. and az. on a bend gobony gu. and . . . Add: *V.*

Gressall.

Gressey. Add: *Harl. MS. 1392.*

Gressy. Arg. a chev. betw. 3 escutcheons sa. each charged with a griffin ramp. or. *V.*

Gresson. Add: *V.*V.*

Grey (Lord Grey of Ruthyn). . . . Add: Sir . . . de Grey of Ruthyn. *S. Y.*

Grey (Enville, co. Stafford). Barry of 6 arg. and az. in chief 3 torteaux and a label of 3 points erm. *Erdeswick.*

Grey (Lord Grey of Groby). . . . Add: Henry de Gray. *K.J.* John de Gray. *E.F.S.* Richard Grey. *A.N.Y.* William Grey, Bishop of Ely 1454, Walter de Grey, Bishop of Worcester 1214.

Gray (Shorland). Barry of 6 arg. and az. a label of 3 points gu. *V.* Reginald Gray, Baron of Ruthin. Same arms. *Nobility Roll. 25 Edw. j.*

Grey. Barry of 6 arg. and az. a label of 5 points gu. Reginald de Gray. *A.E.J.*

Grey. Barry of 6 arg. and az. a label gu. bezanty. Richard Grey. Sandiacre. *Y.*

Grey. Barry of 6 arg. and az. a baton or bendlet compony or and gu. Sire Nicholas de Grey. *N.M.* Barry az. and arg. a baton compony arg. and gu. Sire Nichol de Grey. *O.*

Grey (London 1568). Barry of 6 arg. and az. on a bend gu. a rose of the field. *C.L.*

Grey. Barry of 6 arg. and az. on a canton or a lion ramp. sa. *V.*

Grey. Barry of 6 arg. and az. on a bend gu. 3 martlets or. *V.*

Grey. Barry of 6 arg. and az. on a bend gu. a bezant in chief. Sir Thomas Grey, Norton, Northumberland. *V.*

Grey. Barry of 6 arg. and az. on a bend gu. 3 bezants. *V.*

Grey. Arg. on a bend of 6 fusils conjoined gu. John de Grey. *E.*

Grey (Sir Charles Edward Grey, Knt.). . . . Add: Grey (Newcastle-on-Tyne). *Robson.*

Grey (Essex). Arg. a bend vert betw. 2 cotises indented gu. *V.** Sir Roger Grey. *V.*

Grey (Langley and Donnington, co. Leicester). Add: *V.** Add: The same arms. But on the canton a bear statant arg. Thomas Grey, Donynton Park. *V.*

Grey (Kilay, co. Northumberland). Gu. a lion ramp. within a bordure engr. arg. a martlet for diff.

Grey (Thrandeston, co. Suffolk). Add: Grey (Goldfield Hall, Eye, Suffolk). Same arms. *Cady.*

Grey of Barton. Barry of 6 az. and arg. a baston gu. *V.*

Grey. Barry of six arg. and az. on a bend gu. three leopards faces—insert—*V.* . . . . Add: Grey (Lanfrid). *W.*

Grey Of Rotherfield, co. Oxford. Barry of 6 arg. and az. a bend gu. *S.V.* Mons. Richard Grey. *S.* And with a bendlet gu. Robert de Grey. *E. Harl. MS. 6137.* Sir John Grey, Rotherfield. *V.N.H.Y.* de Grey. *E.F.*

Grey. Barry arg. and az. a bend engr. gu. John de Gray. *K.*

Grey or Gray (Ireland: Patent 1612). Add: Granted by Camden in 1612 to Sir Richard Grey, Secretary in Ireland.

Greyley. Bendy of 8 gu. and or. Sir Thomas Greyley. *I.*

Greyndor. . . . a chev. . . . . betw. 6 crosses crosslet. *Collinson Somerset. j. 142.*

Greylawyers (Company of). Erm. on a chev. sa. betw. 3 squirrels sejant gu. collared lined and ringed or as many roses arg. *V.*

Grice (Brokedisk, co. Norfolk). Add: *V.*

Grice. Purp. a chev. of 7 billets arg. †

Griffinhoofe (Saffron Walden, Essex). Dr. Griffinhoofe, came to England as Physician to King George I. *Notes and Queries. 5.S.ij. 397.*

Griffith (Co. York). Erm. a bend gu. cotised. or. Add: *V.*

Griffith. Gu. a chev. arg. betw. two Saracens heads in chief. . . . Add: *V.** Sir William Griffith, North Wales. *V.*

Griffith. temp. Edw. ij. Az. 3 eagles displ. or beaked and membered gu. *F.Y.*

Gryffythe. Same arms. *Constable's Roll. xj.*

Griffith (Carmarthen, Wales). Gu. a chev. indented arg. betw. . . . 1370. 6 lions ramp. or. *Harl. MS. 2116.*

Griffith. Ap. Or a lion ramp. gu. Crest: . . . Add: Eian ap. Griffit. *F.*

Griffith. Az. a boar betw. 10 trefoils slipped arg. *V.**

Rhys ap Griffith (Derived from Llewyelwyn ap Ynys O'Jel, Lord of Gelligynan, co. Denbigh). Paly of 8 or and gu. a bordure az. bezanty.

Griffith (Port Royal, co. Sligo). Sa. a lion ramp. arg. betw. an orle of 8 roses of the last.

Griffiths (Neath, co. Glamorgan). Gu. a lion ramp. or in a true lovers knot arg. betw. 4 fleurs-de-lis their stalks bending to the centre of the escutcheon. *Nicholas.*

Griffon (Wales). Sa. a chev. betw. 3 fleurs-de-lis arg. *Robson.*

Grigg. Arg. two chevs. sa. Crest: Out of a ducal coronet a dexter hand. . . . Add: *V.*

Grimsby. Per chev. sa. and arg. in chief two chevs. of the second. *Cotton MS. Tiberius. D. 10. fo. 753.* †

Grimsby. Per chev. az. and arg. in chief two chevronels of the second—Add: 'side by side'. *V.**

Griseley. Barry of 6 the 1st. 3rd and 5th traversed in fess erm., and qu. the other three az. *Ferne's Blazon of Gentrie.*

Grizzlehurst. Add: *Shaw.*

Grogan (Harcourt Street, Dublin, bart.). . . . Add: Grogan (Myvore, co. Westmeath), Baronetcy 1859. Same arms.

Gronwy. Lord of Vochnant. Arg. a chev. gu. betw. 3 pheons sa.

Gros. Barry of 6 or and sa. per pile counterchanged. Sir John Gros. *V.*

Grose (Richmond, co. Surrey; granted 1756: the arms of Francis Grose, F.S.A.). Insert— Richmond Herald. . . .

Grosse (Co. Norfolk). Add: *V.* Sir Renaud de Gros. *N.*

Grosvenor. Az. a bend or and bordure erm. quartered by Sneyd.

Grosvenor (London). Az. a garb or betw. 2 bezants in fees. *Vis. Lon. 1633.*

Grove (Co. Bucks). Erm. on a chev. gu. 3 escallops arg. *V.*

Grove (Fernie, co. Wilts). Erm. on a chev. engr. gu. betw. 2 escallops arg. one escallop or. *Hoare.*

Grove (Ferne, co. Wilts., bart.). Insert—1874 . . . Add: *Hoare.*

Grove or Groves (Hull, co. York). Or on a chev. gu. an escallop of the field. *F.Y.*

Grove (Robert Grove, Bishop of Chichester 1691). Erm. on a chev. gu. 3 escallops or.

Groves. Erm. on a chev. gu. 3 escallops arg. *V.**

Groyn. Or on a chev. couched sinister betw. 3 birds sa. 5 mullets arg. But the field arg. *V.**

Grylls (Rev. Richard Gerveys Grylls &c. . . . being required of William Grylls of Tavistocke, co. Devon). Insert—*V.D. 1620.*

Grymer. Add: *V.*

Grys (Wakefield, co. York). Insert—1585 . . . Add: *F.Y.*

Gryse (Co. Norfolk). Add: *Harl. MS. 1404. fo. 131.*

Guales. Insert—(i.e. Wales).

Gualyn (Cornwall). Arg. on a bend gu. betw. 2 cotises az. 3 fleurs-de-lis of the field. *Lysons.*

Gubyon. Insert—(Norfolk). Or a lion ramp. sa. depressed. Add: *V.W.*

Guernsey. Gu. iij. lions pass. guard. or. *Berry.*

Guest (Dowlais, co. Glamorgan, bart.). Insert— 1868 . . .

Guevera (Co. Lincoln descended from Spain). Add: *Guillim.*

Guiness (Ashford, co. Galway. bart.). Insert— 1867 . . .

Gulford or Guildford (Cos. Stafford and York). Add: Sire John de Guldeford. *N.*

Guley. Az. a chev. or betw. 3 crosses moline arg. *V.*

Gulston (Wymondham, co. Leicester; granted by Camden), Insert—1609,

Gulston (Bishop of Bristol 1679–84). Arg. 3 bars nebuly gu. over all on a bend sa. 3 plates. *Guillim.*

Gumars or Gunas. Add: Gumras or Gunnas. *V.V.**

Gumvile. Arg. a chev. betw. 2 couple closes sa. *Randle Holme.*

Gunthorpe (Thomas). *Visitation Notts.* Add: *V.V. p. 189*

Gurlin. Arg. on a bend per pale gu. and az. . . . Crest: . . . Add: *V.*

Gurlen (Gissing, Norfolk). Erm. a bend counter compony arg. and sa. *Blomfield.*

Gurney (Norfolk and London). Or a cross engr. gu. in the dexter chief a 5-foil az. *Vis. Lon. 1633.*

Gurney or Gurnard (Sir Richard Gurney, Lord Mayor of London). . . . Insert—confirmed by Segar 26 July 1633. Add: *Vis. Lon. 1633.*

Gurwood (Colonel Gurwood, Deputy Governor of the Tower of London). Az. a chev. or and for honourable augmentation the shield of the Town of Cuidad Rodrico. viz. Arg. a triangular building with 3 columns, at the back of the shield a sword in pale hilt upwards ppr. for the sword Governor whom Colonel Gurwood took prisoner.

Gussand. Az. a bend fusilly arg. *V.** Sir Peter Gussan. *V. Syl. Morgan.*

Guy (Oundle, co. Northampton and co. Wilts.). Add: Guy of the Collar. Same arms. *V.*

Guy (North Walsham, Norfolk). Same arms. *Cady.*

Guyling. Add: *V.**

Guythold. Add: *V.*

Gwyn. Or a chev. couched sinister . . . Crest: . . . Add: The field arg. *V.V.**

Gwynne (London and co. Berks.). Sa. 3 nags heads erased arg. Crest: A bear pass. sa. towards a rose bush ppr. *Vis. Lon. 1633.*

Gwythold. Add: *V.*

Gybons or Gibbons (Co. Glamorgan, Ditley, co. Oxford and Newhall, co. Warwick). Add: John Gybon DCL. Same arms. *V.* Payne, alias Gybon, confirmed 24 Nov. 1570. Same arms.

Gyll (Granted, about 1586 to Ralph Gyll). . . . Add: Gyll (Mucking, co. Essex). Same arms.

Gyll (Wyrardsbury, co. Bucks). Sa. on 2 chevs. arg. 6 mullets of the first a canton or charged with a lion pass. gu.

Gyl (Co. Hertford). Add: *Harl. MS. 1404. fo. 109.*

Gylwike. Add: *V.*

Gynes. Or a bordure vair. *V.*

Gynes (Much Lees, co. Essex). Vairy or and az. a canton erm. *V.E. 1634.*

Gyse. Barry indented arg. and sa. *Harl. MS. 1404.*

Gyves. Arg. 3 battle axes sa. *V.**

Gyves. Arg. 3 halberts sa. *V.*

H

HABINGDON (Hindlip and Wichenford, co. Worcester). . . . Add: Sir Richard de Habignton. *V.*

Haccombe (Haccombe, co. Devon). . . . Add: Sire Estevene de Haccombe. *N.* John de Haccombe. *Y.*

Hache (Hache . . . co. Devon). Add: *V.*

Hachet. Arg. on a bend gu. betw. 2 cotises sa. 3 fleurs-de-lis or. Sir Richard Hachet. *L.*

Hackett (St. John's Worcester). Add: Sir Walter Hacket. *L.N.* co. Derby *V.*

Hackett. Or 3 bendlets gu. a label of 5 points az. Sir Henry Hakett. *F.*

Hacket. Erm. a bend voided gu. *Randle Holme.*

Hackett (London). Arg. 3 fleurs-de-lis betw. 2 cotises gu. Crest: a lions gamb erased arg. holding a saltire gu. *Vis. Lon. 1633.*

Hackford. Chequy or and vert. Crest: . . . Add: *V.* Add: William de Hakeford, temp. Henry iij. and his son, Thomas. *V.*

Hackluyt or Hackvill (Yetton, co. Hereford and co. Salop). Gu. three hatchets or—add—(or battle-axes).

Hackshaw (Hutton, co. Salop). Add: Hackshaw (Hinton St. George, co. Somerset). Same arms. *V.S.*

Hackwill or Hakewill (Totnes and Exeter, co. Devon). Insert—1620. *Colby.*

Hacote. Add: *V.*

Hadderley. Arg. on a bend gu. betw. 2 lions heads erased sa. 3 crosses crosslet or. *V.*

Haddington (Borough of   ). Az. on a mount in base vert. a goat statant arg. armed horned and bearded or. *Berry.*

Hadey, Haddey or Hadley. Gu. on a bend arg. 3 leopards faces vert. *W.V.*

Hadham. Add: Thos. Haddam. *Y.*

Hadleigh (Town of Suffolk). Granted by Camden 1618. Arg. 3 leopards faces vert. *W.V.*

Hadley (Ireland). Arg. 3 round buckles tongues pendent sa. *Cady.*

Hadley (Ireland). Gu. 3 round buckles tongues to the sinister arg. *V.*

Hadley. Gu. 3 square buckles arg. tongues to the dexter or. *Harl. MS. 1441.*

Hadley (Co. Somerset). Gu. 3 round buckles arg. Add: *V.*

Hadley. Gu. on a chev. or three crosses patonce of the first. Add: *V.*

Hadley. Gu. on a chev. or 3 crosses patonce sa. *V.*

Hadley. Az. a chev. surmounted of a fesse betw. 3 annulets or. Add: John Hadley, Lord Mayor of London. *W.*

Hagar (Batnecast, co. Cambridge). Add: *Fuller.*

Haggerston (Haggerston Castle, co. Northumberland, bart.). Insert—1643. Add: *V.*

Hagh. Arg. a chev. betw. ten crosses crosslet gu. *V.*

Hagthorpe (Co. York). Sa. a chev. engr. or. *V.*

Hagthorpe (Nettleworth). Same arms. *Surtees.*

Haitly. Or on a bend az. 3 boars heads erased arg. *Guillim.*

Hake. Az. 3 bars or a bordure engr. arg. Add: Andrew Hake. *X.*

Hackbeche. Or 2 bars az. Add: Sir Robert Hakebech. *V.* M. Reynald Hakenbeche. *S.*

Hakeluyt (Co. Gloucester). . . . three mullets— delete—of the field another, . . . Add: Sir Reynard Hakeluyt. *S.* Sire Edmon Hakelut. *N.* Sir John Hakeluyt, co. Gloucester. *V.*

Hakelut or Hackluyt. Co. Salop. Arg. on a bend betw. 2 cotises gu. 3 fleurs-de-lis or. Sir Richard Hakelut. *N.*

Hakelute. Arg. on a plain bend betw. two cotises indented gu. 3 mullets or. Sir Edmund Hakelute, co. Salop. temp. Edw. j. *V.*

Halanton. Add: *V.*V.*

Haldane. Insert—Kent. Arg. a bend engr. gu. a chief sa. Crest: a globe ppr. Add: *V.*

Hale. Az. 2 arrows in pale or flighted arg. *X.*

Hale (Kings Walden, co. Hertford). Add: *V.**

Hale (Claybury, Essex). Az. a chev. bretessed or. *V.E. 1612.*

Hales. Gu. 3 arrows double pointed or. *W.*

Hales (Sir Bartholomew H., co. Warwick 1619). Gu. 3 arrows points downwards or feathered arg. quartering arg. a lion ramp. and a bordure engr. sa. *W.*

Hales or Halys (Harwich). Barry of 10 arg. and az. on a canton gu. a lion pass. guard. or. *Z. 206.*

Hales (Mychurch, co. Somerset). Add: Sir Steven de Hales. *S.*

Hales (Nakingdon, Kent). Arg. on a chev. sa. betw. 3 fleur-de-lis each within a chaplet gu. as many estoiles arg. a chief az. charged with 3 writing pens or. *Cotton MS. Tiberius. D. 10.*

Halghton. Add: *V.**

Haliden. . . . on a chev. . . . betw. 3 crows as many boars heads erased . . . **Seal** of John de Haliden. 1361.

Hall (Co. Devon). Sa. a chev. betw. 3 talbots heads erased arg. Add: *W.*

Hall (Co. Devon). Az. a chev. arg. betw. 3 chaplets or. Add: *W.*

Hall (Ireland). Az. a chev. betw. 3 chaplets of roses arg. *Robson.*

Halle (Co. Somerset). Az. a chev. erm. betw. 3 chaplets or. *V.W.*

Hall (Brittly, co. Durham). Arg.—underlined— margin 'or.' . . . as many annulets—underlined —margin 'chaplets'. Add: *Surtees.*

Hall. Sir . . . de Hall. Erm. 2 bars gu. over all 3 escutcheons or. *V.*

Hall (Newsham, co. Durham). . . . 3 talbots heads—insert—erased . . . Crest: . . . Add: Confirmed by St. George, Norroy. Hall (London). Same arms and crest a crescent for diff. *Vis. Lon. 1633.*

Hall (High Meadow, co. Gloucester). Add: *Dingley.*

Hall (cos. Lincoln and Middlesex and Middle-Walton, co. York). . . . as many chaplets— insert—arg. flowered, Add: *V.* Add: Hall (Salford, co. Lancaster). Same arms. *V.* The demi-lions erased.

Hall (Co. Northampton. Granted by Segar, Garter in 1613).

Hall (Co. Lincoln 1640). Arg. on a chev. engr. betw. 3 lions heads erased sa. an estoile or. Add: *Yorke.*

Hall (Serjeant at Law). Vert. 2 bars erm. on a chief arg. a talbots head erased betw. 2 wreaths. †

Hall (London). Arg. 3 talbots heads erased sa. collared or betw. 5 crosses crosslet gu. Add: *Vis. Lon. 1633.* 9 crosslets.

Hall. Arg. a chev. az. betw. 3 talbots heads erased sa. on a chief az. 3 mullets pierced arg.

Hall (Co. Norfolk). Sa. a chev. arg. betw. 3 chaplets or. Crest: a demi-buck saliant . . . Add: *W.*

Hall (Pitcombe   ). Arg. a chev. betw. 3 orles . . . quartering Ruddock. *Collinson Somerset ij. 345.*

Hall (Co. Salop). Arg. on a chev. cotised gu. 3 chaplets or. Add: *W.*

Hall (Co. Somerset). Az. a chev. erm. betw. 3 chaplets or. Add: *W.*

Hall. Az. 3 pole-axes arg. *W.*

Hall. Az. 3 battle axes in fess or. Edward Hall, Bybrook, Kent. Granted by Cooke, 1588. *W.*

Hall (Co. Essex). Sa. on a chev. engr. betw. 3 battle axes or as many eagles displ. of the field.

Hall. Arg. 2 chevs. gu. on a canton of the second a chaplet of the first. *V.*W.*

Hall (Coventry, co. Warwick). Arg. a chev. sa. betw. 3 columbines slipped ppr. Add: *Cady.*

Hall (Burton Abbey, near Oxford). Sa. on a chev. arg. betw. 3 dexter hands each enclosed in an annulet a wreath of laurel . . . betw. 2 roses gu. *Debrett.*

Hall (Redesdale, Northumberland and Otterburn Castle, 1723). . . . a chev. . . . betw. 3 demi-lions ramp. . . . on a chief . . . 3 mullets . . . **Tomb** in Churchyard at Elsden.

Hall. Arg. a chev. sa. fretty or betw. 3 lions ramp. az. *V.**

Hall (Salford, co. Lancaster, Granted in 1532). Same arms. *F.Y.*

Hall (Birtley, Conset and Framwellgate, co. Durham). Add: Hall (Hollenbush, co. Durham Same arms, a martlet for diff. *Robson.*

Halle or Hale. Az. a chev. counter-embattled or. Add: *V.*

Halleley, Hallely or Halliley (Hackney, co. Middlesex). Az. a chev.—insert—arg. . . . —delete—arg. substitute or. . . . Add: *Vis. Lon. 1633.*

Hallestowe. Add: *V.*

Hallewell. Arg. on a chev. sa. three bezants. Add: *V.*

Halliwell. Or on a bend gu. 3 goats trippant arg. . . . Add: *V.**

Hallman (Co. Devon 1607). . . . Add: Granted by Camden.

Hallys. Sa. a chev. betw. 3 lions ramp. arg. Add: and with an annulet sa. on the chev. for diff. Sir Stephen Hallys, Essex. *V.* John Halys, Essex. *V.*

Halontone. Arg. on a bend gu. 3 eagles displ. or Sir Robert de Halontone. *N.*

Halsall. Arg. 2 bars az. a bordure engr. sa. Sir Gilbert de Halsall, co. Lancaster. *V.*

Halsey or Haulsey (London). Arg. on a fess sa. betw. 3 griffins heads erased of the second a 5-foil or. Crest: a griffin sejant arg. *Vis. Lon. 1633.*

Halsham (Co. Suffolk). Arg. a chev. engr. betw. 3 leopards faces gu. Add: Robert Halsham. *V.*

Halsham. Or a chev. betw. 3 lions heads erased gu. Sir Henry Halsham. *T.*

Halsted (Sunning, co. Berks. and London). Granted—insert—by Segar . . . Add: Guillim gives the date of grant by Segar 20 Nov. 1628. The *Visitation of London 1633* gives the chief chequy or and az. and the Crest: a demi-eagle erm. issuing out of a mural crown az.

Halswell (Of Halswell, co. Somerset, Baronetcy 1674). Gu. a lion couchant betw. 6 crosses crosslet arg. 3 and 3 quartering arg. 3 bars wavy az. over all a bend gu. for Tynte. *Guillim.*

Halswell (Wells, co. Somerset). Arg. 3 bars wavy az. a bend gu. *V.S.*

Halthorpe. Sa. a chev. engr. or. *V.*

Halton (Greenthwaite Hall, co. Cumberland). Add: Sir Henry Halton. *V.*

Halton (South Winfield, co. Derby). Add: *Lysons.*

Halton (Co. Lincoln 1640). Add: *Yorke.*

Halton. Arg. 2 bars az. in chief 3 hurts. Robert de Halton. *V.*

Halton. Arg. 2 bars az. in chief 3 escallops gu. Sire de Halton. *Y.* John de Halton 1319. **Seal.**

Halweton. Arg. on a bend gu. 3 eagles displ. or. Sir Robert de Halweton. *G.*

Halyan. Arg. a chev. sa. betw. 3 trefoils slipped vert. *V.V.**

Halyburton (Scotland). Or on a bend az. betw. in chief a crescent and in base a boars head erased sa. 3 mascles arg. *Robson.*

Halyburton (Pitcur, co. Forfar). Add: *Guillim.*

Halyburton (Newmains, co. Roxburgh). Add: quartered by Sir Walter Scott.

Hamborough (Steephill Castle, Isle of Wight and Pipewell Hall, co Northampton, of Hanoverian origin). Add: *A.A.*

Hambrois. Add: *V.*

Hambro (Milton Abbey, Blandford 1868). Az. a chev. or betw. in chief 3 annulets and in base a lion pass. arg. *Debrett.*

Hamel (London). Gu. a fess or betw. in chief a stag courant of the second and in base 3 mullets of 6 points arg. Crest: A demi-stag or. *Vis. Lon. 1633.*

Hamelyn, Hamelen, Hamelin, Hamelyng and Hamelyne. Add: *V.*

Hamelyn (*Ulster's Office*). Add: *S.*

Hamelyn (Quartered by Berkeley, of Wymondham Ley . . . Leicester). . . . Add: Sir John Hamelyn. *I.N.O.V.*

Hamersley (Lord Mayor of London 1687). . . . Add: *Vis. Lon. 1633.*

Hamersley (London, confirmed by Camden 1614). Gu. a chev. betw. 3 rams heads couped or. *Guillim.*

Hamerton (Preston-Jacklyn, co. York 1666). . . . Add: *Dugdale. 354.*

Hamlyn. Chequy arg. and sa. Sire . . . de Hamlyn. *V.*

Hamlyn. Gu. a lion ramp. or goutty de poix. *Y.*

Hamme. Az. a chev. betw. 3 demi-lions or. Sire Johan de Hamme. *N.V.V.**

Hammet. Arg. a lion ramp. sa. on a canton az. 5 fleurs-de-lis or.

Hammet (Somersetshire, granted in 1803). Per fess arg. and gu. counterchanged over all a lion ramp. erminois. on a canton az. 5 fleurs-de-lis. or.

Hammond (Westacre, co. Norfolk). Or on a chev. voided az. 3 martlets of the field. *Dashwood.*

Hamon. Arg. a chev. engr. sa. betw. 3 pierced mullets gu. Anthony Hamon. *Constable's Roll. x.*

Hamon (Co. Kent). Add: *V.*

Hamond (Holly Grove, co. Berks, bart.). Add: *A.A.*

Hamond (Scarthingwell, co. York, 1666). Arg. a chev. engr. betw. 3 mullets pierced sa. Crest: A lion's gamb. gu. betw. 2 bats wings erect ppr. the paw holding an almond slip fructed vert. blossoms of the first. *Dugdale. p. 378.*

Hammond (Co. York). Or a chev. betw. 3 mullets of 6 points sa. Wm. Hammond. *Eliz. Roll. xxxij.*

Hamond (Tuddington, co. Middlesex). . . . 'or, quartering—insert—az' . . . Add: Hamond (Windingham, co. Cambridge, co. Hertford, co. York and Croydon, Surrey). Same arms.

Hampton (London). . . . insert—Certified by Segar, Garter. "Motto" "Fide deo cui vide". Add: *Vis. Lon. 1633.*

Hampton (Wolverhampton, co. Stafford). Add: Sir . . . de Hampton, co. Stafford. *V.*

Hampton. Arg. a chev. componee az. and purp. betw. 3 martlets gu. Crest: A greyhound . . . Add: *V.** chev. counter compony. *V.*

Hamsted. Az. on a bend—insert—'or' fimbriated arg. . . . Add: *V.**

Hamsted. Az. on a bend arg. betw. 3 fleurs-de-lis or as many escallops gu. *V.*

Hamuvile. Sa. crusilly fitchy and a bend or. Henri de Hamuvile. *E.*

Hancett. Gu. 3 bendlets or a label of 5 points arg. Hamund Hancett. *E.*

Hanclow, Hancler or Haneler. Add: *Cotton MS. Tiberius. D. 10.*

Hancoke (Gregory Stoke, co. Somerset). Sa. a chev.—underlined—margin—'But 3 chevs. *V.S. 1623.*'

Handlo. Add: *V.** Nicolas Handlo. *V.*

Hanlo. Or 2 chevs. gu. on a canton of the last a crescent arg. Sir Nicholas Hanlo. *D.A.*

Handlow. Arg. a lion ramp. az. goutty or. Sir John de Hanlo. *L.N.Y.* The lion crowned. *V.*

Hands. Gu. on a chev. arg. three spear heads . . .

Hands (Co. Gloucester). Gu. on a chev. or betw. 3 escallops arg. as many griffins heads erased. . . . *Dingley.*

Hanham. Quarterly or and gu. on a bend sa. 3 crosses formee arg. Add: *V.*

Hanham (Essex). Quarterly or and gu. a chev. sa. betw. 3 crosslets fitchy arg. *Morant's Essex j. 472.*

Haningfield. Or a chev. sa. Add: Sir Wm. Haningfeld. *N.*

Haninvile. Sable crusilly fitchy and a bend or. *E. Harl. MS. 6137.* Henri de Hannivile.

Hankett (Scotland). Or a chev. chequy sa. and arg. betw. 3 bugle horns sa: quartering gu. 3 crescents within a bordure arg. charged with eight 5-foils gu. *Cady.*

Hankford (Co. Devon). . . . another wavy. Add: 'or nebuly' az. *V.*

Hankford (Exeter College). Add: *V.* Add: Hankford. Arg. 2 bends wavy sa. Sir John Hankford. *V.*

Hankeford (Co. Devon). Sa. a chev. wavy arg. *Harl. MS. 1386 fo. 34b.*

Hankwell. Per chev. gu. and erm. 2 chevs counterchanged. *V.V.**

Hankwell. Gu. 3 chevrons erm. *V.**

Hanley (Cos. Devon and Cornwall). Az. 3 goats arg. attired or. Add: *V.*

Hanlow, Hamlow or Handlow. See Handlow.

Hanmer (Hanmer, co. Flint). . . . Arg. 2 lions pass. guard.—insert—'in pale' az. . . .

Hanmer (Baron Hanmer). Arg. 2 lions pass. guard—insert—'in pale' az. Add: *Z. 649.*

Hanrott (London). Add: *Robson.*

Hansard. Gu. a bend betw. six mullets arg. Add: Sir John Hansard, co. Lincoln temp. Edw. j. *V.* Sir Johan Haunsard. *N.*

Hansby or Hans (St. Giles, Beverley and New Malton, co. York). Add: Hansby (Tickhill Castle, co. York). *Hunter j. 234.*

Hanslape. Arg. 2 bars gu. *Dugdale's Baronage. j.*

Hanson (Peckham, co. Surrey and Rastricke and Woodhouse, co. York). Add: *Dugdale. 1665.*

Hansted. Gu. a chief chequy or and az. over all a bend arg. Sir Robert de Hanstede. *L.N.*

Hansted. Gu. a chief chequy or and az. over all a bend erm. Sire Johan de Hanstede. *N.* But a baston erm. Sir John de Hanstede. *O.*

Hansted. Arg. on a bend vert. 3 eagles displ. or. Sir John de Hansted. *L.*

Hansted (Co. Northampton temp. Edw. j. Arg. a chief chequy or and az. a bordure erm. *Harl. MS. 5083.*

Hantvill. Add: *V.* Sir Geoffrey Hanteville, co. Cornwall temp. Edw. ij. *V.*

Hanville. Sa. 2 lions pass. reguard in pale arg. *C.W.*

Hanwell. Arg. 3 crows sa.

Hanway. . . . or chev. betw. 3 demi-lions. Jonas Hanway. 1786.

Harbe or Harbey (Asby, co. Northampton). Sa. —underlined—margin ? gu. ——

Harbenger. Arg. on a chev. sa. three lions heads erased of the first. *V.**

Harborne (St. Olaves, co. Norfolk). Gu. a hawk standing arg. jessed or.

Harborne (Thackley, co. Oxford). . . . . Add: *Vis. Lon. 1633.*

Harborne (Sheen Lane, co. Middlesex). . . . . Add: *W.*

Harcarse (That Ilk, co. Berwick). Add: *Cady.*

Harcote. Arg. fretty az. a bordure of the last. *V.*

Harcourt. Gu. 2 bars or. Sir Robert Harcourt, co. Leicester. *V.* John de Harcourte. *C.L.N.Y.* Gu. 2 bars of a label of 3 az. John de Harcourt, the son. *I.* Gu. 2 bars or on a label of 3 points az. 9 plates. William de Harcourt 1410. **Glass** *in Evreux Cathedral.*

Harcourt. Edward Venables Vernon Harcourt, Bishop of Carlisle and after Archbishop of York. 1 and 4 gu. 2 bars or. 2 arg. a fret sa. 3. or on a fess az. 3 garbs of the field. *Bedford.*

Harcourt (Ellenhall, co. Stafford). Gu. 2 bars or over all a bendlet sinister az. *Erdeswick.*

Harcourt. Arg. on a chev. sa. 3 escallops or. *V.*

Harcourt. Or two bars gu. Wm. Harcourt. *E.* William Harecourt. *Y. F.* Sir John de Harcourt. *G.* Richard de Harcourt. *B.P.* Thomas Harcourt. *S.*

Hardbread (Sheriff of Newcastle 1488). Arg. 2 bars and in chief 3 crosses crosslet gu. *Carr. MS.*

Hardcastle. Insert—Kent, Sa. on a chev. betw. 3 castles arg. as many leopards faces gu. Crest: A lady attired az. . . . .

Hardell (Lord Mayor of London 1253). Or a bend . . . betw. 2 cotises sa. *Harl. MS. 1049. Stow.*

Hardenton. Sa. a bend betw. 6 billets or. *V.V.**

Hardesty. Arg. a chev. betw. 3 crescents gu. *Robson.*

Hardimett. Arg. 2 bars sa. over all an escutcheon az. charged with a plate and a bordure or. *Randle Holme.*

Harding (Lieut, Col. Harding, Upcott House). Insert—co. Devon. Add: *Harding* (London). Same arms. *V.*

Harding (Sheriff of London   ). Arg. on a bend az. three martlets or on a sinister canton of the second a rose or betw. 2 fleurs-de-lis arg. *C.L.*

Harding. (Coaley, co. Gloucester and Rockfields, co. Monmouth). Add: John Harding temp. Henry v. *V.*

Harding (William Harding, citizen of London). Add: *C.L.*

Harding (London). Granted—insert—by Dethick, Garter . . .

Harding (Upcot, co. Devon). Or on a bend sa. 3 martlets of the field. *Lysons.*

Harding (Allowed by Betham, Ulster, 1820 to Henry Harding Esq.). *X.*

Hardinge (Sheriff of Newcastle 1474). Sa. a chev. betw. 3 keys erect arg. *Carr. MS.*

Harding (Kings Newton, co. Derby). Gu. on a chev. arg. 3 escallops of the field. Sir Robt. Harding, Bramscot, co. Notts. *Cady.* 1674. Same arms. *L.N.*

Hardres. Ermine a lion ramp. gu. over all a chev. or. Robert de Hardres. *A.*

Hardrishall. Arg. a chev. sa. betw. three martlets gu. *V.**

Hardreshull. Arg. a chev. betw. 10 martlets gu. Sir John de Hardreshull temp. Edw. iij. *Baker.*

Hardreshull. Arg. a chev. betw. 9 martlets gu. *V.* Sire John Hardreshul. *O.*

Hardworth. Arg. a bend sa. *V.*

Hardy (London). Add: John Hardy, Alderman. *N.*

Hardy (Dunstall Hall, co. Stafford, bart.). Insert —1876 . . .

Hardy. Or a chev. vert. in base an escu. az. a chief of the last. *Randle Holme.*

Hardy (*Ulster's Office*). Add: Gathorne Hardy, M.P. for Oxford University 1868. *Debrett.*

Hare (Earl of Listowel). . . . Add: Francis Hare, Bishop of St. Asaph 1727—31, afterwards of Chichester. *Bedford.*

Hare (Suffolk). Arg. a chev. engr. sa. betw. 3 griffins heads erased az. *Cady.*

Harecourt. Arg. on a chev. sa. 3 escallops of the first. *V.**

Hareford (Bosbury, co. Hereford). Sa. two bends arg. Add: *V.*

Hareman. Arg. a chev. sa. betw. 3 perukes ppr. *Harl. MS. 5860 fo. 8.* Add: *MS. 5507. fo. 311.*

Hareslyn. Arg. on a bend sa. 3 roses or. *V.*

Harewell (Blakenham, co. Suffolk and Bedford Wotton-Shottrey, co. Worcester). . . . 3 hares' heads couped or—insert—Harewell (London). Same arms and crest: *Vis. Lon. 1633.*

Harewood (Thurlby, co. Lincoln and London). Az. a fess compony or and arg. betw. 3 owls of the third. Crest: The bust of a man in male armour ppr. *Harl. MS. 1358.*

Hargonell. Insert—or Hargenill. Add: *Harl. MS. 1458.*

Harington. Or a bend az. and chief sa. *Syl. Morgan.*

Harington (Glaston, co. Rutland). On a chief az. over all a bend engr. gu. quartering Barry of 10 arg. and gu. a canton of the last. *C.R.*

Harington. Arg. a chief gu. over all a bend az. Sir John de Harrington. *N. Harl. MS. 6137.*

Harington. Or a chief gu. over all a bend az. Sir John Harington. *V.N.*

Harington. Or a chief gu. over all a bend engr. az. *C.R. p. 1.*

Harland (Sproughton, co. Suffolk. bart.). Insert—1771. . . .

Harleton. Sa. a chev. or betw. 3 garbs arg. *V.*

Harlewyn. Arg. three lions ramp. gu. crowned or. *V.*

Harley (Earl of Oxford). Add: Sire Richard de Harlee. *N.* Sir Richard Harlegh or Harley, co. Salop. *V.*

Harman (Co. Kent). Add: *Harl. MS. 5860. fo. 8.*

Harneys or Harnous (Co. Bedford). Add: *V.*

Harnoys. Add: Sir Walter Harnoys. *W.*

Harokins. Margin ? Hawkins. Add: *V.*

Harowden. Gu. a lion ramp. bendy wavy of eight arg. and az. Add: *V.*

Harowden. Gu. two bars erm. a canton of the last. Add: *V.**

Harowdon. Gu. 2 bars the upper erm. the other arg. a canton of the second. *V.*

Harpeley (Suffolk). Barry of 8 arg. and or over all 3 chevrons sa. *V.*

Harper (Confirmed to John Harper). . . . Add: *Vis. Lon. 1633.*

Harper (Amerly, co. Hereford). Add: *V.*

Harper (Richard Harper, co. Derby. Justice of the Common Pleas 1572). Per bend sinister arg. and sa. a lion ramp. counterchanged within a bordure compony gu. and or. *W.*

Harpur (Calke, cos. Derby, Devon and Stafford, bart.). Insert—1626 . . .

Harpur. Arg. two bars az. each charged with a lions head erased or. Add: *V.*

Harridge. Arg. on a chev. gu. three crosses crosslet . . . on a chief of the second 3 eagles displ. or. *Robson.*

Harries (Cruckton and Tong Castle, co. Salop, bart). Insert—1623 . . .

Harringwell (Frickley—insert—temp. Edw. ij.) Add: *Foster.*

Harris (Cherston, co. Devon). Add: Harris, co. Cornwall. *W.* Harris of Cherston, co. Devon. *V.D.* 1620. Same arms.

Harris (Maldon, co. Essex). Insert—1612 . . . Add: *V.E.* Add: Harris (Co. Hertford). Same arms. *W.*

Harris (Maldon, co. Essex). Arg. on a chev. engr. sa. betw. 3 hares heads erased gu. a lozenge or betw. 2 roaches of the first. *V.E. 1558.*

Harris (Kent) . . . on a chev. . . . 3 roses . . . a canton.

Harris (Middle Temple, London, granted 10 April 1671). Insert—by Walker. Add: *Guillim.*

Harris. Add:. Harris (London and co. Stafford). Same arms. *Vis. Lon. 1633.* As Harris (Abcot, co. Salop). Add: *V.**

Harris (Worcester). Vert. a chev. erm. betw. 3 urchins . . . *Nash.*

Harris. Alias Prickly (London, allowed by Segar). Or a chev. erm. betw. 3 nails az.

Harris (Cork and Park Grove, co. Kilkenny). Barry of ten az. and erm. three annulets. or.

Harrison (Atcliff, co. Lancaster and Elkington, co. Northampton). Granted—insert—by Segar . . . Crest: . . . pheoned gold. Add: *Vis. Lon. 1633.* Another . . .

Harrison (Acaster, co. York). Az. 3 demi-lions ramp. erased or a canton arg. *Dugdale. 1665. p. 172.*

Harrison (London). Or on a cross az. 5 pheons of the field a chief of the last. Crest: A cubit arm vested and purfled az. cuffed arg. hand holding an arrow gu. pheoned or. *Vis. Lon. 1633.*

Harrison (London). Or on a fess sa. 3 eagles displ. or. Crest: On a cap of maintenance gu. turned up erm. an eagle head or † for diff. *Vis. Lon. 1633.* Granted by St. George, Norroy 7 July 1613.

Harrison. Arg. a chev. gu. betw. 3 escallops sa. within a bordure engr. of the last. *V.*

Harrison (London). Per fesse or and arg. an anchor . . . Crest: Out of a crown . . . Add: confirmed by Segar 17 July 1633.

Harrison (London). *Her. Off.*—insert—Granted by Segar. Add: Crest: as above. *Vis. Lon. 1633.*

Harrison. Arg. a chev. betw. 3 escallops within a bordure engr. sa. Richard Harrison. *V.*

Harrison (Atcaster, Caton and Flaxby, co. York). . . . ramp.—insert—'erased' or. Crest: . . .

Harrison (Thomas Harrison, Mayor of York, Granted 2 Aug. 1592). Same arms.

Harrison (Cayton, co. York 1612). Same arms. *F.Y.* And with a crescent for diff. Harrison of Allerthorpe. co. York 1665. *Dugdale. p. 216.*

Harrison (Cumberland). Arg. two bars gemel sa. betw. three hares courant ppr.

Harrison (Granted by Cooke to John Harrison of London in 1575). Gu. an eagle displ. and a chief or quartering, sa. a chev. betw. 3 hands arg. erased gu. for Ninessor. *Visitation of Northern Counties. fo. xli.*

Harryson. Insert—(Co. Northampton). Gu. an eagle displ. or a chief of the second. Crest: A serpent . . . Add: *W.*

Hart (Boston, co. Lincoln). Add: Hart (London). Same arms, an annulet for diff. Crest: A stag's head erased sa. attired or holding in its mouth a 5-foil arg. stalked and leaved vert. *Vis. Lon. 1633.*

Hart (London). . . . a chev. . . . betw. in chief 2 stags at gaze respecting each other in . . . in base an altar. † *Vis. Lon. 1633.*

Hartagan (Ireland). Az. a lion ramp. or holding in its paw a dagger erect.

Hartford (Thomas Hartford, Badesworth). Arg. on a lion ramp. . . . mascles or. *Y.*

Hartford. Gu. three eagles displ. or (another, arg.). Add: *V.**

Harthell. Barry of six arg. and vert. Add: Sir Richard Harthull. co. Derby temp. Edward j. *V.* Sir Ric. Herthulle. *N.* John Herthill. *Y.*

Harthorp (London). Sa. a chev. erm. betw. 3 spotted cats pass. arg. *Harl. MS. 1404. fo. 130.*

Hartland (The Oaklands, co. Devon). Add: Hartland (co. Gloucester). Same arms.

Hartop (Buckminster, co. Leicester). Insert—Bart. 1619 ext. 1762. Add: Hartopp (co. Cambridge) confirmed in 1617, same arms as Hartopp of Buckminster a crescent gu. on the chev. for diff. *Harl. MS. 6095. fo. 39.*

Hartopp (Co. Leicester). Sa. a chev. erm. betw. 3 otters pass. arg. *W.* Granted 18 May 1596. *Harl. MS. 1359. fo. 32.* Sir Wm. Hartopp, Rotherby, Leicester 1660. *L.N.*

Hartop. Sa. a chev. erm. betw. three tigers arg. Crest: . . . Add: *V.**

Hartshorne. Az. a chev. betw. 3 bucks heads. C. H. Hartshorne, cabossed arg. **Book Plate.**

Harvell. Add: *V.*

Harvey (Co. Suffolk). Gu. on a bend arg. 3 trefoils slipped vert. in chief a fleur-de-lis erm. *Cady.*

Harvey. Insert—Chigwell (co. Essex and London). Add: *C.L.* Add: Harvey, co. Stafford. *V.* Sir James Hervy, Alderman of London. *V.* William Harvey, Clarenceux King of Arms 1560.

Bateson-Harvey (Langley Park   Baronetcy 1868). Gu. on a bend engr. arg. 3 trefoils slipped vert. within a bordure wavy or.

Thursby-Harvey (Abington, Northants). Or a chev. betw. 3 leopards faces gu. for Harvey, quartering: arg. a chev. betw. 3 lions ramp. sa. for Thursby.

Harvey (London). Az. on a chev. embattled or 3 leopards heads sa. Crest: Out of a mural crown chequy or and az. a leopards head gu. *Vis. Lon. 1633.*

Harvey (Middlesex). Or on a chev. betw. 3 leopards faces gu. as many trefoils slipped arg. Crest: A leopard pass. . . . Add: *Vis. Lon. 1633.*

Harvey (London). Gu. on a bend arg. 3 trefoils slipped vert. On a canton or a rose gu.—'rose'. underlined, query a leopards head. *Vis. Lon. 1633.*

Harware (Stoke, co. Warwick). Az. a bend wavy betw. 2 bucks heads couped or. *C.W.*

Haselerton (Great Grimsby, co. Derby). Add: Haselerton, co. York. temp. Edw. j. *V.*

Haselfoot (Boreham Manor, co. Essex). Add: Haselfoot (London). Same arms and Crest. *Vis. Lon. 1633.*

Haselwood (Maidwell, co. Northants, Wickwarren, co. Worcester and co. Oxford). . . . three hazel branches—insert—'with nuts' . . . Add: *V.*

Hashlard. Or a chev. and over all a lion ramp. gu. *V.**

Haslarton. Arg. on a chev. gu. 3 lions pass. guard or. Thomas Haslarton. *X.*

Haslewood. Arg. a chev. sa. betw. 3 blackbirds on a chief az. 3 bur stalks slipped with each 3 burs or. Haslewood of Maydwell who married the heiress of Lazencroft. *L.N. p. 226.*

Haselwood (Co. Northampton). Arg. on a chev. gu. betw. 3 owls heads front faced erased sa. as many lozenges erm. a chief az. charged with 3 hazel branches or. *V.*

Hassett (Pockthorpe, Norwich). Gu. a chev. erm. betw. 3 dolphins embowed arg. *Cady.*

Hastang (Co. Stafford). Add: Sir Robert de Hastang. *G.J.L.N.* and with a label arg. Sir Johan de Hastang. *N.* Sir Thomas de Hastang. *O.* Az. a chief gu. over all a lion ramp. or and a bendlet arg. Sir Richard Hastang, co. Stafford temp. Edw. iij. *V.* But a dexter baston arg. Sir Richard de Hastang. *N.* Sir Nichol de Hastang. *L.*

Hasted (Sunnings, co. Berks.). . . . . Add: Hasted of Canterbury the historian of Kent.

Hasthorpe. Arg. on a bend sa. 3 martlets or. Sire Johan de Hasthorpe. *O.*

Hastings (Elford, co. Oxford and London). Or a maunch gu. a crescent for diff. Crest: A bull's head couped gu. horned or. *Vis. Lon. 1633.*

Hastings. Per fesse vert. and or a bull—insert—'saliant', counter-changed. Add: Sir Drew de Hasting. *V.*

Hatch or Hacche (Hatch, co. Devon). Add: *V.D. 1620.*

Hatcliff. Az. two bars or over all a lion ramp. gu. Crest: . . . Add: *V.*

Hatfield. Erm. a chev. engr. betw. 3 cinquefoils sa. *V.V.**

Hatfield. Erm. a chev. sa. *V.* Thomas Hatfield, Bishop of Durham. 1345–81. *Q.*

Hatfield (Hatfield, co. York 1665). Erm. on a chev. engr. sa. 3 cinquefoils . . . a canton gu. *Dugdale. p. 270.*

Hatfield (Newton Kyme and Laughton). Co. York. Same arms but canton sa.

Hatfield (Willoughby, co. Notts.). Thomas Hatfield . . . Add: *V.*

Hatfield. Paly of six gu. and arg. . . Add: *Randle Holme.*

Hatfield. Sa. on a chev. or betw. three lions ramp. arg. a mullet of the field. Add: Thomas Hatfield. *Y.*

Hatfield (Alexander Hatfield, Esq., of Twickenham, co. Middlesex). Add: Hatfield (Laughton in le Morthing, co. York 1665). Same arms and crest. *Dugdale. p. 185.*

Hatherley (London and Bristol 1442). Arg. on a bend gu. . . . . Add: Sir John Hatherley, Lord Mayor of London. 1442. *Harl. MS. 6860.*

Hathey (Co. Devon). Sa. three birds arg. membered gu. Add: *V.*

Hathye. Sa. a chev. erm. betw. 3 birds arg. beaked and legged gu. in the dexter chief a crescent for diff.

Hathorpe. Sa. a chev. engr. arg. (another, or). Add: *V.*

Hatley (Aylesbury, co. Buckingham &c.). Add: *Vis. Lon. 1633.*

Hatt (Co. Berks, Orsett, co. Essex and London). . . . Add: *Vis. Lon. 1633.*

Hatter, Merchants (Company of, London). Erm. on a chev. betw. 3 felt hats with strings sa. as many escallops arg.

Hatton (Viscount Hatton). . . . . betw. three garbs —delete—gu., substitute 'or'. Crest: . . .

Hatton (Long Stanton, co. Cambridge, bart.). Insert—1641 . . .

Hatton. Arg. a bend gu. charged with three bars indented—insert—or dancetty. *V.** . . . indented or. Add: *V.*

Hatworth. Arg. three hats sa.—insert—(or 3 caps of maintenance). *V.* Crest: . . . .

Hauberk. Arg. on a bend sa. three 5-foils or. Sire John Hauberk. *S.*

Haule or Hale (Co. Devon). Arg. an arrow or feathered gu. betw. three bugle horns stringed sa. and interlacing the lower one. *V.*

Haulsey, See Halsey.

Haunsart. . . . a chief . . . over all a bend . . . **Seal** of Gilbert Haunsart, 14th cent.

Hautevill (Co. Devon). Sa. semee of crosses botonny—insert—(or crosslet) . . . Add: Sire Geffry de Hautcille. *N.O.*

Hautville. Arg. crusilly and a lion ramp. sa. Thomas Hauteville. *V.* Mons de Hautville. *Y.*

Hauton (Pitsford, co. Northants). Or on a bend sa. betw. 2 cotises gu. 3 mullets arg. *Baker.*

Hauteyn (Sheriff of Norfolk 1258). Arg. a bend sa. *Dashwood.*

Hauteyn. Gu. 3 bendlets the chief part of the two adjacent sides of the lower bendlets indented or. Hamo Hauteyn. *F.*

Havellande (Guernsey). Arg. 3 towers sa. portcullised gu. *Harl. MS. 1465. fo. 167.*

Havering (Co. Dorset). Arg. a lion ramp. tail queued gu. collared of the first. Add: *V.* Sir Richard Havering, Halton Park.

Havering (Co. Wilts.). Arg. semee of crosses crosslet a lion ramp. tail queued gu. Add: Sir John Havering. *V.*

Havering. Arg. a lion ramp. tail forked gu. Richard de Havering. *E.* William de Havering. *Y.*

Haveringfield (Essex). Or a chevron sa. *V.*

Havilland (deHavilland Manor, in Guernsey). . . . a branch of this family settled—insert—'Poole', co. Dorset. . . .

Haward (Co. Gloucester). Arg. 3 bars sa. over all as many cotton hanks or. *V.*

Hawberk. Barry nebulee of six or and vert. Add: *V.* Sir Nicholas. *H.*

Hawberke (Co. Leicester). Add: *Syl. Morgan.*

Hawberke. Arg. on a bend sa. nine annulets . . . Crest: . . . Add: *Harl. MS. 6111. fo. 130b.*

Hawe or Hagh. Add: *V.*

Hawe. Arg. on a bend az. 3 lions pass. in bend or. Sire Nicolas Hawe. *T.*

Hawes. Gu. 3 lions pass. gard. arg. on a bend sa. 3 mullets or.

Hawes (London, Ipswich and Belstead, co. Suffolk and Tadworth Court, co. Surrey 1623). Add: Exemplified by Camden, Clarenceux. iv. Jas. I. and *Vis. Lon. 1633.*

Hawes (Sir James Hawes, Knt. Lord Mayor of London, *Visitation 1568*). Add: Granted by Cooke 1573.

Hawes (London). Az. on a chev. or 3 pierced mullets read—5-foils purp. on a quarter arg. a lion statant sa. *V.*

Hawes (London). Gu. a chev. betw. 3 leopards heads arg. *Cady.*

Hawes (London). Sa. on a chev. betw. 3 lions or as many 5-foils pierced gu. *Cady.*

Hawes or Hawse (London). Add: *Harl. MS. 1404. fo. 111.*

Hawes. Insert—(London). Granted by Harvey 1559. Az. on a chev. or 3 cinquefoils gu. a canton arg. . . . Add: *Guillim.*

Hawes. Az. on a chev. or 3 cinquefoils purp. on a canton arg. a lions pass. sa.—underlined— Add: or per pale gu. and sa. *V̄.**

Hawick. Arg. on a bend sa. 3 crosses of the first. *Surtees.*

Hawis. Az. on a chev. or three 5-foils gu. on a canton arg. a lion pass. sa. *Harl. MS. 1404. fo. 111.*

Hawkewood. Arg. on a chev. sa. 3 escallops of the first. Crest: . . . Add: Sir John Hawkewood. *S.V.**

Hawkewood. Arg. on a chev. sa. three escallops or. *V.*

Hawkins (Co. Gloucester and Sherington, co. Hereford). . . . 3 cinquefoils az. as many escallops arg.—underlined—margin ? or. Add: *V.* Add: Hawkins (London). Same arms. *Cady.*

Hawkwood or Haukwood. Az. on a chev. betw. 3 escallops arg. a torteau. *V.**

Hawksworth (Hawksworth). Insert—co. York. Add: *Foster.*

Hawley. Delete—*S.*—insert—co. Devon. Sa. a fret and canton arg. Crest: . . . Add: *V.*

Hawling. Add: *V.**

Hawte. Arg. on a bend az. three lions ramp. or. Add: Sir Nicholas Hawte. *T. Harl. MS. 6137.*

Hawton or Haughton (*Lon. Her. Off. c. 24*). Insert —Granted by Segar. Add: *Vis. Lon. 1633.*

Hawtre. Arg. on a bend cotised sa. four lions pass. guard. of the first. Add: *V.**

Hawtre. Arg. 4 lions pass. guard. in bend betw. 2 double cotises sa. *V.*

Hawtrey (Exeter). Arg. 3 lions pass. guard. sa. crowned or betw. two bendlets of the second. *Colby.*

Hay (Granted by Camden). Sa. a chev. arg. betw. 3 leopards heads or. *W.*

Haydon (Adam Haydon . . .). Add: *C.L. p. 78.*

Hayse (Westminster, co. Middlesex, bart.). Insert—1797 . . .

Hayes (Windsor, co. Berks and London; granted). Insert—by Bysche.

Hayes. Insert—of the Wardrobe and Litley, co. Chester, granted 1615—insert—by Camden . . . Add: *Syl. Morgan.*

Hayes. Az. on a chev. arg. betw. three boars heads erased ermines as many—insert— 'single handled' ewers gu. Add: *V.*

Haylis. Or a chev. sa. betw. three roses of the second a chief of the last. Add: *V.**

Haylis. Or a chev. sa. betw. 3 roses gu. a chief of the second. Sir . . . de Haylis. *V.*

Haylord or Haylard. Add: *V.*

Hayman (Youghal, Ireland). Arg. on a chev. engr. az. betw. 3 martlets sa. as many 5-foils or.

Hayne or Haynes. Add: *Vis. Lon. 1633.*

Haynes (London). Arg. on a fess betw. 3 crescents gu. as many fleurs-de-lis or. *Vis. Lon. 1633.*

Hayton. Arg. three church bells sa. Crest: . . . Add: *V.*

Hayton. . . . billetty . . . a lion pass. . . . Robert Hayton c. 1424. **Brass** *in the Church at Threddelthorpe, co. Lincoln.*

Hayward. Arg. on a bend az. betw. 2. 2. roses gu. a lion pass. or on a chief of the second a rose arg. betw. 2 fleurs-de-lis or. *College of Arms Grants. xxxv.*

Hazelrigg (Nosely Hall, co. Leicester, bart.). Insert—1622. . . . Add: *W.*

Hazelrigg (Sutton Bonnington, co. Notts.). Arg. a chev. sa. betw. 3 hazel leaves vert. *V.N. 1614.*

Hazlewood (Co. Rutland). Arg. a chev. betw. 3 hazel leaves vert. *C.R.*

Head (Hermitage—insert—'Rochester', co. Kent, bart.). Insert—1676 and 1837.

Headlam (Kexby, co. York 1665). Add: *Dugdale. p. 204.* Add: Headlam (Gilmonly Hall, near Barnard Castle). Same arms. *Debrett.*

Heaington. Erminois on a chev. betw. 3. 3. wolves heads erased az. as many crosses crosslet fitchy or. *Eliz. Roll. xxxv.*

Healy. Sa. on a chev. engr. arg. betw. 3 lions ramp. or as many crosses patty gu. quartering vert. on a chief sa. 3 martlets or. *Collinson Somerset. iij. 407.*

Heard. Per fess or and sa. in chief a raven of the last. *Robson.*

Heath (Chester and Weston). Gu. on a bend arg. cotised or 3 heath cocks sa. combs, gills and legs gu. *Randle Holme.*

Hearne. Per pale az. and gu. a chev. betw. three herons arg. *Harl. MS. 1404. fo. 141.*

Heaton or Hayton. Arg. 3 church bells sa. *V.**

Heaton (Claremont, Leeds). Insert—co. York.

Hebbert. Az. a dragon pass. or on a rock, on a chief indented arg. 3 crosses patonce sa. Crest: A talbot pass. ppr. supporting in his dexter paw a caduceus. Motto: "Tenax et fidus". **Book Plate.**

Hebblethwaite } See Heblethwayte.
Hebblewhite }

Hebbs (Corton, co. Dorset). Add: Hebb or Hebbs (London). Same arms. Crest: A lions head erased arg. delete—read 'or', charged with 3 cinquefoils sa. *Vis. Lon. 1633.*

Heber (Marton, co. York . . .). Add: Heber (Hollinghall, co. York). Per fess az. and qu. a lion ramp. or a mullet for diff. Crest: as before. *Dugdale. 1665.* Heber of Stainton, co. York. *1665.* Same arms, as Heber of Marton. *Dugdale. p. 34.*

Heblethwayte (Sedbergh and Malton, co. York). Descended from James Heblethwayte, of—delete—'that place', read—Sedbergh, *F.Y.* Arg. two palets az. . . . a mullet—delete—'pierced', read—sa.—insert—pierced gu.

Heblethwayte (Co. Norfolk). Entirely deleted—Add: *Blomfield.*

Heblethwayt (Of Norton, 1660). Arg. 2 bars az. on a canton or a martlet sa. a torteau. *C.N.*—entirely struck out,—substitute 'same arms'.

Hector. Arg. three bends gu. an estoile az. Add: Sir Hector de Mares, Knight of the Round Table. *Cotton MS. Tiberius. D. 10.*

Hedd (Henry Hedd, Sheriff of London . . .). Add: *C.L.p. 53.*

Hede or Hedesa (Co. Kent and London). Add: *V.* and *Cady.*

Hedingham. Erm. a bend engr. gu. guttee d'eau . . . Add: William Hedingham. *V.*

Hedlam (Stainton, co. Durham). Add: *V.*

Hedley (Newcastle-on-Tyne). Add: *Carr MS. i. V.*

Hedon (Morton Holderness). Insert—1584. Add: *F.Y.*

Heighton. Arg. a chev. betw. 2 paroquets gu. beaked or in chief a mullet for diff. *Carr MS.*

Heland (Co. York). Add: *V.*

Heldt (London, originally of Holstein). Arg. a fess wavy az. over all a nettle leaf stalked and issuing from a tuft of grass vert. Crest: A leaf &c. *Vis. Lon. 1633.*

Hele (John Hele, Serjeant at Law). Gu. on a bend fusilly arg. in sinister chief a mullet or. *Dug. O.J.*

Hele (Hele, co. Devon). Gu. a bend lozengy . . . Sir Roger Hele. *Syl. Morgan.*

Helingsal. Arg. 2 bars within a bordure gu. *V.*

Hellard (Granted to Peter Hellard, Prior of the Canons of Bridlington ix Edw. IV. *1407* by Thomas Holme, Norroy). Sa. a bend betw. 2 cotises and 6 fleurs-de-lis arg. *Tonge. xxxviij.*

Hellard (Ruston, co. York 1612). Same arms. *F.Y.*

Hellard (Kelham, co. York 1665). Same arms. *Dugdale. p. 118.*

Hellard. Sa. a bend betw. 2 cotises flory arg. *V.* The cotises flory and counterflory arg. *V.**

Hellifield. Arg. 2 bendlets wavy sa. William de Hellifield. *Y.*

Helligan (Cornwall). Gu. crusilly or a bend vair. *Lysons.*

Helligan (Cornwall). Gu. on a bend or 3 bucks heads of the first. *Lysons.*

Hellord or Highlord (Woodbury, co. Devon). Insert—and London . . . Add: *Vis. Lon. 1633.* Arms confirmed by Segar 1630.

Hellynes. Arg. on 3 chevs. sa. as many escallops on the centre chev. or. *V.*

Hellnisse (Co. Lincoln, 1640). Same arms as Hellvys, Norfolk. *Yorke.*

Hellynes. Arg. on a chev. betw. 2 couple closes sa. 3 escallops or. *V.*

Helman. Arg. three bendlets az. a bordure gu. Add: *V.**

Helman. Arg. 3 bendlets az. a bordure engr. gu. *V.*

Hellyarde. Sa. a chev. betw. 3 estoiles arg. *Constable's Roll. xj.*

Helmebridge (Co. Gloucester). Add: John de Helmebrige. *V.V.**

Helmebridge or Elmbrigge. Chequy arg. and sa. *V.V.**

Helton (John Helton, Westmorland). Sa. 3 annulets or in chief 2 saltires arg. *X.*

Hellers. Quarterly arg. and az. a bend gu. *V.**

Hellers (Rokelay). Same arms, but a bendlet. *V.*

Helwell. Erm. on a chev. sa. 3 bezants a bordure engr. gu. *C.R. p. 45.*

Helwys (Sheriff of Norfolk 1732). Or a bend gu. over all a fess. az. *Dashwood.*

Hellnisse (Co. Lincoln 1640). Same as Hellvys, Norfolk. *Yorke.*

Heming (Mayor of Worcester 1677). Or on a chev. sa. betw. 3 lions heads erased of the second as many pheons of the first. Impaling per pale indented arg. and gu. *His Monument.* See *N. 2. 3d. 3. V. 489.*

Hemyng (London and co. Herts). Gu. on a fess betw. 3 mascles or as many escallops of the field a bordure engr or. charged with 8 torteaux. Crest: An escallop gu. *Vis. Lon. 1633.*

Hen (Sir Rhys Hen). Or 3 lapwings volant vert. membered gu. a bordure engr. of the second. *Harl. MS. 1441.*

Henchman or Hinchman. Add: Henchman (Norfolk). Or a chev. betw. 3 bugle horns sa. *Blomfield.*

Henden. Add: Sir Edward Henden, Baron of the Exchequer 1639. *Dug. O. J.*

Henden (London). Gu. a lion pass. betw. 3 escallops or. Crest: a demi-lion ramp. az. holding an escallop or. *Vis. Lon. 1633.*

Hendy or Hinde (Co. Lancaster). Add: *V.*

Hendley (Cuckfield, co. Sussex and Courseom, co. Kent). Add: *V.**

Hendwn (Wales). Az. a wolf saliant arg. Meredith ap Hendwn. *Randle Holme.*

Hendy or Hendey. Add: *V.V.**

Heneage (Walker-Heneage, Compton Bassett, co. Wilts.). Or a greyhound courant sa. betw. three leopards faces az.—insert—*V. . . .*

Heneage (Hynton, co. Lincoln). Arg. a greyhound courant sa. betw. 3 wolf's heads erased gu. within a bordure az. charged with 8 cinquefoils of the first. *V.*

Henegan (Cork and Bantry). Arg. a hare courant . . . betw. in chief two 3-foils vert. and in base a crescent gu.

Henkel. Gu. 3 bars enarched arg.

Hendover (Quartered by Bowyer-Smith). Az. a lion ramp. betw. an orle of escallops or.

Henley (Northington, co. Hants). Add: *Vis. Lon. 1633.* Add: Henly (Granted by Camden to Robert Henly Sheriff of Somerset 26 Feb. 1612). *Syl. Morgan.*

Henman (Holkfield, Kent). . . . a lion ramp. betw. 3 mascles . . . *Robson.*

Hennes. Arg. 3 birds close arg. membered gu. a bordure gobony or and az. *Cady.*

Henrickes or Henrike.

Hengsott. Arg. on a chev. betw. 3 leopards heads az. as many bezants each charged with an ogress. *V.**

Henscott (Quartered by Burnby of Bratton, co. Devon). Add: *W.*

Hengs.

Henshaw (Great Marlow, co. Essex and London). Arg. a chev.—read—ermines—betw. &c. Add: *V.E. 1634.*

Hensley (Exeter 1566). Arg. a lion ramp. az. *Cady.*

Hensley (Granted to Richard Hensley Captain of Pioneers at the siege of Kinsale 26 Apr. 1602). Vert. a portcullissed gate in the curtain betw. two spired towers and part of a town wall in base a winding trench arg. *Harl. MS. 1441.*

Henville. Sa. a lion ramp. betw. eight crosses crosslet arg. Crest: . . . Add: Sir   , co. Dorset.

Hepburn (Dr. George Hepburn, Edinburgh 1672). Add: *Nisbet j. 166.*

Herbert (Norbury, co. Derby). Gu. 3 lions ramp. or. *Guillim.*

Herbert (York 1612). Per pale gu. and az. a lion ramp. erminois. *F.Y.*

Herbert (Henry Herbert, Winister). Per pale az. and gu. 3 lions ramp. arg. a crescent and a label of 5 points or. *Z. 348.*

Herbert (York, 1665). Per pale gu. and az. 3 lions ramp. arg. within a bordure compony gu. and or a canton of the last. *Dugdale. p. 148.*

Herbert (Middleton Qhernhow, co. York 1665). Add: Motto: "Pawb-ýn ý Arver". Add: *Dugdale. p. 165.*

Herbert (Calais). Az. a chev. arg. betw. 3 shovellers heads erased of the second ducally gorged or. *V.*

Herbottyll. Add: *V.**

Hercey. Erm. on a chev. sa. three 5-foils or. *V.V.**

Hereford. Gu. 3 eagles displ. arg. a label of 5 points az. Henri d'Hereford. *E.*

Hereward (Sheriff of Norfolk). 1300. Add: *Dashwood.* Add: Sire Robert Hereward. *N.* Sir Robert Hereward, co. Cambridge temp. Edw. j. *V.*

Herice or Heriz. Add: Henry de Herice. *A.*

Herle. Gu. a chev. betw. 3 drakes arg. Sir Robert Herle. *S.*

Hern (Exeter 1502). Gu. a heron or. *Colby.*

Hern. Gu. crusilly or a heron arg. Sir William Hern. *F.* But Hernn. *E.*

Herne. Az. a chev. erm. betw. 3 herons . . . †

Herne (Godmanchester, co. Hunts.). Gu. a chevron betw. 3 herons arg. *V.H. 1613.*

Herne or Heron (Panfield Hall, co. Essex, London and Shacklewell, co. Middlesex 1600). Add: Heron. Treasurer of the Chamber to Hen. viij. *Nicholls. Coll. Top. ij. 166.* Herne (London). A mullet for diff. *Vis. Lon. 1633.*

Heron (Baron Heron . . .). Add: Sir John Heron. *S.X.* Lyonell Heron of Thickley. *Eliz. Roll. xviij.*

Heron (Bokenfield, co. Northumberland). Add: Sir Roger Heron. *N.X.* The herons beaked and legged or with an annulet for diff. Sir Gerard Heron. *S.* And with a † in chief or. Sir Wauter Heron. *S.*

Heron (Chipshaw, Norfolk). Baronetcy 1662. Az. 3 herons arg.

Heron. Gu. 3 herons arg. beaked and legged or in chief a cross crosslet of the last. Sir Wauter Heron. *S.*

Heron (Cos. Essex and Northumberland and Ipswich, Suffolk). Add: Odinel Heron. *B.X.* Sir John Heron. *E.N.V.* Sir Godard and Sir Roger Heron. *M.*

Heron. Heron (Ford Castle). Same arms, quartering. Barry of 6 arg. and az. a bend gu. charged with a plate.

Heron (Co. Northumberland and Scotland). Add: *V.* Add: Heron of London. Same arms. † for diff. *Vis. Lon. 1633.*

Heron (Croydon, co. Surrey). Add: Sire William Heron. *S.V.*

Heron (Essex). Sa. a chev. erm. betw. 3 herons arg. *V.E. 1634.*

Heron (Co. Lincoln). Sa. a chev. erm. betw. 3 herons or. *Yorke.*

Heron (Co. Surrey). Add: Heron, Agecombe, now Addiscombe, Surrey. 1544. Sir John Heron, Chuston. *V.*

Herondi. Gu. billetty and 3 lions ramp. or. John de Herondi. *F.*

Herondon. Insert—(London). Same arms . . . as Herondon, above . . .

Heronvile. Az. three herons arg. Add: Thomas Heronville. *X.*

Heronville (Wednesbury, co. Stafford). Add: John de Herunvile. *F.*

Herren (Sylington, Scotland). Add: *Guillim.*

Herrick or Eyrick (Beaumanor, co. Leicester &c.). Add: *Harl. MS. 1476.*

Herries. Az. a chev. erm. betw. 3 hedgehogs statant or. John Herreys. *V.*

Herring (Lethinby, Scotland). Gu. on a bend arg. two 5-foils and two lions pass. alternately of the first. *Guillim.*

Herriz. Az. a hedgehog or. *V.N. p. 143.*

Herris (London). Or on a bend az. 3 cinquefoils of the field a crescent for diff. Crest: A talbot sejant or. *Vis. Lon. 1633.*

Hertford. Sa. a bend fusilly arg. *V.*V.*

Hertlington. Arg. a lion ramp. crowned gu. Henry Hertlington. *Y.*

Hervey or Harvey (Wangey, co. Essex). Arg. a chev. betw. 3 leopards faces gu. a crescent for diff. *V.E. 1634.*

De Hervill. Arg. 2 lions pass. in pale sa. *V.** The lions reguard. coward tails reflexed over the back. Sir . . . de Hervill. *V.*

De la Hese. Arg. 3 lions ramp. gu. and a fess sa. John de la Hese. *Y.*

Hese. Or 3 eagles displ. sa. Henry Hese. *F.*

Hesill or Hesyll. Add: *V.*

Hesilrigge (Nosely, co. Leicester, bart.). Arg. a chev.—insert—? gu. . . . betw. . . . .

Hesilrigge (Noseby, co. Leicester). Arg. a chev. sa. betw. 3 hazel leaves vert. *C.C. 1619.*

Hesketh (Rufford, co. Lancaster, Baronetcy 1761). Arg. an eagle displ. with 2 heads ppr. *Edmondson.*

Hesketh (Aughton, co. Lancaster 1664). Add: *V.L.*

Hesketh (Poulton, co. Lancaster 1664). Same arms—insert—But a canton sa. Add: *V.L.*

Heskett (*Lancaster Herald 1713*). Add: *Noble.*

Heslerigg. Arg. a chev. betw. 3 trefoils slipped vert. *Eliz. Roll. xxxvij.*

Heslerton (Rotford, &c., co. York). Add: Sir Thomas de Haselartone. *N.* Walter de Heslarton. *Y.*

Hesse (Paddington, Middlesex, confirmed 12 June 1772). Per chev. the upper part per pale erm. and arg. the lower arg. on a chev. sa. betw. in chief on the dexter side an eagle displ. double headed silver holding a gauntlet gu. and a scimitar hovering over an Imperial crown, on the sinister side a turbanned Turk's head in profile couped fesswise face downward, the neck towards the edge of the escutcheon issuing drops of blood over a Turk's banner staff in bend sinister inverted and in base a Z. top and bottom indented sa. enclosed by 2 ash trees vert. from the under part of the chev. a pile az. there on a sun or 6 ostrich feathers each turned towards the centre ppr. a chief az. with a canton gu. charged with a peer's helmet.

Hethman. Az. fretty arg. a bordure engr. or. Sir Rafe Hethman. *L. Harl. MS. 6589. fo. 38.*

Hethersett (Sir John Hethersett of Hethersset, Norfolk). Az. a lion ramp. guard. or armed and langued gu. *Cady*.

Hethersett of Shropham. Az. a lion ramp. guard. or holding in his dexter forepaw a battle axe, and in his dexter hind paw a fire-ball. **Book Plate.**

Heton (Co. Lancaster). Add: James Heton. *V*.

Heton (London 1568). Arg. on a bend engr. sa. 3 bulls heads couped of the field; quartering arg. a Moor's head sa. banded round the forehead of the first and second betw. 3 fleurs-de-lis sa. *C.L.*

Heton. Vert. a lion ramp. arg. (another, a bordure engr. arg.). Add: *V*.

Heuer. Add: Richard Heuer. Cookfield. *V*.

Heveningham. Per saltire or and gu. on a bordure engr. sa. eight escallops arg. Add: *V*.*

Heveningham (Co. Norfolk). Insert—and Suffolk. Quarterly or and gu. on a bordure engr. sa. 8 escallops arg. Add: *V*.

Heveningham (Norfolk). Quarterly or and gu. on a bordure sa. 8 escallops gold. *Dashwood*.

Heveningham (Temp. Edw. ij.). Quarterly arg. and sa. a bendlet gu. *F.Y.*

Heveningham (Co. Stafford). Quarterly or and gu. a bordure engr. sa. bezanty. *Erdeswick*.

Heverley. Add: Wautier de Heverley. *Y*.

Hewe. Add: *V*.

Hewer (Clapham, co. Surrey). Arg. on a chev. engr. betw. three 3-foils vert. as many mullets—delete—substitute, bezants.

Hewis or Hivis (Stowford, co. Devon). The heiress married Hawley. Gu. fretty arg. a canton of the second.

Hewes. Gu. fretty arg. a canton of the last. *V*.*

Hewes (William Hewes &c. . . .). Add: *C.L.*

Hewett (Headley Hall, co. York. bart.). Insert—1621 . . . Add: *Guillim*.

Hewett (Pishiobury, co. Hertford). . . . Same arms. Add: and crest.

Hewett (Viscount Hewett, the 2nd bart. of Pishiobury). . . . Same arms . . . Add: Supporters: Dexter, a falcon or with wings expanded arg. Sinister, a griffin or wings expanded arg. collared az. billetty or. Motto: "Vigilando". **Tomb** in Sawbridgenorth Church.

Hewick or Hewikes. Gu. bezantee a lion ramp. arg. *Y.V.*

Hewish (Co. Cornwall). Add: Sire Richard Hewes. *N.V.*

Hewstas or Eustass. *V*. Az. a bend betw. 6 crosses crosslet fitchy arg. *V*.

Hewston. Gu. on a chev. betw. 3 leopards faces arg. goutee de poix. *V.V.*

Hewya. Arg. fretty and a canton gu. Sir de Hewya. *V*.

Hexstall (Hexstall, co. Warwick and co. Stafford). Add: *V*.

Hexton. Sa. (another, gu.). Insert—*V*.* . . .

Hey (Pudsey, co. York). Per bend nebuly or and sa. a lion ramp. counterchanged quartering sa. a cross betw. 4 fleurs-de-lis or. *Whitaker's Leeds. ij. 3.*

Heyford. Arg. a chev. sa. betw. 3 bucks springing gu. attired or. *V*.*

Heyforde (Lord Mayor of London 1477). Add: *V*.

Heygate (Southend, co. Essex. bart.). Insert—1831 . . . Add: *Vis. Lon. 1633*.

Heygeys. Add: *V*.

Heyland (Co. York). Add: *V*.

Heyliston or Heylston (London). Add: John Heyliston. *V*.

Heyman (Somerfield, co. Kent. bart.). Insert—1641 . . . . Add: Sir Peter Haymon. *V*.

Heynes (Amend to read, Milden Hall, co. Suffolk). . . . confirmed . . . Add: by Cooke . . .

Heyton. Vert. a lion ramp. arg. Sir Adam de Heyton or Heton. *V*.

Heyton. Vert. 3 lions ramp. arg. *Robson*.

Heyton. Vert. a lion ramp. within a bordure engr. arg. Add : *V*.

Hickes (Luxillian, Cornwall). Arg. a tower triple towered betw. 3 battle axes sa. *W*.

Hickes (London and Northants). Az. 2 pales or betw. 9 fleurs-de-lis of the second a martlet for diff. Crest: A griffin sejant or collared gu. on its dexter claw an arrow or. *Vis. Lon. 1633*.

Hickford. Vert. on a chev. betw. 3 bucks heads cabossed as many mullets gu. *V*.

Hickton. Or three eagles displ. sa. Add: *V*.*

Hide. Arg. a chev. betw. 3 lozenges sa. *Cady*.

Hide (Hertford). Az. a chev. betw. 3 lozenges or. *Cady*.

Hide-Abbey (Co. Hants.). Add: *U* and *Tanner*.

Hide (Northbury Hall). Az. a chev. betw. 3 lions ramp. or a † arg. for diff. *Cady*.

Higdn or Hygdon. Per pale az. and vert. a chev. betw. 3 stags heads cabossed or on a chief arg. a rose gu. enclosed by two leopards heads of the first. *Harl. MS. 1404. fo. 109*.

Higford or Hickford (Twining, co. Gloucester). Add: *V*.

Higgat (Co. Suffolk). Insert—and co. Essex. Add: *V.E. 1558*.

Higgins (Worcester: John Higgins). . . . Add: *Nash*.

Higginson (Lisburn, co. Antrim . . .). Add: *A.A.*

Higham (Essex and Cooling, Suffolk). Chevronny of 3 or and sa. a bend engr. arg.

Higham (Cooling, co. Suffolk). Add: Higham (Essex and Goldhanger in Cowling, Suffolk). Same arms. *Harl. MS. 1440. 1560.*

Higham (Co. Kent). Arg. a lion pass. reguard. coward betw. 6 crosses patty fitchy sa. *V*.

Hicklord. See Hellord.

Hicklord or Hellard. Sheriff of London. temp. Charles i. Sa. a bend flory arg.

Hilbeck of Hilbeck, co. Westmorland, the heiress married Blenkinsop. Temp. Edw. ij. Gu. 6 annulets or 3.2. and 1 within a bordure engr. arg.

Hildersham (Co. Cambridge). Add: *V*.

Hildesley (Cromers Gifford; William Hildesley). . . . Add: Hildesley (Barthropp, co. York 1612). Same arms, a mullet for diff. *V.Y.*

Hildesley (Crowmarch Gifford, co. Oxon). Same arms. *V.O.*

Hildyard (Patrington, co. York, bart.). Insert—1660 . . .

Hildyard (Temp. Edw. ij.). Sa. a chev. betw. 3 mullets arg. *F.Y.*

Hills (Confirmed to John Hills of London by Cooke, Clarenceux 1586). Sa. a chev. or betw. 3 cats pass. guard arg. Crest: On a glove fessways or a hawk ppr. belled or. *Vis. Lon. 1633*.

Hill (Hillstope, co. Cornwall). Add: *V.C. 304.*

Hill (Sir Robert Hill) . . . Add: Hill (Shilston in Modbury, co. Devon). Same arms. *V.D. 1620*. A crescent for diff. Hill (Denham, co. Bucks). Sir Roger Hill 1668. *L.N.* Same arms.

Hill (Co. Kent). Az. a chev. betw. 3 fleurs-de-lis arg. Add: *V*.

Hill. Sa. a chev. erm. betw. 3 cats pass. guard arg. *V.V.*

Hill (Stallington Hall, co. Stafford). Sa. a chev. or betw. 3 wild cats pass. guard. quartering Clarke.

Hill (London). Sa. a chev. erm. betw. 3 cats pass. guard or. *W*.

Hill (London, granted by Cooke). Sa. a chev. betw. 3 cats statant guard. or. *W.*

Hill (London). Arg. an eagle displ. . . . 3 roses of the first. Add: *V*

Hill (Sir Rowland Hill, Lord Mayor of London and of co. Salop). Az. 2 bars arg. on a canton sa. a chev. betw. 3 falcons arg. and charged with a griffins (or Wolf's) head enclosed by two mullets gu.

Hill (M.P. for Worcester 1874). Erm. a chev. lozengy or and az. in base on a mound vert. a falcon. *Debrett.*

Hill (Amend to read Teddington, co. Middlesex). Sa. a chev. erm. betw. 3 leopards faces &c. Add: *Vis. Lon. 1633.*

Hill. Preceding—Add: Hill, John Hill of London, Auditor, granted by Cooke. Same arms. *W.*

Hill. Gu. on a chev. betw. 3 garbs arg. a rose gu. *Cady.*

Hill (Co. Somerset, granted by Cooke, 1570). Gu. a chev. engr. erm. betw. 3 garbs or and a bordure arg. *V.S.*

Hill. Alias Hull (Littlepipe, co. Stafford). Add: *W.*

Hill (Middle Temple, London). Erm. a castle gu. with portcullis sa. †

Hill (Axley Manor, Wolverhampton). Or a chev. gu. betw. 3 crosses crosslet fitchy sa. *Debrett.*

Hill (Spakestone, co. Stafford). Gu. on a chev. engr. erm. betw. 3 garbs arg. a 5-foil pierced of the field. *V.*

Hill (Rookwood, Llandaff, co. Glamorgan). Arg. 2 chevs. gu. betw. in chief 2 water bougets sa. and in base a mullet of the second a crescent for diff. *Nicholas.*

Hill (Co. Somerset). Gu. 2 bars or in chief a lion pass. arg. *V.*

Hill. Gu. 2 bars and in chief a lion pass. or. *V.**

Hill Az. a chev. betw. 3 fleurs-de-lis or. *W.*

Hillary (Danbury Place, co. Essex &c.). . . . Add: Hillary (London). Same arms and crest, but arm issuing from a wreath and not from a mural coronet. *Vis. Lon. 1633.*

Hillersdon (Originally of Hillersdon in Collumpton, co. Devon). . . . Add: *V.D. 1620. V.*

Hillersdon (Hoclyfe, co. Bedford). . . . Arg. on a chev.—insert—plain. Add: *W.*

Hilliard (Patrington, co. York. Baronetcy 1660). Az. a chev. arg. betw. 3 mullets or.

Hills (London). Sa. a chev. or betw. 3 cats pass. guard. arg. Crest: On a glove fesswise or a hawk standing ppr. belled or. *Vis. Lon. 1633.*

Hillyard (London).—Az. a chev. arg. betw. three mullets pierced or. *Vis. Lon. 1633.*

Hiltoft or Hiltofte. Add: *V.*

Hilton. Arg. 2 bars az. Le Baron de Hilton. *S.Y.* Le Sire de Hilton. *Y.* Sir Robert Hilton. *V.* Robert de Hilton. *F.F.* Sir Robert de Hiltone. *H.N.*

Hilton (Hilton, co. Durham). . . . one of the great baronial families . . . Add: Motto: "Tant que je puis". *Guillim.*

Hilton (Cos. Lancaster and York). Add: Sire . . . de Hilton. *V.*

Hilton (Co. Lancaster). Arg. semy of mullets sa. a lion ramp. gu. armed az.

Hind (Mayor of Calais 1557). Add: *V.*

Hind (Hedgeworth, co. Bucks). Gu. a chev. betw. 3 hinds statant or. *W.*

Hinde. Arg. on a chev. az. 3 escallops of the first a chief of the second charged with a lion pass. of the field. *V.*

Hinde (Hodgeworth, co. Bucks.). Granted 1583 . . . *Vis. Lon. 1633.*

Hinde (London). Gu. on a chev. betw. 3 hinds trippant or . . . Add: Crest: Out of a ducal coronet or a cockatrice wings expanded or crested and jelloped gu.

Hindle (Co. Lancaster). Vert. a chev. or in chief two greyhounds courant and in base a rabbit also courant.

Hingeston, Hengeston or Heyngeston. Az. a battle axe or headed arg. edge to the sinister. *V.**

Heyngeston. Az. a halbert or edge to the sinister, its lance point arg. *V.*

Hingscot (Co. Devon). Arg. on a chev. betw. 3 leopards az. as many palets or each charged with an ogress. *V.*

Hinstoke. Add: *V.V.**

Hinton. Gu. on a bend arg. cotised or three martlets sa. Add: Hynton, John de Hynton. *Y.* Sir William de Hynton. *V.*

Hirton (That Ilk). Arg. 3 annulets gu.

De Hispanid (Spains Hall, Finchingfield, Essex). Quarterly vert. and or a couped baston of the second.

Hitcham (Confirmed 1604 to Sir Robert Hitcham). Gu. on a chief or three torteaux. Add: Crest: A buck saliant ppr. among leaves and the trunk of a tree. ppr.

Hitching (Carlton, co. York). 1665 . . . a chev. . . . betw. 3 pelicans. *Dugdale.*

Hithman. Az. fretty and a bordure engr. or. Sir Rafe Hithman. *L. Harl. MS. 6589. fo. 44.*

Hizam. Add: *V.V.**

Hobbs (Tooting, co. Surrey). Insert—Granted by Camden 1603 . . .

Hobbs (Trevince, Cornwall). . . . 3 eagles displ. purp. *Lysons.*

Hobildod. Arg. on a plain bend within a bordure engr. gu. 3 martlets or. *V.V.**

Hobleday (Thornton, co. Warwick). . . . Add: *C.W.*

Hobson (Wingwood, Isle of Wight). Add: *V.*

Hobson. Arg. on a chev. engr. az. 3 blocks or each charged with a cross of the second. *Harl. MS. 1404. fo. 118.*

Hobson (Cambridge 1634). Arg. on a chev. az. betw. 3 torteaux as many cinquefoils or a chief vairy or and az.

Hobson (Marylebone Park, co. Middlesex). Add: *V.*

Hobson (Co. Middlesex 1633). Add: *Vis. Lon. 1633.*

Hobury. Gu. a lion ramp. betw. 8 crosses crosslet fitchy arg. *V.*

Hobury. Gu. a lion ramp. or betw. 8 crosses crosslet fitchy arg. *V.*

Hoby. Insert—Hoby, co. Leicester. Az. a bend—delete—(another, a pale). . . . Add: *Burton.*

Hodder (Ireland). . . . a chev. . . . betw. 3 covered cups . . . John Hodder, 1655. *Seal.*

Hoderngo. Gu. 3 lions ramp. or. *Guillim.*

Hodeby. Az. 3 birds arg. armed gu. *V.*V.*

Hodely. Gu. a chev. betw. 3 birds arg. beaked and legged or. *V.*

Hodges (Overne, co. Leicester). Add: *C.C. 1619.*

Hodgetts (Humphry Hodgetts, High Sheriff of Stafford 1720). Per fess gu. and az. a chief 3 birds and in base a fleur-de-lis or. *Shaw.*

Hodgetts (Co. Stafford). Arg. on a crescent az. 3 crescents or. †

Hodgson (Newcastle-on-Tyne). Add: Hodgson (Newhall, co. York). 1612. Same arms. *F.Y.* Hodgson (co. Durham). Same arms. *Surtees.*

Hodgson. 1475. Per fess embattled or and az. three martlets counterchanged. *Carr MS.*

Hodiam. Gu. on a bend erm. three chevronnels of the first Crest: A lions head erased az. Add: *V.*

Hoding. Gu. a bend and bordure vair. Sir J. Hoding, Burnham and Beckonsfield, co. Bucks. time Edw. j. *V.*

Hodeing (Essex). Same arms. *Morant ij. 277.*

Hodisham. Arg. a bend engr. betw. two—delete—(another, three). . . . crescents sa. Add: *V.*

Hodiswell. Gu. 3 square wells arg. water az. *V.*

Hodson (London and co. York). Per chev. embattled or and az. 3 martlets counterchanged † for diff. Crest: On a rock ppr. a martlet or. *Vis. Lon. 1633.*

Hodson. Insert—London, arg. a bend wavy gu. betw. two horseshoes arg. Add: *C.L.* and *W.*

Hodstoke. Add: *V.*

Hoerne. Gu. a chev. or betw. three bugle horns arg. *V.*W.*

Hoey (Dublin). Arg. on a chev. betw. 2 bars gu. 3 crosses patty or; quartering chequy or and gu. a lion ramp. erm. *Robson.*

Hogan (London). Arg. a chev. vairy or and gu. betw. 3 hurts each charged with a lions gamb erased of the first. *C.C.*

Hoggeshon or Hoggesh. Vair a chief or over all on a bendlet 3 mullets . . . *E.*

Hoghton. Erm. a chev. engr. sa. *Harl. MS. 1386. fo. 34b.*

Hogsha. Vairy arg. and gu. a bordure sa. Thomas Hogsha. *V.*

Holele. Arg. two chev. betw. three oak leaves vert. Add: *V.*

Hokeley. Or a lion ramp. gu. overall a bend sa. *V.*

Holand. Az. a bend betw. six mullets pierced arg. Add: *V.*

Holand. Gu. 2 bars or and an orle of martlets arg. Sire John de Holand. *O.*

Holbeame (Holbeame and Coffinswell, co. Devon). The heiress married Marwood . . . Add: *V.*

Holbeche. Insert—co. Somerset. Arg. a chev. engr. sa. Add: *V.V.S.*

Holbrook (Co. Suffolk). Add: Sir James Holbrook. *V.*

Holbrook. 1390 . . . a chev. . . . betw. 3 martlets . . .

Holbrooke (Co. Suffolk). Or a chev. gu. surmounted with a cross formee . . . Add: *V.*

Holbrooke (Co. Kent). Or on a chev. betw. ten crosses crosslet gu. a lions head erased of the field.

Holcam and Holcan. Add: *V.*

Holcam. Az. 3 bars nebuly erm. *V.*

Holcombe (Hull, co. Devon). Add: *V.D. 1620.*

Holden. Arg. a chief sa. over all a bend engr. gu. Add: *V.**

Holden. Gu. a chev. wavy betw. 3 crosses crosslet or. *W.*

Holdenby (Holdenby, co. York and London). . . . a fess . . . betw. 3 covered cups . . . *Vis. Lon. 1633.*

Holder (South Wheatly, co. Notts.). Add: Thomas Holder, Auditor General to the Duke of York. *Guillim.*

Holdich. Az. on a chev. or (another arg.) 3 birds sa. Add: *V.**

Holdich (Granted 1824 to the Rev. Thomas Holdich (Northampton). Add: Holditche (co. Norfolk). Same arms.

Holdiche or Holditch (Read—Ranworth, co. Norfolk). Add: *V.*

Holebrooke. Or a chev. betw. 10 crosses crosslet gu. Crest: . . . Add: *F.* and *N.* Sir Richard de Holebroke.

Holford (Purfleet, co. Essex). Arg. a greyhound statant sa. *V.E. 1612.*

Holford (Co. York). Same arms, a crescent for diff. *F.Y. 639.*

Holford (Alerston, co. York). Same arms, but a mullet gu. for diff.

Holford. Insert—1601. Arg. a chev. betw. three text T's . . .

Holgate (Walden, co. Essex). Add: *V.E. 1634.*

Holirood (Tartoine). Arg. 3 falcons close and belled ppr. *Harl. MS. 1441.*

Holland (Sir Otho . . . first Earl of Kent) . . . Add: Sir Robert Holland. *L.N.* Sir Thomas Holland. *Q.S.* John de Holland. *S.* Henry de Holland. *Y.* And with a cross patty gu. on the shoulder. Sir Otes Holland. *Q.*

Holland. Arg. 2 bars betw. six martlets in orle gu. *Cady.*

Holland (Quidenham and Harleston, co. Norfolk, bart.). Insert—1629 . . . Add: *Guillim,* adds a bordure arg.

Holland (Weare, co. Devon). Az. a lion ramp. betw. 3 fleurs-de-lis or. *Lysons.*

Holland (Recorder of Exeter 1498). Az. a lion salient guard. betw. 5 fleurs-de-lis arg. *Colby.*

Holland (Ipswich, co. Suffolk and London). Az. semy of fleurs-de-lis arg. a lion ramp. guard. of the second over all a bend gu. 3 mullets silver. Crest: A demi-lion ramp. guard. arg. collared gu. charged with 3 mullets arg. *Vis. Lon. 1633.*

Holland (Denton, co. Lancaster 1567). Add: *V.*

Holland (Co. Surrey; William Holland). . . . Add: *C.L.*

Holland. Az. semy of crosses crosslet or a lion ramp. guard. arg. Mons Henry de Holland. *Y.*

Holland. Az. semy of escallops a lion pass. guard. arg. Sir Richard de Houlland. *O.*

Holland-Dance (Wittenham, co. Berks. Baronetcy 1800). Per pale az. and gu. a lion ramp. reguard. erm. betw. 8 fleurs-de-lis alternately arg. and or. *Robson.*

Holland Priory (Co. Lincoln). Add: *Tanner.*

Holleys (Lord Mayor of London 1539). Add: *V.*

Hollinpriest. Or 2 bars engr. az. on an escu. arg. a cross gu. on a chief erm. 3 palets gu. *Randle Holme.*

Hollingsworth (Surrey and Hartlepool, co. Durham). Add: *Robson.*

Hollingworth (Hollingworth, co. Chester). Add: *Vis. Lon. 1633.* Add: Hollingworth (Wheston, co. Leicester 1619). Same arms. *C.C.*

Hollingworth (Co. Chester). Sa. on a bend arg. 3 holly leaves vert. *V.*

Hollingworth (Co. Lincoln 1640). Same arms. *Yorke.*

Holly (Lynn, Norfolk). 1723. Or on a chev. sa. three unicorns heads erased of the field.

Holman (Co. Devon). Granted June 1608. Insert —by Camden . . .

Holman (London). Vert. a chev. arg. goutty de sang. betw. 3 pheons of the second. Crest: a crossbow erect or betw. 2 wings gu. *Vis. Lon. 1633.*

Holman. Vert. a chev. arg. betw. 3 pheons or. *W.*

Holman (London). . . . Crest: On a chapeau . . . Add: *W.*

Holman (Godeston, co. Surrey). Add: *W.*

Holman. Vert. on a chev. or betw. 3 pheons arg. a fleur-de-lis gu. Add: *V.*

Holme or Hulme (Hulme, co. Lancaster). Add: *V.* Add: Holme (London). Same arms. *C.L.*

Holme. Arg. a chev. az. within a bordure engr. sa. *J.*

Holme (Beverley, co. York). Add: *V.*

Holme (Huntingdon, co. York). Insert—1584. Add: *F.Y.*

Holme. Sa. a lion ramp. barry of six arg. and gu. Add: *V.*

Holme (The Revd. Dr. Holme. Fellow of Queen's College, Oxford). Or 3 bars az. on a canton arg. a rose gu. †

Holme (Paull-Holme, co. York). . . . Insert—quartering Wastneys and Rikele. *Dugdale. 1665.*

Holmeden (Co. Kent). Sa. a fess betw. 2 chevs. erm. and 3 leopards faces or.

Holmes. Barry of 6 or and az. on a canton arg. a rose gu. Sir . . . de Holmes. *V.*

Holmes (Co. Lancaster). Barry of 10 or and az. on a canton arg. a chaplet arg. *Carter.*

Holmes. Or a chev. betw. 3 chaplets of roses in chief gu. and in base an anchor sa. *Robson.*

Holmes (North Mymes, co. Herts.). Add: *V.*

Holmes (Hampoll. Visit York 1585). Add: Holmes of Hampole quartered arg. a cross gu. fretty or. *F.Y.*

Holstock (Orsett, co. Essex). Add: *V.E. 1634.*

Holte or Houlte. Arg. a chev. plain betw. 3 saltires engr. gu. *Harl. MS. 1404. fo. 25.*

Holt (Co. Lancaster and London). Add: *Vis. Lon. 1633.* Add: Holt (London and co. Bucks.). Same arms. Crest: A pheon sa. *Vis. Lon. 1633.*

Holt (Stubley, co. Lancaster). . . . Add: *V.L.* Add: Holt (Stoke Lyne, co. Oxford). Same arms. *V.O.* Holt, Lord Chief Justice. 1589.

Holt (Bridge Hall, co. Lancaster 1664). . . . Add: *V.L.*

Holt (Ashworth, co. Lancaster 1664). Add: *V.L.*

Holt. Arg. a chev. betw. 3 fleurs-de-lis gu. Add: *V.*

Holt. Per pale az. and gu. two bars or. Add: John Holte, co. Lancaster. *V.*

Holt. Arg. a chev. betw. three squirrels gu. cracking nuts or. Add: Sir John Holt. *V.* Holt (Brampton, Norfolk). Same arms.

Holte. Az. two bars or. betw. the bars a barrulet environed . . . Add: *V.*

Holtman (Bishop of Bristol 1554–58). Arg. 2 bars engr. az. betw. 3 roses slipped gu. stalked and leaved vert. (cf. below Holyman!).

Holton. Az. on a bend or. 3 eagles displ. gu. Crest: . . . Add: *V.*

Holwell. Per chev. gu. and erm. . . . Add: *V.*

Holyman (Bishop of Bristol 1554–8). Arg. a chev. sa. betw. 3 roses gu.

Holynbrooke (Kent 1375). . . . a chev. . . . betw. 3 estoiles . . . *Robson.*

Holywood. Az. a chev. engr. betw. 3 martlets or. *V.*

Homer. Arg. a crossbow . . . Add: *V.*

Homling. (Homlingstown). Arg. a chev. betw. 3 spaniels sejant gu. *Harl. MS. 1441.*

Hond. Gu. billetty or 3 lions ramp. arg. Joan de Hond. *E. Harl. MS. 6137.*

Hondesacre. Add: *V.* Rauf Hondesacre. *X.* William de Hondishacre. *E.*

Hondon. Insert—'co.' (Lincoln). Add: *Harl. MS. 1404. fo. 109.*

Hondon. Insert—co. Lincoln . . . a lion pass. guard. of the first. Add: *V.*

Honeyman or Honyman. Arg. 3 bendlets each betw. 2 cotises engr. on the outer side gu. *Nisbet. j. 92.*

Honford. Insert—co. Chester. Arg. a chev. betw. three mascles gu. Add: *V.*

Hongate (Of Sakesby). Gu. a chev. engr. betw. 3 hounds sejant arg. *Constable's Roll xiij.*

Honing (Carleton, co. Suffolk). Add: *Coll. Top vij. 395.*

Honner or Honnere. Add: *V.V.**

Honnere.

Honston. Insert—co. Lincoln . . . Add: *V.*

Honychurch (Honychurch, temp. Henry iii). Add: *V.*

Honychurch (Tavistock . . . Devon). Add: *V.D.*

Honywood (Pette &c. . . . Kent). Granted by patent—insert—by Cooke. Add: *Guillim.*

Honywood (Evington, co. Kent, bart.). Add: Honywood (Elmsted, Kent, Baronetcy . . .). Same arms.

Honywood (Marks Hall, Coggeshall, co. Essex). Add: *V.E. 1634.* A † for diff. *Morant's* Essex ij. *169.*

Honywood. Arg. a chev. betw. 3 talbots pass. gu. Add: *V.**

Honywood. Arg. on a chev. bretessed quarterly per chev. gu. and sa. betw. 3 birds heads erased az. ten billets of the first. *Harl. MS. 1404. fo. 149.*

Hoo. Arg. three circles of chain sa. Add: Sir Richard de Hoo, Kent. *V.*

Hoo. Quarterly arg. and sa. a bend gu. Sir Robert de Hoo. *N. Harl. MS. 6137.*

Hoo. Quarterly sa. and arg. a bendlet or. Sir Robert de Hoo. *E.F.*

Hoo (Kent). Arg. a chev. betw. 3 wreathed chaplets sa. Sir Richard de Hoo. *V.*

Hoo. Quarterly sa. and arg. a bordure erminois. John Hoo. Serjeant at Law of Bradley, co. Stafford. *Guillim.*

Hoogan (East Bradenham, Norfolk). Granted by Thos. Hawley, Clarenceux, 1546. Arg. a chev. engr. vairy or and gu. betw. 3 hurts each charged with a lions gamb arg.

Hooke (Richard Hooke, Esq., of Bramshott). Visit. Hants . . . Add: following—Crest: . . . two wings arg. *Vis. Lon. 1633.* . . .

Hooker (Conway   ). Arg. on a chev. betw. 3 owls az. as many bezants.

Hooton (Hooton, co. Chester). Add: Sir William Hooton. *V.*

Hopkins (Oving House, co. bucks and Coventry, co. Warwick). Add: Hopkins (co. Stafford 1583). Same arms.

Hopkins. Sa. a lion ramp. arg. quartering sa. on a chev. arg. 3 roses gu. Evans Hopkins of the Middle Temple. **Book Plate.**

Hopman. Per pale arg. and gu. dexter a flag of the second, sinister a sword in pale . . . on a base sa. 3 human skulls arg. †

Hopton (Hopton, co. Hereford). Add: Wat Hopeton. *E.* Wat de Hopton. *F.* Sire Water de Optone. *N.*

Hopton (Co. Somerset and Blithbon, co. Suffolk). Add: Sir Arthur Hopton. *V.*

Hopton (Ermeley Hall—insert—co. York). Add: *Eliz. Roll. xxiv.*

Hopton (Co. York). Add: Robert Hopton. *X.*

Hopton (Co. York temp. Edw. ij). Arg. on 2 bars sa. 5 mullets 3 and 2. or. *F.Y.*

Hopton (Suffolk). Az. a bend arg. betw. two cotises and 6 crosses patty or within a bordure engr. gu. charged with 8 plates. *V.*

Hopton. Az. a bend cotised arg. betw. 6 crosses pattee or within a bordure engr. gu. platee. Add: *V.**

Hopwood (M.P. for Stockport 1874). Paly of six erm. and vert. on a bend engr. or 3 escallops. *Debrett.*

Horbury. Barry arg. and az. a bend gu. Sire Johan de Horbury. *D.N.*

Horden (Co. Kent). Add: *V.*

Hordentyn. Add: *V.*

Hore (Risford, parish of Chagford, co. Devon). . . . Add: Hore (Chartley, co. Stafford). Same arms. *V.*

Hore (Cos. Devon and Norfolk). Add: Gerard Hore. *V.*

Horlock (Co. Gloucester). Arg. on a bend sa. 3 crosses crosslet of the field.

Hornby (Dalton Hall, co. Lancaster). Add: *F.L.*

Hornby (Poole Hall, Nantwich).

Horne (Oxford). Arg. a chev. engr. gu. betw. 3 unicorns heads erased az. Edmund Horne. *V.*

Horne (Co. Kent). Arg. on a chev. betw. 3 bugle horns sa. as many estoiles of 6 points (another, mullets). or. Add: *V.*

Horne (Quartered by Lambard). Erm. a chev. engr. per chev. gu. and sa. betw. 2 couple closes, the upper one sa. and lower gu. and 3 bugle horns stringed, those in chief gu. that in base sa. *Pedigree 1591.*

Horne. Gyronny of eight or and az. . . . Add: William Horne. co. Lincoln. *V.*

Horne. Arg. a leopard ramp. gu. Add: Sir Gerard Horun. *V.*

Horner (Caleford, co. Somerset; granted). Insert —by Cooke . . . Add: *Harl. MS. 1359 fo. 119.* Sir John Horner. *W.*

Horner. Arg. a chev. betw. 3 bugle horns sa. garnished gu. *Robson.*

Horner. Sa. on a bend betw. 6 crosses . . . Add: *V.*V.*

Horner (Mells, co. Somerset). Add: *Hutchins ij. 667.*

Horniold (Blackmore Park . . .). Az. on a bend crenelly . . . a wolf pass. betw 2 escallops sa. *Nash.*

Hornidge (Barnes Green, Surrey). Az. a chev. . . . betw. 3 spear heads . . .

Horre (Ireland). Arg. an eagle displ. gu. *Robson.*

Horrocks (Preston, Lark Hill, co. Lancaster). Add: Motto: "Industria et spe".

Horsefield. Vert. a chev. betw. three horses heads arg.

Horsham. Az. three bendlets or on each as many mullets gu. Add: *V.*

Horsley (Great Yarmouth, Norfolk). Gu. 3 horses pass. 2 and 1 arg.

Horsman. Arg. a horse barnacle arg. betw. 3 plates, on a chief per pale indented of the first and purp. two estoiles of 16 points of the second in the centre of each a rose arg. *V.*

Horsemayden. Quarterly or and az. on a bend of the second three eagles displ. of the first. *W.V.*

Horspoole (Simon Horspoole). . . . Add: Horsepool, Buckland, Kent. *Vis. 1619.*

Horton (Howle, co. Chester). Add: Horton (London). Same arms, a mullet for diff. Crest: Out of clouds ppr. a demi-stag saliant arg. *Vis. Lon. 1633.*

Horton. Arg. 3 bendlets engr. gu. a canton or. Sir Philip Horton, co. Pembroke. *V.*

Horton (Northumberland). Same arms. *Eliz. Roll. xxxiv.*

Horton. Or a chev. az. betw. 2 wolves pass. in chief gu. . . . Crest: . . . Add: *V.*

Horune (Kent). Arg. on a chev. gu. betw. 3 bugle horns sa. stringed of the second as many mullets or. *Cotton MS. Tiberius. D. 10.*

Horwood (Co. Huntingdon).

Horwood (Co. Huntingdon). Sa. 3 bars erm. closeted compony or and arg. *V.* †

Horwood (Co. Stafford). Add: *V.*

Hoskins (Oxted, co. Surrey). Add: 1668. *L.N.* Add: Hoskins (London). Same arms. *Cady* and *C.L.*

Hoskyns (Harewood, co. Hereford, bart.). Insert —1676 . . . Per pale az. and gu. a chev.— underlined—, margin . . . The chevron engr. *Guillim.*

Host (London 1634). Add: *Vis. Lon. 1633.*

Hosterly. Add: Sir Rauf Hosterley. *V.*

Hotham (Baron Hotham). . . . Add: Hotham of Scarborough, co. York. *Dugdale. 1666.*

Hotham or Hutham. Add: Sir John de Hotham. *Y.* Sir John Hotham. *Y.V.** And with a martlet gu. for diff. Sir John Hothom. *O.* Sir John Hotham of Scarborough in Holderness. *V.* Baronetcy 1641.

Hotham. Arg. on a bend sa. 3 mullets of the field. Sir John Hotham of Scarborough 1558. *Constable's Roll. vij.*

Hotham. Barry of 6 arg. and az. a chief indented ermine a canton or. *V.*

Hotham (Bendley, co. York). Barruly arg. and az. on a canton or a martlet sa. *V.*

Hotham. Az. 2 bars or (another arg.) a chief per fesse . . . Add: *V.**

Hoton (Hardwick, co. Durham). Gu. a chev. betw. 3 trefoils slipped arg. *Robson.*

Hoton or Hooton. Add: *V.*

Hotot. Insert—Gloucester. Add: *V.*

Hotott (Co. Gloucester). Az.—delete—(another gu.) . . . Add: Sire William de Hotot. *N.V.*

Hotot. Az. 2 chevs. or betw. 3 crescents arg. Sire Johan de Hotot, co. Gloucester. *N.*

Hotton. Erm. on a chev. gu. 3 mullets or— underlined—Add: 'arg.' *V.*

Hotton (Holderness, co. York). Gu. a chev. betw. 3 cushions arg. tasselled or. *Constable's Roll. xv.*

Hotun. Or on a bend cotised vert. 3 chessrooks arg. **Seal** of Henry Hotun, Cheshire, temp. Edw. iij. colours from a pedigree of Helsby who quarters Hotun.

Hough (Impalement Fun. Ent. Alderman John Marfen . . . Add: *Ormerod.* Add: Hough (Leighton and Thornton, Hough, co. Chester).

Hough. Arg. 3 bars gu. on a canton az. a martlet or.

Houghbrig. Insert—co. York. Arg. on a bend fimbriated three cocks reguard sa. Add: *Harl. MS. V.*

Houghbrig (Co. York). Arg. 3 cocks reguardant betw. 2 cotises sa. *V.*

Houghton or Haughton (Haughton, co. Chester). Add: Houghton of Houghton Tower, co. Lancaster, Baronetcy 1611. Same arms. Sir Richard de Hoghton. *X. S.* Sire Adam de Houghton, co. Lancaster. *V.* And with a label of 3 points gu. Richard de Houghton. *S.* But with a mullet sa. for diff. John de Hoghton. *X.*

Houghton (Bishop of St. Davids 1361–87). Per pale arg. and purp. 3 bars counterchanged. *Brit. Mus. Add. MS. 12443.*

Houghton (Gunthorpe, co. Norfolk). Add: *V.*

Houghton (Bould, co. Lancaster) . . . 3 bars . . . within a bordure. *Guillim.*

Houn. Vert. on a bend arg. 3 escallops gu. Herei de Houn. *F.*

Hounhill. Vert. a chev. betw. 3 talbots statant arg. Sir John Hownhill. *V.*

Housego. Arg. on 3 chevs. vert. 15 roundels . . . *Cady.*

Houseman (Lincoln). 1714. . . . on a chev. . . . betw. 3 martlets . . . as many mullets . . . **Monument** in Lincoln Cathedral.

Hoveden (Ireland; granted 1585). Add: *Harl. MS. 1359. fo. 90b.*

Hovell (London). Same arms a crescent for diff. Crest: a sea lion sejant erm. *Vis. Lon. 1633.*

Hovile. Arg. a bend az. a label of 5 points gu. Hugo de Hovile. *E.F.*

Howard. Gu. crusilly and a bend arg. Sir John Hauward. *N.* Sir William Hauward. *O.* Sir . . . de Howart. *F.* Gu. crusilly bottony and a bend arg. William Haward. *Y.*

Howard (Lord Howard . . .). Add: Sir John Howard, Admiral of the North Fleet. *Q.* John Howard *S.X.Y.* (*N* the field crusilly). Howard. *Z.* 212. Sire . . . de Howard, Norfolk. *V.* Sir William Howard (the field crusilly). *O.*

Howard (Greystoke, co. Cumberland). . . . line 5.—margin—? a cross moline charged with a crescent.

Hovan (Co. Devon). Arg. a chev. gu. betw. 3 trees vert. *Cady.*

Howard (Lord Howard of Escrick). . . . charged with a mullet—reference at end ? a rose.

Howard (Corby Castle, co. Cumberland). Add: a crescent on a mullet for diff.

Howell (Co. Kent, Stratford and Haley, co. Norfolk). Add: Davy Howells. *V.*

Howes. Arg. a chev. betw. 3 wolves heads couped sa. *C.L. p. 39.*

Howes (Winston, co. Norfolk). Arg. a chev. betw. 3 griffins heads erased sa. *Cady.*

Howghten. Quarterly az. and arg. . . . Add: *V.V.**

Howhitts. Add: *V.V.**

Howley (Archbishop of Canterbury 1828). Az. an eagle displ. erminois, on the breast a—delete —'plain'—cross—insert—'flory'—gu. Add: Granted to William Howley, Bishop of London, by Heard, Garter 25th Sept. 1813. Crest: An eagle as in the arms. *Original Grant.*

Hownd or Hound (Callis, co. Cambridge . . .). Add: John Hownd, Mayor of Calais. 1551. *V.*

Hownhill, Hounehill or Howndhill. Add: Sir John Hownhill. *V.* Add: *V.**

Hownillyard (Co. Devon). Add: *V.**

Hownyll. Sa. a chev. betw. 3 water bougets arg. *V.*

Howorth (Howorth, co. Lancaster). Add: *V.L. 1644.*

Hoynton or Hynton. Erm. on a chev. sa. five martlets arg. *V.*

Hoytren. Arg. 2 bendlets gu. a label of 3 points az. Sir William de Hoytren. *I. Harl. MS. 6589.*

Hubart (Calais). Az. a chev. arg. betw. 3 swans necks erased . . . Add: *V.**

Hubeford. Or an eagle displ. sa. a bee about her neck arg. *Nash.*

Hubert (Extinct in Guernsey). . . . 3 lions ramp. of the—delete—field, substitute 'first'. Add: *V.V.**

Huckford. Add: *V.* Sire Wauter de Hukeford. *N.* Sir Walter de Hukeford, co. Gloucester, temp. Edw. j. *V.*

Huddersfield (Town of, co. York). Or on a chev. sa. betw. 3 rams passant . . . as many towers. Motto "Juvat compegros Deus".

Huddleston (Co. York). Gu. fretty and a bordure or. *Harl. MS. 5803.*

Huddleston. Gu. fretty arg. a bordure indented or. Sire Adam de Hudlestone. *N.*

Huddlestone (Co. York, temp. Edw. j.). *Harl. MS. 5803.*

Hudson (Melton Mowbray, co. Leicester). Add: Hudson (London). Same arms and Crest. *Vis. Lon. 1633.*

Hudson (Ardwick, near Manchester). Sa. a chev. betw. 6 annulets linked together 2. 2. and 2. palewise or. *Harl. MS. 2100. fo. 63.*

Hudson. Per chev. embattled or and az. three martlets counterchanged. Crest: . . . *V.**

Hugford (Dicklestone, alias Dixton, co. Gloucester, Wollas Hall, co. Worcester and co. Warwick). . . . as many mullets—insert— pierced . . . Add: *V.V.**

Hughes (Oxford). Arg. 2 bars betw. 6 crescents sa. 3. 2. and 1. *V.O.*

Hughes (Uxbridge, Middlesex). Gu. a lion ramp. reguard. arg. crowned or. *Drakes York. p. 305.*

Hughes (Middleton Stoney, co. Oxford). Add: *V.O.*

Hughes (Portsmouth, Baronetcy 1773). Az. a lion ramp. or.

Hulbert (Granted March 1639). Insert—by Borough, Garter . . .

Hule. Az. an eagle displ. or armed gu. Sire . . . de Hule, co. Cambridge. *V.*

Hulkeford (Co. Gloucester). Huckford/Hulkford.

Hulke. Per chev. embattled arg. and az. 3 lions ramp. counterchanged. *V.*

Hull (Co. Buckingham &c. . . .). Add: *Vis. Lon. 1633.* Exemplified by Segar, Garter 1624.

Hull (Battersea, co. Surrey). Confirmed 25 Jan —written under—July.

Hull (St. Leonards, co. Cornwall) and Oxford. Add: Hull (Mayor of Exeter 1403). Another 1605. *Colby.*

Hull (Cornwall). Add: *V.*

Hull. Per pale arg. and sa. a chev. betw. 3 dolphins counterchanged. *V.*

Hull. Az. an eagle displ. arg. Joan de Hulle. *E.F.*

Hull (Co. Surrey). Arg. on a chev. az. betw. 3 demi-lions . . . Add: John Hull, Hameldon, Surrey. *V.*

Hulles or Hulls. Az. a chev. betw. 3 fleurs-de-lis or. Add: *V.**

Hulles or Hules. Az. a chev. arg. betw. 3 fleurs-de-lis or. Add: *V.*

Hulleys or Hullers (Co. Cambridge). Add: *V.** Add: Sir Richard Hullys temp. Edw. j. *V.N.*

Hulme (Co. Stafford and London). Barry of 6 or and sa. on a canton arg. rose gu. Crest: A lions head erased arg. gorged with a chaplet of roses gu. *Vis. Lon. 1633.*

Hulson (London and co. York). Add: *V.**

Hulton. Gu. a lion ramp. arg. fretty az. Add: Sir Wm. de Hulton. *V.*

Hulyn (London). Arg. a chev. az. a bordure engr. sa. *V.*

Humble (Stratford, co. Essex and London 1634).

Humble (London, bart.; extinct 1745, created 1660). Same arms. Granted by Dethick. Crest: A demi-buck—insert—'or' . . . *Vis. Lon. 1633.*

Hume (Earl of Dunbar 1605). Vert a lion ramp. arg. quartering 2nd arg. 3 popinjays vert. 3rd arg. 3 escus. vert. 4th as the first, overall. Gu. a lion ramp. arg. The whole within a bordure . . . charged with 8 crosslets . . . *Crawfurd.*

Hume (Earl of Hume, 1605). Vert. a lion ramp. arg. quartering arg. 3 popinjays vert. beaked and legged gu. over all on an escu. or an orle az. *Crawfurd.*

Hummerston (Co. Lincoln 1640). Barry of 6 arg. and sa. in chief 3 ogresses. *Yorke.*

Humez. Quarterly or and az. over all a lion ramp. arg. *MS. 5798. fo. 153.*

Humfines. Arg. three lions pass.—insert—'in pale'. gu.

Humfrey (Ireland). Or on a bend gu. 3 leopards heads of the field. *Robson.*

Humfrey. Or on a chev. betw. 3 fleurs-de-lis sa. as many bezants. Add: *W.*

Humfrey (Dublin . . .). Add: Humphrey (Rishmighes, co. Suffolk and Dublin, confirmed by Preston, Ulster 1638). *Guillim.*

Humphery (Penton Lodge, Andover, Surrey, bart). Insert—1868 . . .

Humphrey. Or a turkey cock in its ire ppr. *Randle Holme.*

Hundescote. Erm. a bordure gu. Sire de Hundescote. *D. Harl. MS. 1441.*

Hune. Gu. 2 bars arg. on a bend sa. an acorn slipped or. *Cady.*

Hungate or Hungatt (Saxton &c. . . . bart.). Insert—1642 . . . Crest: A hound sejant arg.— Add: on a mount vert. Add: *Vis. Lon. 1633.* Add: Hungate (Sand Hutton, co. York). Same arms, a mullet for diff. *F. Y.*

Hungate. Gu. on a chev. engr. betw. 3 talbots . . . Add: *V.*

Hungerford. Sa. 2 bars arg. in chief 3 gloves and another betw. the bars or. Walter Hungerford. *T.*

Hungerford. Az. 2 bars arg. in chief 3 plates. Walter Hungerford. *Y.*

Hungerford. Gu. a chev. betw. 3 crosslets fitchee or. Add: Sir Thomas Hungerford.

Huning. Insert—co. Suffolk. Quarterly az. and gu. . . . Add: *V.*

Huning (Huning, co. Fermanagh; &c. . . . .). Add: Quartered by Flower, co. Notts. *V.N. 1614. p. 121*

Hunt (Chudleigh, co. Devon). Insert—granted 1580. *W.* Add: *V.D. 1620.*

Hunt (London). Same arms, but bend arg. and water bougets arg. No mount in the crest and the talbot gu. *Vis. Lon. 1633.*

Hunt (Romford, Essex). Add: *Vis. Lon. 1633.*

Hunt (Lincolns Inn). Add: *V.*

Hunt (Hermyngtoft, co. Norfolk and co. Suffolk). Add: Hunt (London). Same arms and crest, a martlet for diff. *Vis. Lon. 1633.*

Hunt (Lyndon and Hindon, co. Rutland). Insert—granted in 1585. *C.R.* Add: *W.*

Hunt (Stratford upon Avon). Az. a bend betw. 3 tigers heads or. *Robson.*

Hunt. Az. on a bend or betw. six leopards faces . . . Add: *V.* Add: Hunt (Stoke Danby, co. Rutland). Same arms. *W.*

Hunt. Az. on a bend betw. 6 leopards heads or as many water bougets sa. *V.**

Hunt. Az. a chev. engr. betw. 3 martlets arg. Sir Nicholas Hunt. *V.*

Hunt. Gu. a hind springing arg. . . . Add: *V.*

Hunter (Blackness, co. Forfar). Arg. on a chev. gu. betw. 3 hunting horns vert. a crescent arg. enclosed by 2 cinquefoils or.

Hunter (Mortimer Hill, co. Berks. . . .). Add: *Vis. Lon. 1633.*

Huntercombe (Baron Huntercombe . . .). Add: Sire Walter de Huntercombe *N.G.J.I.H.Y.V.* Rauf de Huntercombe. *E.*

Huntingdon. Arg. 3 lions ramp. ppr. *Ashmole MS. 763.*

Huntingfield (Cos. Bedford and Hertford). Add: Sir John Huntingfield, Norfolk. temp. Edw. j. *V.X.Y.* Sir Walter de Huntingfield. *N.*

Huntingfield (Co. Kent). Quarterly or and gu. a bordure—delete—(another engr.). Sa. Add: Sire Peres de Huntingfield. *N.I.V.*

Huntingfield. Gu. crusilly and a bend arg. Carl de Huntingfield. *A. Harl. MS. 6137.* Jeer d' Huntingfield. *E.* Gu. crusilly fitchy and a bend arg. Cael de Huntingfyld. *A.*

Huntingfield. Or crusilly and a bend gu. Sir William Huntingfield. *I.*

Huntley (Sheriff of Newcastle 1597). Gu. on a bend arg. 3 (? bunches of grapes, or leaves). Vert. † for diff. *Carr MS.*

Huntley (Boxwell, co. Gloucester). Add: *V.* Add: Huntley (Frowcester   ). Same arms. But stags heads couped. *Guillim.*

Hurlock (Essex). Vert. a chev. betw. 3 moors heads couped . . . wreathed or. *Morant's Essex j. 444.*

Hurrell, Hurell or Hurle. Add: *V.*

Hurel or Hurrell.

Hurry (Great Yarmouth, co. Norfolk). Arg. in chief a lion ramp. and in base two mullets or.

Hurstale (   ). Az. 3 axes arg. William de Hurstall. *E.F.*

Hurt (London). Sa. a fess betw. 3 pierced 5-foils or. Crest: A stag statant ppr. an arrow or feathered arg. sticking in the haunch. *Vis. Lon. 1633.*

Hurysse. Add: Thomas Hurysse. *V.* Quartered by Dowriche, co. Devon. *Cotton MS. Tiberius. D. 10. fo. 705.*

Huskisson (Tilghman-Huskisson, Easham, co. Sussex). Add: Huskisson (co. York). Same arms. *Foster.*

Husse. Erm. 3 bars gu. Henry Heuse or Husse. *A.N.V.* Thomas Husse. *X.Y.*

Hussey (Honington, co. Lincoln, bart . . .). Add: Hussey of Hennington, Quarterly 1 and 4. Barry of 6 erm. and gu. 2 and 3 Or a cross vert. *Guillim.*

Hussey (Dean, Kent). Per chev. arg. and vert. three birds counterchanged. *Robson.*

Hussey or Husey. Erm. a chev. az. betw. 3 holly leaves vert. Add: *V.*

Hutcheson (Scotland). Arg. a fesse vert.—margin —? az. *Guillim.*

Hutchinson (Owthorpe, co. Notts. . . .). Add: *V.N. 1614.*

Hutchinson (Co. Lincoln . . .). Add: Hutchinson (Wickham, co. York 1665). Same arms. Hutchinson (Owthorpe, co. Notts.). *V.N. 1614.* Same arms. Hutchinson (Essex and co. York, confirmed by Flower Norroy 1581). Same arms.

Huttoft. Erm. 3 bars gu . . . Crest: . . . Add: Henry Hutoft, co. Hants. *V.*

Huttofts (Co. Hants and Salisbury, co. Wilts). Erm. 3 bars gu. Add: *V.*

Hutton. Quartered by Yorke. Gu. a chev. betw. 3 lozenge cushions erm. tasselled or.

Hutton. Per fess vert and arg. in chief an eagle displ. or in base on each of three hurts a bird of the second, all within a bordure engr. gu. *Harl. MS. 1404. fo. 145.* Thomas Hutton (Dry Drayton, co. Cambridge). Same arms. *Harl. MS. 1392*

Hutton (Hemwick, co. Durham). Add: *V.*

Hutton (Holderness, co. York. temp. Edw. ij). Gu. a chev. arg. betw. 2 goats heads erased within a bordure engr. or. *F.Y.*

Hutton (Glasion, co. Rutland). Add: quartering . . . a cross humetty flory . . . betw. 4 escallops.

Huxley (Huxley, co. Chester). Add: *W.*

Huysh (Confirmed by Cooke . . . Somerset . . . &c.). Add: Huysh (Sidbury, co. Devon). 1620 *V.D.* But *Harl. MS. 1445. fo. 325b.* Gives a mullet in chief for diff.

Huyshe, Hiwis, Huish, Hewish. . . . Add: Huyshe . . . Hewish (Donyford, co. Somerset). 1623. Quartering, barry of 8 or and az. on a bend engr. gu. 3 heads of spears or; and arg. a fess of 5 lozenges conjoined gu. plain cotised sa. *Harl. MS. 1445. fo. 230.* Huysh (Sand, Sudbury, co. Devon). Arg. on a bend az. 3 roaches arg. finned and tailed or; in chief a mullet. *Harl. MS. 1445. fo. 325b.*

Huystock. Add: *V.*

Hwatacre. Add: *V.V.**

Hyde (Co. Dorset). Or a chev. betw. 3 lozenges az. *Cady.*

Hyde (Co. Bedford). Same arms. †

Hyde (Essex). Arg. a chev. gu. betw. in chief 2 mullets sa. and in base a 5-foil of the second. *V.*

Hyde. Az. a chev. betw. 3 lozenges or on a chief arg. a saltire engr. gu. enclosed by two birds sa. *Harl. MS. 1404. fo. 109.*

Hyde (Hydon, co. Dorset). Add: *V.*

Hyde (London). *Her. Office London. . . .* Add: *Vis. Lon. 1633.*

Hyde (London). Gu. 2 chevs. arg. betw. 3 lozenges or. Crest: A lion's head erased or pelletty and charged with a lozenge gu. *Vis. Lon. 1633.*

Hyde. Az. a chev. betw. 3 lozenges or on a canton gu. a lion ramp. betw.—delete—substitute, 'three' . . . Add: The canton is the bearing of Capel.

Hyde. Arg. a lion ramp. ermines langued and armed gu. *Robson.*

Hyde. Az. a chev. betw. 3 lozenges or. John and Thomas Hyde. *V.* Hyde, Earl of Rochester. *Z. 644.* With a mullet gu. for diff. Sir Nicholas Hyde, Chief Justice of the Common Pleas 1626. *Dug. O. J.* And with a crescent on a mullet for diff. Sir Robt. Hyde, Chief Justice of the Kings Bench 1663. *Dug. O. J.*

Hyde. Arg. a chev. betw. 2 mullets in chief and a cinquefoil in base gu. Add: *V.**

Hyde (Co. Norfolk). Or a chev. betw. 3 lozenges az. . . . Add: *Harl. MS. 1404. fo. 109.*

Hyde (Albury, co. Hertford). Baronetcy 1621. The heiress mar. Osborne. Or a chev. betw. 3 lozenges az. on a chief gu. an eagle displ. or. *Guillim* and *Cady.*

Hyde (South Denchworth and Kingston Lisle, co. Berks.) . . .

Hyde (Abingdon, co. Berks). Same arms. *Cady.*

Hyett (Co. Gloucester). Arg. a lion ramp. az. on a chief dancetty sa. two roses arg.

Hygate. Add: *W.*

Hygham or Hyham. Add: *V.V.**

Hyham. Az. a bend betw. 3 lapwings arg. Add: *V.**

Hyll (Glasgow). . . . on a bend . . . betw. 2 crosses crosslet fitchy . . . an escallop . . . enclosed by 2 crescents . . . John Hyll, **Seal.**

Hymners. Arg. a crossbow unbent in pale sa. betw. 3 cocks . . . crested and jelloped gu. Benjamin Hynmers. 1716.

Hynd (Hesore, co. Bucks.) . . . Add: Hynde, co. Notts. Same arms † for diff. *V.N. 1614.*

Hynd (London). Gu. on a chev. betw. 3 hinds trippant . . . Add: Augustine Hynde, Alderman of London. *V.*

Hynde. Arg. on a chev. gu. betw. 3 goats heads erased . . . Add: Sir Francis Hynde, co. Cambridge. *V.*

Hynde. Sa. a lion pass. arg. betw. 3 escallops . . . Add: John Hynde. *V.*

Hynkeley (Co. Chester). Gu. a chev. engr. arg. *Harl. MS. 1386. fo. 34b.*

Hysop (Locheud, co. Kircudbright). Arg. a stag lodged under a holly tree growing out of the base vert. on a chief of the last 3 stars of the field.

Hytte (Co. Worcester). Add: *Nash.*

I

ICHAM. Add: *V.**

Ickworth (Ickworth, Suffolk). Quarterly or and gu. on a bend vert. 3 martlets or. *Cady.*

Idleigh (Penshurst, Kent). Arg. an eagle displ. double-headed . . . .

Ifeld. Add: *V.** Ifeld of the North. Same arms. *V.*

Ilderton. Arg. 3 water bougets sa. *Y.*

Ilderton. Time. Edw. ij. Same arms. *F.Y.*

Ilderton (Northumberland). Sa. 3 water bougets arg. *V. Robson.*

Iliff. Arg. on a chev. engr. sa. betw. 3 estoiles gu. as many stags heads cabossed of the second. *Collinson Somerset ij. 70.*

Iley or Ylee. Erm. 2 chev. sa. Sire John de Ylee. *O.*

Illey. Erm. two chevs. sa. *V.*

Illey. Gu. an eagle displ. or a baston az. Sire Felip de Illeye. *N.*

Illingworth or Illingsworth (Co. Surrey—insert—Bradford co. York). . . . .

Inge. Or on a chev. vert. three leopards faces of the field. Crest: a hand holding a glove ppr. Add: *V.**

Inge (Temp. Edward I). Or a chev. vert. Add: Sir William Inge or Ynge, co. Bedford. *N.V.*

Ingefield or Ingefeld Add: *V.**

Ingledon.

Ingelton. Add: *V** and *Harl. MS. 1386. fo. 36.,* also *V.*

Ingham. Gu. 3 bars vair. *V.**

Ingilbert. Add: *V.*

Ingilton. Add: *V.*

Ingilton. Arg. a chev. sa. betw. 5 crosses.

Inglebert Insert—(Middlesex). Gu. a bend cotised or. Crest: . . . Add: Granted by Camden 1602.

Ingledew. *Robson.*

Inglett (Co. Devon). Sa. a bend arg. betw. 3 escallops. or. *V.D. 1620.*

Inglos or Inglosse. Add: *V.*

Inglose or Inglehose. Gu. 3 bars gemel or on a quarter arg. 5 billets sa. 2.1. and 2. John Ingelhose. *V.* Sir Henry Inglose *V.*

Ingoldsby (Co. Lincoln). Add: *V.*

Ingram. 1629. Az. a chev. or betw. 3 lions pass. of the last goutty de sang.

Inkell. Sa. a bend arg. betw. 6 martlets or. *V.*

Inkpenne. Chequy arg. and sa. *Leland.*

Inns of Court and Chancery. Add: London. Staffords Inn. Or a chev. gu. and canton erm. all within a bordure compony arg. and az. *Syl. Morgan.*

Inverarity. Add: *Seton.*

Ion. Sa. a chev. engr. betw. 3 falcons arg. *Harl. MS. 6829 fo. 50b.*

Ipres (Co. Lancaster). Add: *V.** Sir Ralph Ipres *V.* Sir John de Ipre *S.* a mullet arg. on the chev. for diff. Sir Rauff de Ipre. *S.*

Ipswich. Town of, **Book Plate,** insert, on *wreath: Local Board Office.*

Ipstans, Ipstanes and Ipstones (Co. Suffolk). Add: *V.*

Ireby (Cos. Cambridge and Cumberland). Add: *V.*

Ireby. Arg. fretty sa. on a canton gu. a 5-foil or. Sir Thomas Ireby. Cumberland. *V.*

Ireby. Arg. fretty sa. on a canton gu. a chaplet or. *V.**

Ireland. Or three crowns az. *Cady.*

Iremongers (granted to the "honurable crafte . . ."). Margin—**note:** This is the Company of Ironmongers of London.

Ireton (Little Ireton, co. Derby &c.). Add: *V.*

Irie. Or a bend az. Mathew de Irie. *A.*

Ireys. Arg. a chev. betw. 3 moors heads in profile couped sa. with round caps vert. fretty or. *V.*

Ironmonger (Co. Lincoln 1640) Add: *Yorke.*

Irvine (Borough of   ). Arg. a lion sejant affronty gu. holding in his dexter paw a sword erect ppr. hilted or in his sinister a sceptre of the last. *Berry.*

Irrires or Jerires. Arg. a chev. betw. 3 billets gu. *V.V.**

Irving (Barwhinnock, co. Dumfries). Arg. a chev. sa. betw. 3 holly leaves vert. *A.A.*

Isaac (Boughton, co. Worcester). Add: Isaac or Isake, Kent. Same arms. *V.*

Isbury. Bendy wavy of 6 arg. and sa. *V.*

Ithel-Anwyl (Englefield, in North Wales . . .). Per pale gu. and or in pale a hymoc (mound of earth)—margin—**note:** This hymoc is sometimes described as a Greek Φ.

Ivers or Jevers. Add: *V.**

Ivery. Or 3 chevs. gu. *Harl. MS. 1407 fo. 73b.*

Ivie (Exeter). Gu. a lion ramp. or quartering or a fess engr. betw. 3 ogresses. *Colby.*

J

JACKMAN (Cos. Buckingham and Durham &c.).... Add: *V.E. 1634.* Add: Edw. Jackman, Alderman of London. ob. 1596. *W.*

Jackson (Killingwood, co. York. confirmed in 1613). Gu. 2 bars indented erminois on a chief az. 3 suns or. *F.Y.*

Jackson (Cowling   ). Arg. on a chev. betw. 3 eagles heads erased sa. as many 5-foils arg. *Cady.*

Jackson (Sunderland, co. Durham). Add: *V.*

Jackson (Hickleton, co. York, bart.). Insert—1660. . . .

Jackson (Wakefield, co. York). Gu. a chev. betw. 3 martlets arg. *Cady.*

Jackson (Cowlyng, near Bedale, co. York). Arg. on a chev. gu. betw. 3 griffins heads erased az. 3 pierced 5-foils of the field. *Eliz. Roll. xxix.*

Jackson. Arg. on a chev. betw. three daw's heads. . . . Add: *V.**

Jackson. Arg. a lion pass. betw. three martlets or. *W.*

Jackson. Az. a lion ramp. arg. billettee gu. Add: *V.*

Jacob (Dover, co. Kent). Add: *L.N.*

Jacob (London). Arg. a chev. gu. betw. three 3-foils slipped sa. on a chief of the second an estoile or. Phillip Jacob. *W.*

Jacob (Bromley and Bow, co. Middlesex, bart.). Insert—1665. . . . Add: Jacob (London). Same arms. *V.*

Jacob (Shillingstone, co. Dorset and Salisbury, co. Wilts. . . .). Add: granted in 1633.

Jacobson (Bishop of Chester 1865). Arg. a chev. gu. betw. 3 trefoils slipped sa. on a chief of the second an estoile or. **Seal.**

Jakys. Or two bars tortile of—insert—'6 or' . . . eight . . . Add: *V.V*.*

James (Stroud, co. Gloucester). Chequy arg. and az. on a bend of the first 3 lions pass of the second. *Robson.*

James (Co. Cambridge). Add: *Guillim.*

James (Upminster, co. Essex and co. Kent). Add: *V.** Add: James (Co. Surrey). Same arms. *W.*

James (Park Farm Place, Eltham, co. Kent, bart.). Insert—1778. . . .

James (Wellsborough, co. Kent, and Reigate, co. Sussex). Add: *Guillim.*

James. Az. on a chev. betw. three leopards heads or as many escallops sa. Add: *W.*

James (Reg. Ulster's Office). Add: Sir . . . de James (Ireland). *V.*

Jane or Jann (Bishop of Norwich 1499). Vert. a lion ramp. or over all a fess of the second.

Jarvis (Co. Worcester). Sa. a chev. betw. 3 herons arg. *V.* But lapwings. *V.**

Jason (Broad Somerford, co. Wilts, bart.). Insert—1661. . . . Add: confirmed by Dethick 10 March 1588.

Jaudrell. Sa. 3 round buckles tongues pendent arg. *V.V.**

Jauncey (Whitwick, co. Hereford). Az. 3 chevs. engr. or.

Jay. Insert—co. Salop. Az. a lion saliant and a canton or a bordure engr. of the second. Add: *W.*

Jaye (Sheriff of Newcastle 1443). Arg. a jay vert. beaked and legged gu. in the sinister chief a mullet az. thereon a crescent or. *Carr MS.*

Jaye (London and co. Norfolk). . . . Add: *V.*

Jeane. Arg. 2 chevs. gu. and sa. betw. 3 roses ppr. impaling arg. on a bend sa. 3 bezants. *Collinson Somerset j. 95.*

Jeams (Oxford 1686, granted by Bysche, Clarenceux). Or on a chev. betw. 3 lions pass. reguard. sa. as many escallops of the first. *Guillim.*

Jefferyes or Geffreys (Clifton and Corncastle, co. Worcester 1569). Add: *W.*

Jeffreys (Woodford, co. Stafford). Sa. a lion ramp. betw. 3 scaling ladders or a canton arg. *Dugdale 1664.*

Jeffries (Bulstrode, co. Chester, Baronetcy 1681). Erm. a lion ramp. sa. on a canton of the last a mullet for diff. *Guillim.*

Jeffryes (Priory, co. Brecon). Add: Sir Jeffrey Jeffreys of London. 1699. *L.N.*

Jeffryes (London, Lord Mayor of London 1686). Insert—granted by Bysche 1676.

Jegon. Or two chevs. gu. a canton az. *V.*V*.*

Jekyll. Or 3 asses pass. sa. Sir Joseph Jekyll, Chief Justice of Chester. 1697. *L.N.*

Jen. Or on a lion ramp. vair a fess gu. Sire Richard le Jen. *Y.*

Jene. Erm. a bend betw. 2 cotises sa. *V.*

Jenets. Arg. 2 chevs. gu. 6 martlets, 3.2. and 1. sa. *V.V.**

Jenico. Add: *V.**

Jenicot. Add: Jenicot, Gascoigne. *V.*

Jenings. Add: *V.**

Jenison. Az. a bend or betw. 2 cormorants arg. Sir Ralph Jenison of Elswick, Northumberland 1697. *L.N.*

Jenison. Az. a bend or betw. 2 swans arg. Mayor of Newcastle-on-Tyne 1675.

Jenison or Jenyson (Marneham, co. Notts. . . . .). Add: *V.N. p. 95.*

Jenkins. Sa. a chev. betw. three fleurs-de-lis arg. Crest: A lions gamb erased holding a bezant all or. Add: Sir Lionel Jenkins, Judge of the High Court of the Admiralty.

Jenkyns (York City and Rusby, co. York). . . . Add: also of Grimston, co. York. *Dugdale 1666.*

Jenman (Sussex). Arg. on a bend sa. within a bordure of the last bezanty 3 bezants.

Jennett or Jenet. Arg. 2 chevs. betw. 6 martlets gu. 3.2. and 1. *V.*

Jenney (Great Cressingham, co. Norfolk). Add: *V.**

Jenning. Arg. a chev. betw. three hinds sa. a quarter paly of four or and gu. Add: *V.V.**

Jenninges. Add: *V.E. 1634.* John Jennings, co. Salop. *W.* Jenynges (Wallyborne, co. Salop). *V.*

Jennings. Az. a chev. betw. 3 griffins heads. . . . Add: *V.**

Jennyns or Jennings (Fun. Ent. 1599 . . .). Add: Wm. Jennyns, Lancaster Herald 1485–1556. *W.*

Jenynges or Jenninges. Add: *V.V.**

Jeppe (Sutton's Court, co. Somerset). Add: *Cady.*

Jerard (Pamford, co. Somerset). Add: Jerard (Samford, co. Somerset). **Seal ix Hen. V.** *Visitation of Somerset. Harl. MS. 1385.*

Jereys. Add: *V.**

Jerires. Add: *V.**

Jerkanvile. Add: *D.*

Jermin (Wickham Bishop, co. Essex; granted 9 Aug. 1664). Insert—by Bysche, Clarenceux.

Jernegan or Jerningham (Cossey, co. Norfolk). Insert—Baronetcy 1621 . . . .

Jernegan. Barry of 9 or and az. an eagle displ. gu. *V.**

Jernouthe. Add: *W.*

Jerveaulx, Joreval or Gervis (Cistercian Abbey, co. York). Or 3 water bougets sa. Quartering 2. Barry of 6 arg. and az. a bordure engr. sa. 3. Az. 3 chevrons braced and a chief or. 4. Vair a fess gu. *Tonge p. 45.*

Jervis (Suffolk). Sa. 3 beehives or. *W.*

Jerworth (Meredith ap Jerworth). Or 3 lions dormant in pale sa. *Randle Holme.*

Jerworth ap Gruff ap Heilin. Arg. a bend betw. 6 crosses crosslet az. *Robson.*

Jerworth. Drwyndyn. Sa. a bordure engr. or. *Randle Holme.*

Jevers. Arg. on a bend az. 3 fleurs-de-lis or. *V.**

Jew (Whitfield, co. Devon). Add: Heiress mar. Sir John Hody. *Syl. Morgan.*

Jewell or Jule (Bowden, co. Devon). . . . Add: *V.*

Jobson (Ilford, co. Essex). . . . Add: *Guillim.*

Jobson. Per pale az. and or an eagle displ. counterchanged. . . . Add: *W.*

Joce or Joos. Add: John Joos. *Y.*

Joce. Arg. an eagle displ. sa. a baston gu. Sire Johan Jose. *N.* the baston compony gu. and or. *L.*

Jocelyn (Earl of Roden). Add: Sir Ralph Josselyne, Alderman of London. *V.*

Josselyn (Newhall, Essex). Same arms. *V.*

John. Sa. a chev. betw. three trefoils slipped arg. *W.*

Johnson (Bath, bart.). Margin—Grant.

Johnson (Mayor of Newcastle 1714). Sa. on a bend arg. 3 peascods slipped vert. on a chief dancetty of the second 3 ? hearts gu. *Carr MS.*

Johnson (Burleigh Field, co. Leicester). Arg. 2 chevs. betw. in chief 2 griffins heads erased and in base a palmers scrip gu. *A.A.*

Johnson (Co. Worcester). Az. on a chev. arg. 3 pheons. . . . Add: Johnson (East Ham, Essex). Same arms. *V.E. 1634.*

Johnson (Insert—Willinghall; co. Essex). Arg. on a chev. sa—insert—and revise to read; betw. three lions heads erased gu. an estoile of sixteen points or. Add: *W.* a bordure engr. gu. Add: Johnson (London). Same arms, without the bordure. *W.*

Johnson (Nethercourt and Margate, co. Kent). Add: Add. *MS. 5507 fo. 200.*

Johnson (Gainsborough, co. Lincoln). . . . Add: *Guillim.*

Johnson. Arg. a chev. betw. 3 lions heads erased gu. Edward Johnson. *W.*

Johnson (Preston, originally Walsh Whittle, co. Lancaster). . . . Add: *V.L. 1664.*

Johnson (Norfolk). Or a water bouget sa. *W.*

Johnson (Thomas Johnson, Lothelay, co. York). Sa. on a bend betw. two pairs of manacles arg. three pheons bendwise in bend gu. a chief or charged with a demi-lion ramp issuant enclosed by a pair of lozenges az. *V.*

Johnson (Luffenham, co. Rutland . . .). Add: Johnson (Granted to Robert Johnson, Preacher. North Luffenham, Rutland, by Cooke in 1592). *W.*

Johnson (London). Gu. 3 greyhounds courant in pale arg. collared or. *W.*

Johnson (Recorder of Chichester 1863). Erm. on a chev. az. 3 bezants in the chief point a mullet arg. charged with a label of 3 points sa. *Debrett.*

Jones (Dr. Walter Jones, Rector of Sunningdale, co. Berks. ob. 1672). Gu. a lion ramp . . . within a bordure invected. . . . *Guillim.*

Jones (Sir Saml. Jones, Courtenhall, Northants). Arg. a lion ramp vert. blood dropping from the mouth ppr. *L.N. 1660.*

Jones (Co. Salop and London); granted—insert—by Camden. . . .

Jones (Co. Denbigh). Add: Jones (Co. Salop). Same arms. *W.*

Jones (Abermarles, co. Carmarthen). Bart. 1643. Arg. a chev. az. betw. 3 choughs sa. a bordure of the third bezanty. *Guillim.*

Jones (Revell, co. Wilts.—insert—Granted by Cooke . . . a ducal coronet—delete—of the last; substitute 'or.'. Add: *W.*

Jones (Ramsbury, Wilts, Baronetcy 1774). Per pale az. and gu. 3 lions ramp. arg. 2 and 1. quartering arg. 3 bears heads erased sa. muzzled or for Langham. *Edmondson.*

Joos (Ludlow). Arg. 3 lions . . . az. crescent or. *Leland Coll. j. 232.*

Joos. Arg. a chev. betw. 3 leaves gu. *V.*

Jorcey. Per pale az. and gu. an eagle displ. or. *V.*

Jorcey or Jorcie. Add: Sire Robert Jorce. *Y.* Sir Robert Joce. *V.*

Jorcy. Add: *V.Y.*

Jordan (Co. Somerset and Chittern Whistley, Co. Wilts. . . .). Add: Granted to Sir William Jordan, Co. Wilts. by Camden. Nov. 1604. Add: *Syl. Morgan.*

Jordan (Catwick and Charlwood, co. Surrey). . . . three almond leaves vert.—insert—*V.* Crest: . . . .

Jordan (Co. Wilts.). Per pale az. and or a chev. betw. 3 lozenges. Add: *V.*

Joskyn (Essex). Gu. 3 bird bolts in a parcel arg banded az. one in pale and two in saltire *V.*

Joskyn (   ). Gu. 9 arrows 3 in a parcel 2 in saltire and 1 erect arg. *V.*

Josselyn. See Jocelyne.

Inge or Juge (Co. Leicester). Add: Granted by Borough in 1641.

Julys. Per chief az. and gu. a tower triple towered arg. Dr. Julys. *Harl. MS. 1404. fo. 73.*

K

KANDALE. See Kendall.

Karadoc. Vracheras (Wales). Az. a lion ramp. arg. within a bordure of the last pelletty.

Kardelecke. Az. a castle or. Mons. Thomas Kardelecke. *T.*

Kardoyle. Gu. 6 annulets az. two, two and two. . . . Add: Sir Raufe de Kardoyll. *V.*

Karnabye (Co. Northumberland). Add: *V.*

Kavanagh (Baron of Bellian). Az. a lion ramp. arg. armed and langued gu. within a bordure of the second.

Kaye (Woodesham or Woodsome, co. York . . .). Add: *Dugdale p. 171.*

Kaynes. Vair 3 bars gu. *V.N. p. 123.*

Kebell. Barry wavy of 6 arg. and sa. a canton erm. *V.*

Kebell. Barry nebuly of 6 or. and sa. a canton erm. *V.*

Keble (Lord Mayor of London 1510. . . .). Add: *V.*

Keble (Co. Leicester). Barry nebuly of 6 arg. and sa. on a canton gu. a crescent or. *C.L.*

Keck. Sa. a plain bend betw. 2 cotises wavy or. Sir Anthony Keck 1688. *L.N.*

Keck (Staughton Grange, co. Leicester &c.). Add: Keck (Great Tew, co. Oxford). Same arms. †

Keddell (Sheerness, Kent). Az. a chev. or fretty gu. betw. 3 dragons heads erased of the second.

Kedington (Wilby, co. Norfolk). Arg. on a bend sa. 6 falchions in saltire ppr. *Blomfield.*

Keeling (Co. Essex). Add: *Morant's Essex. j. 415.*

Keene (Co. Devon). Sa. a chev. engr. betw. 3 suns in splendour arg. *Lysons.*

Keigans (Confirmed by Robert, Ulster to Cornelius Keigans &c. . . .).—margin— note: Keigans (Keegan). Arms granted to Cornelius K. Not confirmed, see Grant in Ulster's Office, Dublin. *W. Clare.*

Keirdiff. Arg. a chev. betw. 3 door staples sa. *Harl. MS. 1441.*

Kekebourne. Add: *Cotton MS. Tiberius. D. 10.*

Kekewich. (Peamore, co. Devon originally of co. Lancaster. . . .). Add: *V.*

Kekewiche (Co. Lancaster). Arg. 3 lions pass. guard. sa. betw. 2 bendlets gu. *V.***

Kelk (Co. Lincoln). Sa. a bend flory arg. *Yorke.*

Kelk. Sa. a bend cotised flory or charged with an ermine spot. *V.N. p. 121.*

Kelke. Sa. a plain bendlet or betw. 2 bendlets flory counterflory of the last. Add: *V.*

Kellam. Gu. a double-bodied lion guard crowned or a bordure arg. Add: James Kellam. *V.*

Kellam. Gu. 2 lions ramp. combatant under one head guard. or crowned az. within a bordure arg. James Kellam. *V.*

Kelly. Az. a castle triple towered or betw. 2 lions ramp. combatant arg. William Kelly. Dublin. ob. 1597.

Kelly (Lymston, co. Devon). Arg. a chev. betw. 3 billets gu. quartering arg. a chev. betw. 3 talbots sa. *V.D. 1620.*

Kemeys (Cefn Mably, co. Glamorgan, bart.). Insert—1642. . . .

Kempe. Gu. a bend vair betw. 6 escallops arg. Sir Robert Kempe, co. Devon and Cornwall. *V.*

Kempe (Spain's Hall, co. Essex and co. Suffolk). Add: *V.E. 1612.* Add: Kempe (Finchenfeld, Essex). Same arms. *V.*

Kempe (Pentlow, co. Essex, bart.). Insert— 1636. . . .

Kempston or Kempton. Add: *V.**

Kempstone. Add: *V.**

Kempthorne (Morestow, co. Cornwall). Add: *V.C.*

Kempton (Morden, co. Cambridge and London). . . . Add: *W.*

Kemys (Kiven Mably, co. Glamorgan). Bart. 1662. Vert on a chev. or 3 pheons sa.

Kemys (Co. Gloucester). Vert on a chev. arg. 3 pheons sa. points downwards and outwards. *V.*

Kemys (Co. Gloucester). Same arms and in base a rose of the second. *V.*

Kendale. Arg. on a bend az. 3 pierced mullets or. Sir Robert Kendale. *S.*

Kendall (Pelyn, co. Cornwall &c. . . .). Add: *V.**

Kendall (Ripon, co. York). Per bend dancettee arg. and sa. Add: *F.Y.*

Kendall. Arg. a bend vert. a label gu. Sire Robert de Kendall *N.L.Y.* Richard de Kendale, *Y.* Sir Edmond Kendall, co. Bedford, *V.*

Kendall (Exeter). Add: *V. V.D. 1620.*

Kendall (Co. Hertford). Add: and co. Northumberland. *V.*

Kendall. Arg. a bend dancetty vert. betw. two cotises of the same gu. Sire Edmond de Kendale, *N.* Kendall, Arg. a bend betw. 2 cotises dancetty vert. Sir Edmund de Kendale. *B.* Kendall (Exeter). Arg. a chev. az. betw. 3 dolphins naiant sa. *Colby.*

Kenetts. Gu. 3 hounds courant in pale arg. *P. de Kenetts. V.*

Kenfing or Kensing. Arg. a chev. betw. 3 squirrels sejant gu. cracking nuts or. *V.**

Kenland (Scotland). Az. a goat salient or debruised with a bugle horn vert. *Cady.*

Kenley (Drogheda). *Ulster's Office.* Add: *V.*

Kenley. Per bend embattled sa. and arg. *V.*

Kennedy (Col. Alex. Kennedy &c. . . .). Add: Kennedy (Knockgray, co. Kirkcudbright).

Kensing. Add: *V.*

Kent (County of). Gu. a horse salient arg. *Berry.*

Kent (Thatcham, co. Berks.). Add: Kent (Hemingham, co. Hunts.). Az. a lion pass. guard or a chief erm.

Kent, Smith alias Kent (More End, co. Northampton). Gu. a chev. betw. 3 pierced cinquefoils erm.

Kenton. Sa. a chev. betw. three cinquefoils or. Add: *V.*

Kentwood. Arg. (aliter or), on a bend gu. betw. 3 crosses patty fitchy at the foot az. (aliter sa.), as many pierced 5-foils silver. Nicholas Kentwood. *V.*

Kentwood. Or on a bend betw. 3 crosses crosslet fitchy sa. as many pierced 5-foils of the first. Nicholas Kentwood, co. Berks. *W.*

Kenyon (Peele, co. Lancaster 1664). Add: *V.L.* Sir . . . de Kenyam. *V.*

Ker (Duke of Roxburghe). Add: *Crawfurd.*

Kerby (Essex). Gu. a lion ramp. arg. his feet resting upon garbs or. *Cady.*

Kercher. Or a bend lozengy sa. *Cady.*

Kerr (Scotland). Gu. a chev. . . . in base a buck's head erased. *Cady.*

Kerr (Lord Jedburgh). 1622. Gu. on a chev. arg. 3 mullets of the first. *Crawfurd.*

Kerrison (Sir Roger Kerrison of Brooke, co. Norfolk, Sheriff of Norfolk, 1800). Quarterly gu. and sa. a lion ramp. arg. betw. 3 bezants. *Dashwood.*

Kett (Co. Worcester). Az. on a chev. betw. 3 kites heads erased or as many 3-foils slipped gu. *Nash.*

Kettle. Insert—of the Temple (London)—and Bournemouth, co. Devon. Az. a bend betw. two buck's heads. . . .

Kettleburge. Arg. 3 martlets in bend sa. *Cady.*

Key (Okenshaw). Arg. 2 bends sa. a label of 3 points gu. *Eliz. Roll xxj.*

Key (Co. York). Sa. a chev. arg. in chief a fleur-de-lis per pale or. and az. *Robson.*

Keynes or Keyneto (Tarent, co. Dorset . . .). Add: Sir Robert de Keynes. *V.*

Keynes or Keignes (Winckley Keynes, co. Devon . . .). Add: *V. V.** Add: Keynes or Kaynes (co. Dorset). Same arms. *Dugdale.*

Keynion (—insert—Peele, co. Lancaster . . .). Add: *V.L.1664.*

Keyt. Az. a chev. betw. 3 kites heads erased or. *Collinson Somerset j. 77.*

Kichen. Arg. on a chev. quarterly gu. and sa. betw. 3 bustards of the second as many bezants. *Harl. MS. 1404. fo. 14.*

Kidderminster (Town of). Az. on two chevs. or betw. 3 plates 8 ogresses.

Kidderminster. Az. two chevs. or betw. 3 bezants. . . . Add: Richard Kydermester, Abbot of Winchcomb. *U.*

Kidwally. Az. a wolf ramp. arg. collared and chained gu. Add: Sir Morgan Kidwally. *V.*

Kiffin. Arg. a chev. gu. betw. 3 pheons reversed sa.

Kift. Add: *Robson.*

Kighley (Quartered by Rudston of Boynton, co. York). Gu. a chev. erm. betw. 3 bears heads erased arg. *Dugdale p. 131.*

Kilby (John Kilby, chosen Alderman of York, 1803). Arg. three boars—underlined—margin, read bars. *Robson.*

Kilsh (Aberdeen). Or a chev. betw. in chief two cinquefoils and in base a mullet sa. *Robson.*

Killegrew (Killegrew and Arwennick, co. Cornwall. ... bart,) Insert—1660 ... Arg. an eagle displ.—insert—with 2 heads. ... Add: *V.V.* and *Lysons.*

Killett (Great Yarmouth, co. Norfolk). Or on a mount vert. a boar pass. sa. collared and chained.

Killingbeck (Leeds, co. York). Add: *V.* Killingbeck (Chapel Allerton, Leeds, co. York). Granted 1585. Same arms. *W.*

Killinghall. Gu. a bend raguly betw. 3 garbs arg. *V.*

Killinghall (Myddleton Girg). Sa. a chev. or betw. 3 codfish arg. *Eliz. Roll. xviij.*

Killinghall (Co. Cumberland). Add: *V.*

Killingmarch (Co. Oxford ...). Add: *V.*

Killiowe (Lansallos, co. Cornwall). Add: *V.C. 305.*

Kilmerux ... (another bears a chev.—insert—'az.' ... Add: *Robson.*

Kilnore Add: *V.*

Kimbe Or a chev. gu. within a bordure sa. Sir William de Kimbe. *B.*

Kinardsly Az. a lion ramp. arg. within an orle of crosslets of the second. Add: Sir Hugh Kinardsly, temp. Edw. j. *V.*

Kinardsley. Az. semy of crosses crosslet a lion ramp. arg. Richard de Kinardsley, *E.* Sir Hugh de Kinardsley, *N.*

Kindlemersh (Essex). Per fess erminois and sa. a lion ramp. counterchanged. *Morant's Essex ij. 424.*

King (Co. Essex). Az. a bend engr. erm. betw. 2 double-headed eagles disp. or. *V.E. 1558.*

King (Co. Leicester). Sa. on a chev. arg. 3 escallops ... Crest: ... Add: *V.* Kynge (Suffolk). Same arms. *V.*

King. Arg. a chev. sa. in chief a lion ramp. gu. in base an appletree fructed ppr. Sir John King, Inner Temple 1674. *L.N.*

King (London). Sa. on a chev. arg. 3 escallops gu.

King (London). Sa. on a chev. erm. 3 escallops gu. Crests: ... Add: *V.*

Crests: ... Add: *V.* Alexander Kinge, London. Granted 1592. *W.*

Kingestone. Gu. three eagles displ. or betw. 2 bendlets arg. Add: *V.*

Kingeston or Kingston. Arg. a chapeau or hat az. with a plume of ostrich feathers in front gu. John Kingeston, 1390. *Harl. MS. 1178 fo. 42.*

Kingsfeld. Gu. 2 bendlets erm. *V.*

Kingsmead or Kingesmede—insert—(Co. Salop.). temp. Edw. j. Add: Sir Walter Kingsmede, *V.*

Kingsmead. Barry arg. and gu. on a bend sa. 3 escallops or. Sire Walter de Kyngeshemede. *N.*

Kingsmill (Millbrook, co. Hants.). Arg. crusilly fitchee sa. a chev. ermines betw. 3 millrinds ... Add: Kingsmill (Co. Hants.). Sir William Kingsmill. The field or. *V.V.*

Kingston. Arg. on a bend az. 3 crosses crosslet or. *V.*

Kingston (Co. York). Arg. a bend wavy cotised gu. Add: *V.*

Kingston. Sa. a lion ramp. tail forked or. Sir Nicholas Kingston, co. York. *V.N.* Sir John Kingston, temp. Edw. iij. *V.N.* Thomas Kingston. *Y.* Sir Water de Kingston, Same arms with a dexter baston gu. *N.*

Kingston (Insert—Isle of Wight). Gu. on a chev. or betw. 3 cinquefoils of the second 5 mullets az. Add: *V.*

Kingston (Temp. George III). Add: M.P. for Lymington, c. 1760.

Kingsworth (Kempsing, Kent). Erm. on a bend ... 5 chevrons ... *Robson.*

Kinkley—insert—or Kynkeley. Gu. a chev. engr. arg.

Kinnear (That Ilk, co. Fife). ... three canary birds ppr.—underlined—insert—'vert.'. *Guillim.*

Sneyd-Kinnersley (Loxly Park, co. Stafford). Az. semy of crosses crosslet a lion ramp. arg. quartering arg. a scythe with sneyd in bend sinister sa. in the centre a fleur-de-lis of the second. *Debrett.*

Kinnimouth (Craighall, Scotland). Az. a chev. betw. 3 fleurs-de-lis arg. *Guillim.*

Kirby—insert—Horton, co. Kent. Az. six lions ramp. arg. ...

Kirby. Az. 6 lions ramp. or on a canton of the second a mullet gu. Sir ... de Kirkeby. *V.*

Kirhile or Kirhir (Co. Devon). Or an eagle displ. sa. Add: *V.*

Kirk. Per fess or and gu. a lion ramp. reguard. counterchanged. *V.*

Kirk.

Kirkby (Kirkby, co. York). ... Add: *C.L. p. 46.*

Kirkby Bellers (Augustinian Priory, co. Leicester). Per pale gu. and or a lion ramp. changed. *Tanner.*

Kirkby (Co. Kent; Sir John Kirkby ...). Add: *V.*

Kirkby(Quartered by Mitford through Wharton ...). Add: Kirkby (Kirkby, co. York). Rowcliff, co. Lancaster and Cumberland. Same arms.

Kirkele. Gu. 2 bars or in chief 3 keys wards upwards arg. *V.*

Kirkeby (Heveringham Castle, Essex). Arg. 3 bars gu. on a canton of the second a cross patonce or. *V.E. 1612.*

Kirkeby. Sa. two lions pass. in pale or. Sir Nicholas Kirkeby. *V.*

Kirketon. Arg. 6 eagles displ. 3.2 and 1. sa Raffe de Kirketon *A.*

Kirkham. Arg 3 lions ramp. gu. within a bordure sa. William de Kirkham. *E.* Nichol de Kirkham. *F.*

Kirkham (Ashcombe, temp. Henry iii and Blagdon, co. Devon). ... Add: The field arg. *V.D. 1620.* Sir John Kyrkham, Blakedon, co. Devon. *V.*

Kirkalon. Arg. 3 bars gemel sa. Le Sire de Kyrkalon. *Y.* Sir William Kyrkalane. *V.*

Kirkley. Arg. a chev. az. betw. 3 cocks. gu. *V.*

Kirkloft (Quartered by Bowyer-Smith). Arg. on a chev. gu. 3 crosses crosslet or.

Kirke. Or a chev. az. a label gu. *V. V.*

Kirkton or Kirton. Arg. three eagles displ. sa. Crest: ... Add: Rauf de Kirketon. *E.* Thomas Kirkton. *Y.*

Kirkton. Az. 3 martlets arg. Henry Kirkton. *V.*

Kitchen (Quartered by Banister). Arg. on a chev. per pale gu. and sa. 3 bezants. *V.L.*

Kitchingman (Beeston, Leeds, co. York). Arg. a chev. gu. betw. 3 cranes ppr. *Whitaker's Leeds ij. 256.*

Kite. Az. on a chev. betw. 3 Kites heads erased or as many tulips flowered gu. and leaved vert. *V.* John Kite, Archbishop of Armagh, 1513. Bishop of Carlisle, 1521-37.

Knappe (Woodcot, co. Oxford; granted 2 Sept. 1669). Insert—by Bysche.

Knell (Cos. Oxford and Gloucester). Add: *V.*

Knell or Knelly. Add: *V.*

Kneveson or Nevison. Arg. a chev. betw. 3 eagles displ. az. *V.*

Knevet (Cornwall). Arg. a bend within a bordure sa. a crescent on a crescent for diff. *V.C. p. 305.*

Knevet. Arg. on a bend sa. three trefoils of the first within a bordure engr. of the second. Add: *V.*

Kneysworth or Knesworth (Lord Mayor of London, 1505, cos. Cornwall and Stafford). Add: *V.*

Kneysworth. Erm. a chev. embattled . . . Add: *V.*

Knight (Charwerton and Rowington, co. Northants . . .). Add: *C.W.*

Knight (Norroy King of Arms d. 1593). Add: *V.**

Knight. Vert. a bend of 5 fusils conjoined or. *V.*

Knight (London and Kent granted by Segar). Same arms, a crescent for diff. John Knight, Principal Surgeon to King Charles ij. Vert a bend lozengy or. *Cady.*

Knight (Co. Middlesex). Quarterly 1st and 4th vert. a bend lozengy or 2nd and 3rd per chev. arg. and sa. . . . Add: John Knight, Principal Surgeon to King Charles ij.

Knight (Sir John Knight, Bristol, 1663). Arg. 3 pales gu. on a canton of the last a spur or. *L.N.*

Knight. Arg. on a canton gu. a spur or within a bordure sa. Add: *Cady.* (Another of the second).

Knight. Arg. on a canton gu. a spur leathered or . . . Add: *V.**

Knightley (Fawsley Park, Northants, Baronetcy, 1798). Quarterly 1 and 4. Erm. 2 and 3. Paly of 6 or and gu. all within a bordure az.

Knightley (Off Church, co. Warwick, Baronetcy, 1660). Same arms.

Knightley (Co. York). Same arms.

Knightley (Kingston-upon-Thames, co. Surrey). Add: Sir Robt. Knightley. Astley, co. Surrey, 1676. *L.N.*

Knighton. Barry of 8 or and az. on a canton gu. a tun or. *V.*

Knighton. Barry of 8 arg. and az. on a canton gu. a tun paleways or quartering arg. 6 annulets 3. 2. and 1. gu. *C.L. p. 31.*

Knill. Gu. a lion S crowned g.

Knipell. Az. on two bars or . . . Add: *V.*

Knit (Daneslowne, Ireland). Gu. a chev. betw. 3 round buckles points dexter or. *Harl. MS. 1441.*

Kniveton (Mercaston, co. Derby, bart.). Insert—1611. . . . Add: *V.*

Kniveton alias Gilbert. Add: Kniveton alias Gilbert (Yelgrave, co. Derby).

Knolles. Gu. on a chev. arg. three roses of the field. Add: Sir Robert Knolles. *S.V.X.* Sir Robert Knowls. temp. Ric. ij. (In Church at Harpley, co. Norfolk).

Knottisford. Add: *V.*

Knovile. Gu. 3 water bougets erm. Thomas Knovile. *Y.*

Know (Ford, Kent). Arg. on a bend engr. . . . three 3-foils slipped . . . *Robson.*

Kowles or Knoell. Add: *V.S.*

Knowis (That Ilk). Arg. a chev. betw. 3 roses gu. *Guillim.*

Knowsley. Arg. a chev. betw. 3 martlets gu. *Randle Holme.*

Knyvett (Charlton, co. Wilts.). Arg. a plain bend within a bordure engr. sa. *Z. 398.*

Knyvett (Ashwell Thorpe, co. Norfolk). . . . Add: *V.*

Knocke. Vairy or and vert. and a bend arm. *V.*

Kokerell. Gu. crusilly and 3 cocks arg. *E.*

Kokington. Add: Henry de Kokinton. *F.*

Kotterton. Arg. a chev. betw. 3 cinquefoils sa. *V.*

Koyken. Arg. 3 bendlets gu. a label az. Sir William de Koyken. *I.*

Kromton. Arg. a chev. gu. betw. 3 martlets sa. *Cady.*

Kudford. Add: *V.*

Kullingworth. Add: *V.*

Kychard. Add: *V.*

Kydale or Kendale—insert—co. Devon. Arg. a chev. betw. three dolphins naiant sa. *V.*V.*

Kyffyn. Arg. on a chev. gu. betw. 3 pheons sa. a mullet of the first. Add: *V.*

Kylahy. Arg. two chev. sa. Add: William de Kylaby. *V.*

Kylle (Co. Devon). Arg. a chev. betw. 3 fleurs-de-lis gu. *Cady.*

Kylle or Kylley (Cornwall). Arg. a chev. betw. 3 billets gu. *V.V.**

Kyllingbeck (Chapel-Allerton, co. York). Insert—Granted 1585. Add: *W.*

Kymble. Add: *V.W.*

Kyme (Kesteven, co. Lincoln. temp. Henry ii). Gu. a chev. betw. 10 crosses crosslet or—insert—*V.* (another. . .).

Kyme (Baron Kyme . . . his son, Philip de insert—*A.E.J.G.K.*—William *N.Y.*) In Rolls L. and O. Sir Wm. de Kyme bears a label arg. for diff. But az. in *M.*

Kyme. Arg. a chev. betw. 3 cinquefoils az. stalked. . . Add: *V.* Kyme, Friskeney. *V.*

Kyme. Insert—co. Lincoln. Az. a chev. betw. 3 crosslets or. Add: *V.* Add: Simon de Kyme *G.N.*

Kyme. Az. crusilly and a chev. or. Simon de Kyme *G.N.*

Kymes. Add: *V.*

Kymes (Honour of). Az. a chev. arg. betw. 3 blind 4-foils of the second stalked vert. *V.*

Kynardsley or Keynardsley (Co. Kent). Add: *V.*

Kyndall. Erm. on a bend gu. three chevronels or. Add: *V.*

Kynerby. Arg. three lions pass.—insert—in pale. . . . Add: *V.V.**

Kynnelmarch. Add: *V.V.**

Kynnerton. Arg. a chev. engr. gu. betw. 3 pierced mullets sa. *V.*

Kynsey (Sir Thos. Kynsey, London, 1685). Arg. a chev. betw. 3 conies sejant gu. *L.N.*

Kynsey. Arg. a chev. betw. 3 squirrels sejant gu. *Cady.*

Kynvillem. Gu. a bend betw. 3 spear's heads arg. *V.**

Kyrkby. Arg. two bars gu. on a canton of the second a cross moline or. Add: Richard de Kyrkby. *S.* Sir Roger Krykby, Kirkby, co. York. *V.* Same arms.

Kyrkham (Priory of, co. York). Gu. 3 water bougets arg. over all a Prior's staff in pale or. *Tonge p. 60.*

Kyrle (Much Marcle, co. Hereford, bart.). Insert—1627. . . .

Kyrslow. Add: *V.** See also Kirsklow or Kirkstow.

Kyttfords. Per pale arg. and sa. a lion ramp. counterchanged. *Constable's Roll. xij.*

L

LABORER. Or two bars gemel gu. in chief two crosses couped of the second. Add: *V.*

Lackinglich. Arg. a chev. sa. betw. 3 chaplets of the second flowered gu. *V.V.**

Lacock (Copperthwaite, co. York). Arg. a chev. betw. 3 cocks gu. *Dugdale 1665.*

Lacy (Thornhill, Co. York 1666). Arg. a lion ramp. purp. within a bordure compony or and gu. bezanty. *Dugdale p. 299.*

Lacy (Foulkton, co. York 1645). Same arms.

Lacy. Quarterly or and gu. a bend sa. and a label of 5 points arg. *V.** John de Lacy, Earl of Lincoln and Lord of Pontefract. *D.G.F.V.* Roger de Lacy Constable of Chester ob. 1211. **Seal.**

Lacy (Crombleton, co. York). Quarterly or and sa. a bend gu. a label per pale sa. and arg. *Eliz. Roll. xxiv.*

Lacy. Barry wavy gu. and erm. Sir John de Lacy *N.*

Lacy. Or a lion ramp. purp. Henry de Lacy Conte de Nicole (or Lincoln). *H.J.N.P.V.Z.*

Lacy (Folketon, co. York). Sa. a chev. betw. 3 stags heads cabossed arg. *F.Y.*

Lacy (Beverley, co. York 1612). Same arms. *F.Y.*

Lacy. Arg. on a bend sa. 3 plates. *V.*

Ladbroke (Lord Mayor of London 1748). Add: *V.**

Lagage. Add: *V.**

Laird (Glenhuntly, co. Renfrew 1777).

Laird (Birkenhead, co. Chester). Same arms.

Lake. Sa. a bend betw. 6 crosses bottony fitchy arg. Lancelot Lake. *Eliz. Roll xxj.*

Lake (Castleford, co. York). Same arms. Crest: A seahorse's head couped arg. gorged with 2 bars gu. in the nostrils an annulet of the first. *Dugdale p. 16.*

Lake (Normanton, co. York 1564). Same arms. The crosses called urdée. Quartering; quarterly arg. and sable on a bend gu. 3 mullets arg. † for diff. *F.Y.*

Lake. Sa. a bend betw. 6 crosses crosslet fitchy arg. Sir Lancelot Lake. Middlesex 1660. *L.N.*

Lake (Co. Devon). Arg. a chief gu. overall a bend engr. az. in the centre chief 2 annulets interlaced or.

Lake. Sa. a bend arg. betw. 6 annulets or. Leyke. *V.*

Lake. Sa. a bend betw. 6 annulets or. *V.** Sir de Leke, co. Lincoln. *V.*

Lake (Normanton, co. York 1585). Sa. a bend betw. six 3-foils slipped arg. Quartering Cayley. *F.Y.*

Lake (Stephen Lake, of London. . . . Add: *W.*

Lakenlyche. Add: *V.* Sire John Lakynghithe. *S.*

Lamb (Master of Corpus Christi College, Cambridge. 1827). Arg. a chev. betw. 3 water bougets sa.

Lamb (Lambs Conduit, London). . . . on a chev. . . . betw. two figures 3 in chief . . . and a trefoil in base . . . 3 fleurs-de-lis.

Lambarde (Beechmont, co. Kent).

Lambert (Sheriff of London 1551). Gu. a chev. vair betw. 3 lambs statant arg. *V.*

Lambert (Kingston-upon-Hull 1666). Gu. a chev. betw. 3 lambs pass. arg. a chief chequy or and az. † for diff. *Dugdale p. 367.*

Lambert (Skipton in Craven, co. York). Gu. a chev. betw. 3 lambs statant arg. a chief chequy or and az. *V.*

Lambert (Calton, co. York). Gu. a chev. betw. 3 lambs pass. arg. a chief chequy or and az. quartering, gu. an annulet or betw. 3 chaplets. *F.Y.*

Lambert (Co. York—insert—and co. Durham). Gu. a chev. betw. three lambs pass. arg. Add: *V.** a † for diff. *V.*

Lambert (Richard Lambert, Alderman of London). . . . Add: *C.L.*

Lambourne. Insert—Essex. Arg. two chevs. sa. Add: Lamborn, Monsire William Lamburne. *S.*

Lamborne. Arg. on a bend sa. cotised gu. three lions heads erased or. Add: *V.* Add: Sir William de Lambourne *N.V. A. Harl. MS. 6137)* E. Sir Milo de Lamburn *F.*

Lamburne. Arg. on a bend sa. 3 wolf's heads erased or. *V.**

Lambrun. Arg. on a bend sa. cotised gu. 3 dragons heads erased or. *V.*V.*

Lambton. Gu. a chev. betw. three lambs heads couped arg. Add: *V.*

Lamont (North Burton, co. York 1665). Arg. a lion ramp. vert. *Dugdale*

Lampen (Lampen and Pardardaye, co. Cornwall). . . . Add: *V.C. 305*

Lampet or Lampeth (Co. Suffolk). Add: *V.*V.*

Lamprey (Co. Devon). Sa. a chev. betw. 3 lampreys arg. *Lysons.*

Lanark (Borough of Scotland). Arg. an eagle displ. with 2 heads sa. beaked and membered gu. a bell az. pendant to the dexter leg by a string of the last in chief 2 lions counter passant of the third and in base as many salmons naiant their tails in the middle base point ppr. *Berry.*

Lancaster (Baron Lancaster . . .). Add: Lancaster (Bilton Grange Rugby, M.P. for Wigan 1868). Same arms. Sir John Lancaster *R.V.Y.* Roger de Lancaster *E.X.*

Lancaster (Crackhouse, Cumberland). Same arms.

Lancaster. Barry arg. and gu. on a canton of the second a rose or. Sir Thomas Lancaster. *Q.*

Lancaster. Arg. a chev. betw. 3 eagles legs erased gu. a bordure engr. sa. Sir John de Lancastre. *S.*

Lancaster. Gu. a lion ramp. gard. or collared az. Sir Thomas Lancaster. *Q.* The collar charged with 3 fleurs-de-lis or.

Lancaster. Gu. 3 lions pass guard. in pale or. overall a bendlet (sometimes a baston) az. Sire Henry de Lancastre *H.J.K. Harl. MS. 6317 (sic) N.* Brother of the Earl of Lancaster. *Y.* Henry fils de Lancaster or Henry de Longcastre brother of Thomas Counte de Longcastre *K. Harl. MS. 6589.* Henry son of Edmund Crouchback and afterwards Earl of Lancaster. *Z. 109.*

Lancaster (Fun. Ent. Ulster's Office 1598). . . . Add: Lancaster (Milverton, co. Somerset). Same arms. *V.S. 1623.*

Landon. Or a chev. sa. betw. three wivern-serpents vert. *V.*

Landon. Arg. a chev. sa. betw. three cameleons vert. Add: *V.**

Landsell (Halsted, Kent). Arg. a chevron compony or and sa. *Robson.*

Lane. Gu. a lion pass. guard. betw. 3 saltires or. Sir Richard Lane Attorney General to the Prince of Wales 1634. Lord Keeper of the Great Seal. *Dugdale O.J.*

Lane (Co. Northampton). Add: Sir John Lane. *V.*

Lane (Tulske, co. Roscommon. Baronetcy 1660). Qrg. a lion ramp. gu. within a bordure sa. and for augmentation a canton az. charged with an Irish harp. Imperially crowned ppr. *Guillim.*

Langbergh. Per bend az. and gu. a bend betw. 2 crescents or.

Langdale (Whilbistrond, co. York). Add: Langdale (Ebberston, co. York) 1584. *F.Y.* Langdale (Snainton, co. York 1665). Same arms a mullet az. for diff: quartering gu. 2 chevs. or. *Dugdale p. 82.*

Langetot (Norfolk). Arg. an annulet gu. *Blomfield.*

Langfford. Add: Sir Johan de Langford. *N.* Sir Nicholas Langford. *Q.V.S.O.* But a baston arg. instead of a bend *Y.*

Langford (Sutton Ashfield, co. Notts.). Same arms. *V.N.*

Langford (Selford, co. Bedford); granted—insert —by Camden.... Add: *Syl. Morgan.*

Langford. . . . 3 pales . . . overall a bend. Nichol de Langford in Norton Disney Church, co. Lincoln. *Harl. MS. 6829 fo. 340.*

Langford. Vert. 6 lions ramp. or. Sire Nichol de Langeford. *O.*

Langley. Arg. a weasel sa. langued gu. *Nash.*

Langley. Erm. a bend vert. *V.** Richard Langley, Sawley. *V.*

Langley. Erm. on a bend vert. 3 leopards faces or. Sir John Langley, Lord Mayor of London 1576. *W.*

Langley (North Grimston, co. York 1666). Paly of 6 arg. and vert. a canton gu. *Dugdale p. 301.*

Langley. Per chev. gu. and or a lion ramp. barry nebulee arg. and az. Add: 'or vair'. *V.*W.*

Langley. Insert—Essex, arg. a bend az. betw. three mullets gu. Add: *V.*

Langley (Co. Kent). Quarterly per fess indented gu. and or in the first quarter a lion pass. guard. arg. *V.*

Langlond. Arg. a chev. cotised gu. Add: *V.*

Langrige or Langrich. Arg. 6 billets sa. 3.2. and 1. Add: *V.*

Langston. (quartered by Wayneham. . .). Add: *V.V.**

Langstone. Quarterly az. and arg. a bend or. Add: *V.V.**

Langton (Broughton Tower, co. Lancaster:. . .). Add: *V.L. 1664.*

Langton (Winyard, co. Durham). Add: *Surtees.* Langton (Newcastle-on-Tyne and Berwick). Same arms. *Robson.*

Langton. Quarterly sa. and or a bend of the last. *Harl. MS. 1465 fo. 15b.*

Langton (York). Quarterly sa. and arg. over all a bend of the second. *V.*

Langton (Walton, co. Chester). Add: Langton; Sir de Langton, Baron of Walton, co. Lancaster. *R.* John de Langton, Bishop of Chichester 1305-37.

Langton. Arg. 3 chevs. gu. a label of as many points az. Sir Christopher de Langeton. *S.*

Langton (Langton, co. Lincoln). A family long seated in that county . . . Add: *V.**

Langton (Co. York). Gu. a chev. erm. betw. 3 lions ramp. arg. Sir John Langton. *V.*

Langtree (Langtree, co. Lancaster 1567). Add: *V.*

Lanhergy (Cornwall). Sa. a chev. betw. 3 talbots statant arg. *V.*

Lanine (Co. Cornwall). Add: Lanine (or Lanyon) (Cornwall). *Harl. MS. 4031. fo. 89b.*

Lanleyron, Lanlairon or Langlaron (Co. Cornwall). Add: *V.* Add: Sir Serlo de Lanleyeroun. *N.*

Lansdown. Sa. an eagle displ. or membered beaked and crowned arg.

Lansladron (Co. Cornwall). Amend az. to read arg. and thus 'arg. three chev. sa.'. Add: Sir Serlo de Lansladron of Lansladron, co. Cornwall. temp. Edw. i. *Lysons.*

Lanvaller. Gu. a lion pass. or.

Lanway. Add: *V.**

Lany (Co. Leicester and London). Add: *C.C. 1619.*

Lanyon (Lanyon, co. Cornwall). . . . a square castle in perspective, with a tower at each corner or—underlined, marginal note—The castle arg. underlined. *W.*

Lapley (Lapley, co. Stafford). Chequy arg. and sa. *Erdeswick.*

Large or Lorge. Add: Robert Large, Lord Mayor of London 1439. *Harl. MS. 1439.*

Larfargue (Co. Rutland). Arg. a chev. gu. betw. 3 ogresses.

Larke. Add: *V.*

Laron (Sir Francis Laron). . . . margin c.

Lason. Add: and with an annulet or for diff. Lason of London 1568. *C.L.*

Latham. Quarterly . . . six billets or. Add: *V.*

Lathbury (Holme, co. Derby). Add: *V.*

Lathebury. Add: *V.*

Lathun. Gu. six bendlets 3 sinister and as many dexter vair. Sir Robert de Lathun. *E.*

Latimer (Co. Suffolk). Az. a chev. erm. in chief five cinquefoils arg. pierced or in base 3 crosses. *Cady.*

Laton. Or on a bend gu. 3 greyhounds heads erased of the first collared and luiged of the second. *V.*

Latymer (Freston, co. Suffolk). Add: *V.*

Latymer. Az. a chev. betw. 6 crosses crosslet arg. in the dexter chief a 5-foil or. *V.**

Laud. Add: *W.*

Laudham. Add: *V.*

Launceston-Priory (Cornwall). Add: *Ashmole MS. 763.*

Launtyan (Cornwall). Arg. a bull pass. sa. within a bordure of the second bezanty. *Lysons.*

Laurence. Arg. a chev. betw. three gridirons erect handles downwards sa. *V.*

Lavall. Az. a bend arg. Sir John Lavall. *V.*

Lavenham or Lavingham (Co. Essex). Add: *V.*

Lavenses. Add: *V**

Lavering. Arg. two chevronels sa. betw. three harts' heads cabossed gu. Add: *V.*

Law (Laureston,   ). Arg. a bend gu. betw. in chief a fleur-de-lis and in base a cock. †

Lawndaur. Add: *V.V.**

Lawrence. Sa. a chev. betw. three broken swords arg. on a chief embattled of the second as many martlets gu. Add: *V.*

Lawryn. Add: *V.*

Lawson (Brough Hall, co. York . . .). Add: *Dugdale 1665 p. 90.* Add: Lawson (Nesam,   ). Same arms, a crescent for diff. *Eliz. Roll xviij.*

Lawson (Popleton and Moreby, co. York). Add: *V. F.Y.*

Lawson (Ushworth). Per pale sa. and arg. a chev. counterchanged. Per pale—underlined— and read per fess. *Surtees.* ?

Lawson (Isell, co. Cumberland . . .). Add: Lawson (Thorpe Bulmer). Same arms but in chief a crescent also counterchanged. *Eliz. Roll. xx.*

Layfield (Archdeacon of Essex; confirmed 1639). Insert—by Sir John Borough, Garter.

Layforth. Arg. a bend engr. betw. 4 cotises gu. *V.*

Layton (Delemain, co. Cumberland, temp. Henry iii.). Add: *V.*

Layton. Insert—Co. Devon. Arg. a ram—insert —statant, sa. armed or. Add: *W.*

Lea (Quartered by Framynham, Suffolk). Arg. a chev. betw. 3 crescents ermines. *W.*

Leaby (Shannakiel, co. Cork). Gu. a lion ramp. or armed and langued az. in chief two sceptres in saltire of the second. *A.A.*

Leaf (Park Hill, Streatham). Insert—Surrey. . . .

Leafridge (Kent). Arg. on a chev. sa. betw. as many holly leaves vert. 3 cinquefoils of the field. *Robson.*

Lealle or Leall (Co. Kent). Add: *V.**

Lealle. Gu. a bend or betw. six annulets arg. Add: *V.*

Leirmouth (Darsy, Scotland). Or on a chev. gu. 3 mascles of the first. *Guillim.*

Leathersellers, Company of (London). Add: Granted 7 Nov. 1505. ? Add: Granted 20 May 1479. *Harl. MS. 1359 fo. 74b.* An augmentation as an impalement was granted in 1505 viz. Per fess sa. and arg. a pale and 3 rams salient counterchanged: quartering sa. 3 goats statant affrontes in fess arg. attired or. *Harl. MS. 1359. fo. 75.*

Leaver or Lever. Arg. two bends engr. gu. Crest: An arm embowed holding a club ppr. Add: Leaver (Co. Lancaster). Quartering Cunliffe aliter Bavoyr with Radcliffe and Aylworth. *Harl. MS. 6159. fo. 51b.*

Le Bray. . . . a chev. . . . betw. 3 leopards heads . . . John le Bray (London) 1327. *Cotton MS. Julius C. vij. fo. 184.*

Lechford (Shelwood, co. Surrey). Add: *W.*

Lechford. Ermines a chev. betw. 3 leopards heads arg. *W.*

Lecky (Castle Lecky, co. Derry . . .). Add: Lecky (Co. Londonderry). Same arms.

Le Clerc (Quartered by Rutter). Or 3 books 2 and 1 bendways gu. *Foster.*

Ledgbird (Plumstead, Kent). Quarterly gu. and az. a chev. or in chief 2 eagles displ. . . . *Robson.*

Ledwitch (As borne by Dr. Edw. Ledwitch, author of the antiquities of Ireland). Gu. 3 caps of maintenance or. *A.A.*

Lee (Lee and Darnhall, co. Chester temp. Henry iii.). . . . Add: *V.**

Lee. Az. 3 bars engr. or over all a bend lozengy arg. and gu.

Lee (London; descended from co. Chester). . . . Add: *V.*

Leechford. Ermines a chev. betw. three leopards faces arg. Add: *V.**

Lee (Nantwich and Newport, co. Salop.). Arg. a chev. gu. betw. 3 leopards heads sa. *W.*

Leegh. Barry of 5 az. and arg. a bend chequy or and gu. William de Leegh. *X.*

Leeke. Arg. a chief gu. over all a bend engr. az. in the sinister chief a pierced mullet for diff. Monsire Robert de Leyke *S.*

Leeke. Arg. a chief gu. over all a bend engr. az. in sinister chief an annulet arg. for diff. *Harl. MS. 6829. fo. 58.*

Leeky (Ireland). . . . a chev. . . . betw. 3 mullets . . .

Leer. Arg. a chev. betw. 3 mullets gu. *Cady.*

Le Esterling (Co. Glamorgan). Paly of 6 arg. and az. on a bend gu. 3 cinquefoils or. *Nicholas.*

Leeys or Leys. Sa. on a chev. or betw. 3 lilies arg. two scythe blades crossing each other at the point of the first. *V.*

Legard (Ganton, co. York, bart.). Insert—1660. Add: *C.C.* and *Foster Dugdale p. 111.*

Legat (Cos. Essex, Kent and Norfolk). Add: *V.*

Leggatt. Per saltire az. and arg. in pale 2 lions ramp. or in fess as many roses gu. barbed a. d seeded ppr. *A.A*

Legh. Az 2 bars arg. on a bend or 3 pheons gu. *V.*

Legh (Adlington, co. Chester . . .). Componee gu. and or—insert—*V.*

Legh (Isell, co. York). Az. 2 bars arg. over all a bend counter compony or and gu. *V.*

Legh of the North. Same arms. *V.*

Legh. Az. 2 bars arg. a bend chequy or and gu. William de Leegh *X.*

Le Grice or Le Grys (Co. Norfolk). Add: *Blomfield.*

Le Gros. Quarterly arg. and az. on a bend sa. 3 mullets or. Sir Reginald Le Gros temp. Edw. j. *V.*

Le Gros (Greffier of Jersey 1875). Add: Nicholas le Gros. *A.* Nicholas le Gros. *V.V.**

Leicester. Scroll to **Book Plate**—Borough of Leicester. On a shield gu. a cinquefoil each with an ermine. Crest: A dragon wings displ. and tail nowed sa.

Leicester College (Newark, Co. Nottingham). . . . Add: Newark College in Leicester.

Leigh (Adlington, Sheriff of Cheshire iii Hen. v.). Az. 3 bars arg. a bend company or and gu. *Fuller.*

Leigh (Sutton, Surrey granted by Camden 1609). Or on a chev. sa. 3 lions ramp. arg. in the dexter chief point an annulet of the second. *Guillim.*

Leigh (Cos. Cumberland and Lancaster). Add: *V.* after 3 bezants.

Leigh. Or on a bend gu. a fish arg.

Leigh (Bruch, co. Lancaster 1664). Az. 2 bars arg. in chief 3 ducal coronets or over all a bend compony or and gu. *V.L.*

Leigh (Singleton Grange, co. Lancaster). Arg. a lion ramp. gu. *V.L. 1664.*

Leigh or Lea (Bradley, co. Lancaster). Add: *V.L. 1664.* Adds a label gu.

Leigh (Berthington,   ). Az. 2 bars arg. on a bend gu. 3 pheons of the second. Peter Leigh. *Harl. MS. 1424 fo. 85.*

Leigh (Ashfordby, co. Leicester 1619). Barry of 6 az. and arg. a bend gu. in the dexter chief a mullet for diff. *C.C.*

Leigh (Baggeley). Barry of 5 az. and arg. a bend sa. *Ormerod.* Gerard Leigh author of the Accedence of Armory. Same arms. *Lansdowne MS. 874.*

Leigh (Middleton). Add: Quartering arg. a fess sa. in chief 3 mullets of the last. *Constable's Roll xij.*

Leigh (Ingoldsby, co. York). Arg. a chev. engr. betw. 3 leopards heads sa. *V.*

Leigham. Gu. a swan arg. *Guillim.*

Leighton (Sir Bryan Leyghton temp. Henry viii. . . .). Add: *Cady.*

Lekborne. Arg. crusilly and a chev. sa. Sir Henry de Lekbune. *M.N.*

Leke. Arg. a chief gu. over all a bend engr. az. *V.* Sir Andrew de Leyke. *S.* and with an annulet for diff. Leeke. *Harl. MS. 6827* and with a pierced mullet. Robert de Leyte. *S.*

Lekeborne (Co. Lincoln). Add: *V.*—another 10 crosslets. *V.*

Lakeburne (temp. Edw. ij). Arg. on a bend sa. a lozenge gu. charged with a saltire of the first. *F.Y.*

Lekesworth (Co. Suffolk). Add: *V.**

Lekyborne. Arg. Crusilly sa. a chev. of the last. Add: Sir Henry de Lekborn. *M.N.*

Lemon (Carclew, co. Cornwall bart.). Insert—1774. . . .

Lemesi. Gu. an eagle displ. or a baston of the arms of Montford. Sire Richard de Lemesi. *N.*

Le Moyne or Moncke (Co. Devon). Gu. a chev. betw. 3 lions heads erased arg. *W.*

Lempriere (Seigneurs of Rozel, Jersey). Add: Lempriere, Master of the Grammar School at Exeter. *Colby.*

Len. (Nicholas de Len). Gu. 2 dogs arg. *A.*

Leni. Arg. on a bend gu. 3 lions ramp palewise or. Sir Lawrence Leni. *V.*

Lens (Norwich). Add: **Tomb** *in Winterton Church, Norfolk.*

Lentaigne (Tallaght, co. Dublin . . .). Add: *A.A.*

Lenthall. Sa. a bend fusilly arg. *V.** Sir Rowland Lenthall. *V.* William Lenthall. *Dugdale O.J.*

Lenthall (Co. Dorset). Same arms.

Lenthall (Besselsleigh Manor, Abingdon). Add: The mullets pierced gu. Sir Rowland Lenthall temp. Hen. vj. *V.*

Lenton (Co. Buckingham and Aldwinkle, co. Northampton; granted—insert—by Cooke. . . .

Lepes. Gu. 3 bars gemel or on a canton arg. 5 billets sa. Sir Ingo Lepes. *T.*

Leport. Add: *V.*

Lepull (Gillingham Church, co. Dorset). Pale per sa. and az. a windmill or.

Lerkesworth. Chequy arg. and gu. on a bend az. 3 lions ramp. palewise arg. Sir Robert Lerkesworth, Suffolk. temp. Edw. j. *V.*

Lermouth. Add: *V.*

Leslie. Arg. on a bend az. 3 buckles or quartering . . . 3 lions ramp. . . . for ROS. Walter Leslie, Lord of Ros 1367. *His Seal.*

Leslie (Wardis, co. Moray. Baronetcy 1876). Arg. on a bend az. betw. 2 holly leaves vert. 3 buckles or. Quartering or a lion ramp. gu. debruised by a ribon sa. *Debrett.*

Lessend. Arg. 2 bars wavy sa. Sire Johan Lessend *L.*

Lesquet. Arg. a chev. betw. 3 calves sa. *V.***V.*

Lessington. Add: *V.V.**

Lestrange. Gu. crusilly fitchy and 2 lions pass. arg. Robert le Strange. *E.*

Le Taylor (London). Sa. a lion pass. arg. quartering, or a lion ramp. guard gu. collared arg. and arg. a lion ramp. a chev. gu. betw. 3 eagles displ. sa. *C.L.*

Leton. Add: *V.**

Letster. Gu. a lion ramp. betw. 5 crescents arg. 2.2. and 1. *V.*

Letster. Gu. a lion ramp. betw. three crescents arg. Add: *V.**

Letterington. Add: *V.V.**

Leuker. Arg. a bend raguly az. betw. 6 escallops sa.

Leuger. Arg. a bend raguly vert. betw. 3 escallops gu. *Cady.*

Leukenor. Add: Sir Thomas de Leuknor *N.V.* Sir John Lewknor. *Q.* Sir Roger de Lewknor. *D.H.*

de Leu (Nicole de Leu). Gu. 2 greyhounds arg. *A. Harl. MS. 6137. fo. 96.*

Leventhorpe (Shingey Hall, co. Herts., bart.). Insert—1622 arg. a bend gobony gu. and sa. —Add: betw. 2 cotises sa. *Guillim.*

Leventhorpe (Co. Kent). Add: *Harl. MS. 1414.* Sir . . . de Lenthorp. *V.*

Levensthorpe (Quartered by Comberford, co. Stafford). Arg. on a bend betw. 2 cotises gu. 3 bars az. *Shaw.*

Lever (Arlington, co. Lancaster). Add: *V.*

Lever or Leyver (Co. Lancaster). Arg. a chev. gu. betw. 3 leverets courant sa. *V.*

Leverington. Az. 3 leverets courant in pale arg. *V.*

Leverland (London). Az. a chev. betw. 3 mullets arg. †

Leversedge (Vallis—insert—Frome). . . . Add: *V.V.**

Leversege. Arg. a chev. betw. three matchlocks sa. Add: *V.*

Leversege. Arg. a chev. betw. 3 heads of brown bills sa. *V.*

Levesey or Leviesey. Add: *V.V.**

Levesey (Co. Lancaster). Arg. a lion ramp. gu. betw. 3 trefoils slipped vert. *V.*

Levet or Levett. Add: Sir Walter Levett, First Mayor of Chester. *V.*

Levett. Arg. crusilly gu. a lion ramp. sa. Robert Levet. *A.*

Levett (Salehurst, co. Sussex . . . .). Add: Levett (Petworth, Sussex 1687) Same arms. *Guillim.*

Levins (Eske, co. York 1666). Arg. on a bend sa. 3 escallops of the first. *Dugdale p. 330.*

Levins (Bollington, co. Berks. 1643). Same arms. *Guillim.* Baptist Levinz, Bishop of Sodor &c. 1685. Sir Christopher Levinz, Justice of the Common Pleas 1681.

Lewellyn or Llewellyn. Add: *V.V.**

Lewen (Robert Lewen, Sheriff of Newcastle 1541) Arg. a bend bretessed gu. over all in chief a portcullis az. *Carr MS.*

Lewen (Alderman of London 1555). Arg. on a chev. engr. gu. betw. 3 crescents of the second each charged with a bezant as many estoiles or and betw. them 2 lozenges of the field each charged with a martlet sa. all within a bordure engr. gu. *Harl. MS. 6860.*

Lewes (Sheriff of Norfolk 1440). Sa. a chev. betw. 3 trefoils slipped or. *Dashwood.*

Lewes (Hedon,   ). Gu. a bend erm. betw. 6 owls arg. *V.N. p. 189.*

Lewes. Sa. a chev. betw. three trefoils slipped arg. Add: Sir Richard Lewes temp. Edw. iv. *Harl. MS. 6137 fo. 44.*

Lewin or Lewins. Add: *V.**

Lewis (Bristol and London). Add: Lewis (Langors, co. Brecknock. bart. 1628). Same arms. *Guillim.*

Lewis or Lewys (Ledstone Hall and Marre, co. York bart.). Insert—1660: extinct—insert—1671. Add: *Z. 443. Visitation York 1612.*

Lewkenor. Az. 3 chev. or. Quartering or on a chief gu. 3 bezants. Richard Lewkenor. *Dug. O.J.*

Lewston or Leuston (Wimbledon, Surrey). Gu. 3 pole axes arg. *Cady.*

Lewyne. Add: Sir Richard Lewyne. *X.*

Lewys. Sa. a chev. betw. three trefoils arg. Add: *V.*

Ley (Earl of Marlborough . . .). Marginal note—The heads are shewn as seals heads. *Dug. O.J.*

Ley (Middleton, co. York). Barry of 6 arg. and az. a bend company or and gu. *Eliz. Roll. xxiv.*

Ley (Co. Chester). Az. a pierced billet arg. betw. 3 ducal coronets or. *Harl. MS. 1404. fo. 126.*

Leyborn. Add: *V.**

Leyborne (Co. Kent . . . York). Az.—delete.

Leyborne (Kendal temp. Edw. ij.). Gu. 6 lions ramp. arg. 3.2. and 1. *F. Y.* Sir . . . de Leyborne. *R.* Sire Richard de Leyborne. *N.* Sir James Leybourne, Conswicke. *V.* Sir Thomas Leybourne. *S.* and with a label az. Sir Nicholas de Leyburne. *N.*

Leyburn (Baron Leyburne . . .). Add: William Leborne. *A.D.* Sir William de Leyborne. *N.V.K.E.G.* Roger Leyborne. *A.B.C.* Sir Henry de Leybourne. *L. Harl. MS. 6137.* John Leyburne, Kent. *Y.* Roger Leyburn, Bishop of Carlisle 1504. Az. 6 lions ramp. arg. a label company arg. and gu. Sire Henry Leyborne. *L.* The label of 4 points gu. Roger de Leyburne. *G.* Thomas de Leyburne. *G.*

Leyborne. Az. 6 lions ramp. arg. within a bordure engr. or. Sir John de Leyborne. *R.* Sir Simon de Leyborne. *G.N.* Sir Simon Leyborne, Kent temp. Edw. j. *V.*

Leyborne. Az. 6 lions ramp. arg. a quarter erm. and a bordure engr. or. . . . Layborne du Conte de Salisbury. *V.*

Leyham. Gu. a swan close arg. membered or. *V.*

Lickton. Add: *V.*

Life. Or on a bend betw. 3 martlets . . . as many human hearts of the field. *Robson.*

Ligen. . . . formerly of Hainault: granted—insert —by Camden. Add: *Syl. Morgan.*

Light. Gu. three swans arg. Add: *V.*

Light. Gu. a chev. betw. 3 swans arg. *V.*

Lightborne (Manchester: granted). Insert—by *Dugdale.* . . .

Lightword or Lizthad (London). Arg. a chev. az. betw. 3 tigers statant vert. reguarding a glass or. William Lightword. *V.*

de Ligne (Harlaxton, co. Lincoln). Or a chief chequy or and az. over all a bend gu. *Turner's Grantham.*

Ligne or Lingne of Harlaxton confirmed by Camden to Daniel de Lingne. The chief chequy arg. and az. *Guillim.* Granted 20 Jan. 1619.

Lihou. Add: Capt. John Lihou, R.N. Motto: "Domine dirige me".

Lilburne or Lilborne (Thickley . . .). Add: *V.*

Lilborne. Sa. 3 water bougets arg. Sir John Lilbourne. *S.* John de Lyleburne. *Y.*

Lillebon. Per fess arg. and sa. a chev. counterchanged. Sir William de Lillebon. *F.*

Lilly (Sir William Lilly, London). Arg. a chev. betw. 3 roses gu. *Cady.*

Limesey (Long Iching, co. Warwick). Add: Rauf de Limesi. *F.*

Limsey (Arley, co. Warwick). Add: Sire Peres de Limesi *N.O.* Richard de Limesky. *G.* John Lymesey. *V.*

Limyngton (Co. Chester). Gu. a chev. or fimbriated engr. sa. betw. 3 herons arg. *V.*

Linacre (Linacre Hall, co. Derby). Add: *V.V.**

Lindow (Ingwell, co. Cumberland). Add: *A.A.*

Lindsey (Cumberland). Add: John Lyndesey. *Y.* Sire Felix de Lyndesheye. *N.* and with a baston company az. and arg. Sire Simon de Lyndesheye. *N.*

Lindsey (Co. Warwick.). Add: Rauf de Lindsey. *E.* Geoffrey Lindsay, Baron of Wolverley.

Lindsey. Gu. an eagle displ. or armed sa. *V.**

Lindsey. Or an eagle displ. gu. (another purple) armed az. *V.** Sir Philip Linsey co. Northampton, temp. Edw. j. *V.*

Lindsey. Or an eagle displ. sa. beaked gu. Simon de Lindesie. *G.* and with a baston company az. and gu. Felipe de Lindsseie. *G.*

Lindsey (Gunton, Norfolk). Or an eagle displ. within a bordure gu. charged with ten 5-foils arg.

Linet. Arg. crusilly gu. a lion ramp. sa. Robert Linet. *A.*

Ling (Hockwold, Norfolk). Arg. a chev. engr. gu. betw. 3 whales heads erased sa. *Blomfield.*

Lingaine. Barry of 6 or and az. on a bend gu. escallops arg. Raufe de Lingaine. *E.F.*

Linley (Shegby, Scotland). Arg. on a chev. sa. 3 griffins heads erased of the first. *V.**

Linnet. Sa. a chev. betw. three bears heads couped arg. Crest: . . . Add: *V.*V.*

Linsey. Gu. an eagle displayed or armed az. Monsire de Linsie. *Y.* Sir Peres Linsey, co. Warwick. temp. Edw. j. *V.*

Linsey. Or an eagle displ. purp. (or gu.) armed az. Sir Philip Linsey co. Northumberland, temp. Edw. j. *V.*

Linsey. Or on an eagle displ. sa. 7 or 9 plates in cross Sir   de Linsey. *V.V.**

Linsey. Gu. 6 eagles displ. or 3.2. and 1. Raffe de Linsey. *A.I.* and with a label of 3 points, Sir Richard de Linsey. *I.*

Lippincot (Stoke Bishop, co. Gloucester, bart.). Insert—1778.

Lipton. Arg. 2 bars gu. on a chief az. 3 catherine wheels arg.

Liptrap. Arg. a chev. sa. betw. 3 mullets gu. **Book Plate.**

Lisle (Moxhall, co. Warwick.). Arg. 3 eagles displ. gu. *Cady.* Edward Lisle (Yarwell, co. Northampton). Same arms. *W.*

Lisle. Gu. crusilly or a lion pass guard. arg. crowned gold. Sir Robert del Yle. *N.*

Lisle. Or a chev. betw. three leaves gu. Add: *V.W.* Sir John de Lyle, co. Hants. *N.V.*

L'Isle (Rugemont, co. Bedford . . .). Add: Sir Warren de Lisle *R.O.I.N.V.* Gerard de Lisle or Lile. *A.D.Y.*

de Lisle. . . . semy of 3-foils slipped . . . a lion pass . . . crowned . . . John de Lisle, Lord of Burlee, temp. Edw. iij. Seal. *V.*

Lisley. Gu. a lion pass. guard. arg. crowned with a Marquesses coronet or a crescent for diff. James Lisley of Biddick, Wakefield. *Eliz. Roll. xx.*

Liston (Essex). Arg. on a bend dancetty sa. a cross patty fitchy or. *V.*

Liston. Arg. a bend dancetty—insert—(or indented). Add: Sir Richard Lyston. *V.*

Litcott (Oxford). Arg. 2 bars vairy or and sa. *Syl. Morgan.*

Littleborne. Sa. 3 wicker baskets with handles arg. Sir John Littleborne. *V.*

Littlebury (Fillingham, co. Lincoln). Add: Sir John Littlebury. *S.* Sir . . . de Littlebury, Kirton in Holland, co. Lincoln. *V.*

Littlebury. Arg. 2 lions pass. guard. gu. debruised by a bend vert. charged with 3 eagles displ. or William Littlebury. *Y.*

Littlebury. Arg. on a bend vert. betw. two lions pass. gu. three eagles displ. or. Add: Sire . . . de Littlebury. *Y.*

Littler (Wallerscote, co. Chester). Add: Littler (Wallerscote, co. Chester). Same arms. *Ormerod.*

Littleton. Arg. a chev. betw. 3 escallops az. Sir William Littleton. *V.* and with a crescent on a mullet for diff. Sir Edw. Littleton, Chief Justice of the Common Pleas 1640. *Dug. O.J.*

Littleton alias Lodge. Az. a lion ramp. within a tressure flory arg.

Littleton (Co. Leicester). Add: Sir Thomas Littleton, Justice of the Common Pleas 1466.

Liverpool, Town of **Book Plate.**

Liverpool, Diocese of—*newspaper cutting:* Rouge Croix, Mr Tucker, has "passed" at the Herald's office the seal for the diocese of Liverpool. The body of the seal shows a black eagle with expanded wings on a white ground, the "liver", or "cormorant", or "shoveller duck" having been said by antiquaries to have been originally the eagle of St. John the Evangelist. A yellow nimbus is around its head, and the beak and legs are yellow. In the claws of the right foot, not in the beak, it holds the ancient writing case. Above, is a "chief" or top part of the shield, which is impaled down the centre. On the one half is an ancient galley, gold upon red, with three masts; and on the other half is an open Bible, with the words, "Thy Word is truth". There is no reference, as is customary, to the old diocese of Chester or the Metropolitan See of York.

Livesey (Sutton, co. Lancaster). Arg. a lion ramp. gu. betw. 3 trefoils slipped vert. all within a bordure az. *V.L.1684.*

Livesey (Ifelde, Kent). Or an eagle displ. gu. a bordure of the second charged with 8 cinquefoils arg. *V.*

Lizthed see Lightwood.

Llewellyn (Cardiganshire). Gu. a chev. betw. 3 lions ramp. or. *Robson.*

Lloyd (Bronwydd, Cardiganshire, Kilshue, Pembrokeshire, Baronetcy 1863). Az. a wolf ramp. arg. a bordure erm.

Lloyd (Hardwick, co. York 1665). Per fess arg. and gu. a lion ramp. counterchanged, a canton az. *Dugdale p. 365.*

Lloyd. Gu. a lion ramp. or holding a rose arg. within a bordure of the second pelletty. 1663. *In Woking Church.*

Lloyd alias Resindal. Quarterly or and az. 4 roebucks trippant counterchanged within a bordure of the first. Lloyd alias Resindale, Cheam, Surrey and Denbigh, co. Denbigh. *Z. 424.*

Lloyd (Robert Lumley Lloyd of Cheam). Quarterly or and az. 4 roebucks trippant counterchanged; quartering 2nd arg. a lion ramp. . . . within an orle of mullets . . . 3rd arg. a garb betw. 3 pheons. 4th chequy or and gu. a saltire componcompony . . . and . . . †

Lloyd (Bradenham House, near Wycomb, co. Bucks.). Add: Lloyd (Woking, Surrey), Baronetcy 1662. Same arms.

Locke. Paly of six az. and or 3 falcons of the last. *Ashmole MS. 836.*

Locke (London). Az. 3 pales or on a chev. of the first an eagle rising overt of the second. *Harl. MS. 1404. fo. 144.*

Lockhart (Barr, co. Dumfries). Add: *Guillim.*

Lockwood (1471). Gu. on a bend or 3 padlocks az. in chief a martlet arg. for diff. *Carr MS.*

Lockwood (Sowerby, co. York 1665). . . . . a chev. . . . betw. 3 cinquefoils. . . .

Lodbroc. Add: Sir John de Lodebroke. *S.N.X.E.*

Lofft (Glemham House, co. Suffolk). Granted—insert—in 1864 by Robt. Laurie, Clarenceux.

Loffase. Arg. 10 billets 4.3.2 and 1 gu. *V.*

Loggan (Butler Marsden, co. Warwick). Or a lion pass. and in chief 3 piles sa. quartering 2nd; quarterly per fess indented or and sa. 4 griffins heads erased counterchanged and 3rd az. a chev. betw. 3 kites heads erased or. *Guillim.*

Loketon. Insert—(Co. York). Arg. on a chev. az. a mullet . . . Add: *V.*

Loketon. Arg. a chev. az. within a bordure of the last entoury of mullets of the first. *Harl. MS. 1404. fo. 110.*

Lombard (Whitechurch, co. Cork). Az. an eagle displ. betw. in chief 3 crescents and in base two bugle horns or dimidiated with lozengy sa. and arg. *V.*

London, Twelve First or Principal Companies of: Haberdashers . . . incorporated . . . —insert—1443, Add: Arms granted in 1570. Ironmongers—insert—granted by Lancaster, King of Arms. 1 Sept. xxxiv Hen. vj. (1445). Arg. on a chev. gu.—amend to read—Arg. on a chev. gu. with the line of the chev. three swivels or (the middle one paleways the other two-between. . . . .

London (Albye, co. Norfolk). Add: London (Essex). Same arms. *Morant's Essex ij. 223.*

London. Az. a chev. erm. and a chief or †

Londons. Quarterly, or and az. in chief two cantons, in base a chev. counterchanged, over all an inescutcheon arg. all within a bordure of the last. *V.* †

Londres or Lendres. Add: *V.V.**

Lone or Loan (Kent). Az. a tiger statant or. *V.*

Long (Draycot, co. Wilts. . . .). Add: Long (Semington, co. Wilts.). Same arms.

Long (Sandwich, Kent. Heiress. mar Jacob). Per fess arg. and sa. a lion ramp. within an orle of crosses patty and crosses crosslet alternately all counterchanged. *A.A.*

Long (Edw. Longe, Monkton, co. Wilts. Granted by Cooke). Arg. a lion pass. sa. on a chief of the last 3 crosses crosslet of the first. *W.*

Long (Isle of Wight . . .). Add: *C.L.*

Long (Whaddon, co. Wilts. Granted 1561. Baronetcy 1661). Sa. semy of crosses crosslet and a lion ramp. arg.

Long (Stratton, co. Somerset). Same arms. *V.S. 1623.*

Long (Westminster. Baronetcy 1662). Same arms.

Long (North Molton, co. Devon). Sa. semy of crosses patty a lion ramp. arg. charged on the breast with a martlet. *V.D. 1620.*

Longaster. Paly of 6 (or 7) arg. and gu. on a canton of the last a lion pass. guard. of the first. *V.*

Longendale. Arg. an American diver gu. *Randle Holme.*

Longespee (Reg. Ulster's Office). Add: Earl of Ulster. *Harl. MS. 1407. fo. 74.*

Longespee (Earl of Salisbury). . . . . Add: Nicholas Longespe, Bishop of Salisbury 1291–7. Gul. Longespe. *C.* Sir William Longespee, Conte de Salisbury. *Y. Z. 114–8.* V. Le Conte de Salisbury. *B.P.D.F.G.E.N.* and with a label gu. Estienne Longespe. *B.V.* Stephen Longspey, Earl of Ulster third son of the Earl of Salisbury his heiress m. De la Zouche. *Z. 114–8.*

Longland. Arg. a chev. gu. betw. 3 ogresses on a chief az. a cock enclosed by two crosses crosslet fitchy of the first. Luke Longland. *V.*

Longland (John Longland, Bishop of Lincoln). . . . Add: *Lansdowne. MS. 255.*

Longstaff. Insert—(Co. Durham). Az. a chev. betw. three quarter-staffs arg. Crest: . . .

Longstoder or Longstrother. Add: *V.*

Longevalle. Bendy of 6 vair and gu. Le Sir de Longevalle. *W.*

Longvale. Add: John Longvale. *X.*

Longevillers. Sa. crusilly and a bend arg. Sire Thomas de Longevilers. *O.*

Longvilliers (Baron Longvilliers). . . . . Add: *V.*

Longton. Borough of   . Arms as **Book Plate.** 1865. Motto: Great Industria.

Lonye. Per chev. engr. sa. and erm. John Longe. *V.*

Lopes (Maristow, co. Devon. bart.). Insert—1805. . . . .

Lorene. Or a bend betw. 3 lions ramp. gu. *Eliz. Roll. xxxv.*

Loring or Loringe (Co. Suffolk). Add: *V.* Add: Neel Loring. *S.* Roger Loring. *V.*

Loring. Quarterly arg. and gu. a bend of the last. Sir Neel Loringe K.G., *V.* Sir Peers Loring. *N.* William Loring. *T.*

Loring. Quarterly or and gu. a bend of the last. Neele or Nigel Loringe. *Q.*

Lorks. Az. a bend—delete—double dancette, and substitute down set, arg.

Lorke. Arg. a bend double dancetty arg. *Guillim.* †

Lortie (Axford, co. Wilts.). Arg. a lion ramp. per pale wavy or and gu. *Hoare.*

L'Ospital. Insert—France.

Lotysham (Chiph and Fornington, co. Somerset). Add: *V.S. 1620.*

Loudham. Arg. on a bend az. 3. 5. 7. or more crosses crosslet or. Sir John Loudham. *V.N.*

Lounde or Londe. Az. fretty arg. a bordure or. *V. Harl. MS. 5803.*

Loundres. Sa. a lion ramp. or a bordure engr. erm. Add: *V.V.**

Lountesford (Sheriff of Surrey, time Jas. j.) Az. a chev. betw. 3 boars heads or couped gu. *Fuller.*

Louth or Lowth. Gu. 2 bars arg. on a chief of the last a lion pass. of the first. Sir Adam Lowthe. *V.*

Lowthe (Frense, co. Norfolk). Sa. a lion ramp. or armed gu. *Blomfield.*

Lovayne (Co. Kent). . . . Add: Sir Nicholas Loveyne, Penshurst, Kent. *V.*

Love (Whetlington, co. Stafford). Arg. on a bend az. 3 griffins heads erased of the first. *C.W.*

Love (Broughton, co. Oxford). Add: *V.O.*

Loveday. Az. 3 bars dancetty or. Sire Richard Loveday. *N.* Loveday (Suffolk). *V.*

Loveday (Co. Norfolk and Cheston, co. Suffolk). . . . Add: *V.*

Loveday. Barry dancetty of 6 or and sa. Roger Lovedai. *E.*

Loveday (Williams Cote, co. Oxford). Per pale indented arg. and sa. an eagle displ. with 2 heads armed membered and ducally gorged or. on the breast an escallop.

Loveden (Fyfield and Buscot, co. Berks.). Add: *V.*

Loveis (Cornwall). Or a chev. engr. sa. betw. 3 sea pies ppr. *V.C. p.305.*

Lovell. Barry wavy or and gu. Sir John Lovell. *H.N.* Thomas Lovell, Tichmarsh. *Y.* and with a label of 3 points compony az. and arg. Sir William Lovell. *R.*

Lovell. Or 3 bars nebuly gu. Sir Salathiel Lovell, Baron of the Exchequer 1708. Sir Johan Lovell. *J.* Lovell of Harleston, co. Northampton, the heiress married Badcock in 1742.

Lovell. Barry wavy or and gu. a baston az. Sir Thomas Lovell. *L.N.*

Lovell (London; Thomas Lovell . . .). Add: *C.L.*

Lovell. Or a lion ramp . . . within an orle of crosses crosslet az. *V.**

Lovell (Co. Worcester). *Penn MS.* . . . Add: *V.**

Lovell (Co. Buckingham). Barry nebuly of 6 or and gu. a canton erm. *V.*

Lovell (Barton and Harling, co. Norfolk). Add: Sir Gregory Lovell. *V.*

Lovell or Luvel (Co. Somerset). . . . Add: Sir Richard Lovell. *I.L.N.Y.*

Lovell (Laxfield, co. Suffolk). . . . Add: *V.**

Lovell (Skelton, co. York . . .). Add: *V.*

Lovell (Skelton, co. York). Arg. on a chev. betw. 3 lions heads erased gu. an annulet of the field. *Tonge p. 98.*

Lovell. . . . on a chev. . . . betw. 3 wolves heads erased . . . as many 5-foils . . . . Seal of Thomas Lovell of Skelton. co. York. 1388.

Lovell. Barry nebuly of 6 or and gu. a label of 3 points az. *V.** The label of 5 points John Lovell *E.F.G.*

Lovel. Of Tichmarsh. Barry nebuly (or wavy) of 6 or and gu. *Y.*

Lovell. Barry wavy of 6 or and gu. a label of 5 points az. on each three mullets of 6 points or Joan Lovell. *G.*

Lovell. Barry nebuly of 6 or and gu. a baston arg. John Lovell le filz. *D.* But the baston sa. *F.*

Lovet or Lovett Add: William Lovett. *V.*

Lovetoft, Lovetot or Livetot. Add: Joan de Lovetot. *E.F.V.* Add: De Lovetoft, Lord of Hallam, co. York. *In Sheffield Church.*

Lovetoft. Arg. a lion ramp. gu. crowned sa. Mon de Lovetot. *Y.*

Low. Insert—Preston, co. Lancaster. Arg. an eagle displ. with two heads vert. Add: *V.L. W.*

Lowe (Southmills, co. Bedford). Insert—confirmed by Segar, 1628. *Guillim.*

Lowe (Walden, co. Essex . . .). Add: LeLow. *V.*

Lowe (William Lowe, co. Salop, 1586). Gu. a wolf statant arg. *W.*

Lower (Cornwall). Az. a chev. engr. or betw. 3 roses arg. *W.*

Lower (Trelaske, co. Cornwall . . . Visit. Cornwall, 1620). Sa. a chev. betw. three roses arg. —delete—(another, field az. chev. engr. roses or). Crest: . . . Add: *W.*

Lowis (Co. Devon). Arg. a chev. engr. gu. betw. 3 shovellers sa. breasted arg. *V.D. 1620.*

Lowis. Arg. three bears in pale sa. Add: *V.**

Lowre (Cornwall). Az. a chev. engr. or betw. three roses arg. *W.*

Lowthwick. Add: *Y.*

Lucar (Madenbrook, co. Somerset). Add: *W.*

Lucar (Bridgewater, co. Somerset). Insert— Same arms as above, and quartering. . . . Add: *V.S. 1623.*

Lucar (London). . . . Add: *CL.*

Lucas. Arg. 2 lions ramp. combatant the first az. the second gu. *V.*

Lucas (Co. Cornwall). Arg. on a canton sa. . . . Add: *V.**

Lucas (Newark). Add: *Cady.*

Luccombe. Arg. a chev. betw. 3 lions heads erased gu. *Collinson Somerset iij. 491.*

Lucien. Add: Piers Lucien. *Y.*

Ludbrough. Add: John de Ludburgh. *Y.*

Ludham. Sa. on a bend arg. cotised or. . . . Add: *V.*

Ludlow. Or a lion ramp. tail erect sa. Monsire John Ludlow or de Lolowe *S. Y.*

Ludlow. Or a lion ramp. sa. wounds all over gu. Sir Thomas Lodelowe. *V.*

Ludlow. Azure 3 lions pass. guard. in pale arg. Sir Thomas Ludlow, co. Salop. temp. Edw. j. *V.N.Y.* John de Ludlowe. *Y.*

Luffincote. Arg. an eagle displ. sa. goutty of the field. Sir . . . de Luffincote. *V.*

Lughterburgh. Gu. a chev. arg. goutty de poix betw. 3 leopards faces of the second. *V.V.**

Lulle. Add: *V.*

Lulman (Norwich 1637). Az. a fox sejant arg.

Lumley (Baron Lumley . . . Baron Thweng of Kilton Castle, co. York), the arms of that family, viz:—delete—or substitute—arg.

Lumley. Gu. 6 ringdoves arg. *V.**

Lumley. Gu. 6 popinjays arg. Marmaduke de Lumley. *V.*

Lund (Balgoine, Scotland). Paly of 6 arg. and gu. on a bend az. 3 billets arg; quartering arg. a cross moline gu. *Cady.*

Lunsford. Add: *V.*W.*

Luppingcote (Co. Devon). Add: *V.D. 1620.*

Lupton (Leeds, co. York). Arg. on a chev. betw. 3 dragons heads erased sa. as many lilies arg. on a chief gu. a tau betw. 2 escallops or. *Foster.*

Lupus. Or 3 wolves pass. in pale az. within a bordure per bordure indented or and az. *V.**

Lush. Gu. a chev. erm. cotised engr. arg. and 3 garbs or. *Debrett.*

Lusyon. Arg. a lion ramp. gu. over all a bendlet compony gu. and or. *V.*

Lutburgh. Add: *V.**

Luton or Lucon. Add: Sire . . . de Luton *V.**

Lutton (Cofford, co. Devon . . .). *W.* Add: Lutton (Ken Howton, co. Devon). Same arms. *V.D. 1620.*

Lutton (Mowlish and Cofford, co. Devon, temp. Henry v.). Vert. an eagle displ. double headed or.

Lutton (Knapton, co. York . . .). Add: William Lutton *V.*

Lutton. Sa. on a bend arg. three escallops gu. Add: temp. Edw. ij. *F.Y.*

Lutterell. Or a bend betw. 6 martlets sa. Sir Andrew Loterell. *N.* Loterell, co. Lincoln. *V.* and with a bordure sa. Sire Hewgh Lutterell. *T. Harl. MS. 6137.* But the bordure engr. Sir Hen. Lutrel. *S.*

Lutterell. Arg. a bendlet betw. 6 martlets within a bordure engr. sa. Monsire Hewgh Lutterell. *T.*

Lutterell. Az. a bend betw. 6 martlets arg. Thomas Loterell. *E.* Monsire Loterell. *Y.* Sir Hugh Lotterell. *V.* Sir Andrew Lotrel. *S.* Sire Geffrey Luterell. *J.M.* Robert Lutrel. *Y.*

Lutterell (Co. Somerset). Same arms.

Luxmoore (Kerslake, co. Devon) Add: *A.A.*

Lybb (Co. Oxford). Add: *V.O.* Add: Lybbe, co. Devon. *W.*

Lydwussers (France . . .). Az. a bend arg. on an inescutcheon or a bend engr. sa. Sire Johan de Lydevussers? *O.*

Lye. Arg. a bend of four fusils conjoined sa. and in the sinister chief a crescent of the second. *V.*

Lyfe. Add: *W.*

Lyfeild. Or on a chev. betw. 3 demi-lions gu. as many slipped 3-foils of the first. *V.**

Lygon. Arg. 3 bars sa. on a bend as the second three 5-foils. *Harl. MS. 1407. fo. 42b.*

Lyle (Co. Hants.). Add: with a label az. Sir Walter Lyle. *M.*

Lyle. Arg. on a canton gu. a lion pass. arg. Sir John Lyle, of the North. *W.*

Lylgrave. Add: William Lylgrave, co. York. *V.*

Lymington (Co. Chester). Gu. a chev. or fimbriated and engr. sa. betw. 3 lapwing arg. *V.*V.*

Lyme Regis, Town of (Co. Dorset). Arg. 2 bars wavy az. on a chief gu. a lion of England.

Lynam (Cornwall). Arg. a chev. betw. 3 urchins sa. *Lysons.*

Lynburge. Arg. an inescutcheon sa. within an orle of eight 5-foils gu. John Lynburge. *R.*

Lynch (Groves, co. Kent . . .). Add: Sir Thomas Lynch, Governor of the Island of Jamaica. *Guillim.*

Lynch (Cranbrook, Kent). Sa. 3 leopards ramp. arg. spotted of the field. *C.L. p. 70.*

Lynde. Arg. two bars sa. a bend gu. Add: *V.*

Lynde (Co. Cambridge). Gu. a demi-lion ramp. arg. within a bordure sa. bezantes. *V.*

Lyndey or Lynd (Co. Dorset). Add: *V.*

Lyndowne. Gu. a chev. arg. betw. three crescents or. Add: *V.*

Lyndsey or Lyndesey. Add: *V.*

Lyndwood. . . . a chev. . . . betw. 3 linden leaves. . . . John Lyndewode. **Brass.** *1412 at Linwood, co. Lincoln.*

Lyneham (Fun ent. Ulster's Office . . .). Add: Lyneham (Cornwall). Same arms. *V.C. 305.*

Lingaine. Barry of 6 or and az. on a bend gu. three 5-foils arg. Sir Rauf Lingaine. *V.*

Lyngayne. Barry of six or and az. on a bend gu. three plates—insert—Sir John Lyngayne. *V.* continue . . . (another . . .).

Lynol or Lynell (Co. Worcester . . .). Add: *Nash.*

Lyngen (Sutton, co. Hereford). Barry of 6 arg. and az. on a bend gu. 3 roses or in chief a label of 3 sa. *Guillim.*

Lynn (co. Devon). Gu. a demi-lion ramp. arg. within a bordure sa. bezanty. *V.D. 1620.*

Lyon (Ireland). . . . a lion pass. guard. in chief 7 estoiles. *Robson.*

Lyon (Ireland). Per fess az. and arg. in chief a lion pass. guard. betw. 3 fleurs-de-lis 1 and 2. in base an oak tree vert. *Robson.*

Lyon. Arg. a chev. engr. sa. betw. 3 lions dormant tails coward hanging down, the two in chief respectant gu. Gabriel Lyon, London 1633. *Harl. MS. 1358. fo. 40.*

Lyon (Connaught). Gu. a chev. betw. 3 boars heads erect and erased or. *Robson.*

Lyons. Arg. a chev. sa. betw. three lions dormant cowarded gu. *Collinson Somerset ij. 299.*

Lyonstoppe. Arg. a chev. betw. 3 lions pass. guard. gu. *V.*

Lyssores. Az. 2 chevrons and in the dexter chief a mullet or. Sir John Lyssores. *X.*

Lyston (or Liston). Essex. Arg. a bend indented sa. charged with a cross patty fitchy or for diff. *V.*

Lyttil. Per chev. arg. and sa. in base a tower triple towered or in chief 2 fleurs-de-lis of the second. *W.*

M

MABLETHORPE. Az. a chev. betw. three crosses crosslet arg. in chief (another, on a chief gu.—insert—*V.*) a lion pass. or.

Mabuisson. Arg. semy of martlets gu. on a chev. of the last a crescent of the first. *V.*

Mac Ailin (Ireland). Gyronny of 8 sa. and or a bordure counterchanged. *Robson.*

Mc Alister. Ancient arms. Arg. an eagle displ. in the dexter chief an ancient galley in the sinister chief a cross crosslet fitchy. . . . all within a burdure engr. sa.

Mac Brouder (Ireland). Arg. a bend engr. sa. betw. 2 roses gus. seeded arg. barbed vert. *Harl. MS. 4039 fo. 145.*

Maccarthy (Carbery, co. Hants.). Erm. a buck trippant gu. attired or. *AA.*

Mac Carthy (Cork. M.P. for Mallas, 1874). Arg. a stag trippant gu. in chief a ducal coronet therefrom a hand issuing grasping an otter.

M' Clure (Belmont and Dundela . . .). Insert—1874.

M' Clure (Scotland). Arg. a chev. az. betw. in chief two roses gu. and in base a sword point downwards of the second.

M' Clure (Co. Down, Ireland). Same arms.

M' Combie (Aberdeenshire. M.P. 1868). Or a lion ramp. and a chief gu. *Debrett.*

Mc Donachy (Ballinascreen, 1775-1800). . . . a chev. . . . betw. in chief 2 lions ramp. combat. and in base (a beast) statant.

Macdonald (Moydart, Scotland . . .). Add: Macdonald of Inchkenneth and Gribune, co. Argyle. Same arms. *Burke.*

Macdonald (Largie: . . .). Add: Makdonell. Or 3 lions sa. Sir Duncan Makdonell d'Escoce. *M.*

Mc Donnell (Murlough). Insert—Baronetcy 1872, . . .

Maceldon or Malcedon. Add: *V.*

Machell (Wendover, co. Buckingham). Insert—and co. Essex. Add: *V.E. 1634.*

Machell. Sa. 3 greyhounds courant in pale arg. a bordure compony or and gu. *V.**

Machell (Co. York). Same arms But the greyhounds collared or. *W.*

M' Iver (Asknish, co. Argyll). Add: Mc Iver M.P. for Birkenhead, 1874. *Debrett.*

Mc Kie (Palgown   ). Az. a lion ramp. . . . on a chief arg. 2 crows sa. each holding in its beak an arrow. †

Mc Kinering. Arg. 3 lions pass. in pale gu. armed and langued az. within a bordure of the last. *Harl. MS. 4039 fo. 139.*

Mc Kirdy. Quarterly arg. and sa. in each of the 1st and 4th quarter a mullet of the last.

Mc Kirdy (Birdwood, co. Lanark). Quarterly arg. and sa. in the first and fourth quarter a martlet. All within a bordure az. quartering arg. a fir tree growing out of a mount in base vert. on the dexter side a sword paleways az. ensigned with an antique crown or. *Burke.*

Mackmahon. Arg. an ostrich sa. holding in its beak a horseshoe gu. (*Hybernicus Sylvestris*). *V.*

Mackworth. Per pale indented erm. and sa. a chev. gu. *Harl. MS. 1386 fo. 34b.*

Mackworth. Per pale indented erm. and sa. a chev. gu. fretty or. John Mackworth, Dean of Lincoln, temp. Hen. vj. John Mackworth of Normanton. *Syl. Morgan.*

Mackworth (Bolton Grange, co. Salop.). Per pale indented sa. and erm. on a chev. or 5 crosses patty gu. *Guillim.*

Maclagan (Edinburgh). . . . three martlets—underlined, and margin—'cornish choughs'. *Robson.*

Maclatchy. Per pale gu. and az. 3 lions pass. in pale counterchanged. †

MacLoughlin (Co. Tyrone). Per fess wavy arg. and or in chief a dexter hand appaumy couped . . . in base a lion ramp. holding a flag gu.

MacManus (Co. Antrim). . . . Add: confirmed in 1810. Add: Motto: "Cor et manus".

M' Neill (Baron Colonsay). Insert—created 1867.

Mac Oda (Ireland). Arg. 3 chevs. sa. *Robson.*

Macrea. Arg. a lion ramp. betw. 3 annulets gu. on a chief az. 3 mullets or. quartering sa. a lion ramp. erm. crowned. **Book Plate.**

Macro (Vicar of Great Yarmouth, ob. 1743). . . . 2 bars wavy . . . in chief a lions head erased crowned. *His* **Monument.**

M'Taggart (London, from Scotland . . .). Add: Ellis Mc Taggart (London). *Debrett.*

Madden (Confirmed by Roberts, Ulster, 1647). . . . Add: Madden (Madderton, co. Wilts.). Same Arms. *Guillim.*

Maddeson (Newcastle on Tyne, 1584). Same Arms. *Carr MS.*

Madyson (Funaby, co. Lincoln, granted 1587). Same arms. *Harl. MS. 1539 fo. 109.*

Madesson (Wardale). Same arms. *V.*

Maddock Goch. Arg. a chev. per pale gu. and or betw. 3 sheldrakes ppr. *Randle Holme.*

Madely. Arg. on a chev. az. 3 fleurs-de-lis or. a bordure engr. sa. *V.*

Maddyson of Unthank. Arg. a chev. engr. betw. 3 martlets sa. *Eliz. Roll. xvij.*

Madeworth. Arg. on a bend engr. sa. 3 pheons of the first. *V.*

Madock de la Holme. Sa. a chev. betw. 3 owls arg. *Randle Holme.*

Madock Voell (Wales). Erm. a bordure az. *Randle Holme.*

Madock. Per pale az. and gu. 2 lions pass. or. *V. V.**

Madocks (Co. Middlesex . . .). Add: *Guillim.*

Madocks. Gu. on a bend arg. a lion pass. guard. sa. *Robson.*

Magrath (Ireland). Gu. 3 lions pass. in pale arg. quartering: or a dexter hand couped ppr. lying fessways holding a long cross gu. az. a dexter hand couped ppr. holding a battle axe arg: and arg. a goat trippant sa. *Harl. MS. 4039. fo. 138.*

Mahewe, alias Heller or Mayow (Lostwithiel, co. Cornwall . . .). . . . three ducal crowns or.—insert—*V.** Crest: . . .

Main (Lochwood, co. Stirling). Add: *Guillim.*

Mainwaring (Exeter). Arg. 2 bars gu. within a bordure engr. sa. *Robson.*

Mainwaring (Exeter, 1620). Arg. 2 bars gu. within a bordure compony or and sa. *V.D.*

Mainwaring (Croxton, co. Chester). Arg. 2 bars gu. within a bordure compony sa. and arg. *Ormerod.*

Maisters. Gu. a lion ramp. gard. arg. holding a rose stalked and leaved . . .

Maitland (Dundrennan, co. Kirkcudbright . . .). Add: Maitland (Lord Barcaple, Kirkcudbright, 1862). Same arms. *Debrett.*

Makdelane (Humbie, Scotland). Arg. two chevs. sa. *Cady.*

Malaval (Halstead, Kent). Gu. a lion pass. guard. or crowned arg. *Robson.*

Malbech, Malbesh or Malbish. Add: *V.*

Malbis. Arg. a chev. betw. 3 serpents heads erased gu. Sire William Malbise. *Y.*

Malbys. Add: *Y.*

Males. Gu. 3 round buckles tongues to the dexter or. Sir John Males. *A.*

Malet. Arg. 3 round buckles tongues to the dexter sa. Robert Malet. *E.*

Malet. 1355. Gu. 3 buckles or.

Malet. Sa. 3 round buckles tongues to the dexter arg. Sir Robert Malet. *A.*

Maleverer of Ardsale. Sa. 2 greyhounds courant arg. collard . . . *Constable's Roll xj.*

Maleverer (Arncliffe. temp. Edw. ij.). Same arms, quartering, or a fess gu. in chief 3 torteaux. *F. Y.*

Maleysell. Arg. on a bend sa. 3 martlets or. *V.**

Malford. Sa. three lions pass. in pale or. *V.*

Malham (Elsack, co. York). Gu. three chev. —insert—braced . . . *F. Y. V.*

Malherbe (Fenyton, co. Devon). *V.**

Malherbe. Gu. a chev. betw. three sprigs of mallow leaves. Add: *V.*

Maling (Scarborough—insert—co. York . . . —insert—co. Durham). Add: *Foster.* Crest: A hawk with wings expanded ppr. *Foster.*

Mallepasse. Vair a chev. arg. betw. 3 dogs courant gu.

Mallet (Co. Buckingham and Normanton, co. York). Insert—1585. *F. Y.*

Mallet (Co. York). Sa. a chev. betw. 3 mallets erect arg. *Fairfax's Book of Arms.*

Mallet. Gu. a chev. erm. betw. 6 mullets arg. John Mallet. *Eliz. Roll xxj.*

Mallet (Jersey). . . . or a crescent for diff.—insert—*A.A.* Crest: . . . .

Mallory. Erm. a chev. betw. 3 trefoils slipped arg. a bordure engr. sa. *Harl. MS. 1404. fo. 62.*

Mallory (Sir William Mallory, Knt.). . . . Add: Mons. Antoine Mallory. *S.*

Mallyn (Cornwall). Sa. 3 goats courant in pale arg. *V.*

Malmans. Arg. a bend purp. Sir Nicholas Malmans. *M.*

Malmaynes (Kent). Arg. a bend engr. purp. Nicholas Malmeynes. *Y.* Sir Nicholas Malemeis *N.* Sir Nicholas Malheuveux *L. Harl. MS. 6589.*

Malmeynes. Sa. a bend lozengy arg. Sir Thomas Malmaynes. *X.*

Malmaynes. Arg. a chev. gu. betw. ten crosses crosslet sa. Add: *V.*

Malopasse. Gu. a chev. betw. 3 pheons arg. William de Malopasse. *V.* the pheons or. *V.**

Maloree. Erm. on a chev. gu. a 3-foil slipped or. *V.**

Maloree. Erm. on a chev. gu. a 3-foil slipped or a bordure engr. sa. *V.*

Maloure (Co. Leicester ...). Add: Sir Piers Malory. *V.N.*

Maloysell. Add: *V.*

Malpas (Hampton and Bickerton, co. Chester). ... Add: *V.*

Malt (Co. Somerset). *Harl. MS. 1404.* Add: *V.*

Maltby (Maltby, Cleveland, co. York). Insert—1612. Add: *V.*

Malton Priory. Insert—co. Yorks. . . . . .

Malton. Sa. a lion ramp. arg. . . . . 8 annulets. . . . Add: Henry de Malton. *V.*

Malton. Sa. a lion ramp. arg. crowned or within an orle of 8 annulets of the second. Sir Henry de Malton. *V.*

Maltravers. Sa. fretty or on a canton gu. 3 lions arg. Sir Walter de Maltravers. *A.* Sir Wm. Maltravers. *E.F.* The lions pass. in pale.

Malure. Or 6 lions ramp. sa. Thos. Malure. *Y.*

Malveysin (Cos. Stafford and Lancaster). ... Add: Henry de Malvoisin. *A.* Sir Robt. de Mawvesin. *S.*

Malyn. Sa. on a bend betw. 2 eagles displ. arg. a wreath enclosed by 2 escallops gu. John Malyn, Abbot of Waltham. *U.*

Man. Or a chev. engr. ermines betw. 3 lions ramp. sa. Man (Surrey). *W.*

Mann. Same Arms. *V.E. 1634.*

Man (Hatfield Broadock, Essex). Same arms. *V.E. 1612.*

Manby (Elsham, co. Lincoln and London). Insert—*Visit. Lon. 1633.* Add: *W.* Manby of Elsam and Middleton, co. York. Same arms, quartering 2nd a cross bottony vert. pierced or. for Malkake 3rd Erm. on a fess engr. sa. 3 lozenges or for Arklowe 4th. Sa. a chev. betw. 3 estoiles arg. Mancell, a crescent in fess point for diff. *F.Y. 624.*

Manby—insert—(Co. Lincoln). Arg. a lion ramp. az. on a chief sa. three martlets of the first. Add: *W.*

Manby (Capt. G. W. Manby FRS., Great Yarmouth, co. Norfolk). Add: Manby (Middleton, co. York). Same arms. *Dugdale 1665. p. 84.*

Manby. Arg. three—delete—(another two) . . . Add: Sir Hugh de Manby. *P.Y.* John de Manby. *Y.*

Mancester. Vair a bendlet gu. Sir Guy de Mancester. *O.*

Mancester. Vairy arg. and gu. a bend of the second. *V.** Richard de Mancester. *V.* a bendlet.

Mancester. Vairy arg. and sa. a bendlet gu. Joan de Maincastre. *E. Harl. MS. 6137. E.* Richard de Mancester. *V.* Sir Symon Mancester, co. Warwick. *V.*

Mancester. Vairy arg. and sa. on a bendlet gu. 3 eagles or. Sir Simon de Mancester or Maincester. *N.L.*

Manchester, (City of). On an oval shield per fess arg. and gules in chief a vessel in full sail ppr. in base 3 bendlets enhanced. Crest: On a wreath of the colours a Globe. Supporters: On the dexter side a unicorn ramp. the fore legs resting on the shoulder and bordure of the shield, a rose on the dexter, collared and chained. On the sinister a lion ramp. reguardant and crowned, the fore legs resting on the shoulder and bordure of the shield sinister claws extended and a rose on the shoulder, standing on a scroll. Motto: "Concilio Labore" **Book Plate.**

Manchell. Add: John Manchell. *X.*

Mandere. Erm. 3 annulets interlaced in triangle gu. *V.*

Mandeville (Confirmed to Otho Mandeville, 1393–4). The patent of the grant by Edw. iij. to his father Peter having been lost. Gu. 3 lions pass. guard. or. collared with crowns. sa. *Ashmolean MS. 835 fo. 365.*

Mandit or Manduyt. Add: Sir Thomas Manduit. *E.X.Y.* Thomas Mandyt, Warminster. *V.*

Manduit. Erm. two bars gu. Roger Manduit. *Y.M.* Roger Manduit (Cumberland). Erm. 2 bars purple. *V.*

Manduit. Chequy or and gu. a bend vair Thomas Manduit. *Y.*

Manes. Chequy or and az. a chev. gu. Sir Emeri de Manes. *E.*

Maneward (Quartered by Noah Tookey ...). Add: *C.R. p. 35.*

Maney (Linton, co. Kent). Add: Maney (Biddendon, Kent). Same arms. *V.*

Manfeld (Skirpenbeck, co. York. confirmed). Insert by Flower. Add: *V.* The crosslets fitchy. *V.**

Manfeld. Arg. two bars sa. on the uppermost a wivern volant, tail extended of the field. Add: *V.*

Manfield. Quarterly or and az. 4 caps like Doge's caps counterchanged. *Harl. MS. 1404. fo. 110.*

Manfield (West Leake, co. Nottingham). Add: *V.E. 1634.*

Maningham. Arg. a chev. sa. betw. three moorcocks az. Add: *V.*

Manington (Manington and Combeshed, co. Cornwall). . . . . Add: *V.*

Manlovell. Add: *V. V.**

Mann (Linton, co. Kent). See also Man.

Manners (Ethale or Etall, co. Northumberland). Add: Mon. John Maners. *S.Y.* Sir Robert de Manners. *M.V.Y.*

Mannering (Nantwich, Cheshire). Arg. 2 bars gu. betw. 6 martlets vert. 3 in chief 2 in fess and 1 in base.

Manney. Arg. 3 chevs. sa. *Harl. MS. 1407. fo. 73b.*

Manningham. Arg. a chev. sa. betw. three peacocks az. Add: *V.*

Manny. Or three chevs. sa. *Z. 207. 208.* Sir Walter Manney. *Q. Harl. MS. 6595.* Sir Walter Manney, Essex. *V.* Terry de Manny. *Y*

Manny. Or three chevronels sa. on the uppermost a lion pass. reguard. of the field. Add: Sir Walter Manney, Founder of the Carthusian Monastery of the Salutation of London. But the lion on the centre chev. Sir Walter Manney. *Q. Ashmole MS. 1120.*

Mannyfold or Manyfold—insert—Cornwall. . . . Add: V.

Mansbridge (London). John Mansbridge, citizen and draper. . . . Add: *C.L.*

Mansegles. Arg. on a chev. az. betw. 3 eagles close sa. as many estoiles or. *V.* another herons. *V.*

Manse. Or a lion ramp. sa. within an orle of 8 escallops gu. Sir William Manse, Sussex. temp. Edw. iij. *V.*

Manston or Maston. Sa. a bend counterembattled arg. Crest: A harp or. Add: *V. V.**

Mantaby. Az. three bendlets or. Add: *V.*

Manvers (Holme Pierrepoint, co. Nottingham). Add: *W.*

Manvers. Arg. six annulets sa. 3. 2. and 1. Add: *W.*

Manwike. Sa. an eagle displ. or. Add: *V.*

Maples (Stow, co. Hunts. Baronetcy, 1627. Ext.). Az. a chev. quarterly per chev. or and arg. betw. 3 fleurs-de-lis of the second. *Guillim.*

Maples (Coningsburgh, co. York.). Same arms.

Maplet (Bath). Arg. 3 chevs. az. *S.* Maplet. ob. 1670. *Dingley.*

Mapletoft (Co. Lincoln). Add: Mapletoft (London, 1690).

Marbroke. Bendy of 6 or and az. a bordure gu. *V.*

March . . . on a bend . . . 3 pierced mullets of 6 points. . . . Roger de March. **Seal.**

Marchand (Co. Buckingham, granted). Insert—by Cooke. . . .

Marchant. Sa. a bend cotised or in chief a lion ramp. of the last. *Robson.*

Marchington. Arg. fretty sa. a canton erm. *V.*

Marchington. Arg. fretty sa. on a canton gu. a martlet of the first. Add: *V.*

Marconville. Quarterly or and az. in the first quarter a lion ramp. gu. Raffe de Marconville. *A.*

Marden (Marden, co. Hereford and London). Add: *Vis. Lon. 1633.*

Mardenike. Vert. 3 lions ramp. arg. crowned or. Sir John Mardenike. *V.*

Mare (Baron De la Mare, ext. 1316 . . .). Add: Sir John de la Mare. *S.* Pers de la Mare. *E.F.* Sir Robert de la Mare, co. Hants. temp. Edw. iij. *V.Y.*

Mare or De la Mare. Add: *V.*

de Mares. Arg. 3 bendlets gu. over all an estoile az. Sire Hectore de Mares of the Round Table. *Cotton. MS. Tiberius D. 10. fo. 702.*

Mares. Erm. 3 bars nebuly sa. *V.*

Mareschal. Gu. a bend engr. or. Sir William de (or le) Mareschal. *L.K.N.Y.* Sir Ancel le Mareschal. *O.* But with a label arg. *L.N.*

Mareschal. Gu. a bend of fusils conjoined or. Ancel Mareschal, Rye, Norfolk. *V.* John le Mareschale. *E.A. Harl. MS. 6137.* Sir William le Mareschal. *L.J.*

Mariott (Co. Northants, Avonbank, co. Worcester). Sire John de Meriet. *N.* Meriet, co. Wilts. *V.* Barry of 6 or and sa.

Markaunt. Arg. fretty sa. a canton gu. *V.*

Markes (Co. Essex). Gu. a lion pass. arg. a bordure engr. of the last. Add: *V.*

Markes (Beverly, co. York.). Granted by Dethick in 1560. Gu. a lion ramp. crowned or. armed and langued az. within a bordure erm.

Markeshall (Co. Essex). Arg. on a bend betw. two cotises sa. a bend undy . . . in the sinister chief an estoile sa. pierced of the field. *Morant's Essex. ij. 167.*

Markham alias Cursonne. Arg. a bend gu. 4 bezants. *V.*

Markingfield (Co. York.). Arg. on a bend sa. 3 bezants. Add: Andrew Merkeingefeildede. *Y.*

Markington. Per bend dancetty or and az. *V.*

Marks or Markes (Co. Suffolk). Add: *V.*

Marland. Barry nebulee of six gu. and arg. 7 martlets sa. 3. 3. and 1. on a chief or three pellets. Add: *V.*

Marlborough (College of). Az. an ancient book opened on a chief or a pale az. charged with a mitre . . . on each side of the pale a cross patty fitchy. . . . **Book Plate.**

Marler or Marley (Knavestock, co. Essex and Crayford, co. Kent). . . . Add: *V.E. 1612.*

Marley (Co. York.). Or 3 martlets in pale sa. *Eliz. Roll. xxxij.*

Marling (Stroud, co. Gloucester. M.P. for Stroud, 1875). Arg. 2 bars gu. in chief a label of 5 points of the last charged with 5 roundlets all within a bordure or. *Debrett.*

Marlow or Marlowe. Quarterly az. and or three bendlets gu. Add: *V.*

Marlow. Quarterly sa. and gu. 8 martlets in orle or. Sir Richard Marlowe, Alderman of London. *V.*

Marlowe (Lord Mayor of London, 1409 and 1417). . . . Add: *Harl. MS. 6860.*

Marlyn. Az. an inescutcheon per chev. erm. and gu.—insert—'between'. . . . 8 martlets. . . .

Marlyon. Erm. a chev. gu. within a bordure vert.

Marmion. Arg. 3 lions ramp. sa. crowned or. Roger Marmion. *V.*

Marmyon. Vair a canton gu. Water Marmyon. *V.V.**

Marmyon (Co. Leicester. temp. Edw. j.). Gu. a lion ramp. vair crowned or. Sir William Marmyon. *L.V.*

Marmyon. Gu. a lion ramp. or fretty az.—insert—Sir William Marmyon, co. Gloucester. *V.* another. . . .

Marney (Baron Marney, ext. 1525 . . .). Add: Sir Robert Marney. *S.* Sir Henry Marney. *V.* and with a label of 3 points or. William Marny. *S.*

Maroley (Co. York). Insert—'Sir Edmund Maroley' temp. Edw. 1. . . . Add: *Guillim.*

Marre. Az. billetty and a bend or. Le Counte de Marre, *C.*

Marrior (Navestock, co. Essex). Arg. a chev. purp. betw. 3 escallops sa. *V.E. 1634.*

Marriott (Hardington, co. Northants). Barry indented of 6 arg. and sa. on a bend az. 3 fleurs-de-lis arg.

Marrows. Or a bend betw. 10 billets sa. *V.V.**

Marshal (Earl of Pembroke, ext. 1245). . . . Add: Le Conte Mareschall *B.E.G.F.* Le Conte de Pennebrok. *C.* William Marshall, Earl of Pembroke. *Z. 87. 96.*

Marshall Henry, Bishop of Exeter, 1194–1206. Same Arms.

Marshal. Gu. a bend of 5 fusils arg. Les Armes del Office de Mareschall d'Irland. *X.*

Marshall (Abbots Anne, co. Hants.). *Visitation 1575.* Insert—Tidesmarsh, co. Lincoln. Add: *Harl. MS. 1544. fo. 94.*

Marshall (Aislabie Grange, co. York). Insert—† for diff. Theddlethorpe. . . . Add: *Dugdale. 1665.*

Marshall. Arg. a chev. gu. betw. 3 horseshoes sa. *V.*

Marshall. Arg. a chev. betw. three horseshoes sa. *V.*

Marshall (Co. Northumberland). Add: *V.*

Marshall (Co. York). Arg. 2 chevs. sa. betw. 3 stags heads cabossed gu. *Fairfax's Book of Arms.*

Marshall. Arg. on a chev. betw. 3 bugle horns sa. as many arrows of the field.

Marshall (Bescott and Walsall, co. Stafford . . .). Insert—marginal reference, Dr. G. W. Marshall.

Marshall (Michelham and Lewes, co. Sussex . . .). Add: granted by Camden, 1612.

Marshall (Newton Kyme, co. York). Per pale or and vert. a lion ramp. gu. *Robson.*

Marshall (John Marshall or Martial). Founder in 1671 of Christchurch Church, Surrey. Granted by Camden in 1611). Arg. a chev. betw. 2 couple closes sa. and 3 stags heads embossed gu. Add: *MS. 6049.*

Marshall. Gu. a bend engr. or a label arg. *Cady.*

Marsham (Custon, Kent. Baronetcy, 1663). Arg. a lion pass. gu. betw. 2 bendlets az. on each 3 crosses crosslet or. *V.* Guillim.*

Marsham. Arg. a lion pass. gu. betw. two bendlets az. on each 3 crosses crosslet or all within a bordure engr. gu. *V.*

Martaine or Marten (Bourton, co. Cambridge, allowed by Camden, 1604). Az. on a bend arg. 3 fleurs-de-lis of the field. *Guillim.*

Marten. Arg. an eagle displ. gu. within a double tressure counterflory sa. *V.*

Marten (Harlow, Essex). Az. 3 bends arg. a chief erm. *V.E. 1634.*

Marten. Gu. a chev. erm. in base a rose or. Richard Marten. *V.*

Martham. Gu. a bend betw. 6 lions ramp. arg. *V.*

Martham. Gu. a bend betw. 2 fishes embowed bendwise arg. *V.*

Martham. Gu. a bend wavy betw. 2 dolphins embowed bendwise arg. *V.*

Martin (Scarborough, co. Somerset, 1622). Arg. 2 bars gu. a mullet arg. for diff. *V.S.*

Martin (Long Melford, co. Suffolk) ... Add: Sir Roger Martin Lord Mayor of London, 1568.

Martin (Co. Durham). Add: *Surtees.*

Martin. Gu. an eagle displ. or. *Nash.*

Martin (Cos. Kent and York). Add: *V.**

Martin (Co. York). Add: Sir Walter Martin, co. Gloucester. Same arms. *V.N.*

Martin. Or 3 bars gu. a canton erm. Sir ... de Martin. *V.*

Martin. Or 6 lions ramp. sa. on a chief gu. 3 pierced mullets of the first. John Martine, London, temp. Henry viij. *V.*

Martin (Plymouth, co. Devon). Gu. on a chev. or 3 talbots pass. sa. *W. V.D. 1620.*

Martin. Or on a chev. gu. 3 talbots pass. arg. *Cady.*

Martindale. Arg. 2 bars gu. over all a bend sa. temp. Edw. ij. *F.Y.*

Martindale. Barry of 6 arg. and gu. a baston sa. William Martindale. *X.*

Martindale. Arg. two bars gu. over all a bend az. Crest: A wolf courant ppr. Add: *V.*V.*

Marton (Co. York). Arg. 2 bars gu. on the upper one a bezant.

Marton (Marton, co. York). ... on a chev. .... betw. 3 crosses patonce ... as many fleurs-de-lis. .... Seal of William de Marton xvij. Edw. iij.

Martyn. Arg. 3 martlets sa. on a chief of the second as many escallops as the first a crescent sa. for diff. in the centre point. *V.*

Martyn. Arg. on a bend sa. betw. 2 cotises compony ... and ... 3 cinquefoils or *Dug. O.J.*

Martyn (Co. Kent). Marten. *V.*V.*

Martyn (London). Add: John Martine. temp. Henry viij. *V.*

Martyn. Arg. an eagle displ. gu. Henry Martyn of Staple Mordyn, co. Cambridge, 1619. *W.*

Marwood (Plymouth, co. Devon and Worcester). ... Add: *W.*

Marx. Az. a lion ramp. erm. within an orle of 10 fleurs-de-lis arg. a canton of the second. **Book Plate.**

Maskham. Arg. a chev. betw. 3 butterflies sa. *V.**

Mason (Monkton, Isle of Thanet and Bury St. Edmunds). Per pale arg. and sa. a chev. betw. 3 billets counterchanged. Add: *MS. 5507. fo. 306.*

Mason (Masonbrook, co. Galway). Add: Mason (Great Gransden, co. Hunts.). Sir John Mason. *V.* Robert Mason. *D.O.J.* All same arms.

Masons (Company of, London). Insert—Granted in 1473. .... Add: *Guillim,* gives the field az. and states the grant to be by Hawkston, Clarenceux xiij. Edw. iv.

Masons (Company of, Newcastle-upon-Tyne). Sa. on a chev. engr. betw. 3 towers arg. a pair of compasses extended of the first.

Masons (Company of, Edinburgh). Add: *Berry.*

Massey (Mayor of Chester, 1593). Quarterly gu. and or in the first and fourth quarters a lion pass. arg. quartering 2nd gu. 3 garbs or and 3rd. Per chev. sa. and erm. over all a lion ramp. or **Tomb** in Trinity Church, Chester.

Massey (Sale, co. Chester). Add: *Harl. MS. 1424. fo. 100b.*

Massey (Oborow or Ellerborough). Gu. a lion pass. arg. quartering or a mullet pierced sa. *Harl. MS. 2230. fo. 34. and 1405. fo. 97.*

Masey (Wymingham, co. Chester). 1390. Gu. a chev. betw. 3 lozenges arg. a crescent for diff. *V.*

Massingham (Co. Norfolk). Add: *V.*

Massey (Hoo, co. Chester). Add: *V.*

Massy or Mascy (Timperley, co. Chester). Quarterly arg. and gu. a bendlet of the last. *V.*

Massy (Timperley). Quarterly arg. and gu. a bend az. *Harl. MS. 1424.*

Massy. Quarterly arg. and gu. a bend of the last. *V.**

Massy. Arg. a bend gu. betw. three wiverns heads erased. Add: *V.*

Master (Cirencester and Knole Park, Gloucester). ... originally of Kent. Add: Granted to Richard Master, Physician to Queen Elizabeth by Dethick, Carter, 1568. *Guillim.*

Masters and Mariners (Company of, Newcastle-upon-Tyne). Arg. an anchor pendent az. ring and stock or covering a chief of the second over the stock a boatswain's whistle and a chain supporting the anchor of the third.

Maston (London, 1590). Gu. a fess erm. betw. 3 crescents arg. in chief a fleur-de-lis arg. **Funeral Certificate** of Sir Cuthbert Buckle, 1594.

Matheson (Achany, Sutherlandshire). Baronetcy, 1858. Gyronny of 8 sa. and gu. a lion ramp. or armed and langued az. all within a bordure of the third charged with 3 bears heads 2 in chief and one in base couped az. muzzled arg. and 2 hands fessways in fess holding daggers erect gu.

Mathew (Dodbroke, co. Devon). Add: *W.*

Mathew (Thomas town, Ireland). Sa. a lion ramp. or. *Robson.*

Mathew (London). Gyronny of 8 arg. and gu. a lion ramp. or within a bordure az. charged with 8 crosses patty of the third. *W.*

Mathew (John Mathew, Sheriff of London. temp. Ric. iij. Lord Mayor, 1490). Gyronny of 6 sa. and gu. a lion ramp. or within a bordure az. charged with crosses patty or. *Fuller. Berry.*

Mathew. Per pale gu. and az. 3 lions ramp. erm. *W.*

Mathew (Co. Monmouth). Sa. a martlet arg. *W.*

Mathew. Arg. on a chev. gu. three 4-foils of the first. *V.*

Mathew (Bradden, co. Northampton). .... Desc. from John, Lord Mayor of London, j Ric. iij. Add: *W.*

Matthews (Llandaff). Or a lion ramp. reguard. sa. *Nicholas.*

Mathyn. Az. an eagle displ. double headed arg. armed gu. *V.*

Matoke or Mattick (Cos. Hertford and York). Az. a chev. quarterly—insert—'per fess'. .... Add: *V.V.**

Matson.

Matthews (Co. Hereford). Add: Matthews, M.P. for Dungarvon, 1868.

Mauconant (Co. Lincoln). Arg. a bend sa. cotised gu. Sir Giles Maconant. *V.* Sir Geffry Mauconant. *N.V.Y.*

Maudut. Erm. two bars gu. Sire Roger Maudut. *N.Y.* Sire Roger Maudyut. *O.*

Maulare. Or a demi-lion ramp. enhanced double tailed gu. William Maulare. *E.*

Maule (Melguin). Per pale arg. and gu. on a bordure wavy 8 escallops counterchanged. *Nisbet ij. 52.*

Mauleverer. Gu. a chief or over all a bend comp. az. and arg. Sir John Mauleverer. *M.Y.* But a baston. *N.*

Mauleverer (Arncliffe, co. York). Add: William Maleverer. *F.S.* Joan Mauleverer. *E.Y.* John Mauleverer, Allerton. *V.* Sir Oliver Maulever. *S.*

Mauleverer (Allerton—Mauleverer, co. York. bart.). Insert—1641.

Mauleverer (Wedersun,   ). Sa. 3 greyhounds courant in pale arg.

Mauleverer. Sa. 3 greyhounds pass. arg. collard compony or and sa. Robert Mauleverer. *Y.*

Maleverer (Arncliffe, co. York, 1665). Sa. 3 greyhounds courant in pale arg. quartering or a fess gu. in chief 3 torteaux: and az. a maunch or. *Dugdale p. 97.*

Mauley (Baron de Mauley ...). Or a—read—'bend' for head.... Add: *T.Y.* Pers deMauley. *G.J.N.* Sir Robert Mawley. *Q.*

Mauley. Or on a bend sa. 3 dolphins naiant—insert—arg. *V.V.** (Another ...).

Mauley. Or on a bend sa. 3 eagles displ. arg. Sir Robert Mauley. Sir Robert de Maulee. *G.N.* Co. York, temp. Edw. j. *V.*

Mauley. Or on a bend sa. 3 wiverns arg. Sire Edmon de Maulee. *N.*

Maudefeld. Quarterly or and az. 4 caps like Doge's caps counterchanged. *V.V.**

Maundy (Sandwich, Kent). Arg. 10 (hounds, bears, boars, or wolves,   ?   ). statant az. 3. 3. 3. and 1. and 3 bars gu.

Maunsell (Plasy and Bank Hall, co. Limerick). Add: Sir Richard Mauncel, co. Glamorgan. Same arms. *V.* Maunsoll or Mausel (Margam, co. Glamorgan). Same arms. *Z. 316.*

Maunsell. Arg. a tower sa. having a scaling ladder raised against it in bend sinister or. *Guillim.*

Maunsell. Sa. a chev. betw. 3 mullets pierced arg. Add: *V.* Add: John Maunsell. *X.*

Maure. Arg. semy of escallops gu. a lion ramp. sa. William Maure. *A.N.*

Maurice (Clenenny). Vert. 3 eagles displ. in fess or.

Mautby (Granted by Camden, May 1612). Erm. on a bend gu. betw. 2 cotises or engr. gu. 3 garbs. or. *Syl. Morgan.*

Mawbey (Botley's, co. Surrey). Insert—Granted in 1757....

Mawdley or Maudele (Munney, co. Somerset). Arg. on a chev. az. 3 fleurs-de-lis or a bordure engr. sa. *V.S. 1623.*

Mawdley (Wells, co. Somerset). Same arms.

Mawdesley (Mawdesley, co. Lancaster, 1664). Add: *V.L.*

Mawdesley (Leyland, co. Lancaster, 1664). Add: *V.L. 1664.*

Mawhood (Certified at the College of Arms, London, May 1779). ... Add: This coat is quartered by Thompson of Kirby Hall, co. York.

Mawley (Co. York). Add: Sir Robert Mawley, temp. Edw. ij. *F.Y.*

Mawley (Co. York). Add: Sir John de Maulee. *N.*

Maxe.

Maxfield. Gu. a bend lozengy or. *Syl. Morgan.*

May (Exeter). Granted to Robert May, 1573. Gu. a chev. or betw. 3 roses arg. a chief of the second. *V.S.*

May (Ireland). ... an anchor az. a chief gu.

May. Vert. a chev. betw. 3 crosses crosslet fitchee arg. Add: *V.*

Maycote alias Mackwith (Reculver, Kent). Add: Sir Cavalere Maycott, Kent. *W.*

Maydeley. Arg. on a chev. az. 3 fleurs-de-lis or a bordure engr. sa. Add: *V.*

Maydestone. Arg. three bars az. on the second two annulets interlaced or. Add: *V.*

Maye. Vert. a chev. betw. 3 crosses bottony fitchy arg. Henry Maye. *V.*

Mayell. Add: *V.*

Mayhew (Hemington, co. Suffolk). Add: *V.*

Mayhewe (Clippesby, co. Norfolk, confirmed 9 Nov., 1503). Insert—by Harvey Clarenceux.

Mayn. Add: *V.*

Maynard (St. Alban's, co. Hertford). Add: *Harl. MS. 1404 fo. 156.*

Maynard. Arg. a chev. az. betw. 3 dexter hands gu. *V.**

Maynard (Eston, co. Northampton, Granted 1590). Arg. a chev. az. betw. 3 dexter hands apaumy couped gu. *W.*

Maynard (Estaines, Essex and Wicklow, Ireland, confirmed 1621). Baronetcy, Baronies and Viscountcy. Same arms. But hands *sinister*.

Mayne (Creslow, co. Bucks, granted June 1604). Insert—by Camden.

Mayne (Co. Essex). Add: *Harl. MS. 1404. fo. 94.*

Mayne (Co. Warwick and—read—Rowlston, co. York). Add: Mayne (Rowlston, co. York), with an annulet for diff. *F.Y.*

Maynes. Gu. a chev. betw. 3 hatbands arg. *V.* and *Harl. MS. 1404. fo. 112.*

Mayor (Granted to Rev. Charles Mayor, of Rugby). ... Add: Mayor or Mayer (Jersey), granted temp. Hen. vij. to Mayor of Southampton. Same arms.

Mayott (Ramsden Park, Essex). Arg. a chev. betw. 3 boars heads couped sa. *Robson.*

Maze (Co. Somerset; granted to Peter Maze, Esq., Sheriff of Bristol). Insert—1840.

Mead (Arms confirmed and Crest granted by Hawkins, Ulster, 1706, to Benjamin Mead ...). Sa. on a chev. betw.—insert—'3' pelicans. ...

Meade (Ballintobber ...). Add: *U.A.*

Meade (Co. Essex). Add: *W.* Arms of the famous Dr. Meade who died in 1754, also of Thomas Meade, Judge of the Common Pleas, 1577. *Dug. O.J.*

Meade (Matching, co. Essex). Sa. on a chev. betw. three pelicans or an escutcheon gu. *V.E. 1634.*

Meade (Northborowe, co. Leicester). Add: *C.C. 1619.*

Meadows (Great Yarmouth, Norfolk). Arg. 2 bends ... on a chief of the first 2 crosses patty. ... **Tomb** of Sir Thomas Meadows, Bradwell, Suffolk.

Meadowe. Gu. a chev. erm. betw. 3 pelicans vulning ppr. in chief a label of 3 points. Sir Thomas Meadowe, Great Yarmouth, Sheriff of Norfolk, 1662. *Dashwood.*

Meadows. Az. a chev. erm. betw. 3 pelicans, wings endorsed or. ... Add: The canton was an augmentation granted to Sir Philip Meadows by Walker, 20 Feb., 1662. *L.N.*

Medhurst.

Mede or Meade (Cos. Cambridge and Cornwall). **Brass** of Sir Philip Mede. ...—delete (another, cinquefoils). Add: *V.*

Medley (Co. Warwick). Insert—and co. York. Add: *V.*

Medlicott (Modelicote, co. Salop.). Add: Medlicott (Abingdon, co. Berks: London: and co. Salop., 1634). Same arms. *Harl. MS. 1358. fo. 83.*

Medlycott (Ven House, co. Somerset, bart.). Insert—1808....

Mednerst—marginal note—read Medhurst or Mednerst. Add: *V.**

Meeke (Chaldon Boys, co. Dorset). Sa. a chev. or betw. 2 couples closes erm. and three water bougets of the third. *Hutchin. j. 343.*

Meggs (Whitechapel, co. Middlesex). ... Add: *W.*

Meggs (Darnam, co. Cambridge). Or a chev. arg. betw. 3 mascles gu. on a chief sa. a wolf courant arg. *V.**

Meggs. Or a chev. betw. 3 mascles sa. on a chief of the second a wolf courant arg. *V.*

Mehmet. Az. a greyhound couchant arg. †

Meinmark. Arg. a bend engr. gu. a label az. Lancelot de Meinmark. *C.*

Mekton (temp. Ric. ii). Add: Henry de Mekton. †

Melese or Mellis. Arg. 2 bars and in chief 3 escallops gu. Roger de Melese. *F.*

Mell (Godsall, co. Stafford). Or fretty gu. in the middle an annulet interlaced az. *V.*

Mellington. Or 3 martlets gu. *V.*

Mellish. Az. 2 swans close in pale arg. betw. as many flaunches erm. John Mellish, London, 1634, quartering. Gu. a lion ramp. or betw. 4 crosses patonce vair. *Harl. MS. 1358. fo. 54b.*

Mellish (Blythe, co. Nottingham). Add: *V.**

Mells. Arg. a bend betw. 2 lions heads erased sa. *V.** Mells (Mells, co. Chester). Same Arms. *W.*

Melnehouse. Arg. on a bend sa. 3 fleurs-de-lis of the first *V. Nash.*

Melsanby. Add: Walter de Melsanby. *X.*

Mennes or Menns (Inner Temple, London ...). Add: *W.*

Mennis. Gu. a chev. vair betw. three leopards heads az. *V.**

Menteath (Kerry,   ). Az. a bend chequy arg. and gu. quartering: gu. 3 round buckles arg. *Cady.*

Menvile. ... 3 cinquefoils arg.—insert—'*V.*' another. ...

Mercy. Arg. on a bend gu. 3 lozenges of the field. Add: *V.*

Meredith (Stansley, co. Denbigh, bart.). Insert— 1622. ...

Meredith ap Jerworth. Or 3 lions dormant in pale sa. *Randle Holme.*

Merefield. Arg. a chev. betw. 3 cocks sa. armed gu. *V.**

Merell (Shenford, co. Essex, 1634). Or a bend betw. 6 crosses crosslet gu. a crescent for diff. *V.E.*

Meremone. Or 2 bars sa. in chief a pierced mullet gu. Geffry Meremone. *A.*

Merey or Mereys. Arg. on a bend gu. 3 lozenges of the first. *V.**

Merewether (Henry Allworth Merewether ...). Insert—Granted by Camden, 1607.

Mereworth. Or a chev. gu. betw. 9 crosses crosslet sa. *Cotton MS. Tiberius D. 10. V.*

Mereworth or Merworth. Arg.—delete—(another or) ... Add: *A. Harl. MS. 6137. Y.* Sir John de Mereworth. *R.Y.*

Merfyn. Or on a chev. sa. a mullet arg. quartering Don. *Cotton. MS. Julius. F. 8. fo. 36.*

Merick. Gu. a chev. betw. 3 lions ramp. or. Sir Wm. Merick, Judge of the Prerogative Court, London, 1661. *L.N.*

Merk. Gu. a lion ramp. arg. Ingram del Merk. *C.*

Merifid. Or a chev. gu. betw. 3 cocks sa. armed gu. *V.*

Merks (Co. Essex). Add: Merke, Gu. a lion ramp. arg. within a bordure engr. or. Joan de Merc. *E.V.*

Merland—insert—(Co. Lancaster). Add: *V.*

Merley (Newminster and Morpeth, co. Northumberland ...). Add: Roger de Merley. *B.*

Merling. Or three billets gu. ... Add: *V.*

Merling. Quarterly. ... Add: *W.*

Merrett (London). Granted—insert—by Bysche. ...

Merrifield. Arg. a chev. gu. betw. 3 falcons rising ppr. *C.L. p. 78.*

Merrill. Gu. a bend or in base a cross crosslet arg. †

Mertins (Lord Mayor of London, 1725). Add: *C.N.*

Merton (Merton, co. Devon). Add: *V.*

Merton. Arg. 3 bendlets az. Sir Richard de Merton. *Y.*

Merton. Arg. an eagle displ. within 2 orles gu. the outer one being flory counterflory. *Constable's Roll xvj.*

Mertongale. Arg. 3 American divers ppr. a chief gu. *Randle Holme.*

Merville. Arg. 3 demi-lions ramp. gu. Henri de Merville. *E. Harl. MS. 6137.*

Mervyn. Arg. on a demi-lion ramp. gu. a fleur-de-lis or at the shoulder. *W.*

Mervyn. Per pale or and arg. 3 lions pass. guard. sa. crowned.

Mervyn (Justice of the Common Pleas, 1540). Sa. 3 lions pass. guard. in pale. per pale or and arg. quartering: erm. a squirrel sejant. *Dug. O.J.*

Merwood (Impalement Fun. Ent. Ulster's Office, 1615). Add: *V.*

Meryet. Barry of six or and gu. a bend erm. Crest: Add: *V.**

Meryett. Barry of 6 or and sa. a bend erm. Sir John Meryet. *V.* Sir Johan de Meriet, the nephew. *N.*

Meryfeld. Add: *V.*

Meryfelde. Arg. a chev. betw. 3 birds sa. membered gu. *V.**

Meryng (Co. Nottingham). Add: *V.N. 1569.* Sir Wm. Meryng. *V.*

Meryng. Arg. on a chev. sa. 3 escallops arg. Sir William Merynge. *Harl. MS. 6137. fo. 44.*

Meryton (Castle Leventon, co. York, 1665). Add: *Dugdale p. 107.*

Meriore. Arg. crusilly sa. a chevron gu. Sire William de Meriore. *A. Harl. MS. 6137. Y.*

Meskel (Co. Cork). ... on a chev. ... betw. 6 crosses crosslet fitchy ... as many 3-foils. ...

Le Mesnilwarin (Warmincham, co. Chester). Arg. 6 barrulets gu.

Messarmy. Or a chev. per pale arg.—underlined —insert—'(gu.). *V.**' and vert. betw. three apples—underlined—insert—'cherries. *V.*' gu.

Messiter. Arg. a chev. chequy arg. and az. betw. 3 garbs. or on a canton vert. a cornucopia ppr.

Metcalf (Nappa Hall, Wensleydale, co. York). Add: and with a crescent for diff. Gilbert Medcalfe of Ottrington, co. York. *Eliz. Roll xxiij.* and with a mullet gu. for diff. Capt. Scrope Medcalfe of Yorkshire, Slain at Thame during the Civil War. *Guillim.*

Metcalfe (Nappa, co. York, 1665). Arg. 3 calves pass. sa: quartering Hertlyngton, Pigott, Leedes and Normanville. *Dugdale p. 105.*

Metcalfe (Granted to Matthew Metcalfe by Cooke, Clarenceux in 1581). Arg. 3 calves sa. quartering: Roughton and Jackson. *North County Grants xij.*

Mete (Kent). Az. on a bend or 3 mascles gu. *V.*

Metford. Sa. a lion ramp. double queued arg. .... Add: *V.*

Metringham. Add: *V. Harl. MS. 1386. fo. 95.*

Meuter or Mouter. Add: *V.*

Meynell (North-Kilvington, co. York). Add: Meynell (Hornby, co. York). Same Arms, and with a crescent gu. for diff. Meynell of Kilvington, co. York. *Fairfax's Book of Arms.*

Meynell. Or 3 bars gemel az. Nicholas Meynell. *V.*

Meynell (Thomas Meynell of Stanck, co. York). Az. 3 bars gemel and a chief or over all a bend gu. *Eliz. Roll. xxiij.*

Meynell (Richard Meynell of Aldborough, co. York). Az. 3 bars gemel or on a chief of the last 2 crescents gu. one resting on the other. *Eliz. Roll. xxviij.*

Meynell (West Dalton and Aldborough, co. York). Az. 3 bars gemel and a chief or a canton gu. *Dugdale 1665.*

Meynell or Menell. Az. 2 bars gemel and a chief or. (Sir Nicholas Menell). *I.J.N.* Paly. arg. and gu. on a bend sa. 3 horseshoes or. Sir Gilbert de Menell. *Y.* But the bend az. William Menyll. *Y.*

Meynell or Mennell. Paly of six gu. and or one a bend sa. three horseshoes or. Add: Sir William Meynell. *V.*

Meynell. Paly. of 12 arg. and gu. on a bend az. 3 horseshoes or. Sir Henry Meynyl. *Y.* Sir Hugh Menyl. *Y.*

Meyrick of Cottril, Wales. Sa. a chev. betw. 3 fleurs-de-lis arg. *Nicholas.*

Meyrick (Woodlands, co. Wilts.). Add: *Hoare.*

Michell (Salecombe Regis, co. Devon). Per chev. gu. and sa. a chev. betw. 3 swans arg. *Lysons.*

Michelgrove (Co. Sussex). Insert—'and Essex'. Add: *V.*

Michell (Lord Mayor of London, 1424 and 1436). Add: Michell (Cokefeld, Sussex). Same arms, with a crescent for diff. *V.*

Michell (Stamerham and Horsham, co. Sussex). Add: *V.**

Middlemore. Erm. on a canton sa. a pheon arg. *V.**

Middlemore (Edgbaston, co. Warwick). Add: *V.**

Middlemore (Enfield, co. Middlesex). Add: *Robson.*

Middlesbrough (Co. York). Town of 1853. Arg. a lion ramp. az. armed and langued gu. on a chief sa. 3 two masted ships or with sails of the field.

Middleton. Vert. a chev. betw. three griffins heads erased arg. *Robson.*

Middleton. Arg. on a bend vert. 3 wolves heads erased of the first. Of Hackney, Middlesex. Baronetcy, 1681. Sir Thomas Middleton of Stansted Montfichet, 1675. *L.N.* Middleton (Cherk Castle, co. Denbigh, Baronetcy, 1660, extinct 1718). Same arms.

Midleton (Co. Chester). The heiress mar. Massy. Gu. on a bend arg. 3 lions ramp. sa. *Harl. MS. 1424.*

Midelton. Erm. on a canton or a chev. gu. *V.*

Midelton or Middleton (Stockeld, co. York). Add: Motto: "Regardes mon droit".

Midlemore. Per chev. arg. and sa. in chief two cornish choughs ppr. *V.*

Migat. Az. on a bend or 3 mullets gu. *Cady.*

Mighells (Admiral in 1730 ...). .... a bend ... over all a fess ... *Monument in Lowestoft Church, Suffolk.*

Mignon. Gu. a bend vair bordered or betw. two fleurs-de-lis arg.

Mildmay (St. John-Mildmay, Moulsham Hall, Essex, bart.). Insert—1772. .... Quarterly: ... 2nd. Marginal note *V.E. 1612.*

Mildread. Or a bend sa. cotised and engr. on both sides gu. *Randle Holme.*

Miles (Leigh Court, co. Somerset, bart.). Insert—1859.

Militon (Pengersick, co. Cornwall). Add: Militon. Governor of St. Michaels Mount. temp. Henry viij. *Moule p. 159.*

Milkilly or Mikelly. Gu. 3 chevs. arg. Sire Robert Milkelly. *N.* Mylkelly, co. Herts. *V.*

Millerby. Per chev. undy. arg. and az. *Randle Holme.*

Millers or Milners (Company of, Newcastle-on-Tyne). Arg. a chev. betw. 3 mill picks sa.

Milles. Or a lion ramp. pass. betw. 3 billets sa.

Milles. Arg. a chev. gu. betw. three ink molines sa. **Book Plate** of Jeremiah Milles D.D.

Milles. Az. two ducks in pale arg. betw. as many flaunces erm. Add: *V.**

Millington. Arg. an eagle displ. sa. armed az. *V.*

Millington. Gu. a chev. or betw. 3 salmons naiant arg. *V.V.**

Millom (Cumberland). Arg. a bend betw. two mullet sa. *Lysons.*

Mills (London). Az. a banner without flagstaff or. *B.M. Add. MS. 5535. fo. 71.*

Milluborn. Az. 2 shin bones in saltire the dexter surmounted of the sinister arg. *V.*

Milne (Calverley near Leeds, co. York). Arg. a millrind gu. within an orle of millrinds sa. Crest: On a millrind fesswise sa. a lion ramp. arg. holding in its fore paws a millrind gu. Granted to C. M. Milne, 1878.

Milnehouse. Arg. on a bend engr. sa. 3 fleurs-de-lis of the first. *V.*

Milner (Pudsey, co. York). Sa. three snaffle-bits or. Add: Milner (London, 1633-4). Same Arms. *Harl. MS. 1358. fo. 52b.*

Milton (Milton, near Thame, co. Oxford). Add: *Guillim.*

Minifie (Co. Devon). Vert. on a chev. betw. 3 annulets ... as many eagles displayed. *Guillim.*

Mingay or Mingey (Gymingham, co. Norfolk). Insert—'and Norwich'. .... Add: *Guillim.*

Minors (London). Sa. an eagle displ. or on a chief arg. .... Add: *V.V.**

Minors. Per pale gu. and az. an eagle displ. or—insert—*V.* .... another. ....

Mirfield. Arg. two lions pass. guard. in pale vert. Add: Mirfield (Murcroft, co. York). Vert. two lions pass. in pale arg. *V. Hunter j. 294.* Sir ... de Mirfeld. *V.*

Mitton. Insert—'Weston', co. Stafford. Add: *V.*

Mitton (Shropshire). Per pale gu. and az. an eagle displ. with 2 heads or. *Guillim.*

Moderny (Priory at, co. Norfolk). Or on a bend az. 3 rams heads couped arg.

Moderby. Sa. a bend or on a chief arg. 3 escallops gu. .... Add: *V.*

Modyford (Chiswick and London ...). Add: Modyford (Eastner, co. Kent). Same arms. *Guillim.* Add: Sir John Moels. *I.Y.J.N.H.*

Moels (Baron Moels ...). Roger de Moels. *Y.E.* Add: Moels Arg. 2 bars and in chief three mullets gu. Sir Nicholas de Moels. *B.*

Moels or Mules. Add: Moeles, Moells, Mules, Moyles.

Moigne or Moygne. Or three bars vert. Add: Sir John Moigne. *V.*

Moigns or Moynys (Co. Lincoln). Arg. a chev. betw. 3 taus sa. *V.*

Moldworth or Mudeworth (Co. Chester). Add: *V.V.**

Molent. Sa. a lion ramp. tail forked and nowed arg. *V.*

Molesworth. Arg. on a bend engr. sa. 3 pheons of the first. Richard Molesworth. *Dug. O.J.*

Molington. Arg. on a bend sa. 3 mullets or. *V.*

Molton. Chequy or and gu. Hubert de Molton. *E.F.* Sir Hugh Molton, co. Lincoln. *V.* Sire Thomas de Moltone. *N.*

Molton (Co. Lincoln). Chequy or and gu. (another, or and sa.). x. x. Add: Sir James de Moltone. *N.*

Molton or Moulton. Arg. 3 bars gu. Tibaud de Moletone. *A.* Thomas de Molton. *J.N.B.I.K.* Sire de Moulton, Gillesland. *Y.* Rafe Multon, Egremont. *Y.*

Molton. Arg. 3 bars gu. a label of 5 points az. Multon. Baron of Gillesland temp. Edw. j. the label vert. Thomas Moulton of Gillesland. *Y*. Thomas de Moulton le Forestier, the label sa. *B*.

Mompesson. Arg. 12 pigeons 3. 3. 3. 2. and 1. az. beaked and membered gu. Sir Giles de Monpesin. *G*.

Monboucher. Arg. 3 'possenets' gu. Sir Rauf. Montsoucher. *X*.

Monburnay. Add: *V.V.**

Moncaster. Insert—'co. Devon'. Or a chev. az. betw. 3 pairs of annulets conjoined gu. Add: *Harl. MS. 1386*.

Moncaster. Or a chev. az. betw. 6 annulets linked together 2 and 2 gu. within a bordure of the second. *V*.

Moncaster (Essex). Arg. 3 bars gu. on a bend sa. as many escallops or. Sir Walter Moncaster, temp. Edw. j. *V*.

Moncaster. Barry of 10 arg. and gu. a bendlet az. *V*.

Moncaster. Barry of 10 arg. and gu. a bendlet engr. az. *V.**

Moncaster. Barry or barruly arg. and gu. on a bend sa. 3 escallops or. Sir William Moncaster, Essex. temp. Edw. j. *V*. But the bend az. Sir Walter de Molecaster. *E*.

Monck, Monk or Le Moyne (Potheridge, co. Devon). . . . Add: Monck or Monk (Potheridge co. Devon). Same arms. *Z. 450*.

Moncy or Mouncy. Chequy arg. and gu. Sir Walter de Monci. *K.H.J*. Sir Wauter Mouncy. *Y*.

Monckton or Monketon (Co. Lincoln, Egham, co. Surrey and Cavill, co. York). . . . Add: Monketon (Rebellhall in Howden, co. York). Same arms. *V*.

Monkton (Wharram Grange, co. York). Same arms, a crescent for diff. *F. Y*.

Monkton (Hodroyd, co. York, 1665). Same arms. . . . a canton arg. *Dugdale p. 163*.

Money Coutts. News cutting—*28 Sept. 1880*. "Last night's Gazette contains an announcement that the Queen has been pleased to grant unto Clara Maria Money of Stodham Park, Southampton, widow and relict of James Drummond Money, Clerk, and to her only son and heir apparent, Francis Burdett Thomas Money, of Ancote in the parish of Weybridge, Surrey her royal licence that in compliance with a direction contained in the last will and testament of the most noble Harriott, Duchess of St. Albans, the said Clara Money and Francis Burdett Thomas Money and his issue may take and henceforth use the surname of Coutts in addition to and after that of Money, and may bear the arms of Coutts quarterly, in the first quarter with those of his and their own family."

Mondegon. Per fess indented gu. and arg. 3 annulets counterchanged. *Harl. MS. 1458*.

Money. . . . on a chev. . . . betw. in chief two 6-foils . . . and in base a 6 points mullet . . . 3 slipped 3-foils. . . . Seal of John Money. c. 1315.

Mongodene. Per fess dancetty arg. and gu. three annulets counterchanged. *V*.

Monhalt. Az. a lion ramp. arg. Crest: . . . Add: Sir Roger de Monhalt. *B.D.E.I*. Sir Robert de Monhalt. *H.K.F.N.Y*.

Monhault (West Riddlesden, co. York). Add: Adam de Monhault. *A.E.Y*. Sire James de Monhaut. *N*.

Monhault. Az. a lion ramp. arg. a border or. Add: Sir Andrew Monhault, Messenden. *Q*. Auger de Mohaut. *Q*.

Monington (Co. Cornwall). Add: Monington (Barrington, co. Gloucester). Same arms.

Monk (M.P. for Gloucester, 1868). Gu. a chev. arg. betw. 3 lions heads erased or. *Debrett*.

Monmouth. Or 3 chevs. gu. over all a fess arg. Sir John de Monemuth. *C*. The fess az. Sir John de Monmuth. *F.B.E*.

Monnox or Monnoux (Co. Bedford and London). Add: *V.**

Monox (Co. Nottingham). Add: *V.N .189*.

Monox (Walthamstow, co. Essex. Granted). Insert—by Wriothesley. . . . Add: Sir George Monoux, Lord Mayor of London, 1514. *V*. *Guillim*. Gives 3 bunches of oak leaves 3 in each, and calls the dove a seamew.

Monro (Foulis, Scotland). Or an eagle perching on a helmet gu. *Guillim*.

Monro (Lieutenant General Sir George Monro). The same arms, within a bordure embattled of the second. *Guillim*.

Monsell (Terove, co. Limerick). Arg. a chev. betw. 3 mullets sa.

Montague. Az. a chev. or betw. 3 mullets arg. on a chief gu. a lion pass. guard of the third . . . —insert—Bastian Montagutd. *V*. (another, the lion pass. or.)—insert—V. . . . another. . . .

Montessey. Add: *V.V.**

Montfichett (Stansted-Montfichett, co. Essex . . .). Add: *V*.

Montfichet. Gu. 3 chevs. or a label az. Sir Richard de Montfichet. *B*. But his **Seal** shews a label of 7 points. *Cotton MS. Julius G.7. fo. 136b*.

Montford (London and—insert—co. York). Arg. semee of crosses crosslet gu. a lion ramp. az. Add: *V.** Add: Sire de Montfort. *N*. Thomas de Mountford. *Y.P.V*.

Montford (Kylnhurst, co. York). Add: *V.**

Montford. Az. four bendlets or. Add: *V.**

Montford. Or 4 bendlets az. Sir William Montford. *V*. And with a label of 5 points gu. *F*.

Montford. Az. 6 bendlets or. Pers de Montford. *G*.

Montfort. Bendy of 8 or and az. a label of 5 points gu. Sir Robert de Montfort. *A. Harl. MS. 6137*. Sir Wm. Montfort, but bendy of 6 only. *N*.

Montfort (Tamworth, co. Warwick). Bendy of 8 arg. and az. a bordure of the first.

DeMontfort. . . . semy of crosses crosslet fitchy . . . a lion ramp. tail forked . . . holding in its mouth a child. **Effigy** in Hitchenden Church, co. Bucks. c. 1265.

Montfort (Kilnehurst, co. York). Arg. a lion ramp. az. betw. 8 crosses crosslet fitchy gu. and a bordure erm. *V*.

Montgomery. Or an eagle displ. az. Sire William de Mongomerie. *N.O*. Sir John Montgomery. *Q*. Montgomery, Captain of Calais and Admiral of the Fleet. 1347.

Montgomery (Sir William de Montgomery, one of the knts. of the co. Derby. temp. Edward j). . . . Or an eagle displ. az.—add—armed gu. Add: Sir John Montgomery. *Q*. Sir Nicol Montgomeri. *S*. Sir William Montgomery, Derby. temp. Edw. j. *V*.

Montgomery (Sir Thomas Montgomery, K.G ., .). Add: *V*.

Montgomery (Co. Stafford). Add: *V*.

Montgomery (Earl of Mount Alexander . . .). . . . counterflory gu. on a sur-delete coat, substitute—'tout' . . .

Montgomery. Gu. on a bend or 3 lions ramp. palewise sa. *V*.

Monthermer (Earl of Gloucester and Hereford . . .). Add: Sire Rauf de Monthermer. *N.H.K.F.V*. Sir Edw. Monthermer. *Y*.

Monthermer. Or an eagle displ. vert. Crest: A griffin's head betw. two wings ppr. . . . . repeat above reference.

Monthermer. Same arms, a bordure gu. charged with 8 lions pass. guard, of the first. Add: Sir Edwd. Monthermer. *R.*

Montpinson or Mountpinzo. Add: *V.* Sir Ellis de Montpinson.

Monttyrelle. Arg. a bend engr. gu. betw. 6 escallops az. Eschalard de Monttyrelle. *C.*

Monwike. Sa. an eagle displ. or. Sir Raufe Monwicke. *V.*

Moodie. Per fess wavy gu. and az. in chief a castle in base 3 ships arg. *Nisbet.*

Moon (Portman Square, London, bart.). Insert—1855.

Moorcroft. Add: *Surtees.*

Moorcroft (Kingston, co. Oxford). Az. a mule pass. arg. bridled gu. betw. 3 marigolds or. *V.O. 1634.*

Moore (Exeter, co. Devon, 1454). Erm. on a bend sa. three 5-foils or. *Colby*

Moore (Stockwell, co. Surrey). Add: Sir John Moore, London. *V.*

Moore (Lord Mayor of London, 1682). Add: *L.N.*

Moore (Collumpton, co. Devon). Erm. on a chev. az. three 5-foils or. *W.* The heiress mar. Blackmore.

Moore (Moore Hayes, co. Devon). Same arms. *V.D. 1620.*

Moore (Moorehayes, in Cullompton, co. Devon). . . . Add. *V.*

Moore (Co. York). Az. on a chev. invected per pale or and arg. betw. 3 fleurs-de-lis of the third 3 annulets of the first. *Whitaker's, Leeds ij. 8.*

Moore. Az. on a chev. betw. 3 lions heads erased or as many martlets sa. Crest: . . . Add: Thomas Moore, Newington, Middlesex Granted, 1576. *W.*

Moore. Arg. on a chev. sa. betw. 3 blackamoor's heads in profile. . . . Add: *V.* John Moore, Bishop of Bangor, 1775, Archbishop of Canterbury, 1783.

Moorle. Add: *V.V.*

Morant (Co. Essex). Gu. on a chev. arg. 3 talbots sa. Add: *V.*

Morant, Mordant or Morhant. Gu. a chev. arg. betw. 3 talbots courant—insert—'or pass.' . . . or. Add: Edward Morant of the Exchequer, 1575. *W.*

Morant. Sa. a chev. betw. 3 talbots pass. arg. *W.*

Morby. Arg. on a bend az. 3 pierced mullets of 6 points or over all a label of 5 points gu. Sir Robert de Morby. *V.*

Mordon. . . . a chev. . . . in chief 2 mullets . . . and in base a lion ramp. . . . Thomas Mordon, Hadbury, co. Worcester.

More (Awstrop, co. York). Arg. a chev. betw. 3 fleurs-de-lis and in chief a pile sa. *V.*

More (Barnborough Hall, co. York). Arg. on a chev. betw. 3 unicorns heads erased sa. as many bezants. *Foster.*

More (More Hall and Bank Hall, co. Lancaster, bart.). Insert—1675. . . .

More. Sa. a swan close arg. membered or within a bordure engr. of the last. *V.*

More (Cos. Essex, Lincoln and Stafford and London). Add: *V.E. 1631.* And with a crescent for diff. David Moore, 1693, in Chertsey Church, Surrey.

More (Larden Hall, co. Salop). Add: *V.*

More (Co. Suffolk). Or a chev. engr. ermines betw. 3 Moor's heads couped at the shoulders sa. wreathed about the temples arg. and az. . . . Crest: . . . Add: Moore (Lower Harrop, co. York, 1666). Same arms. *Dugdale p. 54.*

More. Arg. a bend engr. gu. betw. two cotises sa. Sir Robert More. *V.* Roger More. *V.*

More (Anstrop, co. York, 1665). Arg. a chev. and in chief a pile betw. 3 fleurs-de-lis sa. *Dugdale p. 25.*

More (Angram Grange, co. York, 1665). Add: *Dugdale p. 158.*

More (Co. York). Arg. a chev. betw. 3 moorcocks sa. combed and wattled gu. *Eliz. Roll xxxj.*

More. Insert—'co. Cambridge'. Az. three leopards faces or. . . . .

Morele. Az. flory or a demi-lion ramp. arg. and a bend gu. Sir William Morele. *O.*

Morell. See also Murril. . . . Gu. a bend or.

Mores. Ermines 3 bars nebuly arg. William Mores. *V.*

Moreton (Great Moreton, co. Chester). Add: *Ormerod.*

Moreton (Sussex). Arg. 2 greyhounds courant in full course sa. collared gu.

Moreton. Quarterly, 1st and 4th—delete—az. substitute 'arg.' a chev.—insert—'purp' betw. 3 trefoils slipped sa. . . . . . . Crest: . . . Add: Richard Moreton, co. Salop. *W.* But the chev. sa. *V. Cotton MS. Tiberius D. 10.*

Moreyns. Gu. on a bend arg. seven billets sa. —insert—palewise. . . . Add: *V.** Sir de Moryens. *V.*

Morffin. Insert—'Kent'. Or on a chev. sa. 3 crescents arg. Add: *V.*

Morfyn or Murfyn (Cos. Essex and Kent). Add: *V.V.** Add: Sir Thomas Myrfin, London. *V.*

Morgan. Arg. a bend sa. charged with three 5-foils . . . on a chief az. a cross moline betw. 2 fleurs-de-lis. Thomas Morgan, Northampton. *Dug. O.J.*

Morgan (Blackmore, co. Hereford). Per pale . . . and . . . 3 lions ramp. . . . quartering arg. a lion ramp. crowned or for Morgan . . . an estoile of 16 points for Delahay. . . . 2 lions pass. . . . within a bordure . . . for Garnon. *F.Y. p. 627.*

Morgan. Quarterly gu. and az. 3 lions ramp. arg. Sir William Morgan. *V.*

Morgan (Co. Devon and Hambury, co. Worcester). . . . —delete—(another, or.). . . . Crest: . . . Morgan (Morganshays, co. Devon). Same arms. *W.*

Morgan (Co. Kent and Wales). Add: *V.*

Morgan. Gu. three towers arg. Add: *V.*

Morice (Werrington, co. Devon. bart.). Insert—1661. . . . .

Morland. Arg. on two bars sa. three eoplards heads or jessant fleurs-de-lis of the first. *W.*

Morley. Arg. a lion ramp. sa. a label of 3 points gu. Mons Robert de Morlee. *S.*

Morley (Co. Norfolk). Add: William de Morle. *G.* Sir Robert de Morle or Morley. *O.Q.V.* Le Sire de Morley. *S.T.Y.N.* Morley (Droxford, co. Hants. c. 1670). Same arms. George Morley, Bishop of Worcester, 1660. Same arms.

Morley (Manchester, 1664). Sa. a chev. betw. 3 hammers arg.

Morrews or Moriux. Gu. on a bend arg. 7 billets sa. Sir Thomas Morrewes. *S.* Moriux, (Sheriff of Norfolk). *Dashwood.*

Morrice. Gu. a hart trippant or. *Syl. Morgan.*

Morrions. Gu. a bend arg. 8 gouttes-de-poix in pairs. *Cotton MS. Tiberius D. 10.*

Morris. Az. a battle axe in hand sinister surmounted by a tilting spear. . . . Add: Morris. *V.** Sir Christopher Moures, Master of the Ordnance. *V.*

Morris (North Elmsall, co. York, 1660). Add: *Dugdale p. 267.*

Morse (Norfolk, 1807). Per pale arg. and sa. a chev. betw. 3 mullets pierced counterchanged. *Dashwood.*

Morteyn. Az. 3 lions ramp. or. Sir Roger de Morteyn. *J.* But 6 lions, Sir Roger de Morteyn. *N.*

Morteyn. Or 6 lions ramp. az. Sir Roger Morteyn. *I.* Tails forked. *K.* The lions sa. *I.* and *Harl. MS. 6137.*

Morth or Murth (Talland, co. Cornwall). Add: The heiress m. Woolcombe. *V.C. p. 306.*

Mortimer (Baron Mortimer of Wigmore and Earl of March)... Add: Gefrai de Mortimer. The same arms. But over all a saltire gu. *E.* Roger de Mortimer. *E.W.* The escutcheons erm. *E.* But gu. *F.* The inescutcheons arg. charged with 6 billets 3. 2. and 1. sa. Henry de Mortimer. *F.* But the escutcheon arg. charged with 3 nails points in base sa. Robert Mortimer. *V.*

Mortimer. Gu. 2 bars and in chief 3 mullets pierced arg. Sir Constantine Mortimer. *V.*

Mortimer (Baron Mortimer, of Richards Castle). ... Add: William de Mortimer. *V.*

Mortimer. Gu. 2 bars vair. Robert Mortimer. *A.* Hugh de Mortimer. *K.* Robert de Mortimer. *D.E.F.* Sir Hugh de Mortymer. *H.* John Mortymer. *Y.*

Mortimer. Gu. crusilly or 2 bars vair. William de Mortimer. *F.V.*

Mortimer. Arg. 2 bars gu. on a chief of the last three 6-foils of the first. Walran Mortimer. *Y.*

Mortoft (Confirmed by Camden to Valentine Mortoft of Haringham, co. Norfolk, Feb. 1606). Gu. a hart or lying on a bank vert. on a chief or a moorcock ppr. *Syl. Morgan.*

Morton (Sutton, co. Leicester). Add: *C.C.*

Morton. Arg. a raven sa. *V.*

Morton. Gu. 2 bars vair. Hugh Morton. *Y.*

Morton (Wrath House, co. York, 1666). Add: *Dugdale p. 338.*

Moreton (Of Spouthouse, co. York, 1665). Or 3 ravens sa. within a bordure az. *Dugdale p. 175.*

Morton. Arg. a chev. betw. 3 cushions erm.—insert—*V.** ...

Morvile. Az. semy of fleurs-de-lis arg. a demi-lion ramp. or. *V.***W.*

Moryn. Arg. a chev. sa. betw. 3 fleurs-de-lis gu. Add: *V.*

Moryne. Gu. 3 lions pass. guard....... Add: *V.*

Moryan. Gu. a bend betw. 12 billets or. *V.**

Moseley (Moseley and Bilston, co. Stafford). Add: *Guillim.*

Moses (Sir Richard Browne alias Moses, Lord May).

Mosley (Rolleston, co. Stafford, bart.). Insert—1720. ...

Mosley (Newcastle-on-Tyne. Add: Mosley (Rolleston,   ) Baronetcy. Sa. on a chev. betw. 3 millpicks arg. as many mullets gu.

Mosselle. ... a bend engr. ... betw. 3 crescents ... within a bordure engr. ... **Seal** temp. Hen. iv.

Moston (Quartered by Mitford. ...). Add: *V.*

Mostyn (Mostyn Hall, co. Flint, bart.). Insert—1660. ...

Mote. Vair a bend gu. a label arg. William del Mote. *Y.*

Motley or Matley. Az. 3 American divers or. *Randle Holme.*

Mottram alias Mottvane. Add: *Dugdale p. 222.*

Moules (Co. Devon). Gu. 2 bars arg. in chief 3 plates. John Moules. *V.*

Moulso. Insert—Calais. Or a chev. per chev. gu. ... Add: *V.*

Moulson. Gu. a chev. arg. fretty sa. betw. 3 mullets or. Crest: ... Add: Sir Thos. Moulson, London. *Syl. Morgan.*

Moulton (Cos. Gloucester, Kent and York and London ...). Add: *W.*

Moulton. Gu. a chev. arg. fretty sa. betw. 3 mullets pierced or. ... (Another ... of the third). Insert—*V.* ...

Mount (Co. Kent). Arg. on a mount vert. a lion ramp. gu. crowned or. Add: *W.*

Mountain or Montaigne. Add: G. J. Mountain, Bishop of Montreal, 1836. Quebec, 1850. Same arms.

Mountender. Gu. a lion ramp. betw. 8 trefoils slipped or. *V.*

Mountford (Radwinter, co. Stafford and co. Warwick). Add: But of 12. Peres de Mountford. *D.* Pers de Montford. *F.E.* Piers de Mountford, Lord of Beaudesert in co. Warwick. *V.* And with a label of 5 points gu. Robert de Mountford. *D.* Munford. *E.* Sir William Mountford. *J.*

Mountford (Co. Warwick). Barry of 5 arg. and az. a bendlet of the last. *V.V.**

Mountford. Arg. crusilly of crosses crosslet gu. a lion ramp. az. Thomas de Mountfort. *P.Y.* Sire de Mountfort. *N.*

Mountford (Co. York, granted 18 Feb., 1602). Insert—by Camden. ...

Mountford (Co. York). Arg. crusilly and a lion ramp. gu. George Mountford. *Eliz. Roll. xxvij.*

Mountfort. Gu. a lion ramp. tail forked arg. Simon Mountfort, Conte de Leicestre. *Y.Z.V.* Philip de Mountfort. *C.*

Mountforth. Bendy sinister of 10 az. and or. Sir Piers de Mountforth. *A.*

Mountney (Cos. Essex and Leicester and Geswick, co. Norfolk). ... Add: and with a mullet gu. on the bend for diff. Sir John de Mountney. *L.N.* Mountney. Sir Robert Mounconeye. *S.* Sir Ernauf de Mounceney. *N.B.* Sir Ernaud de Mountney. *J.* Sir Robert de Mountney. *E.* Sir Evans de Mountney. *N. Harl. MS. 6137.*

Mounchensy. Arg. a chev. betw. 3 billets sa. Sire John de Mounchensy. *Y.*

Mouncanesy. Arg. a chev. betw. 3 billets az. Sire Richard de Mouncanesy. *O.*

Mounceis. Arg. a bend sa. William de Mounceis. *A.*

Mounford. Az. 3 bendlets or. Sire John de Mounford. *J.*

Mounger or Moungres. Arg. on a bend az. 6 fleurs-de-lis or. *V.V.**

Mountpynson. Arg. on a lion ramp. sa. a pinzon (or chaffinch) or. at the shoulder. Sire ... de Mountpynzon. *N.*

Mountney. Vair a chief gu. a bend of the second. John Mounteney. *Y.*

Mounteney. Vairy arg. and sa. a baston gu. a chief or. Rauf Mounteney. *Y.*

Mounteney. Gu. a bend betw. 2 cotises and † 6 martlets or. Thomas Mounteney. *Y.* Sire Johan de Mounteney. *N.O.*

Mounteney. Gu. a bend betw. 2 cotises and † 6 mullets or. Sir John de Mounteney, Essex. temp. Edw. j. *V.*

Mounteney. Gu. a bend betw. 6 martlets or. Sir Thomas de Mounceney or Mounteney. *O.N.Y.* Sir John Mounceney. *S.* And with a mullet for diff. Sir Thos. de Mounteney. *N.*

Mounz. Or a bend betw. 2 cotises gu. a label az. Sire Eble de Mounz. *N.*

Mouseley (Sheriff of London, temp. Eliz.). Sa. a chev. betw. ... mullets arg. *Fuller.*

Mouter. Sa. 4 martlets arg. 2 and 2. *V.*

Mowbray. Gu. a lion ramp. arg. Sir John de Mowbray. *L.J.N.M.* Robert de Mowbray. *F.* Roger de Mowbray. *A.C.P.Y.*

Mowbray. Gu. 3 lions pass. guard. in pale or. on a label arg. 3 eagles displ. gu. quartering gu. a lion ramp. or a label of 3 az. Sir Thomas Mowbray. *S.*

Mowbray. Gu. a lion ramp. arg. a bend engr. sa. Sir Philip de Mowbray of Scotland. *M.*

Mowbray (Bishopwearmouth, co. Durham). . . . quarterly. 1st and 4th, Mowbray, gu. a lion ramp. erm.—insert—'between' two flaunces or. . . .

Mower (Co. Devon). Add: *V.*

Moyer (Petsey Hall, co. Essex, bart.). Insert— 1701. . . .

Moyer (Bures, Essex). Arg. on each of 2 chevs. gu. a mullet of 6 points or pierced gu. . . . *Morant's Essex. j. 256.*

Moyle (Co. Kent). Same arms. Add: Sir Thomas Moyle. *V.*

Moyle (Lymby, co. Notts.). Gu. a mule pass. within a bordure arg. *V.N.*

Moyne. Arg. 2 bars and in chief 3 mullets sa. William Moyne. *V.S.*

Moyngs (Co. Lincoln). Arg. a chev. betw. 3 crosses tau sa. *V.*

Moyre. Arg. a canton gu. Add: John Moyre. *V.*

Moyser (Farlington, co. York). Add: 1612. *F.Y.* Add: Moyser (Beverley, co. York, 1665). Same arms and crest. *Dugdale p. 212.*

Moyine. Arg. a bend betw. 6 mullets gu. John Moyine. *X.*

Muchgros. Gu. a lion ramp. or a label of 6 points az. John de Muchgros. *G.*

Mucklow (Co. Worcester). Gyronny of 8 or and az. a lion ramp. erm. on a chief arg. an escallop betw. 2 fleurs-de-lis sa. *V.*

Muilman (Debben Hall, Essex). Granted to 10 Dec. 1773. Arg. 2 bars nebuly sa. on a bend engr. sa. a rose betw. as many mullets or.

Muirhead. Arg. on a bend az. betw. two gallies oars in action sa. 3 acorns or.

Mulchester. Arg. 3 bars gemel gu. a bendlet az. *V.*

Muliens. Add: *V.**

Mulleswell. Gu. on a chev. engr. betw. 3 crescents or as many crosses crosslet sa. *V.*

Mulsho or Mulso. Add: *V.V.**

Mulshoe or Mulsho (Gothurst, co. Buckingham. . . .). Add: Sir Edmund Mulso. *V.* Thomas Mulso, co. Northampton. *W.*

Muncels. Arg. a bend sa. Sir William de Muncels. *D.*

Munds, Mouns or Muns (Cos. Cambridge, Essex, Middlesex and Maidstone, co. Kent). Add: *Harl. MS. 1551. fo. 102.*

Muntein. Az. a bend or. Robert de Muntein. *A. Harl. MS. 6137. A.*

Muntrick. Gu. a chev. or goutty de sang betw. 3 billets of the second. *Nash.*

Muntz (Umberslade, co. Warwick). Add: Muntz (Edstone Park, co. Warwick. M.P. for Birmingham, 1868). *Debrett.*

Murch (Recorder of Barnstaple, 1864). az. a chev. countercompony arg. and sa. betw. 3 garbs ppr. *Debrett.*

Murchison (Tarradale, co. Ross). Insert— Baronetcy, 1800. . . .

Murdakes. Gu. 3 bendlets arg. *V.*

Mure. Sa. 3 birds (query swallows) volant recursant arg. beaked and legged or. *V.V.**

Muriell (Scrimby,). Arg. a chev. betw. 3 roses sa. Thomas Muriell. *Y.*

Morrell or Murrill. Or a bend gu. in base a cross crosslet. . . .

Muschgros. Or a lion ramp. gu. Monsire Robert Muschgros. *D.* John Muscgros. *Y.*

Muses (Academy of) London. Arg. 2 bars wavy az. on a chief 2 swords in saltire, beneath them an open book. *Guillim.*

Musgrave (Edenhall, co. Cumberland, bart. . . .). Add.: Query: az. 6 † or.

Musgrave (Sir Thomas Musgrave). Az. 6 annulets 2.2 and 1 or. *V.*

Musgrove (Speldhurst, co. Kent, bart.). Insert— 1851. . . .

Musgrove (Lord Mayor of London, 1850). Baronetcy 2 Aug. 1851. Arg. a bend az. betw. 3 lozenges of the last each charged with a fleur-de-lis or.

Muskham. Arg. a chev. betw. 3 butterflies sa. *V.*

Mustel. Sa. platy and a canton erm. Henry Mustel. *F.*

Musters (Kirklington, co. York). Arg. a bend within a bordure engr. gu. Sir John Musters, 1356. *V.*

Musters (Hornsey, Middlesex). Arg. on a bend gu. a lion pass. or a bordure of the second. Sir John Musters, 1663. *L.N.*

Muston (Gotham and Callis, co. Notts.). Add: *V.N. p. 166.* The field or. *V.N. p. 188.*

Muston. Arg. a chev. betw. 3 crosses flory sa. Crest: . . . Add: William de Muston. *X.*

Muswell (East Herling, co. Norfolk). Add: *Blomfield.*

Muttans. Arg. a bend sa. Walter de Muttans. *A.*

Muttlebury. Sa. two barrulets betw. 3 martlets or. Add: *W.*

Muttlebury or Mutterbury (Co. Somerset). Erm. on a bend within a bordure gu. 3 buckles arg. *V.S.*

Mychell. Sa. a chev. betw. three eagles displ. arg. Add: *V.*

Mychilstan. Gu. 3 gemmed rings arg. (or or.) stones az. *V.* Stoned gu. *W* and *Y.*

Mylbourne. Add: Sir John Mylborne, Alderman of London. *V.*

Myld. Arg. a lion ramp. az. crowned gold depressed by a fess compony or and of the second. *V.**

Mylkeley. Gu. 3 chevs. arg. *Cady.*

Mylles (Lenham, Kent). Per fess sa. and arg. 3 bears counterchanged collared and chained or. *Robson.*

Mynne (Walsingham, co. Norfolk). Arg. on a chev. betw. 3 leopards heads erased sa. as many fliers volant arg. *Cady.*

N

NABB (Co. Lancaster). Arg. on a bend betw. 2 cotises gu. and as many leopards sa. 3 escallops.

Nanby. Add: *V.*

Nanfan. Sa. a chev. betw. three gem rings arg. Add: *V.*

Nanfant. Sa. a chev. erm. betw. three wings arg. Crests: 1 and 2 . . . Add: Sir Thomas Nanfant. *V.*

Nangothan or Nangotham. Add: *Guillim.*

Narbon. Arg. the under parts of 3 belts or garters couped in fess az. buckled and garnished or.

Narvele. Arg. on a chev. gu. 5 bezants. *V.*

Nash. Az. a chev. betw. 3 greyhounds courant arg. *Nash.*

Nash. Insert—'co. Worcester 1634'. Sa. on a chev. betw. 3 greyhounds courant arg. as many sprigs of ashen leaves ppr. Add: *Nash p. 327.*

Nashe. Add: *W.*

Naunton. Insert—'co. Suffolk' (Bartholomew de Naunton) . . . Add: *V.* Bartholomew de Naunton. †

Naylor (Newland, co. Gloucester). Add: Nayler (London). Same arms. *W.*

Neale. (Walhampton, co. Hants.). Insert—Baronetcy 1764 . . .

Neale, Neal or Neyll (Yelden, co. Bedford . . .). Add: John Neale (Wollaston, co. Northants). *W.*

Neale (Dursley, co. Gloucester). Or a lion ramp. gu. overall on a fess . . . 3 dexter hands arg. *Robson.*

Neale (Westminster: granted Nov. 1612). Insert —by Camden to Dr. Neale, Dean of Westminster.

Neale (Leeds, co. York 1666). Or 2 lions ramp. combatant az. holding a sinister hand couped apaumy gu. *Dugdale 234.*

Nedham (Wimeley, co. Hertford). Add: *V.* John Nedeham, London. *V.*

Nedham (Wymondesley, co. Hertford; confirmed). Insert—by Cook.

Needham or Nedham (Nedham in the Peak, co. Derby) . . . Add: Nedham (Bolton, co. Rutland 1618). Same arms. *C.R.* Needham Burton Overy, co. Leicester 1619). Same arms with a crescent for diff. *C.C.* Nedham (Sharington, co. Salop). Same arms. *Z. 320*

Neele. Arg. on a bend sa. 3 pheons or. *V.**

Neeld (Grittleton House, co. Wilts. bart.). Insert —1858.

Neilson (Round Court). Arg. a chev. gu. betw. 3 dexter hands in bend sinister of the last. †

Neirnurst (Co. Buckingham). Gu. a lion ramp. within an orle of billets arg. *V.*

Neketon (Norfolk 1241). Sa. 2 bars humetty in chief as many plates and in base an escallop arg. *Dashwood.*

Nelson (Chaddleworth, co. Berks. . . .). Add: Henri le Nelson. *F.*

Nelson (Bedale, co. York). Add: Christopher Nelson, Grimston, co. York. *V.* Nelson (London and Wanstead, co. Essex). Same arms. *V.E. 1612.*

Nelson (Grimston, co. York). Add: *V.*

Nerford, Neirford, Nereford. Gu. a lion ramp. erm. William Nerford. *A.E.F.V.*

Nerford (Aldborough, co. Norfolk). Gu. a lion ramp. arg.

Nerland. Arg. on a chev. betw. 3 lions ramp. the two in chief respecting each other sa. as many bezants. *V.*

Nermont or Nernewte. Add: *V.*

Nesbitt (Woodhill, co. Donegal). Arg. a chev. gu. betw. 3 bears heads erased sa.

Nesbitt (Lismore, co. Cavan). Same arms.

Nesbitt (Great Yarmouth, Norfolk). Arg. a chev. betw. 3 wolves heads erased gu.

Nesfield. Sa. a chev. betw. 3 mullets arg. Lancelot Nesfield. *Eliz. Roll. xxv.*

Nessfeld. . . . on a chev. . . . betw. 3 estoiles . . . as many fleurs-de-lis . . . **Seal** of Thomas de Nesfeld. temp. Ric. ij.

Neve. Sa. a chev. betw. 3 talbots heads erased arg. *Cady.*

Nevile. Or crusilly sa. a bend gu. John de Nevile le forestier. *B.*

Nevill (Lord Bergavenny . . .). Add: Sir Gilbert Nevill. *V.*

Nevill. Az. a lion ramp. or. Joan de Nevile. *E.Y.* Sir Hugh Nevile, Essex. *C.I.N.V.*

Nevill. Gu. a lion ramp. arg. goutty de poix. John Nevylle le Forester. *Y.*

Nevill (Cos. Huntingdon and Lincoln). Or— underlined, marginal ? arg. Add: Sire Felip de Nevile. *N.*

Nevile. Az. 3 falcons wings expanded arg. *V.*

Nevill. Arg. a chief indented vert. over all a bend. gu. Sir Thomas de Nevile. *N. Harl. MS. 6137.* But a bendlet gu. Sir Thomas Nevill, co. Lincoln. *V.*

Nevill (Faldingworth, co. Lincoln). Add: Sir Thomas de Nevill. *N.*

Nevill (Co. Nottingham). Add: *V.**

Neville. Az. 2 bars gemel and in chief a lion pass. guard. arg. Wat. de Nevile. *E.*

Nevinson or Nevison (Estrey, co. Kent). Add: *V.** Sir Roger Nevison (Kent). *W.*

Newarke (Akham, co. York). Add: *F.Y.*

Newbery (Ireland). Erm. a chev. gu. *Guillim.*

Newborough (Berkeley, co. Somerset and co. Wilts.). Add: *V.S.* Sir Roger Newborough. *V.* Bendy of 6 or and az. a bordure engr. gu. Sir Robert de Nevo or Newborough. *R.*

Newbottle, Newbottell or Newbottel. Add: *V.V.**

Newburgh Abbey (Co. York). Add: Tonge p. 19.

Newcourt (Pickwell, Halesworthy . . . Devon . . .). Add: *V.D. 1620.*

Newcut. Arg. 2 bars counterpotent gu. edged sa. *Randle Holme.*

Newdegate (Harfield, Middlesex). Gu. a chev. betw. 3 lions gambs erased erm. *C.L. p. 34.*

Newdick or Newdyke (Co. Worcester, granted 1 Dec. 1580). Paly of 4 arg. and sa. on a bend gu. five bezants. Thomas Newdick. *V.*

Newenham. Arg. three eagles displ. gu. Add: *V.**

Newenton. Az. three eagles displ. arg. Adam de Newenton. *F.E.Y.*

Newington. Az. six eagles displ. . . . Add: Sire Adam de Newentone. *N.V.*

Newman (St. Giles, co. Middlesex). Add: Newman (London and Norfolk, granted by Camden in 1610). Cauis Newman. Same arms.

Newman (Co. Kent). Add: *W.*

Newman (Dromore, co. Cork). Arg. a chev. gu. betw. 3 lions couchant of the second.

Newnham (Northants). Az. 3 demi-lions ramp. arg. *Baker.*

Newnham. Gu. 3 eagles displ. arg. a label az.

Newport (As borne by Dr. John Newport, Master of Jesus College, Cambridge 1614). Per chev. embattled az. and sa. in base a lion ramp. or in the dexter chief a crescent and in the sinister chief a mullet of the last.

Newport (Co. Stafford). Add: *V.**

Newport. Sa. on a chev. betw. 3 pheons arg. as many mullets gu. *V.*

Newport. Arg. on a bend sa. betw. two lions— insert—ramp. . . . Add: *V.*

Newsom (Co. York). Arg. on a bend az. three roses of the first. *Whitaker's Craven.*

Newton (Essex). Sa. 2 shin bones in saltire the dexter surmounted of the sinister arg. *V.* Sir Isaac Newton, Master of the Royal Mint. President of the Royal Society 1705. Same arms. *L.N.*

Newton (Newton, co. Chester). Add: *V.L.*

Newton (London, Baronetcy 1660, Ext.). Vert. a lion ramp. or langued and armed gu. on his shoulder a cross patty fitchy sa. *Guillim.*

Newton. Arg. a lion ramp. tail forked sa. a crescent in the dexter chief. In East Mascall Church, Sussex 1578.

Newton (Dalcoif, Scotland). Gu. a lion ramp. arg. on a chief az. 3 mullets of the second. *Guillim.*

Newton (Bagdale Hall, co. York). Add: *Dugdale. p. 67.*

Newton. Of Newton. Arg. a chev. sa. betw. 3 popinjays vert. beaked and membered gu. *Sussex Arch. Coll. vol. ix.*

Newton (Norfolk). Arg. 2 chevs. reversed gu. Figured, but no colour, *Harl. MS. 1386. fo. 35.*

Neyrmuyt. Sa. billetty arg. a lion ramp. of the last. Sire John Neyrmyt. *N.*

Neymist. Sa. a lion ramp. or. *V.*

Nichell. Az. on a chev. or betw. two eagles displ. in chief and in base a lion pass. Add: John Nichell. London. *V.*

Nicholson (Sydney and Luddenham, Australia, bart.). Insert—1859.

Nicoll. Gu. a chev. arg. betw. 3 trefoils, stalked, couped and ragulee or. George Nicoll, Southwold, Suffolk. *V.*

Nicoll. Facsimile drawing—insert—not coloured . . . On a fess betw. three lions' heads erased . . . three ravens . . . *Impaling:* Quarterly 1 and 4, a lion rampant, 2, a chevron betw. three eagles' heads erased; 3, . . . on a bend cotised . . . three covered cups. Crest: a lion head erased with a collar charged with three ravens. Mottoes: Above, "Laud panel infanteus pugnam Leo rex animantum". Centre, "Glew ys yr Lew". Below, "Labor ipse voluptas".

Nicolls (Tilney, co. Norfolk). Add: *Harl. MS. 1177. fo. 102.*

Ninesson. Sa. a chev. betw. 3 hands erased gu. quartered by Harrison 1575. *North Country Grants xlj.*

Nixe (Richard Nixe, Bishop of Norwich 1501). Or on a chev. betw. 3 leopards faces gu. a rose of the last. *Lansdowne MS. 255. fo. 7.*

Nixon (Bletchingdon, co. Oxford). Add: *Guillim.*

Noel (Dalby, co. Leicester . . .). Add: Noell (Hayholme, co. York 1665). A crescent for diff. *Dugdales' fo. 70.*

Nonwike. Rauf Richard or Roger de Nonwike. *V.V.*Y.*

Norbury (Norbury, co. Chester . . .). Add: on a chev. a fleur-de-lis sa. John Norbury. *T.*

Norland. Sa. a chev. arg. betw. 3 wolves heads of the second couped gu. Sire Richard Norlande. *S.*

Norman. Arg. on a bend gu. 3 buck's heads cabossed or. *V.*V.*

Norris. Alias Sugar. Sa. in chief a doctors cap in base 3 sugar loaves arg.

Norris. Alias Banks, alias Bank. Add: *V.*

North (Mildenhall, co. Suffolk, bart.). Insert— 1660 . . .

North (Feltham, co. Middlesex). Add: *V.*

North. Gu. 2 chevs. betw. 3 mullets arg. *V.*

Northan. Az. 2 bars arg. in chief a griffin's head erased arg. betw. 2 plates.

Northam. Per pale gu. and az. a lion ramp. arg. crowned or. Sir William Northam. *V.*

Northampton (Lord Mayor of London 1381 . . .). Add: *Harl. MS. 1349. fo. 9.*

Nortoft (Co. Essex). Add: Sir Adam de Nortoft. *N.*

Norton. . . . 3 church bells . . . Stephen de Norton. **Seal.**

Norton. Arg. a chev. betw. 3 buckles sa. Sire Robert de Norton. *O.* But query Morton.

Norton (Abbotsleigh, co. Somerset). Arg. 2 bars gu. on a chief az. an escu. erm. *L.N.*

Norton (Canterbury, co. Kent). Add: Norton (Leigh   ). Same arms. *Collinson Somerset iij. 154.*

Norton (London and Coventry, co. Warwick). Insert—Baronetcy 1661 . . .

Norton (London 1611). Add: This coat was assigned Feb. 1611 to Bonham Norton, the King's printer by Camden, Clarenceux. *Guillim.*

Norton. Norton (Co. Somerset). Arg. on a bend cotised betw.—delete—six, substitute 'two' lions ramp. . . . of the field.—insert—'*V*'. . . .

Norton (Co. Warwick). . . . a lion pass . . . in chief, in base 3 daggers in pattle . . . *Cady.*

Norton. Sa. 3 piles in bend the upper ends flory arg. Robert de Norton. *X.*

Norton. Arg. a chev. gu. betw. 3 barrels standing on their bottoms sa. hooped or. *V.*

Norton. Arg. on a canton vert. a lion ramp. or. Sir Thomas Norton. *W.*

Norton. Arg. a chev. betw. 3 hinds statant sa. *W.*

Norton. Arg. a chev. betw. 3 cushions sa. Sir Roger de Norton. *Y.V.* Sire John de Norton. *Y.*

Norvill or Norvyle. Add: *V.*

Norwich (Cos. Essex, Norfolk, Northampton). Insert—'*W.*' and Suffolk . . . Add: *V.* Sir John de Norwich (Mettingham, co. Suffolk) and with a label or. Sir Johan de Northwyk. *O.*

Noseworth. Add: *V.*

Nott (Kent and London). Add: *V.*

Nowel (Sheriff of Lincolnshire, temp. Hen. viij). Or fretty gu. a canton erm. *Fuller.*

Nuthurst. Add: quartered by Clowes.

Nutshall (Nutshall, co. Lancaster). Add: *V.*W.*

O

OAKES or OKES (Oundle, co. Northampton). Add: *W.*

Oates (Leeds, co. York). Arg. 2 bendlets engr. az. in chief a cock gu. a canton erm. *Whitaker's Leeds j. 96.*

O'Brien (Borris in Ossory, Queen's, co. bart.). Insert—1849 . . .

O'Callane (Ireland). Or on a bend gu. 3 martlets arg. a bordure az.

O'Conor (Co. Roscommon). Arg. 2 lions ramp. respectant gu. supporting an oak tree eradicated vert. on base 3 birds . . . *Debrett.* The O'Conor Don. M.P.

O'Cowick. Arg. 3 pheasant cocks ppr. *Harl. MS. 1441. fo. 40.*

O'Dogherty (Ireland). Az. 2 bends cotised arg.

O'Donagee (Ballinascreen 1775). . . . a chev. . . . betw. in chief two lions ramp. combatant and in base (a beast) statant.

O'Doulee. . . . on a bend vert. fimbriated or a stags head cabossed or. *Harl. MS. 4039. fo. 105.*

O'Dulin. Gu. a bend vert. fimbriated or. *Harl. MS. 4039. fo. 155.*

Offer (Scotland). Az. an anchor arg. *W.*

Offord. Add: *V.*

O'Gara (Coolavin, co. Sligo). . . . Add: *Harl. MS. 4039. fo. 64.*

Oglander (Nunwell, Isle of Wight . . .). Add: The stork arg. *Guillim.*

Ognal. Add: *V.**

O'Grady. Per pale vert. and gu. 3 lions pass. in pale arg. *Harl. MS. 4039. fo. 169.*

O'Hannan. Quarterly gu. and or on a bend sa. 3 crosses patty arg. *Harl. MS. 4039. fo. 221.*

O'Harrell (Princes of Analy in Ireland). Vert. a lion ramp. or. Quartered by Worthington.

Ohenloyne. Or on ground vert. a boar pass. sa (Hybernicus Sylvestris). *V.*

O'Hurley. Arg. on a bend az. betw. 6 crosses patty gu. an armed dexter index hand of the first enclosed by 2 mullets or. *Harl. MS. 4039. fo. 65.*

O'Kearnea. Alias Carney. Arg. 3 lions ramp. gu. armed and langued az. on a chief of the last a dexter hand fesswise couped at the wrist ppr. holding a dagger arg. hilt or in pale betw. 2 pheons of the last. *Harl. MS. 4039. fo. 153.*

Oketon or Okton. Add: *V.V.**

Oldcastle. Arg. a tower triple towered sa. Oldcastle (Lord of Cobham). *V.*

Oldfield. Gu. a lion ramp. arg. over all on a bend sa. 3 crosses crosslet fitchy of the second. Robert de Oldefelde. *Y.W.*

Oldgrave (Sheriff of London temp. Hen. v). Az. a chev. betw. 3 owls arg. *Fuller.*

Oldhall. Per pale az. and purp. a lion ramp. erm. Sir William Oldhall. *V.*

Oldham (Oldham, co. Lancaster). Add: *V.**

Oldham (Manchester). Sa. a chev. betw. 3 owls arg. on a chief of the second as many roses gu. *V. V.L.* 1664. Richard Oldham, Bishop of Sodor &c. 1481. Town of Oldham, co. Lancaster.

Oldliff. Az. a bend betw. 2 cotises and 6 mullets or. *C.R. p. 50.*

Oldmixon. Az. a battle axe or headed arg. the edge to the sinister. Add: *V.**

O'Leary. Arg. a bend engr. gu. Impaling arg. a ship ppr. and on a point per chev. vert. a lion ramp. or. *Harl. MS. 4039.*

O'Learie. Arg. a lion pass. in base gu. in chief— insert—'an ancient' ship . . .

Ollier. Az. a chev. or in base a lion ramp. arg. a chief of the second.

Olney (Sir John Olney, co. Bucks). Barry of 6 arg. and az. a bordure engr. gu. *V.N.*

O'Malley (Recorder of Norwich 1859). Or a boar statant gu. quartering quarterly az. and or a cross engr. sa. in the first and fourth quarters a three masted ship arg. in the second and third quarters a lion ramp. gu. *Debrett.*

O'Meara (Ireland). Or 3 lions pass. guard. in pale gu. within a bordure of the last. charged with 6 crescents of the first. *Harl. MS. 4039. fo. 44.*

O'Meara (The Sept of O'Mearadhaigh . . .). Charged with eight escallops—delete—of the last, and read 'silver'. Add: *Harl. MS. 4039. fo. 44.*

Ones.

Onley. Arg. 3 rams lying down sa. horned or. *V.O. p. 216.*

Opie (Pawton, in St. Breock, co. Cornwall). Add: *V.C. p. 305.*

Orange (Foscott and Mells, co. Somerset) . . . Add: *V.S.*

Orbaston. Arg. a bend and chev. gu. on a canton of the second a lion pass. (another, ramp.) of the first. Add: *Harl. MS. 1404. fo. 110.*

Orbaston. Arg. 2 chevs. gu. on a quarter of the last a lion ramp. of the first. William de Orbaston. *V.*

Orby (Gosworth, co. Chester). Add: *V.** adopted by Fitton on marriage with its heiress.

Orby (Croyland Abbey, co. Lincoln, bart.). Insert—1658, extinct—insert—1724.

Orby. Gu. 2 lions pass. arg. John Orby. *Y.* And with a label or. Sir John Orby, co. Chester. *V.*

Orreby. Arg. 2 chevs and a quarter gu. *V.*

Orchard (Co. Devon). Christian Orchard . . . Add: Orchard (co. Devon). Same arms, quartered by Portman. *Collinson Somerset iij. 275.*

Ore. Barry of six arg. and az. on a bend gu. five bezants. Richard de Ore. *A.*

Orger. Or a chev. gu. betw. 3 water bougets. Crest: Out of a mural crown a horses leg reversed sa. Motto: Per ardua bonum. **Book Plate.**

O'Rian (Ireland). Arg. on a bend gu. 6 ears of wheat 2.2. and 2. or. quartering az. a chev. betw. 3 griffins heads arg. *Harl. MS. 4039. fo. 47.*

Orleston. Or two chevs. gu. on a canton of the second a lion pass. arg. Add: Sir William de Orleston. *A.* Orlandston. Same arms. Sir William de Orlandston. *D.*

Ormesby. Gu. crusilly bottony and a bend arg. *Y.*

Ormesby. Gu. crusilly arg. a bend chequy or and az. Sire William de Ormesby. *N.* and with a mullet sa. for diff. Sire Johan de Ornesby. *N.*

Ormeston or Orneston (Co. Essex). Add: *V.*

Ormsby (Co. Norfolk). Add: *V.*

Ormesby. Gu. a bend (or bendlet) company or and az. betw. 6 crosses crosslet of the second. *V.*V.*

Orr.

Orre. Of Orre. Gu. a bend arg. fretty sa.

Orre. Gu. a bend arg. fretty az. Add: *Visitation Sussex 1634.*

Orreby (Co. Chester). . . . a lion ramp.—underlined—. . . Add: pass. *V.**

Orreby (Gawsworth, co. Chester). Add: Sir Philip Orreby, Justiciary of Chester. temp. Hen. iij.

Orreby (Dalby, Lord of Fulk, Stapleford, co. Chester). . . . Add: The label or. *V.*

Orrebi. Arg. 2 chevs gu. on a quarter of the last so many lions pass. in pale of the first. Sir John de Orrebi. *F.*

Orrock. Sa. on a chev. or betw. three martlets arg. as many chessrooks of the field. *Guillim.*

Orton. Arg. a lion ramp. guard az. crowned or. *Syl. Morgan.*

Orton. Az. a lion ramp. guard. arg. crowned or. John de Orton. *V.*

Osan or Osanne. Add: *V.* Osam or Ossam.

Osbarne. Arg. on a bend betw. 2 cats pass. guard. sa. 3 fishes haurient in pale of the second.

Osborn. Arg. a bend betw. 3 lions ramp. sa. Crest: . . . Add: *V.**

Osborne. Gu. three dolphins or; another, Arg. on a bend betw. two tigers—underlined—margin ? lions . . .

Osborn. Or on a bend betw. 2 greyhounds courant sa. a lion or. *Cady.*

Osgood (Lincoln Inn). Vert. a chev. or betw. 3 garbs. **Book Plate.**

O'Sinan (Ireland). Arg. a bend of 5 lozenges conjoined az. betw. 2 cotises vert. and as many scorpions sa. *Harl. MS. 4039. fo. 235.*

Osman (Quartered by Nayler). Per pale indented gu. and sa. an eagle displ. or in chief two escallops arg.

O'Sullivan (A Sept . . . co. Tipperary . . .). Add: Sullivan (Chesterfield, co. Limerick). *Burke.*

Oswalstre. Add: *V.**

Oteley. Insert—(Pitchford, co. Salop). . . . Add: *W.*

Otoft. Az. a chev. or betw. 3 bezants. *V.*

Ottenbury (Co. York). Gu.—delete—(another, az.). Add: *Harl. MS. 1404.*

Otter (Welham, co. Notts. Granted in 1873). Or on a bend gu. goutty d'or betw. 2 crosses patty of the second 3 crescents of the first.

Otterbourne. Erm. a chev. betw. 3 otters heads couped sa. a chief vert.

Otterbury. Insert—'co. York'. Az. a dunghill cock . . .

Otterby, Otby and Otteby (Co. Lincoln). Add: Sire Randolf de Otterby. *N.*

Ottley (St. Christopher's . . . West Indies . . .). Add: Ottley (Middlesex). Same arms. *A.A.*

Otway (Ingmire Hall and Middleton, co. Westmorland . . .). Add: *Dugdale. 1665.*

O'Twohill (Poors, co. Dublin). Arg. 3 falcons close sa. *Harl. MS. 1441.*

Oughton (Tachbrook, co. Warwick). Baronetcy 1718. Per pale gu. and az. a lion ramp. or.

Oulond, Ouland or Olound. Add: *V.V.** Sir Nicholas Oulond.

Oulpman. Arg. a chev. enarched vert. *Randle Holme.*

Oulton, Olton or Owlton. Per pale gu. and az. a lion ramp. or. *V.V.*W.*

Oundell. Arg. on 2 bars sa. 6 crosses patty or. 3 and 3. *V.V.**

Ousflete. Or on a bend sa. 3 pierced mullets arg. Gerard Ousflete. *V.*

Over Darwen, Town of . . . Or a fess wavy betw. 2 bars wavy azure betw. three hop vines ppr. (2 in chief and 1 in base) fructed dexterwise. Crest: On a wreath of the colours a demi-workman with a pick in the dexter hand resting over his shoulder and in front of him a shuttle charged. Motto: "Absque Labore Nihil". **Book Plate.**

Overton. Insert—'Overton (co. Stafford). *V.*' Arg. a bend sa. in chief a rose gu. . . . .

Ovington. Gu. on a bend arg. 3 martlets sa. *V.*

Owen (Clenneney, co. Carnarvon . . .). Add: Sir Robert Owen. 1678. *L.N.*

Owen (Woodhouse, co. Salop . . .). Add: Sir Thomas Owen Justice of the Common Pleas, 1594. Same arms.

Owen ap Meredith. Add: Sir Davy Owen. *V.*

Owen (Little Bardfield, co. Essex 1634). Az. on a chev. betw. 3 chambers or a pair of compasses sa. betw. 2 squares or on a chief of the second a lion pass. gules. *V.E.*

Owen (Godstone, co. Oxford). . . . Add: *V.O. 1574.*

Owesle. Or a chev. sa. betw. 3 hazel or oak leaves vert. a chief of the second. *V.V.**

Owgan. Arg. 2 bars and in chief 3 mullets sa. William Owgan. *Y.*

Owle. Add: *V.N. p .121.*

Owlerhead. Per chev. engr. per pale counter-changed or and gu. *Randle Holme.*

Ownesley. Az. a bend engr. or betw. four cotises arg. *Randle Holme.*

Oxenbridge (Co. Hants . . .). Add: Sir Godart Oxenbridge. *V.*

Oxenden (Dene, co. Kent) . . . Add: *V.** Oxenden (Wingham, Kent). Arg. a chev. gu. betw. 3 bulls statant sa. *V.*

Oxon. Bendy of 6 arg. and sa. *V.**

Ozanne (The Landes . . . Guernsey . . .). Add: *A.A.*

P

PABENHAM. Barry of six arg. and az. on a bend gu. three mullets of the first—insert—*V.**—delete—(another, or).

Pabenham. Barry of 6 arg. and az. on a bend gu. 3 mullets of the first pierced az. Sir John Pabenham, co. Bedford. *V.*

Pabenham. Barry of 6 arg. and az. on a bend gu. 3 mullets or pierced az. Sir Laurens de Pabenham. *S.* The mullets not pierced. Sir Johan de Pabenham. *N.* and pierced. Sir Johan de Pabenham, the son. *N.*

Packington (Edgeworth, co. Middlesex . . .). Add: *V.*

Paderday. Arg. on a bend sa. three quatrefoils slipped—delete—'and leaved' . . . Add: *V.*

Paganell, Paganel or Painell (Bahuntune . . .). Add: quartered by Sutton, Baron Dudley. *U.*

Page (Donnington, co. Sussex A.D. 1591).—marginal note—the heiresss mar. White.

Page (Gresham Page of Saxthorpe . . .). Add: *Dashwood.*

Pagenham. Add: *V.* Sire Edmon de Pagenham. *N.* John de Pagenham. *Y.* But an eagle displ. vert. in each of the 1st and 4th quarters vert. Sir Edmund de Pagenham, Suffolk. *V.*

Paget (Sheriff of Hampshire 1580). Arg. a chev. vair betw. 3 talbots pass. sa. *Notes and Queries xj. p. 494.*

Painters (Company of 'Peyntours' so first called, granted by Holme, Clarenceux i. Hen. vij). Az. a chev. or betw. 3 phoenix's heads . . . *Walpole's Anecdotes of Painting j. 112.*

Pakeman. Arg. two bars gu. in chief as many pellets . . . Add: *V.** Pakeman (Kirby). Same arms. But † *C.R. p. 17.*

Pakeman. Arg. 2 bars and in chief as many palets gu. on a canton sa. a boar's head couped arg. *V.* Query in error for pellets. *V.**

Pakenham. Gu. a chev. betw. 3 crosses crosslet fitchy arg. Myles Pakenham. *X.*

Palavicini (London 1687). Az. an eagle displ. arg. Sir Peter Palavicini. *L.N.*

Palgrave (Norwood Barmingham, Baronetcy 1641, co. Norfolk). Az. a leopard ramp. guard. arg. spotted sa. *Guillim.*

Palie. Gu. a bend vair betw. 6 crosses potent or. Sir John de Palie. *R.*

Palk (Haldon House, co. Devon bart.). Insert—1782 . . .

Palingham. Arg. a bend gobony gu. and or on the chief point of the bend a lion pass. of the last. Add: Ricd. Palingham. *V. V.**

Palingham. Arg. on a bend gu. 2 bars and in chief a lion ramp. or. Richard Palingham. *V.*

Palingham. Arg. on a bend company gu. and or a lion ramp. in chief of the last. Ricd. Palingham. *V.*

Palley. Gu. on a bend or. betw. three lions ramp. arg. as many mullets az. Add: *V.*

Palliser (Great Island and Portobello, co. Wexford . . .). Add: Palliser (Newby, co. York 1665). Same arms. Crest: Out of a ducal coronet gu. a demi-eagle displ. *Dugdale. p. 95.*

Palmer (Carlton, co. Northampton, bart.). Insert—1660 . . . Add: Sir Geffrey Palmer. Attorney General to Charles ij. *Guillim.* Palmer (Newcastle-on-Tyne). Same arms *Debrett.*

Palmer (Ladibrook, co. Warwick). Az. on 2 bars arg. 3 crosses crosslet gu. in chief a greyhound courant arg. †

Palmer (Howlets, co. Kent 1586). Add: Sir Henry Palmer, Kent. *Syl. Morgan.*

Palmer (co. Leicester). Arg. on a bend sa. five bezants. Add: *V.*

Palmer. Arg. 2 bars gu. on a bend of the second 3-foils slipped arg. (but the trefoils slipped or.). *V.*

Palmer (Lincolns Inn, London. c. 1700). Arg. on a bend sa. betw. 2 ogresses 3 trefoils slipped of the field. **Seal.**

Palmer. Vert. on a chev. erm. betw. in chief 2 palmer's staves and in base a lion ramp. or 3 escallops gu.

Palmer (Earl of Castlemaine, c. branch of Palmer of Wingham). . . . Amend Crest to read 'Motto': Palma virtuti.

Palshed or Polshed. Add: *V.**

Pamphlin (Co. Cambridge). Pally of 6 arg. and gu. on a canton of the first a cross moline sa.

Panell. Arg. two bars sa. betw. 8 martlets gu. . . . Add: *V.**

Panell. Az. 2 lions pass. reguard. coward tails reflexed over the back or. *V.*

Pannell. Arg. 2 bars az. an orle of nine martlets gu. William Pannell. *F.*

Panton. Gu. 2 bars erm. Sir Hugh Pantone, Beaumanton. *V.*

Pantone or Paunton. Sir Hugh de P. Gu. 2 bars and in the dexter chief a millrind erm. *N.*

Panton (Sussex, granted). Insert—by Camden . . .

Panton. Arg. 6 barrulets and a canton gu. James de Pantone. *F.*

Papenham or Pappenham. Barry of 6 arg. and sa. on a bend gu. 3 eagles displ. or. *V.V.**

Papenham. Paly of 6 arg. and sa. on a bend gu. 3 eagles displ. or. *V.*

Papenham. Paly of 6 or and sa. on a bend gu. 3 eagles displ. of the first. *V.**

Parcy. Arg. on a chev. sa. three 5-foils or. Richard Parcy. *V.*

Pardy (that Ilk). Add: *Guillim.*

Pares. Add: Sir Wm. de Pares, co. Lincoln. *V.*

Parham. Revise—to read: co. Wilts, temp. Ric. iij. Arg. on a chev. engr. gu. betw. delete— 'as many', substitute '3' mallets ppr. three lions gambs erased or a bordure engr. sa. bezantee. Add: *V.*

Parham. Arg. on a chev. betw. three mallets gu. as many lions paws erased or. *Collinson Somerset. ij. 377.*

Paris. Sa. crusilly and a chevron arg. Sire William de Paris. *N.O.Y.* Richard Paris. *Cotton MS. Tiberius. D. 10.*

Paris. Sa. a chev. betw. 10 crosses crosslet or. *V.** Richard Paris. *V.*

Paris or Parris. Arg. a bend gobony arg. and gu. Add: *V.*

Park.

Parkby (that Ilk). Az. a chev. betw. 3 crosses crosslet fitchy arg. *Guillim.*

Parke. Sa. an eagle displ. arg. a bordure az. Richard del Parke. *Y.*

Parke (Essex). Az. an eagle displ. arg. goutty de sang. *V.E. 1634.*

Parker (Norton Lees, co. Derby . . .). Add: Parker. *V.** Clopton Hall, Stowmarket, co. Suffolk).

Parker (Baron Morley and Monteagle). . . . Amend 'az.', read 'arg' . . .

Parker (Prior of Gloucester). 1515. Sa. a buck trippant arg. betw. 3 pheons or a bordure engr. of the last. *Ruddes. Hist. p. 139.*

Parker (Shenstone Lodge, Lichfield, bart.). Insert—1844 . . .

Parker (Co. Derby and Whitlet Hall, co. Lincoln). Add: *V.*

Parker (Sandwich, co. Kent . . .). Add: *V.** Parker (Bassingbourn, Essex, Baronetcy 1782). Quartered by Elwes. Same arms.

Parker (London). Arg. a chev. betw. 3 mullets gu. on a chief az. as many stags heads cabossed or. *V.* The chev. gu. *C.L.* 1568.

Parker (Haling). Insert—Croydon . . . Or a buck trippant gu. on a canton of the first a ship az.

Parker (Archbishop of Canterbury 1559–75). Gu. on a chev. betw. 3 keys arg. as many estoiles of the first. *V.*

Parker. Gu. on a chev. betw. 3 keys or as many estoiles of the first. *V.**

Parker (Co. Kent). Gu. on a chev. betw. 3 keys or —delete—(sometimes, arg.) . . . Add: *W.*

Parker (Honyng, Norfolk). Arg. a chev. sa. betw. 3 mascles az. *V.* But lozenges. *Syl. Morgan.*

Parker (London and Hunnington, co. Warwick, Baronetcy 1681). Same arms.

Parker (Hanthorpe House, co. Lincoln). Add: Parker (Erwarton, Suffolk, Baronetcy 1661). Same arms.

Parker (Park Hall, co. Stafford). Gu. a chev. betw. 3 leopards faces or quartering; per fess crenelly or and sa. 3 goats tripping counter-changed: or a bend sa: and sa. a bend betw. 3 spears heads arg. *Guillim.*

Parker (Shenfeld, co. Essex 1612). Arg. 2 bars sa. in chief a talbots head erased gu. betw. 2 torteaux. *V.E.*

Parker (Co. York). Gu. a chev. betw. 3 leopards heads arg. Bryan Parker. *Eliz. Roll. xxv.*

Parker. Gu. a chev. betw. 3 keys within a bordure arg. *V.*

Parker (Lambeth, Surrey). Assigned 28th May 1572 to the eldest son of Parker, Archbishop of Canterbury). Gu. a chev. or betw. 3 keys erect wards upward arg. *Guillim.*

Parker (Woodthorpe, co. York). . . . Add: *Hunter j. 207.*

Parker. Insert—'co. York', confirmed 20 April 1563—insert—by Flower, Norroy. Per pale or and sa. on a chev. betw. 3 annulets . . .

Parker. Insert—'Sussex'. Az. a chev. or betw. 3 cotton hanks . . . Add: *W.*

Parker (Copenhall, co. Chester). Add: *V.*

Parkins (Bramwith, co. York). Vert. a chev. betw. 3 ostrich feathers arg. within a bordure or. *F.Y. 1612.*

Parkley (Scotland). Az. a chev. betw. 3 crosses moline arg. *Robson.*

Parlet (Lynn, Norfolk 1637). Erm. a parrot vert. perched on a scroll . . . on which is written "pense puis parler", in chief a label of 3 points.

Parott. Arg.—delete—(Another, erm.) . . .

Parott (Wales). Erm. on a bend sinister gu. 3 escallops or. *V.*

Parry (Co. Wilts.). Arg. a chev. sa. betw. 3 boars heads couped ppr.

Parry (Co. Salop and Leamington). Arg. a chev. betw. 3 boars heads erased sa. *Debrett.*

E

Parsons (Sir John Parsons, Lord Mayor of London in 1704) . . . Add: Parsons (Great Milton, co. Oxford. 1634). Same arms. *Guillim.*

Parsons (Sherborne, co. Dorset). Az. a chev. erm. betw. 3 slips of parsley ppr. *Robson.*

Partridge (Cirencester . . .). Add: Paltridge or Patriche (Co. Gloucester, from Kendall, Westmorland, confirmed 1561 and 1566. *Harl. MS. 1041. fo. 13b.* Nicholas Pertridge, Sheriff of London temp. Hen. viij. *Fuller.* Sir Miles Pertricn, Sheriff of Gloucestershire. l. Edw. vj. *Fuller.*

Partridge (Horsenden House, co. Bucks.). Add: *A.A.*

Partridge or Partrich. Insert—'London'. Add: Granted to Ashabel Partridge, one of the principal Goldsmiths to Queen Elizabeth by Harvey, Clarenceux 1559. *Guillim.* The Visitation of 1568, gives the bend or.

Parvise (Unsted, co. Surrey). Add: Parvis (co. Essex). Same arms. *V.E. 1634.*

Pashley. Insert—'co. Kent'. Purp. a lion ramp. or another crowned arg. Add: *V.*

Pashley or Pasley (Cos. Lincoln and York). Add: Pashley (Stainton, co. York). *Hunter j. 259.*

Pashley. Purp. a lion ramp. tail forked and nowed or crowned arg. Sir Richard Pashley. *V.*

Passelew. Bendy or and az. on a canton arg. a lion pass. guard. gu. Sir Johan Passeleu. *N.* Passelew, Norfolk. 1241.

Paternoster. Arg. a chev. gu. betw. 3 saltires engr. sa. a bordure sa. *Harl. MS. 1404. fo. 125.*

Pateshull. Insert—'co. Hereford'. Az. on a chev. arg. betw. three hearts or as many escallops gu. Add: *V.*

Patishall. Erm. a lion ramp. gu. (another purp.) crowned or. Add: John de Patishull. *Y.*

Patrick (London). Arg. 3 lions pass. in bend sa. betw. 2 bendlets gu. *C.L. p. 88.*

Patten (Warrington). Lozengy erm. and sa. a canton gu. *V.L. 1664.*

Patton (Bank   ). Fusilly erm. and sa. a canton or quartering 2. . . . 3 mallets . . . 3. erm. 3 estoiles and 4. chequy arg. and sa. a saltire erm. **Book Plate.**

Patteson. Arg. a bend dovetailed on both sides gu. *Randle Holme.*

Paul or Paule (Norfolk and Lambeth, co. Surrey). Add: Paul, Minor Canon of Norwich 1726.

Pauncefote (Hasfield, co. Gloucester). Add: Grynbald de Paucevot. *A.Y.V.E.F.* Sir Gilbert Pauncevod. *N.*

Paunton. Gu. a chev. vair a chief or. Add: Sir Hugh Paunton. *V.*

Paunton. Barry of 10 arg. and gu. a canton of the last. *V.*

Pave, Paven or Pavent. Arg. on a bend gu. 3 eagles displ. of the field. *V.*

Paveley. Gu. 3 lions pass. arg. over all on a bend az. as many mullets or. Sir Walter Paveley. *R.Y.*

Paveley. Barry nebulee of six or and sa. a bendlet arg. Add: *V.* Paveley. Barry or and sa. a bend arg. Sir Walter Paveley. *N.*

Pavell. Az. two wolves pass. reguard. cowarded or. Add: *V.*

Pavent. Arg. on a bend gu. three eagles displ. or. Add: John Pavent. *X.Y.*

Pawne. Arg. three peacocks in pride az. within a bordure engr. gu. Add: William Pawne. *V.*

Pawson (Leeds, co. York). Gu. a chev. betw. three lions—insert—gambs or—amend pass. to read 'paws', or. *Whitaker's Leeds ij. 74.*

Pay (Sussex). Sa. on a chev. betw. 3 spiked maces or as many palets gu. *Berry.*

Payderday. Arg. on a bend sa. three 4-foils of the first. *V.*V.*

Payler (Thoralby, co. York, bart.). Insert—1642 . . . Gu. three lions pass. guard.—insert—in pale . . . Add: *Dugdale 1665. p. 317.*

Payleu. Purp. a lion ramp. or. *V.*

Paylow. Purp. a lion ramp. or. *V.**

Payne (Wallingford, co. Berks. . . .). Betw. two—insert—'plain' cotises . . . of the first—add—barbed vert. Crest: . . .

Payne (Midlow St. Neots, co. Huntingdon). Insert—Granted by Segar 1604.

Payne. Erm. a lion ramp. sa. on a chief gu. 3 crosses crosslet fitchy or.

Payne (Recorder of Buckingham 1866). Sa. on a bend betw. 2 eagles displ. or 3 crosses crosslet purp. *Debrett.*

Payne (Norwich, granted 1670). Or a chev. vair. betw. 3 lions ramp. az.

Payne (East Grinstead and of Newick, co. Sussex; granted). Insert—by Bysche . . .

Payne. Insert—co. Lincoln . . . Per saltire arg. and sa. . . .

Paynell (Baron Paynell, of Drax, co. York). . . . within an orle of—insert—'6 or' eight . . .

Paynell (Co. Hants.). Insert—'6 or' . . . Add: Sir Thomas Paynell Q.V.E.A.

Paynell. Or 2 bars az. betw. 6 martlets gu. 3. 2. and 1. Thomas Paynell. *A.E.Q.X.* William Paynell. *A.*

Paynell. Arg. 2 bars az. an orle of 9 martlets gu. William Paynell. *Y.E.F.*

Paynell (Sir John Paynell . . . co. Leicester). Add: Sire Rauf Paynell. *N.Y.*

Paynell. Gu. 2 chevs. arg. a bordure . . . overall a bend sa. Crest: . . . Add: *V.*

Paynell. Arg. 3 bars az. in chief 3 martlets gu. Sir William Paynell. *I.*

Paynell. Gu. 2 chevs within a bordure arg. Sir John Paynell. *S.*

Paynell (Norfolk). Gu. 2 chevs arg. within a bordure engr. of the last. *V.*

Paynell. Gu. 2 chevs arg. each charged with a martlet of the field. *V.*

Paynter (Twidall, co. Kent). Add: Sir Paul Paynter, Muswell Hill, Middlesex. 1664. *L.N.*

Paynter (Sprole, co. Norfolk). Insert—granted by Segar 1609.

Peachey (Petworth, Sussex, Baronetcy 1736). Az. a lion ramp. double tailed erm. on a canton or a mullet pierced gu. *Edmondson.*

Peche (Kings Thorp, co. Leicester). 1619. Same arms. *C.C.*

Peacock (Burnhall, co. Durham; granted by—delete—Norroy; substitute, St. George, Garter . . .

Peacock (Finchley, co. Middlesex). Add: *W.*

Pearce. Gu. on a bend betw. 2 cotises or, an annulet sa. Add: Major General Thos. Governor of Limerick, quartering arg. on a bend az. 3 mascles . . . †

Peard (Co. Devon). Add: Peard (co. Devon, granted by Camden. May 1606). Same arms.

Pearle. Sa. 2 broad arrows in saltire arg. feathered or in chief a plate. *Harl. MS. 1548.*

Pearse (Court, co. Devon; granted). Insert—by John Borough, Garter.

Pearson. Az. a chev. betw. 3 ostrich feathers arg. in chief as many plates. *Robson.*

Pearson (Co. Chester). Add: *Cady.*

Peart (Co. York). Add: *Cady.*

Pecham. Az. 6 annulets or . . . Add: Sir John de Pecham. *A.*

Peche or Pechey (Co. Oxford). Add: Sire Johan Peche. *N.*

Peche. Az. an eagle displ. arg. a maunch at the dexter wing gu. Sir Thomas Peche. *V.*

Peche. Sa. a falcon rising overt or. Sir Nicholas Peche. *V.*

Peche. Az. a lion ramp. tail forked erm. crowned or. Peche (Lullingstone, co. Kent). Gilbert de la Peche, Baron. xiij Edw. ij. the heiress mard. Hart. Sir John Peache, Kent. *V.S.*

Peche or Pechey. Arg. a chev. gu. within a bordure sa. bezanty. *N.*

Peck (Co. Derby and Wakefield, co. York). Insert—1585. Add: *F.Y.*

Peck (Cos. Leicester and Lincoln). Add: *V.* C.C. 1619.* Serjeant Peck, Norfolk, temp. Charles ij. John Peck. Scole co. Norfolk 1655. John Pike, Wakefield, co. York. *V.*

Peckham (Co. Suffolk). Add: *V.*

Pedegrew. Arg. semy of trefoils sa. an eagle displ. with 2 heads of the last. *Berry.*

Pederton (Cos. Cornwall and Somerset). Add: *V.*

Pedigrew (Co. Cornwall). Add: *V.*

Pedocrew. Insert—Cornwall. Add: *V.W.*

Pedwarden (Co. Hereford). Add: Sir Walter de Pedwardyn. *V.E.S.* William de Pedwardon. *F.* Thomas Pedwardin. *Y.* And with a label of 3 points az. Sir Robert Pedwardyn. *S.*

Peele (Co. Chester), Add: *V.V.**

Peeres or Perse (Westdown, co. Kent). Add: *W.*

Peers (Co. Essex). Sa. a chev. erm. betw. 3 lions heads erased or a chief or the second. *V.E. 1634.*

Peers. Sa. a chev. erm. betw. 3 lions heads erased arg. a chief or. Sir Charles Peers, London 1707. *L.N.*

Peers. Vert. a bend arg. cotised or. Add: *V.* Sir Thomas de Peres. *N.V.*

Peet. Az. a chev. or betw. 3 lions heads erased arg. *W.*

Pegrez or Pegress. Az. 3 pair of backgammon tables open ppr. edged or. *Guillim.* John Pegrez. *V.*

Peirce (Bath, co. Somerset). Sa. a bend nebuly betw. 2 unicorns heads erased or. *Dingley.*

Peirce (Co. York 1612). Az. a pelican in her piety crowned or. *F.Y.*

Peke (Edwd. Peke, Holdchurch Gate, co. Kent; granted by Cooke). Az. 3 talbots statant or. *W.*

Pelham (Laughton, co. Sussex). Az. 3 pelicans arg. vulning ppr. quartering Erm. on a fess . . . 3 crowns or cronels . . . for Crownall. Crest: A cage. Seal of Sir John Pelham. x Hen. vj.

Pelham (Compton-Valence, co. Dorset . . . and Laughton, co. Sussex). Add: Monsire Pelham. *T.* Sir John Pelham. *V.*

Pell (Sir Albert Pell . . . Add: Pell, co. Northampton). Same arms.

Pellett. Add: *V.*

Peltot ? or Pelcot. temp. Edw. i.

Pemarthe (Insert—or). Penarth (Co. Cornwall). Add: *V.*

Pemberton (Pemberton, co. Lancaster). Add: *V.**

Pemberton. Arg. a chev. gu. betw 3 dragons heads couped sa. *V.V.**

Pe?bridge. Barry of 6 or and az. Henry Pembryge. *A.* Sir Fulke de Penbrugge. *V.*

Pembridge. Barry of 6 or and az. a bend (or bendlet) gu. *V.* Sir Richard Pembridge 1375, in Hereford Cathedral. Sir Henry de Pembrige. *E.F.N.* But with a baston gu. *L.*

Pembridge. Arg. a chief az. a bend engr. gu. Sir John Penbrige. *W.V.*

Pembridge. Arg. a chief az. over all a bend fusilly gu. *V.** Sir John Pembrig temp. Edw. vj. *V.*

Pembridge. Arg. a chief az. over all a bend engr. or. Sire Johan de Pembruge. *N.*

Pembridge. Az. a chief gu. a bend engr. arg. Sir John Pembrige. *L.*

Pemerton (Ireland. *Fun. Ent. Ulster's Office* 1651). Add: Pemerton. Arg. a chev. betw. 3 antique dragons sa. *Tonge. p. 56.*

Penbrigg. Barry of 6 arg. and az. on a bend gu. 3 lozenges of the first. *V.**

Penbrigg. Barry of 6 or and az. on a bend gu. 3 lozenges arg. *V.*

Penbrigg. Barry or and az. on a bend gu. 3 mullets arg. Sire Johan de Penbrugge. *N.*

Penarthe (Cornwall). Arg. a chev. betw. 3 bear's heads erased sa. muzzled gu. *V.*

Penceller. Gu. a bend vairy arg. and gu. *V.*

Penceller or Pencoler. Arg. a bend vairy or and gu. *V.*

Pencoler. Arg. a bend vairy gu. and of the first. *Harl. MS. 1386. fo. 35b.*

Pendervis (Cornwall). Sa. a falcon rising between three mullets or. *Fuller.*

Pendergast. Gu. a bend cotised arg. Robert Pendergast. *Y.*

Pendreth (Sheriff of Newcastle 1434). Arg. 3 chevs. braced in base gu. on a chief az. a lion pass. of the field a † sa. for diff. *Carr MS.*

Pengelly. Gu. a lion ramp. arg. betw. 6 trefoils slipped or. *V.*

Peniston (Co. Oxford). Arg. 3 birds sa. beaked and legged gu.

Pennals of Plinton, heiress mar. Stroude of Plimpton, co. Devon. Arg. on a chev. az. 3 fishes ppr. the centre one haurient the others counter-haurient. *Syl. Morgan.* Wm. Pennylles, Brecksham, co. Devon. Same arms. *V.*

Pennarth. Delete—(from Guillim). Substitute, co. Cornwall. Add: *Guillim.*

Penne. Arg. 2 talbots courant gu. *C.L. p. 20.*

Penne (Thomas Penne, Doctor of Physic, London 1574). Erm. 2 greyhounds courant reguard per pale gu. and sa. *W. ij. Harl. MS. 1350. fo. 123.*

Penner. Add: *Cotton MS. Tiberius. D. 10.*

Penneston (Halsted, co. Kent). Insert—Baronetcy. Add: *Guillim.*

Penniles (Lupton, co. Devon). Add: The heiress mar. Upton.

Pennington (Co. Lancaster). Az. 3 falcons or. . . . Add: *V.V.**

Pennyman (Ormsby, co. York), bart. extinct, granted—insert—by Segar . . . Add: Pennyman (Marske, co. York, Baronetcy 1628). Same arms. *Guillim.*

Pennyman (St. Albans, co. Herts, descended from Pennyman of Ormsby, co. York). Same arms within a bordure erm. *Fairfax's Book of Arms.*

Penreth. Add: Richard Penreth. *V.*

Penrose (Co. Cornwall). Erm. on a bend az. 3 roses or. Add: *V.*

Penruddock. Sa. a bend raguly arg. John Penruddock. *Dug. O.J.*

Pensherd. Gu. a bend embattled counter embattled arg. Sir John Pensherd, Cumberland. *V.*

Pentyer. Arg. a chev. sa. betw. three magpies ppr. *Harl. MS. 1404. fo. 14b.*

Penwarn. Add: *V.V. 305.*

Penwortham Priory (Co. Lancaster). Add: *Tanner.*

Penzret. Gu. a bend embattled arg. Sire Johan de Penzret. *N.*

Pepper (Thursmaston, co. Leicester and co. York). Add: *C.C. 1619.*

Pepper. Or 3 bars gu. on a sinister canton . . . a rose . . .

Pepper. Sa. a shoveller duck arg. Sir Cuthbert Pepper, Supervisor of the Court of Wards and Liberties. *Dug. O.J.*

Pepperell. Arg. a chev. gu. betw. 3 pine cones vert. *V.**

Pepenrell, Pepenrill or Perperell (Co. Cornwall). Add: *V.*

Pepwell (Bristol and co. Gloucester). Add: *Harl. MS. 1559.*

Pepys or Pipis (Cottenham, co. Cambridge and Brampton, co. Hunts.). Add: Samuel Pepys of Brampton, Secretary to the Admiralty to Charles ij. Same arms, quartering gu. a lion ramp. within a bordure engr. or. *Guillim.*

Perc. Arg. on a bend gu. 3 pierced lozenges or. Sir William de Perc. *X.*

Perceval. Vert. a horse arg. spancelled or both legs on the near side. *Randle Holme.*

Percivall. Arg. on a chev. sa. three griffins heads erased of the first. *V.**

Percy (Baron Prudhoe . . .). . . . ducally—correct to read 'crowned' or . . .

Percy. Or a lion ramp. az. a mullet of the field at the shoulder. Sire Rauff Percy. *S.*

Percy. Or a lion ramp. az. a bordure 'recersele' i.e. engr. gu. Sir Wm. de Percy. *Y.* Thomas Percy, Bishop of Norwich 1356–69.

Percy. Or on a lion ramp. az. 'ung brize' arg. Sir Piers de Persey. *L.*

Periam (Fulford, co. Devon). Add: Sir Wm. Perian, Chief Baron of the Exchequer 1593. *Dug. O.J.*

Perenton. Gu. a chev. betw. 3 pears pendent or each stalked and with 2 leaves vert. *V.*

Peripons. Arg. 3 wolves courant in pale az. *Nash.*

Perin or Perring (Ashby de la Zouch, co. Leicester). Arg. on a chev. sa. betw. 3 pine apples slipped reversed vert. as many leopards faces or. *C.C. 1619.*

Perkins (Covent Garden, London). Gu. a bend engr. betw. 6 billets arg. †

Perneys. Arg. a chev. az. betw. 3 pears pendent bendwise sinister vert. *V.*

Perpoynt. Arg. a lion ramp. sa. a dexter baton or. Sir Robert de Perpoynt. *L.M.*

Perpund. Barry of 14 or 16 arg. and gu. a lion ramp. sa. over all a bendlet or. Henry Perpund. *E.F.*

Persall. Quarterly 1 and 4 Paly of 6 or and gu. 2 and 3 Erm. all within a bordure az. *V.** Sir Hugh Persall. *V.*

Person (*Fun. Ent. Ulster's Office* 1668, Lady Person). Add: John Person. *V.*

Pert (Arnold, co. Essex). Add: *V.E. 1612.* Sir William Pert. *V.*

Pert. Quarterly az. and gu. 4 lions pass. guard. or on a chief dancetee arg. 3 pellets. Add: Thomas Pert. *V.*

Pery (Co. Worcester). Arg. on a bend sa. 3 pears or. *V.V.**

Pesemarsh. Insert—co. Essex . . .

Peter. Gu. on a bend or betw. 2 escallops arg. a 5-foil az. betw. 2 birds sa. on a chief of the second betw. 2 dimidiated fleurs-de-lis of the first. John Peter. *Dug. O.J.*

Peter (Harlyn, Cornwall). Gu. on a bend betw. 2 escallops arg. as many cornish choughs ppr. *Lysons.*

Peter. Arg. a chev. gu. betw. 3 leopards faces of the second—Add: '*V.** another . . .

Peterkyn. Arg. an eagle displ. double headed per fess gu. and sa. *V.*

Petfyne. Arg. a bend betw. 2 swans arg. ducally gorged and lined or. *V.V.**

Petit (Ardevora, in Filleigh, co. Cornwall). . . . Add: *V.*

Petre (Cranham, co. Essex 1634). Gu. a bend or betw. 2 escallops arg. *V.E.*

Petre (Granted by Dethick to Robert Petre of co. Devon, 1 June 1573). Az. on a bend betw. 2 escallops or a cornish chough ppr. enclosed by as many 5-foils gu. a chief of the second charged with a rose within a pair of dimidiated fleurs-de-lis as the fourth.

Pettet. Az. on a chev. or betw. 3 leopards faces arg. as many cinquefoils vert. Add: *V.*

Pettit (Co. Kent). Add: (or gu. pierced vert.). *V.*

Petty (Ilmington, co. Warwick, *Harl. MSS.*). . . . Add: and with a trefoil slipped az. in chief. Nicholas Petty, Warwick. *V.*

Petyt. Or a fesse sa; another, sa. 3 lions ramp. in fesse betw. 2 bards dancetee arg. Add: see Dandelion.

Petyt (Kent). Gu. a chev. betw. 3 leopards heads arg. *W.* Sir John Petit, Baron of the Exchequer 1527. *Dug. O. J.* Ciriac Petit, Colkins, Kent. 1691.

Pevenly (Kent). Az. 3 chevs. arg. *Robson.*

Pevensey. Az. a chev. or fretty gu. betw. 3 crosses patonce arg. Add: Sir Bartholomew de Pevensi. *A.*

Pevensey. Or an eagle displ. gu. armed az.—insert—'*V.*', another. Gu. an eagle displ. or armed sa. Add: *V.*

Pever (Co. Bedford). Add: Sire John Peyvre. *N.Y.* Sir William Perver. *B.*

Pever. Arg. on a chev. gu. 3 fleurs-de-lis of the first. Sir John Pever, co. Bedford. *Cotton MS. Tiberius. D. 10.*

Peverell (Co. Worcester). Gu. 3 lions ramp. or. *Robson.*

Peverell. Quarterly or and vert. a bend arg. *Harl. MS. 1465. fo. 11b.*

Pew (Galloway, Scotland). Arg. a lion pass. sa. betw. 3 fleurs-de-lis gu.

Pewterer or Pewterwre. Add: *V.*

Peye. Or 10 billets 4. 3. 2. and 1 gu. Sir . . . de Peye of France. *W.*

Peyteven (Co. Lincoln). Erm. 3 chevs. gu. Sir Roger le Peyleven. *V.N.N. Harl. MS. 6589. fo. 39.*

Peyte (Co. Warwick). Barry indented of 6 arg. and gu. per pale counterchanged. *Guillim.*

Peytoe (Chesterton, co. Warwick). Add: *Fuller.*

Peyton (Co. Lancaster). Arg. three magpies ppr. Add: *Harl. MS. 1404. fo. 145.*

Peyvre (Query for Peverall). Arg. on a chev. az. three fleurs-de-lis or. Sir Roger Peyvre. *N.*

Phichdan. Az. 3 boars pass. in pale arg. Philip Phichdan.

Phillips (Norwich 1674). Arg. a chev. betw. 3 roses gu. *Dashwood.*

Phillips (Picton Castle, co. Pembroke, bart.). Insert—1621 . . .

Phillips. Arg. a lion ramp. sa. collared and chained or. *Randle Holme.*

Phillips (London 1568). Or a lion ramp. sa. ducally gorged and chained gold. *C.L.*

Philipps (Aberglasney, co. Carmarthen). Or a ramp. sa. betw. in chief 2 fleurs-de-lis az. and in base a stag's head erased gu.

Philips. Az. 3 birds . . . Wm. Philips. *Dug. O. J.*

Phillips (Barrington, co. Somerset, Baronetcy 1619). Arg. a chev. betw. 3 roses gu.

Phillip (Lord Mayor of London 1463) . . . Add: Sir Matthew Phillip. *V.*

Phillip. Per bend or and arg. a lion ramp. sa. a bordure . . . Add: Sir David Phillip. *V.*

Phillip. Quarterly gu. and arg. . . . Crest: . . . Add: Sir William Phillip. *V.*

Phillipps (Garendon Park . . . co. Leicester). . . . Add: *A.A.*

Phillips. Erminois a lion ramp. sa. collared and chained or betw. 2 crosslets in chief and an escallop in base gu.

Phillips. Arg. a chev. betw. 3 roses gu. Add: Sir Robert Philips of Montacute, Sheriff of Somerset. temp. Jas. j. Philips, Norwich 1674. Same arms. *Dashwood.*

Phillipson. Insert—'London 1568'. Sa. a chev. erm. . . . Crest: A camel's head . . . Add: *V.L.*

Philpot. Sa. a bend erm. Sir John Philpot. *V.* Lord Mayor of London.

Philpot (Tunbridge, Kent; co. Hertford; and of Compton, Thaxton, and Wood Hall, co. Hants.). Same arms.

Pickarell (Roydon, Norfolk). Sa. a swan arg. a chief erm. *Blomfield.*

Pickarell. Same arms. In Burgate Church, Suffolk and *Harl. MS. 1177 fo. 121.*

Pickering (Old Lodge and Clapham, co. Surrey). . . . Add: Pickering (Thirkell). Same arms. *Tonge. p. 97.* Thomas Pickering. *Y.*

Pickering (Kirkby Kendall and Oswaldkirk). Gu. a chev. betw. 3 fleurs-de-lis or. Sir William Pykering. *V.*

Pickering (Oswaldkirk, co. York. temp. Edw. ij.). Gu. on a chev. betw. 3 fleurs-de-lis or as many torteaux. *F. Y.*

Pickering. Arg. a lion ramp. sa. within a bordure gu. bezanty. Sir Thomas de Pickering, Essex. temp. Edw. iij. *N.V.*

Pickingham. Az. a lion ramp. or Add: Pickenham. *V.*

Pickworth. Gu. a bend betw. 6 pickaxes arg. Sir Philip Pickworth. *V.* John Pikeworth. *Y.*

Pickworth. Gu. a bend betw. 6 pickaxes or. Thomas Pikeworth. *X.*

Pie (Herald Painter 1716). Erm. a bend lozengy gu. quartering Wildish.

Pierce (Liverpool). *Her. Coll.* . . . Add: *A.A.*

Pierpont. Sa. semee of cinquefoils a lion ramp. arg. Add: Sir Edmond Perpond. *S.*

Pierrepont or Pierpound. Arg. a lion ramp. sa. within an orle of roses gu. Sir Robert Pirepound. *N.* But an orle of 5-foils gu. *V.V.* * *Y.*

Pierrepont. Arg. a lion ramp. sa. within an orle of 7-foils or 6-foils gu. Thomas Pierrepont. *Y.* Henry Pierrepont. *Y.*

Pierson (Confirmed to Thomas Pierson—insert— Usher of the Star Chamber . . . Add: *Guillim.*

Pigot (Co. Norfolk). Arg. on a bend—insert— 'engr.' betw. . . . Add: Sire . . . de Pygott. *V.*

Pigott (Sir Gillery Pigott, Baron of the Exchequer 1863). Per fess erm. and sa. 3 pickaxes counter-changed.

Pigot (Diddington). Az. 2 bars the upper arg. the lower one in chief a plate betw. 2 bezants. *V.*

Pigot (Dodington, co. York). Add: Monsire John Pigott, Doddington. *Y.* Sire Baudwin Pigot. *N.* Sir John Pigot, Ayton, co. York. temp. Edw. j. *V.*

Pigott. Az. a bend engr. betw. 6 martlets or. Sir Piers Pigott. *C.E.N.X.F.* The bend fusilly. Sir Piers Pigott. *V.* * Sir John Pigott. *V.*

Pigott or Pygott (Co. Bedford). Arg. a bend betw. 6 crosses tau &c. *Harl. MS. 1404. fo. 117.*

Pigott. Arg. a chev. betw. 3 bugle horns sa. *Robson.*

Pigott (Co. Bedford). Arg. a bend betw. six pickaxes sa. Add: *V.* * Sir Randolfe Pigott. *V.*

Pigott. Sa. 3 pickaxes arg. Geoffrey Pigott of Melmoreby. *P.X.* Sr. Randolf Pigott. *S.V.*

Pigott (Weston upon Trent). Sa. 3 pickaxes arg. a mullet for diff. or. *V.N.*

Pigott (Thrumpton, co. Notts.). Sa. three pickaxes arg. handled or. *V.N. 1614.*

Pike (Livericks, co. Kent). Az. three talbots or. Add: *Robson.*

Pikworth. Gu. a bend betw. 6 pickaxes or. Add: Thomas Pykeworth. *X.*

Pilland (Co. Devon). Arg. 2 chevs. wavy betw. 3 fleurs-de-lis sa.—insert—'V.'. (another . . .

Pillesden. Add: *V.*

Pillett (Co. Lincoln). Add: *V.*

Pilsten. Sa. 3 lions pass. in pale arg. *V.*

Pincerna (Cornwall, quartered by Trelawney). Gu. on a chev. sa., 3 goblets or. *Lysons.*

Pinchbeck. Arg. a chev. erm. betw. 3 chessrooks ermines. *V.*

Pinchpoole. Arg. a chev. gu. betw. 3 bugle horns sa. stringed or. *V.*

Pinchpoole. Arg. a chev. engr. gu. betw. 3 bugle horns sa. stringed or. *V.* *

Pindar (Idenshaw, co. Chester, bart.). Insert— 1662 . . . Add: Sir Paul Pindar. Az. a chev. betw. 3 lions heads erased erm. crowned or. *Carter.*

Pinfold (Dunstable, co. Bedford). Add:*Harl. MS. 1359. fo. 22.*

Pinfold (Walton Hall, co. Bucks.). Add: Charles Pinfold, Governor of Barbadoes.

Pink. Arg. 2 chevs. sa. betw. 3 roses gu. Robert Pink, New College, Oxford. ob. 1647. *Guillim.*

Pin. Gu. a chev. arg. betw. 3 pine apples or. Thomas de Pin. *E.*

Pinner. Or on 2 bars sa. 4 leopards faces or. 2 and 2. *Cady.*

Pipard. Quarterly az. and arg. 4 lions ramp. counter changed. Add: Sir William Pipard. *V.*

Pipard. Arg. 2 bars az. on a canton of the last a 5-foils or. Sir Rauf Pipard. *G.J.F. Y.* But a rose or. Sir Ralph Pipard. *F.G.J.* Arg. 2 bars az. on a canton gu. a 5-foil or. Rauf Pipard. *E.*

Pipard or Pipart. Arg. 2 bars sa. on a canton of the second a cinquefoil pierced or—insert— 'Nash' (another . . .

Pipe. Yerdington. Or 2 lions pass. guard. or. *V.*

Piper (Ashden, co. Essex). Add: *Morant's Essex ij. 341.*

Pitfield (Hoxton, co. Middlesex) . . . Add: The chains reflexed over their backs and betw. their legs.

Pytt (Alias Bennett, Pythouse, co. Wilts.). Quarterly arg. and or an Imperial eagle displ. . . . *Hoare iij. 132.*

Pittesford (Pitsford, co. Notts.). Gu. 3 bendlets vair a label arg. ? or. *Baker.*

Pitts. Erm. a chev. gu. betw. 3 peacocks heads erased az. beaked or. *V.*

Pixwell. Add: *V.* *

Place (Yngton, Cornwall). Arg. a chev. sa. betw. 3 ogresses. *V.*

Place (Aughton   ). temp. Edw. ij. Same arms. *F. Y.*

Planche (Co. Bucks.). Add: Sire . . . de la Plaunche. *N.*

Planche or Plaunche (Leicester). Arg. billetty sa. a lion ramp. of the last.

Plance. Arg. goutty de poix and a lion ramp. sa. Jake de la plance. *G.*

Planner. Vert. a chev. erm. betw. 3 annulets or. *W.*

Plantagenet. Az. semy-de-lis or on a bordure gu. 8 lions pass. guard. of the second. Hameline Plantagenet.

Plantagenet (Duke of York). Borne by Edmond of Langley . . . Add: *T.*

Plantagenet (Earl of Lancaster. borne by Edmond, Earl of Lancaster. Add: Papworth Rolls. *E.G.P.Y.H.J.N.K.*

Plasses (Co. Oxford). Arg. 6 annulets gu. 3. 2. and 1. *Harl. MS. 1458.*

Platt (Plastow, co. Essex, granted . . .). Insert— 1578. Add: *W.*

Platt (Wigan, co. Lancaster). Insert—granted 1559. Add: *W.*

Playfair (Meigle, Scotland). Vert. a lion ramp. arg. on a chief or a fleur-de-lis gu. betw. 2 castles ppr. Dr. Lyon Playfair M.P. for Edinburgh 1868. Same arms.

Playse or Plaiz. Add: Sire Richard de Place. *O.Y.* Sir John Place. *S.* Sir de Plaiz, Norfolk, temp. Edw. j. *V.* The lion pass. guard. Sir Giles Plays. *N.*

Playter or Playtor. Add: *V.*

Pleigh (Exeter 1335). Per pale az. and gu. a lion pass. arg. crowned or. *Colby.*

Plesley (At Church at Thribergh, co. York, impaled by Reresby). Gu. on a chev. betw. three 3-foils slipped arg. as many ogresses. *Hunter ij. 43.*

Plessetts. Arg. a chev. gu. betw. 3 mullets sa. *V.*

Plessey or Plessis (Co. Oxford). Add: Sir John de Plessis. *B.Y.* Sir Hugh Plessey. *E.V.* Sire Hugh de Plessis. *J.*

Plescy. Arg. a bend az. betw. 6 annulets gu. Sir Edmond de Plesey. *L.* and *L. Harl. MS. 6137.*

Pley. Or on a bend wavy az. 3 anchors of the field. *Hoare j. 35.*

Plimsoll (Sheffield, M.P. for Derby 1868). Per pale arg. and gu. a lion ramp. counterchanged.

Plokenet or Plunkenet. Erm. a bend engr. gu. Sire Aleyn Plokenet. *D.N.* Adam Plunkenet. *Y.* The bend shewn as fusils conjoined. *E.G.*

Plompton (Co. Lancaster). Add: *V.*

Plonket. Arg. a bend gu. cotised indented sa. Add: Aleyn Plonket. *V.*

Plumbe (Co. Kent, Marston, co. Leicester and co. Norfolk). Add: *C.C.1619.*

Plumme (Essex). Erm. a bend vair betw. 2 cotises vert. *Morant's Essex ij. 300.*

Plumer (Quartered by Plumer-Ward of Gilston, co. Herts.). Per chev. flory counterflory arg. and gu. 3 martlets counterchanged a pile issuant from the centre point of the second.

Plumleigh or Plumley (Dartmouth, co. Devon). Add: *V.D. 1620.*

Plummer (Canterbury, Kent) . . . a chev. . . . betw. 3 griffins heads . . . *Robson.*

Plumptre (Cos. Nottingham and Kent). Add: *V.N.p. 190.*

Pochen or Poching (Barklay, co. Leicester). Add: *C.C. 1619. V.**

Pochin (Barkby Hall, co. Leicester). Add: *V.**

Poincey (Chester). Arg. a canton gu. *Harl. MS. 1078. fo. 24.*

Pointington or Pontington (Pennycott, co. Devon). Add: *V.* and *V.D. 1620.*

Poldegrew. Gu. a lion ramp. guard. or collared arg. depressed by a bend az. Add: *V.*

Pole (Colcomb, co. Devon 1620). Az. demy of fleurs-de-lis and a lion ramp. arg. *V.D.*

Pole. Or a lion ramp. gu. Le Sire de la Pole. *N.* William Poole. *Y.*

Poley. Arg. on a bend gu. 3 crosses formy or. Sir Rauff Poley. *S.*

Polhill (Burwash, Sussex 1634). Arg. on a bend gu. 3 crosses crosslet gu.

Pollard (Trelligh, co. Cornwall; and co. Devon . . . Oxford and Worcester). Add: Pollard Newsham Courtney, co. Oxford. *V.O.*

Pollard (Treleigh, Redruth, co. Cornwall). Arg. a chev. betw. 3 escallops gu. *Lysons.*

Pollard (Co. Devon. Baronetcy 1627). Arg. a chev. gu. betw. 3 mullets sa.

Pollard. Arg. a chev. betw. 3 mullets sa. *V.*

Pollard. Arg. a chev. az. betw. 3 escallops gu. Crest: A stag trippant arg. Add: *V.*

Pollexfen (Kitley, co. Devon). Add: *W.*

Polshed. . . . on a chief az. a 'correct to read "pelican"' insert—"rising", betw. . . . Add: In Thames Ditton Church, Surrey. Richard Polshid or Palshed, Southampton. *V.*

Poltimore. Or a lion ramp. vert. Sir Richard de Poltimore. *V.*

Pomerai (Berle Pomerai, co. Devon). . . . Add: *Lysons.*

Pomeray or Pomeroy. Or a lion ramp. gu. a bordure engr. sa. Sir John Pomeray. *S.* Henry de la Pomeroys. *Y.*

Pomfret. Arg. three cocks sa. armed or. Add: *V.*

Pomys. Barry of 6 arg. and az. a bordure gu. *V.*

Ponpons. Add: *V.*

Ponseyn. Quarterly arg. and az. in the first quarter a lion pass. gu. Sir William Ponseyn. *N.V.* The lion ramp. gu. Sir Wm. Ponseyn, co. Hereford. *V.*

Ponthieu. Add: *Z. 129.*

Pontrel. Or on a bend az. 3 fleurs-de-lis arg. Sire Robert Pontrel. *N.V.*

Poole (Anstey, co. Notts.). Az. a lion ramp. arg. betw. 8 fleurs-de-lis or. *V.N. 1564.*

Poole (Mayfield, co. York). Same arms.

Poole or Pooley (Co. Chester). Add: Sir Lewis de la Poole. temp. Edw. iij. *V.*

Poole. Sir Walter de la Poole. Az. 2 bars wavy or. *Q.*

Poole. Insert—Radburie, co. Derby. Gu. a chev. betw. 3 crescents arg. Add: *V.*

Poole. Arg. a chev. betw. 3 crescents purple. Raufe Poole. *V.*

Poole (Norfolk). Per pale or and az. 2 bars wavy counterchanged. *Cady.*

Poole (Bagley, co. York). Gu. a lion ramp. arg. betw. 7 fleurs-de-lis or quartering arg. a chev. sa. betw. 3 stags heads erased gu. *F.Y.*

Poore (Bishop of Chichester 1215–17, then of Salisbury). . . . on 2 bars . . . 6 crosses patty. *Ashmole MS. 833. fo. 419.*

Pope. Az. a chev. engr. betw. 3 lions heads erased arg. *V.*

Pope. Arg. 2 chevs. gu. on a canton of the last an escallop or. *Collinson Somerset ij. 436.*

Pope. Or 2 chevs. gu. on a canton sa. a mullet arg. *V.*

Pope. Arg. 2 chevs gu. within a bordure or on a quarter of the second an escallop gold. Wm. Pope. *V.*

Pope (Wilcote, Wroxton and Dedington, co. Oxford and Tittenhanger, co. Herts.). Add: Alexander Pope, the Poet.

Pope. Arg. an eagle displ. double headed and in base 3 escallops 2 and 1. or. William Pope. *V.*

Pope. . . . a chev. . . . betw. in chief 2 roses . . . and in base a talbot . . . *Collinson Somerset iij. 404.* John Pope alias Talbot.

Pope (Hendall, Sussex). Or 2 chevs. gu. on a canton of the last a mullet of the first.

Pope (London 1568, Draper to Queen Elizabeth). Arg. 3 popinjays vert. winged or within a bordure engr. az. bezanty: quartering or 3 buckles az. *C.L.*

Popelay (Morehoupe, co. York 1585). Arg. on a bend betw. 2 cotises sa. 3 eagles displ. of the first: quartering arg. on a fess betw. 3 crosses patty gu. a lion pass. or for Stayhton. *F.Y.*

Popkin (Yns-Tawe). Or a stag trippant gu. attired and unguled sa. a bordure engr. of the second. *Nicholas.*

Popler (Cos. Wilts. and York). Add: Poppeler. *V.*

Poppleham. Sa. 3 shovellers in pale arg. *V.*

Popplesham. Sa. 3 seamews arg. *V.**

Poplesham. Sa. a chev. erm. betw. 3 shovellers arg. *V.*

Popley (Bristol, granted 24. Charles II). Insert—by Sir Edw. Walker . . .

Popley (Ketton, co. Rutland). Arg. a bend sa. *C.R.*

Porchester. Or 8 barrulets gu. Sir . . . de Porchester. *R.*

Pors. Add: *V.** Sir James de Pors, temp. Edw. j. *V.*

Port (Poole, co. Dorset). . . . Add: *Hoare j. 242.*

Porter (Co. Cornwall). Sa. 3 church bells and a canton arg. *V.C. p. 306.*

Porter (Lancaster). Sa. 3 bells arg. a canton or. *V.L. 1664.*

Porter (Cos. Lincoln and Kent). Add: *V.*

Porter. Arg. on the trunk of a tree raguly vert. an eagles wings expanded gu. Add: William Porter. *V.*

Porter (Sir John Porter). Sa. 3 broad axes arg. *Harl. MS. 1458.*

Porter (Alfarthing, co. Surrey . . .). Add: *V.*

Portington (Cos. Lincoln and York). Insert— 1666. Add: *Dugdale p. 168.*

Portington (Barnby-Dun, co. York). Gu. on a bend arg. three martlets sa. Crest: . . . Add: 3 cornish choughs. *F.Y.*

Portington. Gu. on a bend or 3 mullets sa. *V.*

Portington (Malton, co. York 1665). Gu. on a bend arg. betw. 2 cotises or 3 martlets sa. *Dugdale. p. 120.*

Portwell. Sa. a chev. betw. 3 estoiles arg. *Nash.*

Pote. Add: *V.D. 1620.*

Pottinger. Per bend sa. and arg. 4 lozenges in bend betw. 6 fleurs-de-lis all counterchanged.

Potts (Mannington, co. Norfolk). Baronetcy 1641. Or 2 bars az. overall a bend or. *Guillim.*

Pouley (Co. Essex). Add: *V.**

Pount or Point. Add: *V.**

Poynt. Az. a covered bridge of 3 arches throughout arg. James Poynt. *V.*

Pourdon (Insert—co. Derby). Erm. a chev. sa. on a chief of the last a leopards face or. Add: *V.*

Pourton or Powrton. Sa. a greyhound ramp. within a bordure engr. arg. *V.V.**

Povey (temp. Charles ii . . .). Add: Thomas Povey, Master of the Requests.

Povey (London: granted Nov. 1614). Insert—by Camden to Justinian Povey of London, Audit-General to Queen Anne. *Guillim.*

Powe (Ewhurst, Surrey). Baronetcy 1661. Gu. a lion ramp. reguard. or: quartering arg. 3 boars heads couped sa. *Guillim.*

Powell. Arg. 2 bars sa. 6 martlets 3. 2. and 1. gu. Sir William Powell. *V.*

Powell (Sir John Powell . . . temp. William iii . . .). Add: *Atkyns.*

Powell (Sandford, co. Oxon 1667). Or a lion ramp. sa. debruised by a fess engr. gu. *Guillim.*

Powell. Paly or and az. on a bend gu. 3 mullets arg. Sire Ovel Powiel. *O.*

Powell (Quartered by Baskerville). Or on a chev. gu. betw. 3 lions gambs erect of the second as many crosses patty of the first.

Power (Edermine, co. Wexford, bart. . . .). Add: Power (Enniscorthy, co. Wexford, Baronetcy 1841 . . .). Same arms.

Power (Co. Devon). Az. a bend betw. 2 cotises indented or. *V.*

Powkeswell. Add: *V.V.**

Powna (Co. Cornwall). Add: *Lysons.*

Pownall (Granted to the descendants of the late Thomas Pownall Esq. of the Parish of St. Paul, Covent Garden, London. Add: The arms within the chief were borne by the Pownall's of Wrexham, co. Salop in 1643 until 1819 when the chief was added in memory of John Fish of Kempton Park, Middlesex.

Powtrell or Poundrell (Co. Derby). Or—delete— (another, arg.). Add: Sir Robert Powtrell. *V.Y.*

Poyer. Az. a bend betw. 2 cotises indented or.

Poyle (Castlezance, co. Cornwall). Add: *V.C. p. 306.*

Poynings (Baron Poynings . . .). Add: Lucas Poynings. *A. Harl. MS. 6137. A.* Sir Michael Poynings. *L.V.N.* Nicolas Poynings. *Q.* Sire de Poynings. *S.* And quartering: gu. 3 lions pass. in pale arg. a bendlet az. *T.*

Poynings (Baron St. John of Basing). . . . Add: *Z. 225.*

Poynings. Barry of 6 or and vert. a baston compony arg. and gu. Sir Christopher (aliter Thomas) Poynings. *R.*

Poynings. Barry of 6 or and vert. a baston gu. Sir John Poynings. *R.Y.* Thomas Poynings. *Y.*

Poynings. Barry of 6 or and vert. on a bend gu. three mullets of the first. Sir Thomas Poynings, Essex. temp. Edw. j. *V.* But the mullets arg. Sir Thomas Poninge. *N.*

Poyntz or Poyns. Barry or and gu. Sir Hugh Poyns. *H.* Sir Nicholas de Poyns. *N.*

Pragell (Kent). . . . a castle triple towered betw. 2 portcullisses . . . on a chief . . . a hand betw. 2 stirrups. *Robson.*

Prall. Sa. a stag springing or overall a fess counter-embattled of the last.

Prale or Prall. Add: *V.*

Prannell or Pranel (Martin Wothy, co. Hants. and London). . . . Add: Henry Prannell, Alderman of London 1584. *V.W.*

Pratt (Ryston Hall, co. Norfolk . . .). Add: *L.N. 1648.*

Pratt (Co. Norfolk). Add: Pratt (Thurloxton). Same arms. *Collinson Somerset j. 77.* Pratt (Coleshall, co. Berks. Baronetcy 1641). Same arms.

Pratt (Ryston, Norfolk). Arg. on a chev. sa. betw. 3 ogresses the 2 in chief charged with a bird of the first and that in the base with an escallop . . . as many mascles or. *V.*

Prayers. Lozengy . . . and . . . a bend raguly . . . Seal of John de Prayers temp. Edw. iij. *Archaeologia. xxix. 406.*

Predius. See Prideoux.

Predieux. Per pale arg. and gu. 3 towers counterchanged. *V.*

Prendergast (Ireland). Gu. a bend cotised arg.

Prenne. Sa. a lion ramp. arg. within an orle of bezants. Add: *V.**

Prentisse. Add: *V.** John Prentysse. *V.*

Prerne. Quarterly sa. and arg. in the first quarter a lion pass. guard. of the second crowned or. Sir Edward Prerne. *V.*

Prescot (Prescot, co. Devon . . .). Add: *V.*

Prescott. Arg. on a chev. sa. 3 owls of the first. *V.*

Prescott. Erm. a chev. gu. on a chief or two leopards heads of the second.

Prescott (Theobald's Park, co. Hert.). . Add: Prescott (Thoby, co. Essex). Same arms, a mullet for diff. *V.E. 1634.*

Prescott (London and cos. Lancaster and York 1627). . . . Add: Granted by Camden 1610.

Presmarch. Az. 3 bendlets or on a chief of the first 2 palets betw. so many squires based as the second an escutcheon arg. Sir Reinold Presmarch. *I. Harl. MS. 6589.*

Preston. . . . Westmorland and co. Lancaster . . . Add: *V.**

Preston (Sir Richard Preston, Westmorland). Erm. 2 bars gu. on a canton of the second a 5-foil or. *V.*

Preston (Holker, co. Lancaster 1613 and 1664) . . . Add: They quartered Benson. *V.L.*

Preston ( ). Gu. 2 bars fusilly arg. *V.*

Preston. Gu. crusilly and a bend or. Sir William de Preston. *A. Harl. MS. 6137. I.* Gu. a bend betw. 6 crosses crosslet or. Sir William Preston. *I. Harl. MS. 6580.* Piers de Preston joust Wendeslawe. *P.*

Preston. Arg. a chev. ermines betw. 3 bugle horns sa. on a chief gu. 3 crescents or. *Robson.*

Prestwich (Holme, co. Lancaster, bart.). Gu.— delete—(Another, vert) . . .

Prestwich (Holme, co. Lancaster). Erm. on a chev. gu. a bezant betw. two leopards faces or. . . . Add: *Harl. MS. 6159. fo. 62.*

Prestwold (Co. Leicester) – delete – 'Sa., (another'; ...az.). Add: *V*.

Prestwold (Co. Leicester). Sa. a chev. or fretty gu. betw. 3 garbs arg. *V*. Hugh de Prestwold. *Y*.

Prestwood (Boterford, in North Huish, co. Devon). . . . Add: Exeter and Totnes, co. Devon. *V.D. 1620*.

Prestwood (Co. Stafford. temp. Henry iv). Add: *Shaw*.

Prettyman (Co. Norfolk and Bawton, co. Suffolk) ... Add: Prettyman (Barnard Castle, Durham). Same arms. *Robson*.

Preuze. Sa. three lions ramp. arg. betw. 9 crosses crosslet or. Add: *V*.

Preuze. Sa. crusilly or 3 lions ramp. arg. Sire William le Preuze. *N*. Sir William Preuz, Cornwall. temp. Edw. iij. *V*.

Preuze. Sa. 3 lions ramp. arg. betw. 9 crosses crosslet or. *V*.*

Price (Charles Price, Lord Mayor of London 1803). Gu. a lion ramp. arg.

Price (The Priory and Fonmon, co. Brecknock). Add: *V*.

Price (Green-Price, Norton Manor, co. Radnor, bart.). Insert—1874. Add: *Debrett*.

Price (Robert Price, one of the Barons of the Exchequer. 1702). Gu. a lion ramp. arg. quartering: 2nd. arg. a rose gu. 3rd arg. a griffin segreant gu. 4th gu. a chev. erm. betw. 3 human heads 5th vert. a hind trippant arg. 6th arg. two trefoils slipped and a chief sa. *Guillim*.

Price (Co. Gloucester. M.P. for Tewkesbury 1868). Erm. a lion pass. guard arg. holding in its dexter paw a caduceus on a chief sa. a cock betw. 2 spear heads. *Debrett*.

Prichard (Sheriff of Monmouthshire temp. Eliz.). Sa. a lion ramp. arg. *Fuller*.

Prichet. Bishop of Gloucester 1672. Erm. a lion ramp. sa. armed and langued gu. within a bordure az.

Prideaux (Orcharton, co. Devon). Add: Prideaux, Sir Thomas Predias. *S*. Recorder of Exeter 1648: quartering az. a roach in pale arg. *Colby*.

Prideaux (Cornwall). Arg. a chev. betw. 3 eagles legs erased gu. *Berry*.

Priestley (Whitewindows, Sowerby, co. York). . . . Add: Prestley (London, granted by Camden 1619).

Pritchard (Ireland). Sa. a chev. betw. three fleurs-de-lis arg. *Robson*.

Pritchard. Same arms with a bordure sa. Crest: a dexter arm ppr. holding a battle-axe handle gu. Add: Sir William Pritchard, London 1672. Same arms. *L.C.*

Probert. Margin reads vide Pritchard.

Probline. Per bend arg. and vert. *Randle Holme*.

Procter. Az. a lion ramp. arg. over all on a fess or 3 torteaux.

Prockter. Arg. 3 water bougets gu. *Eliz. Roll xxxvij*.

Proctor. Arg. a chev. gu. betw. 9 crosses crosslet sa. *Collinson Somerset ij. 345*.

Progers or Ap Roger. Add: William John ap Roger, Sheriff of Monmouthshire. temp. Eliz. *Fuller*.

Prouze (London 1568). Arg. 3 lions ramp. sa.

Prouze. Ermines 3 lions ramp. arg. *V*.* Richard Prouze (Exeter, granted by Cooke). *W*. Prouze, Mayor of Exeter, 1620. *V.D.*

Proude. Or a chev. barry gu. and sa. Lewis Proude at the Charter House, 1619. *Guillim*.

Proude. Insert—or Prude (Egston, co. Kent).

Prous or Prowze (Gidley Castle, co. Devon . . .). Add: *V*.

Prow (Co. Essex). Add: William Prowe. *Harl. MS. 1432*.

Prowse (Oldcliffe, co. Somerset). Add: *V.S.*

Prowse (Mayor of Exeter 1608). Ermines 3 lions ramp. arg. *Colby*.

Pryce. Arg. a chev. betw. 3 spear heads sa.—insert—'*V*', another, sa. . . .

Prye (Horwell, co. Devon). Add: *V.D.*

Pryse (Gogerddan, co. Cardigan). Insert—Baronetcy 1641 and 1866.

Pstrelle. Delete—:margin, substitute Strglley.

Puckering (Weston, co. Hertford). Insert—Baronetcy 1612. Ext. Add: Sir John Puckering, Keeper of the Great Seal of England 1593. *Dug. O.J.* Sir Thomas Puckering, co. Warwick. *W*.

Puckering (Flamborough, co. York). confirmed —insert—by Flower . . .

Pudsey (Bolton near Richmond, York). Add: Sir Richard Pudsey. *V*.

Pudsey (Lawfield, co. York 1665). Add: *Dugdale p. 29*.

Pudsey (Arnforth, co. York 1584). Vert. a chev. betw. 3 mullets pierced or: quartering arg. a fess engr. betw. 6 crosses crosslet sa.: overall a † on a † for diff. *F.Y.*

Pudsey or Puddesey (Barford, co. York). Add: *Eliz. Roll. xxviij*.

Pulham. Sa. a demi-lion ramp. arg. *V*.

Pullein (Killinghall, Carleton Hall and Crake Hall, co. York). . . . Add: *V*.

Pullesburgh. Per fess sa. and gu. an eagle displ. arg. *V*.

Pulley (Leigh, co. Essex). Insert—1634 . . . Add: *V.E.*

Pulleyn (Scotton, co. York). Add: *V*. Sire Rauf Pulleyn.

Pulleyn (Co. York). Az. on a bend or betw. 6 lozenges arg. each charged with a martlet sa. 3 escalⁿps sa. *Eliz. Roll. xxvij*.

Pullison (Lord Mayor of London 1584). Per pale arg. and sa. 3 lions ramp. counterchanged. *Harl. MS. 1349*.

Punchardon. . . . on a bend . . . 3 roundles . . . Richard Punchardon 1441. **Seal.**

Purcell (Ouneslow, co. Salop: granted April 1597). Barry—insert—'wavy or' nebulee . . . Add: *V*.

Purchas (Sir William Purchas, London). Or a lion ramp. sa. over all on a fess az. 3 bezants. *V*.

Purshall. Arg. 2 bars wavy gu. on a bend sa. 3 purses or. *Nash*.

Putland. Az. on a bend wavy or betw. 2 mullets of 6 points pierced arg. 3 rudders sa. **Book Plate.**

Puttenham or Putnam (Co. Beds. and Penn, co. Bucks). Add: *V.V.*

Pykin. Arg. a chev. betw. 3 talbots pass. gu. *V.V.*

Pybus (Thirsk, co. York). Paly of 6 or and gu. a bend vair.

Pye (The Mynde, co. Hereford . . .). Add: Sir Walter Pye. Hereford. *Syl. Morgan*.

Pye or Pyes. Arg. a chev. gu. betw. in chief a bird—query—a magpie ppr. and in base a bar of 3 lozenges conjoined. *Harl. MS. 1404. fo. 110*.

Pye (Hone, co. Derby, bart.). Insert—1604. . .

Pyemont (Lofthouse, co. York). Add: *Foster*.

Pyke. . . . 3 lions ramp. . . . over a . . . a bend of lozenges. Nicholas Pyk. **Seal.**

Pykey (Bramton, co. Devon). Per pale arg. and gu. on a chev. betw. three 3-foils slipped a fish naiant counterchanged. *V*.

Pykenham. Az. a lion ramp. or within a bordure engr. gu. *V.V.*

Pyland. Arg. a chev. gu. betw. 3 garbs vert. Add: *V*.

Pymes or Pynes (Cornwall). Gu. a chev. erm. betw. 3 pine cones slipped pendent or. *V*.

Pyne. Gu. a chev. betw. 3 pine trees eradicated or. *V.**

Pyne or Pine (Ham, co. Cornwall and East Downe, co. Devon). Add: *V.D. 1620.*

Pyne (Co. Cornwall). Arg. a bend betw. six mullets gu. *V.*

Pynk. Erm. two bendlets gu. Add: *Nash.*

Pynsent (Ob. 1668). Gu. a chev. engr. betw. three estoiles arg. In Croydon Church, Surrey.

Pynyll. Insert—co. Devon. Add: *W.*

Pyrley. Per pale arg. and or over all a lion ramp. sa. Add: *V.*

Pyrley. Per pale arg. and gu. a lion pass. counterchanged. *V.*

Pyrton (Co. Essex). Add: *V.E. 1558.*

Pyty. Sa. a chev. betw. 3 shovellers arg. *V.*

Pyvill. Az. an eagle displ. double-headed per pale or and arg. holding in each claw a baston sloped palewise of the opposite metals. *V.*

Q

QUADRING. Arg. a chev. betw. 3 hares—insert— 'courant' sa. *V.V.**

Quaplade. Barry of 6 or and az. a bend gu. *V.** This coat is quartered by Bacon.

Quarm (Nancor, co. Cornwall . . .). Add: *V.C.*

Quarton. Sa. a chev. betw. 3 peacocks (another, griffins) heads erased arg. Add: *V.*

Querton (Westmorland). Az. a bend or. within a bordure arg. *V.*

Quick (quartered by Molton). Arg. a bend wavy betw. 2 badgers—query—moles statant arg. *Harl. MS. 1080. fo. 164b.*

Quinton or Quintin. Insert—Northampton.

Quintridge. Add: Sir Thomas Quitrige. *V.*

Quytlawe. See Whitelaw or Wheateley.

Quithford of that Ilk. Arg. a bend sa. in the sinister chief a garb gu. *Guillim.*

Quixley. Sa. on 3 greyhounds pass. arg. collared compony or and of the first an escallop at the shoulder of each sa. *Y.*

R

RABETT (Dunwich and Bramfield Hall, co. Suffolk). Add: *A.A.*

Raby or Rabey. † error for Raley.

Radcliffe (Radcliffe Tower, co. Lancaster . . .). Add: Sir John Radcliffe de la Tour, co. Lancaster. *V.* Sir William Radcliffe. Sir Richard Radcliffe Smelherle. *V.* And with a fleur-de-lis gu. for diff. William fitz William Radcliffe 1350. *V.* And with a label gu. Sir John Radcliffe Wodeshall. *V.*

Radcliffe (Tunstall, co. York). Arg. a bend engr. sa. a mullet arg. for diff. quartering: arg. a cross moline pierced sa. *F.Y.*

Radcliffe (Rudding Park, co. York). Arg. a bend engr. sa. a crescent on the bend for diff: *Foster.*

Radcliffe (Dr Samuel Radcliffe of Oxford ob. 1648). Arg. a bend engr. sa. in the sinister chief a mullet of the second. *Guillim.*

Radcliffe (Leigh, co. Lancaster 1664). Add: *V.L.*

Radcliffe. Arg. 2 bendlets engr. sa. a fess gu. John Radclif, Chedyrton. *V.*

Radcliffe. Arg. a bend engr. sa. in the sinister chief an escallop gu. Sir Richard Radcliffe. *V.*

Radcliffe (Chappell, co. Essex). Same arms. *V.E. 1612.*

Radclyffe (Todmorden, co. Lancaster). . . . a fleur-de-lis gu.—insert—? sa. Add: *V.* Quartering: Vert. a chev. betw. 3 garbs arg. *V.L. 1664.*

Raen. Thomas ap Madock ap Raen. Sa. a chev. or betw. 3 lures arg. stringed of the second. *V.*

Ragane. Arg. on a chev. sa. 3 stags heads couped or. John Ragane. *X.*

Ragon (Co. Kent). Add: *V.*

Raikes (Walthamstow, co. Essex and London). Add: Raikes (Mold, co. Flint.), M.P. for Chester 1868. Same arms. Quartering: arg. a chev. az. betw. 3 griffins gu. for Whittington. *Debrett.*

Rainwell (Lord Mayor of London 1426). . . . a chev. betw. 3 dolphins embowed. . . . *Moule. p. 31.*

Rakelworthe. Add: Rakelworde. Az. 3 eagles displ. or. Sir Walter de Rakelword.

Raleigh (Raleigh, co. Devon). . . . Add: Henri de Raley. *F.A.E. Lysons.* Gu. crusilly arg. a bend vair. John Raley. *Y.* Monsire de Raley in 1562. *Y.*

Raleigh. Gu. a bend engr. arg. Sir Simon de Ralee. *N.* Sir Simon de Rallee, Cornwall. *V.*

Raleigh (Sir Walter Raleigh . . .). Add: *V.**

Raleigh (Cornwall). Add: Sir John Ralegh *V.*

Raley (Co. Warwick). . . . .—delete—(another, tinctures reversed). Add: Henry de Raley. *F.A.E.*

Ralston (that Ilk, co. Renfrew). Add: John de Ralstone, Lord High Treasurer, Bishop of Dunkeld 1448–52.

Ramesbury. Arg. a chev. betw. 3 martlets sa. *V.*

Rampston. Add: Sir Thomas Rameston. *S.* or Rempston K.G. temp. Hen. iv.

Ramrige. Add: *V.*V.* Thomas Ramrege Abbot of St. Albans, the eagle armed of the first. *U.*

Ramsbery or Ramsbury. Add: *V.*

Ramsden (Byrom, co. York bart.). Insert—1680. . . . as many rams heads couped—underlined—margin, 'erased'. Add: Ramsden (Langley, co. York confirmed by Flower, Norroy 1575). Same arms. *Guillim.*

Ramsey (Hitcham, co. Buckingham . . .). Add: *V.*

Ramsey (Eatonbridge, co. Kent and London . . .). Add: *C.L.*

Ramsey. Insert—Kent. Az. a chev. betw. three rams or. *V.*W.*

Ramsey. Monastery of (Co. Kent). Insert—? Huntingdon, Add: *Tanner.*

Ramstone. Add: *V.N. 188.*

Randall (Kentesbury, co. Devon 1583 . . .). Add: confirmed 1 July 1588, when the lions have tails. *Harl. MS. 1359. fo. 13.*

Rande. Gu. three chevs. arg. a bordure engr. sa. Add: *Y.*

Randes (Radwell, co. Bedford). Add: *V.*

Randes (Insert—Holbeach, co. Lincoln—insert —confirmed by Camden . . .). Add: *W.*

Randolphe. Add: *V.V.**

Rasbotham (Little Hulton, co. Lancaster, High Sheriff in 1769). Arg. a chev. az. betw. 3 antelopes springing ppr. Crest: an antelope couchant ppr. *Baines Lancashire iij. 13.*

Rastricke (Co. York). Arg. a chev. betw. 3 roses gu. seeded or.

Ratcliff. Arg. on a bend engr. sa. a mullet of the field in the sinister chief a crescent of the second. Christopher Ratcliffe of Newton Hansett. *Eliz. Roll. xix.*

Ratcliff (Cokerton). Arg. on a bend engr. sa. an escallop of the first. *Eliz. Roll xviij.*

Ratcliffe (Mowgrave, co. York). Add: Ratcliffe (Chaderton, co. Lancaster. Same arms. *C.W.*

Ratcliff. Gu. bezanty a lion ramp. arg. Maltham Ratcliff. *Y.*

Ratcliffe. Arg. 2 bendlets engr. sa. a label of 3 gu. John Ratcliffe. *Dug. O.J.*

Ratendeen or Ratenden. Add: *V.** Sir John Ratenden. *N.*

Ratford. Per bend sa. and arg. a lion ramp. counterchanged Sir Henry Ratford *V.*

Ratling (Ratling Place, Kent). Sa. a lion ramp. within an orle of tilting spears or. *Robson.*

Raufe. Per bend fracted or and gu. 2 birds in bend sinister counterchanged. *V.*

Raughton (Co. York). Add: *Harl. MS. 1394. fo. 171.*

Raven. Or a raven sa. standing upon a torteaux. *V.* Raven of London, Counsel at Law. *Harl. MS. 1406. fo. 145.*

Raven (Creting St. Mary's, co. Suffolk). Add: Raven of Elsworth. Same arms. *Randle Holme.*

Raven. Or a raven rising ppr. confirmed by Segar to Dr. John Raven, Sworn Physician to King Charles i. He was the son of John Raven, Richmond Herald. *Guillim.*

Ravenhill. Erm. 3 mounts vert. on each a raven sa.

Ravenscroft (Co. Chester, Bretton, co. Flint, co. Lancaster and Horsham, co. Sussex). Add: *V.**

Rathenale. Sa. a chev. betw. 3 foxes heads erased arg. *V.*

Ravensthorpe. Add: *V.*

Ravis. Add: *V.*

Rawdon (Earl of Moira). . . .—correct—'Az.' to read 'Arg.' a fess betw. 3 pheons sa. . . . and 'sheath' to read 'sheaf' of arrows. . . .

Rawles (Fifehide Neville). Insert—co. Dorset. Add: *Hutchins j. 269.*

Rawlings (Saunders Hill, co. Cornwall and co. Hertford). (Padstow, co. Cornwall). (In Morant's hand against these two on p. 841 B.G.A.—"no right").

Rawson (Frystone and Shipley, co. York) Add: *Dugdale 1666. p. 258.*

Rawson (Prior of Kilmancham Priory, Ireland, and Knight of the Order of St. John of Jerusalem). Per fesse sa. and az. a castle with 4 towers arg. Quartering or on a chev. vert. 3 ravens heads erased arg. over both coats, on a chev. gu. a cross arg. *Guillim.*

Rawson (Prior of Kilmainham, Ireland and Knight of the Order of St. John of Jerusalem). Quarterly . . . over—delete—'all' and—insert—'both coats'. Add: *Guillim.*

Rawson. Sa. a castellated portal betw. 2 towers arg. standing on a base barry wavy arg. and az. Richard Rawson, Alderman of London 1746. *W.*

Rawson. Sa. a gateway betw. 2 towers arg. standing on a base barry of 4 arg. and az. Richard Rawson, Alderman of London 1748. *W.*

Rawson (Pickborne, co. York). Add: *Dugdale 1665.*

Rawson. Insert—(Castleford, co. York). Gu. a four-square castle. . . . Add: *V.*

Rawstorne (Penwortham). Insert—and Hutton, . . . Add: *F.L.*

Raygate (Howke,   ). Arg. a bend engr. az. *Y.*

Rayhall (Co. Worcester) Arg. 2 bendlets indented gu. and vert. *Nash.*

Rayle. Arg. 6 lions ramp. gu. *V.*

Rayle. Sa. 6 lions ramp. arg. *V.**

Raymond (Exmouth, co. Devon). . . . betw. two ducks—underlined—margin, read 'swans'. Add: *W.*

Raymond (London, granted 11 April 1687). Add: Sir Jonathan Raymond, Alderman of London. Knighted 1679. *L.N.*

Raymond. Insert—'Essex'. Sa. a chev. betw. 3 eagles displ. . . . Add: *W. V.E. 1612.*

Raymond (Belchamp Hall, co. Essex). . . . on a chief of the second three martlets. . . . Add: *V.E. 1634.*

Raynes (Apleton-in-the-Street). Co. York . . . Add: *Dugdale p. 368.* 3 cranes heads or—delete, read 'arg'.

Raynsford (Bradfield, co. Essex). Add: Sir John Raynsford, Essex. *W.*

Read (Justice of King's Bench 1496 . . . Add: *V.** Sir Robert Reade, co. Lincoln. *V.*

Read (Rougham, Norfolk). Az. on a bend or 3 shovellers sa. *Robson.*

Read (Co. Galway). Gu. a chev. betw. 2 fleurs-de-lis in chief and in base an eagle displ. or.

Read (London; granted 1599). Insert—by Camden.

Reade (Close, co. Northumberland). Insert—1615.

Reade (Cos. Oxford and Somerset). Add: *V.*

Reading. Arg. a chev. betw. 3 bucks heads couped sa. James Reading 1694. In St. Mary's Newington Butts, Surrey.

Reason or Rason (   ). Gu. a lion ramp. or betw. 4 crosses patty vair. the crosses patonce *V.V.**

Reaston-Rodes (Barlborough Hall, co. Derby). Add: *Robson.*

Rebow (Colchester, co. Essex). Granted—insert—by Dugdale . . . Add: Rebow (Essex). Same arms. With a canton or. *Berry.*

Rece (Robert Rece Servd ad arma Regis Hen. viij. Az. a chev. erm. betw. 3 spear heads arg. *Cady.*

Rechewell. Gu. a bend lozengy and a chief arg. in the sinister chief a martlet arg. *V.** Sir John Rechewell *V.*

Red. Add: Sir Pont Red. *V.*

Rede. Gu. a bend fusilly erm. *V.** Nicolas Rede. *V.*

Rede (Ashmans, co. Suffolk). . . . torteaux and hurts—insert—sometimes ogresses.

Redesham. Chequy arg. and gu. Sir Walter de Redesham. *D.*

Redeswell. Arg. a chev. betw. 3 hinds heads couped gu. . . . Add: *V.*

Redham. Gu. an inescutcheon . . . Add: William de Redham. *V.*

Redham. Gu. a chev. engr. betw. 3 reed sheaves arg. Add: *V.*

Redhead. Sa. a bend engr. or betw. . . . Add: Redhead of Sheriff Hutton, co. York. The canton granted in 1598 by Dethick; for services at Bergen Opzoom.

Redhigh. Arg. a chev. sa. betw. 3 cocks heads erased gu. Hugh Redhigh. *V.*

Redland. Or a chev. gu. betw. in chief 2 crosses and in base a saltire sa. a chief az. *Randle Holme.*

Redley or Redleigh. Gu. a chev. betw. three birds. Arg. Add: Hugh Redley. *V.*

Redley. Gu. a chev. betw. 3 goshawks arg. Hugh Redley. *V.*

Redman. (Correct 'T' to read Fulford, co. York). Add: *V.* Quartering, sa. a chev. betw. 3 cross crosslets arg. for Southworth. *F.Y.* Sire Mayes Redman. *S.* without the quartering.

Redmere or Redmore. Delete—(another six). Add: *V.**

Redmore. Sa. a bend arg. betw. 6 fleurs-de-lis or. *V.*

Redness. Sa. a chev. betw. three leopards heads erased arg. Sir William de Redness. *Y.*

Redyke. Or a chev. betw. 3 crosses crosslet fitchy gu. Hugh Redyke, co. Lincoln. *V.*

Reed (M.P. for Hackney 1868). Az. on a bend wavy or within a bordure engr. arg. charged with torteaux 3 shovellers. . . . *Debrett.*

Reed (Mayor of Newcastle 1716). Or a chev. betw. 3 garbs gu. *Carr. MS.*

Reed (Recorder of Bridgewater 1862). Or a chev. gu. betw. 3 boars heads erased ppr. *Debrett.*

Reedham (Sheriff of Norfolk). 1172. Gu. a chev. engr. arg. betw. 3 reed sheaves or. *Dashwood.*

Rees. Az. 2 chevs. or a canton of the last. Add: *V.**

Reeve (Thwayte, co. Suffolk). Insert—Baronetcy 1662 ext.

Regelley. Arg. on a chev. sa. 3 mullets of the first *V.** the mullets pierced. *V.*

Regnold. Add: Robert Regnold (East Barholth, Suffolk). *V.*

Reid (Edinburgh). Arg. an eagle displ. sa. beaked and membered gu. on the breast an escu. az. charged with 3 flames of fire ppr. *Robson.*

Reid (Belfast, Ireland). Az. on a bend wavy arg. within a bordure engr. of the second pelletty 3 birds sa. a sinister quarter arg. divided by a line in pale the dexter side charged with 2 staves couped and reguly in saltire gu. enfiled with a Saxon coronet gold in the sinister a man ppr. habited or in the right hand a sword held over his head in the left a man's head couped ppr. *Robson.*

Remeghers. Az. billetty and a bend or. *V.* W.* Mons John de Remeghers. *W.* Remembrancer of the Exchequer at Westminster, (Office of the). Or a chev. gu. and canton erm. within a bordure compony arg. and az. *Carter.*

Remeville. Add: *V.** The buckles round. *V.*

Rempston or Rampston. Add: Sir Thomas Rempston K.G. temp. Henry iv. Tonge. 3. *V.*

Rempston or Rempton. Quarterly arg. and gu. on a bend vert. betw. 2 cotises or 3 towers arg. *V.*

Remoste or Renoste. Quarterly arg. and gu. on a bend sa. 3 pierced mullets or. *V.*

Remys. Per fess arg. and gu. a martlet sa. *V.*

Renton (Sir Thos. Renton). Az. a lion ramp. arg. on a chief gu. 3 estoiles. . . . *Nisbet. Plate of Subscribers.*

Repley. Per chev. arg. and az. 3 lions ramp. counterchanged. *V.*

Repton (Odell Castle, Bedford 1868). Arg. on a bend sa. 3 covered cups or in chief an annulet gu. *Debrett.*

Repps or Repes (West Walton, co. Norfolk). Delete—(another, arg.). Add: *V.*

Reresby (Thrybergh, co. York bart.). Insert—1642 . . . three crosses-amend to read 'flory'. Add: *Hunter ij. 39.*

Reresby. Gu. on a bend arg. 3 crosses patty sa. Sire Adam de Reresby .*O.* John de Reresby. *X.* William Ryresby. *Y.* And with a label or. William de Reresby, the son. *X.*

Reresby. Gu. a bend betw. 3 crosses patonce arg. *V.*

Reresby. Gu. on a bend arg. 3 pierced mullets sa. Sir Thomas Rersby. *S.*

Resone (Sir John Resone, Essex). Gu. a lion ramp. or on a canton of the second a cross patonce vert. *V.*

Reson or Reason. Add: Sire John de Resoun. *N.*

Retford. Erm. on a chev. sa. three escallops arg. —insert—Thomas de Retford, Asby. *X.* . . . .

Retford. Quarterly arg. and gu. a bordure recercely sa. John de Retford. *Y.* But query Rochford.

Reve (Malden, co. Suffolk). Add: *V.E. 1612. W.*

Reve. Az. a chev. betw. 3 pairs of wings conjoined. . . . Add: Sir Edmund Reve 1639. *Dug. O.J.*

Revell (Co. Derby). Add: *V.N. p. 34.*

Revell. Erm. a chev. gu. within a bordure engr. sa. *V.**

Revelly (Co. Derby). Erm. on a chev. gu. 3 mullets or a bordure engr. sa. *Robson.*

Revers. Sa. on a fess engr. gu. betw. 3 swans swimming in water (barry wavy arg. and az.) their bills in the water; as many roses silver. *V.*

Revett (Co. Suffolk). Add: *Visitation 1656.*

Reygate. Or (another, arg.) 5 foils in fess az; another. Arg. a bend fusily az. Add: Sir Robert Reygate. *V.*

Reymes (Oxstrand, Norfolk). Sa. a chev. betw. 3 lions ramp. guard. arg. langued gu. *Cady.*

Reynes (Cos. Buckingham and Kent). Add: *V.** Thomas and John Reynes (Upton Escudamore). Seal *1416.* Sir John Raynes. *S.* Sir Thomas Reynes. *S.*

Reynes. Arg. fretty sa. over all a bend compony az. and or. *V.*

Reynes or Reymes (Overswood-Kettlestone, co. Norfolk). Add: *V.**

Reynolds (Braunston, co. Leicester . . .). Add: *V. 131.*

Reynolds. Erm. 3 lions pass. guard. gu. *Robson.*

Reynolds (Suffolk). Arg. a chev. lozengy gu. and az. on a chief of the third a cross patty fitchee betw. 2 mullets or.

Reynolds (Colchester, Essex). Sa. a chev. chequy arg. and sa. betw. 3 crosses crosslet fitchy arg. in chief 3 estoiles. . . . .

Reynolds (Carshalton, co. Surrey). Insert—Granted by Camden 1606.

Reys. Or a bend engr. vert. cotised gu. *Randle Holme.*

Rhodes (New Zealand and Kippax, co. York; granted). Insert—20 Oct. 1865.

Rhodes (Barlborough, co. Derby. Baronetcy 1641). Arg. a lion pass. in bend gu. betw. 2. bendlets ermined and 2 acorns az. *Guillim* Francis Rodes, Justice of the Common Pleas. Same arms. *Dug. O.J.*

Rhodes or Rodes (Great Houghton, co. York). . . . Add: *Dugdale p. 266.*

Ribb. Add: *Moule 232.*

Ribblesford of Ribblesford. Erm. a chev. gu. fretty or. *Nash.*

Ribo. Add: Richard Riboo (Newbiggyng). *P.*

Ricard (Granted temp. Henry viii. . . .). Add: Thomas Rycard, Hatfield. co. York. *V.*

Riccard (Hatfield, co. York). Gu. a bend vair betw. 2 garbs placed bendwise or. *Hunter j. 176.*

Ricard (London 1634). Add: *Guillim.*

Rice (Boemer, co. Bucks. temp. Mary i.). Insert—granted by Hawley 2 May 1555.

Rice (London). Insert—Ryce or Ryse. Add: *V.*

Rice (Quartered by Davis). . . . a chev. . . . betw. 3 spear heads. . . . *Collinson Somerset iij. 165.*

Rich (Mulbarton, Norfolk). Gu. on a chev. betw. 3 crosses bottony or a crescent for diff.

Rich of London. Az. in base out of water a swan rising ppr. in chief 2 bars or. In Enfield Church. *Robson.*

Rich. Sir Peter Rich, Alderman of London. Gu. a chev. betw. 3 crosses patonce or. *In St. Mary's Church. Lambeth.*

Rich. Quarterly or and az. a chev. betw. three roundles. . . . Add: Ric. Rich, Sheriff of London ob. 1462.

Richardson (London). Az. a cabled anchor supported by a lion ramp. or on a chief wavy erm. an eastern crown of the second betw. two lions heads erased sa.

Richardson (Tottenham High Cross, Middlesex 1608. Groom of the Privy Chamber, granted by Camden). Gu. on a chev. arg. a 5-foil betw. 2 lions counterpassant of the first.

Richardson (Co. Kent . . . Blackheath . . .). Add: †

Richbell. . . . on a bend . . . 3 bells. . . .

Riches. Arg. 3 annulets az. *V.*

Richmond (Highead Castle, co. Cumberland). . . . Add: Ronald de Richmond. *P.Y.E.V.* Thomas de Richmond. *K.N.*

Richmond. Gu. 2 bars gemel or Roald de Richmond. *Y.*

Richmond (Benedictine Priory of Richmond, co. York). Gu. 4 bars a chief and overall a crozier or.

Richmond. . . . on a bend engr. . . . 3 crosses crosslet fitchy . . . Richard de Richmond. Seal. *W.*

Rickaby (Co. York). Arg. on a chev. engr. az. betw. 3 martlets sa. as many crescents of the first. Quartering or 2 chevs. gu.

Ricksworth

Ricost (Exeter). Arg. a chev. betw. 3 falcons heads erased sa. beaked gu. *Robson.*

Ricroft. Quarterly arg. and gu. on a bend sa. 3 mullets or. Add: *V.*

Ridall or Riddall or Ridhull (Co. Hertford). Insert—? Hereford, delete (another sa.) . . . Add: *V.*

Ridale (Scotland). Arg. a chev. betw. 3 holly leaves vert. *Cady.*

Riddell (Granton, 1731 . . .). Add: *Nisbet.*

Ridell (Co. Bedford). Add: Sire Johan Ridel. *N.*

Rider. Arg. on a bend az. cotised gu. 3 crescents or.

Ridge. (Manchester 1664). Arg. 2 ravens in pale sa. *V.L.*

Ridley (Ridley, co. Northumberland). . . . Add: Ridley (Battersby, co. York 1612). Same arms. *F.Y.*

Ridley (Confirmed by Flower, Norroy in 1581 to Thos. Ridley descended from the Ridleys of Willimonswight, co. Northumberland). Arg. on a mount vert. with rushes ppr. a bull pass. gu. charged on the shoulder with a star. *Guillim.*

Ridley (Nicholas Ridley, Bishop of London). . . . Add: *V.*

Ridley (Co. Surrey). Gu. a chev. betw. 3 falcons arg. . . . Add: *V.**

Ridmedishell. Sa. a chev. or. *V.V.**

Ridmer. Az. a chief arg. over all a bend sa. Reynaud de Ridmer. *P.*

Ridmer. Az. a chief indented arg. overall a bend sa. Reynaud de Ridmer. *P.*

Ridon. Insert—'Suffolk'. Arg. a chev. betw. 3 lions heads erased gu. Add: *Cady.*

Ridware or Ridward. Nethersall, co. Leicester temp. Henry iij. Sire Thomas de Rideware. *N.V.*

Ringwood. Arg. a chev. compony (counter-compony. *V.*) sa. and or betw. 3 moorcocks of the second. *V.**

Riow (London). Az. 2 bars or in base out of water a swan rising ppr. *Robson.*

Ripars. Az. a lion ramp. or Add: ?

Ripley (Kingston-on-Hull 1665). Per chev. or and az. 3 lions ramp. counterchanged. *Dugdale p. 130.*

Ripon (Deanery of). Arg. a paschal lamb pass. ppr. carrying the banner of the last over its head a nimbus or. *Berry.*

Ripon. Town of,—insert—co. York. . . .

Ripon. Gu. a bend erm. a label or Sire William de Ripon. *Y.*

Rishton (Dunnishope, co. Lancaster 1664). Add: *V.L.*

Risleigh (Co. Lancaster, knt.). Add: *R.*

Rissun. Erm. on a bend sa. 3 mullets or pierced arg. *V.*

Ritford. Add: temp. Edwd. ij. *F.Y.*

Ritso (Augusta Ritso dau. of Henry Frederick, Duke of Cumberland, as quartered by Dalton). Arg. on a chev. sa. betw. 3 boars heads couped so many mullets arg.

Rivell. Erm. a chev. gu. a chief indented sa. Monsire John Rivell *Y.*

River. Gu. a bend engr. betw. 6 crescents arg.

Rivers (Pitt-Rivers, Baron Rivers). . . . Supporters: . . . a unicorn—delete—'or' amend to 'arg.' . . .

Rivers. Az. 2 bars dancetty or. Sir William de la River, co. Berks. *V.* Richard de Riveres. *F.* Sir John de la Rivere. *L.N.Y.*

Rivers. Or a lion ramp. az. Baldwin de Rivers, Earl of Devon and Lord of the Isle of Wight. *V.*

Rixton (Rixton, co. Lancaster . . .). Add: *V.**

Rixton. Arg. on a bend sa. 3 covered cups crowned of the first. John Rixton. *V.*

Robartfield. Insert—Northumberland. Or—underlined—margin—'arg.'. *V.** Add: *V.*

Robert. Or 2 chevs. gu. in the dexter chief a mullet sa. Sir William Robert. *W.*

Roberts (Bristol, Westerley, co. Gloucester). Add: *V.*

Roberts. Erm. a lion ramp. az. charged on the breast with a mullet or.

Roberts (Fiddington,   1631). Per pale arg. and gu. over all a lion ramp. sa. **Tomb** in Tewkesbury Abbey.

Robertson. Alias Collyear. Baronetcy 1676. Gu. on a chev. betw. 3 wolves heads erased arg. as many oak trees eradicated ppr. fructed or.

Robertson (Boston). Vert. on a chev. arg. betw. 3 stags those in the chief trippant and that in base statant or a crescent for diff. gu. *V.*

Robinson (Earl of Ripon . . .). Add: Robinson (Newley, co. York). Confirmed 1634. Same arms. *Northern Grants xlix.*

Robinson (Rokeby Park, co. York bart.). Insert—1730. . . . Add: *Dugdale 1665. p. 34.*

Robinson (Cranford, co. Northampton). . . . Add: The augmentation was granted to Sir John Robinson Lieutenant of the Tower of London, created a Baronet 21 June 1660 and is borne quarterly with the paternal coat. *Guillim.*

Robinson (Beverley House, Toronto, Upper Canada. bart.). Insert—1854.

Robinson (Rokeby Hall, co. Louth, bart.). Insert
—1819. . . .

Robinson (Dighton, co. York 1665). Vert. on a
chev. betw. 3 bucks trippant or as many
5-foils gu. a mullet for diff. *Dugdale p. 208.*

Robinson (London, Chief Waiter of the Custom
House . . .). Add: *C.L.*

Robinson (Cowton Grange, co. York). Vert. on a
chev. engr. betw. 3 bucks trippant or as many
4-foils gu. *F.Y.*

Robinson (Ryther, co. York). 1665. Vert. on a
chev. betw. 3 bucks trippant or as many
5-foils gu. in chief a 3-foil slipped arg. Crest:
A buck trippant or palletty gorged with a
chaplet vert. *Dugdale p. 18.*

Robinson (Thormton, Riseborough, co. York).
Same arms. *Dugdale p. 65.*

Robinson (Thicket, co. York 1665). Same arms.
an annulet for diff. *Dugdale p. 142.*

Robinson (Cadgurth, co. Cornwall). Vert. 3
bucks in full course or. *Lysons.*

Robinson (Algburth, co. Lancaster). Add:
Robinson (Sudley, Liverpool). Same arms.

Robinson (Cransley, co. Northampton . . .). Add:
Granted by Camden Nov. 1611 to Henry
Robinson of Cransley.

Robinson (London). Vert. on a chev. betw. 3
roebucks trippant or as many lozenges gu. *W.*

Robinson (Buckton, co. York 1665). Vert. on a
chev. betw. 3 bucks trippant or as many
5-foils gu. a canton arg. *Dugdale p. 117.*

Robinson (York). Per pale gu. and arg. 2 lions
pass. in pale counter changed a canton or.
Thomas Strangeways Robinson. †

Robinson. Sa. a chev. erm. betw. 3 gauntlets arg.
Collinson Somerset iij. 370.

Robinson (York 1612). Vert. a chev. erm. betw. 3
stags trippant or. *F.Y.*

Robsert (Normandy and co. Warwick . . .). Add: *V.*

Robson (Bishop Wearmouth, co. Durham). *V.**

Rocclyfft (Calthorpe). Add: or Rowcliff. *V.*

Roccliff (Colthorpe, co. York). Arg. a chev.
betw. 3 lions heads erased gu. mullet for diff.
F.Y.

Roce. Az. 3 bendlets or a bordure gu. Gwy de la
Roce. *A.* But or 3 bendlets az. a bordure gu.
enoury of fleur-de-lis arg. *A. Harl. MS. 6137.*

Rochdale Borough of (Co. Lancaster). Add:
Motto: "Crede Signo". **Book Plate.**

Roche (Lord Mayor of London 1540). Add:
V.E. 1634.

Rochford. Quarterly or and gu. on a bordure sa.
8 annulets or. *V.N. p. 179.*

Rocheford. Gu. an eagle displ. or quartering
quarterly gu. and or a bordure sa. bezanty.
Sir Raffe Rocheford. *S.*

Roches. Add: *V.* Sir John de Roches. *Y.*

Rochford. Quarterly or and gu. a bordure engr.
arg. Sir Roger Rochford. *L.*

Rochford. Quarterly or and gu. a bordure
indented sa. Sir Robert de Rocheford. *N.L.
Harl. MS. 6137* and with a martlet sa. in the
first quarter. *N.*

Rock (Shrewsbury. Granted by Camden 1603).
Or 3 chessrooks sa. a chief embattled gu.

Rock (Co. Salop.). Or 3 chessrooks and a chief
embattled sa. *W.*

Rockley. Lozengy arg. and gu. a bendlet az.
Richard de la Rokele. *E.*

Rockwood (Kirkby, co. Suffolk). Add: *V.*

Rodbard. Or a chev. betw. 3 oxen sa. *Collinson
Somerset ij. 171.*

Rode. Gu. on a chev. arg. 3 martlets of the first.
Add: *V.*

Rodes. Az. a lion ramp. or. William de Rode. *A.*

Rodes. Az. a lion ramp. or a dexter baston gu.
William de Rodes. *D.*

Rodes (Barlborough, co. Derby). . . . Add: Sir
John de Rodes, co. Notts. *V.* Sir John Rodes,
co. Nottingham. *V.*

Rodgers (Endcliffe Vale, Sheffield, co. York).
Add: *Foster.*

Rodick (Westmorland). Gu. a chev. per pale
wavy arg. and or betw. 3 roses of the second
barbed and seeded vert.

Rodnall or Rothendale. Add: *V.**

Rodney. Or 3 eagles displ. gu. Sir John de
Rodneye. *S.*

Rodney. Or 3 eagles displ. sa. Sir Walter Rodney.
V.

Roe (Co. Devon). Add: *V.D. 1620.*

Rogers. Arg. 3 roebucks courant sa. in chief a
crescent for diff. Sir John Rogers, Comptroller
of the Household, temp. Queen Elizabeth. *V.*

Rogers (Bradford, co. Somerset . . .). Add:
Collinson's Somerset j. 236.

Rogers (Sutton, Kent 1593). Arg. a chev. sa.
betw. 3 roebucks courant of the second
attired or. *W.*

Rogers (London. Granted 1586). Sa. a chev. arg.
betw. 3 roebucks statant of the second attired
or. Rafe Rogers. *W.*

Rogers (Netherthorpe, co. York). Sa. 3 chevs.
betw. as many roebucks trippant arg. *Hunter
j. 311.*

Rogers. Arg. 2 lions ramp. addorsed gu. *V.**

Rogers. Gu. 2 lions ramp. addorsed arg. *V.*

Rogers. Arg. a chev. sa. betw. 3 bucks springing
of the second attired or. *V.**

Rogers (Wisdome, co. Devon). Baronetcy 1698.
Same arms.

Roigate. Arg. a bend engr. az. Monsire Roigate. *Y.*

Rokeby. (Rokeby and Mortham, co. York). . . .
Add: Sir Thomas de Rokeby. *S. Y.* Sir Robert
de Rookby. *R.*

Rokeby (Ackworth, co. York). Same arms, a
crescent for diff. *Dugdale 1665.*

Rokeby (Holtham and Skires, co. York). Same
arms. *Dugdale Vis. 1665.*

Rokeby (Skiers, co. York, bart.). Insert—1660. . . .

Rokeby (Warmsworth, co. York. 1665). Arg. a
chev. betw. 3 rooks sa. a canton gu. *Dugdale
p. 167.*

Rokeby (Maske and Stanningford, co. York). . . .
Add: Rokeby (Manfeld, co. York). Same
arms. Quartering arg. on a cross engr. sa. an
annulet or for Fitz Henry. *F.Y.*

Rokeby (Mortham, co. York). Arg. on a chev.
sa. betw. 3 rooks ppr. beaked and membered
az. a mullet or; quartering arg. 3 chevrons
braced sa. on a chief of the last 3 mullets of
the field for Danby. *F.Y.*

Rokele. Arg. a chev. betw. 3 chessrooks sa.

Rokesborough. Add: *V.V.**

Rokesburgh. Add: *V.**

Rokewood. Arg. three chessrooks sa. a chief of
the last. Add: *V.**

Rockinge. Add: *V.*

Rolph. Add: Granted by Camden to Edmond
Rolph, Goldsmith.

Roleston or Rolston. Bendy of 6 vert. and gu. a
chev. erm. *V.V.**

Rolstone. Same arms, but the chev. engr. *V.*

Romesbury. Arg. a chev. betw. 3 martlets sa. *V.*

Romney (London; granted 16 Dec. 1593). . . .
Add: *W.*

Romey (Middleton, co. Kent; granted 11 April
1615). Insert—by Segar. . . .

Rone (Samborne Hall, co. Essex). Add: *V.E.
1612.*

Roney or Rony. Arg. on a bend betw. 2 cotises
sa. 3 mullets of the first. John Roney. *V.*

Roo. Az. a buck's head cabossed or. . . . See:
Rowe and Roe.

Roo. Gu. on a bend betw. 2 garbs or. 3 crosses crosslet fitchy sa. William Roo, Mercer. London.

Roo (Dartford, Kent). Arg. on a chev. engr. az. betw. three 3-foils slipped vert. as many bezants. *Cady.*

Rooch (Epsom, Surrey). Arg. on a bend betw. 2 cotises sa. 3 mullets of the first. †

Rookeby. Arg. a chev. betw. 3 rooks expanded sa. *V.*

Rookeby (Co. York). Arg. on a chev. betw. 3 rooks sa. as many mullets of the field, a mullet sa. for diff. *Eliz. Roll. xxviij.*

Rookwood (Eveston, co. Suffolk). Add: and with a † for diff. Rookwood (Beston, Norfolk).

Roope. Or a lion ramp. betw. 12 pheons. az.

Roope (Co. Devon). Arg. a lion ramp. gu. betw. 8 pheons sa. *V.D. 1620.*

Roos. Chequy gu. and arg. John de Roos *Y.*

Roos. Or 3 water bougets az.

Roos. Gu. 3 water bougets arg. Robert de Roos. *A.C.D.E.* William de Roos. *B.G.J.K.N.* Robert, son of William de Roos. *B.* And with one bouget charged with a crescent William le Roos. *S.*

Roos (Ashwell, co. Rutland). . . . Add: Roos (Ashwell, co. Rutland 1618). Az. 3 water bougets or a label of 3 points. *C.R.*

Roos. Sa. on a bend arg. 3 roses gu. *V.V.**

Roos or Rosse (Kendal, co. Westmorland). Insert—*Y.* Add: Robert de Roos. Wirke. *B.* And with a mullet sa. for diff. Roos of Cawton of York. *F.Y.*

Roos or Rosse (Co. Gloucester and Swinshead, co. Stafford). Add: Robert de Roos. *S.* Robert Roos de Ingmanthorpe. *V.Y.* Sir William de Ros C.J. and of Yngmanthorp. *N.*

Roos. Erm. 3 water bougets gu. John le Roos. *S.*

Roos. Erm. 3 water bougets sa. Sir James le Roos. *S.* Sir James Roos, Godney. *V.*

Roos. Barry of 6 arg. and gu. a bend fusilly az. John de Roos. Tyd. *V.*

Roos or Ros. Az. 3 water bougets arg. a label or. Sire William de Ros. Youlton. *N.*

Roos. Arg. on a bend sa. 3 water bougets of the field Sir Richard le Roos. *V.*

Roos. Gu. 3 water bougets erm. Sir William Roos. Gedney, co. Notts. *V.E.*

Roos (Co. Derby, Boston, co. Lincoln; Laxton, co. Notts.). Same arms.

Roose (Whetsone, co. Cornwall). Add: *Lysons* gives the field az. and swans ppr.

Ropemakers (Company of, Newcastle-on-Tyne). Arg. a chev. az. betw. 3 rope hooks sa.

Roper (Turndich and Heanor, co. Derby). . . . Sa. an eagle—insert—sometimes called a parrot.

Roringe. Arg. 2 bars gu. 6 martlets 3.2. and 1 of the last. *V.V.**

Ros. Arg. 3 water bougets sa. Sire Johan de Ros. *N.* Sir George de Ros. *O.V.*

Ros. Arg. 3 bars gu. a bend engr. sa. Sire Johan de Ros. *N.*

Ros. Chequy gu. and or. John Ros. *V.*

Roscarrock (Roscarrock, co. Cornwall). Add: *V. V.C. 306.* Add: Roscarrock (Ireland). *V.*

Roscelyn. Gu. 3 buckles, the field crusilly fitchy arg. Sir Thomas Roscelyn. *Willement's Heraldic Notes in Canterbury Cathedral. p. 104*

Rosce or Roscey. Add: Henry Rosce. *V.*

Roscrowe (Roscrowe, co. Cornwall) Add: *V.C. 306.*

Rose (London, Nicholas Rose). Add: *C.L. p.78.*

Rose. Gu. a chev. betw. 3 rose leaves arg. Sir John Rose. *V.*

Rose. Gu. on a chev. or betw. 3 horseshoes arg. as many roses of the first. *V.* William Rosse. *V.* But query the field sa. *W.*

Rossell (Radcliffe, co. Notts. 1614). Arg. on a bend sa. 3 roses or. *V.N.*

Rossellyn. Arg. on a bend gu. 3 square buckles of the first. *V.**

Roscellyn. Arg. on a bend gu. 3 round buckles tongues pendent in bend or. *V.* But the tongues pendent to the sinister. *Cotton MS. Tiberius. D. l0.*

Rosethorne (New Hall, co. Lancaster 1664). Add: *V.L.*

Roshill or Rowsewell. Add: *V.V.**

Rosse. Arg. 3 bars gu. a bend sa. *V.**

Rosse or Roos (Cawton, co. York 1581). Or 3 water bougets within a bordure engr. sa. *F.Y.*

Ross (Rayners, co. Bucks. Baronetcy 1874). Arg. a chev. invected erminois betw. 4 water bougets 3 in chief and 1 in base arg. *Debrett.*

Rosse. Arg. 3 bars gu. a bend engr. sa. Sire Johan de Ros. *S.*

Rosse (Chapel Allerton, co. York). 1666. Az. 3 water bougets or. *Dugdale p. 250.*

Rossial. Purp. a chev. and in base a sinister half chevron arg.

Rossell. Or a chev. az. betw. 3 roses gu. Sire Geffrey Rossell. *N.* Sir Wm. Rossell, Northampton. *V.*

Rosselyne (Co. Norfolk). Amend 'arg.' to read 'az.'. . . .

Rosselyne. (Norfolk) Az. 3 fermails or. Sir William Rosselyne. *N.*

Rosselyne. Gu. 3 square buckles betw. 9 crosses crosslet arg.—insert—*V.*

Rosselyn. Gu. 3 buckles arg. Thomas Rosseline. *Y.* Sir Peres Rosselyn. *N.* The buckles round with tongues to the dexter. Thomas Roseline. *E.* Sir Thomas Rosselyn, Norfolk. temp. Edward j. *V.*

Rosseter (Samerby, co. Lincoln . . .). Add: *W.*

Rosseter (Co. Lincoln 1640). Arg. on a chev. gu. 3 pheons of the field. *Yorke.*

Rosseter (Co. Somerset). Add: *V.*

Rossogan (St. Earme, co. Cornwall). . . . Add: *V.C.*

Roster. Per bend or and gu. on a bend arg. a key wards upwards in the sinister chief a cross patty gu. **Book Plate.**

Rostlings. Arg. a horse pass. sa. bridled and saddled or. *V.*

Rotheley. Arg. on 2 bars humetty vert. 3 fleurs-de-lis or 2 and 1. William Rotherly. *V.*

Rotherham. Vert. 3 bucks at gaze or. . . . Add: *V.** Sir Thomas Rotherham. *V.*

Rothings or Rothinge. Add: *V.*

Rothington. Add: *V.*

Rothwell (Ewerby and Stapleford, co. Lincoln). . . . Insert—1611.

Rothwell (Co. Lincoln). Arg. on 2 chevs. engr. sa. ten plates. *V.*

Rothwell. Arg. 2 chev. engr. sa. on each 5 bezants—insert—*V.** (another 5 plates). Add: *V.*

Rothwell (Sharples Hall, co. Lancaster). Add: Rothwell Bolton le Moors, co. Lancaster. Same arms. *A.A.*

Rotier or Rotyer (Co. Chester). Or in chief a lion pass. and in base 3 garbs arg. *V.*

Rottlewell. Arg. a bend gu. fretty or. William Rotelwell. *V.*

Rouch or De Rouch. Arg. a lion ramp. reguard. purp. tail reflexed over the back. Sir Amand de Rouch *V.*

Roughsedge (Foxghyll, co. Westmorland). Vert. on a bend arg. betw. 2 cotises erm. and 2 covered cups . . . a lion pass. . . .

Rougemont. Or an eagle displ. doubleheaded gu. *V.V.**

Roughton. Sa. a chev. betw. three 4-foils voided arg. *V.**

Roult (Mylton, co. Bedford). Add: Sir Thomas Roult, London. 1682. *C.N.*

Rous or Rowse (Co. Bedford). Add: Sir Richard de Rous. *N.V.*

Rous (Modbury, co. Devon. Sir Anthony Rous . . .). Add: *V.*

Rous. Gu. 2 bars indented or. †

Rous (Co. Gloucester). Add: Jeffrey de Rous. *Y.* Jeffrey de Rous. Sir Johan le Rous. *N.* Sir Roger Rouse, co. Gloucester. temp. Edwd. *j. V.*

Rous. Per pale gu. and az. 3 lions ramp. arg. Gile le Rous. *E.F.*

Rous. Per pale or and az. 3 lions ramp. gu. Sir Roger le Rous. *N.*

Rous. Per pale or and gu. 3 lions ramp. counter changed *V.V.**

Rous. Barry gu. and arg. a chief of the second overall a bend engr. gu. John Rous. Tyde. *Y.*

Rous. Arg. a chev. engr. betw. 3 crescents sa. insert—*V.* . . .

Rousby. Add: *V.*

Rouse (Court yr ala, Glamorgan). Or an eagle displ. pluming its wing az. *Robson.*

Routh or Rowth. Or 3 bars az. on a quarter arg. 2 lions pass. gu. Add: *V.*

Routh. Barry of 6 az. and or a bend compony arg. and az. John de Routhe. *Y.*

Routh. Arg. on a bend betw. 2 cotises sa. 3 mullets of the first. *V.* Sir John de Routhe. *S.*

Routhe. Arg. a chev. sa. betw. 3 lions heads erased gu. Thomas de Routhe. *Y.*

Rowbache (Lytton, co. Herts; confirmed). Insert by Camden. Add: *Guillim.*

Rowcliffe. Arg. on a chev. betw. 3 lions heads erased gu. a chessrook or. Add: Sir Davy Rowcliff. *V.* Geffrey Rowcliff of Carthorp. *V.*

Rowcliffe. Arg. on a chev. gu. a mullet or in chief two lions heads erased gu. Robert de Roucliffe.

Rowcliffe (Colthorp, co. York). Add: John de Roucliffe. *Y.*

Rowe (Macclesfield, co. Chester . . .). Add: *Harl. MS. 1535 fo. 241b.*

Rowe (Co. Devon and co. Kent. Sir William Rowe). . . . Add: *V. C.L.*

Rowe or Roe (Co. Devon: Granted 1595). Arg. a chev. az. betw. 3 trefoils per pale gu. and vert. *V.D.* 1620.

Rowe (Lewes, co. Sussex). Erm. a lion ramp. pass. gu. betw. 3 fleurs-de-lis. az.

Rowe (Bristol). Add: *Guillim.*

Rowley (Maperath, co. Meath). Or on a bend betw. 2 cotises gu. 3 crescents of the first. *A.A.*

Rowton. Or 3 bendlets az. a canton arg. *V.*

Royal Literary Society. Incorporated 1818. Arg. an open book . . . betw. 3 wreaths of laurel . . . on a chief gu. a Prince of Wales coronet and 3 ostrich feathers. . . . **Seal.**

Ruda or Rudd. Arg. on a chev. betw. three stringed bugle horns gu. as many mascles or. Sir Amand de Ruda. *V.*

Royle (Lestwick, co. Chester). . . . Add: *Guillim.*

Royniger or Roynger (Co. Norfolk). Add: Sire Rauf de Royinge. *N.*

Royston. Gu. a chev. betw. 3 keys arg. Add: *V.**

Royton or Ruton. Add: *V.*

Rudd. Az. a chev. betw. 3 bells arg. *V.**

Rudd (Abergavenny, co. Monmouth). Add: Rudd (Aberglasney, co. Carmarthen. Baronetcy 1628. Same arms.

Rudde (London 1634 . . .). Add: *Harl. MS. 1444.*

Rudd (Co. Essex). Same arms. *V.E.* 1634.

Rudinge or Rudings (Martin-Hussingtree, co. Worcester . . .). Add: *W.*

Rue. Add: Sir Oldham de Rue. *Y.*

Rufford (Rufford, co. Buckingham). Add: *V.*

Ruffres. Or a chev. and canton sa. within a bordure indented gu.

Rugge (Felmingham and Billingford co. Norfolk). Add: *Cady.*

Ruggelay. Add: Ruggeley (Shenton and Hawksyard, co. Stafford). Same arms. *W.* John Rugley, co. Warwick. *V.*

Rudnall. Sa. a chev. betw. 3 foxes heads erased arg. *V.V.**

Rus. Arg. on a bend betw. 2 cotises sa. 3 martlets of the field. Sire Dineid de Rus. *Y.*

Rushout. Insert—(Mileham Green, co. Essex. Baronetcy 1661). Sa. 2 lions pass. guard. or.

Rushton (Antley, co. Lancaster). Arg. a lion pass. and a chief sa. *V.L.* 1664.

Ruskyn or Rusken. Add: *V.*

Russell (Brancepeth Castle, co. Durham). . . . Add: Sir William Russell of London, Knighted 20 Oct. 1679. Same arms. *Guillim.*

Russell (Clifton, co. Gloucester, confirmed by Head 1820). Arg. on a chev. betw. 3 crosses crosslet fitchy sa. an eagles head erased or all within a bordure engr. gu. charged with 8 plates.

Russell (Hamilton-Russell). Viscount Boyne. Add: Hamilton-Russell (Baron Brancepeth 1866). Same arms.

Russell of the North. Sa. a chev. betw. 3 roses arg. *W.*

Russell. Or a chev. az. betw. 3 roses gu. Sire Geffrey Rossell. *N.* Sir William Rossell of Northampton. *V.* Sir Thomas Russell. *X.Y.* And with a label arg. Hugh Russell. *X.Y.*

Russell (Co. Rutland temp. Edw. j.). Az. on a chev. or 3 roses gu. *V.*

Russell (Co. Salop.). Gu. on a bend arg. 3 roses of the first. Sir Peter Russell of Russell, co. Salop. *W.*

Russell (Co. Worcester). Arg. a chev. betw. 3 crosses bottony fitchy sa. Sir John Russell. *V.*

Russell. Gu. on a bend or another sa. charged with 2 mullets of the second pierced gu. alternately with as many swans arg. Sir Robert Russell. *S.*

Russell. Or on a bend sa. 3 ducks arg. *V.**

Russell (Co. Wilts.). Add: *V.*

Russell. Arg. a chev. betw. 3 crosses crosslett fitchee sa. Crest: . . . Add: Thomas Russell *X.* Sir John Russell (Worcester). *V.*

Russell. Gu. on a bend sa. bordered or 2 mullets of the last and 2 swans arg. the mullets and swans alternately.

Russell. Gu. on a chev. betw. three mullets arg. as many ducks sa. *V.** But swans. *V.*

Russham. Sa. on a bend betw. 6 martlets arg. 3 roses gu. *V.*

Rusteyn (Co. Norfolk). Arg. a horse pass. sa. bridled and saddled or. *Blomfield.*

Rutlege. Arg. a stag trippant ppr. on a chief az. 3 estoiles or.

Rutter (Cos. Chester and Gloucester and Stratford-upon-Avon, co. Warwick). . . . Add: *W.*

Rychers. Arg. 3 annulets az.

Rydall. Or on a bend gu. 3 wheels of the first. *Nash.*

Rydell. Sir William Rydell. Gu. a lion ramp. within a bordure engr. arg. *L.Y.*

Rydell (Lancaster and Westmorland). Gu. a lion ramp. or within a bordure indented arg. *V.*

Rydewell (Co. York). Add: *V.**

Rye. Gu. a bend erm. a label az. Sir William de Rye. *M.*

Rye (William De Rye, probably son of William de Rye of Swanton, co. Norfolk). . . . Add: de William de Rye. *Y.L.* Sir Nicholas Rye, co. Lincoln. *V.*

Rye (Whitwell, co. Derby . . .). Insert—granted 1575. . . . Gu. on a bend erm. 3 rye stalks—insert—with ears. . . .

Ryed. Arg. a chev. sa. betw. 3 ravens close ppr. Sir Rhys ap Thomas Urian Ryed.

Rykesdon or Rykdon. Arg. on a bend sa. 3 boar's heads bend-wise couped or. *V.V.**

Rykhill. Gu. 2 bars betw. 3 annulets arg. *V.*

Ryland (Clonea Castle near Dungarvon Ireland). Arg. a chev. betw. 3 lions ramp. az. Crest: A cubit arm in armour erect . . . grasping a crescent.

Rylands (Highfields, in the township of Thelwall, co. Chester). . .. and 3rd. erm.—insert—over all. †

Ryman (Sussex). Arg. a chev. sa. betw. 3 escallops erminois. *Berry.*

Rympringden. Gu. on a bend engr. or betw. 3 stringed bugle horns arg. as many ogresses. *V.V.**

Rynell. Erm. a chev. gu. a chief indented sa. John Rynell. *Y.*

Rynge (Norfolk). Arg. 3 bars gu. 8 martlets in orle of the last. *Harl. MS. 5803.*

Ryngwood. Add: *V.*

Ryser. Or a bend sa. a label of 3 arg. *Guillim.*

Ryshworth. Add: *V.V.**

Ryswick. Arg. on a bend sa. 3 billets, blocks or delves pale-wise of the first each charged with a cross gu. *Harl. MS. 1404. fo. 11.*

Ryther (Co. York). Arg. on a bend az. 3 crescents or. Sir John de Ryther. *X.Y.* Sir John Ryder. *V.*

Ryvell or Revell. Erm. a chev. gu. a border engr. sa. Add: Sir John Ryvell. *V.*

Ryvell. Per pale arg. and sa. a chev. gu. *V.**

Ryvell. Per pale indented arg. and sa. a chev. gu. *V. C.L.* another erm. and sa. *V.V.**

Ryver. Sir John de la Ryver co. Berks. Az. 2 bars dancetty arg. *V.*

Rywallon. Add: *V.**

Ryzere. Gu. a bend erm. a label or. Sir William de Ryzere. *N.*

S

SABRAHAM, SAPERHAM or SAPRAM. Arg. a bend embattled counter embattled sa. *V.*

Sachvile or Sachvyle. Az. 3 cross bows bent or with 5 arrows diverse to each arg. *V.V.**

Sackvile. Insert—'confirmed to Thomas Sackville, Gentleman Usher, 1622.' . . . Quarterly or and gu. a bend vair, a border gobonnee arg. and az. Crest: . . . Add: *Guillim.*

Sackville. Quarterly gu. and or a bend vair. Sir Thomas Sakeville. *S.* Geffrey Sakevile, Sussex *X.*

Sackville (Earl and Duke of Dorset . . .). Line 14. Add: Sir Andrew de Sagevile. *N.A. Harl. MS. 6137.* Adam de Sakevile. *A.* Sir Richard Sackvile, Withiam, Sussex. *V.*

Sadellayer (Co. Stafford). Arg. on a beehive sa. a hart lodged arg. attired or *V.*

Sadleir (Granted 34th Hen. viij. to Sir Ralph Sadleir, Secretary of State). Per fess az. and or goutty . . . a lion ramp. counterchanged on a canton or a buck's head cabossed az. *Burke.*

Sadler. Per fess or and az. a lion ramp. counterchanged.

Sadler (Sir Ralph Sadler). Per fess or and az. billetty a lion ramp. all counterchanged. *Dug. O.J.*

Sadler. (Parndon, co. Essex). Az. a lion ramp. arg. over all a saltire gu. *V.E. 1634.*

Sadler (Tipperary). Arg. a demi-lion ramp. couped within a bordure sa. charged with 8 plates.

Safeguard. Sa. a bend engr. arg. treble cotised or. *Randle Holme.*

Safferham or Sayperham. Add: *V.*

St. Alban (Norwich). Arg. a bend sa. betw. in chief a mullet and in base an annulet gu. *Cady.*

St. Albon. Az. a chev. betw. 3 tubs or. John Saint-Albon. *V.*

St. Albons. Arg. two bars gu. on a chief of the last a greyhound courant per pale or and erm. Add: ?

St. Albyn or St. Aubyn (Paracombe, co. Devon and Alfoxton, co. Somerset). Insert—*V.S. 1623.*

St. Barbe (Broadlands, co. Hants. and Aslington, co. Somerset . . .). Add: *V.*V.*

St. Clere. Arg. a lion ramp. gu. within a bordure sa. William St. Clere. *E.*

St. Clere. Az. on a chev. arg. betw. 3 suns or as many pierced mullets sa. *V.*

St. Clere. Or a lion ramp. gu. within a bordure sa. bezanty. Sir John St. Clere. *V.*

Seint Clowe. Arg. a chev. gu. betw. 3 nails sa. *V.*

St. George (Hatley St. George, co. Cambridge). . . . Add: *V.* Add: Sir William de St. Jorge. *N.* Bandoin St. George. *Y.*

St. George. Arg. a lion ramp. sa. collared and crowned or. In Melton Church, co. York.

St. Helens (Lancashire, Town of). Per fess az. and or in chief a lion pass. arg. in base a glass kiln or furnace.

St. Helene. Gu. 6 lions ramp. arg. Joan St. Helene. *E.F.*

St. John (Homeldon). Add: *S.*

St. John. Arg. a bend gu. on a chief of the last two mullets or. Crest: . . . Add: Sir John St. John, Bletsa. *V.*

St. Leger (Annery and Cannonleigh, co. Devon). . . . Add: *V.**

St. Liz (Earl of Huntingdon, 1075). Paly of 6 or and az. a bordure arg. *Harl. MS. 5803.* But paly of 6 or and gu. a bordure arg. *Nisbet System j. 38.*

St. Liz. Arg. 2 bars gu. in chief 3 fleurs-de-lis of the second. Add: *V.*

St. Liz. Arg. 2 bars gu. fretty or. *V.*

St. Lo (Chideock). Add: *V.V.**

Saint Lowe. Or a lion ramp. tail forked sa. Gerard Saintlowe. *Y.*

St. Low (Co. Dorset). Arg. on a bend sa. 3 annulets of the field.

Saintloe. Arg. on a bend sa. 3 annulets or in chief a label of 3 gu. Sir John Seyntloe. *V.*

St. Low. Arg. on a bend sa. 3 annulets or. Crest: . . . Add: *V.** St. Lowe (Oxford, 1675).

St. Maris. Arg. a lion ramp. sa. Sir Herbert St. Maris. *L.*

Sein Martyn. Gu. on a bend arg. 3 escallops vert. Sire Thomas de Sein Martyn. *F.*

St. Martyn (Co. Wilts.). Add: Wm. de St. Martyn. *F.* Laurence de St. Martyn (Bishop of Rochester, 1251). John de St. Martyn. *Y.* William de St. Martyn. *E.* Sir Reginald St. Martyn, co. Wilts. temp. Edw. j. *V.* Renaud de St. Martin. *N.*

St. Maur. Arg. goutty de larmes (query de poix) a chevron voided sa. *Guillim.*

St. Maur (Baron St. Maur . . .). Add: Lawrence de Seintmore. *A. Harl. MS. 6137.* The label of 5 points 3 azure betw. 2 vert. *A.* Nicole de Seinmor the label of 5 points az. charged with 15 fleurs-de-lis. or. *E.*

St. Maur (Co. Gloucester). Add: Sire Nicholas de Seinmor. *N.V.* Lawrence Seymor. *P.E.* Sir Lawrence de St. Maur. *I.*

Seymors. Erm. 2 chevs gu. a label az. Sir Rauf de Seymors. *G.* Seinmore. *N.* Semmaire. *F.* Semure. *J.* The label vert. Sir Rauf de Seinmor. *E.* And charged with 5 fleurs-de-lis or. Nicholas de S. Maure. *F.*

St. Maure or Seymour. Erm. 2 chevs. sa. *V.*

St. Owen. Gu. 3 chevs. or. Sir Gilbert de St. Owen. *N.*

St. Owen Rauf de St. Owen. Or 3 bars gu. *F.*

St. Owen (Co. Gloucester). Gu. 3 chevs. or—insert—*V.* Another. . . .

St. Owen. Barry of 6 gu. and or. John de St. Owen. *E.*

St. Philibert (Baron St. Philibert . . .). Add: Sir John de Seint Fulbert. *O.*

St. Philibert (Co. Norfolk temp. Edw. iii . . .). Add: Sire Johan de Sein Fylebird. *N.* Sire de St. Philibert. *Y.*

St. Philibert (Co. Oxford). Add: *V.*

St. Pierre. Arg. a bend sa. Sir Brian St. Pirre. *I.N.*

St. Pierre (Coole, co. Chester . . .). Add: Urian or Brian de St. Pierre or Pere. *E.F.L.* St. Pier, co. Devon.

St. Quintin (Co. York, 1380). Or on a chev. gu. a greyhound courant . . . a chief vair. *Scrope and Grosvenor Controversy ij. 382.*

St. Quintin. Or on a chev. gu. a martlet arg. a chief vair. Sir John Seint Quintin. *S.*

St. Quintin (Co. York). Or 2 chevs. gu. a chief vair. *V.*

St. Quintin (Baron St. Quintin . . .). Add: Sir Herbert de Seynt Quintyn. *E.F.M.N.* Sir Robert de St. Quintin. *A.*

St. Quintin (Llan Blethian, co. Glamorgan). Or 3 chevs. gu. on a chief arg. a bar wavy az.

St. Quintin. Arg. a lion ramp. reguard. purp. ? sa. Herbert St. Quintin. *Y.*

St. Quintin (Harpham, co. York). . . . Add: *V. Dugdale 1665.* Sir William Seint Quintoyne. *S. Y.* Sir Geffrey Saynt Quintyn. *M.Y.*

St. Quintin (Ganstead and Harswell, co. York). Or a chev. gu. and chief vair a crescent for diff. quartering; gu. a cross vair for Twyre; and . . . 3 chevs. embraced . . . betw. 3 bucks heads erased for Buckton. *F.Y.*

St. Yve. Arg. 3 lions pass. in pale gu. Johan de St. Yve. *F.*

St. Walley or St. Wallery. Add: *V.* Sire Richard de St. Waly. *N.* John de Sein Walleri. *E.*

Sakevill. Erm. 3 chevs gu. Sir Thomas Sakevill. *S.* Sir Bartholomew de Saquevile. *B.*

Sale (Cos. Lincoln and York). Add: Sale (Hope Carr, co. Lancaster, 1664). Same arms. *V.L.*

Salford. Arg. on a chev. gu. 3 escallops or. Sire Neel de Salford. *O.*

Salford. (Town of, co. Lancaster). Or and az. in base a shuttle in the centre fess-wise with three 'garbs' or wheat-sheaves 2. and 1. and a swarm of bees 1. 2. and 2. In chief a corded bale between two mill-rinds. Crest: On a wreath of the colours a demi-lion arg. holding in his paws a blue ensign charged with another shuttle. Supporters: Dexter, a wolf or charged on the shoulder with a mill-rind, and on the sinister side an antelope arg. armed, maned and tail or and similarly charged on the shoulder within a shield gu. the rose of Lancaster. Motto: Integrity and Industry.

Salisbury (Newton Burgelaine, co. Leicester . . .). Add: *C.C. 1619.*

Sall (Co. Devon). Gu. 2 lions pass. guard. arg. within a bordure engr. sa. *W.*

Salle. . . . a bird . . . betw. 3 mullets . . . Johan de Salle. *Seal 14th Cent.*

Sallers. Gu. a chev. betw. 3 covered cups arg. *V.*

Salman (Surrey). Arg. on a eagle displ. double-headed sa. a leopards head or. *W.*

Salomons (Broom Hill, Tunbridge, co. Kent, bart.). Insert—1869, Lord Mayor of London, 1855.

Salt. Arg. a chev. rompu. betw. 3 mullets sa. . . . Add: *Harl. MS. 1404. fo. 28.*

Salt (Saltaire and Crow's Nest both of co. York, bart.). Insert—1869.

Salter (Norwich, 1669). Gu. 10 billets 4. 3. 2. and 1. or. John Salter of Oswestry, Sheriff of Shropshire. temp. Hen. viij. *Fuller.*

Salter (Oswestry). Gu. 10 billets or within a bordure engr. arg. charged with 8 hurts. *V.*

Saltby (Co. Lincoln). Add: *C.R. 29.*

Salter. Arg. a chev. debruised sa. betw. 3 mullets pierced of the last. Add: *V.*

Saltonstall (Co. York). Arg. a bend gu. betw. two eagles displ. sa. *Thoresby.*

Saltonstall (London, Granted by Cooke). Or a bend betw. 2 eagles displ. sa. *V.* Lord Mayor of London, 1597.

Saltonstall (Huntwick Grange, co. York, 1612). Same arms. *F. Y.*

Salveyn. Arg. a chev. betw. 3 boars heads gu. Sire Ankelyn Salveyn. *O.* Sir Amyan Salveyne. *Y.* Wm. Salvayne. *Y.*

Saly. Quarterly arg. and sa. a bendlet gu. Monsire William Saly. *S.*

Samell or Samnell. Add: *V.*

Sames (Co. Essex). Add: 1614. *Guillim* and *V.E. 1612.*

Samford (Bicknoler, co. Somerset . . .). Add: *V.S. 1623.*

Samford. Barry wavy of 6 arg. and gu. William de Samford. *B.* And with a label az. Nicholas de Samford, the son. *B.*

Samoure. Gu. 3 bells betw. as many crosses crosslet 1 and 2. or. *Berry.*

Samplow. Arg. on a bend sa. an annulet in chief or. *V.V.**

Sampson. Or on a mound vert. a windmill sa. William Sampson. *V.*

Samson. Arg. 7 barrulets sa. *Randle Holme.*

Samuda (Rickmansworth, co. Herts. M.P., for Tower Hamlets, 1868). Gu. a lion ramp. or on a chief arg. 3 leaves vert. *Debrett.*

Samuell alias Samwell (Doncaster, co. York). Add: *W.*

Samwell (Co. Cornwall). Add: *V.C. p. 306.*

Sanansez. Gu. billetty and a bend or. Moryan de Sanansez. *W.*

Sanchett. Or a tower triple towered az. *V.*

Sancta Barbara (William de Sancta Barbara, Bishop of Durham, 1143). . . . on a chev. sa. betw. 3 fleurs-de-lis a mitre or.

Sandacre. Arg. a lion ramp. purp. a bend or. another . . . Add: *V.*

Sandacre. Arg. a lion ramp. purp. over all a dexter baston vert. Monsire de Sandacre. *Y.*

Sander. Sa. a chev. engr. betw. 3 bulls heads cabossed arg. Add: *V.**

Sander (Surrey). Sa. a chev. erm. betw. 3 bulls heads cabossed arg. *W.*

Sanderson (Combe in Greenwich, co. Kent, bart.). Insert—1720.

Sanderson. Arg. 3 pales az. over all a bend sa. *Eliz. Roll. xxxvjj.*

Sanderson (1660, Bishop of Lincoln. Granted by Camden, 1603). Paly of 6 arg. and az. a bend sa; quartering, erm. on a canton ... a saltire engr. ... charged with a crescent.

Sanderson (Granted by Dethick in 1594 to Wm. Sanderson, Fishmonger). Paly of 6 arg. and az. a bend sa. ... a crescent for diff. *Guillim*

Sanderson. Paly of 6 arg. and az. on a bend gu. 3 mullets of the first. *Guillim.*

Sanderson. Arg. 3 bendlets gu. *Nisbet. j. 22d.*

Sandes. Arg. on a chev. betw. two couple closes sa. 3 blackamoors heads in profile of the last.

Sandford. Barry nebuly of 6 arg. and az. Gilbert Baron de Sandford. *V.F.*

Sandford. Temp. Edw. ij. Sa. 3 lions ramp. arg. *F.Y.*

Sanford (Exeter, co. Devon). Arg. a chev. betw. 3 martlets sa. *V.D. 1620.*

Sandford (Colchester, co. Essex). Add: *V.E. 1614.*

Sandilands (Lord Abercromby, 1647). Arg. a bend az. quartering Douglas. *Crawfurd.*

Sandiland (Alexander Sandiland, M.D.). Arg. a bend engr. az. betw. 2 hearts gu. each surmounted by 3 mullets az. †

Sandon (Ashby, co. Lincoln). ... 3 bull's heads—insert—'cabossed' arg. Add: *Cady.*

Sands (Co. Lincoln, 1640). Sa. a chev. betw. 3 bulls heads cabossed or armed arg. *Yorke.*

Sandy. Vert. a lion ramp or betw. an orle of leaves arg.

Sanford (Milverton, co. Somerset). Add: an annulet for diff. *C.L.*

Sankey (Co. Bedford, Edesborough, co. Bucks.). ...... three salmon—insert—bendwise. ... Add: *V.*

Sankwell. Per chev. gu. and erm. 2 chevrons counterchanged. *V.*

Sankwell. Gu. 3 chevs. erm. *V.**

Sapcot. Arg. 3 belt-buckles sa. Crest: ... Add: *V.**

Sapcotes (Cos. Cornwall, Herts., and Lincoln). Add: Sir John Sapcott, co. Northampton. *V.* Sapcott of Burleigh, co. Rutland. *C.R.*

Sapcote. ... on a chev. ... betw. 3 dovecotes ... as many escallops. ... *Harl. MS. 6829. fo. 49.*

Sapie (Quartered by Baskerville). Arg. on a bend gu. 3 buckles or.

Sapton. Add: Sir John Saperton or Sapton, co. Hereford. *V.*

Sapy or Sapye. Gu. 3 round buckles tongues in pale or. ... Add: Sir John Sapy. *X.Y.V.*

Sapy. Arg. on a bend az. betw. 2 cotises gu. 3 eagles displ. or. Sir Richard Sapy. *V.*

Sares (Sandwich, co. Kent, Horsham, co. Sussex &c. ...). Add: *C.L.*

Sarley (Co. York, temp. Edw. iij.). Arg. on a bend gu. 3 garbs or. *F.Y.*

Sarnesfield (Sir Nicholas Sarnesfield). Insert—*S.* ...

Sarnesfield. Az. an eagle displ. or. Sir Nicholl Sarnesfeld. *S.*

Sarralt. Barry bendy of 6 counterchanged or and az.

Saul (Dr. Wingate of Fenton Cawthorne House, Lancaster). Quarterly of 6: 1, Arg. a chev. betw. 3 camel heads couped sa.; 2, Erm. on a chev. ermines three crescents; 3, Sa. on a pale cotised or, 3 escutcheons sa.; 4, Sable, a bend cotised erm. betw. six martlets or; 5, Arg. an oaktree ppr.; 6, Of six pieces argent and sa. three herons of the last. Motto: "Fideli certa merces".

Saunder. Inset—London. Arg. a lion ramp. az. crowned gu. on a border of the second 8 fleurs-de-lis. or. Add: *V.*

Saunderson (Saxby, co. Lincoln). Insert—Baronetcy 1612. ...

Saunton. Arg. a bend raguly sa. Add: *V.*

De Sauton (Originally of Alsace and of Hampshire and Worcestershire). Arg. 3 towers 2 and 1. Vert. betw. 3 crosses patty 1 and 2 az. on a chief sa. a bezant. *Gentleman's Magazine, 1866. p. 432.*

Savage (Rock Savage). Insert—Baronetcy 1611. ...

Savage (Earl Rivers ...). Add: Monsire Arnold Savage. S. Sir Arnold Savage, Kent. *V.* Sir Roger Savafe. *N.*

Savage (Bloxworth, co. Dorset). Add: *Hutchin's j. 181.*

Savenses. Arg. a bend betw. 6 billets gu. *L.* Sr de Savenses. *W.*

Savile (Savile Hall, co. York). ... Add: Savile of Howley and Lupset co. York, 1585. Same arms with 8 quarterings. *F.Y.* Sir John Savile. *V.S.*

Savile (Thornhill, co. York, Baronetcy, 1611). Arg. on a bend engr. sa. 3 owls of the first. *Guillim* states that upon the extinction of the elder line the bend was borne plain.

Savile. Arg. on a bend sa. 3 owls of the field a label of 3 points gu. Sir John Savile. *S.*

Savile (Copley, co. York ...). Same arms &c. Add: † for diff. *Dugdale p. 3.*

Savile (Methley, co. York, bart.). Insert—1611. Add: *Dugdale p. 346.*

Savile or Savell (York). Arg. on a bend sa. 3 owls of the field a baton in bend sinister gu. John Savell of Howley. *Eliz. Roll. xxiij.*

Savile (Blaby, co. Leicester ...). Add: *C.C.*

Sawley. Arg. on a bend betw. 2 cotises sa. 3 griffins heads erased of the first. *V.*

Sawney. Arg. an eagle displ. sa. Amys and Henry de Sawney. *D.*

Sawrey (Broughton Tower, co. Lancaster ...). Add: Sawrey (Plumpton, co. Lancaster, 1664). Same arms. *V.L.*

Sawyer. Arg. a chev. betw. 3 woodpeckers. ... "King Charles ij. have added to this coat the rose and crown to his Majesties Cook, one of this name." *Cady.*

Saxby. Barry of 6 or and az. on a bend engr. sa. ... Add: Thomas Saxby, Northumberland. *V.*

Saxton. Sa. on a bend betw. 2 cotises arg. 3 chaplets gu. *V.**

Say (Richards Castle, co. Hereford). Add: *V.*

Say. Quarterly or and gu. in the first quarter a lion pass. guard. az. Sire ... de Say. *N.* Sire Say, Essex. temp. Edward iij. *V.*

Say (Bletchingdon, co. Oxford and Ickenham, co. Middlesex). ... Insert—Sir William Say. *V.* Add: *V.O.* Say (Co. Devon). Same arms. *Harl. MS. 1538. fo. 17b.*

Say (Weston Favell, co. Northants.). Same arms.

Say. Per pale az. and gu. 3 chevs. counterchanged of the field and fimbriated arg. Sir Wm. Say. *V.* But fimbriated or. Sir John Say. **Brass** at Broxbourn, co. Herts.

Say (Essex). Per pale gu. and az. three chevrons couped counterchanged and fimbriated arg. *Harl. MS. 1465. fo. 6b.*

Sayer or Saier (Michaell-Penkevell, co. Cornwall). Add: *V.C. p. 306.*

Sayer. Or a lion ramp. az. over all a bend wavy compony gu. and arg. *Robson.*

Sayer (Pulham, co. Norfolk). Add: *V.*

Sayers (Great Yarmouth). Gu. a chev. erm. betw. 3 sea pies ppr.

Saymell. Per pale indented (sometimes nebuly) or and gu. 6 martlets respectant each other 2. 2. and 2 counterchanged. *V.*

Sayre (Co. Norfolk). Add: *Cady.*

Sayton or Seaton. Az. a bend betw. six mullets arg. Add: *V.*

Scales (Baron Scales ...).... Gu. 6 escallops three two and one or. Add: ? arg.

Scarbar or Scarber (Ireland). Sa. a bend betw. 3 fleurs-de-lis or. Add: *V.*

Scarborough. Or a chev. sa. betw. 3 towers triple towered gu. *V.V.**

Scarborough or Scarburgh (Co. Norfolk). Add: *V.*

Scarbridge (Co. Lancaster). Add: *V.* Scarsburg. Same arms. *V.**

Scarby or Scardby. Add: Scardby, Monsire de Swardly. *Y.*

Scarlett (West Bergholt and Copsford, co. Essex). Insert—Granted by Camden.

Scarlett (East Dereham, Norfolk). Chequy or and gu. a lion ramp. sa. a canton arg.

Scarlton or Scharlton. Arg. a chev. engr. betw. 3 griffins heads erased sa. *V.V.**

Scattergood. Vert. a chev. voided of another engr. arg. *Randle Holme.* Vert. a chev. engr. arg. charged with another plain of the field. *Randle Holme.*

Scawen (Aden, co. Cornwall). Add: *V.C. 306.*

Scawen (Cashalton, Surrey). Arg. a chev. betw. 3 griffins heads erased sa. †

Scerlogg (Wales). See Scowlage.

Scgan (Scotland). Az. a bend arg. *Guillim.*

Scharlow. Sa. 3 bars arg. Sir William Scharlow. *V.*

Scheffield. Erm. a chev. gu. betw. 3 garbs or. Thomas Scheffield. *Y.*

Scherlis. Gu. a bend embattled counter embattled arg. Thomas Scherlis. *V.*

Schipley. Insert—Middlesex. Add: *V.*

Schives (Mureton, Scotland, 1672). Add: *Guillim.*

Schobington (Co. Buckingham). Arg. a chev. gu. betw. 3 squirrels sejant sa. cracking nuts or. *V.*

Schomberg (Recorder of Aldborough, 1845). Gu. 2 chevs. or betw. 12 escutcheons and 4 estoiles arg. in chief and a paschal lamb in base. ppr. *Debrett.*

Schooley (Cadwell, co. Bedford ... confirmed). Insert—by Flower.

Schotbotts. Per pale arg. and az. 2 lions ramp. reguard. addorsed counterchanged. *V.**

Schotbot. Per pale or and az. 2 lions ramp. reguard counterchanged. *V.*

Schorcher. Gu. on a bend arg. 2 bars gemelles of the first. *V.**

Schorcher. Gu. on a bend arg. a fess betw. two bars gemelles of the first. *V.*

Schike. Per chev. gu. and arg. 3 annulets counterchanged. *Harl. MS. 1458.*

Scirland. See Sherland.

Sclergs. Arg. a chev. gu. betw. three 5-foils az. Roger Sclergs. *V.*

Scobington. Add: *V.**

Scocath (Co. Kent). Add: *V.O. p. 165.*

Scopham. Arg. a bend sa. on an inescutcheon or a lion ramp. purp. Sir William Scopham. *V.*

Scopham. Arg. on a chev. betw. 3 crosses crosslet sa. five crescents or. Richard Skopham. *V.*

Scopham or Stopham. Arg. a bend sa. Add: *V.*

Scorah (Doncaster, co. York). 1666. Vair a bend engr. ... *Dugdale p. 168.*

Scorthose (Boroughbridge, co. York). ... a chev. ... betw. 3 escallops. ... Seal of John Scorthose.

Scot. Arg. on a chev. sa. three gauntlets or (another headpieces). Add: *V.*

Scote (Carlisle). Or on a bend az. a mullet of six points betw. two crescents of the field. *Robson.*

Scotney. ... 4 billets in bend ... betw. 2 bendlets ... a bordure dentele ... Peter de Scotney. *Seal c. 1260.*

Scott.

Scott (Thomas Scott alias Rotherham ...). Add: Scott alias Rotherham (Barnes Hall, co. York, 1612). Same arms, a crescent for diff. *F.Y.*

Scott. Arg. a chev. betw. 3 gridirons sa. Add: bendwise handles up. Add: Sir Thomas Scott, Alderman of London. *V.*

Scowlage or Scowrlage. Arg. three bars gu. Add: *V.*

Scoveney. Or a chev. sa. Sir John de Scoveney. *A.*

Scowles (Charlton—insert—nr Wantage, co. Berks. Granted 10 July 1613). Insert—by Segar, Garter. ...

Screen (William Screen, temp. Ric. ij. Hen. iv and Henry v). Az. 3 bars betw. 8 keys or 3. 2. 2. and 1. *Harl. MS. 980. fo. 300.*

Scremby (Scremby, co. Cumberland, temp. Richard ii). ... Add: †

Scrope (Baron Scrope of Bolton, and Earl of Sunderland ...). Add: Richard le Scrop. *S.* Az. a bend or a label of 3 points arg. Henry le Scrope. *S.* 5 points Sir Geoffrey Scrope, Masham and Upsall. *V.* And with an annulet on the bend sa.

Scrope. Sir Thomas le Scrop. *S.* And with a label of 3 points arg. each charged with as many bars gu. Monsire Henri le Scrop. *S.* (4th son of Henry, Lord Scrope of Masham). But the label compony arg. and gu. Sir Geoffrey, eldest son of Henry first Lord Scrope of Masham ob. 1362. The label erm. Monsire John le Scrop. *S.* Az. a bend or in chief a mullet erm. for diff. Monsire Steven le Scrope. *S.* Lord of Bentley, (3rd son of Richard, first Lord Scrope of Bolton).

Scrope. Az. a bend or in the dexter chief a crescent gu. for diff. Henry Scroup, co. York. *Eliz. Roll. xxx.*

Scrope. Az. on a bend or a lion ramp. purple. Sire Henri de Skrop. *N.* or le Scroope. *M.* Sire Henri Scroope, Essex, temp. Edw. iij. *V.* Henry le Scroop, Bolton. *Y.* Monsire William le Scroop. *Y.* Sir Henry Scrope, Chief Justice, First Lord Scrope of Bolton. ob. 7 Sept., 1336.

Scrope. Az. on a bend or 3 crescents of the first a label arg. Sir Thomas, second son of Sir Geoffrey Scrope of Masham 1322. *Scrope and Grosvenor Controversy ij. 105.*

Scrope. Az. on a bend or a lozenge in chief erm. Monsire ... le Scrop. *S.*

Scuteville. Barruly arg. and gu. a bend az. *Randle Holme.*

Searle (London and Plymouth, co. Devon ...). Add: *C.K. 1568.*

Seaver (Heath Hall, co. Armagh). Arg. a chev. gu. betw. 3 doves picking sheaves of wheat ppr.

Secker (Thomas Secker, Bishop . . .). Add: Secker (Feversham, Kent. Confirmed by Camden 1615). Same arms. *V.**

Secroft. Arg. on a chev. sa. betw. 3 mullets gu. a griffins head erased of the first. William Secroft. *V.*

Sedgrave. Arg. on a bend gu. three 3-foils or.

Seedgrew. Insert—(Ireland). Add: *V.*

Sees (Monsire Diggar Sees). Per fess or and az. in chief a lion ramp. iss. sa. in base 6 plates 3. 2. and 1. *D.*

Seger or Segar. Add: *V.** but raven ppr. *V.*

Segar. Or a chev. az. betw. 3 ravens ppr. *V.*

Segar (Confirmed to Robert Segar of the Isle of Sheppey, Kent 1568). Or a chev. betw. 3 mullets az. *Guillim.*

Segrave (William Segrave, co. York). Sa. a lion ramp. arg. tail forked ducally crowned. *Eliz. Roll. xxv.*

Segrave (Cos. Leicester and Lincoln). Add: *Z. 208.* Sir John de Segrave. *H.J.K.N.V.* And with a label gu. Sir Nicholas de Segrave. *H.K.L.N.O.G.J.* And with a dexter baston gu. Henry de Segrave. *G.N.* The baston engr. gu. Sire Johan de Segrave. *N.* The baston or. Sir Symon de Segrave. *N.* And with a fleur-de-lis gu. at the shoulder. Sir Stephen de Segrave. *L.* And over all a baston engr. gu. Sir Henry de Segrave. *L.*

Segrety or Segriti. Add: *V.*

Segrey. Add: Simon de Segre. *E. Y.*

Seint Clowe. Arg. a chev. gu. betw. 3 nails sa. *V.*

Seintclowe. Arg. a chev betw. 3 nails sa. *V.**

Sekynton or Sequinton. . . . a bend charged with 3 chevrons . . . in the sinister chief a pierced mullet . . . Thomas Sequinton. **Seal.** v. Hen. iv. 1403.

Seinttle. Az. 2 bars arg. a chief gu. Hugh Seinttle. *Y.* (But query Deinvile).

Selby (Whitehouse, co. Durham, bart.). Insert— 1663 . . .

Selby (Yearle, co. Northumberland). Barry of eight sa. . . . Add: Sir William Selby. Sheriff of Newcastle 1501. *Carr MS.*

Selby. Insert—The Mote, co. Kent. Barry of fourteen or and sa. Add: *A.A.*

Seldon (Exeter). Az. 3 bendlets arg. *Robson.*

Selley. Erm. 2 chevs. purp. Sir John Selley. *V.*

Selley (Co. Cornwall). Erm. 3 chevs. gu. Add: Sir John Selley "Breton". *Cotton MS. Tiberius D. 10.*

Selley. Arg. three chevs. gu. a bordure engr. sa. Add: Sir Alexander Selley. *V.*

Selling (Co. Kent). . . . wolves heads erased or— insert—*V.* (another . . .

Sellington. Add: *Harl. MS. 1386. fo. 36.*

Selwyn (Co. Essex and Freston, Bechington, co. Sussex; granted May 1611). Insert—by Camden Add: John Selwyn. *V.* Jasper Selwyn. *Dug. O. J.*

Senlis. Chequy arg. and sa. 2 bars gu. in chief 3 fleurs-de-lis or. *V.*

Sentliz. Arg. 2 bars and in chief 3 fleurs-de-lis gu. *V.*

Sennyle. Arg. a bend betw. 6 crosses crosslet fitchy or. Sir Simon de Sennyle. *R.*

Serjant (Co. Kent). Add: *V.*

Serjantson (Hanlith Hall and Camp Hill, co. York). Add: *Foster.*

Sethelston. Or an eagle displ. gu. armed az. *V.**

Seton. Gu. a bend arg. betw. six martlets or. Add: *V.* Add: Sir John de Seton. *S.V.Y.*

Seward. Gu. a chev. erm. betw. 3 escallops or. *Dingley.*

Sewell (Newport, Isle of Wight). Add: Sewale or Sewayll. *V.*

Sewale (Co. Chester and Essex). Sa. a chev. betw. three gadflies arg.

Sewer (Kent). Or billetty sa. 3 bendlets gu. *Cady.*

Sewster (Steeple Morden, co. Cambridge). Add: Sir Robert Sewster (Great Raneby, co. Hunts. 1664. *L.N.*

Seyer (Co. Wilts.). Gu. a chev. arg. betw. 3 birds ? seagulls ppr. *Harl. MS. 1404. fo. 146.*

Seyer (Co. Wilts). Or a chev. az. betw. 3 seagulls ppr. *Harl. MS. 1404. fo. 146.*

Seymer. Sa. on a chev. betw. three cockatrices or 5 mullets gu. *V.**

Seymor or St. Maur.

Seymor. Arg. 2 chevs. gu. a label of 4 points az. Hue de Seymors. *G.*

Seyncks, Seynkes or Scynks. Add: *V.**

Seynner.

Seynes (Newark   ). Sa. on a chev. betw. 3 cockatrices or 5 mullets gu. *V.*

Shadwell (Lyndowne, co. Stafford . . .). Add: *V.V.**

Shafto of Whitworth. Gu. on a bend arg. three mullets az. *Surtees.*

Shafto (Bavington, Northumberland). Gu. on a bend arg. 3 mullets sa. *Eliz. Roll. xxxiv.*

Shafton (Recorder of Newcastle 1670). Gu. on a bend arg. 3 mullets az. in the sinister chief a rose or. *L.N.*

Shakeby. Or a bend erm. betw. 2 cotises indented az. *V.V.**

Shakerley (Shackerly, co. Lancaster). Arg. a chev. betw. 3 tufts of reeds vert. *V.L. 1661.*

Shakesburgh. Alias Shuckburgh . . . Add: *V.*

Shakestaffe. Arg. a chev. removed vert. † *Randle Holme.*

Shambroke. Arg. a chev. betw. 3 congers heads erased gu.—insert—*V.* (another . . .

Shapcote (Co. Devon). Sa. a chev. betw. 3 dovecotes arg. *Visitation 1620. Colby.*

Shapleigh (Totnes, co. Devon . . .). Add: *V.D. 1620.*

Shapter (Exeter). Arg. on a chev. az. betw. in chief 2 chaplets and in base a stork or an escallop betw. 2 martlets or. *Colby.*

Shard (Horsleydown, co. Surrey). Add: Sir Isaac Shard, High Sheriff of Surrey 1707. *L.N.*

Shardelow (Schimpling, co. Norfolk). . . . crosslet fitchee az.—insert—*V.* (another, sa.). Add: *V.*

Sharleton. Sa. 2 bendlets compony or and arg. *V.** But counter compony. *V.*

Shareshill (Shareshill, co. Stafford). Arg. 2 bars wavy gu. within a bordure sa. *Erdeswick.*

Sharnborne (Sharnborne Hall, co. Norfolk). Add: Andrew de Sharingburne. *Y.*

Sharnesfield. Add: *V.*

Sharnfield. Az. an eagle displ. or membered gu. Add: *Y.*

Sharpey (Sharpel, co. Kent . . .). Add: *W.*

Shastow. Gu. on a bend arg. 3 mullets az. *V.* Robert de Shastowe. *B.*

Shaw (Eltham, co. Kent. bart.). Insert—1665 . . .

Shaw (Heath Charnock, co. Lancaster 1664). Add: *V.L.*

Shaw (Preston, co. Lancaster 1664). Add: *V.L.*

Shaw (Colchester, co. Essex and London 1586). Add: John Shawe, Clerk of the Chamber of London. Granted by Cooke. *W.*

Shaw (Sir John Shaw, Lord Mayor of London). Arg. a chev. betw. 3 lozenges ermines. *V.*

Shaw (Alderman of London). 1500. Arg. a chev. betw. 3 lozenges ermines a bordure gu. **Brass** in Hornchurch. *Ogborne.*

Shaw. Arg. a chev. wavy betw. three eagles displ. sa. Crest: A hinds head . . . Add: *V.**

Shaw (Sheppard Castle, co. York. 1666). Vert. a chev. betw. 3 covered cups or. *Dugdale p. 365.*

Shawe (Kesgrave Hall, co. Suffolk). . . . Arg. a chev. erm. —amend to read 'ermines' . . .

Shaw (Arrow Hall, co. Chester). Arg. 2 chevs. betw. 3 lozenges ermines.

Sheafe (London). Erm on a chev. gu. betw. 3 ogresses as many garbs . . . *Guillim.*

Sheepshanks (Leeds, co. York). Add: The Arms of John Sheepshanks who died in 1863 and left his celebrated Gallery of Pictures to the Nation.

Sheer (Exeter). Az. a Pelican feeding on a garb. or. *Robson.*

Sheffield (Duke of Buckingham and Normanby). . . . Add: Sheffield of Mulgrave. *Cady.* Sir Thomas Sheffielde. *V.*

Sheffield. Gu. a chev. betw. three garbs. or. *V.**

Sheffield. Erm. on a chev. gu. 3 garbs or. Thomas Scheffeild. *Y.*

Sheffield (Normanby, co. Lincoln, bart.). Insert— 1755 . . .

Sheil (M.P. for Athlone 1874). . . . a lion ramp. . . . in chief 2 dexter hands appauming couped . . . and in base a mullet. *Debrett.*

Sheild (Co. Rutland). Gu. on a bend engr. or 3 shields. sa.

Sheldon. Arg. on a bend gu. 3 sheldrakes of the first. Dr Gilbert Sheldon, co. Stafford. *Ashmole MS. Wood. 33. fo. 93. V.**

Sheldon (Hampton Court, co. Surrey). . . . Add: Gilbert Sheldon, Bishop of London, granted by Walker 1660. Same arms. *Z. 472.*

Sheldon (Arden, co. Warwick . . .). Add: *Guillim.*

Shelleto (York). . . . a chev. engr. . . . betw. 10 crosses crosslet. *Dugdale 1666.*

Shelleto (Houghton, co. York. Exemplified in 1602 by Dethick, Garter). Same arms. *Northern Grants. xlv.*

Shelton. Arg. a chevron gu. *V.*

Shelton. Arg. on a bend sa. 3 fleurs-de-lis or. Crest: . . . Add: Rauf Shelton. *V.*

Shenloup (Norfolk). Arg. a chev. betw. 3 crosses crosslet fitchy gu. *Cady.*

Shepard or Shepperd (Chelsbury and Roulwright, co. Oxford). Az. on a chev. or —amend to read—betw. as many fleurs-de-lis of the second three estoiles gu. (another . . . Add: *V.O.*

Sheperwast. Add: †

Shepheard (Granted to Alexander Shepheard of Buckingham by Camden Feb. 1615). Gu. 3 poleaxes in fess or a chief erm. *Syl. Morgan.*

Sherard (Baron Sherard) . . . Add: Sherard Whitsonayne, co. Rutland). Same arms.

Sherard (Lopethorpe, co. Lincoln. bart.). Insert—1674 . . . Add: † for diff.

Sherborne (Tower of London). Add: *Guillim.*

Sherborne (Sherborne, co. Lancaster). Vert. an eagle displ. arg. *W.*

Sherborne. Vert. a lion ramp. guard. arg. Sir John Sherborne. *Q.* Sir Richard Sherburne, co. Lancaster. *V.* And quartering Bailey; Sherburne, of Sherborne, co. Lancaster. *Harl. MS. 1549. fo. 86.*

Sherbrooke (Oxton, co. Nottingham). Add: *V.N.*

Sherbrowe. Arg. a chev. gu. betw. 3 oakleaves vert. *W.*

Sherborne (Wolfhouse, co. Lancaster 1664). Arg. a lion ramp. vert. *V.L.*

Sherborne (Little Milton). Same arms, quartering az. 3 mascles or. *V.L. 1664.*

Sherd (Disley, co. Chester). Add: Sherd (Rotherham, co. York). Same arms.

Sherington. Arg. a talbot pass. sa. goutty or. *V.V.**

Sherland (Sheppey, co. Kent and co. Norfolk). Add: Sir Robert de Scirland. *L.N.V.* Sir Roger de Schirlond or Scirland *F.D.A.* Sir Roger de Sirlonde. *E.*

Sherley. Gu. on a bend or three eagles legs sa. Add: *V.*

Sherman (Yaxley, co. Suffolk). Add: Sherman (co. Leicester 1619). Same arms. *C.C.*

Sherwood. Per bend sinister sa. and arg. a bull pass. reguard. erm. and ermines horned gu. *V.*

Sherwood. Arg. a chev. sa. betw. 3 mullets gu. *Collinson Somerset. j. 204.*

Sheseldon. Arg. a chev. sa. betw. 3 chisels or handled of the second. *Harl. MS. 1386. fo. 95.*

Shiers (Slyfield, co. Surrey. bart.). Insert—1684
. . .

Shiffner (Coombe, co. Sussex, bart.). Insert—1818 . . .

Shipley or Schipley (Middlesex). Az. a chev. arg. betw. 3 chessrooks or. *V.*

Shippen (Vice Chancellor of Oxford). Arg. a chev. betw. 3 oak leaves gu. †

Shirland. Az. 5 lions ramp. arg. a quarter erm. Sir Robert de Shirland. *L. Harl. MS. 6589.*

Shirley (Preston, co. Sussex, bart.). Insert—1665
. . .

Shirley. Arg. 2 bars wavy betw. 3 ducks arg. (sic.)[1]. *V.**

Shirley (London). Confirmed—insert—by Segar . . . Add: *V.W.*

Shirley (Astwell, co. Northampton and Stanton Harold, co. Leicester). Paly of 6 or and az. a canton erm. *Z. 237.*

Shoppee. Az. a chev. or betw. in chief of the second and in base a lion ramp. arg. **Book Plate.**

Shore (Baron Teignmouth). Add: Richard Shore. *V.*

Shore (Snifferton 1662). Arg. a bend sa. betw. 3 oak leaves vert. *Dugdale. Vist. Derby.*

Shorthose. Arg. on a chev. sa. 3 crosses crosslet of the field . . . Add: William Shorthose, co. York. *V.*

Shorthose. Az. on a chev. betw. 3 crescents arg. as many escallops sa. *V.*

Shorthose (Temp. Edw. ij). Arg. on a chev. betw. betw. 3 estoiles of 6 points sa. as many crescents of the first. *F. Y.*

Shrigley (Dublin). Gu. a chev. or betw. 3 legs couped below the knee az. in chief a pierced mullet. †

Shrigley. Arg. a chev. betw. 3 soldering irons sa. *V.* and *Harl. MS. 1306. fo. 95.*

Shuckborough (Shuckborough, co. Warwick. Baronetcy 1650). Sa. a chev. engr. betw. 3 mullets arg. *Guillim.*

Shuckforth (Diss. Norfolk). . . . a chev. erm. betw. 3 eagles displ. with 2 heads . . . *Blomfield.*

Shuldham (Shuldham, co. Norfolk. . . .). Add: *V.* Hugo de Schuldam. *Roll of Manor of Marham, co. Norfolk c. 1275.*

Shuldham (Dunmanway, co. Cork . . .). Add: *A.A.*

Shute (Hollington, co. Cambridge). Add: Sir Robert Shute (Justice of the Queens Bench 1584). *Dug. O.J.*

Sibbills. Insert—Kent, Gyronny of eight . . . Add: *V.*

Sibell. Add: 'handled or'. Add: *V.*

Sibsay (Holbeach). Arg. on a bend az. 5 crosses humetty or.

Sibthorpe. Arg. 2 bars gu. within a bordure engr. sa. *V.**

Sibthorpe. St. Albans, co. Herts. Same arms.

Sidebottom (Hadfield, near Manchester). 1874. Or on a chev. engr. sa. 2 bugle horns stringed . . . 3 birds volant towards the base . . . *Debrett.*

Sidey. Insert—Bures St. Mary 1530. Add: *W.*

Sidnam (Co. Somerset). Arg. 3 rams pass. sa. *V.S. 1623.*

Sidney (Shelley-Sidney, Penshurst Place, co. Kent, bart. title vested in Lord de L'Isle and Dudley . . .). Quarterly 1st and 4th—delete 'arg.' substitute 'or'.

Sigden. Arg. a chev. gu. betw. 3 towers sa.

Siggeston, Segheston or Siggestone. Add: John de Siggeston. *V. Y.*

Sillesden. Add: *V.** Thos. Silisdon Figschinfield, Essex. *V.*

Silton. Arg. an eagle displ. vert. a baston compony gu. and arg. Sir John Silton. *L. Harl. MS. 6589.*

Silverlock (Sussex and Essex). Sa. a chev. engr. betw. 3 padlocks arg. *Harl. MS. 1432. fo. 9.*

Simeon. Arg. on a bend sa. 3 dolphins embowed naiant bendwise or. *V.V.**

Siminges (London . . .). Add: Granted to John Siminges of London *MD., W.*

Siminges. Erm. an eagle rising holding in the dexter claw a stone gu. John Siminges. MD., *V.*

Simonds (Co. Worcester). Az. a chev. quarterly or and arg. betw. 3 fleurs-de-lis gold.

---

1. Probably *azure* field but certainly a case for avoiding confusable abbreviations. Az. may be Ar, Gu. may be Sa. etc. Modern armorists have learnt the lesson.

Simon (London and Jamaica 1874). Az. on a chev. erm. betw. in chief two branches of laurel . . . and in base a lion dormant . . . an antique crown. *Debrett.*

Simons. Per chev. embattled gu. and sa. three martlets or. *V.**

Simple (Scotland). Or a chev. chequy arg. and gu. betw. 3 bugle horns stringed sa. *Cady.*

Simpson (Mellor Lodge, co. Derby). Add: Thomas Simpson, co. Rutland. *V.* Simpson (Ryton, co. York). *Dugdale. 1665.*

Singleton. Gu. 3 chevs. arg.

Singleton (Broughton, co. Lancaster &c. . . .). Add: *V.*

Singleton (Co. Essex. temp. Edward iii . . .). Add: Sir Hasbard de Singleton. *V.*

Singleton. Arg. 3 chevs. betw. as many martlets sa. *V.**

Singleton (Steyning, co. Lancaster). . . . Add: *V.L.*

Sipdene. Arg. a chev. betw. 3 leaves gu. *V.* Oak leaves *V.**

Sirr (The Rev. J. D. Sirr). Az. 2 chevs. braced or betw. 3 estoiles arg. in the centre chief a harp surmounted by an Imperial crown. **Book Plate.**

Skenard. Arg. a chev. betw. 3 hawks lures gu.

Skenock (Quartered by Lord de Dunstanville. Arg. a chev. sa. betw. 3 mullets gu. *Lysons.*

Skerne (Portington, co. York). Gu. in the dexter chief and sinister base point a tower and in the sinister chief and dexter base point a lion ramp. or. *F.Y.*

Skeres (Co. York; granted). Insert—by Camden . . .

Skeynert. Sa. a chev. betw. 3 lures or. *V.**

Skewse (Co. Cornwall). Add: *V.*

Skippe (Ledbury, co. Hereford). Add: John Skip, Bishop of Hereford 1539–52. Same arms, But roses stalked and leaves vert.

Skipton (John de Skipton). Arg. a lion ramp. and a base indented purp. *Harl. MS. 1386. fo. 36.*

Skipton. Arg. an anchor gu.

Skipton (Beechill, co. Londonderry). . . . Add: Sir John de Skypton. †

Skipton (Co. Derry). Arg. an anchor in pale sa. in dexter chief a martlet of the last. *A.A.*

Skipwith (Skipwith, co. York . . .). Add: Skipwith Newbold Hall, co. Warwick. Baronetcy 1670). Same arms. *Guillim.*

Skipwith (Prestwould, co. Leicester, bart.). Insert —1622 ext.

Skipwith (St. Albans). Arg. 2 bars gu. on a chief of the last a greyhound pass. per pale or and erm. *V.*

Skirving (That Ilk). Margin—Skirven. *Guillim.*

Skot. Arg. on a chev. sa. three—insert—'esquires' helmets. or. Add: *V.*

Skull (Much Cowarne, co. Hereford). Add: and with a mullet on the bend for diff. Sir Walter Skull, co. Hereford. *V.*

Skynner (Thomas Skynner, Mayor of London). Visit. London—correct to read 1596—amend 'arg.' to 'Or' on a fess . . .

Skynner. Gu. 3 crossbows unbent arg. the stocks or. *V.*

Skynner. Arg. a chev. betw. 3 griffins heads erased sa. Add: *Collinson Somerset. j. 96.*

Skynner. Gu. three crossbows unbent or. Add: *V.**

Skyrmester or Skrymsher (Cos. Nottingham and Stafford). Gu. a lion ramp. or a bend vair. Add: Confirmed by Flower, Norroy in 1584 to Thomas Skrymsoure of Aquilot, co. Stafford. *Guillim.*

Slade (Exeter). Gu. on a chev. arg. betw. 3 falcons heads erased of the second a trefoil slipped vert. *Robson.*

Slaney or Slany (Sir Stephen Slaney . . .). Add: Add: *V.E. 1634.*

Slanning (Ley, co. Devon . . .). Add: *Guillim.*

Slanning (Maristow, co. Devon, bart.). Insert— 1662 . . .

Slaters (Company of, Newcastle on Tyne). Az. a chev. betw. 3 lathing hammers arg. handled or.

Slatter. Or a chev. embattled vert. *Randle Holme.*

Sleggs (Aynesbury, co. Huntingdon). Add: *V.H.*

Sleght. Add: Sir Robert Slight. *S.V.*

Sleghtes (The arms of Robert Sleghtes of Legburn co. Lincoln . . .). Margin—†

Slensly. Add: *V.**

Slie. Add: *V.*

Slingsby (of Scriven, co. York. Baronet of Nova Scotia). Quarterly 1 and 4 Scriven; 2 and 3 Slingsby overall the badge of Nova Scotia baronets. Crest: On a wreath arg. and gu. a lion pass. vert. Supporters: Dexter a unicorn arg. horn mane, hoofs collar and chain or. Sinister a savage ppr. wreathed about his temple and middle with laurel. Motto: "Veritas liberavit."

Slingsby (Co. York). Gu. a chev. or in chief 2 leopards heads of the second. Add: *V.*

Slowley (Slowley-in-Sherwell . . . Devon . . .). Add: *V.D. 1620. W.*

Smalborough. Sa. a chev. betw. 3 bears heads couped or muzzled gu. Sir Wm. Smalborough. *S.*

Smalborough. Sa. a chev. betw. 3 bears heads couped or muzzled gu. *V.V.**

Smalpece or Smallpiece (Worlingham, co. Suffolk). Add: Smallpeece (Hockering, co. Norfolk. Granted 1590). Same arms. *W.*

Smarte (West Chickerel, co. Dorset). Arg. a chev. betw. 3 pheons gu.

Smart. Erm. 3 chessrooks gu. Crest: An ostrich's head . . . Add: *V.*

Smarte. Per bend sinister or and gu. on a bend double cotised 3 lions pass.—insert—bendwise . . . Add: *V.V.**

Smelt (Co. York). Add: Smelt (Kirkby Fleetham and Beverley, co. York).

Smert (Co. Devon). Add: *V.*

Smert (London) . . . Add: Smert (Garter King at Arms in 1450) *V.*

Smert. Arg. on a bend engr. az. betw. 2 demi-greyhounds bendways sa. . . . Add: William Smert, London. *V.*

Smert. Arg. on a bend engr. az. betw. 2 demi-greyhounds ramp. sa. platy and collared arg. 3 marigolds gu. stalked and leaved vert. *V.**

Smerys or Smeys. Sa. 3 chevs. arg. betw. as many mullets or. *V.*

Smethley. Add: *V.*

Smetins. Gu. a chev. betw. 3 crescents arg. The learned Smethins. 1716.

Smethurst (Chorley and Rookwood, co. Lancaster). Add: *F.L.*

Smith (Lenton, co. Beds. Wm. Smith, Yeoman of the Buttery). Erm. on a chev. engr. az. 3 estoiles or in chief a mullet gu. *Harl. MS. 3526.*

Smith (Co. Berks. granted 21 April 1671 to Edward Smith). . . . Add: *Harl. MS. 1172.*

Smith (temp. Henry vij). Arg. 3 greyhounds courant in pale sa. collared or betw. 10 crosses patty fitchy of the second. *V.*

Smith (Hough, co. Chester). Add: Smith (Hough, Cheshire). Same arms; quartering sa. 6 fleurs-de-lis arg. *Harl. MS. 2129. fo. 220b.*

Smith (London). Sa. 3 annulets interlaced or on a chief of the last a lion pass. of the first. *Harl. MS. 3526.*

Smith (West Herrington, co. Durham). Arg. on a bend betw. 2 unicrons heads erased az. armed and maned or. 3 lozenges erminois. *Surtees.*

Smith (Totnes, co. Devon). Add: *Harl. MS. 352b.*

Smith (Durham: granted to John Smith, DD. of Durham . . .). Add: Smith (Burnhall, co. Durham). Same arms. *Surtees.*

Smith (Colpike Hall, co. Durham . . .). Add: *Grazebrook. p. 26.*

Smith (Gloucester and Lambeth, Surrey, co. Surrey; confirmed—insert—by Camden . . .). Add: *W.*

Smith (West Ham, co. Essex and Stoke Prior, co. Worcester). Az. 2 bars wavy erm. on a chief or a demi-lion ramp. issuant ermines. *Visitation of London. 1633.*

Smith (Cheshire). Az. 2 bars wavy erm. on a chief or 3 demi-lions ramp. or. *Harl. MS. 3526.*

Smith. Arg. 2 bars gu. in chief three 5-foils az. *Harl. MS. 3625.*

Smith (Bradbury, co. Chester). Arg. 2 bars wavy erm. in chief 3 bazants. *Glazebrook. p. 10.*

Smith. Arg. 2 bars betw. 3 pheons sa. †

Smith (The Right Hon. John Smith, Speaker of the House of Commons and Chancellor of the Exchequer. temp. Queen Anne.). Az. two bars betw. 3 pheons or and quartering . . . on a chev. . . betw. 3 crosses patty . . . as many roundlets. *Grazebrook. p. 77.*

Smith. Arg. 2 bars gu. each charged with 3 fleurs-de-lis or on a chief az. a lion pass. of the first. *Harl. MS. 3526.*

Smith (Thomas Smith, Bishop of Carlisle 1684). Sa. 3 bars or in chief as many crosses patty fitchy of the second. *Dallaway in MS. in Trinity College, Oxford.*

Smith (Cornwall). Arg. 2 bars gemel sa. on a chief arg. a demi-griffin issuant of the second. *Harl. MS. 3625.*

Smith. Arg. on a bend az. three mullets of the field: quartering or 4 birds sa. †

Smith. Or 2 bendlets engr. ermines. *Harl. MS. 3526.*

Smith (Harwich, Essex). Gu. a chev. betw. 3 crosses crosslet arg. *Grazebrook. p. 49.*

Smith (Nunstainton, co. Durham confirmed by Flower, Norroy 11 Jan, 1567). Arg. a bend betw. 2 unicorns heads erased gu. *Guillim.*

Smith (Thomas Smith, Lord of the Manor of Harnhill, co. Gloucester). . . . Add: *Rudder's Gloucestershire. p. 476.*

Smith (Winell, co. Hereford). Arg. a chev. sa. betw. three ravens ppr. Add: *Grazebrook. p. 74.*

Smith (Water Newton, co. Huntingdon). Margin —? granted by Dethick.

Smith (Co. Kent). Erm. 2 chevs sa. on each 3 fleurs-de-lis or. Add: Granted by Camden. *W.*

Smith (Codenham, co. Kent). Add: *W.*

Smith (Ostenhanger, Kent). Az. a chev. engr. betw. 3 lions pass. guard. or. Crest: An ounces head erased arg. spotted sa. collared of the last edged or chained gold. *Harl. MS. 3526.*

Smith (Co. Lancaster). Or on a chev. gu. betw. three 5-foils vert. as many leopards heads.

Smith (Co. Lancaster). Vert. a chev. betw. 3 mallets or. Add: *Harl. MS. 3526.*

Smith (Granted in 1623—insert—by Segar. Add: *Guillim.*

Smith (Co. Leicester). Gu. on a chev. or betw. 3 plates as many crosses crosslet of the field. *Harl. MS. 3526.*

Smith (Theddlethorpe, co. Lincoln). Add: *Harl. MS. 3526.*

Smith. 1700. Sa. on a mount vert. a lion pass. reguard arg. *Topo. et Geneal. iij. 35.*

Smith (Ireland). Vert. fretty and semy of crosses flory or over all out of a ducal coronet gold a demi-bull salient pied ppr. *Grazebrook. p. 101.*

Smith (Ireland). Gu. a lion ramp. arg. on a chief of the last a mullet az. betw. 2 torteaux. *Grazebrook. p. 62.*

Smith (Mr. John Smith, Merchant of London). Vert. 3 lions ramp. sa. †

Smith (Abraham Smith of London). Add: *W.*

Smith (Hammersmith, co. Middlesex). Add: *Visitation 1663.* Add: Smith. Baronetcy 1694. Extinct 1760. Sir John Smith, bart. quartering gu. 2 chevrons and a bordure arg.

Smith (Parsons Green, co. Middlesex). Add: Sir Thomas Smith, Clerk of the Council. *W.* Same arms.

Smith (London). Arg. a chev. betw. 3 eagles displ. sa. *Harl. MS. 3526.*

Smith. Of London, buried at Christchurch. Sa. a chev. betw. 3 griffins segreant or on a chief of the last as many fleurs-de-lis gu. *Harl. MS. 3525.*

Smith (London. Granted by Walker, Garter 29 Oct. 1667). Gu. on a chev. engr. or 3 crosses patty fitchy sa. *Harl. MSS. 1144 and 1172.*

Smith (London). Arg. on a chev. sa. betw. 3 cinquefoils gu. as many leopards faces of the field. *Harl. MS. 3526.*

Smith (Sir John Smith, Baron of the Exchequer). Arg. on 2 chevs. sa. 6 fleurs-de-lis or a chief az. charged with a lion pass. of the third oppressed on the shoulder by a lozenge gu. *V.*

Smith (Sheriff of London 1509). Sa. on a chev. engr. betw. 6 crosses patty or 3 fleurs-de-lis az. *V.* *

Smith (Richard Smith, Alderman of London, Sheriff in 1509). . . . Add: *Harl. MS. 3526.*

Smith (London). Arg. on a chev. engr. sa. betw. 3 hurts . . . Add: *C.C. p. 79.*

Smith (Sir Walter Smith, Sherford, co. Warwick). Arg. semy of crosses crosslet fitchy sa. 3 greyhounds courant in pale of the second. *Harl. MS. 3526.*

Smith (London). Arg. a chev. sa. on a chief of the second 3 leopards faces or. Granted by Cook. *W.*

Smith (Jenkin Smith of London). Add: *W*

Smith (Middlesex, confirmed 1561). Sa. a bend arg. betw. 7 billets or 4 and 3. *Guillim.* Jenkin Smith, Bury. Same arms. *V.*

Smith. Arg. a chev. betw. 3 griffins heads couped sa. *Harl. MS. 3526.*

Smith (1655 Northants and America). Arg. a chev. betw. 3 griffins heads erased gu.

Smith (Co. Norfolk). Erm. on a bend vert. 3 saltires arg. . . . Add: Authority. *Harl. MS. 3560.*

Smith (Walpole, co. Norfolk). Add: *V.*

Smith (Co. Northampton). Add: *Harl. MS. 3526.*

Smith. Arg. on a bend betw. 2 unicorns heads erazed az. crined or 3 bezants. *Eliz. Roll. xxxv.*

Smith (Co. Oxford). Add: *Plott's Oxfordshire.*

Smith (Oxford). . . . a chev. betw. 3 anvils 1674. *Guillim.*

Smith (Morville, co. Salop). Sa. on a bend betw. 2 cotises arg. 3 martlets gu. *Harl. MS. 3625.*

Smith (Long Ashton, co. Somerset, Baronetcy 1661). Arg. on a chev. sa. betw. 3 leopards faces gu. as many 5-foils or. *Guillim.*

Smith (Boughton, co. Somerset). Add: *Harl. MS. 3526.*

Smith (Co. Devon). Arg. a bend wavy betw. 2 cotises sa. and 3 eagles displ. of the last. *Harl. MS. 3625.*

Smith (Elmsett, co. Suffolk). Add: *Harl. MS. 3625.*

Smith (Co. Surrey). Arg. a chev. cotised betw. 3 crosses pattee gu. Crest: a demi-stag . . . Add: *Harl. MS. 3526.*

Smith (Milford, co. Surrey, confirmed). Insert—by Bysche . . .

Smith (Stratford-upon-Avon, co. Warwick 1838). Gu. 3 crossbows or in the centre point a bezant. Quartering sa. a dolphin embowed arg. *Berry.*

Smith (John Smith, Halesworth, Suffolk). Az. billetty arg. query or/a bend erm. *W.*

Smith (Co. Worcester). Sa. a bend betw. 3 mullets of 6 points . . . Add: *Dingley.*

Smith alias Smithley (Brantingham and Beverley, co. York). Add: the unicorns heads gu. *Harl. MS. 3526.*

Smith (Sneinton, co. York 1665). Arg. on a bend betw. 2 unicorns heads erased az. maned or 3 lozenges erminois in chief a 3-foil slipped gu. *Dugdale. p. 116.*

Smith (Holbeck, Leeds, co. York). Erm. on a bend az. betw. 2 unicorns heads erased of the second 3 lozenges or. Crest: Out of a coronet a demi-bull. *Whitaker's Leeds j. 360.*

Smyth (Marysham and Heath Hall, co. York). Same arms. *James's History of Bradford. p. 435.*

Smith (Co. York). Erm. a chev. gu. on a chief of the last 3 martlets arg.—underlined—and read 'or'. *Harl. MS. 3625.*

Smith (Crabbett, Sussex). Az. on two chevs. arg. ten fleurs-de-lis gu. on a chief of the second a lion pass. of the field. *Harl. MS. 6164. fo. 21b.*

Smith (Major General Sir Sigismund Smith, Knt. K.C.H. ob. 1834). Gu. a lion ramp. or quartering az. a chev. arg. over all on an escu. gu. a helmet . . . *Berry.*

Smith. Az. a chev. betw. ten 5-foils or 6 in chief and 4 in base. *Harl. MS. 3625.*

Smith. Vert. a chev. gu. cotised erminois betw. 3 Turks heads ppr. turbaned a chief arg. for augmentation thereon a mount vert. inscribed with the Greek letters K Y A gold and issuant therefrom a representation of the Silphinus plant ppr. *Grazebrook. p. 71.*

Smith (Edinburgh 1672). Add: *Lyon Register.*

Smith. Sa. on a chev. engr. betw. 6 crosses crosslet fitchee or. 3 fleurs-de-lis az. Add: *V.**

Smith. Sa. on a bend or 3 billets of the first. *W.* Quartered by Viell.

Smith (Milford, co. Tipperary). Arg. on a bend az. betw. 2 unicorns heads erased of the second 3 lozenges erm.

Smith (Annsbrook and Beabeg, co. Meath). Arg. on a bend betw. 2 bulls heads erased az. armed or 3 lozenges of the last.

Smith. Sa. 6 billets erm. 3. 2. and 1. *Harl. MS. 3526.*

Smith. Arg. a chev. gu. betw. 3 turks heads ppr. turbaned or. *Harl. MS. 3625.*

Smith. Arg. a chev. sa. betw. 3 turks heads ppr. *Grazebrook. p. 71.*

Smith. Erm. on a chev. engr. az. three fleurs-de-lis. *Grazebrook. p. 64.*

Smith of Atherstone. Or on a chev. betw. 3 leopards heads gu. as many suns of the first.

Smith. Arg. on a chev. betw. three birds heads erased sa. a 3-foil slipped arg. *Harl. MS. 3526.*

Smith. Arg. a chev. sa. betw. 3 catherine wheels gu. Add: Wm. Smith Bishop of Lincoln 1496. *W.*

Smith. Insert—London. Sa. a bend arg. betw. seven—'inked to read 'six'". Add: *Harl. MS. 3526.*

Smith (Cornwall). Arg. 2 bars gemel sa. in chief a demi-griffin segreant issuant of the last. *Harl. MS. 3625.*

Smith. . . . 2 bars gemel wavy . . . in chief a lion pass. . . . in base 4 mullets 3 and 1.

Smith (London). Az. a bend betw. six billets arg. (another, the bend and billets or.). *Harl. MS. 3526.*

Smith (London). Sa. a bend or betw. 6 billets arg. *Harl. MS. 3526.*

Smith (Quartered by Vernon, Lord Lyveden 1859). Gu. 3 bars gemel arg. a chev. erm. on a chief of the second 3 blackamoors heads ppr. on a canton of the field a battle axe or the whole within a bordure counter compony arg. and az. *Grazebrook. p. 97.*

Smith (Granted in 1803 to Sir Wm. Sidney Smith KCB., the Hero of Acre). Az. on a chev. engr. betw. 3 lions pass. guard. or a wreath of laurel ppr. betw. 2 crosses calvary sa. on a chief of augmentation . . . the interior of an ancient fortification in perspective in the angle a breach and on the sides of the said breach the standard of the Ottoman Empire and the Union Flag of Great Britain. *Grazebrook. p. 39.*

Smithin or Smythwyne (Gissing, Norfolk). Sa. 3 chevs. betw. as many mullets or. *Blomfield.*

Smithley. Arg. a chev. triparted sa.

Smithes. Add: George Smithes, Alderman and Sheriff of London 1611. *W.* Granted by Camden.

Smithes (London and Wike, co. Somerset, exemplified in 1602). *Collinson Somerset. iij. 463.*

Smiths. Company of Smiths, Cutlers, Saddlers, Armourers, Lorenners and Brasiers of the City of Exeter. Or on a chev. sa. betw. 3 esquires helmets ppr. a hammer gold interlaced saltirewise with a pair of pincers arg. betw. 2 manege saddles of the last in the centre chief point a padlock sa. on a chief gu. a hammer surmounted by a ducal crown or interlaced with a pair of pincers in fess arg. betw. 2 pairs of swords in saltire of the last pomels and hilts gold. *V.D. 1620.*

Smithson (Co. Suffolk). Add: Smithson (Monte-wearmouth, co. Durham).

Smyly (Co. Dublin . . .). Add: Smyly (Tyrone, Ireland). Same arms.

Smyth (Long Ashton, co. Somerset, bart . . .). Add: Smyth (co. Wilts.). Same arms. *Collinson Somerset ij. 294.*

Smyth (Isfield, co. Sussex, bart.). Insert—1714 . . .

Smyth. Or a chev. az. betw. three trefoils slipped vert. *Cotton MS. Tiberius. D. 10.*

Smyth (Walsocken, co. Norfolk). Add: Smyth (Cavendish, co. Suffolk). Same arms. *Harl. MS. 3526.*

Smyth (Oxford). Arg. a chev. sa. betw. 3 roses gu. a mullet for diff. quartering arg. a fess dancetty sa. betw. 3 roses gu. a mullet for diff. *V.O.*

Smith (Worcestershire). Sa. a bend betw. 3 mullets of 6 points arg. pierced of the field. *Grazebrook. p. 63.*

Smyth (Bushmills, co. Antrim and Magee College, Londonderry. M.P. for County Londonderry 1874). Az. on a mount in base vert. a castle arg. on a chief or 3 storks heads erased gu. *Debrett.*

Smyth.

Snape (Co. Devon). Arg. a lion ramp. ermines. *Lysons.*

Snassell or Snawsell (Bilton, co. York). Add: Seth Snassell, co. York. *V.* Quartering arg. on a bend sa. cotised gu. 3 fleurs-de-lis of the field. *Dugdale. p. 151.*

Snawsell (Co. York). Arg. on a chev. betw. three leopards faces gu. as many crosses crosslet fitchy of the first; quartering arg. on a bend cotised gu. 3 fleurs-de-lis of the field. *F.Y.*

Snayth. Arg. a chev. sa. betw. 3 falcons heads erased of the second beaked gu. Add: *V.*

Snayth. Arg. a chev. betw. 3 herons heads erased sa. Add: *V.**

Sneap or Snipper. Vert. a chev. betw. 3 snipe *Randle Holme.*

Snelling. Granted by Segar 1611–12. Vert. a chev. betw. 3 hinds heads couped or.

Snow (Kilkenny, Ireland). . . . a chev. or betw. 3 garbs . . .

Snow (Exeter). Gu. on a chev. engr. arg. betw. three plates as many martlets sa. *Robson.*

Snowden (Co. Lincoln 1640). Az. a lion ramp. or. *Yorke.*

Soame (Thurlow, co. Suffolk, bart.). Insert— 1684 . . . Add: *Guillim.*

Sodan (Co. Kent). Az. 3 bends arg. Add: Stephen Sodan. *A. Harl. MS. 6137.*

Sodan. Bendy of 6 arg. and az. Stephen de Sodan. *A.*

Solas. Or 4 pales az. a bendlet arg. *V.*

Solborne. Sa. platy and a canton erm. *V.*

Soleri or Solere. Az. 3 bendlets componee— insert—(or counter compony). . . . Add: *V.V.**

Solers. Paly of 6 or and az. a bend gu. Add: Henri de Solers. *E.*

Solington or Solyngton. Add: *V.*

Soley (Co. Worcester). Per pale or and gu. a chev. counterchanged betw. 3 soles az. and arg. *Moule. 187.*

Somayne. Arg. a lion ramp. gu. within a bordure wavy (?, engr.). az. *V.*

Someri. Or 3 lions pass. in pale az. Sir Johan de Someri. *G.L. Harl. MSS. 6137 and 6589.*

Somerton (Co. Worcester). Add: *V.*

Somerton. Arg. 2 lions ramp. combatant gu. Sir . . . de Somerton. *V.*

Somervile or Somerville (Whichnovre, co. Stafford). Add: *V.*

Somervile (Co. Warwick). Add: Roger de Somervile. *Y.* †

Someri. Sa. a bend betw. 6 martlets arg. Henri de Someri. *F.E.*

Somery. Az. fretty arg. on a canton or . . . fleur- de-lis gu. *A. Harl. MSS. 6137.*

Somery (Co. Bedford). Add: Sire Johan de Someri. *N.* But a bendlet gu. Somery, Counties Bedford, Hertford. *V.* Sir John Somery. *L.*

Somerye. Or 2 lions pass. az. Robert de Someri. *A. Harl. MS. 6137. B.C.E.F.* Sir Johan de Someri. *J.N.* Roger Someri. *Y.* Sir . . . de Someri, co. Warwick. *V.* John de Somery, mar: the heiress of Paganell.

Sonclere. Az. on a chev. arg. betw. 3 suns or as many pierced mullets sa. *V.* (gu. *V.**).

Soothill (Soothill, near Wakefield, co. York). Gu. an eagle displ. arg.

Sorocold (Barton, co. Lancaster 1664 . . .). Add: *V.L.*

Sorre. Add: Sir Mayhugh Sorre, Wales. *V.*

Sorrell (Waltham and Stebbings, co. Essex and Ipswich, co. Suffolk). Add: *V.E. 1634.*

Sorton. Arg. a chev. rompus. sa.

Sorton. Sa. a chev. fracted at the top arg. *Randle Holme.*

Sotherton (Newcastle-on-Tyne 1561). Add: *Carr MS.*

Sothall or Sothehall. Sa. a chev. betw. 3 crosses patty or. *V.*

Sothill. Gu. an eagle displ. arg. (another armed or). Add: Sir Henry de Sodhull. *O.V.* Sir John Sothulle. *N.* Johan de Sothile. *G.* Sir John Sothill, Essex temp. Edw. iij.

Sothill. Gu. an eagle displ. arg. over all a bar az. William de Sothill. *G.*

Sotwell.

Sotwell (Catlinghill, co. York . . .). Add: only two mullets in chief.

Soules. Arg. 3 bars gu. *V.*

South (Ferraby, co. Lincoln). . . . Add: John South, one of the Gentlemen of the Privy Chamber in Ordinary to King Charles ij., son of Sir John South, Kt. *Guillim.*

South. Arg. 2 bars gu. in chief a mullet pierced sa. Granted by Camden to Sir Francis South of Fotherby, co. Lincoln 1602. *Syl. Morgan.*

Southall. Gu. a baston compony arg. and az. a chief or. Sir John Sothall. *Cady.*

Southall (Co. Suffolk). Arg. on a chev. betw. 3 mullets gu. a rose of the first. *Cady.*

Southby (Abingdon, co. Berks.) 1670. Arg. a chev. gu. betw. 3 red cherries slipped ppr. *Guillim.*

Southcott (Bovey, Shillingford &c. . . . co. Devon . . .). Add: Southcott, Justice of the Queens Bench 1563.

Southcote (Southcote, co. Devon). Arg. a chev. betw. 3 coots sa. *V.E. 1634.*

Southerne (Fitts, co. Salop; granted). Insert—by Segar . . . Add: Sotherton. Same arms. *V.*

Southey. Gu. a chev. betw. 3 crosses crosslet arg. Crest: . . . Add: *Cotton MS. Tiberius. D. 10.*

Soureby. Arg. a chev. betw. 3 annulets az. John Soureby. *V.*

Southwell. Arg. a chev. gu. a chief indented vert. *Cady.*

Southwell. Az. a chev. engr. betw. 3 falcons arg. *Cady.*

Southworth. . . . a chev. . . . betw. 3 crosses patonce . . . Seal of Matthew de Sothworth 1394. *V.*

Southworth (Co. Lancaster). Sa. a chev. betw. 3 crescents arg. *V.*

Southworth (Smalesbury, co. Lancaster). Sa. a chev. betw. 3 crosses crosslet arg. *V.V.L.*

Southworth. Sa. a chev. betw. 3 crosses patonce arg. Sir Thomas Southworth. *S.*

Sowray (Co. York). *1666 Visit. Dugdale*—insert— p. 317 . . .

Spalding. Gu. 2 bars arg. in chief 3 annulets of the second. Add: Michell de Spalding. *Y.*

Spark. Arg. on a bend sa. a rose of the field.

Spark (Plymouth, co. Devon 1620). Chequy or and vert. on a bend erm. an annulet gu.

Sparrow (Red Hill, co. Anglesey). Or 3 lions ramp. sa. . . . . quartering arg. 3 hands gu. *Burke.*

Sparshall. Add: Sparsolle (Same arms.). *V.*

Speckard (London; granted). Insert—by Camden . . .

Speke (Anciently Le Espek . . .). Add: Speke (Bere, co. Cornwall). Same arms. *Lysons.* Sir Thomas Speke, co. Devon. Same arms. *Colby.*

Speke (Jordans, near Ilminster, co. Somerset . . .). Add: *V.*

Speke (Hasilbury, co. Wilts, bart). Insert—1660 . . . Add: Sir John Speke. *V.*

Spence (Scotland). Arg. a lion ramp. gu. over all on a bend sa. a round buckle betw. two mascles or. *Cady.*

Spencer. Quarterly arg. with gu. fretty or overall on a bend sa. 3 mullets of the first. Sir Hugh Spencer. *Q.* Gilbert de Despencer. *Q. Harl. MS. 6589.*

Spencer (Yarington, co. York). Quarterly arg. and gu. on a bend sa. 3 mullets of the first. William Spencer. *Eliz. Roll. xxv.*

Spencer (Ashton Hall, co. Lancaster 1664 . . .). Add: *V.L. 1664.*

Spencer (Crediton, co. Devon). . . . and their handles fretty—amend to read 'fretted' or. Add: *V.*

Spencer (Co. Devon). Sa. 2 bars wavy (another nebulee). erm. Add: Sir Robert Spencer. *V. Z. 333.*

Spencer. Arg. on a bend sa. 4 keys endorsed 2 and 2 and interlaced at the bows of the first. *V.**

Spencer. Barry of 6 or and az. a canton erm. Sir Philip Spencer. *S.V.*

Spencer (Wilton, co. Salop. and co. Stafford). Add: *V.*

Speney. Arg. a chev. sa. betw. 3 crescents gu. Add: *V.*

Spenythorne. Add: Thomas de Speneythorne. X.

Spicer (Weare, in Topsham, co. Devon . . .). Add: Spicer (Exeter, co. Devon). *V.D. 1620.*

Spicker. Gu. a chev. or betw. 3 nails points towards the fess point. . . .†

Spiney or De Spineto (Coughton, co. Warwick). Add: Quartered by Throckmorton.

Spittle (Leuchat, Scotland). Arg. an eagle displ. sa. in chief 2 crescents gu. *Guillim.*

Spooner (Co. Norfolk). **Az.** a chev. betw. 3 owls arg. *Cady.*

Spoore or Spoure (Trebartha and Northill, co. Cornwall). . . . Add: *V.C. p. 306.*

Spottiswood (Grunstain, Scotland 1672). Add: *Guillim.*

Sprat (Co. Dorset). Add: *V.** Thomas Sprat, Bishop of Rochester 1684–1713.

Sprotell (Scotland). Arg. a chev. chequy gu. and of the first betw. 3 palmers scrips of the second. *Cady.* (Tinctures also reversed).

Springnell(Highgate, co. Middlesex). Add: Springnell (Coppenthorp, co. York, Baronetcy 1641). Same arms.

Spring (Packenham, co. Suffolk . . .). Insert— Granted by Camden . . .

Spring. Insert—or Springes (Co. Suffolk). Add: *V.*

Spring. Arg. a lion ramp. vert. Sir John Spring, co. York. temp. Edw. j. *N.*

Springham. Gu. a chev. betw. 3 goats heads erased arg. attired or. *W.*

Springhose. Gu. 2 lions pass. arg. a label az. Roger Springhose. *F.* Roger Sprungehose. *E.*

Sprense. Arg. 3 bars sa. over all on a bend gu. 3 escallops or. *V.V.**

Spry or Sprie (Cornwall). Az. in chief a chev. and in base two bars or. *V.C. p. 306.*

Spurcock. Add: *V.*

Spurgeon (Rev. John Norris Spurgeon . . . co. Norfolk). Arg.—marginal note—? 'or'.

Spurway (Spurway and Oakford, co. Devon . . .). Add: *V.D. 1620.*

Spyer—marginal note—Spyre. Add: *V.O. W.*

Spygurnell. Az. 3 bars or. *V.*

Spygornell. Gu. 4 bars and in chief a lion pass. guard. or. *V.*

Squedale. Arg. a bend sa. fimbriated the outer edge engr. gu. betw. 2 eagles displ. vert. *W.*

Squire (Co. Suffolk). Or a squirrel sejant gu. *V.*

Stackpole. Arg. a lion ramp. gu. collared or. *N.* Add: Stackpole. Arg. a lion ramp. gu. collared of the field. Sir Richard Stackpole, co. Gloucester. temp. Edwd. j. *V.*

Stafferton or Staverdon. Arg. a bend engr. betw. two martlets gu. *V.*

Stafford (Earl of Stafford &c. . . . .). Add: Le Baron de Estafforde. *N.* Le Baron Stafford. *I.* Sir Rauf de Stafford. *R.L.* Conte de Stafford. *S.T.Y.* Thomas Stafford. *S.*

Stafford. Or a chev. gu. over all a bendlet az. Monsire Robert de Stafford. *S.*

Stafford (Eyam, co. Derby). Erm. on a bend gu. 3 escallops. *Lysons.*

Stafford. Or on a chev. gu. 3 plates. Le Baron de Stafford. *E.* Sir Robert de Stafford. *X.* And with a label of 5 points az. Robert de Stafford. *E.F.*

Stafford (Bootham Hall, co. Derby). Add: Edmon Stafford. *S.*

Stafford. Or a chev. gu. a chief az. Monsire Nicol de Stafford. *S.* Nicholas Stafford of Froddeswall. *V.*

Stafford (Hook, Suthwyck and Frome, co. Dorset) Delete—(another invected). Add: *V.* Add: Sir Umfrey de Stafford. *S.* Earl of Devon 1469. Stafford of Hook, quartered by Willoughby. *U.*

Stafford (Sydenham, co. Devon). Add: *V.**

Stafford. Or a chev. and bordure gu. Sir Hugh Stafford. *T.*

Stafford. Or on a chev. gu. three bezants— insert—Sire Robert de Estafford. *N.* And with a label of 3 points az. Robert Stafford Egginton and Mogginton. *V.*

Stafford. Or a chev. betw. 9 martlets sa. *V.**

Stafford (Mount Stafford, co. Down &c.). Add: Sir Humphrey Stafford, Codrith, co. Hertford. *V.* Stafford (Grafton). Same arms. *Cady.*

Stainings (Honycott, co. Somerset and Erisone, co. Suffolk). Add: *Syl. Morgan.*

Stainings (Honycott, co. Somerset). Arg. a bat displ. sa. on a chief gu. 3 palets of the field. *V.S. 1623.*

Stainton. Arg. an annulet betw. 3 crosses patonce gu. Crest: . . . Add: *V.*

Stakepowle, Stakepoll or Stakepoole. Add: Sir John Stakepoul. *V.*

Stalebroke (London). Add: *V.* (the heads lapwings).

Staley. Arg. a chev. az. betw. 3 fusils (another lozenges) sa. Add: *V.**

Stallee or Staley. Arg. a plain chev. sa. fimbriated and engr. az. *V.*V.*

Stalket. Add: *V.*

Stallingburgh. Add: †

Stalworth. Arg. on a chev. betw. 3 bundles of faggots sa. as many bezants Add: *V.*

Stamford (Hadley, co. Middlesex). . . . Add: Sir William Stamford, Justice of the Common Pleas 1554. *Dug. O.J.*

Stamford. Az. a chev. betw. 3 geese arg.

Stamp. Gu. on a bend betw. 2 demi-horses erased arg. 3 fleurs-de-lis. **Book Plate.**

Stanard (Laxfield, Sussex). Az. 2 bars dancetty betw. 6 fleurs-de-lis. or 3, 2 and 1.

Stanbery. Per pale az. and or a lion ramp. per fess gu. and sa. Henry Stanbery. *V.V.**

Standelfe. Add: Half spades. *V.*

Standen. Sa. on a bend wavy arg. 3 bendlets wavy az. *V.*

Standen. Arg. an eagle close in trian aspect sa. armed or a bordure engr. of the last. *V.*

Standen. Arg. an eagle wings sa. a bordure engr. of the second. *V.*V.*

Standford. Sa. 3 lions ramp. arg. within a bordure gobony arg. and gu. *Cady.*

Standon. Arg. a bend embattled sa. Sir Henry de Standon. *Y.*

Standon. (Alderman of London) Sa. a chev. erm. betw. 3 lions heads erased arg. *V.*

Stanes. Az. a chev. counter compony arg. and sa. betw. 3 fleurs-de-lis. or. *V.*

Stanford (Packington and Perry Bar, co. Stafford). Add: Stamford or Stanford (Hadlegh, co. Middlesex. Granted 2 May 1542). Stanford (Leicester 1619). Same arms.

Stanford (Rowley, co. Stafford). Arg. 3 bars az. on a canton gu. a dexter hand armed or holding a broken falchion of the third. *Erdeswick.*

Stanford. Az. a chev. betw. 3 birds arg. *V.*V.*

Stanford. Sa. 3 lions ramp. arg. another, Az. a chev. betw. 3 birds arg. Another, sa. a chev. betw. 3 bugle horns stringed arg.—insert— *V.*V.* Another . . .

Stangrave. Erm. a lion ramp. gu. Add: *V.*

Stanhop (John Stanhop, Tuxford in Clay, co. Notts.). Vert 3 wolves pass. in pale or. *V.*

Stanhope (Arms in the Chapel of Balliol College, Oxford . . .). Add: Sir Edward Stanhope. *Harl. MS. 6137 fo. 44. V.*

Stanhope (Co. York). . . . (another, or—underlined—Add: temp. Edw. ij. *F. Y.*

Stanhowe. Barry of 6 or and az. a bendlet erm. Herevi de Stanhowe. *E.*

Stanhowe. Quarterly arg. with gu. fretty or over all a baston sa. Robert de Stanhoue. *F.*

Stanier (Lord Mayor of London 1714). Add: *L.N.*

Stanlaw (Co. Stafford). Add: Sir Raufe Stanlawe temp. Edw. j. *V.*

Stanley. Arg. on a bend betw. 2 cotises az. 3 bucks heads bendwise cabossed or. *W.*

Stanley. Arg. on a bend az. 3 mural crowns or. Crest:... Add: *V.**

Stanley (Grange Gorman, co. Dublin, bart.). Insert—1699 . . .

Stanlow (Co. Stafford). Add: Sir Rafe de Stanlow. *L.N.*

Stanlow. Arg. 2 chevs. gu. on a canton of the second a mullet pierced of the field. Add: *V.**

Stanlowe. Or on a bend gu. 3 mullets arg. on a canton of the second a mullet of the first. *V.*

Stansfield (of Stansfield, co. York). Sa. 3 goats pass. arg. collared and billed or. *V.*

Stansfield (Lewes, co. Sussex, confirmed). Insert—to John Stansfield . . . Add: 2 and 1. *Giullim.*

Stanton. Vairy arg. and sa. a canton gu. Sir Elias de Stanton. *P.V.*

Stanton. Arg. a bend embattled sa. Sir Henry de Stanton. *Y*, but Staunton. *Y.* Steynton. *V.*

Stanton. Arg. 2 chevs. sa. *V.N. p. 189.*

Stanye. Add: *V.*

Stapilford. Insert—of the North. Arg. . . . 3 boars heads—insert—fesswise . . . Add: *W.*

Stapledon (Stapledon, co. Devon). Add: *V. Lysons.*

Staplehill (Exeter and Dartmouth, co. Devon). . . . Add: Mayor of Exeter 1556.

Staplehill. Sa. on a bend arg. 3 staples of the first—insert—*V.* . . . .

Stapleton or Stapylton (Carlton, co. York . . .). Add: Sir Miles Stapelton. *N.* Sir Nicholas Stapelton. *Q.Y.* The following differences were borne on the lions shoulder: Sir Miles Stapleton KG., ob. 1364 a golden mullet. Sir Bryan Stapleton, KG., ob. 1394, a golden annulet. Sir Bryan Stapelton, ob. 1391, a pierced mullet gu. *Tonge's p. 2.* But Sir Bryan Stapleton of Ingham, Norfolk, a pierced mullet gu. *S.*

Stapleton (Myton, co. York. Baronetcy 1660). Arg. a lion ramp. sa.

Stapleton. Az. a lion ramp. tail forked or. Sir Robert Stapleton, co. Stafford. *V.E.N.G.L.* John Stapleton. *Y.*

Starchley. Or a chev. betw. 2 couple closes and three 5-foils sa. *Harl. MS. 1404. fo. 94.*

Starke (Judge of Supreme Court, Ceylon 1848). Add: Stark (Traquair Holm, co. Kircudbright) Same arms. *A.A.*

Starkey (Jarrow Lodge, co. Durham). Az. on a chev. betw. 3 arrows points downwards arg. as many mullets of the first. *Robson.*

Starkey. Arg. a bend engr. vair. betw. 5 storks sa. Crest: . . . Add: Starkey (Wakefield, co. York). Confirmed 1843.

Starkie (Huntroyd, co. Lancaster). . . . Add: *V.L. 1664.* Quartering Parr.

Starky (Aughton, co. Lancaster 1664). Add: *V.L.*

Starling (Stoppesley, co. Bedford, Lord Mayor of London 1670 . . . granted . . .). Insert—by Bysche. Add: *Guillim.*

Starmall. Sa. a lion salient or. *Randal Holme.*

Starmyn. Arg. 3 demi-lions ramp. gu. *V.**

Starne. Az. a stave or starling ppr. *Randle Holme.*

Starton. Or a redstart ppr. *Randle Holme.*

Staunford. Co. Suffolk &c. Add: *V.N. p. 161.*

Staunton (Staunton, co. Notts). Add: *V.N. p. 189.*

Staunton (Longbridge, co. Warwick). Add: Sir Thomas de Staunton. *S.*

Staunton (Co. Lincoln granted). Insert—'in Nov.' 1610. Add: by Camden to Dean Stanton of Lincoln.

Staveley (Bigenhall, co. Oxford . . .). Add: *V.O.*

Staveley or Staley. Arg. a chev. az. betw. two couple closes engr. sa. *V.**

Staveley. Arg. a chev. betw. 3 fusils sa. *V.N. p. 14.*

Stavlay (Stavlay, co. York). Barry of 10 arg. and gu.

Staverdon. Arg. a bend engr. betw. 2 martlets gu. *V.*

Staverton. Arg. a chev. sa. betw. 2 maunches vert. . . . Crest: Add: *V.*

Staverton. Vert. a chev. betw. 3 maunches erm. *V.*

Stayley. Arg. (another or) a chev. engr. az. Add: *V.*

Stayll. Arg. 2 chev. gu. on a chief or three palets —underlined—Add: But billets. *V.*

Stayner (Quartered by Holford). Az. a lion pass. arg. on a chief engr. or 3 mullets sa. *Debrett.*

Steavenson (Sheriff of Newcastle 1458). Arg. on a bend gu. 3 martlets or in the sinister chief a cross crosslet sa. *Carr MS.*

Steed. Sa. 2 lions pass. in pale arg. betw. as many flaunces of the last each charged with a fess az. Add: *V.**

Steele (Hampstead, co. Dublin. bart.). Add: Steele (Great Yarmouth, Norfolk). Same arms.

Stenefeld. Vert. an eagle displ. or Sir Guy de Stenefeld. *N.*

Stensclod. Az. an eagle displ. or. Add: *V.* Sir Guy Stenesclode, Essex temp. Edward v.

Stephen (Barton-on-the Hill, co. Gloucester). . . . Add: Stephens (Co. Worcester). Same arms. *Cady.*

Stephens (Essington, co. Gloucester, Granted by Camden). Per chev. az. and arg. in chief 2 eagles volant or. *Syl. Morgan.*

Stephens (Colchester and Arden, co. Essex). . . . Add: John Stephens, Colchester. *W.*

Stephenson (Henry Frederic Stephenson, Falcon Herald Extra-Ordinary 2 Aug. 1813). Vert. a chev. betw. 2 roses in chief and a lion sejant guard in. base arg. a canton of the last thereon a canton az. charged with the initial A. within a ring of gold gemmed ppr. (being the ring presented to him by the Emperor Alexander). Crest: A falcon rising arg. beaked and legged or within a Herald's Collar of SS. ppr. *Herald and Geneal. vij. 75.*

Stephenson (Granted to George Stephenson, father of Robert Stephenson). Insert—The celebrated Engineers.

Sterchilegh or Strechley. Arg. an eagle displ. sa. beaked gu. Sir John de Sterchileigh, co. Nottingham. *V.*

Sterle or Sterley. Or a chev. betw. 3 estoiles sa. *V.*

Sterling. Az. 2 bars gemel arg. on a chief of the second 3 lozenges gu. Sir Thos. Sterling. *V.*

Stetham. Add: *V.*

Steven. Add: *Nisbet j. 269.*

Stevens. Gu. on a bend arg. 3 roses vert.

Stevens (Smethwick, co. Stafford). Insert—and Exeter . . .

Stevenson (Ounston or Unston, co. Derby . . .). Add: Stevenson (Boston, co. Lincoln). Same arms. *Cotton MS. Tiberius. D. 10.*

Stevenson (Swynflete, co. York 1665). *Dugdale. p. 221.*

Stevenson. Vert. a chev. betw. 3 spear heads arg. **Book Plate.**

Stevenson. Arg. a chev. betw. 3 dexter hands clenched sa. in each a purse of the first. Add: *V.** marginal note—'a stone'. *V.*

Steward. Per chev. gu. and az. a chev. betw. 3 lions heads erased or. Sir John Steward. *V.*

Steward (Norfolk). Arg. a lion ramp. gu. debruised with a bend compony or and vert within a bordure az. *V.*

Steward (Norfolk). Arg. a lion ramp. gu. over all a bend raguly or. *V.*V.*

Steward (Co. Cambridge 1680). Same arms.

Steward of Okhey, Granted by Cooke 1586. Same arms.

Stewart (Lord Downe 1581). Same arms as Lord Evandale with the addition of an escu. of pretence arg. 3 trees eradicated vert. *Cady.*

Stewart (Nova Scotia Baronetcy). Az. a bend or overall a fess chequy or and gu. on an escutcheon arg. a saltire az. overall the Royal arms of Scotland surmounted by an Imperial Crown being the badge of Nova Scotia Baronetcy. †

Stewart (Co. Fife). Or a fess chequy az. arg. surmounted of a lion ramp. gu. all within a bordure engrailed of the second charged with 3 garbs alternating with 3 crescents arg.

Stewins. Az. a chev. or betw. 3 grappling irons each of as many points and double ringed arg. *V. Harl. MS. 1386.*

Steynton (Sir Robert Steynton). Gu. in chief a lion pass. or in base 3 crosses patty arg. 2 and 1. *V.*

Stiklewey. Arg. 3 bulls pass. sa. Thomas Stiklewey. *V.*

Stinte. Erm. on a bend gu. 3 leopards faces or. *V.*

Stiverton. Add: *V.*

Stockbridge, Stokebridge or Stockbreghe. . . . Add: Sir Denis Stokebrige. *V.* And with a crescent gu. for diff.

Stockdale (Lockington, co. York). Robert Stockdale of Lockington. *Eliz. Roll. xxij.*

Stockdale. Add: Stockdale (Bilton, co. York). Erm. on a bend sa. 3 pheons arg. 1665. In the sinister chief an escallop gu. *Hargrove.*

Stocket (Bradstet, co. Kent). Insert—temp. Edw. j. and ij.

Stockhey. Quartered by Sir Walter Raleigh. Az. (? sa.) 6 martlets 3. 2. and 1. or on a canton arg. a mullet gu. *Hoare. V.*

Stockhey (Santon, co. Devon). Sa. a chev. erm. betw. 2 couple closes engr. or. *Lysons.*

Stockley (Yoxall, co. Stafford . . .). Add: *C.L. p. 91.*

Stockton. Letter Crest: A castle entrance dual towered and palewise an anchor the shaft and shackle in chief extending through the entrance to the anchor grips in base, a knotted rope in shackle looped and draped in chief. Inscription: In:Com:Pal; Denelm:Sic:Corp:Stockton.

Stockton. Gu. a chev. vairy sa. and arg. betw. 3 mullets or. *V.*

Stockwith (East Meare, co. Hants. and West Stockwith, co. Notts). Add: The 5-foils arg. *V.N.*

Stodubynt. Barry arg. and az. 3 lions ramp. purp. Rafe Stodubynt. *Y.*

Stodham. Barry of 6 or and az. per pale counterchanged a chev. gu. Sir Simon de Stodham. *E.*

Stody (Lord Mayor of London 1357). Erm. on a bend engr. sa. a leopards head or. *Berry.*

Stoke (Co. Chester). Add: *Ormerod.*

Stoke. Az. a fret arg.; another Arg. a fret az. on a canton of the second a boars head erased or —insert—*V.* Another Az. fretty or on a canton of the first a boars head arg.—insert—*V.* another . . .

De Stoke. Bendy of 10 or and az. a canton gu. Henry de Stoke. *E.*

Stoker. Per saltire vert. and arg. two parrots in fess of the first. *V.*

Stoker. Gyronny of 6 arg. and vert. in chief a popinjay of the last. *Harl. MS. 1469. fo. 30b.*

Stokes (Co. Cambridge). Arg. on a bend engr. sa. 3 dolphins or. *Cole MSS.*

Stokes. Arg. a bend cotised gu. Walter de Stokes.

Stokes. Sa. 2 bars erm. betw. 15 wheat ears or 5. 5. and 5 a bordure of the second. *W.*

Stokes. Erm. on 3 bars humetty sa. 15 wheat ears or 5. 5. and 5. *W.*

Stokes. Gu. a squirrel sejant cracking a nut or on a chief of the last 3 fleurs-de-lis az. *V.*

Stokes (Essex). Sa. 3 eagles displ. and a chief dancetty arg. *V.*

Stokes (Ireland). Per pale vert and arg. a chev. counterchanged. *V.*

Stokes. Per chev. erm. and vert. a chev. engr. counterchanged betw. 3 fleurs-de-lis or. *V.*

Stokes (Watersend, co. Kent). Add: *V.*

Stokes. Arg. on a chev. az. 3 trefoils slipped of the field a bordure gu. bezantee. Add: *William Stokes. V.*

Stokey. Add: *Hoare. j. 117.*

Stone (Wedmore, co. Somerset . . .). Add: Stone, co. Surrey. *V.*

Stone. Arg. a lion pass. guard. sa. William de Stone. *F.*

Stone. Per pale or and az. an eagle displ. double headed counterchanged. *V.*

Stone (Co. Dorset). Add: Stone, co. Somerset. *V.S.*

Stone (Az. crusilly or a bend gu. fimbriated of the second Richard de Stone. *E. Harl. MS. 6137.*

Stone (Streingo Cornwall). Per pale or and vert. a chev. engr. betw. 3 birds counterchanged. *V.C. 1620.* Quartering sa. a fess. betw. 3 bears or.

Stone. Sa. a chev. engr. betw. 3 flint stones arg. *V.*

Stone. Or 2 bars vairy arg. and sa. quartering gu. 2 bars vairy or and sa. and or 3 fleurs-de-lis. *V.**

Stoner. Az. 2 bars dancetty and a chief or. Sir William Stoner. *V.* John de Stonore. *Y.*

Stoner. Sa. a chev. arg. betw. 3 plates. Sir Henry Stoner. *V.*

Stones (Granted to Dr. Christopher Stones of York in 1666 by Dugdale). Gu. on a bend betw. 3 doves arg. as many crosses patty gu. *Northern Grants I. jjj.*

Stoniwell. 1580. Sa. on a chev. arg. betw. three billets . . . as many . . . leaves ppr. *Shaw's Staffordshire.*

Stonyng (Lichfield). Arg. a chev. gu. betw. 3 ogresses each charged with a fleur-de-lis of the first. *V.*

Stopham. Arg. a baston sa. John Stopham. *Y.*

Stopham. Arg. a bend sa. Sir William de Stopham. *N.* And with a label or Sire Johan de Stopham. *N.*

Storey. Arg. a lion ramp, tail nowed purp. Crest: . . . Add: Sir William Storey. *V.*

Stormyn (Co. Chester). Add: *V.* Roger Stormyn. *N.* The mullets pierced.

Stormyn (Co. Suffolk). Quarterly or and gu. on a bend az. three plates. Crest: . . . Add: *V.*

Stormyn. Quarterly or and gu. . . . . another. Gu. a chev. arg. . . . another, Gu. a chev. betw. three pairs of spectacles arg.—insert—*V.*

Stormyn (Co. Chester). Gu. a chev. and in chief 2 mullets arg. *V.*

Story (Arms of William and Richard de Story . . .) With a cross pattee arg. ? 'or'. Add: *S.*

Stotvile. Arg. 6 barrulets gu. Robert de Stotevile. *E.*

Stotevile. Baron of Cotingham. *V.*

Stothall or Stothehall. Sa. a chev. betw. 3 crosses patty or. *V.**

Stott. Vert. 3 conies courant. **Book Plate.**

Stourton (Co. Lincoln 1640). Sa. a bend engr. or betw. 6 fountains ppr. *Yorke.*

Stourton. Sa. a bend or betw. 3 fountains ppr. The Lord of Stourton. *V.* Baron Stourton of Stourton.

Stoutville (Humanby, co. York). Barry of 12 arg. and gu. over all a lion ramp. sa. *Dugdale. 1665.*

Stow or Stowte. Add: *V.**

Stowte. Or 3 bars and in chief as many crosses patty az. *V.*

Strachan (Thornton, Scotland). Az. a stag lodged. or.

Stradley. Add: *V.*

Stradling (St. Donats, co. Somerset, bart.). Insert—1611 ...

Stradling (Wales). Paly of 6 az. and arg. on a bend gu. 3 cinquefoils or. Sir Edward Stradling. *V.*

Strange (of Knockyn). Arg. 2 lions pass. gu. John le Strange. *Y.*

Strange. Arg. 2 lions pass. gu. John l'Estrange. *E.A.B.D.F.J.* or le Strange. Sir Foulke le Straunge. *L.* Monsire le Strange, Blackmere. *Y.Z. 210.* Strange as quartered by Talbot, Earl of Shrewsbury. *U.* And with a label az. John, son of John le Strange. *B.*

Strange (Sir de Strange, Corpham and Frandolph). Arg. 2 lions pass. gu. *V.*

Strange (Baron Strange of Knockyn . . .). Gu. two lions pass. arg.—insert— ?. Crest: ...

Strange. Gu. 2 lions pass. in pale arg. Sire le Strange. *T.S.Y.* John le Strange. *S.* Sir Roger le Strange. *Q.* Strange of Knockyn, quartered by Stanley, Earl of Derby. *U.*

Strange. Gu. 2 lions pass. in pale arg. within a bordure engr. or. Roger le Strange. *E.G.N.* Roger le Strange, Baron of Ellesmere. *Nobility Roll. 25. Edw. j.*

Strange. Gu. on 2 lions pass. arg. a fleur-de-lis at the shoulder of each sa. Mounsyer John Strange. *T.*

Strange. Gu. 2 lions pass. arg. in the dexter chief a fleur-de-lis for diff. Sir John Strange. *T.*

Strange. Gu. 2 lions pass. arg. a bend, bendlet or baston or. Le Strange. *V.** Sir John le Straunge. *S.* Sir Hamond le Strange. *L.V.*

Strange (Walton, co. Warwick). Gu. 2 lions pass. arg. crowned or. *V.*

Strange (London). Gu. 2 lions pass. arg. a border engr. of the last. Add: Sir Roger de le Strange. *J.*

Strange. Gu. demy of martlets of 2 lions pass. arg. Sir Johan de Lestrange. *N.*

Strange. Gu. crusilly fitchy and 2 lions pass. arg. Robert le Strange. *E.F.*

Strangman (Hadley Castle, co. Essex). . . . a bend ragulee—insert—(or counter-embattled). . . . Add: *Guillim.*

Strangways (Melberrie Sampford, co. Dorset:). .. Add: *V.V.**

Strangways (Ormesby, co. York). Sa. 2 lions pass. paly arg. and gu. a crescent for diff. *F.Y.*

Strangways (South House, co. York 1665). Sa. 2 lions pass. in pale paly of 6 arg. and gu. a canton of the second. *Dugdale.*

Stranlay. Paly of 6 arg. and az. on a canton gu. a martlet of the first. *V.** But a mullet on the canton. *V.*

Strasacker. Add: *V.V.**

Stratele. Sa. a chev. betw. 3 heads or eel picks points downwards arg. *Harl. MS. 1386. fo. 95.*

Stratford (Nicholas Stratford, Bishop of Chester 1680). Paly of 8 arg. and az. a lion ramp. gu.

Stratford or Langthorne-at-Bogh Abbey. Co. Essex. Add: *Tanner.*

Stratherne (Scotland). Add: Le Conte de Strathern. *D.Y.*

Stratton. Or 2 bars gu. in chief an escu. of the second. Seigneur le Stratton. *R.*

Straunge. Vert. a chev. or betw. 3 covered cups arg. *V.*

Straunge. Arg. a chev. betw. 3 covered cups gu. *W.*

Straunley. Paly of 6 arg. and az. a canton gu. Sir Sampson de Straunley. *V.*

Stray (Co. York). Add: Thomas Stray, Doncaster co. York. *V.*

Streche. Arg. 2 chevs. az. on a quarter of the last a fleur-de-lis or. Estienne Streche. *X.*

Strecheley. Arg. an eagle displ. sa. armed gu. Add: Sire Johan de Strutheleye. *O.N. V.N. p. 188.*

Stretchley. Or on a chev. sa. another, arg. charged with three 5-foils of the second. *V.*

Straunge or Storauge (Ampton, co. Suffolk). Gu. an eagle displ. arg. a bordure engr. or. *V.V.**

Strelling. Add: John Strelling. *V.V.**

Strethe. Arg. a bend engr. sa. betw. 2 cotises az. and 6 martlets of the second. *V.*

Stretchley (Sir John Stretchley . . .). Add: Thomas Stricheley, the eagle legged gu. *V.*

Stretley (Stripton, co. Northampton). Insert— and co. Oxford ... Add: *V.O.*

Stretley (Kirslowe, co. Bucks). Arg. on a bend sa. 3 owls or. Add: *V.O. p. 177.*

Strettell. Sa. a chev. betw. 3 heads of tridents points ... Add: *V.*

Stretton (Lenton Priory, co. Nottingham). Add: Sir Oliver Stretton. *V.*

Strickland. Arg. 2 bars gu. a canton of the last. Add: Sir Walter de Strickland. *N.*

Strikleway or Stickleway. Add: *V.V.**

Stringer (Enfield, Middlesex). Sa. 2 eagles displ. or. *Robson.*

Stringer (Dover, co. Kent). Add: *Hasted.*

Stringer (Whiston-Sharleston, co. York). Add: Stringer (Grays Inn 1669). Same arms. *L.N.*

Strode (Newnham and Carswell, co. Devon). Arg. a chev. betw. 3 conies sejant sa. *V.D. 1620.*

Strode (Strode in the parish of Ermington: &c. . . .). Add: William Strode, Public Orator at the University of Oxford, ob. 1644. Same arms. A martlet or upon the chev. *Guillim.*

Strode (Co. Devon). Arg. 3 eagles displ. gu. *V.*

Strode. Erm. 3 eagles displ. gu. on a canton of the second a pierced mullet or. *V.**

Strode. Erm. 3 eagles displ. gu. on a quarter of the second a pierced mullet or. *V.*

Strode (Parnham, co. Dorset . . .). Add: *W.* Add: Strode (Westeranmer, co. Somerset. Same arms. *Guillim.*

Strong ( ). Gu. an eagle displ. or a bordure engr. of the last a canton gold charged with a lion ramp. sa. collared gold.

Strongbarr. Arg. 3 palets gu. over all as many bars or. *Randle Holme.*

Strother (Eastfield, co. Northumberland). Add: Strother (Warworth, Northumberland. Same arms. *A.A.*

Strother. Gu. on a bend arg. 3 eagles displ. vert. Sir Thomas de Strother. *V.S.X.*

Strut (Westminster, co. Middlesex . . .). Add: Strut. Belper, co. Derby.

Strudder of Fowberry. Gu. on a bend engr. arg. 3 eagles displ. vert. *Eliz. Roll. xxx.iiij.*

Stryttle. Add: Strytt. *V.V.**

Stuart. Or a bend vert. over all a fess chequy arg. and az. †

Stukeley. Gu. ? or. 3 lions ramp. . . . ? sa. each charged on the shoulder with a mullet. *V.*

Stukeley. Arg. on a bend az. an annulet in the upper part or. Geffrey Stukeley. *V.*

Stukele. Az. a chev. betw. 3 gourds (or pears). *V.** pendent slipped or. *Cotton MS. Tiberius. D. 10.* and *V.**

Sturmye. Sa. a lion salient arg. Add: *V.*

Sturmy or Stormy. Sa. a lion salient arg. *V.* John Sturmy. *Y.* Sturmy of Dromonby, co. York. quartered by Constable. *W.*

Sturmy (Sheriff of Wiltshire temp. Henry v). Arg. 3 demi-lions ramp. gu. *Fuller. V.*

Sturmyn (Suffolk). Quarterly or and gu. on a bend az. 3 plates. *V.*

Sturmyn (Co. Chester). Gu. a chev. arg. betw. 3 plates. *V.*

Sturton (Sturton, co. Nottingham). Add: Sir John Sturton. *T.* Sturton (Co. Leicester). 1619. *C.C.*

Stuth, Stuyth, Stwyth or Stwythe. Add: *V.*

Stutheley. Arg. an eagle displ. sa. armed gu.—insert—*V.* another.

Stutville. Barry of 8 arg. and gu. a bordure gobony or and sa. *Nash.*

Styel. Add: *V.**

Styel. Arg. a bend compony erm. and pean betw. 2 lions heads erased gu. on a chief az. 3 billets or. Sir John Styell. *V.*

Style. Or a bend compony (or counter compony) erm. and sable. *V.V.**

Style. Az. a bordure chevronny of 8 arg. and gu.

Styrly (Lymby). Paly of 6 arg. and az. an annulet. *Constable's Roll. vij.*

Sudbury (Eldon, co. Durham. Baronetcy 1685). Sa. a talbot pass. within a bordure engr. or. *Guillim.*

Sudbery. . . . . (another, the border *or*—underlined—Add: *V.**

Sudeley or Sudley (Sudley Castle, co. Gloucester and co. Warwick). Add: *V.*

Suffolk (Nuneaton). Quarterly . . . and . . . 2 chevs. . . . **Seal** 1624.

Sugar. Sa. in chief a doctor's cap . . . in base 3 sugar loaves arg. *Collinson Somerset iij. 401.*

Sugar alias Norris. Same arms.

Sugg or Sugge. Or a chev. vair—insert—*V.* (another . . .).

Sulley. Or 2 bars gu. Robert Suylly. *Y.*

Sullivan (Dublin, Master of the Rolls in Ireland 1869). Per pale vert. a buck trippant or and per pale arg. and sa. a boar counterchanged over all on a chief or a dexter hand couped at the wrist grasping a sword erect gu. the blade entwined with a serpent ppr. between 2 lions ramp. respecting each other gu. *Debrett.*

Suley or Sulley. Or 2 bendlets gu. Sir Johan de Suley. *J.I.N.E.* John de Suthleye. *G.* Bartholomew de Sully. *A.* And with a label az. Sir Bartholomew de Suleye. *N.* And with a label barruly arg. and az. (or compony arg. and az. Sire William de Suleye. *L.N.*

Sully. Or 2 bends gu. a label az. Crest: a goat pass. arg. Add: Sir John de Sully, co. Worcester *V.*

Summaster (Haynsford, co. Devon . . .). Add: Granted 4 March 1586 by Cooke. *Guillim.*

Sumery. Quarterly az. and or over all a bendlet gu. Sir John de Sumereye. *L.*

Sunderland (Ayleton, co. York 1666). Per pale arg. and az. 3 lions pass. in pale counterchanged. *Dugdale. p. 380.*

Surcott. Arg. on a chev. sa. 3 escallops or . . . a lion pass. of the third—underlined—Add: first. *V.*

Surgan. Az. a wolf pass. arg. Add: Surgeon. *V.**

Sulyard (Suffolk). Arg. a chev. betw. 3 broad arrow heads sa. *Fuller.*

Surrenden (Kent). Arg. a bend gu. betw. two cotises nebuly sa. *V.** But the cotises nebuly on their outer edge. *V.*

Surtees (Dinsdale-on-Tees, co. Durham). Add: *V.V.**

Surtees. Erm. on a canton gu. an orle arg. *Eliz. Roll. xix. V.**

Sunderland (Harden, co. York 1665). . . . . 3 lions pass. in pale . . . a crescent for diff. *Dugdale. p. 21.*

Sustan or Suston. Add: *V.*

Suthes (1625, Lambeth Surrey). Sa. on a bend cotised arg. 3 martlets gu.

Sutton (Sussex). Sa. a chev. or betw. 3 buckets or pails arg. *V.*

Sutton. Arg. a chev. betw. 3 mullets gu. *V.**

Sutton. Gu. a chev. betw. 3 mullets or. George Sutton, Gentleman Usher to the Queen. *V.*

Sutton (Lykelnecher, co. Lincoln). Arg. on a chev. gu. 3 crescents or. *V.*

Sutton (Sutton, co. Chester). . . . . Add: *Ormerod iij. 373.*

Sutton. Erm. a canton sa. Jennes de Sutton, the son. *E.* Sir . . . de Sutton. *F.*

Sutton. Or a lion ramp. vert. quartering, second, arg. a chev. betw. 3 bugle horns sa.; third, Cholmley: 4th Hobart Sir Richard Sutton 1580. *Ormerod iij. 373.*

Sutton. Or a lion ramp. vert. Sir Richard Sutton. *I.* or de Sottone. *N.* And with a label gu. Sire Johan de Sottone. *N.*

Sutton (Boston, co. Lincoln . . .). Add: *V.O. p. 173.*

Sutton. Gu. a bend arg. betw. 6 martlets or. *V.*

Sutton (Co. Essex). Or a lion ramp. az. oppressed with a bend gobony arg. and gu. Add: Sir John de Sutton. Holderness. *V.*

Sutton. Or a lion ramp. az. over all a dexter baston compony gu. and arg. Sir John de Sutton, Holderness. *O.Y.*

Sutton. Or a lion ramp. tail forked vert. over all on a fess arg. 3 torteaux. James Sutton of Chester.

Sutton (Co. Chester). Arg. a chev. betw. three bugle horns stringed sa. *V.*

Sutton (Co. Norfolk). Or three chevs. sa. Add: Sir John de Sutton. *R.S.* Richard Sutton Norfolk). *Y.*

Sutton (Wyvenhall Essex). Sa. 3 chevs. or Sir John Sutton. *V.*

Sutton. Or a chief gu. over all a lion ramp. az. Sir John Sotton, Essex. temp. Edw. iij. *V. N.*

Sutton (Mar. heiress of Somery). Or 2 lions pass. az.

Sutton alias Dudley. Ext. 1643 heiress mar. Ward.

Sutton (Norfolk 1298). Or a chev. gu. on a chief az. 3 mullets pierced of the field. *Dashwood.*

Sutton. Arg. a chev. betw. 3 bugle horns sa. *V.**

Sutton (Sussex). Sa. a chev. or betw. 3 pails or buckets arg. *V.*

Sutton. Az. two chevs. betw. 3 mullets arg. *V.*

Suwardby. Arg. a chev. engr. betw. 3 lions ramp. sa. Sir William Suwardby. *V.*

Swain (London: Samuel . . . William . . . who had the arms confirmed in 1612). Insert—by Camden.

Swaine (Arms impaled with Tregonwell). . . . . Add: Swayne (Co. Somerset). William Swayne. *W.*

Swale (South Stainley . . .). Add: Swale (South Stainley, co. York). Az. a bend nebuly arg. Crest: A passion cross arg. *Dugdale. p. 42.*

Swan (Southfleet, co. Kent, bart.). Insert—1665. Add: *V.E. 1634.*

Swan. Sa. a chev. or betw. 3 swans wings elevated arg. membered gu. *Collinson Somerset. j. 161.*

Swansea. Harbour Trust. Arg. 3 bars wavy over-all palewise an anchor ppr. In chief a castle entrance towered on each side and embattled. Crest: On a wreath of the colours on a rock buildings and a lighthouse ppr. with six rays either side of the light. Supporters: on the dexter side a sailor dressed of the period, hatted and in his right hand a coil of rope and on the sinister side a miner trousered but naked above the belt with a pick in his upraised left hand bendwise behind his neck the point resting on his right shoulder and from the trouser belt a miners torch with 5 rays each side. On a scroll beneath the year 1791 the motto: By Industry we flourish.

Swarland (Quartered by Haselrig . . .). Add: *V.N. p. 153.*

Swaynband. Add: *V.*

Swayne (Co. Somerset and London: . . . confirmed). Insert—by Segar . . . Add: *W.*

Swayne (Cork). . . . a chev. . . . betw. two pheons . . . in chief and a lion pass. . . . in base.

Sweetapple (London). Vert. on a bend arg. 3 roses gu. on a chief of the second as many apples gu. Sir John Sweetapple 1694. *L.N.*

Sweetman or Swetman (Castleleiffe, Kilkenny). Same arms., as Sweetman (Tyrellstown, co. Dublin).

Sweit (Granted 10 April 1665—insert—to Sir Giles Sweit DL., and Dean of the Arches. *Guillim.*

Swellington. Add: *V.*

Swerington (Co. York). Arg. on a chev. az. a fleur-de-lis or a label of 3 points gu. Sir Hugh de Swerington. *Harl. MS. 6137. fo. 22.* Sire Adam de Sueingtone. *N.*

Swettenham or Swetnam (Co. Chester). Arg. on a bend vert. 3 shovels bendwise in bend of the first. *V.*

Swettenham (Somerford, co. Chester). confirmed by Dethick 1568. Same arms. *Harl. MS. 1535. fo. 257.*

Swettenham (Warren-Swettenham of Swettenham co. Chester . . .). Quarterly 1st and 4th Swettenham . . . Add: *V.*

Swift (Roydon, co. Essex). Gu. a chev. erm. betw· 3 tigers heads erased arg. *Harl. MS. 1541.*

Swillington. Arg. a chev. az. a label of 3 points erm. *V.* Sir Robert de Swillington. *S.* But the label gu. Sire Huge de Swillington. *N.* Sir Adam de Swillington. *M.*

Van Swinden. Gu. 3 greyhounds ramp. arg. 2 and 1. **Book Plate.**

Swinford (Co. Huntingdon: . . .). Add: Sir Thomas Swinford, co. Hunts. *V. N.* Norman Swyneford. *Y.* And with a 5-foil in the dexter chief gu. Sir Norman Swynford of Essex. *V.*

Swinglehurst (London). Gu. an arrow in pale point downwards betw. two wings conjoined arg. *Cady.*

Swinhoe (John Henry Swinhoe of Calcutta). Add: Robert Swynehowe. *X.*

Swinnerton. Sir John Swinnerton, Lord of London 1613. Or a chief indented gu. Crest: Out of a ducal coronet a goats head arg.

Swinnerton of Hilton. Arg. a cross flory sa. within a bordure engr. gu. Sir Roger de Swinnerton. ob. 1338. *Harl. MS. 6128. fo. 60.*

Swinnerton of Eccleshall and of Butterton. Arg. a cross flory sa. over all a bendlet gu.

Swinnerton of Suffolk. Erm. a chief gu. fretty or.

Swiny. Arg. a chev. betw. 3 boars sa. *V.**

Swival. Or a bend arg. fimbriated az. *Randle Holme.*

Swymmer (Wm. Sheriff of Bristol 1679). Gu. 3 church bells gold. *MS. 1662/88 of arms of Bristol aldermen. penes W. B. Bannerman.*

Swyne. Arg.—delete—(another, or). . . . Add: *V.**

Swynoe or Swyne. Or 3 boars pass. sa. *Eliz. Roll. xxxvij.*

Swynethwayte. Arg. a chev. betw. 3 boars sa. *Y.*

Swynford (Norfolk 1255). Arg. a chev. betw. 3 boars heads couped gu. *Dashwood.*

Swynford. Arg. a chev. sa. betw. 3 boars heads . . . in dexter chief a 6-foil. Thomas Swynford. *Y.*

Swynford. Arg. on a chev. sa. betw. three 5-foils as many boars heads fesswise couped or. *V.*

Swynnow. Arg. 3 boars pass. sa.

Swynton. Arg. a chev. engr. gu. betw. 3 boars heads couped sa. *V.** John Swynton. *V.*

Swythen. Add: *V.*

Sybelles (Co. Kent). Add: *V.*

Sybthorp (St. Albans, co. Herts. and Ladham—correct—to read Ludham, co. Norfolk).

Sychevile. Erm. 3 crossbows unbent gu. *V.**

Sychevile. Erm. 3 crossbows unbent or. *V.*

Sydall. Arg. a chev. betw. 3 carpenters squares points to the sinister gu. Elias Sydall, Bishop of St. Davids.

Sydemers. Add: *Guillim.*

Sydenham (Sheriff of Nottinghamshire temp. Eliz.). Sa. 3 rams arg. *Fuller.*

Sydenham (Co. Dorset). Arg. five fusils in bend sa. Add: Sydenham of Kittisford, co. Somerset. Same arms.

Sydenham. Bendy paly arg. and gu. *V.**

Sydenham (Langford, co. Somerset). Add: *V.**

Sydinton. Arg. a chev. betw. 5 crosses fitchy 2. 2. and 1. sa. *Harl. MS. 1404. fo. 117.*

Syferwast. Az. 2 bars gemel arg. *V.*

Syferwast. Az. 2 bars gemel and a chief or. Richard de Syferwast. *E.F.V.*

Syferwast or Cyfrewast. Arg. 3 bars gemel az. Sir John Cyfrewast. *V.*

Sylvelney. Insert—Ireland. Arg. on a bend sa. three plates. Add: *V.*

Symer. Sa. a chev. engr. betw. 3 swans necks erased arg. Add: *V.**

Symer. Sa. a chev. engr. betw. 3 shovellers heads erased arg. *V.*

Symkin. Add: *V.**

Synsiwarde. Add: *V.* Roger Synd. *X.*

Syrmington or Sermington. Add: *V.*V.*

Syseley. Insert—Barrow Hall, Essex. granted 31 Dec. 1560. Add: *W.* and at end. *V.**

Susley (Fountains, co. York; Northiam, Sussex; and Sevenoaks, Kent). Same Arms. Add: *MS. 7098. fo. 18.*

Sysley (Barrow Hall, Eastbury, co. Essex). Az. on a chev. betw. 3 goats pass. arg. armed or as many fleur-de-lis of the first.

Sysun or Sysung. Bendy of 6 or and az. *V.V.**

Sywardby. Arg. a bend betw. 2 cotises and 6 lions ramp. sa. John Sywardby. *Y. F. Y.*

T

TABOR (Sir Robt. Tabor, Knt. an eminent physician temp. Charles ij.). Az. on a chev. engr. betw. 3 lions heads erased or 3 leopards faces of the first. *L.N.* Crest: A lions head or. Motto: "Soles occidere et redire possint". Tomb in Holy Trinity Church, Cambridge.

Tadlowe (Cos. Essex and Kent). Add: Tadlowe (co. Warwick). Same arms. *C.W.*

Tailzeter. Erm. a chev. gu. *Guillim.*

Talbot (Bashall, co. York). Add: Sire Edmon Talebot. *N.Y.L.* Sir John Talbot, Bashall. *V.* Sire Thomas Talbot. *S.* Sir . . . Talbott of Bashall. Arg. 3 lions ramp. az. *R.*

Talbot (Carr, co. Lancaster 1664). Add: *V.L.*

Talbot (Thornton, co. York). Arg. 3 lions ramp. purp. *Dugdale. p. 38, 236.*

Talbot (London 1633). Arg. 3 lions ramp. purp. in the centre a fleur-de-lis for diff. *Harl. MS. 1358. fo. 67b.*

Talbot. Gu. a lion ramp. within a bordure engr. or Sir Gilbert Talbot, co. Gloucester temp. Edw. iij. *L.V.* Talbot of Goodrich Castle and Blackmere. *Z. 242. 448.* Richard le Talbot, Steward of the King's house. *Q.* Sir Richard Talbot quartering Arg. 2 lions pass. in pale gu. *S.*

Talbot. Sir John Talbot. Gu. a lion ramp. and a bordure engr. or over all a bendlet az. *R.*

Talbot. Or a lion ramp. gu. collared gold a bordure vert. bezanty. Richard Talbot. *C.*

Talbot. Gu. a lion ramp. or charged on the shoulder with a mullet . . . a bordure engr. of the second. John Talbot. *Y.*

Talbot (Ireland). Or a lion ramp. within a bordure gu. *V.*

Talbot (Wymondham, co. Norfolk, granted 1581). Arg. a chev. gu. betw. 3 talbots pass. sa. *W.*

Talbot. Arg. a chev. betw. 3 talbots statant sa. Sir William Talbot. *V.*

Talbot (*Ulster's Office*). Arg. 4 bendlets gu. Add: *V.V.**

Talbot. Or 5 bendlets gu. Sir Richard Talbot. *E.* But the bendlets enhanced gu. Sir Gilbert Talbot. *V.*

Talbot. Bendy of 10 arg. and gu. Sir Gilbert Talbot of Salwarp, Master of the Jewel House to King Charles ij.

Talbot. Gu. 2 bars vair. Add: Talbot. Talbot of Castle Richard. *V.* William Talbot. *Y.* Sir Richard Talbot. *O.* And with a pierced mullet in the dexter chief for diff. *M.* Gilbert Talbot. *S.*

Talebot. Vairy gu. and or a bordure az. Gilbert Talebot. *F.*

Tallant. Paly of 8 or and sa. on a canton arg. a griffin segreant gu. Add: *V.*

Tallet. Arg. a chev. betw. 3 heathcocks gu. *V.V.**

Tallet. Or a chev. betw. 3 heathcocks gu. *V.**

Talliate. Vert. a bordure indented or. *Randle Holme.*

Tallow Chandlers, Compony of . . . three doves of the last—insert—membered gu. . . . Add: Arms granted by John Smart, Garter 24th Sept. 1456. Confirmed by Camden and the Supporters granted 19 Jan. 1602. *Grants.*

Tallowe. Marginal note—Query Callowe.

Tallum. Arg. on a chev. sa. 3 crescents of the first. *V.**

Talstock. Or a demi-lion ramp. az. in a mural crown reversed arg. Add: *V.*

Talworthe. Or two bars az. over all on a chev. gu. 3 mullets of 6 points arg. *V.**

Talworth. Barry of 6 or and az. a chev. gu. Sir Piers Talworth. *V.*

Talworth. Barry of 6 or and az. on a chev. gu. 3 mullets or—insert—*V.* (another, arg.). Add: *V.**

Tancre. Az. 2 bendlets arg. Bartram de Tancre. *A.*

Tancred (Boroughbridge, co. York, bart.). Add: Tancred (Whixley, co. York.). Same arms.

Tane. Or 3 eagles displ. sa. Richard Tane. *T.*

Taney or Tany (Co. Essex). Add: Sir Richard de Tany, Essex. *V.J.N.* Richard Tamy. *A.* Richard Thani. *E.*

Tanfield or Tansfield (Copswood, co. Essex). Add: Sir Robert Tanfield. Tanfild, temp. Edw. iv. *Harl. MS. 6137. fo. 44.* Sir Laurence Tanfield, Chief Baron of the Exchequer 1607 and quartering arg. a chev. sa. betw. 3 griffins heads erased gu. *Dug. O.J.*

Tanfield. Gu. a chev. or in chief a lion pass. arg. *V.V.**

Tankard or Tankert (Co. York). Add: *V.V.** Tankard (Pannell, co. York). Same arms. *F.Y.*

Tankard (Whixley, co. York 1665). Arg. a chev. betw. 3 escallops gu. *Dugdale. p. 56.*

Tankard (Boroughbridge co. York). Baronetcy 1662. Arg. on a chev. betw. 3 escallops gu. as many annulets or.

Tankersley. Insert—co. York. Arg. on a bend gu. 3 escallops or. Add: *V.*

Tanket (Arden co. York). Arg. a chev. betw. 3 escallops gu. a crescent for diff. *Eliz. Roll. xxiij.*

Tankesley and Tankisle. Add: *V.* Tankersley of of Tankersley co. York.

Tansley (John Tansley . . .). Add: *C.R. p. 29.*

Tarsell. Or a chev. sa. betw. 3 hazel nuts erect slipped gu. John Tarsell. *V.*

Tasburg (St. Andrews in Ilkensall, Suffolk). Arg. on a chev. betw. 3 swords points downwards each supporting a pouch or purse sa. pomels and tassels or. a crescent of the last. *Harl. MS. 155. fo. 25.*

Tasbrough or Tasborough (Southelman, co. Suffolk). Add: Tarburg (St. Andrews in Ilkensall, Suffolk). Same arms with a crescent for diff. *Harl. MS. 1103. fo. 83b.*

Tasker. (Robert Adams, alias Tasker 1590), granted by Cooke. Erm. 3 cats pass. guard. in pale az. *W.*

Tatershall or Tatersall. Add: *V.V.**

Tatershall. Per chev. or and gu. two chevrons counterchanged a chief erm.

Tatlock. Insert—of Canscogh, co. Lancaster 1664. *V.L.*

Tattercombe (Co. Devon). Purp. 3 birds (? eagles) displ. arg. *V.*

Tanyers (Company of London). Erm. on a chev. sa. betw. 3 squirrels sejant gu. ppr. with beads and chains of gold about their necks as many roses arg.

Tavenor (Uxminster, co. Essex). Add: *V.E. 1634.* Tavernor (Gorleston, Suffolk). Same arms.

Taverner (Hoxton, co. Hertford and co. Kent . . . and by patent). Insert—by Camden . . .

Tawell (Norwich). Az. on a chev. . . . . betw. three plates 5 trefoils . . . **Tomb** in Norwich Cathedral.

Tay (Co. Essex). Arg. a chev. az. on a chief of the second three martlets—delete. 'of the first (another,' or). and further delete 'another erm.'

Tay. Arg. a chev. az. on a chief of the second 3 martlets of the first Sir Henry Tay. *V.*

Tay (Essex). The same arms but the martlets erm.

Taylor. Per pale sa. and arg. in base a lion pass. and in chief 3 annulets all counterchanged.

Taylor (Bradley, co. Hants). Sa. a lion pass. arg. quartering sa. a chev. erm. betw. 3 ram's heads erased arg. armed or for Ramsey. *Guillim.*

Taylor. Stechworth and Lidgate, co. Cambridge). Arg. a chev. sa. betw. in chief two lions pass. and in base an annulet of the second. *Coll. MS. xj. 219.*

Taylor (Lingfield, co. Surrey). Add: *V.*

Taylor. Insert—Dublin. Az. a lion ramp. arg. depressed by a bend gu. charged with three escallops of the second. Add: Taylor of the North. *W.*

Taylor (Great Yarmouth, co. Norfolk 1731). Sa. a leopard pass. or.

Taylor (Dublin). Arg. a lion ramp. az. overall on a bend gu. 3 escallops of the field. *W.*

Taylour. Az. on a chev. engr. arg. betw. 3 dolphins naiant embowed as the second finned or a fleur-de-lis enclosed by two greyhounds courant respectant of the first. Thomas Taylour. *W.*

Tee or Tye. Add: *V.N. 189.*

Teed (London). Erm. a chev. engr. az. betw. in chief 2 griffin heads erased and in base a griffin pass. gu. *Debrett.*

Tegalle. Add: *W.*

Telmaston. Gu. 6 lions ramp. erm. Roger de Telmaston. *A.*

Temperley. Erm. on a chev. az. 3 leopards faces or. Add: *V.V.*

Tempest (Bracewell, co. York. . . .). Add: Sir Richard Tempest. *S.V.* William Tempest. *Y.*

Tempest (Heaton, co. Lancaster, bart.). Insert—1866 . . .

Tempest (Tong Hall, co. York . . .). . . . Arg. a bend—delete—'engr.' betw. 6 martlets sa. Add: 'a crescent for diff.' *Dugdale 1666. p. 319.* Add: Tempest (Holmside and Studley, co York). Arg. a bend engr. betw. 6 martlets sa. *Tonge p. 103.* Thomas Tempest. *Dug. O. J.*

Tempest. rg. a bend indented betw. 6 martlets sa. Richard Tempest. *Y.*

Tempest. Arg. a chev. gu. betw. 3 martlets sa. Monsire Tempest. *Y.*

Tempest (Broughton Hall, co. York . . .). . . . † for diff. *Dugdale 1666. p. 360.* Crest: . . . beak gu. Add: † for diff.

Temple. Arg. on a chev. sa. five birds of the first beaked and legged gu. *V.*

Tench (Low Leyton, co. Essex, bart.). Insert—1715 . . .

Tencreek of Tencreek. Arg. a chev. supporting on its point a cross patty sa. *A.A.*

Tennant (York and Essex). Erm. on each of 2 bars sa. an annulet or. *V.E. 1634.*

Tenant (Norfolk). Erm. 2 bars gu. each charged with a bezant. *Cady. j.*

Tennant (Scotton, near Richmond, co. York). Confirmed 1613. Erm. on 2 bars sa. 3 bezants 2 and 1. *Northern Grants. xlvij.*

Tennant (M.P. for Leeds 1874). Erm. on 2 bars sa. 3 bezants 2 and 1 in base an escallop . . .

Tenison (Kilronan Castle, co. Roscommon). Gu. a bend engr. or betw. 3 leopards heads jessant de lis.

Tenton. Sa. a chev. betw. 3 tents arg. Add: *V.*

Tenvise (Scotland). Or on a bend az. 3 crescents of the field. *Cady.*

Terett. Gu. 3 towers with cupulas or. *V.*

Terrick (Co. Stafford). Add: *Randle Holme.*

Terrick. Gu. 3 martlets or. In York Minster.

Terrick (London 1633). Vert a chev. couped betw. 3 fleurs-de-lis or in chief on an escu. unj. as many in bend sa. *Harl. MS. 1358. fo. 83.*

Terry (Ireland). Sa. 2 bars or charged with 3 crosses crosslet . . . in chief a demi-lion . . . *Robson.*

Teshe. Per pale or and gu. a chev. couped and voided betw. 3 cinquefoils on a chief two escallops all counter changed. *Cady.*

Tessington. Add: *C.R. p. 29.*

Tetlow. Arg. a bend engr. gu. betw. 2 cotises sa. *Randle Holme.*

Tey (Essex). Arg. a chev. surmounted by a fess az. in chief 3 martlets of the last.

Tey (Co. Northumberland). Add: Peter Tey. *V.*

Teyes. Arg. a chev. gu. Dominus Teyes. *V.* Monsire Henry Ties. *Y.H.N.J.Q.I.K.* or Tyes.

Teys. Gu. a chev. betw. 8 crosses crosslet arg. *V.N. p. 105.*

Thackeray (Granted by Leake, Garter . . .). Add: Arms of Thackeray, the novelist.

Thame (Chinnor, co. Oxford and co. Leicester . . .). Add: *C.L. 1619.*

Therkeston. Or on a bend double cotised . . . 3 fleurs-de-lis . . . **Book Plate.**

Thewarct ap Robert (Wales). Sa. a bordure gu. *Randle Holme.*

Thwested. Gu. a chev. betw. 3 leopards heads arg. *V.*

Thickness (Co. Warwick). Az. on a plain bend or within a bordure engr. arg. two 5-foils gu. *C.W.*

Thicknesse. Arg. a chev. sa. fretty or in chief the blade of a scythe barwise az. *V.* and *Harl. MS. 1386. fo. 94.*

Thicknesse (Beech Hill, co. Lancaster . . .). Add: *A.A.*

Thirkwald. Add: Ralph de Thirkewald. †

Thirlwall (Co. Norfolk). Add: *V.*

Thirwall. Insert—co. Norfolk. Add: *V.*

Thirwall. Gu. a chev. betw. 3 boars heads erased arg. Add: *F.Y.*

Thistlethwayte (Cos. Wilts). Insert—confirmed by Segar 1607 . . . and Hants . . . Add: *V.E. 1634.*

Thomas (Llwyn Madoc, co. Brecon; granted 6 Edward vi). Insert—by Hawley Clarenceux.

Thomas (Danygraig, co. Glamorgan). Sa. a chev. betw. 3 fleurs-de-lis arg. *Nicholas.*

Thomas (Carmarthen). Az. a stag trippant arg. collared and lined or betw. the attires an imperial crown ppr.

Thomas (London). Arg. a chev lozengy or and sa. —insert—(or chequy). Add: Granted by Camden 1606. *Syl. Morgan.*

Thomas (temp. Henry vii). Add: *V.** Sir Rhys ap Thomas. *V.*

Thomason (London). Per fess embattled arg. and sa. 3 falcons counterchanged in chief a † sa.

Thompson (Lord Mayor of London). 1828. Az. a lion pass. guard. or within a bordure arg.

Thompson (Samuel Thompson. Windsor Herald). Sa. a lion pass. guard. or betw. 3 saltires couped arg. *W.*

Thompson (Streatham, Surrey). Same arms.

Thomson (Shalfield, co. Essex and co. Lincoln). . . . Add: John Thomson. Auditor to Queen Elizabeth. Same arms. *W.*

Thomson. Quarterly, 1st gu. a lion pass. guard. betw. three crosses crosslet; 2nd . . . —insert —*V.* Crest: . . . .

Thomson (Kent 1660). Per pale or and arg. an eagle displ. gu. *Syl. Morgan.*

Thomson. Per pale or and arg. an eagle displ. gu. a canton erm. This canton was granted by Charles j. for services in Ireland to James Thomson. Motto "Lucem virtus amat". *Syl. Morgan. p. 61.*

Thomson (Esholt, co. York). Per fess embattled arg. and sa. 3 falcons counterchanged bells and beaks or. *F.Y.*

Thoresby (Hay, co. Brecon . . .). Add: *V.* Hugh de Thoresby. *P.Y.* John Thoresby, Keeper of the Privy Seal. *Q.*

Thorley. Arg. on a bend flory counterflory sa. . . . . Add: *V.** William Thorle. *V.*

F

Thornbery (Windsor Herald 1735). Arg. a demi-lion ramp. erased az. betw. in chief 2 chaplets vert. and in base a garb. ppr.

Thornbury. Per chief or and arg. overall a lion ramp. az. debruised by 2 bendlets gu. Sir John Thornbury. *S.*

Thornbury.

Thornell. Gu. 2 chevs. or a border of the last. Add: *V.V.**

Thorntonrust. Sa. 3 battle axes arg. Elys de Thorntonrust. *P.*

Thornetonrust. Gu. 3 martlets or. Rauf Fitz-Stephen de Thornetonrust. *X.*

Thornetonsteward. Gu. 3 martlets arg. Mathew de Thornetonsteward. *X.*

Thornhagh (Fenton, co. Nottingham: confirmed 4 Feb. 1582—insert—by Flower.

Thornhill (Thornhill, co. York . . .). Add:

Thornhill (Co. Lincoln 1640). The same arms with an annulet or on a crescent sa. for diff. *Yorke.*

Thornhill (Suffolk). Barry of ten arg. and gu. *V.*

Thornton (Kirkland Hall, co. Lancaster). Add: *F.Y.*

Thornton (Brockhall and Newnham, co. Northampton). . . . Add: Sir Peirse Thornton, co. Chester. *V.* Sire Piers de Thornton. *R.*

Thornton (Co. Lincoln 1640). Arg. on a bend gu. within a bordure sa. 3 escarbuncles pommetty and floretty or. *Yorke.*

Thornton (Greenford, co. Hertford). Add: also Thornton of Birdforth, co. York 1584. *F.Y.*

Thornton (Newcastle upon Tyne). Sa. a chev. arg. and a chief dancetty of the last. *V.*

Thornton (Tyersal, co. York . . .). Add: *Dugdale p. 250.*

Thorold (Marston, co. Lincoln . . .). Add: Thomas Thorold, London 1633–4. Same arms. quartering Hough, Marston and Berehaugh. *Harl. MS. 1358. fo. 87b.*

Thorold (Rector of St. Martin's, Ludgate, London). Gu. 3 goats salient arg. †

Thorold (Boston, co. Lincoln; confirmed 10 Nov. 1631). Insert—by St. George, Clarenceux.

Thorold. Barry of 6 sa. and or on a canton of the first a martlet of the second. *Constable's Roll. xvj.*

Thorp (Thorp, co. York). Add: Thorpe (Danthorpe, co. York 1665). Same arms. *Dugdale p. 134.*

Thorpe (Holderness, co. York). Arg. 2 lions ramp. gu. betw. 8 fleurs-de-lis az. *V.* Sir Stephen Thorpe 6th Hen. iv. Same arms **His Seal.**

Thorp. Quartered by Stockdale of Wilton Park, co. York). Gu. a chev. betw. 3 stags heads erased arg. *Guillim.*

Thorp. Barry of ten arg. and gu. a bend engr. sa. *Cady.*

Thorpe (Co. York). Az. a chev. engr. arg. betw. 3 lions ramp. arg. —delete—(another, tinctures reversed). Add: *Fairfax's Book of Arms.*

Thorpe (Birdsall, co. York). Sa. on a chev. engr. arg. betw. 3 lions ramp. or as many martlets of the field. *Eliz. Roll. xxxj.*

Thorpe. Arg. on a chev. az. betw. 3 eagles displ. sa. crowned gu. as many crescents or. Add: *V.*

Thorpe. Arg. three bars gu. a bend sa. Add: *V.**

Thorpe. Arg. 3 bars gu. a bend engr. sa. *V.*

Thornton (Co. Chester). Arg. a chev. sa. within a bordure erm. over all a chief dancetty sa. *Harl. MS. 1535 fo. 28.*

Thory (co. Lincoln 1640). Arg. on a bend sa. 3 maunches of the first. *Yorke.*

Thowested (Co. Kent). Add: *V.**

Throckmorton (Coughton Court, co. Warwick, bart.). Insert—*V.*

Throckmorton (Burnebutts, co. York 1665). Gu. on a chev. arg. 3 bars gemelles sa. a canton or. *Dugdale. p. 84.*

Thurston (Bobshead, co. Kent). Arg. on a bend gu. 3 mullets or. *Robson.*

Thurgryn. Add: *V.*

Thurkill. Arg. a chev. betw. 3 leopards heads sa. In Sprotborough Church, co. York. *Hunter j. 346.*

Thurkingham. Arg. 2 bars gu. betw. three torteaux over all a baston sa. Sire Walter de Thurkingham. *O.*

Thursbie. Sa. a chev. betw. 3 estoiles within a bordure arg. Thomas Thursbie. *Eliz. Roll. xxx.*

Thurston. Arg. 3 bars sa. on the first a lion pass. guard. betw. 2 martlets . . . Add: *V.**

Thwaites (temp. Henry vj.). Arg. a lion ramp. sa. over all on a fess of the second three bezants. *V.*

Thweng (Co. York). Arg. a chev. gu. betw. 3 popinjays vert. collared gu. *Eliz. Roll. xxxj.*

Thweng (Over Helmsley, co. York). Same arms a mullet for diff. *F.Y.*

Thynne (Sir Egremont Thinne, Serjeant at Law. Same arms. An annulet for diff.

Thynne. Insert—co. Kent. Gu. on a chev. arg. betw. 3 martlets or . . . mullets sa. . . . as many mascles of the first. Add: *Cady.*

Tibbett. Sa. 3 bars triple gemels arg.

Tidemarsh. Purp. a lion ramp. or betw. 8 crosses crosslet fitchy arg. Sir . . . de Tidemarch. *V.*

Tildesley (Garret, co. Lancaster). Arg. a chev. betw. 3 molehills ppr. with grass each charged with an annulet of the first. *V.L. 1664.*

Tillesley (Burham, co. Buckingham). Arg. a chev. vert. betw. 3 pomeis on each a hand lodged of the first. *V.*

Tillesworth (Henry Tillesworth, temp. Henry viii . . . .). Add: *C.L. p. 22.*

Tillington or Tyllington. Add: *V.*

Tillioll. Gu. a lion ramp. a bendlet az. Add: Piers Tillioll. *X. Y.* Sir Robert Tillioll. *M.N.V.*

Tilney (Wisbeach, co. Cambridge and co. Norfolk). Add: *V.V.**

Tilson. Or on a bend cotised betw. 2 garbs az. a mitre . . . Crest: . . . Add: *V.** Tilson (Dewsbury, co. York). Same arms.

Tilston or Tilson (Huxleigh, co. Chester; confirmed 28 Aug. 1580). Insert—by Flower . . .

Tiltington. Gu. a chev. betw. 3 goats heads erased arg. *V.**

Tinker. Arg. 2 chevs. sa. on a canton of the last a church bell . . . **Book Plate.**

Tipper (Impalement *Fun. Ent. Ulster's Office* 1609). . . . betw. three—insert—'r' (for 'round') see:

Tipper (Co. Kildare: *Ulster's Office*). . . . betw. three—insert—'round' wells arg. Add: *Harl. MS. 1441.*

Tipping (Draycott, co. Oxford). Arg. on a bend engr. vert. 3 pheons of the field. *V.O.*

Tipping (Wheatfield, co. Oxford, bart.). Insert—1698 . . .

Tippingwell. Or a bend sinister gu. betw. two cantons az. † *Randle Holme.*

Tirington. Arg. on a bend sa. 3 escallops or—insert—*V.*

Tirrell (Co. Hertford). Add: Sir Roger Tyrrell. *L.V.N.*

Titesbury or Tittesbury. Arg. a bend lozengy or (?,) betw. 6 lions ramp. sa. Baudwine Titesbury. *V.*

Tissington (Co. Rutland). . . . on a bend . . . 3 roundlets . . . quartering, arg. a chev. sa. betw. 3 fleurs-de-lis. *V.R.*

Titmarsh. Gu. a lion ramp. tail coward elevated over the back arg. betw. 7 crosses crosslet fitchy or. *V.*

Titemarch. Gu. a lion salient arg. within an orle of crosses crosslet fitchy or. *V.**

Titton. Arg. two chevs. gu. a canton of the last. Add: *V.** Query error for Fitton.

Titteller. Arg. a bend gu. cotised vert. *Randle Holme.*

Tocketts. Az. a lion ramp. arg. over all a bend gu. Roger Tocketts, co. York. *Eliz. Roll. xxvj.*

Todd (Buncrana Castle, co. Donegal). Arg. a chev. gu. betw. 3 foxes heads erased . . .

Todenham. Barry dancettee of six az. and arg. Add: Oliver Todenham. *E.*

Todenham. Arg. 3 bars fusilly az.

Todenham. Barry dancetty of 6 gu. and arg. *Y. Randle Holme.*

Tofeild. Gu. a chev. erm. betw. 3 martlets arg.

Toft or Tofte. Arg. a chev. betw. 3 crosses formee fitchee sa. (another, crosses gu.). Insert—*V.** Crest: . . .

Tolimond. Add: *V.*

Toll (Grewell, co. Hants.). Add: Christopher Toll, co. Gloucester. *V.*

Tolley (London John Tolley . . . Add: *V.N. 140.*

Tolley or Tollye. Insert—of Ramessey . . . Add: *V.*

Tolmond. Add: *V.*

Tomkins (Monington, co. Hereford). Az. a chev. betw. 3 birds or. Sir Thomas Tomkins 1661. *L.N.*

Tomkins (Middlesex). Arg. a chev. betw. 3 oak leaves slipped vert. *Cady.*

Tomlin. Arg. a chev. betw. 3 oak leaves vert. Crest: . . . Add: Sir Richard Tomlins Kt. *1628.*

Tomlinson (Leeds and London). Add: *Whitaker's Leeds ij. 26.* Tomlinson (Thorgamby, co. York 1665). *Dugdale. p. 376.*

Tompson. Sa. a chev. betw. 3 martlets arg. Add: *V.**

Tompson (Witchington, Norfolk 1827). Gu. a lion pass. guard. or quartering arg. a lion ramp. gu. *Dashwood.*

Tonds. Add: *V.*

Tong (Manningham, co. York and Newark, co. Nottingham . . . Add: Thomas Tonge *Constable's Roll. x.* Tong (Newark, co. Notts. 1614.). Same arms with a mullet for diff. and quartering arg. a fess counter flory gu. betw. 3 escallops sa. for Illingworth. *V.N.*

Tonge (Tonge, co. Lancaster 1664). Add: *V.V.L.* Tong of Tong, co. York. Same arms.

Tonge. Az. a bend per bend or and arg. betw. 2 cotises and 6 martlets those in chief of the second, those in base of the third. Richard Tonge. London. *V.*

Tonge (Thickley   ). Az. a bend betw. 4 cotises or and 6 martlets arg. George Tonge. *Eliz. Roll. xviij.*

Tonge. Az. a bend per bend or and arg. cotised of the last betw. six martlets of the second. Add: *V.**

Tonkes. Or 10 billets 4. 3. 2. and 1. sa. a canton erm. Sir Walter Tonkes, co. Notts. temp. Edw. j. *W.* But sa. 10 billets or a canton erm. *I. V.*

Tonke. Arg. a bend lozengy betw. two bendlets sa. *V.*

Tonkes (Co. Cambridge). Bendy of 6 arg. and sa. *V.*

Tonke. Or billetty sa. a canton sa. *V.** Sir Walter Tonke, co. Nottingham, temp. Edw. j. *W.*

Tonke. Sa. billetty or a canton erm. Sir Walter Tonke, co. Nottingham. temp. Edw. j. *V.I.N.*

Tonnis or Tonnes (Cos. Northampton and Nottingham). . . . Add: William Tonnes. *V.*

Tooley (Co. Lincoln 1640). Add: *Yorke.*

Topcliff (Topcliffe, co. York). Per pale or and sa. three crescents counterchanged.

Topcliffe. . . . a chev. . . . betw. 3 pegtops . . . In Topcliffe Church, co. York. 1391.

Topham (Grays Inn, London and Calverley). Insert—Aglethorpe, co. York. Add: 1665.

Topps or Towpis. Sa. on each of two bars arg. a water bouget vert. in chief 2 tops of the second. *V.*

Topsfield (Cos. Norfolk and Suffolk). Add: *V.E. 1634.*

Topsfield. Vert. a bend or Add: *V.**

Torell. Arg. a bull statant gu. armed or. Sir William Torell. *V.*

Torner (Tableheart, co. Sussex; confirmed). Insert—by Cooke.

Torpigni. Az. an inescutcheon within an orle of 9 escallops argent. William de Torpigni. *A. Harl. MS. 6137.*

Torr (Eastham, Cheshire. M.P. for Liverpool 1873). Gu. 3 towers triple towered or. *Debrett.*

Torre (Abbey of Premonstralensian Canons, co. Devon). Gu. a chev. betw. 3 pastoral staves or. *Ashmole MS. 763.*

Torrens. Arg. 3 candlesticks or. *Robson.*

Torrington (Co. Devon). Gu. two bars or in chief a lion pass. of the last. John Torrington. *V.*

Toste. Arg. on a chev. betw. 3 crosses patty fitchy gu. a crescent for diff. Robert Toste. *V.*

Totenham. Gu. four bars dancettee arg. *V.*

Tothill (Peamore, co. Devon Henry Tothill . . .). Add: *V.D. 1620.* Add: Tothill granted 1561. *W.* Tothill quartered by Harvey. *V.*

Totehyll. Az. 2 bars and in chief a leopards head arg. *V.*

Tottehul or Toutehill. Or on a chev. sa. 3 crescents arg. *V.*

Tothill.

Totleworth. Sa. on a chev. arg. 3 martlets of the field.

Toty. Arg. on a chev. az. a mullet (another, pierced) of the field. Add: *V.*

Touchet (Nether Whitley and Buglawton, co. Chester). . . . Add: Sir Thomas Touchet. *N.* Sir William Touchet, co. Northants. *V.* Sir Robert Tuchet. *X.* And with a label az. Sire Robert Touchet the son. *N.*

Touchet (Earl of Castlehaven . . .). Add: Roll. *U.*

Touchet. Gu. 6 martlets or. Sir William Touchet. *I.K. Harl. MS. 6589.* But 10 martlets. *N.*

Touke. Add: *N.*

Touke. Sa. 2 bars arg. Sir Robert Touke, co. Cambridge. *V.*

Tourney. Arg. fretty and semy of castles gu. *Harl. MS. 1407. fo. 156.*

Tournay. Arg. a chev. gu. betw. 3 oxen pass. sa. armed or. *Fuller.*

Tournay. Arg. a chev. betw. 3 bulls statant sa. Crest: . . . Add: *V.** William Tournay. *V.*

Tours. Arg. three towers gu. Add: *V.*

Toutson. Sa.—delete—'on' a chev. . . . Add: *V.*

Towergyes or Tourgeis (Co. Dorset). Add: *V.*

Towers or Towres. Gu. 3 castles or. *Harl. MS. 1386. fo. 66.*

Towers (Sowerby, co. Lincoln). Add: Thomas Towers 1352, quartered by Topcliff. *W.*

Towers. Of Thymock, co. Lincoln. 1640. Same arms. *Yorke.*

Tower. Huntsmore Park, co. Bucks. Same arms.

Towne. Arg. on a chev. sa. 3 crosses crosslet of the first. *V.*

Townsend. Az. a chev. engr. betw. 3 escallops erm. Granted by Walker, Garter in 1663 to Sir Robert Agborough alias Townsend. *Guillim.*

Townsend (Ludlow, co. Salop). Add: *V.*

Townshend (Raynham, co. Norfolk . . .). Add: Sir Roger Townshend, Norfolk. *V.*

Towpis. Sa. on each of 2 bars arg. a water bouget vert. in chief 3 tops of the second. *V.*

Tozer (Recorder of Bury St. Edmunds 1861). Arg. a chev. gu. betw. 3 bridges with towers ppr. *Debrett.*

Tracy (Sir John Tracy, Barnstaple). Or a lion pass. sa. betw. 2 cotises gu. *V.*

Tracy. Or 2 bendlets gu. in chief an escallop sa. Sir William Tracy. *L.N.* The escallop betw. the bendlets and over all a label of 5 az. Sir John Tracy. *R.*

Tracy (Co. Worcester). Or two bend gu. Add: Sir Ralph Tracy. *V.*

Tracy or Tresse. Add: *V.* William Trasi. *E.*

Treheron (Granted by Camden to John Treheron, Porter to Queen Elizabeth and King James). Arg. a chev. betw. 3 herons sa. a canton arg. with 3 bars or and a lion ramp. gu. *Syl. Morgan.*

Traherne (Somerset Herald to Hen. viij). Same arms but canton erm. with 4 bars az. and a lion ramp. gu. *Noble.*

Traisens. Or 3 bendlets az. a bordure gu. Sir Otes Traisene. *A. Harl. MS. 6137.*

Traner.

Transquillet (Cornwall). . . . a chev. . . . betw. 3 squirrels . . . *Lysons.*

Trappes (London . . .). Add: *V.E. 1634.*

Traseme. Bendy of 6 or and az. a bordure engr. gu. Sir Otes Traseme. *A.*

Trasaher (Trevethan, co. Cornwall). Add: *V.C. 1620.*

Travell (Sir Thomas Travell, London 1684). Per pale az. and gu. on a bend or 3 mullets pierced sa. on a chief arg. 3 garbs az. (or vert). *L.N.*

Travell. John Travell, London descended from Travell, Wenlock, co. Salop. 1633. *Harl. MS. 1558. fo. 75.*

Travers (Co. York). Arg. 3 bars pass. in pale sa. Add: *V.* *

Travers (London 1633–4). Arg. 3 bears statant in pale sa. in the dexter chief a mullet for diff. *Harl. MS. 1358. fo. 34b.*

Travers. Arg. a chev. betw. four butterflies sa. Sir John de Travers. *S.*

Travers. . . . a chev. . . . betw. . . . 3 boars heads fesswise couped . . . Laurence Travers. *Seal. V.*

Travers (Monkstown Castle, co. Dublin . . .). Add: *V.*

Traves. Az. 3 bears pass. arg. muzzled gu. *V.V.* *

Travieur. Arg. 2 chevs. counterpointed az.

Trayfray. Sa. a chev. betw. 3 trefoils slipped arg. *V.*

Trayner. . . . a chev. engr. betw. 3 martlets . . . *Robson.*

Trayton. Arg. on a bend sa. a helmet of the first. Crest: . . . Add: *W.*

Trayton (Lewes, co. Sussex; granted). Insert—by Segar . . .

Treage (Cornwall). Arg. a chev. betw. 3 crosses crosslet fitchy sa. *V.*

Treage (Co. Cornwall). Arg. a chev. betw. three crosses crosslet sa. Add: *V.*

Treantone (Co. Lincoln). Add: *V.* Raf de Tirentone. *F.* Rauf de Trahampton. *P.* Sire Rauf de Trauntone. *N.* Rauf de Trehampton. *B.*

Treby (Goodamoor and Plympton House, co. Devon). Add: Sir George Treby, Speaker of the House of Commons. ob. 1700.

Treckingham. Add: *Y.*

Threckingham or Trekingham. Arg. 2 bars gu. in chief 3 torteaux over all a bendlet sa. *V.* * Walter de Treckingham, co. Lincoln. *V.*

Tregarth (Cornwall). Arg. a chev. betw. 3 escallops sa. *V.*

Tregewe (Harlyn, Cornwall). Arg. on a chev. sa. betw. 3 torteaux 5 bezants. *Lysons.*

Tregian (Quartered by Woollcomb . . .). Add: Tregian. *V.* and *Harl. MS. 1392.*

Tregold. Gu. 3 battle axes arg. . . . pierced of the last. Add: Thomas Tregold. *V.*

Tregoose or Tregooze. Add: *V.* *

Tregoz. Robert Tregoz. Gu. 2 bars and in chief a lion pass. or. *V.*

Tregoz. Az. 3 bars gemel and in chief a lion pass. or. Henry Tregoz. *A.*

Tregoz. Or 3 bars gemel and in chief a lion pass. gu. Robert de Tregoz. *B.* Sir John Tregoz. *D.F.H.Y.* Geffrey Tregoz. *C.*

Tregos (Hylford, co. Cornwall). Add: Henry Tregoz. *A.F.E.N.Y.*

Tregos (Co. Cornwall). Arg. a chev. sa. betw. 3 cornish choughs ppr. Add: *V.* *

Tregos (Co. Cornwall). Arg. three foxes pass. gu. Add: *V.*

Tregosse. Sa. 2 swans in pale arg. that in base reguard. Add: *V.V.* *

Tregoz. Arg. a chev. betw. 3 cornish choughs ppr. *V.*

Trehampton. Arg. on a bend gu. 3 cinquefoils pierced or—delete—(another, of the field). Add: *V.Y.*

Trehawke. Add: *Lysons.*

Trehington. Erm. (another, arg.)—insert—*V.* * . . .

Treise. Arg. 3 bars az. in chief as many cinquefoils per fess gu. and sa. Add: *Lysons.*

Trelamer. Add: *V.*

Trelansard. Arg. 3 bendlets gu.

Trelawarren (Quartered by Beville). Arg. a lion couchant tail reflexed betw. the legs over the back gu. on a chief of the first 2 bendlets of the second betw. 3 fleurs-de-lis bendwise in bend sinister az. *Harl. MS. 1079. fo. 37b.*

Trelawny (Shotwick, co. Chester). Add: Trelawney (Cornwall). Same arms. *V.*

Trellowe. Az. a chev. betw. 3 escallops arg. Sir John Trellowe. *S.*

Tremayne (Cos. Cornwall and Devon). Add: *V.*

Tremenet (Hennock, co. Devon). Add: *Lysons.*

Tremouille. Or a chev. gu. betw. 3 eagles displ. az. *Z. 542.*

Trench (Cornwall). Arg. 3 chevs. sa. *Lysons.*

Trench. Insert—Essex—Paly of 6 arg. and sa. a bend or. Add: *V.E. 1634.*

Trencheld (Walden, Kent). . . . a chev. . . . betw. cinquefoils . . .

Trenchfield or Trenchfoyle. Sa. a chev. betw. 3 cinquefoils arg.

Trenchard (Collacomb, co. Devon). Add: *Lysons.*

Trenethin. Arg. a raven sa. memberd gu. Add: *V.* *

Trent. Az. 3 chevs. or in chief 2 roses arg.

Trennorth *Collinson Somerset. ij. 264.*

Trentham. . . . 2 bars . . . in chief three 5-foils. Thomas de Trentham 15th Edwd. ij. **Seal.** *Cotton MS. Julius. F.*

Trenwith (Co. Cornwall). Add: *Lysons.*

Trerice (Trerice, Newlyn, co. Cornwall). . . . Add: *V.*

Treryge. Add: *V.* *

Tresawell (Cornwall). Arg. (query or) on a bend betw. 2 cotises sa. 3 mullets . . . *Lysons.*

Treshar (Co. Devon). Gu. a chev. betw. 3 boars heads couped arg. *V.* *W.*

Tresley. Add: John Tresley. *V.*

Tretheke. Arg. a chev. betw. 3 moors heads in profile erased sa. wreathed another of the first and az. *V.V.* *

Trethewy (Brannel, co. Cornwall). Add: *Lysons.*

Trethewy (Co. Cornwall). Add: *V.C. p. 306.*

Trethewy. Sa. a chev. engr. betw. 3 goats statant arg. *Collinson Somerset ij. 130.*

Treunwith. Add: *V.C. 306.*

Trevarthian (Trevarthian, co. Cornwall). . . . Add: *V.*

Trevenor (Appledore, co. Cornwall). Arg. a chev. gu. betw. three sea-pies-insert—'rising' ppr. Add: *Harl. MS. 1404. fo. 147.*

Trevenouthe. Add: *V.**

Treverne (Quartered by Carnsew, Cornwall). Gu. a bull pass. sa. *Lysons.*

Trevers. Quartered by Baskerville. Gu. a chev. betw. 3 escallops arg.

Trevery. Arg. 3 bars gemel sa. Add: *V.**

Trevery. Arg. 3 bars sa. *V.*

Treveyston. Add: *V.*

Trevillian. Gu. a demi-horse ramp. issuant arg. issuing from a base barry wavy of ten arg. and az. *V.** Sir William Trevillian, co. Devon. *V.*

Trevithin (Cornwall). Arg. a cornish chough ppr. *V.*

Trevory. Insert—co. Devon. Arg. 3 bendlets sa. Add: *V.*

Trewarthen. Gu. a lion ramp. arg. betw. 3 square buckles of the same a bordure az. bezanty. *Robson.*

Trewent. Add: *V.* Estienne de Trewent. *X.Y.*

Trewin (Co. Devon). Arg. on a bend vert. betw. 6 crosses crosslet fitchy gu. 3 crosiers gu. *Lysons.*

Trewithian. Add: *Shaw.*

Trewola. Add: *V.C. p. 306.*

Trewren. Add: *V.C. p. 306.*

Trewyn. Add: *V.**

Trewyn. Az. a chev. arg. betw. 3 trees eradicated or. Sir John Trewyn. *V.*

Treyge. Arg. four bars sa. Add: *V.*

Trice. Add: *V.H. 1613.*

Triconie. Arg. a chev. betw. 3 martlets sa. Sire William Trionie. *Y.*

Trollop of Thornley. Vert. 3 bucks trippant arg. attired or. John Trolop. *Eliz. Roll. xix.*

Trollop. Vert. 3 bulls courant arg. Andrew Trollope. *V.*

Trollope. Insert—Casewick, co. Lincoln, Baronetcy 1641. Baron Kesteven—insert—1868 . . .

Trompington. Add: Roger de Trompington. *V.*

Trott (Laverstoke, Hampshire, Baronetcy 1660). Paly of 6 or and gu. on a canton arg. a cross flory sa. *Guillim.*

Trott. Sa. a horse arg. bridled gu. Add: *W.*

Trotter (Helmden, now Helmington Hall . . .). Trotter (Skelton Castle, co. York). Same arms.

Trotter (Raheen, co. Galway . . .). Add: Trotter Queensborough, co. Galway). Same arms. *A.A.*

Troughton (Great Lindford, co. Buckingham . . . granted). Insert—by Hervey . . . ducally—over written—'gorged' or . . .

Trowbridge (Modbury, co. Devon). Add: *V.D. 1620.*

Trowbridge (Co. Devon). Arg. a bridge of 3 arches masonry gu. water az. on the bridge a flag or. *V.* This coat is quartered by Halliday.

Trowert. Arg. a chev. gu. betw. 3 eagles double headed displ. sa. *V.*

Troys. Arg. a bend betw. 5 crescents sa. Add: *V.*

Truelove or Trelow.

Trusbut. Arg. 3 water bougets gu. Add: *F.* Robert Trusbutt. *E.* Robert le Ussebut. *Harl. MS. 6137.*

Truss (Rev. William Nicholas Truss). . . . Per Pale—underlined—in margin ? Per bend *A.A.*

Trussell. Same arms. With a border sa. Add: Roger Trussell. *V.*

Tryerman (Cumberland). Vert. a bend chequy or and gu. *Lysons.*

Tryot. Arg. a chev. betw. 3 crosses crosslet sa.

Tryot. Quartered by Thornhill of Fixby, co. York. Same arms.

Trigot (South Kirkby, co. York). Same arms. *Hunter ij. 447.*

Tubb (Trengoff, co. Cornwall . . .). Add: *V.C. p. 306.*

Tubby (Brockdish   ). Sa. a chev. erm. betw. 3 swans arg. *Dashwood.*

Tuck (Co. Kent and London . . .). Add: *C.L.*

Tuck (Mayor of Norwich). 1665—corrected to read 1865.

Tucker. Az. a chev. embattled or betw. 3 sea-horses naiant arg. *Syl. Morgan.*

Tucker (Dublin . . .). Add: Tucker (Co. Devon). Same arms . . . *Visitation 1620.*

Tooker. . . . a chev. . . . betw. 3 estoiles . . . In Romney Church, Kent. *Robson.*

Tucker. Vert. on a bend arg. 3 hearts gu. *W.*

Tucker (Moddington, co. Wilts, Baronetcy 1664). Same arms. *Guillim.*

Tucker (Moorgate, Rotherham, co. York). Vert. on a bend engr. arg. 3 hearts gu. *Hunter ij. 25.*

Tudenham. Arg. 3 bars fusilly gu.

Tudenam. John de Tudenham. Barry indented arg. and gu. *Harl. MS. 1386.*

Tudor (Duke of Bedford . . .). Add: Tudor (Ellen bastard daughter of Jasper Tudor, she married William Gardener). Same arms with a baston sinister . . . *Tonge. p. 36.*

Tudor Maur. Gu. a bordure indented or. *Randle Holme.*

Tudor (Duddington, Northants). Per pale wavy vert. and gu. a lion pass. erm. betw. 3 annulets arg.

Tudor (Harpwell, co. Northampton). Or on a lion pass. betw. 3 annulets sa. a martlet. *W.*

Tudor. Gu. a chev. betw. 3 helmets arg. Owen ap Meridith ap Tudor. *Z. 285.*

Tuke (Cressing Temple, co. Essex, bart.). Insert—1666 . . . 3 lions pass.—insert—in pale or. Add: *V.E. 1634.* Add: Sir Bryan Tuke. *V.*

Tullby. Add: *V.V.**

Insert—**Tumly or Tumlyn.** Add: *V.V.**

Tupigney. Az. an inescutcheon arg. Add: Sir Walter de Tupigni. *A.*

Turberville. Arg. a lion ramp. gu. *F.D.E.* Hugh de Turberville. *A. Harl. MS. 6137.*

Turberville (Bishop of Exeter 1555). Erm. a lion ramp. gu. ermined or armed and langued az.

Turberville. Sa. 3 lions ramp. or. Add: Geffrey Turberville. *E.*

Turgeis. Insert—co. Devon. Add: *V.*

Turgis (Co. Somerset). Add: *V.*

Turing (Fovercan   ). Arg. on a bend sa. 3 boars heads couped bendwise or. *Guillim.*

Turke (London temp. Edw. iii). Add: *V.* Sir Robt. Turk. *S.*

Turk (Waltr. Turk, Alderman of London 1352). Gu. a chev. betw. 3 lions heads erased or on a chief of the second a griffin pass. az. armed gu. *Lansdowne MS. 874 fo. 8.*

Turner (London; desc. from Halberton, co. Devon). . . . Add: Oliver Turner. *V.*

Turner (Sussex). Per pale gu. and az. 3 talbots pass. arg. *W.*

Turner (Thorreton, co. Devon). Sa. a chev. erm. betw. 3 ink molines or on a chief arg. a lion pass. gu. *V.D. 1620.* Sir John Turner (Lyme Regis, Norfolk 1684). Same arms. *L.N.*

Turner (Co. Worcester, granted by Heard, Garter 1785). Arg. a lion ramp. gu. betw. 3 millrinds sa. a bordure engr. az. charged with 8 annulets or.

Turpin (Cos. Cambridge and Leicester). Add: *V.V.**

Turpinton. Arg. on a bend betw. 2 cotises sa. 4 mullets or on an escutcheon the arms of Mortimer. Sire Hugh de Turpington. *O.*

Turroplere. Arg. on a bend gu. 3 lions ramp. palewise or. *V.*

Turvile (Normanton Turville, co. Leicester). . . . Add: *C.C. 1619.* Add: Sire Nicolas Torvile. *N.V.*

Turvile. Gu. a chev. vair betw. 3 mullets arg. *V. C.C.p. 55.*

Turvill. Gu. a chev. vair betw. 3 mullets of 6 points or. *V.*

Tuttall (Co. Norfolk). Insert—and Essex. Add: *V.E. 1634.*

Tuystale. Add: *V.V.**

Twenge. Arg. on a bend cotised gu. 3 fleurs-de-lis of the field. Add: John Twenge or Thwoing. *V.*

Twiford or Twyford (Co. Leicester). Arg. 2 bars sa. on a canton of the last a cinquefoil or (another, arg.). Add: John de Twyford. *Y.L.* Richard Twyford. *Y.* Sir Robt. Twyford. *V.*

Twisleton (Barley, co. York . . .). Insert— Granted 22 Nov. 1602 . . . and d.s.p.—insert— 1635 . . .

Twyford (Co. Leicester and Frostdyke, co. Lincoln). Add: *V.** Sir Johan de Twyford. *N.*

Twyford. Arg. 2 bars and a quarter sa. Monsire de Twyford. *Y.*

Twyneho. Arg. a chev. betw. 3 heronshaws sa. *V.*

Tyas or Tyes (London). Add: *W.*

Tychewell. Arg. a chev. sa. betw. 3 leopards heads az. *V.*

Tyddeswall. Az. a bend betw. 6 escallops or. *V.*

Tyldesley (Garrett, co. Lancaster . . .). Add: *V.L. 1664.* each hill charged with † arg.

Tyldesley. Arg. a chev. betw. 3 molehills . . . each charged with an annulet of the field. Add: *1563 Guillim.*

Tyler. Arg. a bend gu. betw. 6 nails sa. Add: John Tyler, Bishop of Llandaff 1706–24.

Tyler. Vert. a bend arg. betw. 6 nails or. *V.*

Tylioff. Sa. 3 demi-greyhounds in pale arg. Sir Pearse Tylioff. Kt.

Tynwike. Add: *V.*

Tyrell (Springfield, co. Essex, bart.). Insert—1666 . . .

Tyrell (Boreham House, co. Essex, bart.). Insert —1809 . . .

Tyrell (Thornton, co. Bucks . . .). Add: *V.*

Tyrell (Hanslape, co. Bucks, bart.). Insert—1665 . . .

Tyreman (Lord Mayor of York 1668). Sa. (arg.) 2 chevs. betw. 3 lions (ramp.) pass. arg.

Tyrington or Tyryngton. Add: *V.V.**

Tyrrell (Stanford, co. Berks). Add: Tyrrell (Hanslap and Castle Thorpe, co. Bucks, Baronetcy 1665). Same arms.

Tyrrell (Thornton, co. Bucks, Baronetcy 1638). Same arms.

Tyrrell (Stanford, co. Berks). Add: Heiresses mar. Hatch and Nicholl.

Tyrrell (Baron of Castlekeswick 1370). Arg. a lion pass. sa. armed and langued gu. betw. two bars of the last.

U

UAIRME (Oxdrortoun, Scotland). Gu. 3 martlets or within a bordure arg. *Cady.*

Udney (Of that Ilk). Gu. 2 greyhounds arg. leaning against a tree eradicated or with a harts head in the tree. *Guillim.*

Uffleet. Or a bend betw. 6 martlets gu. Add: Sir Gerard Ufflett quartering arg. on a fess az. 3 fleurs-de-lis or. *S.*

Ulterton. Quarterly or and az. a bend gu. *V.** Ulterton (Norfolk) a bendlet gu. *V.*

Umeler or Umener. Add: *V.*

Undercourt. Az. 3 bars indented on the underside arg. *Randle Holme.*

Underhill (Wolverhampton, co. Stafford). Add: *V.*

Underhill (Stratford-upon-Avon. Add: Underhill, Bishop of Oxford, 1589. Same arms.

Underhill (Idlicote, co. Warwick). Add: *Fuller.*

Unnester, Umeler or Umler. Add: *V.V.**

Upwell. Gu. a lion ramp. arg. within a bordure erm.

Urmestone (Westley, co. Lancaster and co. York) Add: *V.L. 1664.*

Urren. Alias Currence (Wales . . .). Insert— granted by Segar . . . .

Urswick (Cos. Cumberland, Lancaster and York). Add: Robert Urswick. *Y.* Robert de Urswicke. *S.* Sir William Urswick. *V.* And in the sinister chief a crescent of the second for diff. Sir Wauter Ursewycke. *S.*

Usher (Dublin). Az. a chev. or betw. 3 batons of the second. *Harl. MS. 1425. fo. 220.*

Usher (Eastwell, co. Galway, Mount Usher, co. Wicklow . . .). Add: James Usher, Bishop of Meath 1621. Bishop of Carlisle 1641.

Uverey. Add: *V.*

V

VACHE. . . . 3 lions ramp. guard. Philip de Vache. **Seal.**

Vachell. Erm. 3 bendlets az. John Vachell, co. Berks. *V.*

Valeman. Gu. a bend betw. two cotises and as many birds (? pheasants) arg. Monsire Rusten Valeman. *T.*

Valence (Earl of Pembroke . . .). The number of bars vary from 10 to 20.

Valentine (Bentcliffe, co. Lancaster 1664). Add: *V.L.*

Vale-Royal, or Dernhall-Abbey (Co. Chester). Add: *Tanner.*

Valletort (Quartered by Monck, of Potheridge). . . . Add: Valletort (Trematon Castle, co. Cornwall). Same arms. *Lysons*

Valoines. Barruly arg. and az. on a bend gu. three mullets of 6 points or. Richard de Valognes. *E.*

Valoyns. Paly wavy of 6 or and gu. a bordure erm. Ralph de Valoyns. *X.*

Valomys. Gu. a lion pass. or within an orle of 8 martlets arg. *V.*

Vampage. Az. an eagle displ. within a double tressure flory counterflory arg. Sir John Vampage. *V.*

Van (Marcross, Wales). Sa. a chev. betw. 3 butterflies volant arg. *Nicholas.*

Vane. Arg. a chev. sa. betw. 3 pellets. Add: Sir Henry Vane. *V.*

Vannell. Or two chevs. gu. within a bordure sa. bezanty. *V.**

Vannell (Co. Norfolk). Add: *V.*

Vans (The Honb. Col. Patrick Vans of Barnbarroch). Or a bend gu. †

Van Swinden. Gu. 3 greyhounds ramp. arg. 2 and 1. **Book Plate.**

Vanys. Add: *V.*

Varen. Gu. 2 lions pass. guard. or. Richard de Varen *Z. 76.*

Vaughan (Gwynne-Vaughan . . .). Add: *A.A.*

Vaughan. Bishop of St. Davids 1509. Per pale sa. and arg. a lion ramp. *C.C.*

Vaughan (Lloydcarth, co. Montgomery). Sa. a goat pass. arg.

Vaughan (Wales). Sa. a goat salient feeding on an ivy bush.

Vaughan. Insert—co. Montgomery. Arg. 2 lions pass. guard. gu. crowned or. Add: *V.*

Vaulx (Co. Kent). Add: Sir William Vaux. *L.*

Vaulx or Vaux. Insert—co. Northumberland arg. a bend counter compony or and gu.—insert—*V.* Crest: . . .

Vaulx. Arg. a bend compony gu. and or. *V.**

Vaulx (Lord Vaulx, Harrowden, co. Northants). Chequy arg. and gu. on a chev. az. three 5-foils or. *V.*

Vauncy. Arg. an eagle displ. az. membered—delete—'or' read gu. Add: *Y.*

Vaux. Arg. a bend chequy or and gu. Roland Vaux. *X.*

Vaux. Erm. a bend chequy . . . and . . . Sir Nicholas Vaux. c. 1400.

Vaux. (Harrowden, Northants). Chequy gu. and arg. on a bend az. 3 roses or. *Berry.*

Vaux. Chequy arg. and az. a label gu. *Berry.*

Vaux (Fringford, co. Oxford . . .). Add: Sir John de Vaux *A.D.E.P.F.Y.* Sir Robert de Vauxl. *C.* And with a label az. Sir Joan de Vaus. *N.*

Vaux (Harrowden,   ). Chequy arg. and az. on a chev. arg. 3 roses gu. *Cady.*

Veale (Winneheys, co. Lancaster 1664). Add: *V.L. 1664.*

Vele. Arg. on a bend sa. 3 calves passant (or statant) of the field. Robert le Vele. *A. Harl. MS. 6137.*

Vele. Arg. on a bend sa. 3 calves passant bendwise or. Sir Pierse Vele. *V.*

Venables (Newbold, co. Chester temp. Edward III . . . Add: **Seal** 15th Edw. iij.

Venables. Arg. 2 bars az. on a bend gu. 3 arrows of the field. Sir Richard de Venables. *S.*

Venables (Co. Lancaster). Az. 2 bars arg. on a bend gu. 3 arrows of the second. Add: M. Richard de Venables. *S.*

Venables. Az. 2 bars arg. a bend gu. Add: Sir Alexander Venables temp. Edw. iij. and iiij. *V.*

Venner (Dr. Tobias Venner, Bath, co. Somerset ob. 1660).Gu. 2 lions pass. guard. in pale or. *Dingley.*

Venour. Or a lion ramp. double queued gu. an orle of crosses crosslet of the last. Add: Sir Robert Venour *V.V.**

Venour. Arg. crusily a lion ramp. tail forked gu. Sire Robert le Venour. *N.*

Venour. Per bend sinister wavy or and az. a lion ramp. counterchanged. *V.*

Verdon. Sa. a lion arg. Sir Thos. de Verdon. *N.* Sir Thos. de Verdon, co. Northampton temp. Edw. j. *V.* Sir John Verdon. *R.*

Verdon. Sa. on a lion ramp. arg. a chessrook gu. at the shoulder. Sir Christopher de Verdon. *R.* Sire Thomas de Verdon. *Y.*

Vere. Quarterly or and gu. a bordure vair. Sir Richard de Vere. *R.*

Verli or Verley. Or on a bend gu. betw. 6 eagles displ. sa. Felip de Verley. *N. Morant Essex. j. 423.*

Verman (Lamorran, co. Cornwall . . .). Add: *V.C. p. 306.*

Verman (Cornwall). Sa. 3 eagles displ. in bend betw. two cotises arg. *Lysons.*

Vernal (Fairfield,   ). . . . a chev. . . . betw. 3 bugle horns. . . . *Collinson Somerset j. 258.*

Verney. Arg. 3 standards sa. in an orle gu. *V.*

Vernon (London). Arg. a fret sa. a canton gu. Add: Sr. Ric. Vernon. *S.*

Vernon (Horningham. co. Wilts.). Az. 2 bendlets or betw. 6 lions ramp. arg. *Hoare.*

Vernon. Or a bend az. Add: Geo. Vernon, Justice of Common Pleas 1631.

Vidion (Half-Yowke, Maidstone, co. Kent; granted). Insert—by Walker. . . .

Vieleston. . . . a chev. . . . betw. 3 fishes hauriant . . . *Baker.*

Vigor (Co. Somerset). Arg. 6 lions ramp. gu. 3.2. and 1. †

Villers or Vilers. Add: Sir Payne Villers. *V.*

Villiers (Crosby, co. Lancaster). Arg. 6 lions ramp. gu.

Villet or Violet (Co. Kent). . . . Add: *C.L. 1568.*

Vincent (Baronsborough, co. York 1665). Arg. 2 bars gu. on a canton of the second a trefoil slipped or quartering Gu. on a chief indented arg. 3 lions ramp. az. Crest: A trefoil slipped. *Dugdale p. 202.*

Vincent. Arg. two bars and a canton gu. charged with a trefoil slipped or all within a bordure az. *Eliz. Roll. xxlij.*

Vincent. Az. 2 bars betw. six 4-foils arg. *V.*

Vintners (Company of, London). Granted in 1447 confirmed in 1530. Sa. a chev. betw. 3 tuns arg. *Cotton MS. Tiberius. D. 10.*

Vipont. Gu. 6 annulets or. John de Vipount. *P.B.* Sir Nicholas Vipount. *I.* Gu. 6 annulets or a label az. Sir John de Vipount. *M.*

Vipount. Gu. 6 annulets or 2. 2. and 2. Sir Robert de Vipount, co. York. *V.*

Vipont (Westmorland). Or 6 annulets gu. John Vipont. *Y.* Sire Nicholas de Vipound. *N.M.L.* De Vipointe. *Y.* And with a label az. Sir John de Vipont. *L.*

Vivian (St. Colomb, co. Cornwall . . .). Add: *V.L. p. 307.* Granted by Sir John Borough, Garter 1663. *Guillim.*

Vivian (Bodmin, co. Cornwall . . .). As many martlets or underlined—add: 'arg.'. *V.O.p.307.*

Vivian (Exeter). Or on a chev. az. betw. 3 lions heads erased ppr. as many annulets of the field. *Colby.*

Vivian (Glanafan, co. Glamorgan). Same arms. *Nicholas.*

Vivian (Trelowsen, co. Cornwall, Baronetcy 1644). Arg. a lion ramp. gu.

Vivian (Cornwall). Arg. a lion ramp. gu. facing to the sinister. *V.*

Vivian (Sheriff of Cornwall temp. Hen. vij). Arg. a lion ramp. gu. in base two bars wavy az. *Fuller.*

Vivian (St. Colomb Minor, Cornwall). Or on a chev. az. betw. 3 lions heads erased as many annulets . . . on a chief embattled gu. a cock betw. 2 birds. . . . *Debrett.*

Vivian. Arg. a chev. sa. betw. 3 lions heads erased ppr. in chief gu. Crest: . . . Add: *V.**

Vode (Scotland). Sa. on a bend arg. 3 mascles of the field. *Cady.*

Voell. Az. a chev. betw. 3 cocks arg. armed &c. gu. Jevan Voell quartered by Eyton 1674.

Voss. Or on a bend sa. 3 lions ramp. arg. *Nicholas.*

Vowell (Co. Essex). Add: *V.*

Vynne (Norfolk). Vert. 3 eagles displ. in fess or.

W

WACES (Norfolk). Or 2 bars gu. in chief 3 torteaux over all a bendlet az. *V.V.**

Wadcote. Arg. a bend gu. on a chief vert. two 5-foils of the first.

Wade (London). Add: *Harl. MS. 1404. fo. 127.* Wade. Az. a bend betw. 3 lures or within a bordure sa. bezanty. *Harl. MS. 1404. fo. 127.*

Wade (London). Az. on a bend or within a bordure gu. bezanty 3 lures palewise of the first, wings of the third. *V.*

Wade. Az. on a bend or within a bordure gu. bezanty 3 lures of the first. *V.**

Wade. Az on a bend or two roses gu. stalked and leaved vert. *V.**

Wade (Leeds, co. York). Az. on a bend or 2 gilly flowers ppr. a bordure arg. *Whitaker's Leeds ij. 154.*

Wade. Az. on a bend or three falcon's lures of the field a border—delete—(another, engr.) gu. bezantee. Add: *V.**

Wadesley. Arg. on a bend betw. 6 martlets gu. 3 escallops or. Sir Robert de Wadesle. *N.*

Wadesdon. Add: *V.** Wadeson (London). *W.*

Wadeson (Yafford, co. York. Granted by Ric. St. George, Norroy Nov. 1612). Gu. a chev. arg. betw. 3 eagles displ. erminois. *F.Y.*

Wadham (Merefield, co. Somerset). Add: Sir Nicholas Wadham. *V.* and *Collinson Somerset j. 8.* with quartering, ob. 1609.

Wadripount. Or 2 lions ramp. addorsed in fess gu. Sire . . . de Waderipount. *A.D.*

Waffir. Add: Sir . . . de Waffir, Ireland. *V.*

Wagstaffe (Co. Warwick; confirmed). Insert—Feb. 1616. . . .

Wait ( ), granted by Camden in 1611 to Thomas Waite. Arg. a chev. betw. 3 bugle horns sa. Sir Nicholas Waite, London 1699. *L.N.*

Wake (Baron Wake . . .). Add: Le Sire de Wake *Y.* Baldwin Wake. *A.D.E.* Sir Hugh de Wake *B.P.V.* John Wake. *G.H.J.N.*

Wake (Clevedon, co. Somerset Baronetcy 1621). Same arms.

Wake. Az. a chev. wavy arg. *Randle Holme.*

Wake (co. Kent). Or 2 bars gu. a bend az.—insert—*V.* . . .

Wake (Deeping, co. Lincoln). Add: Sir Thomas Wake (Blisworth). *V.*

Wake. Arg. 2 bars gu. a bordure indented sa. in chief 3 torteaux. Sir Thomas Wake of Blisworth. *O.Y.*

Wakefare. Arg. a lion pass. sa. *V.**

Wakefield (Kingston-upon-Hull, co. York). Add: *V.V.**

Wakeford (Co. Norfolk). Add: Sir Robert Wakeford. *V.*

Wakelyn. Barry of six—insert—(or 9). . . . Add: *V.**

Wakering (Co. Essex). Add: *V.E. 1634* and of Co. Stafford. *Syl. Morgan. 59.*

Wakers. Company of (Edinburgh). Add: *Berry.*

Walborne. Gu. water bougets or in chief a bezant, quartered by Lassells of Brakenborough, co. York. *W.*

Walch. Gu. 2 bars gemelles a bend arg. John Walch of Grimsby, Sheriff of Lincolnshire Ric. ij. *Fuller.*

Walcot (Co. Lincoln). Add: *V.*

Walcot (Walcot, co. Salop. . . .). . . . 3 chessrooks erm—read—ermines. Add: *V.V.**

Wallcott (Co. Lincoln). 1640. Arg. a chev. betw. 3 chessrooks sa. *Yorke.*

Walcot. Az. an inescutcheon within an orle of 8 martlets arg.—insert—Walter Walcote. *Y.* (Another, or.)

Waldby of Walbie. Arg. on a chev. sa. 3 crosses patty or. *Eliz. Roll. xxxj.*

Walden-Abbey (Co. Essex). Az. on a bend—delete 'gu.' read 'arg. . . .' 3 escallops—delete —'arg.' read 'gu.'. *Reyner j. 215.*

Walden (Buckworth, co. Huntingdon and co. Norfolk). . . . . 6 martlets of the second three—insert—'dexter', wings—insert—'elevated' arg. Add: Sir Richard Walden. *V.*

Walden. Sa. 2 bars erm. in chief 3 5-foils arg. *M.* Alexander Walden. *S.*

Walden. Sa. 2 bars arg. (another, erm.) in chief 3 cinquefoils pierced of the second. Add: *V.* Ralph Walden, Bishop of London 1405.

Waldeschef (Quartered by Umpton or Unton). Add: *V.* And with a label of 3 az. *V. Nash.*

Waldescuf. Gu. 2 chevs. arg. on a label of 5 points az. as many fleurs-de-lis or. Sir Edmund de Waldescuf. *F.A.*

Waldren (Lord Mayor of London 1412 and 1422). Add: *V.*

Walerand. Arg. a bend engr. gu. *Hoare iij.*

North Wales. Arg. 3 lions pass. reguard. in pale gu. *Harl. MS. 4199 fo. 22b.*

North Wales. Quarterly gu. and or 4 lions pass. guard. counterchanged. *Archaeologia xxix 412.* Le Prince de Gales. *Y.*

Wales, Principality of: . . . to the last Prince Llewelyn, viz.: Quarterly or and gu. 4 lions pass.—insert—guard. . . . Add: Owen Glendwr. **Seal** 1404.

South Wales. Gu. 3 chevs. arg. in chief 2 lions ramp. or. *Archaeologia xxix p. 413.*

Waleys. Erm. a bend gu. Sir John de Waleys. *L.N.*

Waleys. Quarterly arg. and gu. a bend or. Sire Richard de Waleys. *N.*

Waleys. Or 3 bars gu. on a canton erm. a bend engr. of the second. Add: Stephen Waleys. *V.*

Walkeden (Hadley, co. Middlesex). Insert—and London Add: *C.C.*

Walkenton see Walkington.

Walker. Arg. a chev. sa. surmounted by the ring and stock of an anchor of the same.

Walker (Studley Castle, co. Warwick). 1874. Arg. a chev. betw. 3 crescents sa. *Debrett.*

Walker ( ). Arg. on a chev. gu. betw. 3 ogresses as many crescents of the first.

Walker (Depperhaugh, Scole, co. Suffolk). . . . Add: Walker (Oakley House, Suffolk, Baronetcy 1856. Same arms.

Walker (Co. York granted 11 March 1654 . . .). Add: Walker (Granted to Anthony Walker, co. York 1563). Az. a chev. engr. erm. betw. 3 bezants on each a 3-foil slipped vert. *W.*

Walker (Sand Hutton, co. York and Beachampton, co. Bucks., bart.). Insert—1868. . . .

Walker (Rotherham, co. York). . . . Add: Granted in 1778.

Walker (Dr. Thomas Walker, Master of University College Oxford, ob. 1665. Granted by Walker, Garter). Arg. on a chev. ringed at the point betw. three crescents sa. an estoile. . . . *Guillim.*

Walker. Arg. on a bend betw. 3 leopards faces gu. as many dexter hands clenched arg. Add: *V.**

Walker. Insert—co. Derby—Or on a chev. sa. 3 garbs of the first. Add: *W.*

Walkfare (Co. Norfolk). Arg. on a lion ramp. sa. a mullet or at the shoulder. Sir Robert de Walkefare. *N.*

Walkingham (Fareham, co. York). Add: Alain de Walkingham of Redmer. *Y.* John de Walkingham. *Y.M.N.*

Walkington (Co. Chester). Add: *Z. 340.*

Walkington. Gu. a chev. betw. 3 mullets of 6 points pierced arg. Add: *V.*

Walkington. Insert—temp. Edw. iij. Gu. on a chev. betw. 3 martlets arg. a crescent of the first. Add: *V.V.**

Walkington. ? or, on a chev. az. 3 mullets arg. pierced of the field. Sir William Walkington. *R.*

Wall (Crich, co. Derby). Add: *V.*

Wall (Preston and Wallrush, co. Lancaster). Add: *V.L. 1664.*

Walleis (Co. Leicester, temp. Edw. j.). Arg. a lion ramp. double tailed gu. *Burton.*

Waller (Braywick Lodge, co. Berks., bart.). Insert—1814. Same arms.—insert—Sa. on a bend engr. betw. 2 plain cotises or 3 walnut leaves ppr. *Debrett.*

Waller (Cambridge 1635). Arg. on a bend gu. betw. 2 cotises sa. as many dexter hands couped ppr. *V.*

Waller (Boklesham, co. Suffolk). Add: *V.*

Waller alias Warren (Baningbourne, co. Cambridge and Ashwell, co. Hertford a branch of Warren of Poynton). Chequy or and az. a bordure engr. sa. overall on a canton gu. a lion ramp. double tailed and nowed arg. *Harl. MS. 1546. fo. 114.*

Walles or Walleys. Co. Somerset. Erm. a bend sa. Sir John Walleys. *V.V.**

Wallesey. Az. a bend masculy or. *Randle Holme.*

Walleys. Gu. a bend erm. Sir John Walleys. *R.*

Walleys. Gu. a billet or within an orle erm. surmounted by billets gold. *Harl. MS. 1404.*

Walley. Or on a chev. sa. 3 crosses patty arg.

Walleys. Quarterly gu. and arg. a bend or—delete—(another, of the second.) Add: Steven le Waleis. *E.* Richard Walleys. *Y.*

Walleys. Quarterly gu. and arg. a baston engr. or. Richard Wallays. *Y.*

Wallop (Sir Henry Wallop . . .). Quarterly 1st and 4th—insert—*V.*

Wallpool (Co. Sussex). Add: *V.*

Walpoole (Co. Lincoln 1640). Add: *Yorke.*

Walpole. Sa. a chev. arg. betw. 3 martlets or. Add: *V.*

Walrand. Arg. a bend engr. gu. Robert Walrand. *B.*

Walrond. Arg. a bend of 5 lozenges conjoined gu. Robert Walrond. *F.*

Walrand. Arg. a bend indented gu. John Walrant. *Y.*

Walrond. Sir John Walrond, co. Wilts. Barry of 6 or and az. an eagles displ. gu. *V.*

Walsalle. Arg. a wolf statant sa. *V.*

Walsh (Wanlip, co. Leicester, Sheriff iij. Hen. vj.). Gu. 2 bars gemelles a bend arg. *Fuller.*

Walsh. Arg. a chev. betw. 3 fleurs-de-lis sa. Sir John Walsh. *S.*

Walshage (Co. Lancaster). Arg. a chev. engr. sa. betw. 3 bugle horns of the last stringed az. *V.*

Walshage. Arg. a chev. engr. sa. betw. three bugle horns gu. *V.**

Walshagh (Co. Lancaster). Arg. a chev. engr. gu. betw. 3 bugle horns sa. stringed az. *V.*

Walshage. Arg. a chev. engr. betw. three bugle horns gu. *V.**

Walshe. Gu. 3 bars arg. a canton erm. *V.*

Walsham. Gu. an eagle displ. arg. beaked az. a bordure engr. or. *V.*

Walshall. Arg. a fox pass. sa. Sheriff of Staffordshire. temp. Ric. iij. *Fuller.*

Walsham (Cambridge). . . . a chev. . . . betw. three roses. . . . *Cole. MSS. Vol. iij.*

Walsham for Walsingham. Sa. a chev. arg. betw. 3 pierced cinquefoils or. Sir Roger de Walsham. *S.*

Walshe. Arg. 4 bars gu. on a canton of the first a bend fusilly of the second. *V.*

Walshe (Co. Leicester). Add: Monsire Thomas Walshe. *S.*

Walshe. Gu. 3 bars gemel arg. over all a bend of the last. *V.**

Walshe.

Walshe. Barry of 6 gu. and arg. a canton erm. Add: *V.*

Walsingham (Co. Kent). Add: *V.* Roger de Walsingham. *Y.S.* Sa. a chev. arg. betw. 3 cinquefoils or.

Walsingham. Arg. three chessrooks gu. Add: *V.**

Walsingham. Gu. 3 chessrooks arg. Sir Richard de Walsingham. *N.* of Norfolk temp. Edw. j. *V.*

Walsy (Norfolk). Or on a chev. betw. 3 woolsacks az. as many garbs of the field. *Cady.*

Walter. Or on a bend sa. betw. 2 cotises gu. 3 boars heads bendwise couped arg. a bordure engr. sa. *V.*

Walter (Co. York). Insert—Granted to Sir Robt. Walter, Lord Mayor of York. . . .

Walter (temp. Edw. iiij.). Arg. on a bend betw. 2 leopards heads gu. as many dexter hands clenched of the same. *V.*

Walters. Insert—co. Glamorgan. Or a lion ramp. sa. thrust through with 2 swords. . . .

Walthall (Wistaston, co. Chester). Add: *Randle Holme* calls them Cornish choughs.

Walthall (Co. Essex). Same arms. An annulet for diff. *V.E. 1612.*

Waltham. Sa. a chev. betw. 3 suns arg. Sir John Waltham. *V.*

Waltham. Sa. a chev. betw. 3 cinquefoils arg. (another, or). Add: *V.*

Walthew (Deptford, co. Kent, granted). Insert—'10 Jan.' 1611,—insert—by Camden. . . . Add: Robert Walthew, Sergeant of the Confectionery to King James j.

Walton (Clifton, co. Gloucester . . .). Add: *A.A.*

Walton (Walton, co. Lancaster and Lacock, co. Wilts.). Add: *V.V.**

Walton (Walton on the Hill, co. Lancaster, 1664). Add: *V.L.*

Walton. Arg. a bend betw. 6 escallops sa. Add: *V.*

Walton. Arg. a chev. betw. 3 buglehorns Add: 'gu.'. *V.**

Walworth (Lord Mayor of London 1373 and 1380). Add: *V.*

Walworth. Sa. a bend raguly arg. betw. six bezants. *V.*

Walwyn. Arg. a bend erm. in the sinister chief a talbot pass. . . . all within a bordure of the second. *Dug. O.J.*

Walwyn (Witham co. Sussex). Add: *V.**

Waney or Wancy. Gu. an eagle displ. arg. armed or. *V.** and *Harl. MS. 1392.*

Wandesford (Kirklington, co. York . . .). Add: Sir Richard Wandesford, Attorney General of the Court of Wards, quartering 2nd arg. a bend and bordure engr. gu. 3rd . . . a fess and chief 3 lozenges . . . 4th az. a pair of wings elevated. *Dug. O.J.*

Wandford. Arg. a chev. betw. 3 quatrefoils voided sa. *V.V.**

Wandlesworth. . . . on a chev. betw. in chief two letters 'W' and in base a cross patty another chevron charged at the bottom with a pair of annulets. . . . **Seal.**

Wangford (Priory at co. Suffolk). Per pale or and vert. a lion ramp. gu. *Taylor.*

Wankford (Berwick Hall, co. Essex granted). Insert—by Byshe. . . .

Wanton (Co. Essex). Add: Sir William de Wanton. *A. Harl. MS. 6137.*

Wanton. Arg. a chev. sa. in the dexter chief a martlet gu. Sire Thomas de Wanton. *Y.* Sire William Wanton. *R.*

Wanton (Co. Gloucester). Add: Sir Wm. de Wanton. *L.N.V.X.*

Wantone. Arg. on a bend sa. 3 round buckles tongues in chief or. John de Wantone. *E.* The tongue in fess. Johan de Wantone. *F.*

Wapail. Arg. 2 chevs. and a quarter gu. Roger de Wapail. *E.* Roger Wappayle. *X.*

Waplott. Quarterly sa. and or a bend az. *Harl. MS. 1465. fo. 15b.*

Waplode. Sa. on a chev. gu.—insert—fimbriated arg. . . . Add: *V.*

Warberton. Arg. 3 birds (query swans) sa. *T.*

Warburton (Warburton and Arley, co. Chester, bart.). Insert—1660.

Warburton. Add: *Guillim. V.* Warburton (Whitbeck, Cumberland). Same arms. *Guillim.* John Warburton, Somerset Herald. Same arms.

Warburton. Arg. 3 birds sa. *T.*

Warburton of Arley, Sheriff of Cheshire time Hen. vj. Arg. 2 chevs. gu. on a canton of the last a mullet or. *Fuller.*

Warburton (Co. Salop.). Add: Warburton (Co. Suffolk). Same arms. *Cady.*

Warcop (Co. Cumberland; quartered by Lowther of Lowther). Insert—and Allanson of London. Add: *Vis. Lon. 1633.*

Warcup. Sa. a chev. betw. 3 covered cups arg. Add: Thomas de Warcop. *Y.*

Ward (Co. Berks.). Add: *V.* Ward the Harbinger. *V.*

Warde (Co. Berks.). Arg. on a chev. sa. 3 wolves heads erased of the first a chief az. charged with on a cross patonce betw. 2 martlets or 5 (ogresses. *W.*) hurts. Thomas Warde, Benhams co. Berks. *Cotton. MS. Tiberius. D.10.*

Ward. Arg. on 2 bars gu. 4 martlets of the first 2. and 2. John Warde. *V.*

Ward (Brockton, co. Stafford). . . . Add: Ward (Newton Baschurch, co. Salop.). Same arms.

Ward (Witley Court and Dudley, co. Worcester). . . . Add: Henry Ward Esq. 1547. *Dug. O.J.*

Ward. Arg. 2 bars betw. 3 martlets gu. 2. and 1. Robert Warde. *V.*

Ward. Az. a bend within a bordure engr. arg. *V.N. p. 117.*

Ward. Barry wavy sa. and arg. Robert de la Ward. *Y.*

Ward or Ware. Add: Sir . . . de Warde. *V.*

Wardall. Arg. a chev. betw. 3 boars heads fesswise couped sa. on a chief of the last as many gourds or. *V.*

Warde. Gu. a bend vairy . . . and . . . within a bordure vair. *V.*

Warde. Arg. a chev. betw. 3 wolves' heads erased sa. Add: *V.*

Wardell or Wardle. Add: *V.*

Wardour (Oxford 1645). Sa. on a chev. betw. 3 talbots heads erased arg. as many fleurs-de-lis. az. *Guillim.*

Wardwike. Add: John Wardwicke. *Y.*

Ware. Gu. a lion ramp. arg. a dexter baston sa. William de Ware. *G.*

Ware, Were, Wey, Vaus, Wayez or Wazz. Or 2 lions pass. guard. az. within a bordure gu. charged with martlets of the first. Sir John Ware. *L.*

Waren. Arg. a chief chequy or and az. Sir John Wareyn. *V.*

Waring (Coventry, co. Warwick). Chequy or and az. on a canton gu. a lion ramp. arg. a martlet for diff. *C.W.*

Waring (Waringstown, co. Down . . .). Add: *V.*

Waring. Sa. a chev. betw. 3 storks heads erased arg. *Shaw's Staffordshire.*

Warmington. Add: Robert Warmington of Calais, temp. Edw. iv. *V.*

Warmoth (Sheriff of Newcastle 1598). Or on a bend betw. 2 lions ramp. az. 3 pierced mullets of 6 points of the field. *Carr MS.*

Warner (Waltham, co. Essex and co. Sussex . . .). Add: *V.* Add: Warner (Parham) Baronetcy 1660. Same arms.

Warner (Knaresborough, co. York). Same arms.

Warner (Co. Kent). Quarterly, 1st and 4th per pale-margin pencil ? 'bend' *V.*

Warner (Wolston, Sheriff of Warwickshire temp. Charles i.). Arg. a chev. betw. 3 boars heads sa. couped gules. *Fuller.*

Warner (Strowd, co. Middlesex . . .). Add: *C.L.*

Warner (Ratcliffe and Rowington, co. Warwick). Add: *W.*

Warner (Walthamstow, co. Essex). Add: *A.A.*

Warner (Brandon Parva, co. Norfolk). Sa. 3 bars gemel and in chief or. *Blomfield.*

Warnett (Framfield, co. Sussex). Add: *V.*

Warram (Mudeley, co. Salop.). Erm. on a bend counter-embattled az. 3 mullets or.

Warr (Hestercomb, co. Somerset). Gu. Crusilly a lion ramp. arg. within a bordure engr. of the same. *Guillim.*

Warren (Aldenham, co. Herts). Insert—and Harrow, Middlesex. . . . Add: *Harl. MS. 1234. fo. 136.*

Warren (Ashwell, co. Herts.). Add: *Harl. MS. 1234 fo. 142.*

Warren (St. Albans, co. Herts.). Insert—Poynton, co. Chester and London. Add: *Harl. MS. 1546. fo. 54.*

Warren (London). Granted by Camden to John Warren in 1613. Chequy or and az. on a canton erm. a lion ramp. double queue. *Syl. Morgan.*

Warren (Bygrave, co. Hertford). Arg. a chev. engr. counter compony az. and or betw. 3 squirrels sa. each holding a branch vert. and cracking a nut or. *W.*

Warren (Hopton, co. Suffolk). Add: Saml. Warren, QC. Recorder of Hull and Author of Ten Thousand a Year &c.

Warren. Chequy az. and or on a bend gu. 3 lions pass. guard. arg. Crest: . . . Add: *V.**

Warren. Insert—(Co. York). Chequy or and az. on a bend gu. 3 lions pass. guard. of the first. Add: *V.V.**

Warren (Mespil, co. Dublin . . .). Add: *A.A.*

Warrington, Borough of, Incorporated 1847. **Seal. Book Plate.** Arg. six lioncels, three, two and one. betw. two flags in saltire, the dexter shewing three lions pass. guard. palewise; sinister three red roses of Lancaster. The shield surmounted by a sceptre bearing an imperial crown and a sword crosswise the point piercing the overall scroll through the dexter a wreath ppr. The wording on the scroll: Anno Decino Victoria Regina.

Warter or Watre (Priory of, co. York). Gu. 3 water bougets arg. that in base transfixed by a Prior's Staff in pale or. *Tonge p. 67.*

Warton. Or on a chev. az. a martlet betw. 2 pheons of the field, on a chief sa. a lion pass. guard enclosed by 2 crescents arg. Crest: . . . Add: Thomas Warton. *V.*

Washington (Cos. Lancaster, Leicester, Northampton, Buckingham, and Kent). Add: Washington Adwick, co. York 1666. Same arms a crescent for diff. *Dugdale.*

Wass (Kirkhill, co. York). Add: *V.* Sire William Wasse. *N.*

Wassington. Add: *V.** William de Wassington. *S.*

Wastell (Co. Northampton and Wastell-Head, co. Westmorland). Add: John Wastell, Prior of Dunstable and his brother Thomas Wastell. *V.*

Wasthouse. Add: Wasthose. *V.V.**

Wastlay. Arg. 3 pairs of angles interlaced palewise with a ring at each end gu. *V.*

Wastneys of Stowe temp. Edw. ij. Sa. a lion ramp. arg. vulned gu. *F.Y.*

Wasteney. Sa. a lion ramp. arg. Sir William Wasteney. *I.*

Wasteneys. Sa. a lion ramp. arg. collared gu. Sir William le Wasteneis. *E.F.L.N.* Sir William de Wasteneys, co. Stafford temp. Edw. j. *V.*

Wastney of Stow. Sa. a lion ramp. double tailed arg. langued and armed gu. collared or and charged with a fleur-de-lis. *Constable's Roll xij.*

Watenald. Sa. a bend fusilly arg. Sir William de Watenald. *R.*

Waterfall. Or a bend wavy az. *Randle Holme.*

Waterhouse (Coningsborough, co. York) (Antient Arms). Gu. 3 wells or waterhouses arg. doors sa. water undy arg. and az.

Waterlow (Fairseat, co. Kent and Highgate, co. Middlesex, bart.). Insert—1873. . . . .

Waters. Gu. a bend wavy waved arg. and az. *Randle Holme.*

Waters. Arg. on a chev. engr. gu. betw. 3 birds az. 5 bezants. *V.S.*

Wateville. Arg. 3 chevs. gu. a martlet sa. in the dexter chief for diff. Sir Roger Wateville. *L.N.*

Wateville. Sa. semy of crosses crosslet and a lion ramp. arg. Sir Geffrey Wateville. *L. Harl. MS. 6137.*

Wateville. Arg. 3 chevs. gu. within a bordure engr. sa. Sir Robert de Wateville. *L.N.V.*

Wateville. Arg. three chevs. gu. Add: Sire John de Wateville. *N.*

Watker. Add: *V.**

Watringbury (Co. Kent). Add: Sir Bartholomew de Watringbury. *A.*

Watson (London   ). Or a chev. engr. az. betw. 3 martlets sa. on a chief of the second 3 crescents of the first. *C.L. p. 86.*

Watson (Erstage, co. York 1666). Arg. on a chev. az. betw. 3 martlets sa. as many crescents or. Crest: A griffins head erased sa. holding in its beak a rose branch. *Dugdale p. 283.*

Watson (Sheriff of Newcastle on Tyne 1514). Arg. on a chev. engr. sa. betw. 3 martlets vert. as many crescents or a mullet for diff. *Carr MS.*

Watson (Lidington, co. Rutland). Add: *V.*

Watson (Kilmanahan Castle, co. Waterford . . .). Add: *A.A.*

Wattes (Shunks, co. Somerset, Granted by Segar. 1626). Az. 3 arrows or plumed arg. points downwards on a chief of the second 3 man's heads couped full faced ppr. and crined sa. *Guillim.*

Watts. Az. 2 bars az. in chief 3 pellets. Add: Granted in 1596. *W.* Sir John Watts, Lord Mayor of London 1603.

Watur. Or on a bend betw. 3 leopards heads gu. as many dexter hands clenched arg. *V.*

Waulkerne. Add: Mark Waulkerne. *V.*

Wauton. Arg. a chev. gu. William de Wauton. *A.*

Wauton (Shepreth, co. Cambridge). Add: Sir William de Wauton. *N.S.*

Wauton. Arg. a chevron and in the dexter chief an annulet sa. Sire Thomas Wawton. *S.* And quartering gu. a lion ramp. arg. crowned or with creting; and sa. on a bend or 3 goats pass. gu. In Great Staughton Church, co. Hunts.

Waverley. Add: Robert de Waverey. *W.*

Wax Chandlers, Company of . . .. Add: The Arms were granted and also the Crest by Thomas Hawley, Clarenceux in 1484.

Way (Co. Devon). Gu. a chev. or betw. 3 lucies haurient arg. Add: *Moule 119. V.V.**

Way. Sa. 2 bars wavy arg. each charged with 3 pales wavy gu. Add: (or sa. 2 bars wreathed arg. and gu.). *V.*

Wayd. Az. on a bend or within a bordure engr. arg. 2 roses gu. stalked with as many leaves to each vert. *V.*

Wayer (London . . . Thomas Wayer, gent and citizen of London). . . . Add: *C.C.*

Waynard (Co. Devon). Add: Waynard (Recorder of Exeter 1404). *Colby.*

Wayne (Quorndon House, co. Derby). Add: *V.*

Wayney. Add: *V.*

Waynforth (Roydon, co. Norfolk). Or a lion ramp.—insert—az. betw. . . . Add: *Blomfield.*

Wayte (Co. Hants.). Arg. a chev. betw. 3 bugle horns stringed sa. Add: *V.*

Wayte (Southampton 1612 . . .). Add: *V.*

Weale (Co. Salop.). Gu. a bend compony or and az. betw. 6 crescents arg.

Weare alias Brown (Denford, co. Berks. and Boxton, co. Wilts.). Add: also Marlborough, co. Wilts. *V.*

Weavers, Company of. Add: Weavers (Company of, Newcastle on Tyne). Same arms.

Webber (Co. Devon). Add: *Lysons.*

Webber. Insert—co. Cornwall. Arg. on a chev. engr. az. betw. 3 hurts as many annulets or. Crest: . . .

Webster (Edwd. Webster, Principal Secretary to the Lord Lieutenant of Ireland). Az. a lion ramp. or betw. 3 pierced mullets ar. Impaling gu. 5 bezants in saltire a chief arg. †

Webster (Flamborough, co. York . . .). Add: Webster (Flamborough, co. York 1590). *Lansdowne. MS. 865.*

Webster (Pallion Hall, co. Durham). Add: Webster (Copthall, Essex, Baronetcy 1703). Same arms. *Guillim.*

Weddell (Earswick, co. York 1665). Gu. on a chev. counter-embattled or betw. 3 martlets arg. an eagle displ. betw. 2 escallops sa. *Dugdale p. 164.*

Wede. Barry or and gu. fretty arg. Hernol de la Wede. *C.*

Wedderburn (Baron Loughborough 1780). Arg. on a chev. gu. betw. 3 roses of the last a † arg. Crest: An eagles head couped ppr. Supporters: 2 eagles ppr. gorged with collars arg.

Wedgwood. Sa. a chev. fretted with another reversed both arg.

Wednissop. . . . 3 nuns' heads—insert—'bend-wise' . . . Add: *V.*

Weelsteed. . . . a chev. . . . . betw 3 fleurs-de-lis. . . . *Collinson Somerset ij. 231.*

Weems or Weemys. Earl of Weemys 1633. Or a lion ramp. gu. quartering arg. a lion ramp. sa. *Crawfurd.*

Welarge or Welause. Arg. on a bordure 3 pheons of the first. *V.V.**

Welbeck. Insert—Co. Derby. Arg. on a chev. gu. betw. 3 lozenges—delete—(another, mullets) . . . Add: *V.*

Welbeck. Arg. on a chev. gu. betw. 3 mullets sa. as many martlets or. *V.*

Wele. . . . on a bend betw. a Roman letter W . . . and an annulet . . . 3 hurts. . . . Walter de Wele ob. 1388. Great Grimsby Church. *Harl. MS. 6829. fo. 3.*

Welington. Add: *V.*

Welle. Arg. 2 bars gu. in chief 3 torteaux. Add: Sir Robert Welle. *V .*

Welle. Gu. a bend gobony or and az. betw. 6 crescents arg. Add: Sir John de Welle Kent. *V.*

Welle. Arg. on two bastons gu. bezants. . . . Sir Robert de Welle. *B.*

Welles (Baron Welles . . .). Add: Sir Adam de Welles. *K.N.H.S.T.Y.V.* John Lord Welles. *Z. 417.* And with a dexter baston gu. Sire Felip de Weles. *N.*

Welles (Lord Mayor of London 1431). Lozengy erm. and vert. A lion ramp. gu. *V.*

Welles. Arg. on a bend sa. betw. 6 roses gu. 3 mullets pierced or. Add: *V.*

Welles. Az. a bend embattled counter-embattled arg. Add: *V.*

Welles. Paly of 6 or and gu. on a canton arg. a mullet sa. Add: *V.**

Wells (Buckstede, Sussex). Arg. a chev. ermines betw. 3 martlets sa. *W.*

Wells (Holme, co. Derby). Ermines on a canton or a buck's head—insert—'cabosses'. . . . Crest: . . . Add: *Lysons.*

Wells (Piercefield, Chepstow, co. Monmouth). Add: *Guillim.*

Wells. Arg. a chev. erm. betw. 3 martlets sa. Add: *V.**

Wells. Arg. a chev. az. betw. 3 bulls heads cabossed gu. Add: William de Wells. *V.*

Wells. Arg. a chev. sa. betw. 3 fleurs-de-lis gu. *F.Y.*

Welton of Welton. Arg. a lion ramp. dismembered gu. *Eliz. Roll. xxxv.*

Wellysand. Add: John Wellysand. *V.*

Welnborn. Add: *V.V.**

Welston. Per pale sa. and az. a bend chequy (another, componee) arg. and gu. Add: *V.**

Weltes. Per pale az. and arg. a chev. betw. 3 fleurs-de-lis counterchanged Add: *V.*

Weltes. Per pale or and az. a chev. betw. 3 fleurs-de-lis counterchanged. *Nash.*

Wenard (Co. Cornwall). Arg. on a bend az. 3 pierced mullets of the first. *V.*

Wendesley (Quartered by Verney, of Compton, co. Warwick). Add: *V.** Sir Thomas Wendesley (Wendesley, co. Derby). *V.* Sir Thomas Wennesley. *S.*

Wendy (Co. Norfolk). Or a chev. betw. 3 lions heads erased az. Add: *V.V.** Wendy (Wendy and Haslingfield, co. Cambridge). Same arms. *L.N.*

Wenington (Co. Lincoln). Insert—Lancaster Add: *V.*

Wenlock (Baron Wenlock . . .). Add: Sir John Wenlock KG., *V.*

Wenlock (Wenlock, co. Salop). Add: *V.*

Wenlock. Gu. a chev. or betw. 3 lions ramp. arg. Crest: . . . Add: *V.*

Wentlas. Add: *V.*

Wentwage. Az. a lion ramp. arg. crowned or. Sir Walter Wentwage. *Q.*

Wentworth (Earl of Stafford . . . the third earl . . . d.s.p. 1799)—insert—*V.*

Wentworth. Gu. on a bend arg. 3 escallops az. Sir Roger Wentworth. *Harl. MS. 6137. fo. 44,* But query Bissett; quartered by Sir Roger Wentworth. *V.*

Wentworth (Woolley, co. York). . . . Add: *Dugdale p. 10.*

Wentworth (South Elmsall, co. York . . .). Add: *Dugdale p. 288. Constable's Roll p. v.*

Wentworth (South Elmsall, co. York 1666). Sa. on a chev. betw. 3 leopards faces or as many mullets gu. *Dugdale p. 284.*

Wentworth (Bretton, co. York, bart. . . .). Add:

Wentworth (West Bretton, co. York 1666). Sa. a chev. betw. 3 leopards faces or a bordure arg. *Dugdale p. 307.*

Wentworth (Gosfield, co. Essex). Sa. a chev. betw. 3 leopards heads or † for diff. *V.E. 1612.*

Wenunwin. Or a lion ramp. gu. Griffith ap Wenunwyn. *E.* Griffith le fitz Wenonwen. *Y.* Ap Wenonwin, Lord of Powis. *V.*

Werdon. Sa. 3 chessrooks arg. Add: *V.*

Werdissaller. Arg. on a chev. az. 3 rams heads couped or. *V.V.**

Werfield. Sa. crusilly and a bend of 5 lozenges conjoined arg. Robert de Werefield. *A. Harl. MS. 6137. fo. 93.*

Wescombe. Sa. 2 bars arg. a canton erm. †

Wessington. Gu. a lion ramp. arg. a bordure gobony of the second and az. Add: Walter de Wessington. *Y.*

West (Co. Suffolk). Sa. a lion ramp. arg. collared or quartered by Gresley of Colton, co. Stafford. *Z. 341.*

West. Sa. a chev. betw. 3 crescents erm. Add: *V.*

Westby (Westby, co. York and Moberly, co. Lancaster granted 1560). Arg. on a chev. az. 3 5-foils of the first. *W.*

Westby (Mowbreck and Rawcliffe, co. Lancaster . . .). Add:

Westby (Murescough, co. Lancaster 1664). Same arms. *V.L.*

Westby (Ravenfield, co. York 1665). Same arms and Crest. *Dugdale p. 174.*

Westerdale. Bendy sinister of 6 gu. and vert. a chev. erm. *V.*

Western (Rivenhall, co. Essex, bart.). Insert—1864. . . .

Westlake (Kirkhampton, Cornwall). Per pale az. and or a chev. engr. betw. 3 lions ramp. counterchanged *Lysons.*

Westlemore. Add: John Westlemore. *V.*

Westles. Arg. a chev. betw. 5 billets and 3 crosses crosslet fitchy sa. Sir John Westles. Norfolk. *V.*

Westmacott. Gu. 3 anchors arg. 2 and 1. **(Book Plate).**

Weston. Quarterly per fess indented az. and gu. a bend arg. Add: *V.V.**

Weston. Sa. a chev. betw. 3 holly leaves arg. Add: *V.*

Weston. Erm. on a bend gu. 3 lions heads erased or. Add: *V.*

Weston. Arg. a chev. engr. per pale or and gu. Sir William Weston, Chief Justice in Ireland. *Dug. O.J.*

Weston (Collen Weston, co. Dorset). Per chev. gu. and az. a chev. engr. betw. 3 roses counterchanged.

Weston. Gu. crusilly fitchy or a lion ramp. arg. over all a dexter baston engr. of the second. Monsire Roger de Weston. *Y.*

Westropp (Co. York). Or. on a chev. sa. 3 escallops. *Fairfax's Book of Arms*

Westroppe (Corneburgh, co. York). 1585. Sa. a lion ramp. erm. crowned or quartering on a fess gu. betw. 3 popinjays vert. collared gu. as many escallops of the first for Thwenge. *F.Y.*

Wetherall, Wyrall or Wyrrall (Lovesall, co. York. confirmed 1537). Arg. 2 lions pass. guard. in pale. sa. on a chief sa. 3 covered cups. or. *Harl. MS. 1359.*

Wetherby. Vert. a chev. erm. betw. 3 rams or. *V.V.**

Wetherton or Whetarton (Co. Northumberland). Add: *V.*

Wettenhall (Heming, co. Rutland . . .). Add: *C.R. 1589.*

Wetwang (Sheriff of Newcastle 1462). Gu. a chev. betw. 3 lions gambs erect and erased arg. on a chief sa. 3 escutcheons of the first *Carr MS.*

Weye. Gu. a chev. or betw. 3 fishes. . . .

Weyland (Co. Suffolk). Az. a lion ramp. arg. debruised with a bendlet or. Add: Sire Richard de Weylande. N.

Weyland. Az. a lion ramp. arg. over all a bendlet gu. Sir John Weyland. Suffolk. temp. Edwd. iij. V.L.N. Roger de Welonde. E.

Weymouth (Town of, co. Dorset). Barry wavy of 10 or and sa. quartering a lion ramp. double queued gu. Lewis Topo. Dict.

Whaddon (Plymouth, co. Devon . . .). Add: Guillim. gives the crosses crosslet fitchy.

Whaley (Dalton, co. York). Add: F.Y. 1584.

Whalisburgh. Insert—Cornwall. Add: V.

Whalley (Cos. Lancaster and Sussex). Add: V.* The harts springing. V.

Whannell (Co. Ayr, Scotland). Add: Granted 4 Aug. 1778.

Whaplod. Per pale sa. and arg. 2 lions combatant counters changed (another adds, on a chief sa. 5 bezants in saltire). Add: V.

Whatton (Whatton, co. Nottingham . . .). Add: V.N. 199.

Wheateley Robert alias Quytlaire of Toneby, co. Cumb. gent. xv cent. Sa. 2 hands conjoined supporting a heart or. Beds. visitation.

Wheeler or Wheler (Burbury, co. Warwick . . .). Add: Wheeler (London, granted by Cooke). Same arms. W. Wheeler (Westminster, Baronetcy 1660). Same arms.

Wheeler (Co. Worcester). Per bend az. and gu. a fish weel. . . . Add: V.

Wheeler or Wheler. Arg. on a chev. engr. sa. betw. 3 buckles az. as many martlets or. Nash.

Wheler. Or a camel sa. betw. 3 half-wheels. . . . Add: John Wheller, Stoke, Surrey 1543. V.

Wheeler (Thames Ditton, Church Surrey). Or a camel betw. 3 half wheels sa. on a chief az. a catherine wheel or enclosed by 2 bezants.

Wheller (Tunbridge, Kent). Sa. 2 chevs. . . betw. 3 cones arg. Robson.

Wheling. Add: V.V.*

Whelpdale (Skirsgill and Penrith, co. Cumberland . . .). Add: V.

Whelpdale (Bishop of Carlisle 1420). Arg. 3 wolves pass. gu. on the shoulder of the first a mullet or.

Whelpdale. Arg. a chev. betw. 3 greyhounds courant sa. V.V.*

Whelple. Or 3 chevs. az. Sir . . . de Whelple. V.

Whelpenton (Mayor of Newcastle 1435). Gu. a chev. arg. in base a mullet or a chief vairy or and gu. on the chev. a crescent for diff. Carr MS.

Wheterton Add: V.*

Whetonhall (Richmond, co. York). Add: F.Y.

Whetstone (Woodford Row, co. Essex). Add: V.E. 1634.

Wheywell. Add: V.

Whichcote (Aswarby Park, co. Lincoln, bart.). Insert—1660. . . . Add: Charles Whichcoot, London 1633-4. Same arms, in dexter chief a crescent for diff. Harl. MS. 1358. fo. 12.

Whiddon (Chagford, co. Devon . . .). Add: Dug. O.J.

Whight. Insert—(Co. Hants.). Gu. a chev. betw. 3 goats heads erased arg. armed or. Add: Thomas Wight. V.

Whistelford. Quarterly, 1st and 4th, per bend— insert—'dancetty or'. . . . Add: V.

Whiselford. Per fess az. and arg. 3 annulets counterchanged. Harl. MS. 1458.

Whistmormead or Whiztozmead. Add: V.V.*

Whitbread (Whittenobley, co. Essex). Arg. a chev. sa. betw. 3 hinds heads erased gu. V. V.E. 1634.

Whitbread. Arg. a chev. betw. 3 antelopes heads erased gu. V.E. 1634.

White. Gu. on a bordure sa. 8 mullets or on a canton erm. a lion ramp. of the first. V.* (another the canton arg. and lion sa. V.*

White (Hampshire). Gu. on a canton arg. a lion ramp. sa. crowned gold a bordure sa. charged with 8 estoiles or. Harl. MS. 1404. fo. 110.

White (Anglesea). Sa. a chev. betw. 3 fluers-de-lis arg. Z. 320.

White (St. Stephens, co. Cornwall . . .). Add: V.C. 307.

White (Truro, co. Cornwall). Add: V.*

White (St. German's and Ince, co. Cornwall). Add: Lysons.

White (Exeter, co. Devon . . .). Add: Guillim.

White (Mayor of Exeter, 1646). Gu. on a canton erm. a lion salient sa. within a bordure of the last charged with estoiles arg. Colby.

White (Hutton, co. Essex). . . . Arg. a chev. 'gu.' underlined—marginal, ? az. V.E. 1612. Add: V.E. 1634.

White (South Wainborough, co. Hants. and of Okingham). Add: and London † for diff. Add: V.V.*

White (Earl of Bantry 1816). Gu. an annulet arg. within a bordure sa. charged with 8 estoiles or on a canton erm. a lion ramp. of the second.

White (London). Or a chev. vert. betw. 3 goats heads erased sa. Crest: . . . Add: V.* Same arms with crescent for diff. John White of London. Granted by Cooke. W.

White (Co. Norfolk). Gu. a chev. betw. 3 boars heads couped arg. tusked or. Crest: . . . Add: Sir John Whyte (Norfolk. temp. Edw. j. V. Sir John White of Nottingham ob. 1407.

White (Shottesham, Norfolk). Gu. a chev. betw. 3 boars heads couped and a bordure engr. arg. Cady.

White (Tuxford, co. Nottingham . . .). Add: V.N. p. 189.

White (Ireland). Arg. a lion salient gu. in chief 3 mullets sa. W.

White (Granted 1 March 1467 to William White). . . . Add: White (Ashford, co. Kent). Same arms. V. White (Beverley, co. York). Same arms.

White or Whiet. Add: V.V.*

White (Ireland). Arg. a chev. betw. 3 wolves heads erased sa. V.

White (Rathgonan   ). Arg. a chev. engr. betw. 3 roses gu.

Whyte (Ireland). Same arms. V.

Whitehead (Uplands Hall, co. Lancaster). Add: F.L.

Whitelaw or Quitlaw. Sa. a chev. betw. 3 boars heads couped or. Guillim.

Whitelock. Az. a chev. engr. betw. 3 eagles close or. Crest: . . . Add: Whitelock (Justice of the Kings Bench 1624). Same arms, quartering . . . on a bend . . . 3 bucks heads cabossed. Add: Dug. O.J.

Whitenhall or Whitnall (Co. Kent). Add: Sir Thomas Whitenhall, Kent. V.

Whitewell. Insert—or Whitwell. Gu. a chev. betw. 3 well-buckets or. Add: V.V.*

Whitfeld (Sheriff of Newcastle 1585). Or 2 bendlets sa. Carr MS.

Whitfield (Whitfield Hall, co. Northumberland . . .). Add: Harl. MS. 1386. fo. 34. Ralfe Whitfield, Serjeant at Law 1634. Dug. O.J.

Whitfield. Sa. semee of crosses crosslet a bend engr. or. Add: (or fusilly or.) Robert de Wytefeld. E.

Whitfield. Sa. a bend engr. or. Sire William de Wytfeld. O. But fusilly or Sir William de Witevelde. V. Robert de Witefelde. A. Richard de Wittevelde. F.

Whitfoot (   ). Sa. on a chev. or betw. 3 eagles legs erased arg. a tower gu. betw. two annulets sa. *Cady.*

Whithede. Add: *V.**

Whithede. Az. a chev. betw. 3 bugle horns stringed arg. *V.*

Whythede. Az. a chev. or betw. 3 bugle horns stringed arg. *V.*

Whithorse. Per chev. arg. and gu. a chev. per chev. counterchanged. Add: *V.*

Whitlebury (Co. Warwick). Barry of 4 az. and arg. on a chief of the second 3 hurts. Add: 'Error see † Arg. 2 bars az. in chief 3 hurts'.

Whitney. Arg. a lion ramp. sa. on a chief of the last 3 mullets arg. Add: *V.**

Whitney (Ireland). Arg. a lion ramp. gu. on a chief sa. 3 mullets of the first. *V.*

Whittall. Add: *A.A.*

Whitte. Add: *V.*

Whitteley. Insert—Co. York. Add: *V.*

Whittingham (Potton, co. Bedford). Az. a lion ramp. arg. betw. 3 crosses patty fitchy or on a chief of the second 3 bees volant ppr.

Whittle (London). Granted 1587. Gu. a chev. erm. betw. 3 talbots heads erased or. *W.*

Whittle (Over Helmsley, co. York). Same arms.

Whitton (Nethercote, co. Oxford . . .). Add: *V.O.*

Whitton. Paly of 4 arg. and sa. 3 eagles displ. counterchanged. Add: *V.V.**

Whitwang. Arg. a chev. erm. betw. 3 lions gambs erased and erect or armed gu. *Harl. MS. 1404. fo. 120.*

Whitwike (Co. Stafford; granted). Insert—by Camden. . . .

Whitwong. Add: George Whitewong. *V.V.**

Whitworth (Co. Nottingham . . .). Add: *V.N. p. 179.*

Whitworth. Arg. a bend betw. two cotises sa. in chief a garb gu. †

Whitworth. Insert—of Stancliffe, co. Derby . . . (bart.). Insert—1869.

Whizt. Insert—Ireland. Arg. a chev. gu. Add: *V.*

Whorwood (Co. Oxford). Arg. a chev. betw. 3 bucks heads cabossed sa. Crest: . . . Add: Whorwood (Holton, co. Oxford). Same arms with a crescent for diff. *V.O.*

Whyte (Ireland). Arg. a chev. betw. 3 foxes heads erased gu. collared or. *Cady.*

Whyte (Redhills, co. Cavan). Sa. on a chev. betw. 3 crescents arg. a leopards head betw. 2 5-foils gu.

Wiard (London). Add: *V.*

Wickens (Stochtbrewen, co. Northampton; confirmed). Insert—by Sir J. Borough. . . .

Wickens. Per chev. vert. and or on a chev. . . . Add: *V.**

Wickham (Swalcliffe, co. Oxford and Welton, co. Northampton). . . . Add: *V.O. 1634.*

Wickham. Arg. 3 chevs. sa. betw. as many roses gu. *Harl. MS. 1407. fo. 74.*

Wickins. . . . a chev. betw. 3 trefoils . . . a † for diff. Thomas Wickins 1694, Banstead Church.

Wicksted (Wicksted, co. Chester). Add: Wicksted (Crownest, Cheshire). Same arms. *Randle Holme.*

Widowson (Loudham, co. Notts.). Gu. on a chev. betw. 3 5-foils 5 billets of the field. *V.N. p. 96.*

Wiffold (Sir Nicholas Wyffold, Lord Mayor of London 1450). Per chev. embattled gu. and or 3 lions ramp. counter changed. *Harl. MS. 1349.*

Wigmer. Arg. a bend sa. charged with another wavy of the first. *Guillim.*

Wigmore. Arg. 3 greyhounds courant in pale sa. collared or. Sir Thomas Wigmore. *V.*

Wigmore in Ingham Church, Norfolk 1315. *Gough. Sep. Mon. ij. 121.*

Wigmore (Co. Norfolk, granted 1586 . . .). *Cady.*

Wignall. Gu. a bend arg.—delete—(another, or). . . .

Wignall. Gu. a bend or betw. 3 escallops arg. *V.*

Wigston. Insert—Wigston (Lennerlyde, co. Leicester). *V.* Add: *V.**

Wigston (Co. Leicester). Erm. a chev. per pale sa. and arg. betw. 3 estoiles or. *Harl. MS. 1404. fo. 78.*

Wigton or Wigston (Co. Worcester). Erm. on a chev. per chev. sa. and az.—underlined—margin ? arg. *C.W.*

Wigton. Or 3 moles statant within a bordure engr. sa. Thomas Wigton. *V.*

Wike. Arg. 3 chevs. sa. a fleur-de-lis of the last—insert—in the dexter chief. Add: *V.V.**

Wilberfoss or Wilberforce (Wilberfoss, co. York). . . . beaked and legged—delete—ppr. read 'gu.'. Add: *Dugdale p. 121.*

Wilbornham (Co. Norfolk). Arg. 3 bendlets wavy az. *V.*

Wilbraham (Woodhey, co. Chester . . . was ancestor of Wilbraham of Delamere). Insert—*W.*

Wilbraham. Az. 3 bendlets wavy arg. on a canton sa. a greyhounds head erased of the second. Ralph Wilbraham. (*Dug. O.J.*).

Wilbraham (   ). Az. 2 bars arg. quartering az. 3 bends wavy arg. *F.L.*

Wilbroughton. Vert. 2 lions ramp. addorsed. *Randle Holme.*

Wilbury. Sa. semee of crosses crosslet fitchee or 3 lions ramp. arg. Add: *V.*

Wilby. Arg. a chev. sa. Crest: . . . Add: Sir Robert de Wileby. *E.F.G.*

Wilcocks (Brightlingsea, co. Essex . . .). Add: *V.E. 1634.*

Wilcotts. Az. an eagle displ. arg. Add: *V.* Wilcotts alias Sparks. *V.* The eagle ducally collared or. Wilcotts. *V.*

Wild (Canterbury and Lewisham, co. Kent . . .). Of the second 3 martlets of the first—insert—*V.* Crest: . . .

Wilde (Lowestoft, co. Suffolk). . . . on a chev. . . . betw. 3 lions heads erased . . . as many martlets. . . . **Slab** in Lowestoft Church.

Wilde (bart. extinct; . . .). Add: Sir J. P. Wilde, Judge of the Probate and Divorce Court 1863.

Wilde.

Wilford (London). Insert—and Enfield. Per pale or and gu. on a chev. betw. 3 leopards faces. . . . Add: *V.*

Wilkes (John Wilkes, the politician). . . . Crest: On—read **Book Plate** a mount vert. . . .

Wilkins. Arg. on a bend engr. betw. 2 plain cotises sa. 3 martlets or and with a crescent in the sinister chief for diff. Timothy Wilkins, Capt. in the Parliamentary Army, but afterwards one of the defenders of Pontefract Castle against Cromwell's Army ob. 1671. Younger brother of Wilkins, Bishop of Chester. *Guillim.*

Wilkinson (Sheriff of Newcastle 1555). Sa. a chev. betw. 3 whelk shells or. *Carr MS.*

Williard (Eastbourne, co. Sussex . . . betw. 3 flasks or jars ppr.). Insert—also described as fish baskets, weels or eel pots.

Willason (Slugwas, co. Hereford). Add: *W.*

Willes (Sir James S. Willes, Justice of the Common Pleas 1855). Per fess gu. and arg. 3 lions ramp. *C.C.* within a tressure flory counterflory az. quartering arg. a chev. betw. 3 lozenges ermines.

Willes. Az. a lion ramp. arg. Richard de Willes. *F.*

Willesthorp or Wolsthorp (Co. York). Add: John Willesthorpe. *X.* The lion pass. guard. Sir Oswald Willestrop. *V.*

Willestrop. Az. a chev. gu. betw. 3 lions pass. guard. arg. *V.*

Willey. Erm. on 2 bars vert. 3 martlets or 2 and 1. Add: *W.*

Williams (Guernavet, co. Brecknock, Baronetcy 1643). Arg. 3 cocks gu. *Guillim.*

Williams (Wales). Arg. a chev. gu. betw. 3 perukes sa. *Randle Holme.*

Williams (Reurhim, co. Carnarvon Bart. 1661). Gu. a chev. arg. betw. 3 man's heads couped ppr. *Guillim.*

Williams (Dyffryn Ffrwd, co. Glamorgan). Vert. a chev. betw. 3 cockatrices heads erased or. quartering Lewis sa. a lion ramp. arg. *Nicholas.*

Williams (Herringstone, co. Dorset). Add: Williams (Marnehull, co. Dorset, Baronetcy 1642). Same arms. *Guillim.*

Williams (Bristol, co. Gloucester). Add: Sir David Williams, Justice of the Kings Bench 1603. *Dug. O.J.*

Williams (Chichester, co. Sussex, Baronetcy 1746). Gu. a wolf issuing out of a rocky cave from the sinister side of the shield all arg. Quartering; arg. 3 boars heads erect and erased sa. for Booth. *Edmondson.*

Williams. Per pale gu. and or 2 lions ramp. addorsed counterchanged. *Randle Holme.*

Williams alias Cromwell. Gu. 3 chevs. arg. over all as many lions rampant or. Richard Williams *V.*

Williams (Dean of Llandaff). Arg. a chev. gu. betw. 3 bulls heads sa. *Nicholas.*

Williamson (Keswick, co. Cumberland). Add: *V.E. 1634.*

Williamson (Melbeck Hall, co. Cumberland . . .). Add: Sir Joseph Williamson, son of His Majesty's Principal Secretary of State. *Guillim.*

Williamson (New Hall, co. Cumberland). Add: *Guillim.*

Williamson (Co. Middlesex and Denford, co. Northampton). Add: Williamson (Tusmore, co. Oxford). Same arms. *V.O.*

Williamson. Arg. a chev. betw. 3 trefoils slipped vert. all within a bordure engr. sa. *Eliz. Roll. xix.*

Williamson (Tusmore, co. Oxford . . .). Add: *V.O.*

Williamson. Insert—(Hackness, co. York). Arg. on a chev. engr. az. betw. 3 trefoils slipped sa. as many crescents or a border engr. of the second. Add: *Cady.* Williamson (Scarborough, co. York. granted 1557). *W.*

Willie. Arg. a chev. betw. 3 greyhounds salient sa. those in chief face to face. *V.O. p. 199.*

Willington (Co. York). Arg. a chev. betw. 3 martlets gu. Thomas Willington. *Eliz. Roll. xxv*

Willington. Erm. 3 bends az. Add: *V.*

Williscot (Co. Salop). Sa. a bend betw. 6 martlets or. *W.*

Willison (Co. Hereford). Add: *V.**

Willmescott. Or 3 bars az. a lion ramp. gu. crowned or. Sir Henry Willmescott, co. Gloucester temp. Edwd. iij. *V.*

Willock. Az. a lion ramp. or a fess gu. Crest: . . . Add: *V.*

Willock. Arg. a lion ramp. sa. ducally crowned or a fess chequy of the third and az. Add: The fess counter compony. *V.*

Willoughby (Wollaton, co. Nottingham . . . Sir Francis . . . of this line). Insert—Sir Henry Willoughby, co. Notts. *V.* Mon. Edmund Willoughby. *S.*

Willoughby (Normanton, co. Notts.). Arg. 2 bars gu. charged with 3 water bougets or. *V.N.*

Willoughby. Az. fretty or on a canton gu. a cross moline arg. Add: William Fitz Robert de Willoughby *V.*

Willoughby. Arg. 2 bars az. charged with three 5-foils or. Richard de Willoughby. *Y.*

Wills (Saltash and Boatesfleming, co. Cornwall). . . . Add: *V.C. 307.*

Wilmer. . . . . a chev. vair betw. 3 ducal coronets. *C.W.*

Wilmer (Sywell, co. Northampton and Meriden and Starton, co. Warwick). Add: Sir Wm. Wilmer. *W.*

Wilmescott. Add: Sire Henri de Willemescotte. *N.*

Wilmescott or Willemscott. Or 3 bars az. over all a lion ramp. gu. crowned or. Sir Henry Willmescott, co. Gloucester temp. Edw. iij. *V.*

Wilsford (Hateridge and Dover, co. Kent). Add: Sir James Wilsford, Knight, Bannerette 1547. quartering; arg. 3 bugle horns sa. Portrait in Lord Stafford's Gallery at Costessy.

Wilson (Melton and Rudding Hale, co. York). Sa. a wolf salient or in chief 2 estoiles arg. on a canton or a cross patty gu. quartering Fountayne.

Wilson (Dulwich, co. Surrey). Or a wolf salient sa. betw. 3 escutcheons of the last each charged with a walnut leaf of the first. *A.A.*

Wilson. Arg. on a chev. betw. 3 mullets az. and in the dexter fess point a bears head erased . . . muzzled . . . in the sinister an anchor erect . . . cabled . . . a talbots head of the first.

Wilter. Add: *V.*

Wilton. Gu. on a chev. arg. 3 crosses crosslet fitchy of the first. Sir John de Wilton. *S.V.*

Wiltshire or Wiltechire. Add: *V.*

Winckley (Brockholes and Collerall Hall, co. Lancaster). Add: Winckley (Preston, co. Lancaster). Assigned by Dugdale on account of a **Seal** of Winckley, co. Lancaster. *Harl. MS. 1637. fo. 93.*

Wincoll (the town of Leicester and the Middle Temple . . .). Add: *C.C.*

Windesbanke. Vert. a chev. betw. 3 hawks standing wings expanded or.

Windibanke. Vert. on a chev. betw. 3 falcons volants or as many trefoils slipped sa. Add: Windebanke (Haynes, co. Wilts., Baronetcy 1645. Same arms. But trefoils vert. *Guillim.*

Winesbury (Sheriff of Shropshire temp. Ric. ij.). Az. on a bend betw. 2 cotises or 3 lions gu. *Fuller.*

Winford (Glasshampton-in-Astley, co. Worcester, bart.). Insert—1702. . . .

Wingar or Winger (Lord Mayor of London 1504). Add: *V.** Add: Wynger (Co. Leicester). Same arms. *W.*

Wingfield (Letheringham, co. Suffolk . . .). Add: Sir Thomas Wingfield. *V.* Wingfield (Goodwins, Suffolk, Baronetcy 1627). Same arms.

Wingfield (Co. Norfolk). Add: Wingfield (Upton co. Northampton and co. Rutland). Same arms. *C.R.*

Wingham. Gu. a chev. betw. 3 falcons lures or. Add: *V.*

Winnington (Co. Chester). Add: *Randle Holme.*

Winniffe. Arg. a chev. betw. 3 escallops sa. Thomas Winniffe, Bishop of Lincoln 1642–54. But the chev. charged with another invected az. *Harl. MS. 2275. fo. 20.*

Winslade or Wirdeslade, (Co. Devon). Arg. a chev. vairy sa. and or betw. 3 herons wings expanded sa. *V.*

Winslow. Erm. on a bend gu. 3 escallops or. *Morant's Essex ii. 529.*

Winslow. Erm. a chev. engr. ermines. *V.V.**

Winslow. Erm. on a chev. engr. sa. three 4-foils or. *V.*

Winter (Worthington and Northington, co. Leicester). . . . . Add: *C.C. 1619.*

Winterfall. Az. a chevron fracted arg. † *Randle Holme.*

Wintersells. Arg. a chev. betw. 3 bulls pass.—insert—or statant. . . . Crest: . . . Add: *V.*V.*

Winteringham (Dover Street, Hanover Square, London, bart.). Insert—1774. . . .

Wirdeslade (Co. Devon). Arg. a chev. vairy sa. and or betw. 3 herons wings expanded sa. *V.*

Wire Drawers. Company of, Gold and Silver, London). Az. on a chev. or betw. in chief 2 coppers of the second and in base 2 points in saltire arg. a drawing iron betw. 2 rings sa.

Wise (Sydenham, co. Devon . . .). *Visit. Devon 1620.* Insert—Mr John Wise of the City of London, Master Plumber, to the Office of His Majesty's Ordnance. Same arms. *Guillim.* . . . in the dexter paw a mace or . . . Add: a mullet for diff. *V.D.*

Wise (Ireland). Sa. a chev. erm. Wysse. *V.*

Wiseman (Canfield Hall, co. Essex, bart.). Insert—1628. . . .

Wiseman (Riven Hall and Upminster, co. Essex, bart.). Insert—1660. . . . Crest: . . . Add: *V.E. 1612.*

Wiseman. Per pale . . . and . . . a chev. . . . betw. 3 coronels arg. Symon Wysseman.

Wiseman (Felsted, Essex, granted 1574). Sa. a chev. betw. 3 coronels arg. *W.*

Wiseman (Felstead, Essex). Sa. a chev. betw. 3 spur rowels arg. † for diff. *V.E. 1552.*

Wiseman (Waltham, co. Essex. . .). Add: *V.E. 1612.*

Wiseman (Berningham, Norfolk). Az. a chev. betw. 3 cronels. . . . *Cady.*

Wistowe. Arg. a chev. gu. in chief 3 torteaux. Sire William de Wistowe. *Y.*

Witchingham. Add: *Guillim.*

Witham (Co. York). Or a bend gu. betw. 3 cormorants sa. *Whitaker's Leeds ij. 240.*

Witham (Garforth, co. York 1666). Or 3 ravens sa. overall a bendlet gu. *Dugdale p. 374.*

Witham (Ledston, co. York 1585). Same arms. *F.Y.*

Witham (Cliffe, co. York 1665). Or 3 eagles sa. overall a bendlet gu. *Dugdale p. 109.*

Witham (Goldesborough, co. York, bart.). Insert—1682 . . . betw. 3 eaglets—insert—close—Add: *V. Guillim.*

Wither (Manydown, co. Hants.). Add: Sir Thomas Wither. *V.*

Wither (Colchester, Essex). Same arms. † for diff. *V.E. 1612.*

Withering (Nelmes, co. Essex . . .). Add: Confirmed by Segar to Edwd. Withering, co. Stafford. *Guillim.*

Witherington. Quarterly arg. and gu. a bend sa. *V.** Monsire Gerrard de Witherington. *S.* But a baston sa. John de Wyderington. *Y.*

Withie. Per pale erm. and gu. a lion ramp. counterchanged. *W.*

Withie. Per pale erm. and or a lion ramp. gu. John Withie, London, "Armes Painter". *W.*

Withines. Gu. a chev. embattled counter embattled erm. betw. 3 martlets or. John Withines, Dean of Battle, Sussex. 1615. His **Brass** in Battle Church.

Withers. Arg. a chev. gu. betw. 3 torteaux. George Withers "the Polt". *Cady.*

Witneill. Add: *V.** Sir William Wytnyll. *V.*

Wittal or Witwell (Co. York). Arg. on a bend gu. 3 men's heads horned or. *Carter.*

Wittie (City of York 1665). Gu. a chev. betw. 3 scorpions erect nowed or. Crest 2 serpents in pale embowed and interlaced. *Dugdale p.221.*

Witton (Witton, Sheriff of Salop. . . .). Add: *Fuller.*

Wytton. Sa. a water bouget arg. *V.*

Witton (London 1678). Sa. a water bouget arg. in chief 3 bezants; quartering arg. a fess gu. betw. 3 bulls heads cabossed sa. *C.L.*

Wixston. Arg. a chev. gu. in chief 3 torteaux. Sir William de Wixston. *V.* Sir Robert de Wixstoon. *Y.*

Wlathaw. Gu. a chev. betw. 3 birds heads erased arg. *Harl. MS. 1404.*

Woburn Abbey, Co. Bedford. Az. 3 bars wavy arg. *Tanner.*

Wobrew. Arg. 2 bars gu. in chief 3 wolves heads couped of the second. *V.**

Wodam (Thomas Wodam, co. Leicester . . .). Add: *V.N. p.131.*

Wodebith or Wodebinch. Barry of 10 arg. and az. 3 lions ramp. gu. crowned or. Raffe de Wodebith. *A.*

Wodehouse (Earl of Kimberley . . .). Sa. a chev. gu. or gutte de sang . . . insert—*V.*

Woderowe. Arg. on a chev. betw. 3 crosses patty fitchy gu. a crescent arg. for diff. Thomas Woderowe. *V.*

Wodey. Gu. a chev. engr. arg. betw. 3 birds or. *V.*

Wodilston. Arg. a chev. compony or and gu. betw. 3 bugle horns sa. *V.**

Wodnester (Bromyard, co. Hereford. Granted by Cooke 1588). Sa. a bend arg. betw. 2 eagles displ. or. *V.*

Wodrington or Witherington. Quarterly arg. and gu. a bend sa.—insert—*V.** Add: Sir John Wodrington. *V.* Wodrington of Wodrington, Northumberland. *V.*

Wokingdon. Gu. a lion ramp. arg. crowned or. Sir Nicholas Wokingdon. *L.N.G.*

Wold. Or on a quarter az. a pale engr. erm. betw. —insert—'6 or' . . . Add: *V.*

Wolf (Madeley, co. Salop). . . . on an escutcheon of pretence—insert—as an augmentation. . . .

Wolf. Barry of 10 or and vert. a wolf ramp. or. Add: *V.V.**

Wolf. Arg. a chev. betw. 3 wolves heads erased sa. each gorged with a ducal coronet or. *V.*V.*

Wolf. Sa. a chev. or betw. 3 wolves heads erased arg. *V.*

Wolfe (Kentisbury, co. Devon). . . . 3 wolves pass. 'arg.' amend to read 'az.'. Add: *Lysons.*

Wolfe. Gu. 3 bars arg. on a chief of the last 3 wolves heads erased of the first. Add: *V.*

Wolfe. Or 3 wolves pass. in pale az. a border per bordure indented gu. and az. Add: Anthony Wolfe co. Devon. *V.*

Wolfe. Sa. 2 wolves pass. arg. *V.** Sir William Wolfe. *V.*

Wolfedon. Insert—Cornwall sa. a chev. or betw. 3 wolves heads erased arg. Add: *V.*V.*

Wollacombe (Wollacombe, co. Devon). Insert—Granted by Camden 1611. . . .

Wolley (Comberworth, co. Lincoln). Add: Sir John Wolley (Chancellor of the Order of the Garter). Same arms.

Wolley. Arg. a chev. sa. *Dingley.*

Wolrich. Sir Toby Wolrich, Cowling, Suffolk, 1661. Gu. a chev. betw. 3 swans wings elevated arg. *L.N.*

Wolrington (Hacke, co. Devon). Gu. 2 demilions pass. guard. or. *Lysons.*

Wolsey (Curate of Hornsey 1664). Az. on a bend or 3 eagles displ. sa. *Cole MSS.*

Wolston.

Wolston (Staverton, co. Devon). Add: *V.D. 1620.*

Wolston. Arg. a chev. betw. 3 bucks lodges gu. Add: *V.V.**

Wolston. Quarterly sa. and or a bend gu. Sir John Wolston. *Harl. MS. 1465. fo. 15b.*

Wolston. Arg. a wolf pass. sa. Add: (Sir George Wolston 19 Edw. IV). Quartering arg. 3 turnstyles sa. a mullet for diff. and arg. on a chev. sa. betw. 3 rams heads erased az. as many billets or. *C.L. p. 84.*

Wolton. Or a lion ramp. supporting a saltire engr. couped gu. John Wolton, Bishop of Exeter 1579.

Wolunston. Quarterly or and sa. a bend gu. *V.*

Woleridge. Gu. a chev. erm. betw. 3 swans rising arg. Sir James Wolveridge. *Dug. O.J.*

Wolverton (Wolverton. co. Buckingham . . .). Add: Sir John de Wolvertone. *N.*

Wolwardington or Walrington (Co. Warwick). Add: Sir Peers de Wolwardingtone. Bendy of 10 arg. and sa. *N.*

Wombwell (Wombwell, co. York, bart.). Insert— 1770 . . . 6 unicorns heads—delete—'erased' read 'couped' arg. Crest: . . .

Wombwell. Arg. on a bend betw. 6 martlets gu. gu. 3 bezants. Thomas Wombell. *X.*

Wombwell (Northfleet, co. Kent). Add: *W.*

Wombwell (Silvercliff, co. York). Insert—1585. . . Add: a crescent for diff. *F.Y.*

Womwell. Or—delete—(another, arg.). Add: *V.*

Wood (Stapleford, co. Essex). Add: *V.**

Wood (Kent). Sa. on a chev. betw. 3 pine cones slipped or as many martlets of the first. *V.*

Wood (Co. Lancaster 1582). Insert—Granted by Flower. . . .

Wood (Islington, co. Middlesex; granted Feb. 1606). Insert—'to Wood, Serjeant at Law, by Camden'. . . .

Wood. Arg. on a bend sa. 3 fleurs-de-lis of the first in the sinister chief a crescent for diff. or in the crescent gu. Thomas Wood, Kelnwike, co. York, granted by Flower. *W.*

Wood (Co. Stafford and West Cutton and Thorp, co. York). A crescent on a crescent for diff. *F.Y.* Arms and first crest granted—insert— by Harvey.

Wood. Arg. 2 squirrels sejant affrontant gu. betw. an orle of crosses crosslet sa. *V.V.**

Wood (Co. Warwick). Arg. a chev. betw. 3 bulls heads cabossed sa. armed or. Add: *V.*

Wood. Az. 3 doves arg. legged gu.

Wood. Per pale or and sa. 2 eagles displ. counter-changed. Crest: On a ducal coronet or. . . . Add: Granted in 1592 to Thomas Wood, M.D. of Suffolk. *W.*

Wood. Insert—Granted to Thos. Wood of Kelnwike, co. York. Arg. on a bend sa. 3 fleurs-de-lis of the first in the sinister chief a crescent—amend—'or', read 'gu.'; on a crescent—amend 'gu,', read 'or'. Crest: . . . Add: Granted by Flower. *W.*

Wood. Sa. on a chev. betw. 3 pine trees or as many martlets of the first. *V.**

Wood. Gu. on a bend arg. three—insert—'elm'. . . . Add: *V.*

Woodborne. Barry of 12 arg. and az. 3 lions ramp. gu. Sir . . . de Woodborne. *V.*

Woodburgh. Barruly of 15 arg. and az. . . . Add: Rauf de Wodeburgh. *E.Y.* William de Wodeburgh. *E.* John Wodeburgh. *Y.* Thomas Woodburgh. *Y.*

Woodcock (Co. Essex). Add: *V.E. 1634.* Sir John Woodcock (Lord Mayor of London 1405). *Harl. MS. 1349.*

Wooderton. Gu. a chev. betw. 3 lions gambs . . . Add: *V.V.**

Wooderton. Sa. a chev. arg. betw. 3 lions gambs erased gu. *V.*

Woodhall. Az. a chev. chequy arg. and gu. *Constable's Roll xij.*

Woodhouse (Co. Norfolk). Add: *V.*

Woodhouse or Woolhouse (Glapwell, co. Derby). Per pale az. and sa. a chev. engr. erminois betw. 3 plates. *Harl. MSS. 1486. fo. 57: 1537. fo. 111.*

Woodland (Woodland and Bockington, co. Devon). Add: *V.** Sir Walter Woodland *V.*

Woodliston (Wolverston,). Arg. a chev. counter compony gu. and or betw. 3 bugle horns stringed sa. *V.*

Woodmongers (Company of, London). Arg. a chev. sa. betw. 3 bundles of laths vert. *V. Cotton MS. Tiberius. D. 10. fo. 885.*

Woodnester (Bromyard, co. Hereford). Add: *V.*

Woodrofe. Add: Sir Richard Woodroffe. *V.*

Woodroffe (Hoope, co. Derby and co. York). Add: *Lysons.*

Woodstock, De. Add: Edmund of Woodstock, son of Edward ij. *V.Y.*

Woodthorpe. Arg. a bend az. betw. 6 crosses crosslet fitchee vert. Crest: . . . Add: *V.*

Woodward. Arg. a chev. gu. betw. 3 delves of the second. Add: *V.**

Woodward. Az. a chev. engr. erm. betw. 3 fleurs-de-lis arg. Add: John Woodward, Kent. *V.*

Woodward (Norfolk). Az. a chev. betw. 3 billets or. *W.*

Woolfall (Co. Lancaster). Arg. an erm. spot betw. 2 bends gu. Add: *V.L. 1664.*

Woolfe (Confirmed 1 July 1588). Or 3 wolves statant in pale az. *Harl. MS. 1359. fo. 13.*

Woolhouse (Glapwell, co. Derby). . . . a chev. engr. erm.—read—'erminois. Add: *Harl. MS. 1093. fo. 111.*

Woolley. Az. a chev. vairy or and sa. betw. 3 female heads and busts arg. †

Woolmerston. Vert. a chev. betw. 3 lions ramp. or. *Collinson Somerset j. 256.*

Woolridge (Garlenick in Creed, co. Cornwall . . .). Add: Woolrich (Dunmore, co. Hereford). Same Arms. *Dingley.*

Woore (Richard Woore of London . . .). Gu. a bend arg. fretty sa.—underlined—marginal note ? az. Add: *C.L.*

Worcel. Add: *V.**

Worley. Ermine a lion salient tail forked gu. Henry Worley, Alderman of London. *V.*

Worley. Arg. a chev. engr. betw. three bugle horns sa. tipped and chained or. *Nash.*

Wormegrey (Norfolk). Barry of 8 or sa. arg. az. or. sa. arg. az. *Cady.*

Worship (Great Yarmouth) co. Norfolk). Add: *V.V.**

Worsley (Worsley Mains co. Lancaster, 1613 . . .) Add: Sir Thomas Worceley. *V.*

Worsolley. Add: *V.**

Worth. Erm. an eagle displ. double headed sa. armed gu. Sir . . . de Worthe, Devon. *V.*

Worth (Co. Devon). Erm. an eagle displ. sa. membered gu. standing on the trunk of a tree raguly arg. *Syl. Morgan p. 60.*

Wortham. Insert—Co. Devon. Gu. a chev. erm. betw. 3 lions gambs of the second, the two in chief bending to each other. Add: *V.*

Worthington or Wrightington. Insert—Co. Lancaster. Add: *V.*

Worthivale (Worthivale, co. Cornwall . . .). Add: *Lysons.*

Wortley (Wortley, co. York, bart.). Insert— 1611. . . . Add: *F.Y.* Sir Nicholas Woteley, co. York. *V.N.* Wortley (Chelmsford, co. Essex 1612). Same arms with a crescent on a crescent for diff. *V.E.*

Worvil (Braunceford). Or on a bend gu. treble cotised sa. 3 crescents arg. *Nash.*

Wotshall. Add: *V.*

Wotshall. Arg. on a bend gu. 3 square buckles or. *Cole MSS.*

Wotton-Waven College. Insert—Co. Warwick....

Wotton. Insert—Tuddenham, Norfolk, Gu. a chev. betw. in chief 2 crosses crosslet and in base an annulet or. Crest: ... Add: *Cady.*

Wotton. Az. 3 martlets arg. *V.*

Wouton (Chester). Arg. a chev. sa. *Cady.*

Wray (Co. York). Az. on a chev. erm. betw. 3 falchions bendwise arg. handled or a crescent sa. on a chief of the fourth 3 martlets gu. *Fairfax's Book of Arms.*

Wray (Trebitch, Cornwall. Baronetcy 1626). Sa. a chev. betw. 3 hatchets arg. handles gu. *Guillim.*

Wray (Wensleydale, co. York). Az. a chev. erm. betw. 3 helmets ppr. on a chief or 3 martlets gu.

Wray (Co. York). Az. a chev. erm. betw. 3 scimitars arg. hilts and pomels gold on a chief or three martlets gu. *Eliz. Roll. xxjx.*

Wren (Bilby Hall, co. Durham). Add: *V.* Matthew Wren, Bishop of Hereford, Norwich and Ely. *Parentalia.*

Wren (Bynchester, co. Durham). Arg. a chev. betw. 3 lions heads erased az. langued gu. on a chief of the last 3 crosses crosslet or. *Eliz. Roll xviij.* Sir Christopher Wren 1632–1722.

Wrenne. Arg. on a chev. az. 3 wrens of the first a chief charged with as many horses heads erased brown. *Harl. MS. 1404. fo. 111b.*

Wren. Per pale indented arg. and sa. 6 martlets counterchanged 2.2. and 2. Add: *V.*

Wrenbury. Arg. a chev. sa. betw. 3 wrens ppr. *Harl. MS. 1404. fo. 147.*

Wrenne (Worlingham, Suffolk). Per pale indented or and gu. 6 martlets counterchanged. **Brass** in Worlingham Church.

Wrey. Arg. on a bend engr. az. betw. 2 demi-lions ramp. gu. bezantée 3 mullets of 6 points pierced or. Add: John de Wrey, Sussex. *V.*

Wriallie or Wriley. Add: *F.*

Wright (Nantwich, co. Chester). Per pale or and arg. on a chev. az. betw. 3 boars heads couped fess wise sa. as many bezants. *Harl. MS. 1535. fo. 29.*

Wright (Longstone Hall, co. Derby). Add: *Lysons.*

Wright (Dagenhams, co. Essex, bart.). Insert—1660. ... Add: Wright (Dennington, co. Suffolk, Baronetcy 1645. Same arms. Sir Nathan Wright, Serjeant at Law 1696. Same Arms. *L.N.* Ensely Wright. Same arms. *Dug. O.J.*

Wright (Co. Hants.). Insert—Baronetcy 1772; Sa. a chev. betw. 3 fleurs-de-lis arg. on a chief of the second as many spearheads az.

Wright (Co. Kent; granted by Segar, Garter). Insert—1603. ...

Wright. Arg. 3 bars gemel gu. on a chief az. 3 leopards faces or.

Wright (Co. Lincoln 1640). Add: *Yorke.*

Wright. Gu. on a chev. engr. arg. betw. 3 unicorns heads erased ... as many spearheads sa. Crest: A lamb pass. bearing a flag. Richard Wright, M.D. **Book Plate.**

Wright (Gola, co. Monaghan . . .). Marginal 'pencil' note ... 'only in trick in *Rec. Ped.*'

Wright (Compsey Cottage, co. Tipperary . . .). Marginal 'pencil' note. '*Grt. 1833.* Grts. E'.

Wright (Guayaquil, South America . . .). Marginal 'pencil' note 'Conf. 1862. *Gts. F*'. Add: *A.A.*

Wriothsley, Wryotesley or Wristeley. Add: Hugh de Wryotesley KG., *S.V.*

Wrokeshall (or Wroxhall). Erm. 2 bars gu. Sir Geffry de Wrokeshall. *Y.*

Wroth (Woodbery and Youngs, co. Herts. . . . and co. Essex). Insert—*V.E. 1612.* Add: Sir Thomas Wroth, Blinden Hall, Kent. Baronetcy 1660 ext. 1722. Sir Robert Wroth, Middlesex. *V.*

Wrotheley. Arg. on a bend betw. 6 martlets gu. 3 bezants. Sir Thomas Wrotheley 1558. *Constable's Roll. vij.*

Wrothe. Add: John Wroth. *V.*

Wroughton (Stowell Lodge, co. Wilts.). Add: *V.*

Wryne. Per fess arg. and gu. a lion ramp. counterchanged. Add: *V.*

Wryttle Add: *V.V.**

Wyard. Arg. a chev. betw. 3 roses gu. *Nash.* Philip Wyard. *V.*

Wyatt (Sherwell, co. Devon and Bexley, co. Kent). Add: *V.*

Wybaston Add: *Shaw.*

Wybury. Sa. semee of crosses crosslet or 2 lions pass. in pale arg. Add: John Wybury. *V.*

Wybury. Sa. crusilly fitchy and 3 lions ramp. or. *V.*

Wyche (Salisbury). Confirmed in 1587. Antient arms. Arg. on a chev. gu. betw. 3 4-foils vert. as many plates. *Hoare.*

Wycliff (Thorp, co. York). Arg. a chev. betw. 3 crosses crosslet sa. *Dugdale p. 195.*

Wycliff. Arg. a chev. betw. 3 crosses crosslet sa. Add: Wycliff of Wycliff, co. York. Arg. a chev. sa. betw. 3 crosses bottony gu. Add: *V. Eliz. Roll. xxviij.*

Wycliff. Arg. a chev. betw. 3 crosses crosslet gu. Robert Wycliff. *P.*

Wycliffe of Wycliffe. Arg. on a chev. sa. betw. 3 crosses crosslet bottony gu. 7 stags heads cabossed arg. with 5 bucks heads. *Tonge p. 40.* John Wycliffe of Wickliff, co. York. *V.*

Wycombe. Or 2 lions ramp. combatant gu. armed and langued az. Crest: ... Add: *V.*

Wydent. Add: Bartholomew Wydent (Radiswell, co. Hertford, granted 1515). *V.*

Wyke (Minehead, co. Somerset 1400). Add: *Cotton MS. Tiberius D. 10.*

Wyke. Arg. 3 chevs. and in the dexter chief a fleur-de-lis sa. *V.*

Wyke. Arg. a chev. erm.—read—'ermines'. Add: *Harl. MS. 1078. fo. 40.*

Wykeham. Arg. 2 chevs. sa. betw. 3 roses gu. Sir Thomas Wykham. *V.*

Wykes. . . . a chev. ermines betw. 3 barnacle birds. ppr. *Harl. MS. 1078. fo. 40b.*

Wykes (Co. Gloucester). Gu. a bend erm. cotised indented or Add: *V.*

Wykes. Az. a lion ramp. chequy arg. and gu. Richard Wykes. *E.* Nicholas Wikes, Sheriff of Gloucestershire. temp. Hen. viij. *Fuller.*

Wykes (temp. Hen. iij.). Arg. a chev. compony az. and vert. betw. 3 gannapyes az. membered gu. *V.*

Wyldbore (Stamford, co. Lincoln 1674). Add: *Guillim.*

Wylde. Arg. 2 bends gu. on each 3 crosses crosslet or. Add: *V.**

Wylde (Nettleworth Hall and Southwell, co. Notts. . . .). Add: *V.N. 189.*

Wyle. Add: *V.*

Wymarke (North Luffenham, co. Rutland . . .). Add: *V.R.*

Wymor. Add: *V.*

Wynard. Or on a bend az. 3 pierced mullets arg. *V.*

Wynchcombe (Bucklesbury, co. Berks.). Add: Baronetcy 1661. extinct. Add: *Guillim.* describes the eagles as lapwings.

Wyndeslade or Wynslade. Add: *V.**

Wyndham (Orchard-Wyndham, co. Somerset ...). Add: *Collinson Somerset ij. 285.*

Wyndham (Baron Leconfield). Insert—1859. . . .

Wyrall. Arg. 2 lions pass. guard. the first gu. the second sa. on a chief of the last 3 covered cups or. Add: Hugh Wyrall, co. York. *V.*

Wyrcestre. William Wyrcestre, calling himself by his mother's name Botoner. Arg. on a chev. betw. 3 lions heads erased gu. crowned or as many bezants.

Wyreley. Insert—Co. Stafford. Add: *V.*

Wyrley De (Co. Stafford; granted ii. Edw. iij). Add: *Harl. MS. 1116. fo. 1.*

Wyreley. Arg. a chev. engr. betw. 3 bugle horns sa. stringed or. *V.**

Wysse (Ireland). Sa. a chev. erm. *V.*

Wystowe (John de Wystowe, temp. Richard ij). Arg. a chev. gu. betw. 3 torteaux. †

Wytchers. Gu. a chev. or betw. 3 goats heads erased arg. armed of the second. *V.*

Wyter. Erm. a bull statant sa. armed gu. *V.*

Wythens (Wantaway, co. Berks., Eltham, co. Kent and London; granted). Insert—by Dethick—delete 1649, read '1594'.

Wythepoll or Wethypoll. Per pale or and gu. 3 lions pass. in pale within a bordure all counterchanged. *V. V.**

Wytte. Add: *V.**

Wyvell (Croydon, co. Surrey). Add: Wyvell (Bellarby, co. York 1665). Same arms. quartering 2 arg. 3 pickaxes sa. † for diff. 3. Sa. a chief indented arg. and 4 az. a bend or a label of three points arg. *Dugdale p. 37.*

Wyvill (Osgodby, co. York 1664). Same arms with a 3-foil slipped az. on the chief for diff. *Dugdale p. 329.*

Wyvell. Arg. 2 bars sa. a border engr. gu. Add: William de Wivile. *E.V.*

Wyvill (Osgodby co. York. *Ancient Arms*). Gu. 3 chevs. each embattled on the top arg. a chief or. *Harl. MS. 1487. fo. 322b.*

Wyvill (Co. York). Gu. 3 chevs. braced compony arg. and sa. on a chief or a mullet of the third. *Harl. MS. 1404. fo. 103.*

Wyvill (Burton Constable, co. York . . .). Add: *Dugdale p. 89.*

Y

YALDWIN (Blackdown, co. Sussex; granted 1651). Insert—by Byshe . . .

Yarborough (Wilmsby, co. Lincoln). Add: Yarborough (Doncaster, co. York 1665). Same arms and crest. *Dugdale. p. 186.*

Yarborough (Appleton, co. York 1665). Per chev. arg. and az. a chev. betw. 3 chaplets all counterchanged, a canton gu. *Dugdale. p. 169.*

Yarborough (Campsmount, co. York). . . . quarterly . . . —2nd and 3rd or. a chev. gu. betw. 2 lions pass. guard sa.—insert—for Cooke. . . .

Yard (Cosby, co. Leicester). . . . Add: Yard, Mayor of Exeter 1695. *Colby.*

Yardley (Upbery, co. Kent and Yardley, co. Stafford). Add: *V.** Yardley (Calcott, co. Chester). Same arms.

Yarmouth (Co. Norfolk and Blondston, co. Suffolk). Add: *V.*

Yarmouth (Gt. Yarmouth, Norfolk 1300 to 1570). Sa. a chev. betw. 3 bears feet erased or. Add: *MS. 5524.*

Yatton. Or a chev. gu. (another sa.). betw. 3 garbs az. Add: *V.*

Yatton. Or a chev. betw. 3 garbs az. Add: *V.*

Yaxley (Yaxley and Bawthorp, co. Norfolk). Add: *V.*

Yaxley. Erm. a chev. betw. 3 mullets sa. Crest: . . . Add: Yaxley (Bickarton, co. York). Same arms. *Fairfax's Book of Arms.*

Yeland (Seaham, co. Durham). . . . 2 bars . . . and in chief 2 mullets . . . **Seal** of John de Yeland 1295. *Surtees.*

Yelverton (Rougham, co. Norfolk, bart.). Insert —1620. Add: *V.* Yelverton (Easton Manduit, co. Northampton, Baronetcy 1641). Same arms.

Yelverton (Earl of Sussex . . . third son of William Yelverton of Rougham). Insert—*Dug. O. J.*

Yelverton. Arg. 3 lions ramp. guard. gu. on a chief of the second as many lions ramp. guard of the first. Add: *V.V.**

Yeo (Heampton Sachville, co. Devon . . .). Add: *V.D. 1620.*

Yeo. Arg. a chev. betw. 3 shovellers az. *V.**

Yeo or Yoo. Or a chev. sa. betw. 3 shovellers az. *V.*

Yeo. Arg. on a chev. sa. betw. 3 gannapies az. membered gu. as many plates. *V.* But shovellers instead of gannapyes. *V.**

Yeo. Or a chev. sa. betw. 3 garbs az. *V.**

Yerde. Add: *V.*

Yerde (Co. Devon). Sa. a chev. betw. 3 water bougets arg. *V.*

Yeton or Yeaton. Or a bend sa. Add: *V.*

Yhedingham. Arg. a chev. betw. three fleurs-de-lis erm. Richard de Yhedingham. *Y.*

Yeverey. Arg. on a bend gu. 3 oak—insert— (or walnut) . . . Add: *V.*

Ylee. Erm. 2 chevs. sa. Sire John de Ylee. *O.*

Yively. . . . 2 chevs. . . . betw. 3 dexter wings erect. **Seal** of Richard Yvelly. 1357. *V.*

Ynge. Or a chev. vert. Add: Sire William Yngee. *N.*

Yngfeld. Barry of 14 arg. and gu. on a canton like the second a mullet as the first. *V.*

Yoard (Stokesby, co. York). . . . 2 chevs. . . . *F.Y.*

Yoe. Or a chev. betw. 3 garbs az. *T.*

Yoe. Or a chev. sa. betw. 3 garbs az. *V.*

Yong (Lord Mayor of London 1466). Lozengy arg. and vert. on a bend az. an annulet betw. 2 griffins heads erased or. *Harl. MS. 1349.*

Yonge or Young (Bassildon, co. Berks., granted). Insert—by Segar.

Yonge (Co. Wilts.). Lozengy arg. and vert. on a chevron az. 3 bezants. *Harl. MS. 1404. fo. 102.*

Yonge (Wittenham, co. Berks.). Lozengy arg. and vert. on a chev. az. 3 bezants on a chief gu. a boars head erased. betw. two 5-foils or. *V.*

Yonge (Co. Devon; granted by Camden, Clarenceux). Add: *Lysons.*

Yong (Co. Wilts.). Lozengy arg. and vert. on a bend az. . . . Add: Sir John Yong, Lord Mayor of London 1466. *Harl. MS. 1439.*

Yong. Paly bendy or 6 arg. and vert. on a bend az. two unicorns heads bendwise erased arg. *V.*

Yonge (Co. Worcester). Arg. on a bend sa. 3 griffins heads erased palewise or. *V.*

Yonge (Dr. Edwd. Yonge, Rithsons Lecturer, Cambridge 1614). Arg. on a bend sa. within a bordure engr. of the second 3 griffins heads erased or.

Yonge. Arg. a chev. componee counter-componee or and sa. betw. 3 griffins heads erased gu. on a chief . . . Add: *V.*

York (Fillack, co. Cornwall . . .). Add: *V.C. p. 307.*

York. Arg. a chev. sa. betw. 3 hind's heads couped gu. Add: Roger Yorke, Serjeant at Law *V.*

Young (Plymouth, co. Devon). Per saltire or and az. a lion pass. betw. 2 fleurs-de-lis in fess arg. †

Young (Kingerby, co. Lincoln). Add: Sir Richard Young, one of the Privy Council to King Charles j. Baronetcy 1627. *Guillim.*

Young (Co. York 1612). Arg. on a bend sa. 3 griffins heads or erased gu. *F. Y.*

Young (Culleton, co. Devon Baronetcy 1661). Arg. on a bend betw. 2 cotises sa. 3 griffins heads erased or. *Guillim.*

Young (Stancombe, England). *Ulster's Office* . . . Add: ? granted 1583. *W.*

Young. Arg. 3 bars sa. over all a lion ramp. gu. †

Younge (Buckhorne). Insert—co. Dorset and Colbrooke co.—delete—Dorset, read 'Devon'. Add: *V.D. 1620.*

Younge (Buckhorne Weston, co. Dorset). Arg. 3 lions ramp. guard. sa.

Younge (Raxwell and Roxhall, co. Essex). Add: *V.E. 1634.*

Younger. Arg. on a bend sa. betw. 2 dolphins haurient and embowed . . . Add: *Harl. MS. 6829. fo. 47.*

Younghusband (Sheriff of Newcastle 1492). Arg. on a bend sa. 3 griffins heads erased or. on a chief az. 3 plates. *Carr. MS.*

Younghusband (Berwick-upon-Tweed). Az. on a chev. or 3 mullets pierced of the field.

Z

ZAKESLEY. Arg. the upper half of a sickle blade serrated on the under (dexter) edge erect sa. *V.*

Zeketh. Gu. a chev. betw. 3 heathcocks—insert—or pheasants Add: *V.**

Zenelton. Sa. 2 bars arg. a label of 3 points gu. *V.*

Zerman. Add: Peter Zerman. *V.*

Zevelton. Arg. 2 bars nebuly sa. a label of 3 points gu. M. Robert de Zevelton. *S.*

Zingel. Gu. an arrow point upwards betw. two—insert—'conjoined' wings arg.

Zorke. Per pale az. and arg. on each side a bend counterchanged. Add: *V.*

Zorke (Called York). Az. a bend arg. impaling arg. a bend az. *V.*

Zorke. Arg. a bend arg. (*sic* ? for Az.) impaling the same. *V.*

Zouch (Cos. Derby and Leicester).

Zouch (Cos. Derby and Leicester). Add: Sire William La Souche. *N.* Baron Zouche. *U.* Le Sire de Zouch. *T.* Sir Roger la Zouche, co. Leicester. *V.* And quartering arg. on a fess dancetty sa. 3 bezants. Sire John Souche. *T.*

Zouch (Co. Leicester). Gu. a chev. erm. betw. 10 bezants 4. 2. 1. 2. and 1. Add: Sir Oliver Zouche. *V.*

Zouch (Gosberkirke, co. Lincoln). Add: Sire Oliver la Souche. *N.*

Zouch. Gu. bezanty and a canton indented in the bottom. erm. Sr. William la Zouche. *R.*

Zouch. Zouch (Codnor, co. Derby). Gu. bezanty on a canton erm. a crescent for diff. Sir John Zouch. *V.*

Zouch. Gu. bezanty on a canton arg. a mullet sa. Sire Thomas la Souche. *N.* Sir Thomas Zouche, co. Leicester. *V.*

Zouch. Gu. bezanty a bend arg. Sire Amory la Souche. *N.O.*

Zouch. Gu. bezanty a bend erm. Sir Amory de la Zouch. *L. Harl. MS. 6137.*

Zouch. Gu. a bend arg. betw. 6 bezants. Monsire le Zouche. *Y.*

Zouch. Gu. a bend arg. betw. 8 bezants. Sir Amory de la Zouch. *L.* But with 10 bezants. *V.L.*

APPENDIX

Ababrelton: FD2–
Abbadie: Ne 5/319–
Abbey: Mt 178–FD2–
Abbott: Bn 1–FD2–
Abdy: FD1–FD2
A Beckett: FD1–FD2–
Abercrombie: Ne 2/107–Bn 1–FD2–
Abercromby: FD1–FD2–
Abel: FD1–
Abell: Ne 3/168–
Abercorn: FD1–
Aberdare: FD1–
Aberdeen: FD1–
Abergavenny: FD1—FD2–
Abernethy: Bn 1–
Abingdon: FD1–
Abinger: FD1–
Abney: Mc 2/3–FD1–
Abrahall: Bn 1–VH 9–
Abraham: FD1–FD2–
Abrahams: FD2–
Abrahamson: FD2–
Abram: FD2–
Accorrett: W2/21–
Acheson: FD1–FD2–
Ackers: FD1–FD2–
Ackland: FD2–
Acland: FD1–FD2–
Acland-Hood-Reynardson: FD2–
Acland-Court-Repington: FD2–
Acklom: Bn 1–
Ackroyd: FD1–
Acton: FD1–FD2–
Adair: FD1–FD2–
Adam: Bn 1–FD1–FD2–
Adams: Ne/23–Mt(A) 3–Bn 1–Mc 1/3, 2/8–
    VH 7–W2/21–FD1–FD2–
Adamson: FD1–FD2–
Addenbrooke: FD1–FD2–
Adderley: FD1–FD2–
Addington: Bn 1–FD1–
Adeane: FD1–FD2–
Addison: Bn 2–Mc 1/6–FD2–
Adkins: FD2–
Adlercrow–FD2–
Adlam: FD1–
Adlington: FD1–
Affleck: FD1–FD2–
Agar: FD2–
Agar-Ellis: FD1–
Agar-Robartes: FD2–
Agassiz: Ne 6/382–
Aglionby: FD1–
Agnew: Mt 202–Bn 2–FD1–FD2–
Ahmuty: Bn 2–
Aiken: FD1–FD2–
Aikenhead: FD1–FD2–
Aiken-Sneath: FD2–
Aikins: FD2–
Aikman: Mt(A) 3–FD2–

Ailesbury: FD1–
Ailsa: FD1–FD2–
Ainsworth: FD1–
Aird: FD2–
Airey: FD2–
Airlie: FD1–
Aitchison: Bn 2–VH 9–FD2–
Aitken: FD2–
Akerly: Mt(A) 3–
Akers-Douglas FD1–FD2–
Alban: W2/22–
Albany: FD1–FD2–
Albemarle: FD1–
Albright: FD2–
Albro: Mt/149–
Albu: FD2–
Alcester: FD1–
Alcock: FD2–
Alcock-Beck: FD2–
Alcott: Bn 2–
Alden: Mt(A) 3–Bn 2–
Alder: FD1–
Aldersey: FD1–FD2–
Aldis: Mt 160–
Aldovisi: W2/22–
Aldous: FD2–
Aldrich: Bn 2–
Aldridge: FD2–
Aldwell: FD2–
Aldworth: FD1–FD2–
Alexander: Ne 2/158–Bn 2–VH102–Ah3,17–
    FD1–FD2–
Alexander-Sinclair: FD2–
Alington: FD1–FD2–
Alford: FD2–
Algar: FD2–
Algeo: FD2–
Algei: FD2–
Alison: FD1–FD2–
Alkin: FD2–
Allan: Bn 2–FD1–FD2–
Allanby: FD2–
Allanson: FD2–
Allanson–Winn:FD2–
Allardyce: FD2–
Allcock: Bn 2–
Allcroft: FD1–FD2–
Allder: FD2–
Allen: Bn 2 & 3–VH7–W1/9–W2/22–FD1–FD2–
Allenby: FD2–
Allerton: Mt(A) 4–Mc 2/10–
Alleyne: Bn 3–FD1–FD2–
Allfrey: FD2–
Allgood: FD2–
Allhusen: FD1–FD2–
Alling: Mt(A) 4–
Allison: Bn 3–FD2–
Allisrow: FD2–
Allix: FD2–
Allott: FD2–

Allpress: FD2–
Allsopp: FD2–
Allyn: Bn 3–
Almey: Mt 20 7–
Almy: Bn 3–
Alofsen: Bn 3–
Alsop: Ne 3/169–Bn 3–
Alsopp: Mt (A) 4–
Alston: Bn 3–FD2–
Alston-Roberts-West: FD2–
Altenklingen: Ne 7/400–
Altham: FD2–
Alward: Bn 3–
Ambler: Mt(A) 4–Bn 3 & 4–VH103–AH91–
   FD2–
Abrose: FD1–FD2–
Ames: Mt 23–Bn 4–FD2–FD1–
Amcotts–Ingilby: FD1–
Ameer–Ali: FD1–
Amherst: Ne 2/128–FD1–; FD2–
Amory: Mt 161–Mt(A) 4–Bn 4–AH4, 17–FD
Amphlett: FD1–FD2–
Ampthill: FD1–
Anable: Mt 141–
Ancaster: FD1–
Anderson: Bn 4–AH5–FD1–FD2–
Anderson–Pelham: FD1–FD2–
Anderton: FD2–
Andrewes: FD1–
Andrews: Mt(A) 5 & 4–Bn 4–VH10–FD2–AH6–
Andros: Ne 4/253–Bn 4–
Andrus: Mt(A) 5–FD2–
Angas: FD2–
Ann: FD2–
Anne: FD2–FD1–
Annesley: FD2–FD1–
d'Anglade de Malevas et de Maleure: W2/22
Angst: AS 8–
d'Anselm: W2/23–
Anglesey: FD1–
Angus: FD1–
Annaly: FD1–
Ansbacher: FD2–
Ansell: FD1–FD2–
Anson: FD1–FD2–
Anson-Morton: FD2–
Anstice: FD1–
Anstruther: FD1–
Anstruther-Duncan: FD2–
Anstruther-Gough-Calthorpe: FD2–
Anthonisz: FD1–
Anthony: Bn 4–Mc 2/13–FD2–
Anterroches: Ne 4/260
Antill: BN4–
Antrim: FD1–
Antrobus: FD1–FD2–
Appleton: Ne 1/2–Mt(A) 5–Bn 5–AH 1–FD2–
Appach: FD2–
Apperley: FD2–
Ap Roger: FD2–
Apsey: W1/9–W2/23
Apsley: Ne 6/439–
Apthorpe: Mt(A) 5–Bn 5–
Aranegui: W1/10–W2/24–
Arbuthnot: W2/25–FD1–FD2–
Archdale: FD2–
Archdeacon: Bn 5–
Arcedeckne-Butler: FD2–
Archer: Bn 5–Mc 2/19–VH 71–AH 1–FD1–FD2–
Archer-Houblow: FD2–
Archer-Shee: Ne 8/545–FD2–
Archibald: FD1–FD2–
Ardagh: FD1–
Arden: FD2–
Ardilaun: FD1–
Ardley: FD2–
Argenti: FD2–

Arding: FD2–
Argyll: FD1–
Argyll of the Isles: FD1–
Arkwright: FD1–FD2–
Armistead: Mc 1/12–VH 96–FD2–
Armit: FD2–
Armitage: FD2–FD1–
Armstrong: Bn 5–Ne 8/553–FD1–FD2–
Armstrong of Gallen: FD2–
Armstrong-MacDonnell: FD1–FD2–
Armstrong-Lushington-Tolloch: FD2–
Armytage: FD1–FD2–
Arnold: Mt 76–Bn 5–AH 4–
Arnold-Foster: FD1–FD2–
Arnall-Thomson: FD2–
Arnott: FD2–
Arran: FD1–
Arrol: FD1–FD2–
Arthur: FD1–FD2–
Arthur of Glanomera: FD2–
Artindale: FD2–
Arundell: FD1–FD2–
Ascroft: FD2–
Asbolt: FD2–
Ash: FD2–
Ashbrooke: FD1–
Asburnham: FD1–FD2–
Ashburton: FD1–
Ashby: FD2–
Ashcombe: FD1–
Ashdown: FD2–
Asher: FD2–
Ashfordby-Trenchard: FD2–
Asfordby: Ne 6/381–
Ashenden: Bn 6–
Ashhurst: Mt(A) 5–FD1–FD2–
Ashley: FD2–
Ashley-Cooper: FD1– FD2–
Ashmead-Bartlett: FD1–FD2–
Ashton: Bn 6–VH 11–FD1–FD2–
Ashton-Gwatkin: FD1–FD2–
Ashtown: FD1–
Ashwell: Bn 6–
Ashwin: FD2–
Ashworth: FD2–
Ashwell: Bn 6–
Aske: FD2–
Askew: FD2–
Askew-Robertson: FD2–
Askwith: FD1–FD2–
Aspinwall: Bn 6–
Aspinall: FD2–
Assheton: Bn 6–Ne 8/566–FD1–FD2–
Asseton: FD1–
Aston: Ne 5/308–VH 66–
Astell: FD1–FD2–
Astley: FD1–FD2–
Astley-Corbett: FD1–
Asquith: FD2–
Astor: FD2–
Atcherley: FD2–
Athawes: Bn 6–FD1–
Atherley: FD1–
Atherley-Jones: FD1–
Atherton: Mt(A) 5–FD2–
Athill: FD1–FD2–
Athlumney: FD1–
Atholl: FD1–
Athorpe: FD2–
Atkey: FD1–FD2–
Atkin-Roberts: FD1–FD2–
Atkinson: Mt 65–BN 6–VH 97–AS 10–W1/11
   W2/25 FD1–FD2–
Atkinson-Clark: FD2–
Atlee: Mt 170–Bn 6–
Attenborough: FD1–
Attree: FD1–FD2–

Attwick: Bn 6–
Atwill: Mt 81–
Atwood: Bn 6–FD1–
Attwood: FD2–
Aubertin: FD2–
Auchmuty: Bn 6–
Auckland: FD1–
Auden: FD2–
Augustan Society: AS6–
Austen-Carthell: FD2–
Austen-Leigh: FD2–
Austin: Mt 231–Mt(A) 6–Bn 6–FD1–FD2–
Averill: Mc 1/15
Avery: Ne 4/268–Mt195–Bn 6–
Avonmore: FD1–
Avis: Bn 7–
Awdry: FD1–FD2–
Aykroyd: FD2–
Aylesbury: FD2–
Aylesford: FD1–
Aylmer: FD1–FD2–
Aylwen: FD2–
Aylwin: Bn 7–

Babington: FD2–
Bacchus: FD2–
Bache: FD2–
Bachert: Bn 7–
Back: FD2–
Backhouse: Bn 7–FD1–FD2–
Backus: Mt 87–Bn 7–
Bacon: Ne 7/472–Bn 7–Mc 2/31–VH 58–AH9–
    FD1–FD2–
Baddeley: FD2–
Baden-Powell: FD2–
Badham-Thornhill: FD2–
Baer: Bn 7–
Bagenal: FD2–
Baggall: FD2–
Baggallay: FD2–
Bagge: FD1–FD2–
Bagley: Mt(A) 6–Mt 34–
Bagnall-Wild: FD1–FD2–
Bagnell: FD2–
Bagot: Fd1–FD2–
Bagot-Chester: FD2–
Bagshawe: FD1–FD2–
Bagwell: FD1–
Bagwell–Purefoy: FD2– ˙
Baikie: FD2–
Bailey: Bn 7–FD1–FD2–
Baillie: Bn 7–FD1–FD2–
Baillie-Gage: FD2–
Baillie-Hamilton: FD1–FD2–
Bain: FD1–FD2–
Bainbrigge: FD1–FD2–
Bainbridge: Mt(A) 6–Bn 7–W1/11–W2/26–FD2–
Baines: FD2–
Bainton: Ne 7/508–
Baird: Bn 7–FD1–FD2–
Baker: Mt 96–Bn 7–VH 11–FD1–FD2–
Baker-Cresswell: FD2–
Baker-Wilbraham: FD2–
Balch: Mt 31–Bn 8–
Balche: AH 13–
Balck-Foote: FD2–
Baldwin: Mt(A)6, 92, 131, 153–Bn 7–FD2–
Balfour: FD1–FD2–
Balfour-Melville: FD1–FD2–
Balfour-Paol–FD1–
Ball: Ne 6/418–Bn 8–Mc 2/36–VH86–FD1–FD2–
Ball-Acton: FD1–
Ball-Antine-Dykes: FD2–
Ballagh: Bn 8–
Ballingall: FD2–
Ballord: Bn 8–

Ballou: Bn 8–
Balmanno: BN 8–
Balston: FD2–
Baly: FD2
Bamford: FD1–FD2–
Bamphfylde: FD2–
Banbury: FD2–
Bancker: Bn 8–
Bancroft: Ne 5/338–Bn 9–FD2–
Bandon: FD1–
Banham: FD2–
Bankes: FD2–
Bangor FD1–
Bangs: Mt(A) 6–Bn 9–
Banister: Bn 9–
Banks: Mt(A) 6–Bn 9–FD1–FD2–
Bannerman: FD1–FD2–
Banon: FD2–
Bantry: FD1–
Barbenson: FD2–
Barber: Bn 9–AS 12, AS 14–FD2–
Barber-Starkey: FD2–
Barberie: Bn 9–
Barbour: FD1–FD2–
Barclay: Ne 2/124–Mt(A) 7–AH3–Mt 59–Bn 9–
    Mc 2/50–FD1–FD2–Ne 8/543
Barclay-Allardice: FD1–FD2–
Barberton: W1/11–W2/26–
Barboglio de Gaioncelli: W1/12–W2/27–
Barbey: Bn 9–
Barclays Bank Ltd: W2/27
Barcroft: FD2–
Bard: Bn 9–AH 15–
Bardswell: FD2–
Barham: Ne 7/451–FD2–
Barker: Bn 9–AH 15–
Barksdale: Bn 9–
Baring: FD1–FD2–
Baring-Gould: FD1–FD2–
Barker: FD2–
Barkworth: FD1–
Barling: FD2–
Barlow: Mt(A)7–Bn9–FD1–FD2–
Barlow-Hussicks: FD2–
Barlowe: Ne 6/431
Barnard: Bn 9–FD1–FD2–
Barnardiston: FD1–FD2–
Barnato: FD2–
Barne: FD2–
Barnes: Mt(A)7–FD1–FD2–
Barneby: FD2–
Barnett: FD1–FD2–
Barnewall: FD1–FD2–
Barnston: FD2–
Barney: Bn 10–
Barnwell: Bn 10–
Barr: FD2–
Barradall: Bn 10–VH 11–
Barran: FD2–
Barrell: Bn 10–
Barrett: Ne 7/490–Bn 10–FD2–
Barrett-Hamilton: FD2–
Barrett-Lennard: FD1–FD2–
Barrie: FD2–
Barrington: Bn 10–FD1–FD2–
Barrington-Ward: FD2–
Barrington-White: FD2–
Barron: Bn 10–
Barrow: FD1–FD2–
Barry: Mt 25–Bn 10–FD1–FD2–
Bartenbach: Ne 7/512–
Barthe: Ne 4/302–
Bartholomew: Mt 203–
Bartlett: Mt(A)7–Bn 10–AH 15–FD1–FD2–
Bartlett-Burdett-Coutts: FD1–
Barton: Mt 222–Mt(A)7–Bn 10–FD1–FD2–
Bartow: AH 5–

Bartram: Bn 11–
Barttelot: FD1–FD2–
Barwick: FD2–
Bascom: Mt 66–
Basile: W2/27–
Basing: FD1–
Bashford: FD2–
Baskerville: Ne 5/334–VH11–
Bass: FD1–FD2–
Bassano: FD1–
Basset: FD1–FD2–
Bassett: Bn 11–VH 96–FD1–
Bastard: FD2–
Batcheldor: Bn 11–VH10–
Batchelor: FD2–
Bate: FD1–FD2–
Bateman: FD1–FD2–
Bateman-Hanbury: FD1–FD2–
Bateman-Hanbury-Kincaid-Lennox: FD1–
Bates: Ne 4/285–Bn 11–FD1–FD2–
Bateson: FD2–
Bath: FD1–FD2–
Bathurst: Bn 11–VH12–FD1–FD2–
Batt: Mt(A)8–VH 15–
Batte: Ne 4/298–
Batte-Lay: FD2–
Batten: FD2–
Battersby: FD2–
Battersea: FD1–
Battenberg: FD1–
Batterson: Bn 11–
Battie–Wrightson: FD1–FD2–
Battiscombe: FD1–
Battye-Trevor: FD1–
Bay: Bn 11–
Bayard: Mt(A)8–Bn 11–AH11–
Bayless: Mc 2/53–
Bayley: Bn 11–FD2–
Bayne: AS 186–
Baynes: FD1–FD2–
Bax: FD2–
Bax-Ironside: FD2–
Baxendale: FD2–
Baxter: FD2–
Baynton: Bn 11–
Bayer: FD2–
Bayford: FD2–
Bayley-Worthington: FD2–
Bayliss: FD2–
Bazalgette: FD1–FD2–
Bazeley: FD1–FD2–
Beal: Mt(A)8–Bn 11–Mc 2/56–66–
Beale: Bn 12–VH 13–FD2–
Beamish: FD1–FD2–
Beach: FD2–
Beadnell: FD2–
Beale-Browne: FD2–
Bean: FD2–
Beardmore: FD2–
Beare: Mt 221–
Beardoe-Grundy: FD1–
Beart: FD1–
Beatson: FD1–Fd2–
Beatty: Ne 3/226–Bn 12–FD2–
Beauchamp: FD1–FD2–
Beauclerk: FD2–
Beaufort: FD1–
Beaumont: FD1–FD2–
Beaver: FD2–
Bearley: FD2–
Beazley: FD2–
Beck: Bn 12–FD1–
Becket: Bn 12–
Beckett: FD1–FD2–
Beckett-Turner: FD1–FD2–
Beckford: FD2–

Beckwith: Mt 38–Ne 6/392–Bn 12–Ne 8/392A–
  BN 8/588–VH72–FD1–FD2–
Beddington: FD2–
Bedell: Bn 12–
Bedell-Sivright: FD1–FD2–
Bedford: Bn 12–FD1–FD2–
Bedlow: Bn 12–
Bedon: Bn 12–
Beeby: FD2–
Beech: FD2–
Beecham: FD2–
Beeching: FD2–
Beekman: Ne 2/95–Mt(A)8–Bn 12–AH 3, 17–
(de) Beelen: Mt 142–
Beeman: Bn 12–
Beetham: FD1–FD2–
Beevor: FD1–FD2–
Begbie: FD2–
Behrens: FD2–
Beit: FD2–
Belcher: Ne 4/283–Mt(A)8–Bn 12–13,–AH4,–
  FD1–
Belchier: Bn 13–
Beley: AS 16–W1/12–W2/27, W2/28–
Belhaven: FD1–
Belilios: FD2–
Belknap: Mt 45–
Bell: Bn 13–Mc 2/78, 82–AH6–FD1–FD2–
Bell-Clothier: FD2–
Bellairs: FD1–FD2–
Bellamy: FD2–
Bellasis: FD1–
Bellew: FD1–Fd2–
Bellingham: Mt 204–Bn 13–FD1–FD2–
Bellwood: W1/12–W2/29–
Belmont: Bn 13–
Belmore: FD1–
Belper: FD1–
Belt: Mc 2/106–
Bemrose: FD2–
Benbow: FD2–
Bence: FD2–
Bence-Lambert: FD1–FD2–
Bendall: FD2–
Bendyshe: FD2–
Benett-Stanford: FD2–
Benger: Bn 13–
Bengough: FD2–
Benham: Mt(A)9–
Benison: FD2–
Benjamin: Mt(A)9–Mt 199–Bn13–Mc 1/18–
Benn: FD1–FD2–
Bennett: Mt 146–Bn 14–VH82–W1/13–W2/29–
  FD2–
Bennitt: FD1–FD2–
Bennow: Ne 2/78–
Benson: Bn 14–FD2–
Bentinck: FD2–
Bentley: FD1–FD2–
Benyon: FD2–
Bere: FD2–
Berens-Dowdeswell: FD2–
Beresford: Bn 14–FD1–FD2–
Beresford-Peirse: FD1–FD2–
Berger: FD2–
Bergman: Ne 5/359–
Bergne-Coupland: FD2–
Beridge: FD2–
Berington: FD2–
Berkeley: Ne 4/263–Bn 14–FD1–FD2–
Berkeley-Portman: FD1–
Berkeley-Weld: FD2–
Bernard: Ne 3/195–Ne 2/130–Mt(A)9–Bn 14–
  VH 13/71–FD1–FD2–
Berners: FD1–
Berney: FD1–Fd2–
Bernon: Bn 14–

Berridge: FD2–
Berry: Bn 14–Mc 1/23–Mc 2/112–FD2–
Bertie: FD1–Fd2–
Bertram: FD2–
Bertrand: FD2–
Bertrand de la Grassiere: W2/175–
Berwick: FD1–
Bessborough: FD1–
Besseher: FD1–
Besanot: FD2–
Best: W1/13–W2/30–FD1–FD2–
Best Dalison: FD2–
Beswick-Boyds: FD1–
Betham: FD2–
Bethell: FD1–Fd2–
Bethel: FD1–
Bethune: Bn 14–AH4–FD2–
Betton: Bn 14–
Betts: Mt(A)9–Bn 15–AH16–FD2–
Bevan: Mt 89–FD2–
Beveridge: FD2–
Beverley: Ne 4/300–Bn 15–VH 74–
Bewes: FD2–
Bewicke: FD1–FD2–
Bewicke-Copley: FD1–Fd2–
Bewley: FD2–
Benyon: FD1–FD2–
Bibby: Mt(A)9–FD2–
Bickerton: Bn 15–
Bickersteth: FD2–
Bicket: FD2–
Bickford-Smith: FD1–
Bickley: Ne 7/500–VH16–
Bicknell: FD2–
Bidder: FD2–
Biddle: Mt(A)10–Bn 15–
Biddulph: FD1–FD2–
Bidie: FD2–
Bigelow: Mt(57), 34–Bn 14–
Biggar: Bn 15–
Bigge: Ne 6/428–FD2–
Bigger: Bn 15–
Bigham: FD2–
Bigland: FD2–
Biles: FD2–
Bill: Bn 15–FD1–
Billiat: FD2–
Billings: Bn 15–Mc 2/119–
Billingsley: New 7/520–
Bilsland: FD2–
Bingham: Bn 15–FD1–FD2–
Bingley: FD2–
Binney: Bn 15–FD1–FD2–
Bindloss: FD1–
Birch: FD1–
Birch-Reynardson: FD1–FD2–
Birchall: FD1–
Birchenough: FD2–
Bird: FD2–
Birdwood: FD1–Fd2–
Birkbeck: FD1–FD2–
Birkin: FD2–
Birkmure: FD2–
Birley: FD2–
Birnie: Mt(A)9–
Birrell: FD2–
Birt: FD2–
Biscoe: FD1–FD2–
Bishop: FD1–FD2–
Bishop-Culpeper-Clayton: FD2–
Bispham: Bn 15–
Bisset: FD2–
Blachford: FD1–Bn 16–
Black: FD2–Bn 15–
Blackborn: FD1–
Blackburn: FD2–
Blackburne: FD2–

Blackburne-Haze: FD1–
Blachly: Bn 15–
Blackden: FD2–
Blacker: FD2–
Blacker-Douglas: FD2–
Blackett: FD1–FD2–
Blackett-Ord: FD2–
Blackie: FD2–
Blackman: FD2–
Blackstock: Bn 16–
Blackwell: Ne 6/409–Bn 16–
Blackwood: FD1–FD2–
Bladen: Bn 16–
Blades: FD2–
Bladon: W1/14–W2/30–FD2–
Blagg: FD2–
Blaine: FD1–
Blair: Bn 16–FD1–FD2–
Blake: Mt 43, 139–Mt(A)10–AH15–Ne 5/354–
    Bn 16–Mc 2/121–FD1–FD2–
Blake-Deburgh: FD2–
Blake-Humfrey: FD2–
Blakiston: Ne 8/552–Ne 8/526–FD1–FD2–
Blakiston-Houston: FD2–
Blanchard: Mt 41–Bn 16–
Bland: FD2–Ne 6/445–Bn 16–VH17–
Blanckensee: Ne 8/581–
Blandford: FD1–
Blandy: FD2–
Blane: FD1–FD2–
Blatchford: Bn 16–
Blantyre: FD1–
Blathwayt: FD2–
Blaxland: FD2–
Blayney: Bn 16–
Blee(c)ker: Mt(A)10–Bn 16–AH3–
Blencowe: FD2–
Blenner-Hassett: FD1–FD2–
Blick: FD2–
Bligh: FD1–FD2–
Blight: Bn 16–FD2–
Bliss: Bn 16–
Bliven: Mt(A) 10–
Block: FD2–
Blodgett: Bn 17–
Blofeld: FD2–
(de) Blois: Ne 5/310–FD1–FD2–
Blomefield: FD1–FD2–
Blomfield: FD1–
Blood: FD2–
Bloodgood: Bn 17–
Bloomfield: Bn 17–FD1–FD2–
Bloss: Mt 27–Mc 2/133–
Blossom: Mt 65–
Blount: Mt 57–Bn 17–FD1–FD2–
Blundell: FD2–
Blundell-Holinshead-Blundell: FD2–
Blunden: FD1–FD2–
Blunt: FD1–FD2–
Blyth: FD2–
Blythswood: FD1–
Boadle: FD2–
Boag: FD1–
Board: FD2–
Boardman: Mt 156–Bn 17–
Boas: Bn 17–
Boase: FD2–
Boddington: FD2–
Boddy: FD1–
Boden: FD1–FD2–
Bodfish: Bn 17–
Body: FD2–
Boehm: FD1–
Boerum: Mt(A)10–
Bogart: Bn 17–
Boger: FD2–
Boileau: FD1–FD2–

Boilead: FD2–
Boker: Bn 17–
Bolckow: FD1–
Boldero: FD2–
Bolding: FD2–
Boles: FD2–
Bolingbroke: FD1–
Bolitho: FD1–FD2–
Bolles: Mt(A)10–Ne 1/16–Bn 17–
Bolling: Bn 17–Mc 2/136–VH18–
Bolognese: W2/31
Bolton: FD1–FD2–Bn 17 & 18–AH5–
Bolster: FD2–
Bonaparte: Ne 5/321–
Bonar: W2/31–FD2–
Bond: Bn 18–FD1–FD2–
Bonham: FD1–FD2–
Bonner: Mt 148–Bn 18–AH 90–
Bonsor: FD2–
Bontein: FD1–FD2–
Bonython: Mt(A)11–Ne 1/53–FD2–
Booker: Mc 2/142–FD2–
Bonney: FD1–
Booker-Blakemore: FD2–
Boone: Bn 18–
Booraem: Mt/129–
Boord: FD1–FD2–
Boot: FD2–
Booth: Bn 18–Mc 1/26–VH14–FD1–FD2–
Boothby: FD1–FD2–
Bootle-Wilbraham: FD1–FD2–
Borch: W1/14–W2/31–
Borden: FD2–
Boreel: FD1–
Borland: Ne 5/314–Bn 18–
Borlase-Warren-Venables: FD1–
Borley: FD2–
Borough: FD2–
Borrer: FD1–FD2–
Borrowes: FD1–FD2–
Borthwick: W1/15–W2/31–FD1–FD2–
Borton: FD1–
Borwick: FD2–
Bosanquet: FD1–FD2–
Bosca di Roveto: W2/175–
Boscawen: FD1–FD2–
Bossom: W2/32–FD2–
Bostock: FD2–
Boston: Mt(A)11–FD1–
Bosville: FD1–FD2–
Boswell: FD2–
Bostwick: Mt(A)11–Bn 18–
Both: W2/33–
Botha: W1/15–W2/33–
Botry-Pigott: FD1–
Boucher: Bn 18–FD2–
Boughey: FD1–FD2–
Boulton: FD2–
Bourchier: Ne 7/451–Bn 18–
Boudinot: Bn 18–
Bourbon: W2/35–
Bourbon-Two-Scilies: W2/35–
Bourke: FD1–FD2–
Bourke-Borrowes: FD2–
Bourne: Bn 19–W2/37–FD1–FD2–
Bournes: FD2–
Bousfield: FD2–
Boush: Bn 19–
Boutcher: FD2–
Boutelle: Mt(A)11–
Bouth: FD1–
Bouverie-Pusey: FD2–
Bouwens: FD2–
Bowater: FD2–
Bowden: Ne 6/437–FD2–
Bowden-Smith: FD1–
Bowditch: Ne 1/22–Bn 19–

Bowdoin: Bn 19–
Bowen: Ne 1/3–Mt(A)11–Bn 19–FD1–FD2–
Bowen-Colthurst: FD2–
Bower: FD1–FD2–
Bowers: Bn 19–
Bowes: Ne 2/119–Mt(A)11–Bn 19–FD1–FD2–
Bowes-Lyon: FD2–
Bowie: Mt 108–Bn 19–VH19–
Bowker: FD2–
Bowlby: FD1–FD2–
Bowles: VH97–FD1–FD2–
Bowly: Bn 20–
Bowman: Bn 20–FD1–FD2–
Bowring: FD1–FD2–
Bowring-Hanbury: FD2–
Bowyer: FD1–FD2–
Bowyer-Smith: FD1–FD2–
Boxall: FD2–
Boyce: FD2–
Boyd: Mt(A)12–Bn 20–Ne 8/577–W1/16–W2/37–
    FD1–FD2–
Boyd-Rochfort: FD2–
Boyes: FD2–
Boyle: FD1–FD2–
Boylston: Bn 20–AH 92–
Boyne: FD1–
Boynton: FD1–FD2–
Bozman: Bn 20–
Brabazon: FD1–FD2–
Brabourne: FD1–
Brace: FD2–
Bracey: Ne 1/55–
Brackenbury: FD2–
Brackett: Bn 20–
Bradbrooke: FD2–
Bradburn: FD2–
Bradbury: Ne 2/139–Bn 20–FD1–FD2–
Braddick: FD1–FD2–
Braddon: FD1–
Bradford: Mt 12–Bn 20–AH 13–FD1–FD2–
Bradish-Ellames: FD2–
Bradjurst: Mt 30–
Bradley: Mt 94–Bn 20–
Bradney: FD1–FD2–
Bradshaw: Bn 20–FD2–
Bradstreet: Mt 12, 62, 134–AH 14–Ne 2/145–
    Bn 20–FD1–
Brady: FD1–FD2–
Bragdon: Bn 21–
Bragge: FD1–
Braithwaite: FD1–FD2–
Brampton: FD2–
Bramston: FD2–
Bramwell: FD1–
Branch: VH 104–
von Brancovan: AS 18–
Brand: FD1–FD2–
Brandram: FD2–
Brandreth: FD1–
Brandford: Bn 21–
Branton-Day: FD1–
Branfill: FD2–
Branston: FD2–
Brasher: Bn 21–
Brasier: FD2–
Brasier-Creagh: FD2–
Brassey: FD1–FD2–
Brattle: Bn 21–AH 14–
Braund: FD2–
Bray: Bn 21–VH 7–
Braybrooke: FD1–
Braye: FD1–
Brayton: Bn 21–
Brazer: Bn 21–
Breadalbane: FD1
Brearly: Bn 21–
Breck: Bn 21–

Breed: Bn 21–
Breese: Mt(A)12–AH 14–
Bredin: FD2–
Bredon: FD2–
Brent: Mt(A) 12–Bn 21–Mc 1/30–VH20–
Brenton: Mt(A)12–Ne 2/91–AH 120–
Brereton: Mt 32–Bn 21–
Bretherton: FD1–FD2–
Brett: Mt(A)13–Bn 21–FD1–FD2–
Brevitt: FD2–
Brew-Mulhallen: FD2–
Brewer: Mt(A)13–Ne 7/514–Bn 21–
Brewer-Williams: FD2–
Brewin: FD1–
Brewster: Mt 11, 109, 116, 123, 154, 225–Bn 21
   & 22–AH4–
Brice: Mt(A)13–
Bridge: Bn 22–FD1–FD2–
Bridgen: Bn 22–
Bridgeman: FD1–FD2–
Bridger: Ne 4/287–FD2–
Bridges: FD1–FD2–
Bridgford: FD2–
Bridgman: Bn 22–
Brigden: Bn 22–
Bridport: FD1–
Bridson: FD2–
Brierly: FD2–
Brigg: FD2–
Briggs: Ne 3/221–Mt(A)13–Bn 22–FD1–
   Brigham: Bn 22–
Brigham: Bn 22–
Bright: Mt(A)13–Bn 22–AH 6–FD1–FD2–
Brightley: Bn 22–
Brigstocke: FD2–
Brimacombe: FD2–
Brimage: Bn 22–
Brinatti: W2/38–
Brinckerhoff: Bn 22–
Brinckman: FD1–FD2–
Brine: FD2–
Brinkley: FD2–
Brinley: Ne 4/248–Bn 22–AH6–
Brinton: FD1–FD2–
Brisbane: Bn 22 & 23–FD1–FD2–
Brisbin: Ne 8/544, 8/575, 8/576–
Briscoe: Mt 107–FD1–FD2–
Bristol: FD1–
Bristow: VH 22–
Brittain: W1/16–W2/38–
Britton: FD1–FD2–
Broadbent: FD1–FD2–
Broadhead: Bn 23–FD2–
Broadhurst: FD2–
Broadrick: FD1–FD2–
Broadwood: FD2–
Brock: FD2–
Brockett: Mt 119–Bn 23–
Brocklebank: FD1–FD2–
Brocklehurst: FD1–FD2–
Brodhurst: FD1–
Brodie: FD1–FD2–
Brodnax: Bn 23–VH75–
Brodribb: FD1–FD2–
Brodrick: FD1–FD2–
Brogan: FD2–
Brogdew: FD2–
Brogden: FD2–
Broke: FD1–FD2–
Brome: Mc 1/35–
Bromfield: Mt(A)13–Ne 6/410–Bn 23–
Bromhead: FD1–FD2–
Bromley: FD1–FD2–
Bromley-Wilson: FD2–
Brook: FD2–Ne 5/349
Brook-Hitching: FD2–
Brooke: FD1–FD2–Mt 189–Mc 1/40–

Brooke-Pechell: FD2–
Brooke-Popham: FD2–
Brookes: FD2–
Brookfield: FD1–FD2–
Brookings: Bn 23–
Brookman: FD2–
Brooks: FD1–FD2–Mt(A)14–Mt 232–Bn 23–
Brooksbank: FD1–FD2–
Broome: Mt 206–Bn 23–
Brotherton: FD2–Mt 230–
Brough: FD1–
Brougham: FD1–FD2–
Broughton: FD1–FD2–Mt(A)14–Ne 2/109–Bn
   23–
Broughton-Adderley: FD2–
Brown: FD1–FD2–Mt 205–Bn 23 & 24–Mc 1/46–
   AH5–W1/17–W2/39–
Brown-Morison: W2/38–
Brown-Westhead: FD1–FD2–
Browne: FD1–FD2–Mt(A)14–Ne 1/54, 5/361–
   Bn 24–Mc 2/148–V.H.23/24–AH8, 17–
Brown-Lecky: FD2–
Browne-Synge-Hutch: FD2–
Brownfield: FD2–
Brownhill: FD2–
Brownlow: FD1–FD2–
Brownell: Mt 29–Bn 24–
Brownrigg: FD1–FD2–
Bruce: FD1–FD2–Ne 5/323–
Bruce-Hiller: FD2–
Bruce-Porter: FD2–
Brudenell: FD2–
Brudenell-Bruce: FD1–FD2–
Bruen: FD2–
Brun: Mt 210–
Brune: Mt(A)14–Bn 25–Mc 1/50–
Brunner: FD2–
Bruns: AS 20–
Brunton: FD2–
Brush: AS 24, AS 26, AS 28–
Bryan: FD2–
Bryant: FD2–Mt 37–Mc 2/150–
Brysdon: FD2–
Brymer: FD2–
Buccleugh: FD1–
Buchan: FD1–FD2–
Buchan-Hepburn: FD1–FD2–
Buchanan: FD1–FD2–Bn 25–
Buchanan-Jardine: FD2–
Buchanan-Dunlop: FD2–
Buchanan-Riddell: FD1–FD2–
Buchannan: FD1–FD2–
Buck: W1/17–W2/40–
Buckingham: FD2–
Buckinghamshire: FD1–
Buckland: FD2–
Buckle: FD1–FD2–Bn 25–W1/18–W2/40–
Buckler: FD1–FD2–Bn 25–
Buckley: FD1–FD2–
Buckmaster: FD2–
Buckner: FD1–FD2–V.H. 108–
Buckworth-Herne-Soame: FD1–FD2–
Budd: FD2–
Buddicom: FD2–
Bude: Bn 25–
Budgett: FD2–
Buek: Ne 1/63–
Bulfin: FD2–
Bulfinch: Bn 25–
Bulkeley: FD1–Ne 1/4–Bn 25–
Bulkley: Mt(A)–Bn 25–AH1–
Bull: FD2–Bn 26–Ne 8/580
Bullard: Bn 26–
Buller: FD1–FD2–
Buller-Fullerton-Elphinstone: FD2–
Bullock: FD2–Mc 2/157
Bullough: FD2–

Bulman: FD1–FD2–
Bullmore: FD2–
Bult: Bn 26–
Bulwer: FD1–FD2–
Bulwer-Lytton: FD2–
Bunbury: FD1–FD2–
Bunbury-Tighe: FD1–FD2–
Bunten: FD1–
Burbridge: FD2–
Burch: FD2–Mt 183–
Burchardt-Ashton: FD2–
Burden: Bn 26–
Burder: FD2–Bn 26–
Burdett: FD1–FD2–Bn 26–
Burdett-Coutts: FD2–
Burdick: FD2–
Burdon: FD1–FD2–
Burdon-Sanderson: FD1–FD2–
Burdwan: FD2–
Burges: FD2–
Burgess: Bn 26–
Burgoyne: FD1–FD2–
Burgoyne-Wallace: FD2–
Burke: FD1–FD2–
Burkett-Gottwaltz: FD2–
Burleigh: Mt(A)15–
Burlton: FD2–
Burman: FD2–
Burn: FD2–
Burn-Murdock: FD2–
Burn-Callander: FD2–
Burnaby: FD1–FD2–
Burnard: FD1–FD2–
Burne: FD2–
Burne-Jones: FD1–
Burnes: FD2–
Burnet: Ne 5/312–Bn 26–AH6–
Burnett: FD1–FD2–
Burnett-Stuart: FD2–
Burney: FD1–FD2–
Burnham: Mt 29–Bn 26–AH14–
Burnley-Campbell: FD2–
Burns: FD1–FD2–
Burns-Hartopp: FD2–
Burns-Lindow: FD1–FD2–
Burnyeat: FD2–
Burr: FD2– Bn 27–
Burra: FD1–FD2–
Burrard: FD1–FD2–
Burrage: Mt 16–
Burrel: FD1–
Burrell: FD2–
Burrill: Bn 26–
Burrill-Robinson: FD2–
Burrough: FD1–FD2–Ne 3/220–
Burroughes: FD2–
Burroughs: FD1–
Burrow: FD2–
Burrowes: FD2–Mt(A)15–
Burrows: FD1–FD2–Bn 26–
Burt: FD1–Mt 40–Bn 27–
Burt-Marshall: FD2–
Burtchaell: FD1–FD2–
Burton: FD1–FD2–Mc 1/56–
Burton-Lingen: FD2–
Burton Mackenzie: FD1–FD2–
Bury: FD2–
Burry-Barry: FD2–
Burwell: Mt 160–Mt(A)15–Bn 27–V.H.33–
  AH121–
Busfield: FD2–
Bush: FD1–FD2–Mt(A)15–
Bushby: FD1–FD2–
Bushe: FD1–FD2–
Bushnell: Mt(A)16–Mt 154–
Busk: FD1–
Bussey: Mt(A)16–

Butcher: FD2–Bn 27–
Bute: FD1–
Butler: FD1–FD2–Ne 5/369–Mt(A)16–Bn 27–
  V.H.79–AH12–
Butler-Bowdon: FD2–
Butler-Fitzgerald: FD2–
Butler-Kearney: FD2–
Butt: FD2–Mc 1/62–
Butt-Gow: FD2–
Butter: FD2–
Butterfield: FD2–
Butterwick: FD2–
Butts: FD2–
Buxton: FD1–FD2–
Byass: FD2–
Byfield: Ne 2/137–Bn 27–
Byington: Mt 68–
Byng: FD1–FD2–
Byrd: FD2–Ne 3/174–Bn 27–V.H.103–
Byrne: FD2–
Byron: FD1–FD2–
Bythesea: FD1–
Bywater: FD2–
Byworth: FD2–

Cabell: Mt 217–Mt(A)16–Bn 28–V.H.104–
Caborne: FD2–
Cabot: Bn 28–
Caddy: FD2–
Cadell: FD2–
Cadena: Bn 28–
Cadman: FD2–
Cadogan: FD1–FD2–
Cadwalader: Mt 184–
Cafe: FD2–
Caffey: AS 32, AS 34–
Cahill: FD2–Bn 28–
Caillard: FD2–
Caillaud: Bn 28–
Cain: FD2–
Cairnes: FD2–
Cairns: FD1–FD2–
Caithness: FD1–
Calcraft: FD1–
Calder: FD2–Ne 2/100–
Caldwell: FD2–Bn 28–
Caledon: FD1–
Caley: FD2–
Calhoun: Mt 213–Bn 28–
Call: FD1–
Callaghan: FD2–
Callard: FD2–
Callaway: Bn 29–
Callender: Bn 29–
Callender-Brodis: FD2–
Calley: FD2–
Calmady: FD1–
Calmady-Hamlyn: FD2–
Calthorp: 7/492–
Calthorpe: FD1–V.H.26–
Calverley: FD2–
Calvert: FD1–FD2–Mt 128–Ne 2/147–Bn 29–
  Mc 2/163–V.H.63–
Cambridge: FD1–FD2–Bn 29–
Camden: FD1–
Cameron: FD1–FD2–
Cameron-Head: FD2–
Camm: Bn 29–V.H.68–
Cammell: FD1–FD2–
Cammock: Ne 3/176–
Camoys: FD1–
Camp: Bn 29–
Campbell: FD1–FD2–Mt 150–Mt(A)16– Bn 29–
  Ne 4/306, 6/396, 400–W1/19–W1/20–W2/42–
  W2/43–
Campbell-Bannerman: FD1–

Campbell-Meiklejohn: FD2–
Campbell-Orde: FD1–
Campbell-Swinton: FD1–FD2–
Camperdown: FD1–
Candee: Mt(A)17–
Candler: FD2–Bn 29–
Cane: FD2–
Canfield: Mt(A)17–
Cannan: FD2–
Canning: FD1–FD2–
Cantelupe: FD1–
Canterbury: FD1–
Cantley: FD2–
Cantrell-Hubberstry: FD1–FD2–
Cantwell: FD2–
Capel: FD2–FD1–
Capel-Carnegy-Arbuthnot: FD2–
Capell: FD1–FD2–
Capen: Mt(A)17–
Capper: FD2–
Capron: FD2–
Carbery: FD1–
Carbutt: FD1–
Carden: FD1–FD2–
Cardew: FD2–
Carew: FD1–FD2–
Carey: FD2–
Carey-Thomas: FD2–
Carfrae: FD2–
Cargill: FD2–
Cargill-Thompson: W2/43–
Carhart: Mc 2/168–
Carington: FD1–FD2–
Carleton: FD1–FD2–Mt(A)17–Mt 216–
Carlile: FD2–
Carlingford: FD1–
Carlisle: FD1–
Carlton: FD2–
Carlyon: FD2–
Carlyon-Britton: FD2–
Carmichael: FD1–FD2–Bn 30–
Carmichael-Anstruther: FD1–FD2–
Carmichael-Ferrall: FD2–
Carnarvon: FD1–
Carnduff: FD2–
Carnegie: FD1–FD2–
Carnegy: FD2–
Carnegy-Arbuthnot: FD2–
Carnegy-de-Balinhard: FD2–
Carnwath: FD1–
Carpendale: FD2–
Carpenter: FD2–Mt 230–Mt(A)18–Bn 30–AH16–
Carpenter-Garnier: FD1–FD2–
(de) Carpenteir: Ne 6/424–
Carr: FD1–FD2–Mt(A)18–Bn 30–
Carr-Ellison: FD2–
Carr-Gomm: FD1–FD2–
Carrick: FD1–
Carriere: W1/20–W2/44–
Carrington: FD1–FD2–Bn 30–V.H.95–
Carritt: FD1–Mt 57–
Carroll: FD1–FD2–Mt 231–Mt(A)18–Bn 30–
Ne 3/234–Mc 1/66, 2/170–AH9–AS 36–
Carroll-Irwin: FD2–
(de) Carron: Mt 177–
Carruthers: FD2–
Carson: FD2–Mc 1/73–
Cart: FD2–
Carter: FD1–FD2–Mt 111, 188–Bn 30–V.H.87/
97–
Carteret: Ne 2/117–
Carthew: FD2–
Carthew-Yorstoun: FD1–FD2–
Cartier: FD1–
Cartland: FD2–
Cartwright: FD1–FD2–Bn 30–AS 38–W1/21–
W2/44–

Carus-Wilson: FD1–FD2–
Carver: Ne 3/198–Bn 31–
Cary: FD1–FD2–Ne 7/458–Bn 30–Mc 1/80–
V.H.104–AH9–
Cary-Caddell: FD2–
Cary-Elwes: FD1–
Carysfort: FD1–
Case: FD2–Bn 31–
Casement: FD2–
Casey: FD2–
Cass: FD1–FD2–
Cass-Tewart: FD2–
Cassan: FD2–
Cassel: FD2–
Cassels: FD2–
Casteel: Ne 7/459–
Castello: FD2–
Castle: FD2–Bn 31–
Castlehow: FD2–
Castlemaine: FD1–
Castle-Stuart: FD2–
Castletown: FD1–
Cater: FD2–
Cathcart: FD1–
Catherwood: Bn 31–
Catlin: Bn 31–
Caton: FD2–
Cator: FD2–
Catt: FD2–
Catto: FD2–
Caulfield: FD1–FD2–
Causton: FD1–
Cautley: FD2–
Cavalleri: W1/21–W2/44–
Cavan: FD1–
Cave: FD1–FD2–
Verney-Cave: FD2–
Cave-Browne-Cave: FD1–FD2–
Cave-Brown: FD2–
Cave-Orme: FD2–
Cavendish: FD1–FD2–
Cavendish-Bentinck: FD1–FD2–
Cavenagh: FD2–
Cavenaugh-Mainwaring: FD2–
Caverly: Bn 31–AH9–
Cawdor: FD1–
Cawley: FD2–
Cawston: FD2–
Cawthorne: FD2–
Cawthra: FD2–
Cay: Bn 31–V.H.9–
Cayley: FD1–FD2–
Cayne: Ne 3/205–
Cayzer: FD1–FD2–
Cazalet: FD1–FD2–
Cazenove: FD2–
Cecil: FD1–FD2–
Cely-Trevilian: FD2–
Chads: FD2–
Chadwick: FD1–FD2–
Chadwyck-Healey: FD2–
Chaffee: Mt(A)18–
Chafy-Chafy: FD1–
Chalice: FD2–
Chalker: FD2–
Challinor: FD2–
Chalmers: FD2–FD1–Bn 31–
Chaloner: FD1–FD2–Bn 31–AH6–
Chamberlain: FD1–FD2–Mt(A)18–Bn 32–
Chamberlayne: FD2–
Chamberlin: FD2–
Chambers: FD1–FD2–Bn 32–
Chambre: FD2–
Chambres: FD2–
Chamier: FD1–FD2–
Chamney: FD2–
Champernowne: Ne 2/138–

Champion: FD2–Bn 32–
Champion-de-Crespigny: FD1 -FD2–
Champley: FD1–
Chance: FD1–FD2–
Chancellor: FD2–Mt(A)18–
Chandlee: FD1–
Chandler: Mt(A)19–Bn 32–AH16–
Chandos-Pole: FD2–
Channell: FD2–
Channer: W1/21–W2/44–
Channing: FD1–
Chapin: Bn 32–
Chapman: FD1–FD2–
Chaplin: FD2–
Chapline: Mc 2/174–
Chapman: Mt(A)19–Bn 32–V.H.16–
Chapman-Purchas: FD2–
Charlemont: FD1–
Charles: FD2–Bn 32–
Charlesworth: FD2–
Charleville: FD1–
Charley: FD1–FD2–W2/45–
Charlton: FD2–
Charnock: Bn 32–
Charrington: FD2–
Charteris: FD2–
Chase: Mt 104–Mt(A)19–Bn 33–AH4–
(de) Chastel: Ne 7/459–
Chatfield: Ne 2/134–
Chatterton: FD2–Bn 33–
Chattock: FD2–
Chatwin: FD2–
Chaunc(e)y: Mt(A)19–Ne 2/86–Bn 33–AH6–
Chauvel: FD2–
Chavasse: FD2–
Chaworth-Musters: FD2–
Chaytor: FD1–FD2–
Cheape: FD1–FD2–
Checkland: FD1–FD2–
Checkley: Mt(A)20–Bn 33–
Cheetham: FD1–FD2–
Cheever: Bn 33–
Cheevers: AS 40–
Chelmsford: FD1–
Chenoweth: Mt 132–Mc 1/86, 2/179–
Cherry-Garrard: FD2–
Chesebrough: Bn 33–
Chesham: FD1–
Chester: FD1–FD2–Mt(A)20–Ne 1/48–Bn 33–
Chester-Master: FD2–
Chesterfield: FD1–
Chetwode: FD2–
Chetwood: Ne 4/246–
Chetwood-Aiken: FD1–FD2–
Chetwynd: FD1–FD2–
Chetwynd-Stapylton: FD2–
Chetwynd-Talbot: FD1–FD2–
de la Chevalerie: W1/22–W2/46–
Chevers: FD2–
Chevreul: W1/22–W2/46–
Chew: Mt(A)20–Bn 34–Mc 2/181–V.H.33–
  AH113–
Chewton: FD1–
Cheylesmore: FD1–
Cheyne: FD2–
Chibnall: FD2–
Chicheley: V.H.79–
Chichester: FD1–FD2–V.H.77–
Chichester-Constable: FD2–
Chidson: Bn 34–
Chignell: FD2–
Chilcott: FD1–FD2–
Child: FD1–FD2–Bn 34–
Child-Villiers: FD1–FD2–
Childe: FD2–
Childe-Freeman: FD2–
Childs: Mt 103–

Chilton: Mc 1/89–
Chinnery-Haldene: FD2–
Chisenhale-Marsh: FD2–
Chisholm: W1/23–W2/46–
Chisholm-Batten: FD1–FD2–
Cholmeley: FD1–FD2–
Cholmeley-Jones: Mt 47–
Cholmondeley: FD1–FD2–
Chovil: FD2–
Christian: FD2–
Christie: FD1–FD2–
Christie-Miller: FD2–
Christison: FD1–FD2–
Christmas: Mt 161–
Christopher: FD2–
Christopherson: FD2–
Christy: FD2–
Chrystie: Mt 161–Bn 34–
Chubb: FD2–
Chumasero: Mt 86–
Church: FD2–
Churchill: FD2–FD2–Mt 133, 192–Bn 34–V.H.
  17–
Churchman: FD2–
Churnside: FD2–
Churston: FD1–
Chute: Ne 1/46–Mt(A)20–Bn 34–AH6–
Cinnamond: FD2–
Clagget: Bn 34–Ne 8/525–
Claghorn: Bn 34–
Claiborne: Ne 7/466–Mt(A)21–Bn 34–V.H.95–
Clancarty: FD1–
Clanmorris: FD1–
Clapp: Bn 34–
Clapton: FD2–
Clare: FD2–
Clarendon: FD2–FD1–
Claricarde: FD1–
Clanwilliam: FD1–
Clarina: FD1–
Clark: FD1–FD2–Mt(A)20–Bn 35–Mc 2/187–
  W2/47–
Clark-Kennedy: FD2–
Clark-Lloyd: FD2–
Clarke: FD1–FD2–Ne 1/33–Mt(A)20–Bn 35–
  V.H.75–Nc 8/571–
Clarke-Butler-Cole: FD2–
Clarke-Jervoise: FD1–FD2–
Clarke-Thornhill: FD2–
Clarke-Travers: FD1–
Clarkson: Ne 7/503–Mt(A)21–Bn 35–AH14–
Clauson: FD2–
Clavering: FD1–
Clay: FD1–FD2–Mt(A)21–
Clay-Ker-Seymer: FD2–
Clayborne: AH9–
Clayhills-Henderson: FD2–
Claypoole: Bn 36–
Clayton: FD1–FD2–Bn 36–V.H.32–Ne 8/538–
Clayton-East: FD1–FD2–
Cleborne: Bn 36–
Clegg: FD1–FD2–
Clegg-Hill: FD2–
Cleghorn: FD2–
Cleland: FD2–
Henderson-Cleland: FD2–
Clement: Ne 1/37–Bn 36–Mc 1/97–
Clements: FD1–FD2–
Clemison: FD2–
Clench: FD1–
Clerk: FD1–FD2–Bn 36–
Clerk-Rattray: FD1–
Clerke: FD1–
Clermont: FD1–
Cleveland: FD1–Mt(A)21–AH141–
Clifden: FD1–
Cliff-McCullough: FD2–

Cliffe: FD2–
Clifford: FD1–FD2–Bn 36–
Clifford-Constable: FD1–
Clifton: FD1–FD2–
Clifton-Hogg: FD2–
Clifton-Robinson: FD2–
Clinton: FD1–FD2–Ne 3/224–Mt 157–AH3–
  Mt(A)21–Ne 2/80–Bn 36–
Clippingdale: FD2–
Clive: FD2–
Cloete: FD2–
Clonbrock: FD1–
Cloncurry: FD1–
Clonmell: FD1–
Clopton: Ne 5/341–Bn 36–V.H.21–
Close: FD2–
Close-Brooks: FD1–FD2–
Closieres: W2/47–
Clothier: FD2–Mt 16–
Clough: FD1–FD2–
Clough-Taylor: FD2–
Clover: FD2–
Clowes: FD2–Bn 36–
Clutterbuck: FD2–
Coakley: Mt(A)21–
Coale: Mc 2/189–
Coape-Arnold: FD1–FD2–
Coats: FD2–
Coates: FD2–
Cobb: FD1–Bn 36–
Cobbe: FD2–
Cobham: FD1–FD2–
Cochran: FD2–Mt(A)22–Bn 36–
Cochran-Patrick: FD2–
Cochrane: FD2–Mt 59–
Cochrane-Baillie: FD2–
Cock: FD2–Bn 36–V.H.83–
Cockayne: Bn 36–
Cockayne-Cust: FD1–FD2–
Cockburn: FD1–FD2–
Cockburn-Campbell: FD1–FD2–
Cockburn-Hood-Shapland: FD2–
Cockbron-Campbell: FD1–
Cocke: Bn 36–V.H.23–
Cockerell: FD2–
Cockle: W1/23–W2/47–
Cocks: FD1–FD2–
Cocquiel: Ne 7/500–
Codd: FD2–V.H.23–
Coddington: FD2–Bn 36–AH14–
Codman: Bn 37–
Codrington: FD1–FD2–
Coe: Ne 5/337–
Coffey: FD2–
Coffin: FD2–Mt(A)22–Bn 37–AH4–
Coggeshall: Ne 1/10–Bn 37–AH14–
Coggin: FD2–
Coghill: FD1–FD2–
Coghlan: FD2–
Cohen: FD2–Bn 37–
Cokayne: FD1–FD2–
Coke: FD1–FD2–
Coker: FD2–
Colborne: FD1–
Colburn: Bn 37–
Colby: FD1–FD2–
Colchester: FD1–
Colcock: Mt 6–
Colden: Bn 37–AH7–
Coldham-Fussell: FD1–FD2–
Coldstream: FD2–
Cole: FD1–FD2–Bn 38–V.H.25–W1/23–W2/48–
Colebrook: FD1–FD2–
Coleman: Mc 2/196–
Colepepper: Ne 2/98–
Coleridge: FD1–FD2–
Coles: FD2–Mt 134, 196–Bn 38–

Coley: Mt(A)22–
Colfox: FD2–
Colgate: Mt 5, 182–
Colhoun: FD2–
Collacutt: Bn 38–
Collet: FD1–FD2–
Colleton: Bn 38–
Collett: Ne 5/343–Bn 38–
Colley: FD2–
Collier: FD1–FD2–Bn 38–
Collinge: FD2–
Collings: FD2–
Collingwood: FD1–FD2–
Collins: FD2–Mt 67–Mt(A)22–Bn 38–
Collinson: FD2–
Collis-Sandes: FD2–
Collison: FD2–
Collyer: FD2–
Collynge: Mt 107–
Colman: FD1–FD2–Bn 38–
Colquhoun: FD1–FD2–
Colquhoun-Farquharson-MacDonald: FD2–
Colquitt-Craven: FD2–
Colston: FD2–V.H.65–
Colt: FD1–FD2–Bn 38–
Colthurst: FD1–FD2–
Coltman-Rogers: FD2–
Colton: Bn 38–
Colton-Fox: FD2–
Colvile: FD2–
Colvill: FD2–
Colville: FD1–FD2–
Colvin: FD1–FD2–
Combe: FD1–FD2–Bn 38–
Comber: FD1–FD2–
Combermere: FD1–
Combes: Bn 38–
(del) Commoda: W2 48–
Compston: FD2–
Compton: FD1–FD2–
Compton-Bracebridge: FD2–
Compton-Thornhill: FD2–
Compton-Vyner: FD2–
Comstock: Mt(A)22–Bn 38–
Comte: Mt(A)7–
Conacher: FD2–
Conant: FD2–Bn 38–
Concanon: FD2–
Conarroe: Bn 39–
Conder: FD1–FD2–
Cone: Mt 129–
Congreton: FD1–
Congreve: FD2–
Congleton: FD1–
Conlan: FD2–
Connaught: FD1–
Connellan: FD2–
Connemara: FD1–
Conney: Ne 1/17–
Connolly: Bn 39–
Conolly: FD2–
Conover: AH162–
Conran: FD2–
Conroy: FD1–
Constable: Bn 39–
Constable-Maxwell-Stuart: FD1–FD2–
Constantine: FD2–
Contee: Bn 39–Mc 2/199–
Converse: Bn 39–
Conway: FD2–Bn 39–V.H.68–
Conway-Gordon: FD1–FD2–
Conybeare: FD2–
Conyers: FD1–
Conyngham: FD1–FD2–
Cooch: FD1–
Coode: FD1–FD2–
Coode-Adams: FD2–

Cook: FD1–FD2–Mt(A)22–Mt 39–
Cooke: FD1–FD2–Mt 65, 71–Mt(A)23–Bn 39–
Ne 3/181, 209–Mc 1/104–V.H.30–W1 24–W2
46–
Cooke-Collis: FD2–
Cooke-Cross: FD2–
Cooke-Hurle: FD1–FD2–
Cooke-Yarborough: FD2–
Cookes: FD2–
Cookman: FD2–
Cookson: FD1–FD2–
Cooley: Bn 29–
Coolidge: Bn 39–AH8–
Coombe: FD2–
Coope: FD2–
Cooper: FD1–FD2–Mt 42–Bn 40–
Cooper-Deam: FD1–FD2–
Cooper-Horsfall: FD2–
Coote: FD1–FD2–Ne 2/161–Bn 40–
Cope: FD1–FD2–Mt 207–Ne 6/395–
Copeland: FD2–
Copeman: FD2–
Coppen: FD2–
Coppin-Straker: FD2–
Corah: FD2–
Corbally Stourton: FD2–
Corbet: FD1–FD2–
Corbett: FD1–FD2–
Corbett-Winder: FD2–
Corbin: Bn 40–V.H.87–W1/24–W2/50–
Corble: FD1–W2/50–
Corbould: FD2–
Corbould-Warren: FD1–FD2–
Corbusier: Mt 60–Mc 1/109–
Corby: FD2–
Corcoran: FD2–
Cordeaux: FD2–
Cordes: FD2–
Corey: Bn 40–
Corfield: FD1–FD2–
Cork & Orrery: FD1–
Corlet: FD2–
Corlies: Mt 170–
Cornbury: Bn 40–
Cornette: Ne 5/329–
Cornewall: FD1–FD2–
Corning: Mt 194–
Cornwall: FD2–Mt 33–
Cornwall Legh: FD2–
Cornwall-Brady: FD2–
Cornwallis: FD2–Ne 7/481–
Cornwallis-West: FD2–
Corrie: FD2–
Corrigan: FD1–
Corry: FD1–FD2–
Corsar: W1/25–W2/51–
Corsi Di Torre-Montanara: W1/25–W2/51–
Corstorphine: FD2–
Corwin: AH6–
Cory: FD2–Bn 40–
Cory-Wright: FD2–
Cosby: FD2–Mt 106–
Coslell: FD2–
Costello: FD2–
Costobadie: FD2–
Cottenham: FD1–
Cotter: FD1–FD2–
Cotterell: FD1–FD2–
Cotes: FD2–
Cottesloe: FD1–
Cottingham: FD2–
Cotton: FD2–Bn 40–AH10–
Cotton-Jodrell: FD1–FD2–
Cotts: FD2–
Coulson: FD2–
Couper: FD1–FD2–
(de) Courcy: Ne 5/358–

Courtenay: FD1–FD2– Bn 40–
Courtown: FD1–
Cottier: FD2–
Courtauld: FD2–
Courthorpe: FD2–
Courtis: FD2–
Coutant: AH5–
Coutant de Saisseval: W2/51–
Covel: Bn 40–
Covelle: Bn 40–
Coventry: FD1–FD2–Ne 5/371–
Cowan: FD1–FD2–
Cowans: FD2–
Cowen: FD2–
Cowell: FD1–Bn 40–
Cowell-Stepney: FD1–
Cowper: FD1–FD2–
Cowper-Essex: FD1–FD2–
Cox: FD1–FD2–Mt 11–Bn 41–
Coxe: Ne 3/230–Bn 41–
Coxon: FD2–W1/26–W2/52–
Coxwell-Rogers: FD2–
Coytmore: Ne 6/408–
Cozens-Hardy: FD1–FD2–
Crabb: Bn 41–
Crabbie: FD2–
Crackawthorpe: FD2–
Cracroft: FD1–
Cracroft-Amcotts: FD2–
Cradock: Mt(A)23–Bn 41–AH8–
Cradock-Hartopp: FD1–FD2–
Cragg: FD1–
Craggs: FD2–
Craig: FD2–Bn 41–
Craigie: FD2–
Craigie-Halkeit: FD1–FD2–
Craignish: FD1–
Craik: FD2–
Crailshein: FD2–
Cram: Bn 41–
Cramer: FD2–
Crampton: FD2–
Cramsie: FD2–
Cranbrook: FD1–
Crane: Mt(A)23–
Cranmer-Byng: FD1–FD2–
Cranston: Ne 1/27–Bn 41–
Cranstoun: FD1–AH13–
Cranstoun-Day: FD2–
Cranwell: Mt 77–
Craster: FD2–
Craven: FD1–FD2–Bn 41–
Crawford: FD1–FD2–Bn 41–V.H.107–
Crawford & Balcarres: FD1–
Crawford-Pollok: FD1–
Crawford-Stirling-Stuart: FD2–
Crawfurd: FD1–FD2–
Crawhall: FD2–
Crawley: FD2–
Crawley-Boevry: FD1–FD2–
Crawshaw: FD1–
Crawshay: FD1–FD2–
Creagh: FD2–Bn 41–
Cregaw: FD2–
Cregoe-Colmore: FD2–
Cresswell: FD2–
Crewdson: FD2–
Crew-Milnes: FD2–
Crewe: FD1–
Crewe-Read: FD2–
Creyke: FD2–V.H.79–
Crichton: FD1–FD2–
Crichton-Stuart: FD2–
Cripps: FD1–FD2–
Crisp: FD1–FD2–
Crispin: FD2–Ne 2/155–
Critche: FD2–

Critchley: FD2–
Crocker: Bn 41 & 42–
Croft: FD1–FD2–
Crofton: FD1–FD2–
Crockatt: Mt 15–
Croke: FD1–
Croker: FD2–
Croly: FD2–
Cromartie: FD1–
Crombie: FD2–Mt 15–
Crome: Bn 42–
Cromelien: Bn 42–
Cromer: FD1–
Crompton: FD1–FD2–
Crompton-Roberts: FD1–FD2–
Cromwell: AH11–
Crone: AS 42–
Cronlund: Ne 7/488–W1/26–W2/53–
Cronshaw: FD2–
Crooke: Bn 42–
Crookes: FD2–
Crooks: FD2–
Crookshank: FD2–Bn 42–
Cropper: FD2–
Crosbie: FD1–FD2–
Crosby: Ne 6/388–Bn 42–
Crosfield: FD1–FD2–
Crosland: FD2–
Cross: FD1–FD2–Mt 163–
Crosse: FD1–FD2–
Crossfield: FD2–
Crossing: FD1–
Crossland: Mt 128–
Crossley: FD1–FD2–W1/26–W2/53–
Crosshaw: FD2–
Crossman: FD2–Mt(A)23–
Crosthwait: FD2–
Crosthwaite-Eyre: FD2–
Crosweller: FD2–
Crothers: FD2–
Crouch: FD2–
Crowe: FD2–
Crowfoot: FD1–FD2–
Crown(e): Ne 5/328–Bn 42–
Crowninshield: Bn 42–
Crowther: FD2–
Crowther-Benyon: FD1–FD2–
Cruwys: FD1–FD2–
Croxton: FD2–
Crozier: FD2–
Cruddas: FD2–
Cruger: Bn 42–AH5–
Cruikshank: FD2–
Cruise: FD2–
Crump: FD2–
Crumpe: FD2–
Crutchley: FD2–
Cruttenden: Bn 42–
Cruttwell: FD2–
Cryan: FD2–
Cubitt: FD2–
Cuffe: FD2–
Cull: FD2–
Cullen: FD2–
Culley: FD2–
Cullum: FD1–
Culme-Seymour: FD1–FD2–
Culverden School: W2/53–
Cumberland: FD1–
Cumberlege-Ware: FD2–
Cumming: Ne 2/301–
Cummings: Bn 42–
Cummins: FD2–
Cunard: FD1–FD2–
Cuninghame: FD2–FD1–
Cunliffe: FD1–FD2–
Cunliffe-Owen: FD2–

Cunningham: FD2–Mt(A)23–Bn 42–
Cunninghame: FD2–
Cunynghame: FD1–FD2–
Cure: FD1–
Curle: FD2–Bn 43–V.H.37–
Currey: Bn 43–
Currie: FD1–FD2–
Currier: Mt 36–Bn 43–
Curry: Bn 43–
Curteis: FD1–FD2–
Curtin: Bn 43–
Curtis: FD1–FD2–Mt 110–Bn 43–AH8–
Curtler: FD2–
Curwen: FD2–Mt(A)24–Bn 43–Ne 8/541–
Curzon: FD2–Bn 43–
Curzow: FD1–FD2–
Curzow-Howe: FD1–FD2–
Cusack: FD2–
Cusack-Smith: FD1–FD2–
Cushing: Mt 218–Bn 43–Mc 1/114–AH6–
Cushman: Bn 44–
Cussans: FD1–FD2–W1/26–W2/54–
Cust: FD1–FD2–
Custance: FD2–
Custis: Bn 22–V.H.44–
Cutbush: Bn 44–
Cuthbert: FD1–FD2–Mt(A)24–
Cutlack: FD2–
Cutlar-Fergusson: FD1–FD2–
Cutler: Mt(A)24–Bn 44–
Cutting: Bn 44–
Cutts: Bn 44–
Cuyler: FD1–FD2–Bn 44 & 45–AH5–

Dacre: Mt 230–
Dadabhoy: FD2–
Dadd: FD2–
Dade: Bn 45–Ne 6/398–
Daggett: Mt(A)24–
Dahlgren: Bn 45–
Dakin: Ne 6/379–
Daintry: FD2–
D'Albani: FD1–FD2–
Dalby: FD2–
Dale: FD1–FD2–Bn 45–V.H.69–
Dalgety: FD2–
Dalgleish: FD1–FD2–
Dalglish-Bellasis: FD2–
Dalhousie: FD1–
Dalison: FD1–FD2–
Dall: Mt 196–
Dallett: Ne 8/608–
Dalrymple: FD2–FD1–
Dalrymple-Hay: FD2–FD1–
Dalrymple-White: FD2–
Dalton: FD2–
Dallas: FD1–
Dalton-Fitzgerald: FD1–
Dalway: FD2–
Daly: FD1–FD2–
Dalywell: FD2–
Dalzell: FD1–FD2–
Dalziel: FD2–
Dame: FD2–
Damon: Bn 45–
Dampier: FD1–
Dampier-Bide: FD2–
Dampier-Whetham: FD2–
Dana: Mt 48–Bn 45–
Dancer: FD1–FD2–
Dancy: Mt 26–
Dandrige: Bn 45–Mc 1/117–V.H.30–
Dane: FD2–
Danforth: Bn 45–
Dangar: FD1–FD2–
Daniel: FD2–Ne 7/497–

Daniell: FD1–FD2–
Daniell-Jenkins: FD2–
Danson: FD2–
Danvers: FD2–
Darbishire: FD1–FD2–
Darby: FD1–FD2–
Darby Griffith: FD2–
D'Arcy: FD2–
Darell: FD1–FD2–
Darell-Blount: FD2–
Darling: FD1–FD2–Bn 45–
Darlington: FD2–
Darnley: FD1–
Darnton: FD2–
Darroch: FD2–
Dart: Bn 46–
Dartmouth: FD1–
Dartrey: FD1–
Darwin: FD1–FD2–
Dasent: FD1–
Dashwood: FD1–FD2–
Daubeney: FD1–FD2–
Daubeny: Ne 5/366–
Dauglish: FD2–
Daunt: FD1–FD2–
Dauntesey: FD2–
Davenport: FD1–FD2–Ne 1/20–Mt 17–Bn 46–
  AH6–
Davenport-Handley: FD1–
Davenport-Handley-Humphreys: FD2–
Davey: FD1–FD2–
David: FD2–
Davidson: FD1–FD2–Mt 203–Bn 46–W1/27–
  W2/55–
Davie: FD1–Ne 2/150–Mt(A)24–Bn 46–
Davies: FD1–FD2–Mt 151–Ne 8/612–
Davies-Cooke: FD2–
Davies-Evans: FD2–
Davies-Gilbert: FD2–
Davies-Scourfield: FD2–
Davis: FD1–FD2–Mt 163, 185–Bn 46–Mc 1/121–
Davis-Goff: FD2–
Davison: FD2–Bn 46–V.H.85–
Davson: FD2–
Davy: FD2–
Dawes: FD2–Bn 46–
Dawkins: FD2–Mt 46–Bn 46–
Dawnay: FD1–FD2–
Dawson: FD1–FD2–
Dawson-Grove: FD2–
Dawson-Lambton: FD2–
Day: FD1–FD2–Mt(A)24–Bn 47–
Dayrell: FD1–FD2–
Deacon: Bn 47–
Deane: Bn 47–AH8–FD1–FD2–
Deane-Drake: FD1–FD2–
Deane-Drummond: FD2–
Deane-Freeman: FD2–
Deane-Morgan: FD2–
Deas: Bn 47–
Dease: FD2–
Deasy: FD2–
Debarry: Mt 29–
De Bathe: FD1–FD2–
De Beelen: Mt 142–
Debenham: FD2–
De Berdt: Bn 47–
De Blaquiere: FD1–
De Blois: Bn 47–
De Bruyn: Ne 8/540–
De Burgh: FD2–
De Burgh-Lawson: FD1–
De Burgho: FD1–
De Burton: FD1–FD2–
De Capell-Brooke: FD1–FD2–
De Carron: Mt 177–
De Cetto: FD2–

De Carteret: FD2–
Decies: FD1–
De Clifford: FD1–
De Courcy: FD1–FD2–Bn 47–
De Courcy-Wheeler: FD2–
Deeley: FD2–
Defreyne: FD1–
De Fonblanque: FD2–
De Forest: FD2–
De Frece: FD2–
Degen: Bn 47–
De Grasse: Bn 47–
De Grey: FD1–FD2–
De Hauley: FD1–
De Hochepied-Larpent: FD1–FD2–
De Houghton: FD1–FD2–
De Horsey: FD2–
De Iturbide: Ne 8/567–
De Jersey: FD2–
De Jersey-Vavassour: FD2–
De Keyser: FD1–
De Kierzkowski-Steuart: FD1–FD2–
De La Bere: FD1–FD2–
De La Cherons: FD2–
De La Cherons-Crom-Melin: FD2–
Delacour: FD2–
Delafield: FD2–Ne 3/170–Mt(A)25–Bn 47–
De La Ferte: FD2–
De La Fontaine: Mt(A)33–
Delamare: Bn 47–
Delamere: FD1–
De Lancey: Bn 47–
Delano: Mt(A)25–Bn 47–AH7–
Delany: FD2–Bn 47–
Delap: FD2–
De La Poer: FD1–
De La Rue: FD1–FD2–
De La Vergne: Mt 105–
De Lavis-Trafford: FD2–
Delawarr: FD1–
Delcambre: Mt 214–
Delfau: Ne 7/453–
De Lisle: FD1–
De L'Isle & Dudley: FD1–
Della Rafia: FD2–
Delme-Radcliffe: FD2–
De Luze: Mt(A)25–
De Longueuil: FD1–
Delmege: FD2–
De Losada: FD2–
De Metriadi: FD2–
De Moleyns: FD1–
De Montalt: FD1–
De Montfort: FD2–
De Montmorency: FD1–FD2–
Dempsey: FD2–
Dempster: Bn 47–
Denbigh: FD1–
Dendy: FD2–
Dene: FD1–
Denham: FD2–
Denis-Tottenham: FD2–
Denison: FD1–FD2–Mt(A)25–Bn 47–AH8–
Denman: FD1–FD2–
Denn: Ne 2/154–
Dennington: FD2–
Dennis: FD2–Mt 204–
Dennistoun: FD2–
Denny: FD1–FD2–Bn 48–
Dennys: FD1–
De Normandie: Bn 48–
Dent: FD2–
Denton: FD1–
Denys: FD1–
Deodate: Ne 7/504–
De Pass: FD2–
Depew: Bn 48–

De Peyster: Bn 48–Mt 112–
Deramore: FD1–
De Ramsey: FD1–
Dering: Bn 48–
De Reuter: FD2–FD1–
Derby: FD1–
De Renzy: FD1–
Dering: FD1–FD2–
D'Erneville De Launcy: Ne 8/554–
De Ros: FD1–
De Rosset de Fleury: Bn 48–
Derry: FD2–
Derwent: FD1–
Desart: FD1–
De Saumarez: FD1–
Despard: FD2–
De Stackpoole: FD2–
Des Voeux: FD1–FD2–
De Tabley: FD1–
Detcher: Bn 48–
De Teissier: FD2–
De Tonge: FD1–FD2–
De Trafford: FD1–FD2–
De Uphaugh: FD1–FD2–
Devas: FD2–
Devenish: FD2–
De Vere: FD1–FD2–
Devereux: FD1–FD2–Bn 48–
De Vesci: FD1–
De Villiers: FD2–
Devitt: FD2–
Devlin: Bn 48–
Devon: FD1–
Devonshire: FD1–
Devotion: Mt(A)25–Bn 48–
Dewar: FD2–W1/27–W2/55 & 56–
Dewar-Harrison: FD2–
Dewhurst: FD2–
Dewey: FD2–Mc 1/128–
De Winton: FD1–FD2–
De Witt: Mt 7–
De Wolf: Mt 66–
De Worms: FD1–FD2–
Dewrance: FD2–
Dexter: Bn 48–
Dey: FD2–
De Yarburgh-Bateson: FD1–FD2–
De Zeng: Mt(A)25–
Diamond: FD2–
Diasbandaranike: FD2–
Dick: FD1–FD2–AS44–
Dick-Cunyingham: FD1–FD2–
Dicken: FD2–
Dickenson: FD2–AH13–
Dickie: FD2–
Dickins: FD2–
Dickinson: FD2–Bn 49–
Dick-Lauder: FD1–
Dickson: FD1–FD2–Ne 6/397–Bn 49–
Dickson-Poynder: FD1–FD2–
Digby: FD1–FD2–
Digges: Ne 5/320–Mt(A)26–Bn 49–AH15–
Diggles: Bn 49–V.H.32–
Dighton: Ne 2/111–
Dilke: FD1–FD2–
Dillman: Bn 49–
Dillon: FD1–FD2–
Dillon-Lee: FD1–
Dillon-Trenchard: FD2–
Dillwyn-Llewelyn: FD1–
Dillwyn-Venables-Llewelyn: FD2–FD1–
Dimsdale: FD1–FD2–
Dingwall-Fordyce: FD1–FD2–
Dinham-Peren: FD2–
Dinwiddie: Ne B/353–Bn 49–
Diodati: Ne 7/504–Mt(A)26–
Disbrow: Mt(A)26–AH5–

Disney: FD2–Bn 49–
Disraeli: FD1–FD2–
Ditchfield: FD1–
Dix: Bn 49–
Dixie: FD1–FD2–
Dixon: FD1–FD2–Ne 3/175–
Dixon-Johnson: FD2–
Dixon-Hartland: FD1–
Dixson: FD2–
Dixwell: Ne 1/18–
Doane: Bn 49–
Dobbin: FD2–
Dobie: FD2–
Dobbs: FD2–
Doble: FD2–
Dobtree: FD1–FD2–
Dobson: FD1–FD2–
Dockrel: FD1–
Dodd: FD2–Mt(A)26–
Dodge: FD1–Mt 50, 121, 186–Bn 49–AH4–Mc
  1/113–
Dods: FD2–
Dodson: FD1–FD2–
Dodsworth: FD1–
D'olier: FD1–
Dolling: FD2–
Dolmage: FD2–
Domville: FD1–FD2–
Don: FD2–
Donald: FD2–
Donaldson: FD2–W2/56–
Donaldson-Hudson: FD2–
Donelan: FD2–
Donegall: FD1–
Doneraile: FD1–
Dongan: Ne 5/322–Mt(A)26–Bn 50–
Donington: FD1–
(Van der) Donk: Ne 7/468–
Donne: FD1–
Donnek: FD2–
Donnel: W2/56–
Donnell: Ne 6/444–W1/28–
Donnellan: FD2–
Donovan: FD2–
Donoughmore: FD1–
Doodes: Bn 50–V.H.39–
Doolette: FD2–
Dooner: FD2–
Dopping-Hepenstal: FD2–
Doran: FD2–
Dorchester: FD1–
Dorman: FD1–FD2–
Dormer: FD1–
Dorcy: FD2–Mt 172–
Dorington: FD2–
Dorling: FD2–
Dormer: Ne 7/471–V.H.42–
Dorr: Mt(A)26–Bn 50–
Dorsey: Bn 50–
D'Osten-Moller: FD2–
Doty: Mt 118–
Doughty: FD1–Mt 205–
Doughty-Tichborne: FD1–FD2–
Douglas: FD1–FD2–Mt 55–V.H.38–
Douglas-Campbell: FD2–
Douglas-Hamilton: FD2–
Douglas-Home: FD2–
Douglas-Pennant: FD1–FD2–
Douglas-Scott: FD2–
Douglass: Ne 8/524–W1/28–W2/57–
Doulton: FD1–FD2–
Dous: Bn 50–
Douw: Bn 50–
Dove: Bn 50–
Dowdall: FD2–
Dowdeswell: FD1–
Dowland: FD2–

Downe: FD1–
Downer: FD2–
Downes: FD1–FD2–
Downing: FD2–Ne 2/131–Bn 50–
Downshire: FD1–
Dowse: FD2–Bn 50–
Doxat: FD2–
Doyle: FD1–FD2–W1/29–W2/57–
D'Oyley: Mt 84–Mt 24–
D'Oyly: FD1–FD2–
Doyne: FD2–
Draffen: W1/29–W2/58–
Drake: Ne 1/36, 6/447–Bn 50–Mt(A)27–Mc 1/ 135–AH4–
Draper: Mt 158–Mt(A)27–Bn 50–
Drayton: Bn 51–
Drew: FD2–Bn 51–
Drew-Mercer: FD2–
Drexel: Bn 51–
Dreyer: FD2–
Drinkwater: FD1–FD2–
Drogheda: FD1–
Dron: FD2–
Drought: FD2–
Drower: FD2–
Drughorn: FD2–
Drummond: FD1–FD2–
Drummond-Hay: FD1–
Drummond-Wolff: FD2–
Drury: FD2–
Drury-Lowe: FD2–
Dryden: FD1–FD2–
Duane: Mt(A)27–Bn 51–
Duberly: FD2–
Du Bois: Mt(A)27–AH13–
Dubs: FD2–Bn 51–
Du Cane: FD1–FD2–
Ducat-Hamersley: FD2–
Ducie: FD1–
Duckett: FD1–FD2–
Duckett-Stewart: FD2–
Duckworth: FD1–FD2–
Duckworth-King: FD1–FD2–
Ducros: FD2–
Dudgeon: FD2–
Dudley: FD1–Mt 41–Ne 2/87–Bn 51–AH8–
Dudley-Janns: FD2–
Duer: Mt(A)27–Bn 51–
Duff: FD2–
Duff-Assheton-Smith: FD1–FD2–
Duff-Gordon: FD1–FD2–
Duff-Sutherland-Dunbar: FD2–
Dufferin & Ava: FD1–
Duffey: FD2–
Duffield: Mt(A)27–Bn 51–
Dugdale: FD1–FD2–
Duggan-Cronin: FD2–
Dugon: FD2–
Duguid: FD2–
Duguid-H'Combie: FD1–FD2–
Duignan: FD1–FD2–
Duke: FD1–FD2–Mt 167–Bn 51–Mc 1391/– V.H.19–
Dulany: Bn 52–
Dumaries: FD2–
Dumas: FD2–
Dumarsque: Mt(A)28–
Dumbleton: FD2–
Dumbrille: W2/59–
Dumbreck: FD2–
Dumersq: Ne 1/5–Bn 52–AH4–
Dummer: Ne 3/227–Mt(A)28–Bn 52–AH8–
Dumont: Bn 52–
Du Moulin-Browne: FD1–FD2–
Dunalley: FD1–
Dunbar: FD1–FD2–Bn 52–W1/30–W2/58–
Dunboyne: FD1–

Duncan: FD2–Ne 2/94–Bn 53–
Dunch: Ne 4/273–
Duncombe: FD1–FD2–Bn 52–V.H.46–
Duncombe-Anderson: FD2–
Dundas: FD1–FD2–
Dundonald: FD1–
Dungan: Ne 5/322–
Dunkin: FD2–Bn 52–
Dunleath: FD1–
Dunlop: FD2–
Dunmore: FD1–Mt(A)28–
Dunn: FD1–FD2–
Dunne: FD2–Bn 52–
Dunnell: FD2–Mt 187–
Dunn-Gardner: FD2–
Dunning: FD2–
Dunnington-Jefferson: FD1–FD2–
Dunraven & Mountearl: FD1–
Dunsandle & Clanconal: FD1–
Dundany: FD1–
Dunscombe: FD2–
Dunsford: FD1–
Dunsmure: FD2–
Dunston: FD1–FD2–
Duntze: FD1–
Dun-Waters: FD2–
Dupee: Bn 52–
Dupont: Bn 53–
Du Pont: Bn 53–
Dupre: FD2–
Dupree: FD2–
Durand: FD1–FD2–Bn 53–
Durant: FD2–
D'Urban: FD2–
Durham: FD1–FD2–
Durrant: FD1–FD2–
Duryea: Bn 53–
Duryee: Bn 53–
Dusgate: FD2–
Duthie: FD2–
Dutton: FD1–FD2–
Duval(l): Bn 53–Mc 1/142, 146–
Duveen: FD2–
Duvernoy: Ne 8/563–W1/30–W2/60–
Dwight: Mt(A)28–Bn 53–
Dwyer-Hampton: FD2–
Dyce: FD1–FD2–
Dyckman: Bn 53–
Dyer: FD1–FD2–Mt 136–Bn 53–
Dyke: FD1–FD2–
Dymond: Bn 53–
Dymore: FD1–
Dynevor: FD1–
Dyott: FD2–
Dysart: FD1–

Eade: FD1–
Eady: FD2–
Eagar: FD2–
Eager: Mt(A)28–
Eales: FD1–FD2–
Eames: FD2–Mt(A)28–
Eardeley: Mt(A)29–
Eardley-Wilmot: FD1–FD2–
Earle: FD1–FD2–Mt 218–Bn 53–
Earp: FD2–
Eastbrook: Bn 53–
D'Este-East: FD2–
Eastcott: FD2–
Easten: FD1–
Eastice: FD2–
Easton: Bn 53–
Eastwick: Bn 53–
Eastwood: FD1–FD2–
Eaton: FD1–FD2–
Ebble-White: FD2–

Ebden: FD2–
Ebrahim: FD2–
Ebsworth: FD2–
Ebury: FD1–
Eby: Bn 53–
Ecceleston: Bn 53–
Eccles: FD2–
Eccles-Williams: W2/61–
Eccroyd: FD1–
Echlin: FD1–FD2–
Eckersley: FD2–
Eckley: Mt(A)29–Bn 53–
Eckstein: FD2–
Ecroyd: FD2–
Eddleston: FD2–
Eddy: Mt 191–AH164–
Edelen: AS46–W1/31–W2/61–
Eden: FD1–FD2–Ne 4/247–Bn 54–
Edes: Bn 54–
Edgar: FD1–FD2–
Edgcumbe: FD1–FD2–
Edge: FD1–FD2–
Edgecomb: Ne 1/66–
Edgell: FD2–
Edgerley: Bn 54–
Edgeworth: FD2–
Edlin: FD1–
Edmands: Bn 54–
Edmeades: FD1–FD2–
Edmondes: FD2–Mt 18–Bn 54–
Edmondstone: FD1–
Edmondstone-Montgomerie: FD2–
Edmonstoune-Cranston: FD1–
Edward: FD2–
Edwardes: FD1–FD2–
Edwards: FD1–FD2–Bn 54–V.H.17–W1/31–
 W2/61–
Edwards-Moss: FD1–FD2–
Edwin: FD2–
Edwin-Cole: FD1–
Eelles: Mt(A)29–
Eels: Bn 54–
Effingham: FD1–
Egan: W2/62–
Egerton: FD1–FD2–Mt(A)29–
Egerton-Warburton: FD1–FD2–
Egginton: FD2–
Egginton-Ernle-Erle: FD1–
Egleston: Mt(A)29–
Eglinton: FD1–
Egmont: FD1–
Ehrmann: FD2–
Eills: FD2–
Eisenhower: Ne 8/565–
Elam: Bn 54–
Elburne: FD2–
Eld: FD2–
Elder: FD2–
Eldon: FD1–
Eldredge: Mt 100, 206–Bn 54–
Elers: FD2–
Eley: FD2–
Elgin: FD1–
Elgood: FD1–FD2–
Elibank: FD1–
Eliot: FD1–FD2–Mt(A)30–Bn 54–AH2, 17–
Eliott: FD1–FD2–
Eliott-Drake-Colborne: FD2–
Eliott-Lockhart: FD1–FD2–
Elkington: FD2–
Elkins: Mt 220–
Ellenborough: FD1–
Ellerman: FD2–
Ellerton-Thorp: FD2–
Ellery: Bn 55–AH108–
Elles: FD2–
Ellesmere: FD1–

Ellicot: Mt 180–
Elliman: Mt(A)30–
Elliot: FD1–FD2–Mt 35–Bn 55–
Elliot-Murray-Kynynhound: FD2–
Elliott: FD2–
Ellis: FD1–FD2–Ne 6/421–Bn 55–
Ellis-Griffith: FD2–
Ellison: FD2–
Ellison-Macartney: FD1–FD2–
Elliston: Bn 55–
Ellsworth: Bn 55–
Elmhirst: FD1–FD2–
Elmsall: FD2–
Elphinstone: FD1–FD2–
Elphinstone-Dalrymple: FD2–
Elphinstone-Stone: FD1–FD2–
Elsmie: FD2–
Elton: FD1–
Elwes: FD2–
Elwon: FD1–
Elwood: Mt(A)30–Bn 55–
Elwyn: Ne 3/207–
Ely: FD1–Mt(A)29–Bn 55–
Emeris: FD1–FD2–
Emerson: FD1–FD2–Mt(A)30–Bn 55 & 56–
 AH2–W1/31–W2/62–
Emerton: FD1–
Emery: Mt(A)30–Bn 56–Mc 1/152, 156–W1/–31
 W2/62–
Emly: FD1–
Emmet: Mt(A)30–Bn 56–
Emmett: FD2–
Emmons: Mt 30–
Emmott: FD2–
Emory: Mc 1/159–
Empson: FD1–
Endecott: Bn 56–
Endicott: Bn 56–AH14–
Engleheart: FD1–
English: FD1–FD2–Bn 56–V.H8.–
Enniskillen: FD1–
Enroor: FD2–
Ensign: Bn 56–
Entwisle: FD2–
Enys: FD1–FD2–
Eppes: Bn 56–V.H.91–
Erle: FD1–
Erne: FD1–
Errington: FD1–Ne 3/222–
Erroll: FD1–
Erkine: FD2–
Erskine: FD1–FD2–Ne 8/535–
Erskiney: FD2–
Erving: Bn 56–
Esdaile: FD2–
Eshelby: FD2–
Esher: FD1–FD2–
Esmonde: FD1–FD2–
Espin: FD1–
Esplen: FD2–
Essex: FD1–
Estcourt-Oswald: FD2–
Ethelston: FD2–
Etherton: FD2–
Etting: Bn 56–
Ettrick: FD2–
Eustace: FD2–Bn 56–
Eustis: Bn 56–
Evans: FD1–FD2–Mt 63, 75–Mt(A)31–Bn 56–
Evans-Freke: FD1–FD2–
Evans-Gordon: FD2–
Evans-Lloyd: FD1–
Evans-Lombe: FD2–
Eveleigh-de-Moleyns: FD1–FD2–
Evelyn: FD2–V.H.11–
Even: Ne 7/489–
Everard: FD2–Ne 3/217, 231–

Everest: FD2–Bn 57–
Everett: FD2–Bn 57–
Everitt: FD2–
Everitt-Heath: FD2–
Eversfield: FD2–
Every: FD1–FD2–
Every-Clayton: FD2–
Every-Halstead: FD1–FD2–
Eves: FD2–
Ewart: FD1–FD2–
Ewing: FD1–FD2–Bn 57–
Exeter: FD1–
Exmouth: FD1–Ne 7/502–
Exshaw: W2/63–
Eykyn: FD2–
Eyre: FD2–Mt(A)31–Bn 57–AH15–
Eyre-Hatcham: FD2–
Eyres: FD1–
Eyston: FD2–
Eyton: FD2–

Faber: FD2–
von Faerber von Augusta: AS188–
Fagan: FD2–Bn 57–
Fagge: FD1–FD2–
Fair: FD1–FD2–
Fairbairn: FD1–FD2–
Fairbanks: Mt 107, 210–Bn 57–
Fairchild: Bn 57–
Fairclough: FD2–
Faire: FD2–
Fairfax: FD1–FD2–Ne 5/347–Mt(A)31–Bn 57–
    V.H.93–AH1, 17–
Fairfax-Cholmeley: FD1–FD2–
Fairfield: Mt(A)31–
Fairholme: FD2–
Fairlie: FD1–FD2–
Fairlie-Cuninghame: FD1–
Fairweather: AH10–
Falcon-Cooke: FD2–
Falconar-Stewart: FD2–
Falcon-Steward: FD2–
Falconer: FD2–Bn 57–
Falkiner: FD1–FD2–
Falkner: FD2–
Falkland: FD1–
Falle: FD2–
Fallon: FD2–
Falls: Mt(A)31–
Falmouth: FD1–
Falshaw: FD1–
Fancourt: FD2–
Fane: FD1–
Fane-de-Salis: FD2–
Faneuil: Bn 57–Ne 8/529–
Fanshawe: FD1–FD2–
Fardell: FD1–FD2–
Farie: FD1–FD2–
Farish: FD2–
Farewell: FD2–
Farkas de Kisbarnak: W2/64–
Farley: FD2–Ne 5/324–
Farlow: Bn 57–
Farm: FD1–
Farmar: Ne 8/560–
Farmbrough: FD2–
Farmer: FD1–FD2–Mt(A)31–Bn 58–
Farncombe-Tanner: FD2–
Farnham: FD1–FD2–Bn 58–
Farquhar: FD1–FD2–
Farquharson: FD1–FD2–
Farr: Bn 58–
Farragut: Bn 58–
Farran: FD2–
Farrar: Ne 5/342–V.H.20–
Farrer: FD1–FD2–

Farrington: FD1–FD2–Bn 58–
Farrow: Bn 58–
Farsyde: FD2–
Farwell: FD1–Mt(A)32–
Faudel-Phillips: FD2–
Faulkner: FD2–
Faunce-de-Laune: FD2–
Fauntleroy: Ne 7/470–Mt(A)32–V.H.12–
Fauquier: Bn 58–
Faussett: FD2–
Favria: W2/64–
Fawcett: FD2–
Fawconer: Mt(A)32–
Fawkes: FD2–
Fawkener: Bn 58–
Fawknor: Ne 1/26–
Fay: Bn 58–
Fay Maubourg: Bn 58–
Fayerweather: Bn 58–
Fayle: FD2–
Fayrer: FD2–
Feachem: FD2–
Feake: Ne 6/402–
Fearn: Mt(A)32–
Fearney-Whittingstall: FD1–FD2–
Fearon: Bn 58–
Feetham: FD2–
Fehr: FD2–
Feilden: FD1–FD2–
Feilding: FD1–FD2–Bn 58–V.H.78, 80–
Fell: FD2–
Fellowes: FD2–Bn 59–
Fellows: FD1–FD2–
Fels: Bn 59–
Felt: Bn 59–
Felton: Ne 1/15–
Fendell: Bn 59–
Fenner: Mt(A)32–
Fenton: FD1–FD2–
Fenton-Livingstone: FD1–FD2–
Fenwick: FD1–FD2–Ne 1/34–Mt(A)32–Mt 7–
    Bn 58–
Fenwick-Owen: FD2–
Fenwick-Palmer: FD2–
Fenwick-Clennell: FD2–
Fenwyke: Bn 59–
Ferguson: FD1–FD2–Mt(A)33–Bn 59–
Ferguson-Dane: FD2–
Fergusson: FD1–FD2–
Fergusson-Buchanan: FD2–
Fergusson-Pollock: FD2–
Fermor-Hesketh: FD1–FD2–
Fermoy: FD1–
Fernandez de Lima: AS48–
Ferrand: FD1–FD2–
Ferrar: FD2–
Ferrers: FD1–FD2–
Ferrier: FD1–FD2–
Ferrin: Bn 59–
Ferris: FD2–Mt 174–
Fetherston: FD1–
Fetherston-Dilke: FD2–
Fetherstonhaugh: FD2–
Feversham: FD1–
Ffarington: FD2–
Ffinden: FD1–FD2–
Ffennell: FD2–
Ffooks: W1/32–W2/65–
Ffrench: FD1–
Ficklin: FD1–FD2–
Field: FD1–FD2–Ne 6/420–Mt(A)33–Bn 59–
    AH12–W1/32–W2/65–
Fieldeny: FD2–
Fieldhouse: FD2–
Fielding: Bn 59–
Fieldson: W1/33–W2/65–

Fife: FD1–FD2–
Fife-Cookson: FD1–
Filgate: FD1–
Filleol: FD2–
Filmer: FD1–Ne 6/423–V.H.31–
Finch: FD1–FD2–
Finch-Hatton: FD1–FD2–
Findlater: FD2–
Findlay: FD1–FD2–
Findlay-Hamilton: FD2–
Findlay: Mt 45–
Findlayson: FD2–
Fingall: FD1–
Finny: FD1–FD2–
Firbank: FD2–
Firebrace: FD2–
Firman: FD1–FD2–
Firth: FD2–
Fisc: Bn 59–
Fish: Mt 199–Bn 59–Mc 1/165–
Fisher: FD2–Bn 60–
Fisher-Rowe: FD1–FD2–
Fishwick: FD1–
Fisk: Bn 60–
Fiske: Ne 1/19–Mt 193, 229–AH10–
Fison: FD2–
Fitch: FD1–FD2–Ne 1/62–Mt(A)33–Bn 60–
    AH8–W1/33–W2/65–
Fitzalan-Howard: FD1–FD2–
Fitz-Ancher: FD2–
Fitz-Clarence: FD1–FD2–
Fitz-Gerald: FD1–FD2–Mt 113–
Fitz-George: FD2–
Fitz-Herbert: FD1–FD2–
Fitz-Herbert-Brockholes: FD1–FD2–
Fitzherbert-Stafford: FD2–
Fitzhugh: FD2–Ne 5/360–Bn 60–V.H.65–
Fitzjames-Stuart: FD2–
Fitz-Maurice-Deane: FD1–
Fitzroy: FD1–
Fitz Patrick: FD2–
Fitz Randolph: FD2–
Fitz Simon: FD2–
Fitz William: FD1–
Fitz-Wygram: FD1–
Fitz-Williams: FD2–
Flannery: FD2–
Flavel: FD1–
Flavelle: FD2–
Fleet: V.H.107–Ne 8/583–
Fleetwood-Hesketh: FD2–
Fleming: FD1–FD2–
Fleming-Parsons: Ne 8/609–AS50–W2/66–
Fletcher: FD1–FD2–Bn 60–
Fletcher-Campbell: FD1–
Fletcher-Twemlow: FD2–
Fletcher-Vane: FD1–
Flint: FD2–Mt 35–
Floebeckher: Bn 60–
Flood: Bn 60–
Flory: FD1–FD2–
Flournoy: V.H.52–
Flower: FD1–FD2–Bn 60–V.H.18/24–
Floyd: FD1–FD2–Mt 110–
Floyer: FD2–
Floyer-Acland: FD2–
Fludyer: FD1–
Fogg: Bn 61–
Fogo: FD2–
Foley: FD1–FD2–
Folliott: V.H.110–
Foljambe: FD1–FD2–Bn 61–
Fonnereau: FD2–
Fongs: Ne 6/407–
Fontaine: Mt(A)33–V.H.90–
Fooks: FD2–
Foot: FD2–Ne 6/405–Mt 46–Bn 61–V.H.84–

Forbes: FD2–FD1–Bn 61–
Forbes-Leith: FD1–FD2–
Forbes-Robertson: FD2–
Forbes-Sempill: FD2–
Forbush: Mt(A)33–
Ford: FD1–FD2–
Fordham: FD1–FD2–
Forensic Medicine, The British Association in:
    W2/66–
(de) Forest: Ne 4/270–
Forester: FD1–FD2–
Forman: Bn 61–
Forrest: FD1–FD2–
Forsaith: FD2–
Forsdike: FD2–
Forster: FD1–FD2–
Forster-Coull: FD1–FD2–
Forster-Morris: FD2–
Forsyth: FD2–Mt(A)33–Bn 61–AH16–
Fort: FD1–
Fortescue: FD1–FD2–Bn 61–
Forth: FD2–
Fortune: FD2–
Forty: FD2–
Forward: Bn 61–
Forwood: FD1–FD2–Mc 1/168–
Fosbery: FD2–
Foster: FD1–FD2–Ne 4/245–Mt(A)34–Bn 61 &
    62–AH16–
Foster-Melliar: FD2–
Foster-Versey-Fitzgerald: FD1–FD2–
Fothergill: FD2–
Foulds: FD2–
Foulke: Mt 11, 36–
Found: FD2–
Fountain: AH11–
Fountaine: FD2–
Fowke: FD1–FD2–Bn 62–AH15–
Fowle: Bn 62–V.H.85–
Fowler: FD1–FD2–Mt 152–Bn 62–
Fowler-Butler: FD2–
Fownes: FD2–
Fownes-Luttrell: FD2–
Fox: FD1–FD2–Bn 62–V.H.9–
Foxcroft: Bn 62–AH13–
Fox-Strangways: FD2–
Fox-Davies: FD2–
Foy: FD2–
Foyster: FD2–
Frampton: FD2–
France-Hayhurst: FD1–FD2–
France-Lushington-Tulloch: FD2–
Francine: Mt 144–
Francis: FD1–Bn 63–
Francis-Miller: AS52–
Francklin: FD1–AH1–
Franey: FD1–FD2–
Frankfurt: FD1–
Frankland: FD1–FD2–Ne 2/132–
Frankland-Russel-Astley: FD2–
Franklin: FD2–Mt(A)34–Bn 63–
Fraser: FD1–FD2–Bn 63–
Franks: FD2–
Fraser-Mackenzie: FD2–
Fraser-Mackintosh: FD1–
Fraser-Tytler: FD1–FD2–
Fraunces: Bn 63–
Frazer: Mt(A)34–Mt 225–Bn 63–Mc 1/171–
Freake: FD1–FD2–
Frederick: FD1–FD2–
Freehoff: Ne 7/473–W1/33–W2/67–
Freeling: FD1–FD2–
Freeman: FD1–FD2–Mt 138, 175, 178–Bn 63–
Freeman-Mitford: FD1–FD2–
Freeman-Thomas: FD2–
Freemantle: FD1–
Freer-Smith: FD2–

Freese: FD2–
Freese-Pennefather: FD2–
Freestone: Ne 2/76–
Freke: Bn 63–
Fremantle: FD2–
Fremlin: FD2–
French: FD2–Mt 33–Bn 63–
Frere: FD1–FD2–
Freshfield: FD1–FD2–
Freston: FD2–
Frewen: FD2–
Frewen-Layton: FD2–
Friedland: Ne 3/212–
Friestedt: AS 54–
Frisby: FD2–
Friswell: FD2–
Frith: FD2–
Frith-Lowndes: FD2–
Frizell: Bn 63–
Frost: FD2–Bn 63–
Frothingham: Bn 64–
Fry: FD1–FD2–Mt(A)34–Bn 64–
Frye: Bn 64–
Fryer: FD1–FD2–
Fulford: FD2–
Fuller: FD1–FD2–Mt(A)34–Bn 64–
Fuller-Acland-Hood: FD1–FD2–
Fuller-Eliott-Drake: FD1–FD2–
Fullerton: FD1–FD2–Bn 64–
Fulton: FD2–
Furley: FD2–
Fursdon: FD2–
Fyers: FD2–
Fynes-Clinton: FD2–
Fysh: FD1–FD2–

Gabbett-Mulhallen: FD2–
Gabriel: FD2–
Gade: Ne 7/491–
Gage: FD1–FD2–Ne 3/165–
Gago Da Camara De Medeiros: W1/34–W2/68–
Gaillard: Mc 1/175–
Gainsborough: FD1–
Gainsford: FD2–
Gair: W2/68–W2/69–W2/70–
Gaisford: FD2–
Gaisford-St.-Lawrence: FD2–
Gait: FD2–
Gaitskell: FD2–
Galbraith: FD2–
Gale: FD1–FD2–Ne 5/334–Bn 64–Mc 1/178– W1/34–W2/71–
Galea: W1/35–W2/71–
Gallaher: Mt 116–
Gallatin: Mt 93–Ne 7/498–Bn 64–AH13–
Gallaudet: Bn 64–
Gallini: FD2–
Gallishan: Bn 64–
Galloway: FD1–FD2–
Gallway: FD2–
Galpin: FD2–
Galt: FD1–FD2–
Galton: FD2–
Galvez: Bn 64–
Galway: FD1–
Gambier: FD2–
Gamble: FD1–FD2–Bn 64–Mc 1/182–As 190–
Gammell: FD1–FD2–
Gandolfi: FD2–
Gantt: Mc 1/186–
Gape: FD2–
Garden-Campbell: FD1–
Gardiner: FD2–Mt(A)34–Bn 64–AH3–
Garden: FD2–
Gardner: FD1–FD2–Bn 65–
Gardner-Brown: FD2–

Gardner-Medwin: FD2–
Gardyner: Ne 8/537–
Garfit: FD1–FD2–
Garforth: FD2–
Garland: Bn 65–
Garlick: Bn 65–V.H.9–
Garnett: FD1–FD2–Bn 65–Mc 1/190–
Garnett-Botfield: FD1–FD2–
Garnett-Orme: FD2–
Garrard: FD2–Mt 191–
Garratt: FD2–
Garrett: FD2–Bn 65–
Garrod: FD1–FD2–
Garstin: FD2–
Garthwaite: FD2–
Garton: FD2–
Gartside-Tipping: FD1–
Gartside-Spaught: FD2–
Garvagh: FD1–
Garvan: FD2–
Garvey: FD2–
Gascoigne: FD2–
Gascoyne-Cecil: FD1–FD2–
Gaskell: FD1–FD2–
Gaskins: FD2–
Gaston: Mt 40–
Gatacre/Gataker: FD1–FD2–
Gatehouse: FD2–
Gathorne-Hardy: FD2–
Gates: FD2–Ne 2/104–
Gatti: FD2–
Gatty: FD1–FD2–
Gauld: FD2–
Gault: FD2–
Gaunt: FD2–
Gause: Bn 65–
Gavit: Bn 65–
Gay: Mt(A)35–Bn 65–
Gayer: Ne 1/67–Mt(A)35–
Gayre of Gayre & Nigg: W1/36–W1/37–W2/72– W2/73–
Gazzam: Mt 142–
Geach: FD2–
Geary: FD1–FD2–
Geddes: FD2–
Gedney: Mt(A)35–Bn 65–Ne 8/589–
Gee: FD2–Bn 66–
Geer: Mt 154–Bn 66–AH15–
Geijer: FD2–
Gell: FD1–
Gemmell: FD2–
Genoese: W2/73–
di Genova: AS 56–W1/37–W2/74–
Gentleman: FD2–
Geoghedan: FD2–
George: FD2–Mt 10–
Gepp: FD2–
Gerard: FD1–FD2–Bn 66–
Gerard-Dicconson: FD2–
German: FD2–
Geron: FD2–
Gerrard: FD2–
Gerrish: Mt(A)35–Bn 66–
Gervais: FD2–Bn 66–
Gethin: FD1–FD2–
Getting: FD2–
Gibb: FD2–
Gibbes: Bn 66–
Gibbon: Ne 2/136–
Gibbons: FD1–FD2–
Gibbs: FD1–FD2–Ne 2/74–Mt 125–Bn 66–
Gibson: FD1–FD2–Mt(A)35–
Gibson-Craig: FD1–
Gibsone: FD2–
Gidley: FD2–
Giffard: FD2–
Gifford: FD1–FD2–Bn 66–

Gignilliat: Bn 66–
Gilbert: FD1–FD2–Mt 14, 126, 171–Bn 66–
Gilbey: FD1–FD2–
Gilchrist: FD1–FD2–Bn 67–
Gilchrist-Clark: FD2–
Gildea: FD1–FD2–
Giles-Puller: FD2–
Giles: FD2–Mt 226–Bn 67–AH8–
Gill: FD1–FD2–AS 58–W2/74–
Gillespie: FD1–Bn 67–
Gillette: Bn 67–
Gillies-Smith: FD2–
Gillman: FD2–
Gillon: FD2–
Gilman: Mt 79–Bn 67–Mc 1/193–AH4–
Gilmer: Bn 67–V.H.111–
Gilmour: FD2–
Gilpin: FD2–Mt(A)35–Bn 67–AH13–
Gilpin-Brown: FD2–
Gilroy: FD1–
Gilstrap: FD1–
Gipps: FD1–
Gisborne: FD1–FD2–
Gist: FD1–FD2–
Gladstone: FD1–FD2–
Glasbrook: FD2–
Glasgow: FD1–FD2–
Glasspoole: FD2–
Glatfelter: Bn 67–
Glazebrook: FD1–FD2–
Gledstaines: FD1–FD2–
Gleason: Bn 67–
Glegg: FD2–
Gleim: Bn 67–
Glen: FD2–
Glen-coats: FD1–FD2–
Glencross: FD2–
Glenn: FD2–Mt 17, 191–
Glidden: Mt 168–Bn 68–
Glossop-Harriss: FD1–
Gloucester & Bristol: FD1–
Glover: FD2–Bn 68–
Glyn: FD1–FD2–
Goddard: FD1–Bn 68–
Godden: FD2–
Godfrey: FD1–FD2–Bn 68–
Godlee: FD2–
Godley: FD2–
Godman: FD2–
Godson: FD1–
Goelet: Bn 68–
Goetchius: Ne 7/486–
Goff: FD2–
Gogarty: FD2–
Going: FD2–
Gold: FD2–AH111–
Goldie: W1/38–W2/75–
Goldie-Scot: FD2–
Goldie-Scott: FD1–
Golding: Ne 3/173–
Goldman: FD2–
Goldney: FD1–FD2–
Goldsborough: Bn 68–Mc 1/196, 199–
Goldsmid: FD1–FD2–
Goldsmid-Montefiore: FD2–
Goldsmith: Bn 68–
Gooch: FD1–FD2–Ne 4/255–Bn 68–V.H.34–
Goodacre: FD2–
Goodden: FD2–
Gooden-Chisolm: FD2–
Goodeve-Erskine: FD1–FD2–
Goodfellow: FD1–FD2–
Goodford: FD2–
Goodhart-Rendel: FD2–
Goodman: Bn 69–
Goodrich: Mt(A)36–Bn 68–
Goodridge: FD1–Bn 68–

Goodsell: AH12–
Goodson: FD2–
Goodwin: FD1–Mt 181–Bn 68–V.H.29–
Gookin: Mt(A)36–Ne 1/39–Bn 69–V.H.88–AH9–
Goold: FD1–FD2–
Goolden: FD2–
Goold-Verschoyle: FD2–
Gordon: FD1–FD2–Ne 5/313–Ne 7/480, 519–
Mt(A)36–Bn 69–V.H.10/17/35–W1/38–W1/39–
W2/76–
Gordon-Canning: FD2–
Gordon-Cumming: FD2–
Gordon-Cumming-Skene: FD2–
Gordon-Duff: FD2–
Gordon-Lennox: FD1–FD2–
Gordon-Oswald: FD2–
Gore: FD1–FD2–Ne 1/6–Bn 69–
Gore-Booth: FD1–FD2–
Gore-Browne: FD2–
Gore-Langton: FD1–
Gorge: Mt(A)36–
Gorges: FD1–FD2–Ne 2/93–Bn 69–
Goring: FD1–FD2–
Gormanston: FD1–
Gorst: FD1–FD2–
Gorsuch: Ne 3/193–
Gort: FD1–
Gorton: Ne 1/65–
Goschen: FD2–
Gosford: FD1–
Gosling: FD2–
Gosnold: Ne 6/430–
Goss: FD1–FD2–
Gostwyck: FD2–
Gottsichi: Ne 7/486–
Gottwaltz: FD2–
Gough: FD1–FD2–Bn 69–
Gough-Calthorpe: FD1–FD2–
Gould: FD1–FD2–Mt 179–Bn 69–
Goulding: FD1–FD2–
Goulter: FD2–
Gourgas: Bn 70–
Gourlay: FD1–FD2–
Gove: Mt(A)36–Bn 70–
Grace: FD1–FD2–
Gradwell: FD2–
Graeme: FD1–FD2–Bn 70–
(de) Graffenreid: Ne 7/464–
Grafton: FD1–
Graham: FD1–FD2–Ne 7/511–Bn 70–V.H.35–
Barns-Graham: FD2–
Graham-Clarke: FD2–
Graham-Montgomery: FD1–FD2–
Graham-Toler: FD1–FD2–
Graham-Stewart: FD1–
Graham-Wigan: FD2–
Grahame: FD2–
Granard: FD1–
Grange: FD2–
Granger: FD2–Mt 100–
Grant: FD1–FD2–Mt 51–Bn 70–
Grant-Duff: FD2–
Grant-Dalton: FD2–
Grant-Ives: FD1–FD2–
Grant-Suttie: FD1–FD2–
Grant-Thurold: FD2–
Grantham: FD1–FD2–
Grantley: FD1–
Granville: FD1–FD2–
(de) Grasse: Ne 5/377–
Grattan-Bellew: FD1–
Graumann: FD2–
Gravely: FD2–
Graves: FD1–FD2–Bn 70–AH10–
Graves-Knyfton: FD2–
Graves-Sawle: FD1–FD2–
Gray: FD1–FD2–Ne 3/206–Bn 70–V.H.40–

Gray-Buchanan: FD2–
Gray-Cheape: FD2–
Grayson: FD2–
Greathead: FD2–
Greaves: FD1–FD2–Bn 71–
Greaves-Bagshawe: FD1–
Greaves-Lord: FD2–
Green: FD1–FD2–Bn 71–
Green-Price: FD1–FD2–
Green-Thompson: FD2–
Greenall: FD1–FD2–
Greene: FD1–FD2–Ne 2/97–Mt(A)36–Bn 71–
    Mc 1/209–AH8–
Greenhalgh: FD2–
Greenfield: FD2–
Greenham: FD2–
Greenleaf: Bn 71–
Greenlees: Mt(A)37–
Greenly: FD2–
Greenough: Bn 71–
Greenshields: FD2–
Greenshields-Leadbeater: FD2–
Greenway: FD2–Bn 71–
Greenwell: FD2–
Greenwood: FD2–Mt(A)37–Bn 71–AH13–
Greer: FD1–FD2–
Greg: FD1–FD2–
Gregorie: Bn 72–
Gregory: FD1–FD2–Ne 2/125–Mt(A)37–AH16–
Gregson: FD2–
Greig: FD1–FD2–
Greenfell: FD1–FD2–
Gregory-Hood: FD2–
Gren: Ne 8/598–
Grenfell: FD1–FD2–
Gresham: Ne 6/442–
Gresley: FD1–FD2–
Greswolde: FD2–
Gretton: FD2–
Greville: FD1–FD2–
Greville-Nugent: FD1–FD2–
Greville-Smith: FD2–
Grew: Bn 72–
Grey: FD1–FD2–
Grey de Ruthyn: FD1–FD2–
Grey-Egerton: FD1–FD2–
Greystoke: Mt 230–
Gribble: FD1–
Grierson: FD1–FD2–
Griffin: FD1–FD2–Bn 72–V.H.105–
Griffith: FD1–FD2–Mt 138–Bn 72–
Griffiths: FD2–Bn 72–
Griggs: FD1–FD2–
Grigson: FD2–
Grimaldi: FD2–
Grimes: W1/39–W2/77–
Grimke-Drayton: FD1–FD2–
Grimshaw: Bn 72–
Grimston: FD1–FD2–
Grimthorpe: FD1–
Grimwood: FD2–
Grindle: FD2–
Grinlington: FD2–
Griscom: Mt 96–
Grissell: FD1–FD2–
Griswold: Mt 214–Bn 72–AH3–
Grogan: FD1–FD2–
Gromditch: FD2–
Gross: Mt 208–Bn 72–
Grosschmid-Zsogod of Visegrad: W2/78–
Grosvenor: FD1–FD2–Bn 72–AS60–
(de) Grouchy: Ne 7/516–
Grout: Bn 72–
Grove: FD1–FD2–
Groves: FD1–FD2–Bn 72–
Grubb: FD1–FD2–
Grubbe: FD1–FD2–

Grundy: Bn 72–
Grylls: FD2–
Grymes: Bn 73–V.H.45/66–
Gubbay: FD2–
Gubbins: FD2–
Guerin: W1/40–W2/78–
Guerrant: Bn 73–
Guest: FD2–
Guild: Mt(A)37–Bn 73–
Guilford: FD1–
Guillamore: FD1–
Guinand: Bn 73–
Guinnes: FD2–
Guines: FD2–
di Guira: W1/38–W2/75–
Guion: AH107–
Guise: FD1–FD2–
Gull: FD1–FD2–
Gun-Cunninghame: FD1–FD2–
Gundry: FD2–
Gunn: FD2–W1/40–W2/79–
Gunning: FD1–FD2–
Gunter: FD2–
Gunther: FD2–
Gurden: Ne 3/219–
Gurdon: FD2–
Gurdon-Rebow: FD2–
Gurney: FD2–Bn 73–
Gutch: FD2–
Guscotte: FD2–
Guthe: FD2–
Guthrie: FD1–FD2–
Guyon: FD2–
Gwatkin: FD1–FD2–
Gwydyr: FD1–
Gwilt: FD2–
Gwyer: FD2–
Gwynne: FD2–
Gybrow-Honneypenny: FD2–

Hackett: FD2–
Hackforth-Jones: FD2–
Hacking: FD2–
Haddington: FD1–
Haden-Best: FD1–
Hadfield: FD2–
Hadley: FD2–Bn 73–
Hagart-Speirs: FD2–
Haggard: FD2–
Haggerston: FD1–FD2–
Hagon: FD2–
Haig: FD1–FD2–Bn 73–
Haig-Bovey: FD2–
Haig-Thomas: FD2–
Haigh: FD2–
Haight: Bn 73–
Hain: FD2–
Hains: Bn 73–
Haire: FD2–
Haire-Forster: FD2–
Hairston: Bn 73–
Hakim: W2/80–
Halahan: FD2–
Halcrow: W1/41–W2/80–
Haldane: FD1–FD2–
Haldane-Duncan: FD1–FD2–Ne 8/551–
Haldon: FD1–
Hale: FD2–Mt(A)37–Mt 120–Bn 73–AH12–
Hales: FD2–
Halford: FD1–Bn 74–
Halifax: FD1–
Halkett: FD1–
Hall: FD1–FD2–Mt 94, 140–Bn 74–V.H.30–
    W1/41–W2/80–
King-Hall: FD2–
Hall-Dare: FD1–FD2–

APPENDIX

Hall-Dempster: FD2–
Hall-Say: FD2–
Hallen: FD1–FD2–
Hallet: Ne 3/171–
Hallifay: FD2–
Hallowell: Ne 7/517–Mt 51–AS62–
Hallowes: FD2–
Halsbury: FD1–
Halsey: FD2–Mt 139–
Halswell: FD2–
Hambledon: FD1–
Hambleton: Mt(A)38–
Hambling: FD2–
Hambro: FD2–
Hambrough: FD2–
Hamersley: FD2–Mt(A)38–Bn 74–AH15–
Hamill-Stewart: FD2–
Hamilton: FD1–FD2–Mt(A)38–Mt 141–Bn 74 & 75–Ne 8/559–
Hamilton-Campbell: FD2–
Hamilton-Dalrymple: FD1–FD2–
Hamilton-Gordon: FD1–FD2–
Hamilton-Grace: FD2–
Hamilton-Russell: FD2–
Hamilton-Starke: FD1–
Hamilton-Wedderburn: FD2–
Hamilton-Temple-Blackwood: FD2–
Hamlyn: FD1–FD2–
Hammick: FD1–FD2–
Hammond: FD1–FD2–Bn 75–
Hammond-Davies: FD2–
Hamond: FD1–FD2–
Hamond-Graeme: FD1–FD2–
Hampden: FD2–
Hampson: FD1–FD2–
Hampton: FD1–
Hampton-Lewis: FD2–
Hanbury: FD1–FD2–Ne 2/140–Mt(A)37–
Hanbury-Tracey: FD1–FD2–
Hanbury-Sparrow: FD2–
Hanchett: Bn 75–
Hancock: FD2–Ne 3/229–Mt(A)38–Bn 75–AH2–
Hancocks: FD1–FD2–
Hand: FD1–FD2–Mt(A)38–
Handcock: FD1–FD2–
Handford: FD2–
Handley: FD2–Bn 75–
Handley-Seymour: FD2–
Hanford: FD2–
Hanham: FD1–FD2–
Hankey: FD2–
Hankinson: FD2–
Hanmer: FD1–FD2–
Hannay: Bn 75–
Hannen: FD2–
Hansard: FD2–
Hansell: FD2–
Hansford: FD2–V.H.40–
Hanson: FD1–FD2–Bn 75–Mc 1/215–
Hapgood: Bn 75–
Harben: FD1–FD2–
Harberton: FD2–
Harbord: FD1–FD2–W1/42–W2/81–
Harbord-Hamond: FD2–
Harcourt: FD2–
Harcourt-Vernon: FD2–
Hardcastle: FD2–
Hardenbrook: Bn 75–
Hardenbergh: Mc 1/219–
Hardie: Mc 1/224–
Harding: FD1–FD2–Bn 76–
Hardinge: FD1–FD2–Bn 76–
Hardwicke: FD2–
Hardy: FD1–FD2–Bn 76–
Hare: FD1–FD2–Mt 126–Mt(A)38–
Harewood: FD1–
Harford: FD2–

Hargrave: FD2–
Hargreaves: FD2–
Harington: FD1–FD2–
Harington-Stuart: FD1–
Harison: Bn 76–
Hark: Bn 76–
Harkness: FD2–
Harkness: FD2–Bn 76–
Harlakenden: Ne 2/144–Mt 75–Bn 76–
Harland: FD1–Bn 76–
Harlech: FD1–
Harman: FD1–FD2–Bn 76–
Harmer: FD2–
Harmon: Bn 76–
Harmood-Banner: FD2–
Harmsworth: FD2–
Harnage: FD1–
Harold: Bn 76–
Harold-Barry: FD2–
Harpending: Bn 76–
Harper: FD2–
Harraton: FD2–
Harrel: FD2–
Harries: FD2–
Harrington: FD1–FD2–
Harris: FD1–FD2–Bn 76–Ne 8/597–
Harris-Burland: FD2–
Harris-St. John: FD2–
Harris-Temple: FD1–
Harrison: FD1–FD2–Mt(A)39–Bn 76–V.H.22/102–
Harrison-Broadley: FD2–
Harrison-Topham: FD2–
Harrison-Wallace: FD2–
Harrow School: W2/81–
Harrowby: FD1–
Harrowing: FD2–
Hart: FD1–FD2–Mt 86–Bn 77–
Hart-Davis: FD1–
Hart-Synnot: FD2–
Hartcup: FD2–
Harter: FD2–
Hartigan: FD2–
Hartley: FD1–FD2–
Hartill: FD2–
Hartstonge-Weld: FD2–
Hartwell: FD1–FD2–Bn 77–AS64–
Harty: FD1–FD2–
Harvent: FD2–
Harvey: FD1–FD2–Bn 77–
Harvie-Brown: FD2–
Harward: Bn 77–V.H.28–
Harwood: FD1–FD2–Mt(A)39–V.H.94–
Hasbrouck: Mt(A)39–
Hasegawa: AS66–
Hasell: FD2–Bn 77–
Haskell: Mt 20–Bn 77–
Haskins: Bn 77–
Haslam: FD1–FD2–
Hasler: FD2–
Haslewood: FD1–
Hassell-Haw: FD2–
Hastings: FD1–FD2–Mt(A)39–Bn 77–
Hatch: FD2–Bn 77–AH12–
Hatfield: FD2–
Hatherell: FD2–
Hatherton: FD1–
Hathorn-Johnston-Stewart: FD2–
Hatry: FD2–
Hatton: FD2–
Hatton-Ellis: FD2–
Havelock-Allan: FD1–FD2–
Havemeyer: Bn 78–
Haviland-Burke: FD2–
Havinden: FD2–
Hawarden: Ne 3/180–
Hawes: FD2–Ne 3/197–Mt(A)39–Bn 78–

Hawke: FD1–FD2–
Hawkes: Mt(A)39–Bn 78–
Hawkes-Cornock: FD1–FD2–
Hawkesbury: FD1–
Hawkins: FD1–FD2–Bn 78–
Hawks: Bn 78–
Hawkshaw: FD2–
Hawksley: FD2–
Hawley: FD1–FD2–Mt(A)40–
Haworth: FD2–
Haworth-Booth: FD2–
Haworth-Leslie: FD1–
Hawtrey: FD2–
Hay: FD1–FD2–Mt 6–Bn 78–AH5–W1/42–
 W2/82–
Hay-Drummond-Hay: FD2–
Hay-Drummond: FD2–
Hay-Gordon: FD1–FD2–
Hay-Newton: FD1–FD2–
Haycraft: FD2–
Hayden: AH8–
Haydock: Ne 1/72–
Hayes: FD1–FD2–Mt 160–Bn 78–
Hayne: FD2–Bn 78–
Haynes: Ne 3/191–Mt(A)40–Bn 78–
Hays: Bn 78–
Hayter: FD1–
Hayter-Hames: FD2–
Hayward: Bn 78–
Hazard: Mt(A)40–
Hazelhurst: Bn 78–
Hazelton: AS68–W2/82–W2/83–
Hazierigg: FD1–
Head: FD1–FD2–Ne 5/330–Bn 78–
Headfort: FD1–
Headlam: FD2–
Headley: FD1–
Heald: FD2–
Heap: FD2–
Heape: FD2–
Heard: FD1–FD2–Bn 78–
Hearn: FD2–Bn 78 & 79–
Hearnsey: FD2–
Heaslett: FD2–
Heath: FD2–
Heathcoat-Amory: FD1–FD2–
Heathcote: FD1–FD2–Ne 2/85–Bn 79–AH1–
Heathcote-Drummond-Willoughby: FD1–FD2–
Heathcote-Hacker: FD2–
Heaton-Armstrong: FD1–FD2–
Heaven: FD1–FD2–
Heazell: FD2–
Heber-Percy: FD2–
Heberden: FD2–
Hedley-Dent: FD2–
Hedley: FD2–
Hedstrom: FD2–
Heesom: FD2–
Heigham: FD2–
Helme: FD2–Ne 5/348–
Helm: FD2–W1/42–W2/83–
Helmershausen: Ne 1/9–Bn 79–
Helsham-Jones: FD1–
Hely-Hutchinson: FD1–FD2–
Helps: FD2–
Helmore: FD2–
Helsham: FD2–
Helyar: FD2–
Hemingway: FD2–
Hemming: FD2–
Hemphill: FD2–
Hemraj: FD2–
Hemsworth: FD2–
Henchman: Bn 79–
Henchy: FD2–
Henderson: FD1–FD2–Ne 7/467–Bn 79–V.H.72–
Hendrick: Mt 150, 176–

Hendrick-Aylmer: FD2–
Heneage: FD2–
Henkel: Bn 79–
Henley: FD2–FD1–
Henn: FD2–
Henn-Gennys: FD2–
Hennessey: FD2–
Henniker: FD1–FD2–
Henniker-Heaton: FD2–
Henniker-Hughan: FD2–
Henniker-Major: FD1–FD2–
Henry: FD2–Mt 88–Mc 1/227, 229–
Henry-Batten-Pooll: FD2–
Henryson-Caird: FD2–
Henshaw: Ne 5/365–Mt(A)40–Bn 79–
Henty: FD2–
Henwood: FD2–
Hepburn: FD2–Bn 79–
Hepburn-Stuart-Forbes: FD2–
Hepburne-Scott: FD2–
Hepton: FD2–
Hepworth: FD2–FD1–
Herburne-Scott: FD1–
Herbert: FD1–FD2–Bn 79–V.H.39–
Herbert-Huddleston: FD2–
Hercy: FD2–
Herd: FD2–
Herdman: FD2–
Hereford: FD1–FD2–
Heriot: FD2–
Hermon-Hodge: FD2–
Hernandez Vinceza y Soto: AS70–
Herndon: Mt(A)40–Ne 7/501–
Heron: FD2–
Heron-Maxwell: FD1–FD2–
Herries: FD1–
Herries-Crosbie: FD2–
Herrick: Mt(A)40–Mt 138–Bn 79–AH14–
Herringham: FD2–
Herrman: Bn 79–
Herron: FD1–FD2–
Herschel: FD1–
Herschell: FD1–FD2–
Herter: Bn 80–
Hertford: FD1–
Hervey: FD1–FD2–
Hervey-Bathurst: FD1–FD2–
Heseltine: Bn 80–
Hesilrige/Hazlerigg: FD2–Ne 4/284–
Hesketh: FD2–
Hewart: FD2–
Hewes: Bn 50–
Hewett: FD1–FD2–
Hewitt: FD2–
Hext: FD1–
Heycock: FD2–
Heygate: FD1–FD2–
Heyman: Ne 7/456–Bn 80–V.H.44–
Heys: FD2–
Heytes: FD1–
Heyward: Bn 80–
Heywood: FD1–FD2–Bn 80–
Heywood-Jones: FD2–
Heywood-Lonsdale: FD2–
Heyworth: FD1–FD2–Ne 7/455–
Heyworth-Savage: FD2–
Hibbert: FD2–Bn 80–
Hibbins: Bn 80–
Hickey: FD2–
Hickie: FD2–
Hickling: FD2–
Hickman: FD1–FD2–
Hicks: FD1–FD2–Ne 2/148–Bn 80–AH16–
Hicks-Beach: FD1–FD2–
Hickson: FD2–
Higginbotham: FD2–
Higgins: FD1–

Higgins-Bernard: FD2–
Higginson: FD2–Ne 2/73–Mt(A)41–Bn 80–
Higgs: Bn 80–
Higham: FD2–
Highmore: FD2–
Hight: Bn 81–
Higinbotham: FD2–
Hignett: FD2–
Hilborne: FD2–
Hildreth: Bn 81–
Hildyard: FD2–
Hill: FD1–FD2–Mt 12, 53–Mt(A)41–Bn 81–Mc
   1/238–V.H.36/46–W1/42–W2/83–
Hill-Lowe: FD1–
Hill-Trevor: FD1–FD2–
Hill-Wood: FD2–
Hillegas: Bn 81–
Hillhouse: Mt 91, 159–
Hilliard: Bn 81–
Hillingdon: FD1–
Hills: Bn 81–
Hills-Johnes: FD1–FD2–
Hilton: Bn 81–
Hilton-Johnson: FD2–
Hilton-Simpson: FD2–
Hinchcliffe: FD2–
Hinckes: FD2–
Hinckley: Mt(A)41–
Hincks: Bn 81–
Hind: FD2–
Hindlip: FD1–
Hinds: FD2–
Hindson: FD2–
Hines: Bn 81–
Hingley: FD1–FD2–
Hingston: FD2–
Hinman: AH 168–
Hinton: Mt(A)41–Bn 81–
Hippisley: FD1–FD2–
Hirch: FD2–
Hires: AS72–W2/84–
Hirsch: FD2–
Hirst: FD2–Mt 137–
Hislop: FD2–
Hitchin-Kemp: FD2–
Hitchcock: Mt(A)41–
Hite: Mt 5–
Hoadley: Mt(A)41–
Hoar: Bn 81–AH2–
Hoare: FD1–FD2–Mt(A)42–
Hobart: FD2–Mt 209–Bn 82–
Hobart-Hampden: FD1–FD2–
Hobhouse: FD1–FD2–
Hoblyn: FD1–FD2–
Hobson: FD2–
Hockin: FD2–
Hodder: FD2–
Hodge: FD1–FD2–Mt(A)42–
Hodges: FD2–Bn 82–
Hodgson: FD2–Bn 82–
Hodsden: Bn 82–
Hodson: FD1–FD2–
Hoffman: Mt(A)42–Bn 82–Mc 1/242–
Hoffnung-Goldsmid: FD2–
Hog: FD1–FD2–
Hogg: FD1–FD2–
Hoggson: Bn 82–
(von) Hohenzollern: Ne 6/440–
Hohler: FD2–
Holbech: FD2–
Holbrook: Bn 82–
Holbrow: FD2–
Holcroft: FD2–
Holden: FD1–FD2–Mt(A)42–
Holder: FD2–Mt 166–
Holdich: FD2–
Holdich-Hungerford: FD2–

Holdsworth: FD2–
Hole: FD1–FD2–
Holford: FD2–V.H.43–
Holland: FD2–
Holland:Hibbert: FD1–FD2–
Holland-Martin: FD2–
Holliday: Bn 83–
Hollins: FD2–Mt(A)42–
Hollinsworth: Mt 189–Bn 83–
Hollis: FD2–
Hollister: Mc 1/247–
Holloway: FD2–
Holloway-Calthrop: FD2–
Hollist: FD2–
Holmden: FD2–
Holme: FD2–Bn 83–
Holmes: FD2–Mt 117–Bn 83–
Holmes A Court: FD1–FD2–
Holstein: Ne 2/110–
Holt: FD2–Bn 83–
Holyoke: Mt(A)42–Bn 83–
Homan-Mulock: FD2–
Homans: Bn 83–
Home: FD1–FD2–
Home-Purves-Hume-Campbell: FD2–
Home-Spiers: FD1–
Homer: FD2–
Honan: FD2–
Hone: V.H.91–
Honyman: FD1–
Honywood: FD1–FD2–
Hood: FD1–FD2–
Hooke: Ne 2/123–Bn 83–V.H.42–
Hooker: Ne 3/213–Bn 83–
Hoole: FD2–
Hooper: FD1–FD2–Bn 83–
Hope: FD1–FD2–Bn 84–
Hope-Dunbar: FD2–
Hope-Edwards: FD2–
Hope-Vere: FD2–
Hopetown: FD1–
Hopewell: Bn 84–
Hopgood: FD2–
Hope-Wallace: FD2–
Hopkins: FD2–Mt(A)43–Bn 84–AH14–
Hopkinson: FD2–Bn 84–
Hopkirk: FD2–
Hopley: AH168–
Hopton: FD2–
Hopwood: FD1–FD2–
Hord: Mc 1/249–
Horder: FD2–
Horder-Despard: FD2–
Hordern: FD1–FD2–
Hore: FD2–
Horlick: FD2–
Horn: FD2–
Hornby: FD1–FD2–
Horncastle: FD2–
Horne: FD2–
Horner: FD2–
Hornor: FD2–Mc 1/253–
Hornyold: FD2–
Horridge: FD2–
Horrocks: FD2–
Horry: Bn 84–
Horsey: Mc 1/259, 256–
Horsfall: FD2–
Horsford: FD2–Bn 84–
Horsley-Beresford: FD2–
Horsmanden: Ne 5/325–
Hort: FD1–
Horton: FD2–Bn 84–
Horton-Smith: FD2–
Horton-Starkie: FD2–
Horwitz: Mt 227–Mt(A)43–
Hoskins: FD1–Bn 84–

Hoskyns: FD1–FD2–
Hoste: FD1–FD2–
Hotblack: FD2–
Hotchkiss: Bn 85–
Hotham: FD1–FD2–
Hothfield: FD1–
Hotson: FD2–
Hotuny: FD2–
Hough: FD2–Mt(A)43–Bn 85–
Houghton: FD1–FD2–Ne 6/149–Mt(A)43–Bn 85–
Houldsworth: FD1–FD2–
House: FD2–
Houston: FD2–Ne 4/289–Bn 85–
Houstoun-Boswall: FD1–FD2–
Hovell-Thurlow-Cumming-Bruce: FD2–
Hovell: FD2–
Hovenden: FD2–
How: FD2–Bn 85–
Howard: FD1–FD2–Ne 4/265–Mt 230–Mt(A)43, 44–Bn 85–Mc 1/263, 266–AH9–
Howard-Brooke: FD2–
Howard-M'Lean: FD2–
Howard-Bury: FD2–
Howard-Martin: Mc 1/271–
Howard-Stepney: FD2–
Howard-Vyse: FD2–
Howatson: FD2–
Howe: FD1–FD2–Mt 121–Bn 85–
Howell: Mt(A)43–Bn 86–V.H.97–AH12–
Howes: Mt 59–Bn 86–
Howland: Mt 74, 83–Bn 86–AH16–
Howlett: FD2–
Howth: FD1–
Hoyle: FD2–
Hoyt: Bn 86–
Hozier: FD1–FD2–
Hubard: Bn 86–
Hubbard: FD1–FD2–Mt(A)44–Bn 86–
Hubbell: Mt(A)44–
Huckel: Bn 86–
Hudson: FD1–FD2–AS74–
Hudson-Kinahan: FD1–FD2–
Huband: FD2–
Huchet: FD2–
Huddleston: FD2–
Hudleston: FD2–
Hudnut: Bn 86–
Hugel: Bn 86–
Huger: Ne 4/243–Bn 86–AH9–
Huggett: Bn 87–
Hughes: FD1–FD2–Bn 87–
Hughes-Buller: FD2–
Hughes-D'Aeth: FD2–
Hughes-Hughes: FD2–
Hughes-Morgan: FD2–
Hughman: FD2–
Huidekoper: Mt 114–
Huidekooper: Ne 2/127–
Huie: Mt(A)108–
Hull: FD2–Mt(A)44–Ne 2/133–Bn 87–
Hulbert: FD2–
Hulburd: FD2–
Hulse: FD1–FD2–
Hulley: FD2–
Hulton: FD2–Bn 87–
Hulton-Harrop: FD1–FD2–
Humble: FD1–FD2–
Humble-Burkitt: FD2–
Hume: FD1–FD2–Mt 125–Ne 1/14–V.H.45–
Humfrey: FD2–Ne 2/113–Bn 87–
Humphery: FD1–FD2–
Humphreys: Bn 87–
Humphreys-Johnstone: FD2–
Humphreys-Owen: FD1–FD2–
Humphries: FD2–Bn 87–
Sidney-Humphries: FD2–
Humphry: FD2–

Humphrys: FD2–
Hunlock: Ne 2/153–Mt(A)44–
Hunloke: FD2–
Hunnewell: AS76–
Hunt: FD1–FD2–Bn 87–
Hunt-Grubbe: FD2–
Hunter: FD1–FD2–Mt(A)44–Bn 87–
Hunter-Arundell: FD2–
Hunter-Blair: FD1–FD2–
Hunter-Marshall: FD2–
Hunter-Weston: FD1–FD2–
Huntingdon: FD1–Mt(A)45–Bn 87–
Huntingfield: FD1–
Huntington: FD2–
Huntington-Whiteley: FD2–
Huntingtower: FD1–
Huntley: FD2–
Huntly: FD1–
Hunton: Bn 87–
Huntshaw: FD2–
Hurd: Ne 4/261–Mt 172–Bn 87–
Hurly: FD1–FD2–
Hurry: Mt 119–Bn 87–AH15–
Hurst: FD2–
Husey-Hunt: FD2–
Hurt: FD1–
Hut-Sitwell: FD1–
Huson: FD2–
Hussey: FD1–FD2–
Hussey-Freke: FD1–FD2–
Hussey-Walsh: FD1–FD2–
Hustler: FD2–
Hutchins: Mt(A)45–Bn 88–
Hutchinson: FD1–FD2–Ne 1/42–Mt(A)45–Bn 88–AH2, 17–
Hutchings: FD2–Bn 88–
Hutchison: FD1–FD2–
Huth: FD1–FD2–
Hutson: Bn 88–
Hutton: FD1–FD2–Bn 88–
Huxtable: FD2–
Huyshe: FD2–
Hyatt: Mt 73–
Hyde: FD2–Ne 4/293–Mt 3, 193–Ne 6/413–Mc 1/278–
Hyett: FD2–
Hylton-Joliffe: FD1–
Hynson: Mc 1/280–
Hyslop: Bn 88–

I'Anson: FD1–FD2–
Iddesleigh: FD1–
Ilbert: FD2–
Ilchester: FD1–
Inchiquin: FD1–
Illingworth: FD2–
Imthurn: FD2–
Image: FD2–
Imbert-Terry: FD2–
Imlay: FD2–
Imperiali: W1/43–W2/85–
Impey-Lovibond: FD2–
Ince: FD2–
Inderwick: FD2–
Ing: FD2–
Inge: FD2–
Ingersoll: Bn 88–
Ingham: FD2–
Inglesby: FD2–
Ingilby: FD1–
Ingle: FD2–
Inglis: FD2–Bn 88–V.H.29–AH11–
Ingraham: Bn 88, 89–
Ingram: FD1–FD2–
Ingverdsen: AS78–W1/43–W2/85–
Inman: FD2–

Innes: FD1–FD2–Ne 7/475–Bn 89–Ne 8/584–
Innes-Cross: FD2–
Innes-Ker: FD2–
Insole: FD2–
Institute of Heraldry: AS80–
Instone: FD2–
International Congress of Genealogy and
    Heraldry 1962: W2/85–
Inverarity: FD2–
Inwood: FD2–
Irby: FD1–FD2–
Iredell: FD2–Bn 89–
Ireland: Ne 8/592–
Ironside: Bn 89–
Irvine: FD1–FD2–Bn 89–AH10–
Irvine-Fortescue: FD2–
Irving: FD2–Bn 89–AS82–W1/43–W1/44–
    W2/85 & 86–
Irwin: FD1–FD2–Mt 3, 101–
Isaacs: FD2–
Isaacson: FD2–
Iselin: Ne 7/496–Bn 89–
Isham: FD1–FD2–Ne 5/309–Mt 53–Bn 89–
    V.H.47–
Ishay: FD1–
Isherwood: FD2–
Iveagh: FD1–
Iverach: FD2–
Ives: Mt 15–Bn 89–
Ismay: FD2–
Iveson: FD2–
Ivey: FD2–
Ivimey: FD2–
Ivrea: FD2–
Izard: Bn 89–
Izzard: Bn 89–

Jackman: W1/45–W2/87–
Jackson: FD1–FD2–Mt 116–Bn 90–W1/45, 46,
    47, 48–W2/87, 88, 89, 90–
Jackson-Barstow: FD2–
Jacob: FD1–
Jacobs: FD2–Bn 90–Ne 8/548–AS84–
Jacobsen: Bn 90–
Jacoby: FD1–FD2–
Jacquelin: Bn 91–V.H.28–
Jacquet: Ne 6/443–Mt 7–Bn 91–
Jadwin: V.H.107–
Jaeger: Bn 90–
Jaffe: FD2–
Jaffray: FD1–FD2–Ne 8/587–
Jaffrey: Mt(A)45–Bn 90–
Jagemann: Bn 90–
Jago-Trelawny: FD1–
Jalland: FD2–
James: FD1–FD2–W2/90–
James: Mt(A)45–
Jameson: FD2–Bn 90–V.H.33–
Janney: Bn 90–
Janvrin: Bn 91–
Jardine: FD1–FD2–
Jarrett: FD2–
Jarvis: FD2–Bn 91–
Jary: FD2–
Jatia: FD2–
Jaudon: Mt(A)45–
Jauncey: Bn 91–
Jauregui: AS86–
Jay: Bn 91–AH3–
Jayne: FD2–Bn 91–
Jebb: FD2–
Jeffcoat: FD2–
Jefferds: Bn 91–
Jeffers: Bn 91–
Jeffock: FD2–
Jeffery: Bn 91–

Jeffray: Ne 4/249–
Jeffrey: Mt(A)46–
Jeffreys: FD2–
Jeffries: Ne 4/251–Mt(A)46–Bn 91–AH4–
Jehanghir: FD2–
Jejeebhoy: FD1–FD2–
Jekyll: FD1–FD2–Bn 91–
Jelf: FD2–
Jelf-Petit: FD2–
Jelf-Sharp: FD2–
Jellett: FD2–
Jellicoe: FD2–
Jenings: FD2–Bn 92–V.H.26–
Jenkins: FD1–FD2–Mt 50–Bn 92–Mc 1/284, 287,
    290–
Jenkinson: FD1–FD2–
Jenks: Bn 92–
Jenner: FD1–FD2–Bn 92–
Jenner-Fust: FD1–FD2–
Jenney: FD2–
Jennings: FD1–FD2–Mt 88–
Jephson: FD1–
Jerdone: Bn 92–V.H.29–
Jerningham: FD1–FD2–
Jersey: FD1–
Jervis: FD1–FD2–
Jervis-White-Jervis: FD2–FD1–
Jervois: FD2–
Jervoise: FD2–
Jessel: FD1–FD2–
Jessop: FD1–FD2–
Jes(s)up: Mt 70–Bn 92–
Jett: Bn 92–V.H.8–
Jeune: FD1–FD2–
Jex-Blake: FD2–
Jewers: FD1–
Jewett: Bn 92–
Joachimsen: Bn 92–
Jocelyn/Josselyn: FD1–FD2–Mt(A)46–
Jodrell: FD1–FD2–
Joel: FD2–
John, Venerable Order of St., in the Briksle
    Realm: W2/91–
Johnes: AH13–W1/48–W2/91–
Johns: FD2–Mt(A)46–
Johnson: FD1–FD2–Ne 2/162, 3/167, 4/272,
    5/326, 7/485–Bn 92, 93–Mt 52–Mt(A)46, 47–
Johnston: FD1–FD2–Mt 126–Bn 93–
Johnston-Gerrard: FD2–
Johnston-Stewart: FD1–
Johnstone: FD1–FD2–Ne 2/82–AH13–W1/49–
    W2/91–
Johnstone-Scott: FD2–
Johonnot: Bn 93–
Joicey: FD1–FD2–
Joicey-Cecil: FD2–
Jolian: FD2–
Joly de Lotbiniere: FD2–
Jolliffe: FD2–
Jones: FD1–FD2–Ne 7/476–Mt 64, 76, 135–Bn
    93, 94–Mc 1/296–V.H.26/46/51–
Jones-Parry: FD1–FD2–
Jones-Williams: FD2–
(de) Jongh: Ne 5/336–
Jordan: FD2–Bn 94–
Jorkin: AS88, 90–
Joseph: FD2–
Joseph-Watkin: FD1–
Joslin: FD2–
Josselyn: FD1–Ne 2/99–Bn 94–
Jossilyn: Mt(A)46–
Jouet: AH16–
Joy: Bn 94–
Joycliffe: AH170–
Joynson: FD1–FD2–
Jockes-Clifton: FD1–
Jourdain: FD2–

Jowett: FD2–
Joyce: FD2–
Joynt: FD2–
Judah: Bn 94–
Judd: FD2–Mt 47–Bn 94–
Judge: FD2–
Judkin-Fitzgerald: FD1–FD2–
Judson: Mt 73, 154–Bn 94–
Jump: FD2–

Kaitenborn (von): Ne 6/433–
Kane: FD1–FD2–Mt(A)46–
Karnezis: AS92–
Karras: AS94–
Karslake: FD1–
Kasson: Mt(A)47–
Kater: FD1–FD2–
Kavanaugh: FD2–
Kay: FD1–FD2–Mt(A)47–Bn 95–
Kay-Menzies: FD2–
Kay-Shuttleworth: FD1–FD2–
Kaye: FD2–
Kealy: FD1–FD2–
Keane: FD1–FD2–
Kearley: FD2–
Kearney: FD2–Bn 95–
Keates: FD1–FD2–
Keating: FD2–
Keayne: Ne 3/205–Mt(A)47–Bn 95–
Keeble: Bn 95–V.H.8–
Keeling: FD1–FD2–
Keegan: FD2–
Keene: Bn 95–
Keese: Bn 95–
Keevil: FD2–
Keighly-Peach: FD2–
Keith: Bn 95–
Keith-Falconer: FD2–
Kekewich: FD2–
Kelham: FD2–
Kelhead: FD1–
Kelk: FD1–
Kelker: Ne 8/595–
Kellett: FD1–FD2–Bn 95–
Kelley: Mt(A)47–
Kellogg: Bn 95–
Kelly: FD2–Bn 95–
Kelso: FD1–FD2–
Kelvin: FD1–
Kemeys-Tynte: FD1–FD2–
Kemmis-Steinman: FD2–
Kemball: FD2–
Kemble: Bn 95–
Kemp: FD1–FD2–
Kempe: Bn 95–V.H.34–
Kemper: Mt 194–
Kempton: FD2–
Kemsley: FD2–
Kendall: FD2–Mt 47, 80–
Kendrick: Bn 95–
Kenhare: FD1–
Kenna: FD2–
Kennard: FD1–FD2–
Kennaway: FD1–FD2–
Kennedy: FD1–FD2–Ne 5/327–Bn 95–Mc 1/296–
   Ne 8/586–
Kennedy-Erskine: FD1–FD2–
Kennedy-Crauford-Stuart: FD2–
Kennett-Barrington: FD1–
Kenney: FD2–
Kenney-Herbert: FD1–
Kent: FD2–
Kensington: FD1–
Kenworthy: FD2–
Kenyon: FD1–FD2–Ne 2/79–
Kenyon-Slaney: FD1–FD2–

Tyrell-Kenyon: FD2–
Keppel: FD1–FD2–
Ker: FD2–
Kerby: FD2–
Kery-Seymer: FD1–
Kerr: FD1–FD2–Mt(A)18–Bn 95–
Kerr-Pearse: FD2–
Kerrich-Walker: FD2–
Kerrison: FD1–
Kerry: FD1–
Kersey: FD2–
Kershaw: FD2–
Kesteven: FD1–
Ketchum: Bn 96–
Kettle: FD1–Bn 90–
Kettlewell: FD1–FD2–
Keutcheoglu: W1/49–W2/92–
Key: FD1–FD2–Mc 1/299, 302–
Keyes: FD2–
Keyser: FD1–Bn 96–
Keyworth: FD2–
Kezdy Vasarhelyi de Kezd: W1/49–W2/92–
Kidd: FD1–FD2–
Kidston: FD2–
Kienbusch: Bn 96–
Kiggell: FD2–
Kilburn: FD2–
Kilby: Bn 96–
Kilham: Bn 96–
Killik: FD2–
Kilmaine: FD1–
Kilmorey: FD1–
Kilpin: FD1–FD2–
Kimball: Mt(A)48–Bn 96–FD2–
Kimber: FD1–FD2–
Kimberley: FD1–
Kimberly: Bn 96–
Kincaid: Ne 8/557–
Kindersley: FD2–
King: FD1–FD2–Ne 1/68–Mt(A)48–Bn 96–Mc
   1/305, 308–V.H.50–
King-Fane: FD2–
King-Harman: FD2–
King-King: FD2–
King-Tenison: FD2–
Kingan: FD2–
Kingerlee: FD2–
Kingsale: FD1–
Kingsburgh: FD1–
Kingscote: FD2–
Kingsford: FD2–
Kingsford-Lethbridge: FD2–
Kingshill: FD1–FD2–
Kingsmill: V.H.36–
Kingston: FD1–Bn 97–
Kingstone: FD2–
Kington-Oliphant: FD1–
Kinloch: FD1–FD2–
Kinloch-Smyth: FD2–
Kinlock: Bn 97–
Kinloss: FD1–FD2–
Kinmond: FD2–
Kinnaird: FD1–FD2–
Kinnool: FD1–
Kinsman: AH170–
Kinsolving: Ne 2/115–
Kintore: FD1–
Kip: Mt(A)48–Bn 97–AH1–
Kippen: FD2–
Kipshaven: Mt(7)–
Kirby: FD2–
Kirk: FD1–FD2–
Kirkpatrick: FD1–FD2–
Kirkpatrick-Caldecot: FD2–
Kirkpatrick-Howat: FD2–
Kirkwood: FD2–
Kirlew: FD2–

Kirsopp: FD2–
Kirsopp-Reed: FD2–
Kirwan: FD2–
Kirton: FD2–
Kissam: Bn 97–
Kitchener: FD2–
Kite: Bn 97–
Kitson: FD1–FD2–
Kittelle: Mt(A)48–
Kleinworth: FD2–
Klock: Bn 97–
Knapp: FD2–
Knapton: FD2–
Knatchbull: FD1–FD2–
Knatchbull-Hugessen: FD1–
Klock: Bn 97–
Knauth: Me 1/61–
Kneeland: Bn 96–
Knight: FD1–FD2–Mt 60–Bn 97–
Knight-Erskine: FD1–FD2–
Knight-Gregson: FD2–
Knightley: FD1–FD2–
Knights: FD2–
Knill: FD1–FD2–
Knocker: FD2–
Knott: FD2–
Knowles: FD1–FD2–Bn 97–
Knowlton: Mt 48, 138–
Knox: FD1–FD2–Bn 97–
Know-Browne: FD2–
Knutsford: FD1–
Knyvett: FD2–
Koe: FD2–
Koecker: Bn 97–
Kona: AS96–
Konig: FD2–
Korda: W1/50–W2/93–
Krumbhaar: Bn 97–
Kuhne: Mt 150–
Kunkel: Mt 44–
(von) Kupferberg: W1/50–W2/93–
Kyle: FD2– Ne 4/237
Kyd: FD2–
Kyllachy: FD1–
Kynaston: FD1–FD2–
Kynnersley: FD1–
Kyrke: FD1–

Labadie: Ne 4/303–
Labberton: Bn 98–
Labouchere: FD1–
Lacey: FD2–
Lacon: FD1–FD2–
Lacy: FD2–
Ladd: Bn 98–
Laery: FD2–
Lafayette: Ne 2/157–
Laffan: FD2–
La Fleur: AS98–
Lafone: FD1–FD2–
Laidlay: FD1–FD2–
Laing: FD1–FD2–
Lake: FD1–FD2–Ne 1/41–Bn 98–
Lakin: FD2–
Laking: FD2–
Lamar: Bn 98–V.H.19–
Lamb: FD1–FD2–
Lambarde: FD2–
Lambart: FD1–FD2–
Lambe: FD2–
Lambert: FD1–FD2–
Lambton: FD1–FD2–
Lamington: FD1–
Lamont: FD1–FD2–
Lamplugh: FD1–FD2–

Lamprey: Bn 98–
Lampson: FD1–FD2–
Lancaster: FD2–
Landon: V.H.25–
de Lancey: AH3–
Landale: FD1–
Lane: FD1–FD2–Ne 7/454–Mt(A)48–Bn 98–
Lane-Fox: FD1–
Lanesborough: FD1–
(von) Lang: Ne 7/478–
Langborne: Bn 98–V.H.9–
Langvin: FD1–
Langford: FD1–
Langham: FD1–FD2–
Lansdale: FD2–
Landon: FD2–
Langdale: FD2–
Langley: FD2–FD1–
Langleg: FD1–
Langman: FD2–
Langmore: FD2–
Langrishe: FD1–FD2–
Lanigaw-O'Keefe: FD2–
Langton: FD2–Bn 98–
Lansdowne: FD1–
Lansing: Mt(A)49–
Lanyon: FD2–
Lapage: FD2–
Larcom: FD1–FD2–
Lardner: Bn 98–
Larken: FD2–
Larkin: FD2–
Larking: FD1–
Larrabee: Bn 98–
Lascelles: FD1–FD2–
La Serre: Mt(A)49–
Lasinby: Bn 98–
Lash: Bn 98–
Laszlo de Lombos: FD2–
Latane: Bn 98–V.H.24–
Latham: FD2–Ne 1/68–Bn 98–
Lathame: Mt 76–
Lathom: FD1–
Lathrop: Mt 148–AH2–Ne 8/606–W2/94–
La Touche: FD2–
La Trobe-Bateman: FD2–
Latter: FD2–
Latta: FD2–
Latting: Mt(A)49–
Lauder: FD2–Bn 98–
Lauderdale: FD1–
Laughlin: Bn 99–
Laurens: Bn 99–
Laurie: FD1–FD2–
Lavalle: W1/52–W2/94–
Law: FD1–FD2–Bn 99–W1/53–W2/94–
Laward: AS104–
Lawder: FD2–
Lawes: FD1–
Lawes-Wittenwronge: FD2–
Lawless: FD2–
Lawley: FD1–FD2–
Lawlor-Huddleston: FD2–
Lawlor: FD2–
Lawrence: FD1–FD2–Ne 6/393–Bn 99–Mt(A)49–
   AH4–
Lawson: FD1–FD2–Bn 99–V.H.59–
Lawson-Smith: FD2–
Lawton: FD2–Mt(A)49–
Lay: AS100–
Layard: FD1–
Laycock: FD2–
Layland-Barratt: FD2–
Layon: Ne 6/432–
Lazarus, Military & Hospitaller Order of St.:
   W2/95–
Lazarus: FD2–

Lea: FD1–FD2–Ne 5/339–
Leach: FD2–Bn 99–
Leadbetter: FD2–
Leadbitter: FD2–
Leadbitter-Smith: FD2–
Leader: FD2–
Leahy: FD2–
Leake: FD1–
Leaper: Ne 8/533–W1/53–W2/96–
Learned: Mt 82–Mt 44–
Leatham: FD1–FD2–
Lean: FD2–
Leask: FD2–
Leather: FD2–
Leavenworth: Bn 100–
Le Breton: FD2–
Le Brun: Mt 210–
Leche: FD2–
Lechmere: FD1–FD2–Ne 5/363–
Leckie: FD2–
Lecky: FD1–FD2–
Leikie: FD2–
Leconfield: FD1–
Leddel: Bn 100–
Ledlie: FD2–
Ledyard: Mt(A)49–Mt 217–
Lee: FD1–FD2–Ne 2/105–Mt(A)50–AH9, 17–
    Bn 100–Mc 1/311–V.H.94–
Lee-Dillon: FD2–
Lee-Elliot: FD2–
Lee-Gratton: FD2–
Lee-Norman: FD2–
Lee-Warner: FD1–FD2–
Leech: FD2–
Leeds: FD1–FD2–Ne 2/58–Mt(A)50–
Leeming: FD1–FD2–
(van) Leer: Ne 5/362–
Lees: FD1–FD2–
Lees-Milne: FD1–FD2–
Leese: FD2–
Leeson: FD2–
Leeson-Marshall: FD2–
Leete: Ne 2/143–Mt(A)50–Bn 100–
Le Fanu: FD2–
Lefferts: Bn 100–
Le Fleming: FD2–
LeFroy: FD1–FD2–
Leftwich: Bn 100–V.H.89–
Legard: FD1–FD2–
Legg: FD2–Bn 100–
Legge: FD1–FD2–Ne 8/600–
Leggett: Mt 176–AH7–
Legh: FD2–
Le Hunte: FD2–
Leicester: FD1–FD2–
Leicester-Warren: FD2–
Leigh: FD1–FD2–Ne 4/258–Bn 100–Ne 5/339–
Leigh-Bennett: FD2–
Leigh-Clare: FD2–
Leigh-Mallory: FD2–
Leigh-White: FD2–
Leigh-Wood: FD2–
Leighton: FD1–FD2–W1/53–W2/96–
Leinster: FD1–
Leir: FD2–
Leir-Carleton: FD2–
Leith: FD2–
Leith-Buchanan: FD1–FD2–
Leith-Ross: FD1–FD2–
Leitrim: FD1–
Le Merchant: FD1–FD2–
Le Mesurier: FD2–
Le Mee-Power: FD2–
Lemmon: Bn 100, 101–
Lemon: Bn 101–
Le Mottee: FD2–
Lempriere: FD1–

Lendrum: FD2–
Leng: FD2–
Lennard: FD1–FD2–
Lenney: Bn 101–
Lennox: FD1–FD2–
Le Noble: Bn 101–
Lenox: Bn 101–
Lentaigne: FD2–
Lenthall: FD2–Bn 101–
Leonard: Mt 75, 117–Bn 101–
Leon de La Barra: AS102–
Le-Poer-Trench: FD1–FD2–
Lepper: FD2–
Lermitte: FD1–FD2–
Lescher: FD1–FD2–
Leslie: FD1–FD2–
Leslie-Duguid: FD2–
Leslie-Ellis: FD2–
Leslie-Melville: FD1–FD2–
L'Estrange: FD2–
L'Estrange-Malone: FD1–FD2–
Letchworth: FD2–
Lethbridge: FD1–FD2–
Letts: FD2–
Leven & Melville: FD1–
Leveson: FD1–FD2–
Leveson-Gower: FD1–FD2–
Lever: FD2–
Leverett: Bn 101–AH4–
Levering: Mt 8, 74–
Levett: FD2–
Levett-Prinsep: FD2–
Levick: FD2–
Levinge: FD1–FD2–
Levis: FD2–
Levy: FD2–Bn 101–
Levy-Lawson: FD2–
Lewes: FD1–
Lewin: FD2–
Lewis: FD1–FD2–Ne 1/52–Mt 142, 233–Bn 101,
    102–V.H.53–W2/96–
Lewis-Barned: FD2–
Lewthwaite: FD1–FD2–
Ley: FD1–FD2–
Leycester: FD2–
Leyland: FD2–
Leyton: FD2–
Liddell: FD2–FD1–
Lidget: Bn 102–
Lidwill: FD2–
Lichfield: FD1–
Liddel: FD1–
Liebenrood: FD2–
Lifford: FD1–
Lighton: FD1–FD2–
Lightfoot: Bn 102–V.H.36–
Ligon: Ne 6/415–
Lilburn: W1/53–W2/97–
Lilford: FD1–
Lilley: FD2–
Lillie: Bn 102–
Lillingston: FD2–
Lillington-Johnson: FD1–
Limerick: FD1–
Lincoln: FD1–Bn 102–
Lind: FD2–
Lindley: FD1–FD2–
Lindsay: FD1–FD2–Ne 4/296–Mt 111–Bn 102–
    Mc 1/323–V.H.43–AH14–
Lindsay-Hogg: FD2–
Lindsay-Smith: FD2–
Lindsey: FD1–
Lindsey-Brabazon: FD2–
Lindesay: Ne 4/276–
Lindgren: W1/54–W2/97–
Lindly: Mt(A)50–Mc 1/320–
Lindsley: Bn 102–

Lindstedt: Bn 102–
Lingard: FD2–
Lingard-Monk: FD1–
Lingen: FD1–
Lingen-Burton: FD1–
Linker: Ne 7/499–
Linkletter: FD2–Ne 6/406–
Linnard: Mt 125–
Linthorne: FD2–
Linzee: Bn 102–AH94–
Lippincott: Mt 56–Bn 102–
Lippitt: FD2–
Lipton: FD2–
Lisburne: FD1–
Lisle: FD1–Ne 4/242–Bn 102–
Lismore: FD1–
Lister: FD1–FD2–Bn 102–V.H.13/22–
Lister-Empson: FD1–
Lister-Kaye: FD1–FD2–
Liston: FD2–
Liston-Foulis: FD1–FD2–
Listowel: FD1–
Litchfield: FD2–
Litchfield-Speer: FD2–
Lithgow: FD2–Bn 103–
Little: FD2–Mt(A)50–Bn 103–
Little-Gilmour: FD2–
Littleboy: FD2–
Littledale: FD1–FD2–
Littlefield: Bn 103–
Littlejohn: FD2–
Littleton: FD1–FD2–Ne 7/484–V.H.38–
Litton: FD2–
Livermore: Bn 103–
Liverpool: FD1–
Livingston: FD1–FD2–Ne 2/96–Mt 159–
  Mt(A)50–Bn 103–AH1, 17–
Livingstone-MacDonald: FD2–
Livingstone-Learmouth: FD2–
Livius: Bn 103–
Llandaff: FD1–
Llangattock: FD1–
Llanoover: FD1–
Llewellin: FD2–
Llewellyn: FD2–Bn 103–
Lloyd: FD1–FD2–Ne 3/179–Mt 57, 74–Bn 103,
  104–V.H.41–AH16–AS106–
Lloyd-Baker: FD2–
Lloyd-Moston: FD1–FD2–
Lloyd-Jones: FD2–
Lobnitz: FD2–
Loch: FD2–
Locker: FD2–
Lockett: FD1–FD2–
Lockhart: FD1–
Lockley: FD2–
Lockton: FD2–
Lockwood: FD2–Mt 122–Bn 104–
Lockyer: FD2–
Locock: FD1–FD2–
Loder: FD1–FD2–
Loder-Symonds: FD1–FD2–
Lodge: FD1–Bn 104–
Loftus: FD1–FD2–
Logan: Mt 13–Bn 104–
Logan-Home: FD2–
Logie: FD2–
Lomar: FD2–
Lombard: FD2–Bn 104–
Lomax: FD2–
Lombe: FD2–
Londesborough: FD1–
London: FD1–FD2–
Londonderry: FD1–
Long: FD2–Bn 104–V.H.38–
Longbottom: Bn 105–
Longcroft: FD2–

Longfield: FD2–
Longford: FD1–FD2–
Longley: FD2–Bn 104, 105–
Longman: FD2–
Longmore: FD1–FD2–
Longrigg: W1/55–W2/98–
Longstaff: FD1–FD2–
Longueville: FD1–FD2–
Longworth: FD2–
Lonsdale: FD1–
Loomis: FD2–Bn 105–
Lopes: FD1–FD2–
Lopez: Bn 105–
Loraine: FD1–
Lord: FD2–Ne 2/159–Mt(A)51–Bn 105–AH2–
  AS104–
di Lorenzo: W1/55–W2/98–
Loring: Bn 105–AH8–
Lorne: FD1–
Lort-Phillips: FD2–
Loscombe: FD2–
Lotbiniere: Bn 105–
Lothian: FD1–
Lothrop: Bn 105–
Lott: Bn 105–
Loudoun: FD1–
Louis: FD1–FD2–
Louth: FD1–
Lovat: FD1–FD2–
Loveday: FD2–
Lovelace: FD1–Ne 3/194–
Loveland: FD1–
Lovell: FD2–
Lovett: FD2–
Low: FD2–
Lowdell: FD1–FD2–
Lowe: FD2–
Lowdell: Ne 1/30–Mt 104–Bn 105–AH2–
Lowndes: FD1–FD2–Ne 6/380–Mt(A)51–
  Bn 106–AH9–
Selby-Lowndes: FD2–
Lowndes-Stoke-Norton: FD2–
Lowry-Corry: FD1–FD2–
Lowry: FD2–
Lowsley: FD1–
Lowson: FD2–
Lowther: FD1–FD2–
Lowthorpe: FD2–
Lowthorpe-Lutwidge: FD2–
Lowth: FD2–
Loyd: FD2–
Luard: FD1–FD2–
Lubbock: FD1–FD2–
Lubienski: FD2–
Lucan: FD1–
Lucas: FD1–FD2–Ne 6/394–
Lucas-Calcraft: FD2–
Lucas-Scudamore: FD2–
Lucas-Shadwell: FD2–
Lucas-Tooth: FD2–
Lucifero: W1/56–W2/99–
Luckin: Bn 106–V.H.42–
Luckock: FD2–
Lucy: FD2–
Luddington: FD2–
Ludlow: FD2–Ne 2/156–Mt 102–AH3–Mt(A)51–
  Bn 106–V.H.48–
Ludlow-Bruges: FD1–
Ludlow Hewitt: FD2–
von Ludman: Ne 8/579–
Ludwell: Mt(A)51–Bn 106–V.H.10–AH9–
Lufkin: Bn 106–
Lugard: FD2–
Luke: V.H.49–W1/56–W2/99–
Lukens: Bn 106–
Lukey: FD2–
Lukin: FD2–

Lukis: FD2–
Lumb: FD2–
Lumley: FD2–
Lumley-Saville: FD2–
Lumsden: FD1–FD2–W1/57–W2/100–
Lund: FD2–
Lunn: FD2–
Lunsford: Bn 106–V.H.40–
Lunt: Bn 106–
Luquer: AH3–
Lurgan: FD1–
Luscombe: FD2–
Lushington: FD1–FD2–
Lusk: FD1–FD2–
Luxmore: FD2–
Lydall: FD2–V.H.27–
Lyde: FD2–Bn 106–
Lydig: Bn 106–
Lydius: Bn 106–
Lyell: FD1–FD2–
Lyle: FD2–
Lygon: FD2–
Lyman: Mt 184–Bn 106–AH8–
Lunch: FD2–
Lunch-Blosse: FD2–
Lynch: Bn 107–AH13–
Lyncker: Ne 7/499–
Lynch-Staunton: FD1–FD2–
Lynde: FD2–Ne 3/211–Bn 107–
Lyndhurst: FD1–
Lynes: FD2–
Lyon: FD2–Bn 107–
Lyon-Dalberg-Acton: FD2–
Lyons: FD1–FD2–
Lysaght: FD2–
Lyseley: FD2–
Lysons: FD1–FD2–
Lyster: FD1–FD2–
Lyster-Todd: FD2–
Lyte: FD1–
Lyttelton: FD1–FD2–
Lytton: FD1–

Macadam: FD2–
MacAndrew: FD1–
McAlester: FD2–FD1–
MacAlister: FD2–
McAllister: Bn 111–
McAlpine: FD2–
Macara: FD2–
MacArthur: FD1–FD2–
MacArtey: Bn 107–
Macartney: FD2–FD1–
Macartney-Filgate: FD2–
Macaulay: W1/58–W2/101–
M'Aulay: FD2–
Macaulay-Anderson: FD2–
MacAusland: FD2–
McAuslane: FD1–FD2–
McBain: Ne 8/550–
M'Barnet: FD2–
MacBeth: FD2–
MacBrayne: FD1–FD2–
MacCabe: FD2–
McCaffrey: Ne 6/389–
McCall: FD1–FD2–Bn 111–
M'call: FD2–
McCalla: Mt 51–
McCalmont: FD1–FD2–
McCammond: FD2–
McCance: FD2–Bn 111–
McCandlish: Bn 111–
McCarter: Bn 111–
McCarthy: FD1–FD2–
MacCartie: FD2–
McCaskie: FD2–

McCaughan: AS108–
McCauley: AS110–
McCausland: FD2–
Macchi Del Sette: W2/101–
McClain: Ne 3/166–
McClary: Mt(A)51–
Macclesfield: FD1–
McClean: Mt 153–
McClellan: Bn 111–
McClelland: Mt(A)52–
McClintock: FD1–FD2–
M'Clintock: FD1–FD2–
M'Clure: FD2–
McClure: Mt(118)–Mt 204–
McComb: Bn 111–
McConnel: FD2–
M'Connel: FD2–
McCoun: Bn 111–
MacCormick: FD2–
McCormack: FD2–Bn 111–
M'Corquodale: FD2–
McCoy: FD2–
McCulloch: Bn 111–
McCulloh: Bn 111–
McCullough: Mt(A)52–
McCracken: FD2–
McCready: FD2–
M'Creagh-Thornhill: FD2–
M'Culloch: FD2–
MacDermot: FD2–
MacDermott: FD2–
MacDonald: FD1–FD2–Mt 24–W2/101–
MacDonald-Millar: FD2–
M'Donnel: FD2–
McDonnell: FD1–FD2–
Macdonell: FD1–FD2–
MacDougald: W1/58–W2/102–
McDougall: FD1–FD2–
Macdowell: FD1–FD2–
MacDowell: FD1–FD2–
McDowell: Mt 164–
MacDuff: FD1–FD2–
MacDuffie: Mt(A)52–
McElroy: Mt 21–
MacFarlane: FD1–
MacFie: FD1–FD2–
M'Eacharn: FD2–
McEvers: Bn 111–
Macevoy-Netterville: FD2–
McEwen: FD2–
McFarlan: Bn 111–
McFarland: FD2–
MacFarlane-Grieve: FD2–
McFerran: FD2–
MacGeough: FD1–
McGarel-Hogg: FD2–
McGarrity: Bn 112–
McGavin: FD2–
McGee: Ne 3/208–
M'Gee-Russell: FD2–
MacGeough-Bond: FD2–
McGillycuddy: FD2–
MacGillivray: FD2–
McGough: AS112–
M'Grady: FD2–
MacGregor: FD1–FD2–Bn 112–
McGrigor: FD1–
M'Grigor: FD2–
McGuffie: FD2–
McGuire: Mt(A)52–
McHaffie-Gordon: FD2–
McHard: Bn 112–
McHardy: FD1–
Maciver: FD1–FD2–Bn 112–
Maciver-Campbell: FD1–FD2–
Machell: FD2–
Machin: FD2–

McIntosh: Bn 112–
McGusty: FD2–
MacIlraith: FD2–
Mack: FD2–
Mackain: FD2–
Mackarness: FD2–
MacKarty: Ne 5/352–Bn 107–
Mackay: FD2–
McKay: FD2–Bn 112–
Hay-Mackay: FD2–
MacKean: FD2–
McKean: Bn 112–
McKechnie: FD2–
M'Kee: FD2–
Mackell: FD2–
Mackenzie: FD1–FD2–Ne 5/351–Mt 70, 95–
  W1/58–W2/103–
Mackenzie-Ashton: FD2–
Mackenzie-Grieve: FD2–
Mackenzie-Gillanders: FD2–
McKenzie: Bn 112–Mc 1/335–
McKerrell: FD1–FD2–
McKernan: FD2–W1/59 & 60–W2/103, 104, 105–
McKerrell-Brown: FD2–
McKerrow: Bn 112–
Mackesy: FD2–
McKetchnie: Bn 112–
M'Kie: FD2–
Mackey: FD1–Bn 107–
Mackie: FD1–FD2–W1/60–W2/105–
McKim: Mc 1/344–
Mackinder: FD2–
MacKinnon: FD1–FD2–W1/60 & 61–W2/105 &
  106–
Mackintosh: FD1–FD2–
Mackirdy: FD2–
Mackworth: FD1–Ne 4/295–
Mackworth-Praed: FD2–
McLachlan: FD2–
Maclachlan: FD2–FD2–
Maclagan: FD1–FD2–
Maclaine: FD1–FD2–
McLanahan: Bn 112–
M'lardy: FD2–
M'Laren: FD2–
McLaren: FD2–
MacLaren: FD2–
MacLaurin: FD2–
Maclay: FD2–
Maclean: FD1–FD2–
M'Lean: FD2–
McLean: FD2–Bn 112–
McLellan: Bn 112–
Macleod: FD1–FD2–Bn 107–W1/62–W2/107–
MacLulich: FD2–
MacLure: FD1–FD2–
McMahon: FD2–
MacMahon: FD1–FD2–
MacManaway: FD2–
McMillan-Scott: FD2–
M'Mordie: FD2–
MacMillan-Scott: FD1–
MacMurran: FD2–
McMullen: FD2–
MacMurrough-O'Murchoe: FD2–
MacNaghten: FD1–
Workman-MacNaghton: FD1–
McNair: Bn 112–
MacNamara: FD2–
MacNeal: FD1–FD2–
MacNeale: FD2–
MacNeece: FD2–
McNeight: FD2–
MacNeil: FD2–
McNeill: FD2–
MacNeill: FD1–FD2–
Macomber: Bn 107–

Maconochie: FD1–FD2–
Maconchy: FD2–
Maconochie-Wellwood: FD2–
MacPherson: FD1–FD2–Bn 108, 113–W1/62 &
  63–W2/108–
McPherson: Bn 112–
McPhillips: FD2–
MacPherson-Grant: FD2–
McQueen: Bn 113–
McQuillan: AS114–
MacRae: FD2–
Macrae-Gilstrapp: FD2–
McRickard: FD2–
MacRitchie: FD1–
MacRobert: FD2–
McRobbie: W2/109–
MacRory: FD2–
MacSwiney: FD2–
MacSwinney: FD2–
MacTaggart: FD2–
McTavish: Bn 113–
McTurk: FD2–
M'Veagh: FD2–
MacVickar: AH16–
M'Vittie: FD2–
MacWilliams: Bn 108–
Macy: Bn 108–
Madden: FD1–FD2–
Maddick: FD2–
Maden: FD2–
Madge: FD2–
Madison Township High School Heraldry and
  Genealogy Club: AS116–
Magan: FD2–
Magenis: FD2–
Magheramorne: FD1–
Magill: FD2–Bn 108–
Magnay: FD1–FD2–
Magnus: FD2–
Magrath: FD1–
Magruder: Mt 173–Mc 1/348–
Maguth: FD2–
Maher: FD2–
Mahler: W1/64–W2/110–
Mahon: FD1–FD2–
Mahony: FD1–FD2–
O'Mahony: FD2–
Maidstone: FD1–
Maillet: Mt 7–
Mainwaring: FD1–FD2–
Mainwaring-Ellerker-Onslow: FD2–
Maitland: FD1–FD2–Mt(A)52–
Maitland-Makgill-Crichton: FD2–
Major: FD2–
Makant: FD2–
Makgill: FD2–
Makins: FD2–
Malbone: Bn 108–
Malcolm: FD1–FD2–
Malden: FD1–
Malet: FD1–FD2–
Malet De Carteret: FD2–
Maling: FD2–
Mallaby-Deeley: FD2–
Mallalieu: FD2–
Mallinson: FD2–
Mallock: FD2–
Mallory: Ne 4/299–V.H.69–
Malmesbury: FD1–
Malone: FD2–
Malta, Sovereign Military Order of: W2/110–
Maltby: W1/64–W2/110–
Man: FD2–
Manby-Cole-Grave: FD2–
Manbey: FD2–
Manchester: FD1–
Mander: FD2–

Manfield: FD2–
Mandleberg: FD2–
Manierre: Mt 68–
Manisty: FD2–
Mann: FD2–Mt(A)52–Bn 108–V.H.50–Ne 8/607–
Manners: FD1–FD2–
Manners-Sutton: FD1–FD2–
Manigault: Bn 108–
Manning-Kidd: FD2–
Mannigham: Ne 6/403–
Manningham-Buller: FD1–FD2–
Mansel: FD1–FD2–
Mansergh: FD1–FD2–
Mansfield: FD1–FD2–Mt 11–
Mansfield-Hausom: FD2–
Manson: Bn 108–
Mant: FD1–FD2–
Manton: Mt 2–
Manvers: FD1–
Manwaring: Ne 1/32–
Mapes: Mt 182–
Maple: FD1–
Maples: FD2–
Mapother: FD2–
Mappin: FD1–FD2–
Mar: FD1–
Mar & Kellie: FD1–
Marbury: Ne 2/81–
March: Bn 108–
March-Phillips: FD2–
Marchant: Bn 108–
Mardon: FD2–
Maresca Donnorso Correale Revertera: W2/110–
Marion: Bn 108–
Marjoribanks: FD1–FD2–
Margary: FD2–
Marindin: FD2–
Marix: W1/65–W2/111–
Mark: FD1–
Markham: FD1–FD2–Mt(A)53–Bn 108–AH172–
Markoe: Bn 108–
Marks: FD2–
Marlborough: FD1–
Marling: FD1–FD2–
Marmaduke: AS118–
Marples: FD1–FD2–
Mars: FD2–
Marr: FD2–
Marriott: FD2–
Marriott-Dodington: FD2–
Marrow: FD2–
Marryat: FD2–
Marsden: FD1–FD2–
Marsh: FD2–Mt 4–
Marshall: FD1–FD2–Ne 1/60–Bn 109–
Marsham: FD1–FD2–
Marsham-Townshend: FD1–FD2–
Marson: FD2–
Marston: FD2–Bn 109–
Marten: FD1–FD2–
Martin: FD1–FD2–Mt 9, 19–Bn 109–V.H.53–
Martin-Edmunds: FD1–FD2–
Martin-Harvey: FD2–
Martin-Holloway: FD1–
Martin-Leake: FD2–
Marton: FD2–
Martyn: FD2–Bn 109–
Martyn-Linnington: FD1–FD2–
Marwick: FD1–FD2–
Marwood: FD2–
Marwood-Elton: FD1–
Maryon-Wilson: FD1–FD2–
Mascaren(ne): Mt(A)53–Bn 109–Ne 3/232–AH4–
Masham: FD1–
Mason: FD2–Ne 1/50–Bn 109, 110–V.H.42–
Massereene: FD1–
Massey: FD1–FD2–

Massey-Mainwaring: FD1–
Massie: FD2–
Massingberd: FD2–
Massingberd-Mundy: FD2–
Massy: FD1–FD2–
Massy-Beresford: FD1–FD2–
Master: FD2–Ne 4/250–
Master-Whitaker: FD2–
Masters: FD2–
Masterton: Bn 110–
Mather: FD2–Mt(A)53–Bn 110–AH96–
Matheson: FD1–FD2–W1/65–W2/112–
Mathiesen: W2/112–
Mathieson: FD2–
Matthews: FD1–FD2–Bn 110–
Mathias: FD2–
Matterson: FD2–
Matthew: FD2–
Mattinson: FD2–
Maturin: FD2–
Maturin-Baird: FD2–
Maude: FD1–FD2–
Maule: FD1–
Maundy-Gregory: FD2–
Maunsell: FD1–FD2–
Mauran: Bn 110–
Maverick: Bn 110–
Mawdsley: FD1–FD2–
Max-Muller: FD2–
Maxcy: Bn 113–
Maxtone-Graham: FD1–FD2–
Maxwell: FD1–FD2–Bn 110, 113–
Maxwell-Gumbleton: FD2–
Maxwell-Heron: FD2–
Maxwell-Lyte: FD2–
May: FD2–Mt 228–Bn 110–
Maye: Mt(A)53–
Mayer: Bn 110–
Mayhew: FD2–Ne 2/126–Bn 110–
Maynadier: Mc 1/361–
Maynard: FD1–FD2–
Otway Mayne: FD2–
Mayne: FD2–
Mayo: FD1–FD2–Bn 110, 111–V.H.51–
Maywood-Strutt: FD2–
Mazyck: Bn 111–
MacGwire: FD2–
Mead: FD2–Bn 113–
Meade: FD1–FD2–
Meade-King: FD1–FD2–
Meade-Waldo: FD2–
Meadmaker, Company of: W2/113–
Meadows: FD2–
Means: Bn 113–
Meany: FD2–
Meares: FD2–Bn 113–
Measom: FD1–
Meath: FD1–Bn 113–
Mecham: FD2–
Medlycott: FD1–FD2–
Mee: FD2–
Meek: FD2–
Meeking: FD2–
Meeks: FD2–
Meigh: FD2–
Meikle: FD2–
Meiklejohn: FD2–
Warford-Mein: FD2–
Melba: FD2
Meldon FD2
Meller: FD2–
Melles: FD1–FD2–
Mellon: Bn 113–
Mellor: FD2–
Melville: FD1–FD2–Bn 113–
Mends: FD2–
Meng: Mt 74–

Menifie: Bn 113–V.H.56–
Menzies: FD1–FD2–
Steuart-Menzies: FD2–
Mercer: FD2–Ne 7/506–Bn 113–V.H.85–
Mercier: Ne 7/506–
Meredith: FD2–Mt 69–Bn 113–
Meredyth: FD1–
(von) Mering: Ne 6/438–
Meriwether: Mt 77–V.H.106–
Merrick: Mt 201–Bn 114–
Merrill: Mt 211–Bn 114–AH16–
Merriman: FD2–
Merritt: Bn 114–W1/65–W2/113–
Mersick: Bn 114–
Mesham: FD1–FD2–
Mesier: Mt 215–
Meston: FD2–
Messchert: Bn 114–
Messel: FD2–
Messinger: Mt(A)53–Bn 114–
Metcalf: Mt(A)54–
Metcalfe: FD1–FD2–V.H.53–
Metge: FD1–
Methuen: FD1–
Methven: FD2–
Meux: FD1–
Mexborough: FD1–
Mewburn: FD2–
Meyer: FD2–Bn 114–
Meymott: FD2–
Meynell: FD1–FD2–
Meynell-Ingram: FD1–
Meyrick: FD2–FD1–
Tapps-Gervis-Meyrick: FD2–
Williams-Meyrick: FD2–
Meysey-Thompson: FD1–FD2–
Michell: FD2–
Michie: Bn 114–
Mickel-Saltonstall: Mt 221–
Middlebrook: FD2–
Middlecott: Bn 114–
Middlemore: FD2–
Middleton: FD1–FD2–Bn 114, 115–AH9–
    W2/113–
Midgley: Bn 115–
Midleton: FD1–
Mifflin: Bn 115–
Milbank: FD1–FD2–
Milbanke: FD1–FD2–
Milbanke-Huskisson: FD1–
Milborn: Bn 115–
Milborne-Swinnterton-Pilkington: FD1–FD2–
Miers: FD2–
Mieville: FD2–
Milburn: FD2–
Mildham: FD1–FD2–
Mildmay: Ne 4/281–
Miles: FD1–FD2–
Milhau: Mt(A)54–
Millais: FD1–FD2–
Millar: FD2–
Millear: FD2–
Miller: FD1–FD2–Bn 115–V.H.55–
Miller-Cunningham: FD2–
Milles: FD1–FD2–
Milles-Lade: FD2–
Millet: Ne 4/262–Mt 18–AS120–
Milligan: Bn 115–
Milliken-Napier: FD1–
Millington: Bn 115–
Mills: FD2–Bn 115–
Milltown: FD1–
Milman: FD1–FD2–
Milman-Mainwaring: FD1–FD2–
Milne: FD1–FD2–Mt(A)54–
Milnes: FD2–
Milner: FD1–FD2–Mt(A)54–Bn 116–V.H.44–

Milner-Gibson: FD1–
Milroy: FD1–
Milson: FD2–
Milvain: FD2–
Milward: FD1–FD2–
Minchin: FD2–
Miner: Ne 1/24–Mt 86–AH4–
Minet: FD1–FD2–
Minoprio: FD2–
Minnoch: FD2–
Minns: Bn 116–
Minor: Bn 116–V.H.100–
Minot: Mt 6–Bn 116–
Minshull: Bn 116–
Minto: FD1–
Minton: FD2–
Minton-Senhouse: FD2–
Minturn: Bn 116–
Mires: AS122–
Misa: FD2–
Mistruzzi Di Frisinga: W1/66–W2/114–
Mitchell: FD1–FD2–Ne 4/304–Bn 116–
Mitchell-Carruthers: FD2–
Mitchell-Gill: FD2–
Mitchell-Innes: FD2–
Mitchell-Thomson: FD2–
Mitchelson: FD2–
Mitford: FD2–
Mitter: FD2–
Mitton: FD2–
Mixon: Ne 6/611–
Moat: FD2–Bn 116–
Mockler: FD2–
Moffat: FD2–Mt 83–
Moffett: Mt(A)54–
Moir: FD2–
Moir-Byres: FD2–
Molesworth: FD1–FD2–
Molesworth St. Aubin: FD2–
Molineux: Bn 116–
Crisp-Molineux-Montgomerie: FD2–
Molloy: FD1–FD2–
Molony: FD2–
Molyneux: FD1–FD2–
Molyneux-Seel: FD1–FD2–
Monash: FD2–
Monck: FD1–FD2–
Monckton: FD1–FD2–Bn 116–
Monckton-Arundell: FD2–
Moncreiff: FD1–FD2–
Moncreiffe: FD1–FD2–
Moncreiffe of that Ilk: W1/66–W2/115–
Mond: FD2–
Money: FD2–
Money-Coutts: FD2–
Money-Kyrle: FD1–FD2–
Monier-Williams: W1/67–W2/115–
Monk: FD1–FD2–
Monkswell: FD1–
Monins: FD2–
Monnet: Bn 116–
Monro: FD1–FD2–Bn 116–
Monsell: FD2–
Monson: FD1–FD2–
Montagu: FD1–FD2–Ne 5/350–Bn 117–V.H.87–
    AH10–
Montagu-Douglas-Scott: FD2–
Montagu-Pollock: FD1–FD2–
Montagu-Stuart-Wortley: FD1–FD2–
Montaldi: FD2–
Monteagle: FD1–
Montefiore: FD1–FD2–
Montejoye: Ne 4/236–
Montford: Bn 117–
Montgomerie: FD1–FD2–
Montgomerie-Charrington: FD2–
Montgomerie-Fleming: FD2–

Montgomery: FD1–FD2–Ne 7/477–Mt(A)54–
  Bn 117–AH1–
Montgomery-Cunninghame: FD1–
Monti Della Corte: W1/67–W2/115–
Montresor: FD2–
Montrose: FD1–
Monypenny: FD2–W2/116–
Moody: Ne 4/274–Bn 117–Ne 6/411–
Moon: FD1–FD2–
Moor: FD2–
Moore: FD1–FD2–Mt 216–Bn 117–V.H.105–
Moore-Brabazon: FD2–
Moore-Gwyn: FD2–
Moore-Stevens: FD2–
Moral: FD2–
Moran: Bn 117–
Moray: FD1–
Mordaunt: FD1–
Mordecai: Bn 117–
More: FD2–
More-O'Ferrall: FD2–
Moreduck: Bn 117–
Morehead: Bn 117–V.H.101–
Moresby: FD2–
Moreton: FD1–FD2–
Moreton-MacDonald: FD1–
Morewood: FD1–
Morgan: FD1–FD2–Mt 56, 181–Bn 118–
Morgan-Grenville: FD1–
Morgan-Tighe: FD1–
Moriarty: FD1–Ne 2/118–
Morison: FD2–Bn 118–W1/68–W2/117–
Morkill: FD2–
Morley: FD1–FD2–
Morony: FD2–
Morrell: FD1–FD2–
Morrice: FD1–
Morris: FD1–FD2–Ne 2/101, 6/449–AH1–Mt
  190–Mt(A)55–Bn 118–Mc 1/375–W1/68–W2/
  117–
Mooris-Eyton: FD2–
Mooris-Marsham: FD2–
Morrison: FD1–FD2–Ne 7/495–
Morrison-Bell: FD2–
Morrison-Low: FD2–
Morrison-Scott: FD2–
Morrough-Bernard: FD2–
Morse: FD1–Mt 144–Bn 118–
Morse-Bycott: FD1–FD2–
Morshead: FD1–
Mortimer: FD1–FD2–Bn 118–
Morton: FD1–Mt 187–Mt(A)55–Bn 119–
Moryson: V.H.49–
Moseley: FD2–Ne 1/45–Mt 67–Mt(A)55–Bn 119–
  V.H.57–
Mosley: FD1–FD2–
Mosman: FD2–
Moss: FD2–Bn 119–
Mosse: W1/69–W2/117–
Mostyn: FD1–FD2–
Mostyn-Owen: FD2–
Motion: FD1–FD2–
Motley: Bn 119–
Mott: FD2–Mt 190–Bn 119–
Motte: Bn 119–
Moulton: FD2–Bn 119–
Moultrie: Bn 119–
Moubray: FD2–
Mounsey-Heysham: FD2–
Mount: FD2–
Mountain: FD2–
Mountbatten: FD2–W2/118–
Mountcashell: FD1–
Mount-Edgclimbe: FD1–
Mountford: Bn 119–AH14–
Mountgarret: FD1–
Mount Morres: FD1–

Mount Stephen: FD1–
Mount-Temple: FD1–
Movius: Bn 119–
Mowbray: FD1–FD2–Mt 230–
Mowll: FD2–
Moynihan: FD2–
Moysey: FD2–
Muhlenberg: Bn 119–
Muir: FD1–FD2–
Muir-Mackenzie: FD1–FD2–
Muirhead-Murray: FD2–
Muirhead: FD2–
Mulchinock: FD2–
Mulholland: FD2–
Mullens: FD2–
Mullery: Ne 7/493–
Mullins: FD1–FD2–
Mulloy: FD2–
Mulock: FD1–
Mulvey: FD2–
Mumford: Mt(A)55–
Munby: FD1–
Muncaster: FD1–
Mundy: FD1–FD2–
Monro: FD1–FD2–AH5–
Munro-Ferguson: FD1–FD2–
Munro-Spencer: FD2–
Munsell: AH5–
Munster: FD1–
Muntz: FD1–FD2–
Murdoch: FD1–FD2–Bn 119–
Mure: FD1–FD2–
Murphy: FD2–
Murray: FD1–FD2–Ne 4/264–Bn 120–W1/69–
  W2/118 & 119–
Murray-Aynsley: FD1–FD2–
Murray-Graham: FD2–
Murray-Prior: FD2–
Murray-Stewart: FD2–
Murton: FD2–
Muscat: AS192–
Musgrave: FD1–FD2–Bn 120–
Muskerry: FD1–
Muspratt: FD2–
Musters: FD2–
Mutter: FD1–FD2–
Myatt: FD2–
Myddelton-Biddulph: FD2–
Mylchreest: FD2–
Myers: FD2–
Mylne: FD1–FD2–
Mynors: FD2–
Myers: FD2–
Mytton: FD2–

Naesmyth: FD1–FD2–
Nagel: Bn 120–
Nainby-Luxmoore: FD2–
Nairn: FD2–
Nairne: FD1–
Nall: FD2–
Nall-Cain: FD2–
Nanfan: Ne 7/510–
Naper: FD2–
Napier: FD1–FD2–
Nash: FD2–
Nayler: FD2–
Naylor-Leyland: FD2–
Neal: FD2–
Neale: FD2–Bn 120–
Neame: FD2–
Neave: FD1–FD2–
Need: FD2–
Needham: FD1–FD2–Bn 120–
Neeld: FD1–FD2–
Neill: Mt 171–

Neish: FD2–
Nelson: FD1–FD2–Ne 5/317–Bn 120–Mt(A)55–
   V.H.31–
Nepean: FD1–
Netterville: FD1–
Neumann: FD2–
Neven-Spence: FD2–
Nevile: FD2–
Nevill: FD1–Bn 121–
Neville: FD1–FD2–V.H.64–
Neville-Grenville: FD2–
Neville-Rolfe: FD1–FD2–
Newall: FD1–FD2–
Newbolt: FD2–
Newberry: Mt 74–Bn 121–
Newbery: FD2–
Newbold: Bn 121–
Newborough: FD1–
Newburgh: FD1–
Newcastle: FD1–
Newcastle-under-lyme: FD1–
Newce: V.H.37–
Newcomb: Bn 121–
Newdigate: FD2–
Newell: FD2–
Newhall: Mt 39–Bn 121–
Newland: FD2–
Newman: FD2–FD1–Bn 121–
Newenham: FD1–
Newport: FD2–
Newry: FD1–
Newson: FD2–
Newsum: FD2–
Newnes: FD2–
Newton: FD1–FD2–Ne 5/316–Mt(A)56–Bn 121–
   V.H.89–AS194–
Newton-Deakin: FD1–FD2–
Nias: FD1–FD2–
Niblett: FD2–
Niblock-Stuart: FD2–
Nicholas: FD2–Mt(A)56–Bn 121–
Nicholl: FD1–
Nicholl-Carne: FD2–
Nichols: FD2–
Nicholson: FD1–FD2–Ne 7/507–Bn 121–
   Mt(A)56–V.H.82/86–AH9, 17–W2/120–
Nickels: FD2–
Nickerson: Bn 121–
Nicklin: Bn 121–
Nickisson: FD2–
Nicol: FD1–FD2–
Nicolas: FD1–FD2–
Nicoll: Ne 3/116–Mt 140–Bn 122–AH7–
Nicolls: FD2–Bn 122–
Nicolson: FD1–FD2–
Nield: FD2–
Nightingale: FD1–FD2–
Nisbet: Ne 2/114–
Nisbet-Hamilton-Ogilvy: FD1–
Nivision: FD2–
Noakes: FD2–
Noailles: Ne 7/483–
Noble: FD1–FD2–
Nixon: FD2–
Nocton: FD2–
Noel: FD1–FD2–
Noel-Hill: FD1–FD2–
Nolan: FD2–
Norbury: FD1–FD2–Mc 1/381–
Nordeck: Bn 122–
Norden: Bn 122–
Norfolk: FD1–
Norman: FD1–FD2–
Normanby: FD1–
de Normandie: AH15–
Normanton: FD1–
Norris: FD2–Mt 22–Bn 122–Mc 1/385–

North: FD1–FD2–Bn 122–
North-Bomford: FD2–
Northcote: FD2–FD1–
Northcroft: FD2–
Northampton: FD1–
Northbourne: FD1–
Northbrook: FD1–
Northesk: FD1–
Northey: FD2–
Northmore: FD2–
Northomberland: FD1–
Northridge: FD2–
Northumberland: FD1–
Northwick: FD1–
Norton: FD1–FD2–Ne 3/200–Mt(A)56–
   Ne 4/279–Bn 122–AH15–
Norton-Griffiths: FD2–
Norwood: Bn 122–
Nott: FD2–Bn 122–V.H.15–
Nottage: FD1–
Nourse: Mt 119–
Nowell: FD2–
Nowell-Usticke: FD1–FD2–
Noyes: FD2–Ne 6/434, 435–Bn 122–Mt 124–Mc
   1/389–
Nugent: FD1–FD2–Bn 123–
Nugent-Dunbar: FD2–
Nussey: FD2–
Nunn: FD2–
Nuttall: FD2–
Nutting: FD2–

Oakeley: FD1–FD2–
Oakes: FD1–FD2–
Oakley: Mt(A)57–
Oates: FD2–
Obre: FD2–
O'Brien: FD1–FD2–Ne 4/294–Bn 123–
O'Callaghan-Westropp: FD1–FD2–
O'Carroll: FD1–FD2–
Ochterlony: FD1–FD2–
O'Connell: FD1–FD2–
O'Conner: AS124–
O'Connor: FD1–FD2–
O'Conor: Bn 123–
Odell: FD2–Bn 123–AH174–
Odingselle: Ne 4/278–
Odling-Smee: FD2–
Odlum: FD2–
O'Donnell: FD2–Mt 185–Bn 123–
O'Donoghue: FD2–W1/70–W2/120–
O'Donovan-O'Farrell: FD2–
O'Fflahertie: FD2–
Offley: Mt(A)57–Bn 123–V.H.12–
Ogden: Mt 74–Bn 123–AH16–
Ogg: FD1–
Ogilby: FD2–Bn 123–
Ogilvie: FD2–
Ogilvie-Forbes: FD1–
Ogilvie-Grant: FD2–
Ogilvy: FD1–FD2–
Ogilvy-Dalgleish: FD2–
Oglander: FD2–
Ogle: FD1–FD2–Bn 123–
Oglethorpe: Ne 4/282–
O'Grady: FD1–FD2–
Ogston: FD2–
O'Hagan: FD1–W1/70–W2/120–
O'Halloran: FD1–FD2–
O'Hara: FD2–
O'Hea: FD2–
O'Hilson: FD2–
O'Kelly: FD2–
Okeover: FD2–
Olcott: Bn 123–
Old: FD1–FD2–

Oldfield: FD2–
Oldnall: FD2–
Oliphant: FD1–FD2–
Oliphant-Ferguson: FD1–
Oliver: FD1–FD2–Ne 4/240–Mt 24–Bn 123, 124–
Oliver-Bellasis: FD2–
Olive: FD2–
Oliverson: FD2–
Olivney: FD2–
Olliffe: FD1–
Olmsted: Mt(A)57–
O'Loghlen: FD1–FD2–
O'Lundy: W1/71–W2/121–
Olyphant: Ne 5/355–
O'Malley: FD2–W1/71–W2/122–
O'Malley-Keyes FD2–
O'Mond: FD2–
Onderdonk: Mt 165–
O'Neal: FD2–
O'Neill: FD1–FD2–Mt(A)57–
O'Neill-Power: FD1–
Onslow: FD1–FD2–
Oppenheim: FD2–
Oppenheimer: FD1–FD2–
Oram: FD2–
Oranmore: FD1–
Orde: FD1–FD2–
Orde-Powlett: FD1–
O'Reilly: FD2–
Orford: FD1–
Oriel: FD2–
Orlebar: FD2–
Orkney: FD1–
Ormanthwaite: FD1–
Orme: FD2–
Ormerod: FD2–
Ormonde: FD1–
Ormsby: FD2–Ne 8/582–
Ormsby-Blake: FD1–
Ormsby-Gore: FD2–
Ormsby-Hamilton: FD2–
Ormiston: FD2–
Orpen: FD2–
Orr: Ne 2/112–
Orr-Ewing: FD1–FD2–
Orr-Lewis: FD2–
Orr-Owens: FD2–
Osborn: FD1–FD2–Bn 124–
Osborne: FD1–FD2–
Osborne-Gibbs: FD1–
Osborne-Gibbes: FD1–
Osgood: Mt(A)57–Bn 124–
O'Shee: FD2–
Osler: FD2–
Oshaston: FD2–
Osmond: FD2–
Oswald: FD1–FD2–
Oswald-Brown: FD2–
Oswell: FD2–
Otis: Mt 228–Mt(A)57–Bn 124–
Otter: FD2–
Ottery-Barry: FD2–
Otway: FD1–FD2–
Otway-Ruthven: FD1–FD2–
Fielding-Ould: FD2–
Oulton: FD2–
Outhwaite: FD1–FD2–
Outram: FD1–FD2–
Ouvry: FD1–
Overing: Bn 124–
Overton: Mt(A)58–
Overtown: FD1–
Ovey: FD2–
Owbridge: FD2–
Owen: FD1–FD2–Bn 124–
Owings: Ne 6/384–W1/72–W2/124–
Owsley: Mt(A)58–

Oxenbridge: FD1–Ne 7/452–Bn 124–AH174–
Oxenden: FD1–
Oxford: FD1–
Oxley: FD2–

von Pabst: Ne 8/573–
Paca: Mc 1/395–
Pack-Beresford: FD1–FD2–
Packe: FD2–
Paddison: FD2–
Paddock: Ne 3/199–
Paddy: Bn 124–
Padelford: Bn 124–
Page-Turner: FD2–
Page: FD2–Mt(A)56–Bn 124–V.H.106–AH9–
Paget: FD1–FD2–Mt 200–
Paget-Tomlinson: FD2–
Paige: Bn 125–
Pain: Bn 125–
Paine: Mt 5–Mt(A)58–Bn 125–
Paint: FD2–
Pakenham: FD1–FD2–
Pakenham-Mahon: FD2–
Pakington: FD2–
Palethorpe: FD2–
Paley: FD2–
Palgrave: FD2–Ne 6/401–
Palitana: FD2–
Palk: FD2–
Palles: FD2–
Palliser: FD2–
Palmer: FD1–FD2–Ne 7/465–Mt(A)58, 59–
    Bn 125, 126–
Palmer-Morewood: FD1–FD2–
Palmer-Samborne: FD2–
Palmes: FD2–Ne 2/77–Mt(A)54–Bn 126–
Palumbo Fossati: W2/125–
Panton: Bn 126–
Panzera: FD2–
Papillow: FD2–
Parent: W1/72–W2/126–
Paris: W2/126–
Parish: FD1–FD2–AS196–
Paric: FD1–
Park: FD2–Mc 1/398–
Parke: FD2–Bn 126–
Parker: FD1–FD2–Mt 2–Mt(A)59–Bn 126–
    V.H.98–AS126–W2/127–
Parker-Hutchin: FD2–
Parker-Jervis: FD1–FD2–
Parkes: FD2–
Parkes-Buchanan: FD1–FD2–
Parkin: FD1–FD2–
Parkin-Moore: FD2–
Parkinson: FD2–
Parkman: Bn 126–
Parks: Bn 126–
Parkyns: FD1–
Parlane: FD2–
Parmele: Mt(A)59–Bn 126–
Parnell: FD1–FD2–
Parr: FD2–
Parrington: FD2–
Parrott: Bn 126–
Parry: FD1–FD2–Ne 1/58–Bn 126–
Parry-Evans: FD2–
Parry-Hawkshaw: FD2–
Parry-Mitchell: FD2–
Parsons: FD1–FD2–Mt 165, 210–Bn 126, 127–
    Mt(A)59–W2/127–
Paschall: Bn 127–
Pasley: FD1–FD2–Bn 127–
Pasley-Dirom: FD1–FD2–
Paston-Bedingfield: FD1–FD2–
Pastorius: Ne 2/116–
Partington: FD2–

Patridge: Mt 62–
Paske: FD2–
Passingham: FD2–
Passmore: FD2–
Paston-Cooper: FD2–
Patridge: FD2–
Patchett: FD2–
Paterson: FD1–FD2–Bn 127–
Pateshall: FD2–
Paton: FD1–FD2–
Patrick: FD1–FD2–
Patterson: FD2–
Patteson: FD2–
Pattison: FD2–
Patton-Bethune: FD1–FD2–
Paul: FD1–FD2–
Paulet: FD1–FD2–
Paulin: FD2–
Paull: FD2–
Pauncefort-Duncombe FD1–FD2–
Pawle: FD2–
Pawlett: V.H.50–
Pawson: FD2–
Paxton: FD2–Bn 127–
Payne: FD2–Ne 1/70–Mt(A)58–Bn 127–
    Mc 1/401–
Payne-Frankland: FD1–
Payne-Gallwey: FD1–FD2–
Paynter: FD1–FD2–
Payson: Bn 127–
Peabody: Mt(A)60–Bn 127–
Peachey: Bn 127–V.H.51–
Peacock: FD2–
Peake: FD2–
Pearce: FD1–FD2–Bn 127–
Pearce-Edgcumbe: FD1–FD2–
Pearce-Serocold: FD1–FD2–
Pearks: FD2–
Pearmain: Bn 127–
Pearse: FD1–FD2–
Pearson: FD1–FD2–V.H.52–
Pearson-Gee: FD1–
Pearson-Gregory: FD2–
Pease: FD1–FD2–Mt(A)60–Bn 128–
Peatling: FD2–
Pechell: FD1–
Peck: FD2–Ne 3/202–Mt 179, 211–Bn 128–
    AH14–
Peckham: FD2–Bn 128–
Peckover: FD1–
Pedder: FD2–
Peek: FD1–FD2–
Peel: FD1–FD2–Bn 128–
Peers-Adams: FD1–
Pegge-Burnell-Smith-Milnes: FD2–
Peerbhoy: FD2–
Pegler: FD2–
Peirce: Mc 1/403–
Peirse-Duncombe: FD2–
Pelham: FD1–FD2–Ne 1/43–Mt(A)60–Bn 128–
    AH2–
Pelham-Clinton: FD1–
Pelham-Clinton-Hope: FD2–
Pell: Ne 1/40–Mt 10, 155–Bn 128–Mc 1/409–
Pellew: FD1–FD2–Ne 7/502–Bn 128–
Pellatt: FD2–
Pelletier: W2/127–
Pelly: FD1–FD2–
Pemberton: FD2–Ne 5/356–Mt(A)60–Bn 128–
Pember: FD2–
Pemberton-Barnes: FD2–
Pembroke: FD1–
Pendarves: FD2–
Pendleton: Bn 128–V.H.54–
Pender: FD1–FD2–
Penfold: FD2–W1/72–W2/128–
Pengelly: Bn 128–

Penhallow: Ne 2/135–Mt(A)60–
Penington: Ne 6/386–Bn 128–
Penn: Ne 3/177–Bn 128–AH5–
Pennefather: FD1–FD2–
Pennington: FD1–Bn 129–AH12–
Penny: FD2–
Pennyman: FD2–
Pennypacker: Bn 129–
Penrhyn: FD1–
Penrhyn-Hornby: FD2–
Penrose: Mt(A)60–Bn 129–
Penruddocke: FD1–FD2–
Penton: FD2–
Penzance: FD1–
Peperell: Ne 1/28–Bn 129–Mt 27, 133–
Peploe: FD2–
Pepper: FD2–Bn 129–
Pepys: FD1–FD2–
Perceval: FD2–
Perceval-Maxwell: FD2–
Percival: Bn 129–
Percy: FD2–Ne 3/214–W1/73–W2/128–
Perine: Bn 129–
Perkins: FD1–FD2–Ne 3/233–Mt(A)61–Bn 129–
Perks: FD2–
(de) Pernay: Ne 7/497–
Peronneau: Bn 129–
Perot: Mt(A)61–Bn 129–
Perowne: FD2–
Perrier: FD2–
Perrine: Mt(A)61–
Perring: FD1–
Perrins: FD2–
Perrot: FD1–
Perrott: Bn 130–V.H.55–
Perry: FD1–FD2–Bn 130–
Perryman: FD2–
Persse: FD2–
Perth & Melfort: FD1–
Peruzzi: Mt 100–
Pery: FD1–FD2–
Pery-Knox-Gore: FD2–
Peter: Mt(A)61–Bn 130–
Peter-Hoblyn: FD2–
Peterburough: FD1–
Peters: Mt 173–Bn 130–
Petherick: FD2–
Petigru: Bn 130–
Petit: FD1–FD2–
Petley: FD2–
Peto: FD1–FD2–
Petre: FD1–FD2–
Petrie: FD2–
Pettiward: FD2–
Pettus: V.H.61–
Petty: Bn 130–
Petty-Fitz-Maurice: FD1–FD2–
(de) Peyster: Ne 5/375–AH3–
Peyton: FD1–FD2–Bn 130–V.H.91–AH9–Ne
    8/5–
Pharo-Tomlin: FD2–
Phayre: FD2–
Phelips: FD2–
Phelps: Mt 71–Bn 130–AH11–Ne 8/602–
Philipps: FD2–
Foley-Philipps: FD2–
Philips: FD1–FD2–
Philipps: FD1–
Philipse: Bn 130–AH1–
Philipson: FD2–
Philipson-Stow: FD2–
Phillimore: FD1–FD2–
Phillips-Wolley: FD2–
Phillips-Treby: FD2–
Phillips: FD2–Mt 76–Bn 130–W1/73–W2/129–
Phillips-Conn: FD2–
Philippin: Mt 7–

Phinney: Bn 130–
Phippen: Ne 1/12–Mt(A)61–AH9–
Phipps: FD1–FD2–Ne 7/469–Mt 43, 139–Bn 130, 131–
Phips: Bn 131–
Phythian-Adams: W2/129–
Piatt: Mt(A)61–
Pickard-Cambridge: FD2–
Pickering: FD1–FD2–Bn 131–
Pickersgill-Cunliffe: FD2–
Pickman: Bn 131–
Pickstone: FD2–
Picoley: Ne 2/121–
Pidock-Hensell: FD2–
Piddocke: FD2–
Pierce: Bn 131–
Piercy: FD2–
Pierrepont: FD2–Mt 38–Bn 131–
Piers: FD1–FD2–
Pierson: Bn 131–
Pietz: Bn 131–
Pige-Leschallas: FD2–
Pigeon: Bn 131–
Piggot: FD2–
Pigot: FD1–FD2–
Pigott: FD1–FD2–
Pike: FD1–FD2–
Pilkington: FD2–
Pillsbury: Ne 8/547–
Pilter: FD2–
Pinchon: Mt(A)62–
Pinckney: FD2–Bn 131, 132–
Pine: AS128–
Pine-Coffin: FD2–
Pini Di San Miniato: W2/175–
Pinnell: FD2–
Pintard: Bn 132–
Pipe-Wolferstan: FD2–
Pirie-Gordon: FD2–
Pirie: FD2–
Pitcher: FD2–Mt(A)62–
Pitkin: Mt 78, 229–Bn 132–
Pitmans: FD1–
Pitreathly: FD2–
Pitt: FD1–Mt(A)62–
Pittman: Bn 132–
Pixley: FD2–
Place: Mt 197–V.H.39–
Plaisted: Bn 132–
Platt: FD1–FD2–
Platt-Higgins: FD1–FD2–
Platts: FD2–
Player: FD2–
Playfair: FD1–FD2–
Plender: FD2–
Plenderleath: FD1–FD2–
Pleydell-Bourverie: FD1–FD2–
Plowden: FD2–
Plowes: FD2–
Plumb: Ne 6/391–Mt 162–
Plumer: FD1–FD2–
Plummer: FD2–
Plumptre: Bn 132–
Plumste(a)d: Ne 5/345–Bn 132–
Plumtre: FD2–
Plunkett: FD1–FD2–
Plunkett-Ernle-Erle-Drax: FD2–
Plympton: Mt 61–
Poate: FD2–
Pochin: FD2–
Pocklington: FD2–
Pocklington-Senhouse: FD2–
Pocock: FD1–FD2–
Pode: FD2–
Poe: Mt(A)62–
De La Poer: FD2–
Poisson: Bn 132–

Pole: FD1–FD2–Ne 1/12–Mt(A)62–
Pole-Carew: FD2–
Polhemus: AH11–
Polhill: FD2–
Pollard: FD1–FD2–
Pollard-Urquhart: FD2–
Pollen: FD1–FD2–
Pollitt: FD2–
Pollock: FD1–FD2–Mt(A)62–Bn 132–
Polson: FD2–
Poltimore: FD1–
Polwarth: FD1–
Polwhele: FD2–
Pollok: FD2–
Pomeroy: FD1–FD2–Mt 101–Bn 132–
Pomfret: FD2–
Pond: Mt 61–
Ponsonby: FD1–FD2–
Ponsonby-Fane: FD1–FD2–
(du) Pont: Ne 5/332–
Pontifex: FD2–
Poole: FD2–Ne 2/75–Mt(A)63–Ne 4/291–Bn 132–
Poore: FD1–FD2–Mt(A)63–
Pooler: FD2–
Poor: Mt 49–Bn 132–
Popham: Mt(A)63–
Porcher: Bn 132–
Portarlington: FD1–
Porter: FD1–FD2–Mt 19, 134, 156–Bn 132–AH175–
Pope: FD2–
Porch: FD2–
Portal: FD2–
Portland: FD1–
Portman: FD1–FD2–
Portman-Dalton: FD2–
Portsmouth: FD1–
Post: Bn 133–
Potier: Ne 6/389–
Pott: FD1–
Potter: FD1–FD2–Bn 133–
Pottinger: FD1–
Poulett: FD1–FD2–
Poultney: Bn 133–
Pound: FD2–
Powell: FD1–FD2–Mt 126–Bn 133–Mc 1/418–
Powell-Edwards: FD2–
Power: FD1–FD2–Bn 133–W1/73–W2/129–
Power-Lalor: FD2–
Powerscourt: FD1–
Powis: FD1–FD2–
Pownall: Ne 4/256–Bn 133–
Powys: FD1–FD2–
Powles: FD2–
Pownall: FD2–
Powney: FD2–
Powys-Keck: FD1–FD2–
Powys-Lybbe: FD2–
Poyen: Ne 6/436–
Poynter: FD2–
Pountz-Stewart: FD2–
Poyser: FD2–
Prain: FD2–
Prasad Singh: FD2–
Pratt: FD1–FD2–Mt(A)63–Bn 133–V.H.21–Ne 8/549–W1/74–W2/130–
Preble: Mt(A)63–Bn 133–AH176–
Prendergast: FD2–
Prentice: FD1–FD2–
Prentis: Bn 133–V.H.32–
Prescot: FD1–
Prescott: FD1–FD2–Bn 134–AH14–
Prescott-Decie: FD2–
Presswell: W1/74–W2/130–
Prestige: FD2–
Preston: FD2–Mt(A)63–Bn 134–

Preston-Hillary: FD2–
Pretor-Pinney: FD1–FD2–
Pretyman: FD2–
Prevost: FD1–FD2–Bn 134–AH5–
Price: FD1–FD2–Ne 6/390–Mt 57–Bn 134–
Price-Davies: FD2–
Prickett: FD2–FD1–
Pride: Bn 134–
Prideaux-Brune: FD2–FD1–
Pridham: FD2–
Priestley: FD2–Bn 134–
Priestman: FD2–
Prime: Mt 52–Bn 134–
Primrose: FD2–FD1–
Prince: FD2–Bn 134–
Pringle: FD1–FD2–Bn 134–
Prioleau: Bn 134–
Prior-Wandesford: FD1–FD2–
Priston: FD2–
Pritchard: FD2–
Prittie: FD1–FD2–
Privett: FD2–
Probert: FD1–
Proby: FD2–Bn 134–
Probyn: FD1–FD2–
Proctor: Bn 134–
Proctor-Beauchamp: FD1–
Prodgers: FD2–
Proger: FD2–
Pronay: Ne 8/572–W2/130–
Provoost: Mt(A)64–Bn 135–AH148–
Prower: FD2–
Pruett: AS/130–
Pruyn: Mt 48–
Pryce: FD1–FD2–Bn 135–
Pryce-Jones: FD1–FD2–
Pryce-Jenkins: FD2–
Pryke: FD2–
Pryse: FD1–FD2–
Puddy: W1/74–W2/132–
Puleston: FD1–FD2–
Pullan: FD2–
Pullar: FD2–
Pulley: FD2–
Pumpelly: Mt(A)64–Bn 135–
Punchard: FD2–
Purcell: FD1–FD2–
Purcell-Fitzgerald: FD1–FD2–
Purefoy: FD2–
Purves: FD1–
Purvis: FD2–
Putman: Bn 135–
Putnam: FD2–Ne 1/35–Mt(A)64–Bn 135–Mc
   1/421–
Puttock: W1/74–W2/132–
Puxley: FD2–
Puxon: FD2–
Pybus: Bn 135–
Pyddoke: FD2–
Pye: W1/75–W2/133–
Pyke: FD1–FD2–
Pyke-Nott: FD2–
Pym: FD2–
Pynchon: Ne 1/8–Mt(A)62–Bn 135–AH12–
Pyne: FD2–Ne 7/513–Mt(A)64–Bn 135–

Quain: FD1–FD2–
Quarles: Ne 4/286–
Quayle: FD1–FD2–
Queensberry: FD1–
Quilter: FD1–FD2–
Quincy: Mt 180–Bn 135–AH2–
Quintard: Bn 135–
Quisenberry: Mc 1/423–V.H.111–

Radcliffe: FD1–FD2–
Radclyffe: FD2–
Radetzky von Radetz: AS132–
Radford: FD1–FD2–W1/76–W2/134–
Radford-Norcop: FD2–
Radnor: FD1–
Radstock: FD1–
Rae: Bn 136–V.H.54–
Raeburn: FD2–
Raffles: FD1–FD2–
Raffles-Flinty: FD2–
Ragland: FD1–
Raikes: FD2–
Raines: FD1–
Rainey: FD1–FD2–
Rainey-Robinson: FD2–
Rainsborough: Ne 5/376–
Rainsford: FD2–
Rait: FD1–
Raitt: FD1–
Ralli: FD2–Mt 92–
Rakowski: FD2–
Ralston-Patrick: FD2–
Ram: FD2–
Ramage: FD2–
Ramio Sole: AS134–
Ramsay: FD1–FD2–Bn 136–V.H.56–
Cameron-Ramsay-Fairfax: FD2–
Ramsay-Denny: FD1–
Ramsay-Fairfax: FD1–
Ramsay-Gibson-Maitland: FD1–
Ramsay-L'Amy: FD2–
Ramsden: FD1–FD2–W1/76–W2/134–
Ramsden-Jodrell: FD2–
Rand: Bn 136–
Randall: FD2–
Randles: FD2–
Randolph: FD2–Ne 3/178–Mt 64–Bn 136–
   V.H.15–AH9–
Ranfurly: FD1–
Rankin: FD1–FD2–Mt(A)64–Bn 136–
Rankine: FD2–
Ranking: FD1–FD2–
Rapaljie: AH7–
Raphael: FD2–
Rasay: AH16–
Rasch: FD1–FD2–
Rashleigh: FD1–FD2–
Ratcliffe: FD2–
Ratcliffe-Ellis: FD–2
Rathbone: FD1–FD2–Bn 136–
Rathborne: FD2–
Rathbun: Bn 136–
Rathdonnell: FD1–
Ratford: FD2–
Ratlifee: FD2–
Ratton: FD1–FD2–
Rattray: Bn 136–
Ravenel: Bn 136–
Ravenshaw: FD2–
Ravensworth: FD1–
Rawle: Bn 136–AH147–
Rawlins: FD2–
Rawlinson: FD1–FD2–
Raw: FD2–
Rawnsley: FD2–
Raworth: FD2–
Rawson: FD2–Ne 2/120–Bn 137–Ne 4/239–
   AH12–
Rawstorne: FD2–
Ray: FD2–Bn 137–
Rayden: FD2–
Rayer: FD2–
Rayleigh: FD1–
Raymond: FD2–Bn 137–
Raymond-Barker: FD2–
Rayner: FD2–

Rea: FD2–W1/77–W2/135–
Read: FD1–FD2–Mt 4, 69, 177–Bn 137–
Reade: FD1–FD2–Ne 3/196–Bn 137–V.H.95–
  Ne 8/532–AH7–
Readett-Bayley: FD2–
Readhead: FD2–
Reay: FD1–
Reckitt: FD1–FD2–
Reading: FD2–
Redmond: FD1–FD2–Bn 137–
Redwood: FD2–Bn 137–
Reddaway: FD2–
Redford: FD2–Bn 137–
Reece: AS136–
Reed: FD1–FD2–Bn 137–
Reekie: FD2–
Rees: FD2–
Rees-Hogg: FD2–
Reeve: FD2–Bn 137–
Reeves: FD2–
Reichel: FD1–FD2–
Reichert: Mt(A)65–
Reid: FD1–FD2–Bn 138–V.H.13–W1/77–
  W2/135–
Reid-Cuddon: FD1–FD2–
Relton: FD2–
Remington: Ne 3/203–Bn 138–
Remsen: Bn 138–
Renals: FD1–FD2–
Rendall: FD2–
Rendel: FD1–
Rendlesham: FD1–
Rendtorff: FD2–
Renshaw: FD1–FD2–Bn 138–
Rensselaer: Ne 5/378–
Renton: FD2–
Rentool: FD1–
Renwick: FD2–Mt 41–
Rettie: FD2–
Reveley: Bn 138–
Revelstocke: FD1–
Revere: Bn 138–
Reynard: FD2–
Reynell: FD2–
Reynolds: FD2–Bn 138–
Reynolds-Moreton: FD1–
Rhett: Bn 138–
Rhinelander: Mt 99, 145–Mc 1/431–
Rhiner-Waring: FD2–
Rhoades: Mt(A)65–Bn 138–
Rhodes: FD1–FD2–Mt 215–Bn 138–
Riall: FD2–
Ribblesdale: FD1–
Ribton: FD1–
Ricarde-Seaver: FD2–
Ricardo: FD2–
Rice Rhys: FD2–
Rice: FD1–FD2–Mt 51–Bn 138 & 139–V.H.34–
Rice-Trevor: FD1–
Rich: FD1–FD2–Bn 139–V.H.49–
Richards: FD2–Ne 3/204–Mt(A)65, 147–Bn 139–
  V.H.31–W1/77–W2/135–
Richardson: FD1–FD2–Mt(A)65–Bn 139–W1/
  78–W2/136–
Richardson-Brady: FD2–
Richmond-Gale-Braddyll: FD2–
Richmond: FD1–FD2–Mt 164–Bn 139–
Rickards: FD2–
Rickets: Bn 139–
Rickett: FD2–
Ricketts: FD1–FD2–
Riddell: FD1–FD2–
Riddell-Blount: FD2–
Riddell-Carre: FD2–
Ridgel(e)y: Mt(A)65–Bn 13–
Ridg(e)way: Mt(A)65–Bn 13–FD2–

Ridley: FD2–
von Rieben: Ne 8/568–
Rigby: W2/136–
Rigg: FD1–FD2–
Rijker: AH7–
Riky: FD2–
Riley: FD1–FD2–
Rimington-Wilson: FD2–
Ripley: FD1–FD2–Bn 140–
Ripon: FD1–
Ring: Bn 139–V.H.49–
Risley: Bn 140–
Ritchie: FD1–FD2–W2/137–
Ritson: FD2–
Rivett-Carnac: FD2–FD1–
Rivington: FD1–FD2–
Rix: FD2–
Rixon: FD2–
Roane: Bn 140–V.H.111–
Robartes: FD1–
Robbins: Mt(A)66–
Roberdeau: Bn 140–AH11–
Robert: Bn 140–
Roberts: FD1–FD2–Bn 140–Mc 1/434–W1/77
  W2/137–
Roberts-Gawen: FD2–
Roberts-West: FD2–
Robertshawe: FD2–
Robertson: FD1–FD2–Bn 140–Mc 1/44–AS13
Robertson-Fullerton: FD2–
Robertson-Glasgow: FD1–FD2–
Robertson-Luxford: FD2–
Robertson-MacDonald: FD2–
Robertson-Ross: FD2–
Robertson-Shersby: FD2–
Robeson: Bn 140–
Robinson: FD1–FD2–Ne 6/412, 7/474–Mt(A)66–
  Bn 140–V.H.14–
Robinson-Montagu: FD1–
Robson-Scott: FD2–
Robson: FD2–
Roby: FD1–
Roche: FD1–FD2–
Rochester: FD1–
Rochfort: FD2–
Rochfort-Boyd: FD2–
Rocke: FD2–
Rockwell: Ne 3/187–Bn 141–Ne 8/603–
Rockwood: Mt 132–
Roddam: FD2–
Roden: FD1–
Rodes: Mt(A)65–V.H.79–
Rodger: FD1–FD2–
Rodney: FD1–FD2–Ne 4/292–Bn 141–
Rodman: Bn 141–
Roe: FD1–
Rodrigue: Mt 130–
Roeder: Bn 141–
Roeding: Bn 141–
Rogers: FD1–FD2–Mt(A)66–Mt 78, 229–
  Bn141–Ne 8/610–
Rohde: FD1–FD2–
Rokeby: FD2–
Rolfe: V.H.20–
Roll: FD2–
Rollason: FD2–
Rolleston: FD2–
Rollins: Mt(A)66–Bn 141–
Rollo: FD1–
Rolt: FD2–
Romanes: FD2–
Romanis: FD2–
Rombulow-Pearse: FD2–
Rome: Ne 2/160–
Romilly: FD1–FD2–
Romney: FD1–
Roney-Dougall: FD2–

Rooke: FD2–
Rookwood: FD1–
Roope: FD2–
Rooper: FD2–
Roome: Bn 141–AH12–
Roose: FD2–
Roosa: Ne 5/335–
Roosevelt: Mt 1–Bn 141–Mc 1/447–AH11–
Rootenburgh: FD2–
Rootes: Bn 142–V.H.92–
Roper: FD2–
Roper-Curzon: FD2–
Ropner: FD2–
Rorie: FD2–
Rorison: Mc 1/451–
Rosati: W2/137–
Roscow: Bn 142–V.H.64–
Rose: FD1–FD2–Mt 217–Bn 142–
Rosebery: FD1–
Rose-Innes: FD2–
Roskell: FD2–
Ross: FD1–FD2–Mt 36, 39–Bn 142–W1/78–
   W2/138–
Ross-Lewin: FD1–FD2–
Ross-of-Bladensburg: FD1–FD2–
Rosse: FD1–Mt(A)66–
Rosslyn: FD1–
Rossmore: FD1–
Rostron: FD1–FD2–
Rotch: Bn 142–
Roth: FD2–
Rothband: FD2–
Rothe: FD2–
Rotheram: FD2–
Rothes: FD1–
Rothschild: FD1–FD2–
Rothwell: FD2–
Rothwell-Jackson: FD2–
Round: FD1–FD2–
Round-Turner: FD2–
Roundell: FD2–
Roupell: FD2–
Rous: Bn 142–
Rousby: Bn 142–
Rouse: Bn 142–
di Roveto: W2/139–
Rouse-Boughton: FD1–FD2–
Rouse-Boughton-Knight: FD1–FD2–
Routh: FD1–
Routley: FD2–
Rowan: FD2–
Rowbotham: FD2–
Rowcliffe: FD2–
Rowe: FD2–Ne 4/738–Bn 142–
Rowell: FD2–
Rowett: FD2–
Rowland: FD2–Mt 170–
Rowlands: FD1–FD2–
Rowley: FD1–FD2–
Rowley: FD1–FD2–
Rowley-Conway: FD1–FD2–
Rowton: FD1–
Roxburgh: FD1–FD2–
Roxburghe: FD1–
The Royal Bank of Scotland: W2/139–
Royall: Bn 142–
Royden: FD2–
Royds: FD1–FD2–
Royse: FD2–
Royster: Mt(A)67–
Rubie: FD2–
Rucker: FD2–
Rudd-Clarke: FD2–
Rudder: W1/79–W2/139–
Rudge: FD2–
Rudkin: FD2–
Rudyerd: FD2–

Rudyerd-Halpman: FD2–
Rugge-Price: FD1–FD2–
Ruggles: FD1–Mt 20, 28, 146, 217–Bn 143–Mc
   2/633–
Ruggles-Brice: FD1–
Ruiz de Bustamente: AS140–
Rulon: Mt 208–
Rumbold: FD1–FD2–
Rumsey: Bn 143–
Runchorelal: FD2–
Runchman: FD2–
Rundle: FD2–
Ruscombe-Emery: W2/140–
Rush: Bn 143–Mc 6/406–
Rushbrooke: FD2–
Rushout: FD1–FD2–
Rushton: FD2–
Russell: FD1–FD2–Ne 4/267, 277–AH2–Mt(A)
   67–Bn 143–
Purvis-Russell-Montgomery: FD2–
Russell-Pavier: FD2–
Ruston: FD2–
Rutgers: Bn 143–
Rutherford: FD1–FD2–
Rutherfurd: Ne 2/92–AH3–
Ruthven: FD1–FD2–
Ruthven-Stuart: FD2–
Rutland: FD1–
Rutledge: Bn 143–
Rutson: FD2–
Ruttledge: FD2–
Ruttledge-Fair: FD2–
Ruvigny: FD1–
Ruxton: FD2–
Rycroft: FD1–FD2–
Ryan: FD2–Mt 28–
Ryder: FD1–FD2–
Rye: FD2–
Ryland: FD1–FD2–
Rylands: FD1–FD2–
Rymer: FD2–
Rynd: FD2–

Sabine: Bn 143–
Sackett: Mt 106–
Sackville: FD1–FD2–
Sackville-West: FD1–FD2–
Sadleir: FD2–
Sadler: FD2–
Saffin: Ne 2/149–Bn 143, 144–
Sagar-Musgrave: FD1–FD2–
Sahler, von: Mt (A) 78
St. Albans: FD1–
St. Asalph: FD1–
St. Andrew-Vaugham of Leicester: FD2–
St. Aubyn: FD2–
St. Barbe: Bn 144–
St. Clair: Bn 144–Mc 1/453–
St. David's: FD1–
Sainter: W1/80 W2/140
St. George: FD1–FD2–
St. Germans: FD1–
St. John: FD1–FD2–
St. John-Mildmay: FD1–FD2–
St. Lawrance: FD1–
St. Leger: FD1–FD2–
St. Leonards: FD1–
St. Levan: FD1–
St. Maur: FD1–
St. Oswald: FD1–
St. Paul: FD2–
St. Quintin: FD2–
St. Vincent: FD1–
Sainz de la Maza: As 198–
de Saisseval: W1/80–
Sale: FD1–FD2–

Sale-Hill: FD1–FD2–
Salisbury: FD1–Bn 144–AHZ–
Salmon: FD1–
Salomons: FD1
Salt: FD1–FD2–
Salter: FD1–Mt 133–Bn 144–
Saltmarshe: FD1–
Saltonstall: Mt 219, 221–Bn 144–Ne 1/13–
   Mc 6/410–AH 6, 17–
Saltoun: FD1–
Salusbury: FD1–FD2–
Salusbury-Trelawny: FD1–FD1–
Saltza: Ne 4/244–
Salvesen: FD2–
Salvin: FD2–
Salwey FD2–
Sampson: FD1–
Samuel: FD1–FD2–
Samuel-Montagu: FD1–FD2–
Samuels: FD2–
Samuelson: FD1–FD2–
Sanborn: Bn 144–Mc 3/462–
Sandars: FD1–FD2–
Sandau: FD2–
Sandbach: FD2–
Sandem: FD1–
Sandeman: FD1–FD2–
Sanders: FD2–Ne 4/290–Mt (A) 67–
Sanderson: FD1–FD2– Bn 144–
Sandes: FD2–
Sandford: FD1–FD2–
Sandhurst: FD1–
Sandilands: FD1–FD2–
Sandoz: Ne 7/494–
Sands: Mt 99–Mc 1/461–AH7–
Sandwich: FD1–
Sandys: FD1–FD2–V.H.61–
Sanford: Ne 1/38–Bn 144–
Sangusko-Formhals: AS 142–
Sankey: FD2–
Sant: FD1–FD2–
Sapwell: FD2–
Sargant: FD2–
Sargeant: FD2–
Sarge(a)nt: Mt 217–Mt (A) 67– Bn 144, 145–
Sargent: FD2–
Sargood: FD2–
Sarsfield: FD2–
Sassoon: FD1–FD2–
Satterlee: Mt(A)67–
Satterthwaite: Bn 145–
Sattig: Bn 145–
Saumarez: FD1–
Saunders: FD2–
Saunderson: FD1–FD2–
Saunders-Know-Gore: FD2–
Saurin: FD2–
Sausse: FD1–
Sauvage-Nolting: FD2–
Savage: FD1–FD2–Ne 4/141–Mt(A)67–
   Bn 145–AH 12–
Savile: FD1–FD2–
Saville: Bn 145–
Savill-Onley: FD1–FD2–
Savory: FD1–FD2–
Sawbridge: FD2–
Sawbridge-Erle-Drax: FD1–FD2–
Sawrey-Cookson: FD1–FD2–
Sawyer: FD2–
Saxe-Coburg-Gotha: FD1–
Sayedsele: FD1–
Sayer of Pett Place: FD2–
Sayle: FD2–
Sayre: Mc 1/463–
Sayres: Mc 1/466–
Sayward: Bn 145–
Scantlebury: FD2–

Scarborough: Ne 5/364–Bn 145–V.H. 62–
Scarbrough: FD1–
Scarburgh: Ne 5/364–
Scarisbrick: FD2–
Scarlett: FD1–FD2–
Scarsdale: FD1–
Schank: FD1–FD2–
Scheffer: W1/81–W2/40–
Schenck: Mt(A)68–Bn 145–AY 7–
Schermerhorn: Bn 145–Mc 3/483–
Schieff(e)lin: Mt 127, 175–Bn 145–AH 13–
Schilizzi: FD2–
Schindel: Mt 151–
Schimberg: FD2–
Schlegal: Ne 8/604–
Schleswig-Holstein: FD1–
Schofield: FD2–Bn 145–
Schomberg: FD2–
Schröder: FD1–
Schuster: FD2–
Schuyler: Ne 3/163–Mt(A)68–Bn 145, 146–
   AH 1–
Schwarzenberg: W1/81 W2/141–
Schweder: FD2–
Scicluna: FD2–
Scobie: FD2–
Scot: Ne 2/83–
Scotland: FD1–
Scott: FD1–FD2–Ne 4/288, 297–Bn 146–
   V.H. 67–AH 11, 15–W1/82–W2/142–
Scott-Chad of Pynkney: FD2–
Scott-Douglas: FD1–
Scott-Elliot: FD2–
Scot-Ellis: FD2–
Scott-Gatty: FD1–FD2–
Scott-Kerr: FD2–
Scott-Moncrieff: FD1–FD2–
Scott-Nickolson: FD2–
Scottow: Bn 146–
Scottowe: Bn 146–
Scott-Plummer: FD1–FD2–
Scourfield: FD1–
Scratchley: FD2–
Scratton: FD2–
Screven: Mt(A) 68–
Scribner: Bn 146, 147–Mc 4/446–
Scripps: Bn 147–
Scriven: FD2–
Scrymgeour-Wedderburn: FD1–FD2–
Scrymsoure-Steuart-Fothringham: FD2–
Scudamore-Stanhope: FD1–FD2–
Scudder: Mt 21–
Scully: FD1–FD2–
Seabury: Mt 8–Bn 147–AH 16–
Seafield: FD1–
Seager of Cardiff: FD2–
Seale: FD1–FD2–
Sealy-King: FD2–
Seaman: Mt 19–
Searles: Bn 147–
Sears: Mt(A) 68–Bn 147–
Seaton: FD1–
Sebastian: FD2–
Sebright: FD1–FD2–
Seccombe: FD2–
Secretan: FD2–
Sedgwick: Bn 147–
Seeds: FD2–
Seely: FD1–FD2–
Seelye: Bn 147–
Sefton: FD1–FD2–
Segar: Ne 3/164–
Segar-Owen: FD2–
Segrave: FD2–
Segur: Ne 8/593–
Selborne: FD1–
Selkirk: FD1–

Selby: FD2–Bn 147–
Selby-Bigge: FD2–
Selden: Mc 1/471–
Sellar: W1/83–W2/142–
Selle: FD2–
Sellers: Mt 7–
Sempill: FD1–
Semple: Bn 147–
Sener: Bn 147–
Sennett: FD2–
Sergison: FD2–
Sergison-Brooke: FD2–
Seton: FD1–FD2–Bn 147–
Seton-Karr: FD1–FD2–
Seton–Steuart: FD1–
Seton-Stevar: of Allanton FD2–
Severne: FD2–
Sewall: Bn 147–AH 100–
Sewell: FD2–Mt 143, 169–Bn 147–
Seymer: FD2–
Seymour: FD1–FD2–Mt 216–Ne 4/275–Bn 148–
Shackleton: FD2–
Shaffer: Mt 120–
Shaftesbury: FD1–
Shafto: FD2–
Shairp: FD1–FD2–
Shakerley: FD1–FD2–
Shakerley-Ackers: FD2–
Shand: FD1–
Shanks: FD2–W1/83–W2/143–
Shann: FD1–FD2–
Shannon: FD1–
Shapleigh: Mt (A)68–Ne 5/307–Mc 3/489
Sharer: FD2–
Sharman-Crawford: FD2–
Sharp: FD2–Bn 148–
Sharpbethone: FD2–
Sharpe: FD1–FD2
Sharpless: Ne 6/383–Bn 148–
Shattuck: Bn 148–
Shaughnessy: FD2–
Shaw: FD1–FD2–Bn 148–W1/38–W2/143
Shawcross: FD2–
Shawe-Sturey: FD2–
Shaw-Hamilton: FD2–
Shaw-Hellier: FD2–
Shaw-Kennedy: FD2–
Shaw-Lefevre: FD1–
Shaw-Lefevre-St. John-Mildmay: FD2–
Shaw-Mackenzie: FD2–
Shaw-Stewart: FD1–FD2–
Shaw-Yates: FD2–
Shead: FD2–
Sheaffe: Bn 148–
Shearer: FD2–
Shearman: FD2–
Shed: Mt(A)68–
Shedden: FD1–FD2–
Sheepshanks: FD2–Bn 148–
Sheffield: FD1–FD2–Bn 148–
Shelburne:W2/176–
Shelby: Mc 2/652
Sheldon: Mt (A)69–Bn 148–
Shelley: FD1–FD2–Bn 148–
Shelley-Mills: FD2–
Shelley-Rolls: FD2–
Shelton: Bn 148–
Shennan: FD2
Shenstone: FD1–
Shenton: Bn 148–
Shepard: FD2–W1/84–W2/143–
Shepherd: FD2–
Shepherd-Cross: FD2–
Shepley: W2/144–
Sheppard: FD2–Ne 6/448–Bn 148–
Shepperd-Folker: FD2–
Shepstone: FD1–

Sherard: FD1–
Sherborne: FD1–
Sherbrook: FD2–
Sherbrooke: FD1–FD2–
Sherbrooke-Walker: FD2–
Sherburne: Mt 85–Bn 148, 149–
Sherd: Mt(A)68–
Sherlock: FD1–FD2–
Sherman: Ne 3/216–Mt(A)69–Bn 149–
Sherson: FD2–
Sherston: FD2–
Sherston-Baker: FD2–
Sherwood: FD2–Bn 149–
Sherwood-Hale: FD2–
Shields: FD2–Mt 89–
Shiffner: FD1–FD2–
Shipman: Bn 149–W2/144–
Shippen: Mt 22–Bn 149–Mc 2/658–AH 11–
Shipstone: FD2–
Shipton: FD2–
Shipway: FD2–
Shipwright: FD2–
Shirley: FD1–FD2–Ne 4/254–Mt 115–Bn 149–
    AH 16–
Shober: Bn 149–
Shoemaker: Mt 109–Mc 1/478–
Shoolbred: FD2–
Shore: FD1–FD2–
Shorrock: FD2–
Short: FD2–Mt(A)69–Mt 57–Bn 149–Mc 5/446–
Shortall: FD2–
Shorting: FD2–
Shrewsbury: FD1–FD2–
Shrimpton: Bn 149–
Shriver: Mc 2/665, 673
Shrubb: FD2–
Shubrick: Bn 150–
Shuckburgh: FD1–FD2–
Shufeldt: Mt 31–Mc 5/451–
Shuldham: FD2–
Shute: FD1–
Shuttleworth: FD2–
Sibbald: FD2–
Sibthorp: FD2–
Sidebotham: FD2–
Sidmouth: FD1–FD2–
Sidney: FD2–Bn 150–
Siemers: Ne 2/90–
Sievier: FD2–
Sill: Mt(A)69–Bn 150–
(de) Sille: Ne 5/331–
Sillifant: FD2–
Sillitoe: W1/84–W2/145–
Silsbee: Bn 150–
Silver: Mc 2/683
Silvertop: FD2–
Silvester: Bn 150–
Sim: FD2–
Simcox: FD2–
Simeon: FD1–FD2–
Simes: Bn 150–
Simmons: FD1–FD2–Bn 150–
Simons: FD2–
Simpson: FD1–FD2–Bn 150–
Simpson-Hinchliffe: FD2–
Sims: FD2–Bn 150–
Sinaver: FD2–
Sinclair: FD1–FD2–Bn 150–AH3–Ne 8/601–
Sinclair-Lockhart: FD2–
Singer: FD2–
Singleton: FD1–FD2–
Sinma: FD2–
Sinnott: FD2–
Sirr: FD2–
Sismey: FD2–
Sisterson: FD2–

Sitwell: FD1–FD2–
Skeats: Bn 151–AH 139–
Skeet: FD2–
Skeffington: FD1–FD2–
Skeels: FD2–
Skelton: Mt(A)69–Bn 151–VH 84–
Skene-Tytler: FD2–
Skinner: FD2–Ne 3/215–Mt 222–Bn 151–
   Mc 6/418–
Skipwith: FD1–Ne 3/183–Bn 151–Mc 3/496–
   VH86–AH15–
Skrine: FD2–
Slack: FD2–
Slacke: FD2–Bn 151–
Slade: FD1–FD2–Mt 3–
Sladen: FD1–FD2–
Sladden: FD2–
Slagle: Mc 4/453–
Slater: Bn 151–
Slaughter: FD1–FD2–Mt(A)69–Bn 151–
Slazenger: FD2–
Sleight: FD2–
Slevin: W1/85–W2/145–
(van) Slichtenhorst: Ne 6/416–
Sligo: FD1–
Slingsby: FD1–FD2–
Sloan: FD2–
Sloane: FD2–
Sloane-Stanley: FD2–
Slocum: Mt(A)70, 78, 229–
Sloggett: FD1–FD2–
Sloper: FD2–
Smallman: FD2–
Smallwood: FD2–
Smart: FD1–
Smiles: FD2–
Smiley: FD2–
Smith: FD1–FD2–Mt(A)70–Mt 51, 74, 199,
   209–Bn 151, 152, 153–Mc 5/457–Ne 2/151–
   Ne 5/370, 6/441, 2/84–Ne 3/190, 218–
   Mc 3/499–Mc 3/515, 4/460, 466–
   V.H. 14/60/79–AHY–W1/85–W1/86–W2/146,
   147–
Smith-Barry: FD2–
Smith-Bosanquet: FD1–FD2–
Smith-Carington: FD2–
Smith-Chatterton: FD2–
Smith-Cuningham: FD2–
Smith-Dodsworth: FD1–FD2–
Smith-Dorrien: FD1–FD2–
Smith-Dorrien-Smith: FD1–FD2–
Smith-Gordon: FD2–
Smith-Marriott: FD1–FD2–
Smith-Masters: FD2–
Smith-Rewse: FD1–FD2–
Smith-Ryland: FD1–FD2–
Smith-Shand: FD2–
Smith-Sligo: FD2–
Smithers: FD2–
Smollett: FD1–
Smyly: FD1–FD2–
Smyth: FD1–FD2–Bn 153–
Smyth-Pigott: FD2–
Smythe: FD1–FD2–Bn 153–
Smythies: FD1–
Snagge: FD1–
Sneadcox: FD2–
Snell: Bn 153–
Snelling: Ne 2/142–Mt 167–Bn 153–Mc 3/523
Sneyd: FD2–
Sneyd-Kynnersley: FD1–FD2–
Snook: FD2–
Snow: FD2–Mc 4/474–
Snowden: FD2–Mc 1/487, 491–AH 179–
Soames: FD2–
Sodor & Man: FD1–
Sohier: Mt 37, 90–Bn 153–Mc 3/526–

Solart: Bn 153–
Solly: Bn 153–
Solly-Flood: FD2–
Soltau: FD2–
Soltau-Symons: FD1–FD2–
Somerby: Bn 153–
Somers: FD1–FD2–
Somerset: FD1–FD2–
Gelderd-Somervell: 2/1811
Somervell: FD2–Bn 154–Mc 2/691–3/533
Somerville: FD1–FD2–
Sondes: FD1–
Soote: FD2–
Soper: FD2–
Sopper: FD2–
Sopwith: FD2–
Sorley: FD2–
Sotheron-Estcourt: FD2–
Sourton: Bn 154–
Sousa-Deiro: FD2–
Southack: Bn 154–
Southampton: FD1–
Southar: Mt 152–
Southesk: FD1–
Southey: FD2–
Southwark: FD1–
Southwell: FD1–FD2–
Southworth: Ne 2/152–Mt 138–Bn 154–
Sowden: FD2–
Sowler: FD2–
Spafford: FD2–
Spaight: FD1–FD2–Bn 154–
Spalding: FD2–
Sparkawk: Bn 154–
Sparks: FD2–Bn 154–
Sparrow: FD1–FD2–Bn 154–
Spaulding: Bn 154–
Speaight: FD2–
Spearman: FD1–FD2–
Spears: FD2–
Speed: Mc 6/12–
Spedding: FD2–
Speer: FD2–
Speir: FD2–
Speirs: FD1–FD2–
Speke: FD1–FD2–
Spelman: V.H.51–Ne 8/528–
Spenceley: Bn 154–
Spencer: FD1–FD2–Ne 7/461–Mt 97, 232–
   Bn 154–Mc 2/687–Mc 3/536–V.H. 25–
Spencer-Churchill: FD1–FD2–
Spencer-Cooper: FD2–
Spencer-Stanhope: FD1–FD2–
Spens: FD2–
Sperling: FD2–
Speyer: FD2–
Spicer: FD2–Mc 4/480, 6/425–
Spinney: Bn 155–
Spitzer: Mt 164–Mc 5/463–
Spokes: FD1–FD2–
Spooner: Bn 155–
Spotswood: Mt(A)70–Ne 1/31–V.H.47–Bn 155–
   Mc 1/496–AH100–
Spottiswoode: FD1–
Sprague: Bn 155–
Sprigg: Mc 2/694–
Springer: Ne 605–
Springmann: FD1–
Spring-Rice: FD1–
Sproat: Bn 155–
Sprot: FD1–FD2–
Spry: FD2–Bn 155–
Sprules: FD2–
Spurgeon-Farrer: FD2–
Spurway: FD2–
Staats: BN 153–
Stabb: FD2–

Stable: FD1–FD2–
Stables: FD2–
Stack(e): FD2–
Stacpoole: FD1–
Stacy: Ne 3/223
Stafford: FD1–Bn 153–
Stafford-Jerningham: FD1–
Stafford-King-Harman of Rockingham: FD2–
Stainer: FD2–
Stainforth: FD2–
Stair: FD1–
Stalbridge: FD1–
Stallard: FD2–
Stamer: FD2–
Stamford: FD1–W1/87–W2/147–
Stamford & Warrington: FD1–
Stancliffe: FD2–
Stancomb: FD1–FD2–
Standish: FD2–Ne 2/102–Mt(A)70–Bn 155–
  AH 15–
Stanford: Bn 155–
Stanham: FD2–
Stanhope: FD1–FD2–
Stanier: FD2–2/1826–
Staniland: FD2–
Stanley: FD1–FD2–Mt 166–Bn 155–
Stanley-Cary: FD2–
Stanmore: FD1–
Stannus: FD1–FD2–
Stansfield: FD2–
Stansbury: Mt 11–
Stanton: FD2–Bn 155–
Stanwood: Bn 155, 156–
Stanyforth: FD2–
Staples: FD1–FD2–
Staples-Browne: FD2–
Stapleton: FD1–
Stapleton-Bretherton: FD2–
Stapleton-Cotton: FD2–
Stapley: FD1–
Stapylton: FD2–
Stark: Bn 156–
Starke: FD2–
Starkey: FD2–
Starkie: FD2–
Starky: FD2–
Starr: Bn 156–Mc 4/488
Startin: FD1–FD2–
Stauffer: Bn 156–
Staunton: FD1–FD2–
Staveley: FD1–FD2–
Stavert: FD2–
Stawell: FD2–
Stead: FD2–
Stearns: Mt(A)70–Bn 156–Mc 1/500, 4/493–
Stebbing: Mt(A)70–
Stecher: Ne 8/596–
Stedman: FD2–Bn 156–
Steel: FD1–FD2–Bn 156–AH 179–
Steele: FD1–FD2–Mt(A)71–
Steele-Nicholson of Ballow: FD2–
Steenwyck: Bn 156–
Steer: FD2–
Steere: FD1–FD2–
Stein: AS 144–
Steiner: Mc 1/503–
Stenhouse: FD2
Stenning: FD2–
Stephen: FD1–FD2–
Stephens: FD1–FD2–
Stephenson: FD1–FD2–
Steptoe: Bn 156–VH 86–
Sterling: Ne 5/333–Mt(A)71–
Stern: FD2–
Sterry: FD1–FD2–
Stetson: Mt(A)71–Bn 156–AH 10–
Steuart: FD1–FD2–

Steuart-Fotheringham: FD1–
(von) Steuben: Ne 1/56–
Steven: FD1–FD2–
Stevens: FD2–Mt(A)71–Mt 54–Bn 156, 157–
Stevenson: FD1–FD2–
Stevenson-Hamilton: FD1–FD2–
Steward: FD1–
Stewart: FD1–FD2–
Stewart-Bam of Ards: FD2–
Stewart-Liberty: FD2–
Stewart-Mackenzie: FD2–
Stewart-Murray: FD2–
Stewart-Robertson: FD1–FD2–
Stick: AS 148–
Stickney: Bn 157–Mc 5/472–
Stiffe: FD1–
Stileman: Be 6/427–AH 133–
Stiles: FD2–
Stilgoe: FD2–
Still: FD2–
Stille: Bn 157–
Stilwell: FD1–FD2–
Stirling: FD1–FD2–
Stirling-Maxwell: FD1–
Stith: Bn 157–
Stitt: FD2–
Stobe: Bn 157–
Stock: FD2–
Stockbridge: Mt 162–
Stockenström: FD2–
Stockley: FD2–
Stockman: Ne 3/188–
Stockton: FD2–Mt 227–Mt(A)71–Bn 157–
  Mc 6/428–AH 13–
Stoddard: Mt 34–Bn 157–
Stoddart: Bn 157–AH 8–
Stoker: FD2–
Stokes: FD1–FD2–Mt(A)72–Bn 158–W1/87–
  W2/148–
Stoll: FD2–
Stonard: Bn 158–
Stone: FD1–FD2–Mt 85–Mt(A)72–Bn 158–
  V.H. 48–W2/148–
Stonehouse: FD2–
Stoner: Mt 202–
Stoney: FD1–FD2–
Stonhouse: FD1–FD2–
Stonor: FD1–FD2–
Stopford: FD1–FD2–
Stopford-Sackville: FD2–
Stops: FD2–
Storer: Bn 158–
Storey: FD2–
Story: FD2–Mt 64–Bn 158–
Story-Maskeltyne: FD2–
Stott: FD2–Bn 158–
Stouge: W2(149–
Stoughton: FD2–Ne 6/385–Bn 158–AH 142–
Stourton: FD2–
Stoveld: FD2–
Stowe: Mt(A)72–Bn 158–
Stowell: Mc 1/507–
Stracey: FD1–FD2–
Stracey-Clitherow: FD1–FD2–
Strachan: FD2–VH 112–
Strachey: FD1–FD2–Ne 8/523–VH 28–
Stradbroke: FD1–
Strafford: FD1–
Strakoscp:FD2–
Strange: FD2–
Strangman: FD1–FD2–
Strangs: AH 7–
Strangways: FD2–
Stratford: FD2–
Strathallan: FD1–
Stratheden: FD1–FD2–
Strathmore & Kinghorne: FD1–

Tenison: FD1–FD2–
Tennant: FD1–FD2–
Tennyson: FD1–FD2–
Tennyson-D'Eyncourt: FD1–
Tenterden: FD1–
Teofani: FD2–
Ternan: FD2–
Ternay: Bn 162–
Terry: FD2–Bn 162–
Tetly: FD2–
Teynham: FD1–
Teulow: FD2–
von Tevenar: W1/89–
Thacher: Ne 1/59–Mt(A)74–Bn 162–
Thackeray: FD2–
Thackwell: FD1–FD2–
Thairlwall: FD2–
Thatcher: Bn 162, 163–AH 117–
Thaxter: Bn 163–
Thayer: Mt 183–Bn 163–
Thebald: Bn 163–
Thellusson: FD1–FD2–
Theobald: FD1–Mt(A)75–
Thesigner: FD1–FD2–
Thicknesse: FD2–
Thicknesse-Touchet: FD1–
Thiselton-Dyer: FD1–FD2–
Thistlethwayte: FD2–
Thomas: FD1–FD2–Mt 62, 145, 181–Bn 163–
　Mt(A)75–Mc 4/513–AH 14–
Thomas-Ferrand: FD2–
Thomas-Stanford: FD2–
Thomas-Treherne: FD2–
Thom-Postlethwaite: FD2–
Thompson: FD1–FD2–Ne 1/29–Mt 192, 212–
　Mt(A)75, 91–Bn 163–
Thompson-Butler-Lloyd: VH27–AH 7–
　W2/152, W2/176, W2/177–
Thoms: FD2–
Thomson: FD1–FD2–
Thomson-Walker: FD2–
Thorburn: FD1–FD2–
Thornburgh-Cropper: FD2–
Thorndike Ne 1/11–Mt(A)75–Bn 164–
Thorndyke: AH 2–
Thorne: FD1–
Thorneycroft: FD1–
Thornelow: FD2–
Thornewill: FD2–
Thornhill: FD1–FD2–
Thorn-Pudsey: FD2–
Thornton: FD1–FD2–Bn 164–VH 99–W2/153–
Thornycroft: FD2–
Thorold: FD1–FD2–Ne 1/71–
Thoroughgood: V.H. 60–
Thorowgood: Bn 164–
Thorp: FD1–FD2–
Thorpe: V.H. 61–
Thowless: W1/89–W2/154–
Thoyts: FD2–
Thrall: Mc 5/504–
Threlfall: FD2–
Thring: FD1–FD2–
Throckmorton: FD1–Ne 2/103, 1/21–Bn 164–
　V.H. 55–
Throop: AH 7–
Thruston: FD2–Bn 164–Mc 4/530–V.H. 54–
Thunder: FD2–
Thurlow: FD1–
Thursby: FD1–FD2–
Thursby-Pelham: FD2–
Thursfield: FD2–
Thurston: FD1–FD2–
Thwaites: FD2–
Thynne: FD1–FD1–
Tiarkes: FD2–
Tickell: FD2–

Tickle: FD2–
Ticknor: Mt(A)75–
Tidswell: FD1–FD2–
Tiernan: Mt 97–
Tierney: FD1–
Tighe: FD2–
Tilden: Mt(A)75–Ne 8/564–
Tilestone: Bn 164–
Tilghman: Ne 5/368–Mt(A)76–Bn 164–
　Mc 6/437–AH 147–
Till: W2/154
Tillard: FD2–
Tilley: Ne 8/599–
Tillinghast: Bn 164–
Tillotson: Bn 164–
Tilney: FD2–
Tilton: Bn 164–Ne 8/536–W1/90–W2/154–
Timins: FD2–
Timms-Hervey-Elwes: FD2–
Timpson: FD2–Ne 7/482–Mt(A)76–
Timson: Bn 164–V.H. 45–
Tindal: FD2–
Tindal-Carill-Worsley: FD1–FD2
Tinker: FD2–
Tirrey: Bn 165–V.H. 64–
Tisdall: FD2–Mt 198–Mt 130–
Titcomb: Bn 165–Ne 8/531–
Tittle-Hamilton: FD2–
Tobey: Bn 165–
Tobin: FD2–
Todd: FD2–Mt(A)76–Mt 83–Bn 165–
Todd-Mercer: FD1–FD2–
Todd-Thornton: FD1–FD2–
Toepfer: AS 154–
Toke: FD2–
Toker: FD2–
Toland: Bn 165–
Tolcher: FD2–
Toler: FD2–Bn 165–
Toler-Aylward: FD2–
Toler-Rowley: FD2–
Tolhurst: FD1–FD1–
Tollemache: FD1–FD2–
Tolson: FD2–
Tomkinson: FD1–FD2–
Tompkins: Mt 26–Bn 165–
Tonge: FD1–FD2–
Toohey: FD2–
Tooker: Bn 165–V.H. 62–
Toomey: FD2–
Tooth: FD2–
Toppin: FD2–
Torkington: FD2–
Torphichen: FD1–
Torr: FD2–
Torrey: Bn 165–
Torrington: FD1–
Tory: FD2–
Tottenham: FD2–
Touche: FD2–
Touteville: Ne 5/373–
Tower: FD1–FD2–
Towers: FD2–
Towers-Clark: FD2–
Towle: FD2–
Towles: Bn 165–VH 94–
Towne: Mt(A)76–
Towneley-O'Hagan: FD2–
Townley: Ne 4/269–
Townley-Balfour: FD1–
Townsend: FD2–Mt 3–Mt(A)76–Bn 165–AH 6–
Townsend-Farquhar: FD1–
Townshend: FD1–FD2–
Towry-Law: FD1–
Towsey: FD2–
Tozer: FD2–
Tracy: Mt(A)76–Bn 165–

Trafford: FD1–FD2–Ne 6–
Trafford-Rawson: FD2– /450–
Tragett: FD2–
Trail: Bn 166–
Traill: FD2–Ne 8/574–
Trapp: Ne 6/399–
Trappes-Lomax: FD1–
Trask: FD2–
Travers: FD2–Bn 166–
Travis: Bn 166–
Trayner: FD1–FD2–W1/91–W2/155–
Trebarne: FD2–
Tredegar: FD1–
Tredgold: FD2–
Treffry: FD2–
Trefusis: FD1–
Tregarthen: FD2–
Tregoning: FD1–FD2–
Treherne: FD2–
Tremayne: FD2–
Trench: FD1–FD2–
Trench-Gascoigne: FD2–
Trenchard: FD2–Mt 200–
Trevelyan: FD2–
Trevenen: FD2–
Trevor: FD1–
Trevor-Battye: FD1–FD2–
Trevor-Roper: FD2–
Trew: Bn 166–
Trimlestown: FD1–
Tringham: FD2–
Tripp: FD1–
Trippe: Mc 6/443–
Trist: FD1–FD2–
Tritton: FD1–FD2–
Trollope: FD1–
Trollope-Bellew: FD2–
Tronberg: Bn 166–
Trotman: FD2–
Trotman-Dickenson: FD2–
Trotter: FD1–FD2–
Trotter-Cranstoun: FD1–FD2–
Trottman: Bn 166–
Troubridge: FD1–FD2–
Trowbridge: Mt 169–
Trower: FD2–
Troyte: FD2–
Troyte-Chafyn-Grove: FD2–
Truell: FD2–
Truesdell: Bn 166–
Truman: Mt 81–Mc 2/714–
Trumbull: Bn 166–
Truro: FD1–
Turndle: Mc 2/718–
Truscott: FD1–FD2–
Trustram: FD2–
Trye: of Harlshill: 2/1968–
Tryon: Ne 4/266–Bn 166–
Tubby: FD2–
Tuck: FD2–Mt(A)77–
Tucker: FD2–Bn 166–Mc 5/509–V.H. 98–
Tuckerman: Bn 167–AH 147–
Tudor: Bn 167–
Tudor-Craig: FD2–
Tufnell: FD1–FD2–
Tufnell-Tyrell: FD1–
Tufton: FD1–FD2–Bn 167–
Tuite: FD1–FD2–Bn 167–
Tullis: FD2–
Tully: FD2–
Tunnard: FD2–
Tunnard-Moore: FD1–
Tupper: FD1–FD2–Bn 167–
Turberville: Bn 167–V.H. 22–
Turing: FD2–
Turnbull: FD1–FD2–
Turnbutt: FD2–

Turner: FD1–FD2–Bn 167–Mc 2/724–V.H. 65–
Turnley: FD2–
Turnor: FD2–
Turnour: FD1–FD2–
Turnour-Fether-Stonhaugh: FD2–
Turton: FD2–
Turville-Petre: FD2–
Tuthill: Bn 167–
Tutte: Mt(A)77–
Tuttle: Bn 167–Mc 4/542–AH 10–
Tweeddale: FD1–
Tweedie: FD2–
Tweedmouth: FD1–
Tweedy: FD2–
Twemlow: FD1–FD2–
Twentyham: FD2–
Twigg: FD2–
Twisleton: FD1–
Twisleton-Wykeham-Fiennes: FD1–FD2–
Twyford: FD2–
Twysden: FD1–
Tyack: FD2–
Tydd: FD2–
Tylden: Bn 167–AH 16–
Tylden-Wright: FD2–
Tylden-Pattenson: FD2–
Tylee: FD2–
Tyler: FD1–FD2–Mt 120–Bn 168–Mc 3/568–
    AH 2–
Tyndale: FD2–
Tyng: Mt(A)77–Bn 168–AH 2–
Tynte: FD2–
Tyringham: FD1–FD2–
Tyrrell: FD2–
Tyrwhitt: FD2–
Tyrwhitt-Drake: FD2–
Tyrwhitt-Wilson: FD1–FD2–
Tyser: FD2–
Tyson: FD1–FD2–Bn 168–Mc 2/729–
Tytler: FD2–

Udny: FD2–
Ulster Transport Authority: W2/156–W1/93–
Underhill: Ne 2/108–Bn 168–Mt(A)77–V.H. 110–
    AH 10–
Underwood: Bn 168–
Uniacke: FD1–FD2–Bn 168–
Uniacke-Penrose-Fitzgerald: FD2–
Unthank: FD2–
Unwin: FD2–
Upcher: FD2–
Upcott: FD2–
Updike: Ne 4/252–Bn 168–
Uppleby: FD2–
Upton: FD1–Bn 168–
Upton-Cottrell-Dorner: FD1–FD2–
Urquhart: FD1–Ne 8/555 & 556–
Usborne: FD2–
Usher: FD2–Mt(A)77–Bn 169–AH 101–
Ussher: FD2–
Utermarck: FD2–
Uthwatt: FD2–

Vacher: FD2–
Vade-Walpole: FD2–
Vail: Bn 169–
Vaile: FD2–
Vaisey: FD2–
Vaizey: FD2–
Vale: FD2–
Valentia: FD1–
Valentine: Bn 169–
Vallance: FD2–
Valpy: FD2–
Van Allen: Bn 169–

Van Alst: AH 11–
Van Berckel: Bn 169–
Vanbrugh: Ne 3/184–
Van Brunt: Bn 169–
Van Buren: Bn 169–
Vance: Bn 169–
Van Cortlandt: Mt(A)77–Bn 169–AH 1, 17–
Van Cutsem: FD2–
Vandeleur: FD2–
Vanderbilt: Bn 169–
Van Der Kemp: Bn 169–
Van Derlip: Bn 169–
Van Der Poel: Bn 169–
Van Duyn: AH 108–
Vane: FD1–FD2–Ne 2/129–
Vane-Tempest: FD2–
Vane-Tempest-Stewart: FD2–
Van Guysling: Bn 170–Mc 5/522–
Van Halen: FD2–
Van Hulsteyn: FD2–
Vann: Mt 49–
Vanneck: FD2–
Van Nest: Bn 170–Mc 2/737–
Van Nort: AH 11–
Van Notten-Pole: FD1–
Van Rensselaer: Mt(A)78–Bn 170–
Van Raalte: FD2–
Van Santvoord: Mt 2–
Van Schaick: Bn 170–
Vansittart: FD2–
Van Sittart: Bn 170–AH 11–
Van Sittart-Neale: FD2–
Van Vleck: Ne 7/518–
Van Voorhis: Bn 170–
Van Vorhees: AH 5–
Van Vorst: Mt 143–
Van Wenckum: Ne 6/417–
Van Wyck: Mt(A)78–AH 5, 17–
Van Zandt: Bn 170–
Varian: FD2–
Varick: Bn 170–
Varnum: Bn 170–
Vassal: Ne 5/351–Mt(A)78–
Vassall: AH 12–2/1994–
Vassar-Smith: FD2–
Vaughan: FD1–FD2–Mt 51, 201–Bn 171–
Vaughan-Lee: FD2–
Vaughan-Morgan: FD2–
Vaughan-Pryse-Rice: FD2–
Vaughton: FD2–
Vaux: FD1–FD2–Bn 171–
Vavasour: FD1–FD2–
Veale: FD2–
Veazey: Mt 72, 188–
Vealsques: Bn 171–
Venable: Mc 6/452–
Venables-Vernon: FD2–
Venn: FD2–
Venning: FD2–
Veno: FD2–
Ventry: FD1–
Verastequi: AS 156–
Verdin: FD2–
Verdon: FD1–
Vereker: FD1–FD2–
Verity: FD2–
Vermont: FD2–
Verner: FD1–FD2–
Verney: FD1–FD2–
Vernon: FD1–FD2–M(A)78–Ne 4/280–Bn 171–
Vernon-Harcourt: FD1–FD2–
Vernon-Wentworth: FD2–
Verrall: FD2–
Verschoyle: FD1–FD2–
Verster: Bn 171–
Versturme-Bunbury: FD2–
Verulam: FD1–

Vesey: FD1–FD2–
Vesey-Fitzgerald: FD1–
Vestey: FD2–
Vicars: FD1–FD2–
Vicars-Miles: FD2–
Vick: FD2–
Vickers: FD2–
Vigors: FD1–FD2–
Villiers: FD1–FD2–
Villiers-Stuart: FD2–
Vincent: FD1–FD2–
Vine: FD1–
Vint: FD2–
Vipont: FD2–
Visegrady: AS 158–
Visinet des Presles: W2/156–
Vivian: FD1–FD2–
Vivian-Neal: FD2–
de Voil: W1/92–W1/93–W2/157–W2/158–
Von Haupt-McLeod: FD2–
Von Herkomer: FD2–
Von Peyer: FD2–
Von Stieglitz: FD1–FD2–
Von Volborth: Ne 8/562–AS 160, 162–
  W1/94–W2/158–W2/159–
Voorhees: Mc 6/456–
Vose: Mt(A)78–Bn 71–
Voules: FD2–
Voultsos: AS 164–
Vowler-Simcoe: 2/2012–
Vyvyan: FD1–

Waddell: Ne 5/361–Bn 171–
Waddingham: FD2–
Waddington: FD2–Bn 171–
Waddy: FD2–
Wade: FD2–Ne 5/315–Bn 171–
Wade-Dalton: FD2–
Wade-Gery: FD1–FD2–
Wade-Palmer: FD2–
Wadham: Bn 171–
Wadswort(h): Mt(A)79–Bn 171–
Waechter: FD2–
Wailes-Fairbairn: FD2–
Wainwright: Bn 172–AH 14–
Wait: Mt 79–Mc 5/530
Wake: FD1–FD2–
Wakefield: FD1–FD2–
Wakely: FD2–
Wakeman: FD1–FD2–
Walcot: FD2–
Walcott: Bn 172–
Waldegrave: FD1–FD2–
Waldie-Griffith: FD1–
Waldo(e): Bn 172–VH112–
Waldron: Mt(A)79–Bn 172–
Wale: FD2–
Wales: FD1–FD2–
Walford: FD2–
Walke: VH 21–
Walker: FD1–FD2–Bn 172–Mc 5/533, 537–
  Ne 8/578–AS 166–
Walker-Heneage: FD2–
Walker-Heneage-Vivian: FD2–
Walker-Morison: FD1–FD2–
Walkinshaw: FD2–
Wall: Bn 172–
Wallace: FD1–FD2–Bn 172–V.H. 54, 67–
  W1/95–W2/160–W2/161–
Waller: FD1–FD2–Ne 7/462–Bn 173–V.H. 37–
Waller-Bridge: FD2–
Walley: Bn 173–
Wallington: FD2–
Wallis: FD2–
Wallis-Wright: FD2–
Wallscourt: FD1–

Walmesley: FD1–FD2–
Walmisley: FD2–
Walmsley: Mt(A)79–Bn 173–
Walpole: FD1–FD2–
Walrond: FD1–FD2–W1/95–W1/96–W2/160–
Walsh: FD2–
Walsham: FD1–FD2–
Walsingham: FD1–
Walston: FD2–
Walter: Mt(A)79–Bn 173–
Walters: FD1–FD2–Bn 173–
Walthall: FD2–
Walton: FD2–Mt(A)79–Bn 173–
Walworth: Mt(A)79–Bn 173–AH13–
Wanton: Bn 173–AH 136–
Wantage: FD1–
Warburton: FD1–FD2–
Ward: FD1–FD2–Mt 28, 219–Bn 173–AH 12–
Ward-Boughton-Leigh: FD2–
Ward-La Touche: FD2–
Warde-Aldam: FD1–FD2–
Wardell-Yerburgh: FD2–
Wardlaw: FD1–FD2–
Wardlaw-Ramsay: FD2–
Wardlow: Bn 174–
Wardwell: Bn 174–
Ware: Bn 174–2/2039–
Waring: FD1–FD2–Bn 174–
Warmington: FD2–
Warner: FD1–FD2–Mt 80–Bn 174–V.H. 58–
Warrack: FD2–
Warrand: FD1–FD2–
Warren: FD1–FD2–Ne 7/479–Bn 174–
  Mc 3/570, 573–Mt 131, 137, 224, 230–
  Mt(A)80–V.H. 63–AH 3–
Warren-Darley: FD2–
Warren-Swettenham: FD1–FD2–
Warrender: FD1–FD2–
Warrington: FD2–
Warry: FD1–FD2–
Warry-Stone: FD1–FD2–
Warwick: FD2–
Washbourne: Ne 5/311–
Washburn: Mt(A)80–Bn 174–
Washington: Ne 1/1–Bn 174–Mt 55, 102–
  Mc 2/740–V.H. 109–
Wason: FD1–FD2–
Waterfall: FD2–
Waterford: FD1–
Waterhouse: FD2–
Waterlow: FD1–FD2–
Waterman: Bn 175–
Waterpark: FD1–
Waterton: FD2–
Waters: Bn 175–V.H. 101–
Watkins: FD1–Bn 175–
Watmough: Bn 175–
Watney: FD1–FD2–
Watson: FD1–FD2–Ne 7/487–Bn 175–
  AS 168–W1/96–W2/161–
Watson-Armstrong: FD2–
Watson-Gandy: FD2–
Watson-Taylor: FD1–FD2–
Watt: FD2–
Watts: FD1–FD2–Mt 112–AH 15–
Watts-Jones: FD2–
Watts-Russell: FD1–FD2–
Wauchope: FD1–FD2–
Waudby: FD2–
Waugh: FD2–
Way: FD2–
Wayne: FD2–Mt 7–Bn 175–
Weare: FD1–
Wearing: FD2–
Weaver: FD1–Mt(A)80–
Weaver-Hazelton: W2/162–
Webb: FD2–Mt 197–Bn 175–V.H. 64–

Webb-Johnson: FD2–
Webber: FD1–FD2–Bn 175–
Webster: FD1–FD2–Mt(A)80–Bn 175–
Wedder-Burn: FD2–
Wedderburn: FD1–FD2–
Wedderburn-Maxwell: FD2–
Wedgwood: FD2–
Weed: Mt 157, 177–
Weeks: Bn 176–
Wegg-Prosser: FD1–FD2–
Weil: FD2–
Weir: FD2–Mt(A)80–
Welby: FD1–FD2–Ne 8/585–
Welby-Everard: FD2–
Welby-Gregory: FD1–
Welch: FD2–Bn 176–
Welchman: FD2–
Welch-Thornton: FD2–
Weld: FD1–FD2–Ne 1/64–Mt(A)80–Bn 176–
Weld-Blundell: FD2–
Weld-Forester: FD1–FD2–
Weldon: FD1–
Weller: AS 170–
Welles: Mt(A)81–
Wellesley: FD1–FD2–
Wellington: FD1–
Wellman: Bn 176–
Wells: FD1–FD2–Mt(A)8k–Mt 201–Bn 176–
Welman: FD2–
Welsh: Bn 175–
Welsh-Anderton: FD2–
Welsteed: Bn 176–
Wemyss: FD1–FD2–
Wemys-Charteris-Douglas: FD2–
Wendel: FD2–Mt(A)81–Bn 176–AH 7–
Wenlock: FD1–
Wensley: Bn 177–
Wentworth: FD1–Be 1/44–Mt(A)81–Bn 177–
  AH 10–
Wentworth-Fitzwilliam: FD1–FD2–
Wentworth-Shields: FD2–
Wenzal: As 171–
Wernher: FD2–
Wessel: FD2–
Wesselhoeft: Ne 2/89–Bn 177–
West: FD2–Ne 3/201–Mt(A)81–Bn 177–
  V.H. 48, 57–
West-Erskine: FD1–
Westbrook: Bn 177–
Westbury: FD2–
Westby: FD2–
Westbury: FD1–
Westenra: FD2–
Western: FD1–
Westervelt: Mt(A)81–
Westmacott: 2/2066–
Westmeath: FD1–
Westminster: FD1–
Westminster Bank Ltd: W2/162–
Westmorland: FD1–
Weston: FD1–FD2–
Weston-Webb: FD2–
Weston-Smith: Bn 177–
Westropp: FD1–FD2–
Westropp-Dawson: FD2–
Westwood: Bn 177–V.H. 26–
Westworth: FD2–
Wetherall: FD1–
Wethered: FD2–AH 182–
Wethey: FD2–
Wetmore: Ne 6/422–Mt 135–Bn 177–AH 12–
Wettenhall: FD2–
Whalley: FD1–FD2–Ne 2/122–
Wharrie: FD2–
Wharncliffe: FD1–
Wharton: FD1–FD2–Ne 6/426–Mt(A)82–
  Bn 178–

Whatley: Bn 178–
Wheatley: FD2–
Wheble: FD2–
Wheeler: FD2–Mt 27, 226–Mt(A)82–
Wheeler-Cuffe: FD1–
Wheelock: Mt 90–Bn 178–Mc 2/747–
Wheelwright: FD2–Mt 82–Bn 178–
Wheildon: Bn 178–
Wheler: FD2–
Wheler-Galton: FD2–
Whewell: FD2–
Whichcote: FD1–FD2–
Whieldon: FD1–FD2–
Whineray: FD2–
Whinney: FD2–
Whinyates: FD1–FD2–
Whipple: Mt 85–Bn 178–Mc 6/465–
Whistler: Mt(A)82–Mt 127–
Whiston: FD2–
Whitaker: FD1–FD2–
Whitburn: FD2–
Whitcomb: Bn 178–
White: FD1–FD2–Ne 3/172, 5/340–Bn 178–
   Mt 78, 229–Mt(A)82–
White-Smith: FD2–
White-Thomson: FD1–FD2–
Whitebread: Bn 179–
Whitehead: FD1–FD2–Bn 179–V.H. 27–
   Ne 8/558–
Whitehorn: FD2–
Whitehouse: Bn 179–
Whitelaw: FD1–FD2–
Whiteley: FD2–Mt(A)83–Mc 4/550–
Whitelocke-Lloyd: FD1–FD2–
Whitfield: FD2–Ne 4/241–
Whitgreave: FD1–FD2–
Whitin: Bn 179–
Whiting: Ne 3/210–Mt(A)83–Bn 179–V.H. 59–
   AH 10–
Whitley: FD2–
Whitman: Bn 179–Mc 6/488–
Whitmore: FD1–FD2–Bn 179–
Whitney: FD2–Mt 143–Bn 179–Mc 6/495–
   AH 7–
Whitson: FD2–
Whiton: Mt(A)83–
Whittaker: FD2–
Whittingham: FD2–Bn 180–
Whittington-Ince: FD2–
Whittle: Bn 180–
Whitwell: Bn 180–
Whitworth: FD1–FD2–
Whyte: FD2–
Whyte-Venables: FD2–
von Wichmann-Eichhorn: W2/162–
Wickes: FD2–
Wickham: FD1–FD2–Bn 180–Mc 4/552,
   5/549–
Wicklow: FD1–
Wickman: W2/163–
Widdrington: FD2–
Wiener: FD2–Bn 180–
Wigan: FD1–FD2–
Wiggett-Chute: FD2–
Wiggin: FD1–FD2–
Wiggins: FD2–
Wigglesworth: Bn 180–
Wight-Boycott: FD1–FD2–
Wigley: FD2–
Wignall: FD2–
Wigram: FD1–FD2–
Wilbraham: FD2–
Wilbur: Mt(A)83–Bn 180–
Wilby: FD2–
Wilcox: Mc 5/552–
Wilde: FD1–FD2–
Wilder: FD1–FD2–AH 182–

Wildman-Lushington: FD2–
Wilgus: Mt(A)83–
Wilkes: FD2–Ne 7/522–Bn 180–
Wilkie: FD2–
Wilkin: FD2–
Wilkins: Mt(A)83–
Wilkins-Leir: FD2–
Wilkinson: FD2–Mt 168–Bn 180–AH 10–
   2/2091–
Willans: FD2–
Willard: Mt(A)84–Bn 180–
Willding-Jones: FD2–
Willet: Mt(A)84–
Willett: FD2–
Willey: FD2–Bn 181–
William-Stephens: FD2–
Williams: FD1–FD2–Ne 1/51–Bn 181–
   Mc 3/594, 4/555, 573–Mc 5/558, 564–Mt 76–
   Mt(A)84–AH 8–AS174–W2/163–W2/164–
Williams-Bulkeley: FD1–FD2–
Williams-Drummond: FD1–FD2–
Williams-Freeman: FD2–
Williams-Treffgarne: FD2–
Williams-Wynn: FD1–
Williamson: FD1–FD2–Bn 182–
Williamson-Napier: FD2–
Williamson-Noble: FD2–
Williamson-Ross: FD2–
Willington: FD1–
Willis: FD2–Mt(A)84–Bn 182–V.H. 49–
Willis-Bund: FD1–FD2–
Willis-Fleming: FD2–
Willoughby: FD1–FD2–Ne 1/49–Mt 122–
   Bn 182–V.H. 83–AH 12–
Wills: FD1–FD2–
Wills-Sandford: FD2–
Wills-Sandford-Wills: FD2–
Willshire: FD1–FD2–
Willson: FD2–
Willyams: FD2–
Wilmer: Bn 182–
Wilmot: FD1–FD2–
Wilson: FD1–FD2–Ne 1/25, 6/404–Mt 124–
   Mt(A)84, 85–Bn 182–V.H. 103–AH 10–
Wilson-Barkworth: FD1–FD2–
Wilson-Filmer: FD2–
Wilson-Fitzgerald: FD1–FD2–
Wilson-Haffenden: FD2–
Wilson-Patten: FD1–
Wilson-Slator: FD2–
Wilson-Todd: FD1–FD2–
Wilton: FD1–FD2–
Wimble: FD2–
Wimborne: FD1–
Winans: FD1–
Winch: FD2–
Winchell: Bn 182–
Winchester: FD1–
Winchilsea: FD1–
Winckley: Bn 182–
Windeyer: FD1–
Windham: FD2–
Windle: FD2–
Windley: FD2–
Windsor: FD1–W2/164, 165, 166–
Windsor-Clive: FD1–FD2–
Wing: FD2–
Wingate: FD2–
Wingfield: FD2–Ne 6/446–Bn 182–
Wingfield-Stratford: FD2–
Winlaw: FD2–
Winn: Bn 182–
Winnicott: FD2–
Winnington: FD1–
Winslow: Ne 2/185–Bn 183–Mc 3/610, 615–
   AH 6–W2/166–Ne 8/534–AS 176–W1/96–
Winsor: Bn 183–

Winston: Bn 183–
Winter: FD2–
Winter-Irving: FD1–FD2–
Winterbotham: Bn 183–
Winterton: FD1–
Winthrop: FD2–Ne 1/7–Bn 183, 184–AH 2, 17–
Winwood: FD1–FD2–
Wirgman: FD2–
Wisden: FD2–
Wise: FD1–FD2–VH 89–
Wiseman: FD1–FD2–Bn 184–
Wiskin: W1/96–W2/167–
Wistar: Mt 209–Bn 184–
Wister: Mt 25–
Witham: FD2–V.H. 31–
Withers: Bn 184–V.H. 62–
Witt: Mt 7–
Witthaus: Bn 185–
Witts: FD2–
Wodehouse: FD1–FD2–
Wogan-Browne: FD2–
Wolcott: Mt 21, 98–Bn 184–Mc 6/499–AH 7–
Wolff: FD2–
Wolff-Barry: FD2–
Wollaston: FD1–FD2–
Wolley-Dod: FD2–
Wolrige-Gordon: FD2–
Wolryche-Whitmore: FD1–FD2–
Wolseley: FD1–FD2–
Wolseley-Jenkins: FD1–
Wolverton: FD1–Mt(A)85–
Wombwell: FD1–FD2–
Wood: FD1–FD2–Bn 184–
Wood-Acton: FD1–FD2–
Wood-Martin: FD2–
Woodbridge: Bn 185–
Woodbury: Mt(A)85–Bn 185–
Woodd: FD1–FD2–
Woodford: Mt(A)85–Bn 185–V.H. 18–
Woodgate: FD2–
Woodhead: FD2–
Woodhouse: FD2–V.H. 81–
Woodhull: Ne 4/235–AH 1–
Woodman: Bn 185–
Woodroffe: FD2–
Woodruff: Mc 3/616, 5/573, 581–
Woods: FD1–FD2–
Woodward: FD1–FD2–Mt(A)85–Mt 131–
   Bn 185–Mc 3/630–
Woollan: FD2–
Woollcombe: FD1–FD2–
Woollcombe-Adams: FD2–
Woollcombe-Boyce: FD2–
Woolls: FD2–
Woolrabe: FD2–
Woolrych: FD2–
Woolsey: Bn 185–AH 11, 17
Woon: FD2–
Woosnam: FD1–FD2–
Wooten: Bn 185–
Worcester: FD1–Bn 185–
Wordsworth: FD2–
Workman-Macnaghten: FD1–FD2–
Worley: FD2–
Wormald: FD2–
Wormeley: Bn 185–VH 83–
Worrall: FD2–
Worsfold: FD2–
Worsley: FD1–FD2–
Worsley-Taylor: FD2–
Worthing: AS 178–
Worthington: FD1–FD2–Mt 13–Mt(A)86–
   Bn 185–
Worthington-Evans: FD2–
Worthington-Eyre: FD2–
Wotherspoon: FD2–
Wottrich: AS 180–

Wragg: FD2–
Wraxall: FD1–
Wray: Bn 185–V.H. 61–
Wreford: Ne 5/346–
Wren: FD2–
Wrey: FD1–FD2–
Wright: FD1–FD2–Ne 4/251–Mt(A)86–
   Bn 185–W1/97–W2/98–
Wright-Armstrong: FD2–
Wrightson: FD1–FD2–
Wrigley: FD2–
Wrixon-Becher: FD1–FD2–
Wrottesley: FD1–FD2–
Wurtemberg: W2/167, 168, 169–
Wust: Ne 7/463–
Wyatt: FD1–FD2–Ne 3/192, 7/515–Mt(A)86–
   V.H. 60–
Wybergh: FD2–
Wyche: V.H. 90–
Wykeham: FD2–
Wykeham-Martin: FD2–
Wykeham-Musgrove: FD2–
Wyllys: Ne 1/47–
Wyndham: FD1–FD2–
Wyndham-Quin: FD2–
Wynford: FD1–
Wynkoop: Bn 186–
Wynn: FD1–FD2–
Wynne: FD2–W1/98–W2/170–
Wynne-Jones: FD2–
Wynne-Marriott: FD2–
Wyse: FD2–
Wythe: Bn 186–
Wythes: FD2–
Wyvill: FD2–

Yale: FD2–Ne 2/146–
Yarborough: FD1–
Yarde-Buller: FD1–FD2–
Yardley: Bn 186–Mc 3/636–
Yarnall: Bn 186–
Yarrow: FD2–
Yate: FD2–
Yates: Bn 186–
Yeamans: Bn 186–Ne 8/542–
Yeardley: V.H. 47–
Yeatman: FD2–
Yeatman-Biggs: FD1–FD2–
Yeoman: FD2–
Yeoward: FD2–
Yerburgh: FD2–
Yockney: FD2–
Yonge: Bn 186–
York: FD1–FD2–
Yorke: FD1–FD2–
Young: FD1–FD2–Mt(A)86–Bn 186–
Younger: FD1–FD2–
Youngs: Bn 187–
Ypina: AS 182–
Yuille: FD1–FD2–Bn 187–V.H. 55–
Yule: FD2–

Zeppelin: W2/172–
Zetland: FD1–
Ziegler: W2/173–
Zinzendorf: Ne 7/521–
Zollikofer: Ne 7/460–
Zouch: FD1–FD2–Ne 5/318–V.H. 59–

APPENDIX

List of Abbreviations

Bn. Charles Knowles Bolton's American Armory published Boston, The F. W. Faxon Company 1927.

Mt. Matthew's American Armory and Blue Book published by John Matthews, 93 & 94 Chancery Lane, London, 1907.

Mt(A). Matthew's American Armory Appendix.

Mc. Mackenzie's Colonial Familes.

Ne. New England Historical & Genealogical Society Roll of Arms; published 1928 (corrected issue 1950), 1932 (corrected issue 1950) 1936, 1940, 1946, 1954, 1958, 1968–71 (& parts).

AH. Vermont's American Heraldica (BM Press Mark 9902 1.15).

W. William and Mary Quarterly–reference gives Vol. no., series (in brackets) & page number (BM Press Mark Ac 8543).

VH. W. A. Crozier, Virginian Heraldica (1908) (BM 9903–15).

As. The Augustan Society Roll of Arms 1967 & Addenda for 1968 ed.

WI. The Armorial Who Is Who 1961-2, first edition.

W2. As above, 2nd edition 1963–4.

FD1. Arthur Davies Fox-Davies Armorial Families 1895 edn.

FD2. As above (pt. 1 1929, pt 2 1930).

BIBLIOGRAPHY

REFERENCES

Archaeologia. xxix.

Aubrey's. Surrey, London 1719.

Baines. Lancashire, iij, 1836.

Baker. History & Antiquities of the County of Northampton, London, 1822–38.

Banks. Baronage, 5 vols. 1807–37.

Bedford. The Blazon of Episcopacy, London, 1858.

Berry. County Genealogies, Berkshire, Essex, Hampshire, Sussex. 1830.

Blom(e)field. History of the County of Norfolk, 1805.

Brit. Mus. Add. Ms. 12443.

Burke. Heraldic Illustrations, 3 vols. London, 1845.

Burton. Description of Leicestershire, fo: London, 1622.

Cady. A manuscript "Alphabet of Arms" apparently compiled by William Cady, a clerk in the Herald Office, c. 1630. The chief part of the work seems temp Henry VIII & the additions made by Cady. The volume also contains copies of Grants of Arms & it is in the possession of A.W.M.

Camden Grants. Brit. Mus. Harl. Ms. 6095.

Carr Ms. Catalogue of the Mayors & Sherrifs of Newcastle-on-Tyne. Surtees Society, XLI.

Colby. The Heraldry of Exeter, F. J. Colby, *Arch. Inst.* XXXV, 1880.

Coll: Top. Collectanea Topographica et Genealogica by J. G. Nichols, 8 vols. London, 1834.

College of Arms Grants.

Collinson's. Somerset, Bath, 1791.

Constable's Roll. Lansdown MS 205, Published by the Surtees Society, vol. 41.

Cotton Mss. Tiberius, Julius, Cleopatra. B.M.

Dashwood. Vicecomities Norfolciae. Norfolk, 1843.

Debrett. Peerage, Baronage, House of Commons, Judicial Bench & for various years. 13 large folio sheets, each containing 56 coats of Arms "Subscribers to this work" but I cannot ascertain to what work it refers. The date is however clearly between 1712 and 1714 as appears by the names of some of the nobility and Bishops and George II being only Prince of Wales.

Dingley. History from Marble by Thos. Dingley, 2 vols. Camden Society 1867.

Drake's. York, History and Antiquities of the City of, London 1736.

Dugdale. The Visitation of the County of York 1665–1666 by W. Dugdale. Surtees Soc. 1859.

Dug: O. J. Origines Juridiciales, by William Dugdale, Norroy. fol. London 1671.

Edmondson. Baronagium Genealogicum. Brit. Mus.

Eliz: Roll. Elizabethan Roll of Northern Heraldry, Surtees Soc. xli. p. xvii.

Exerpta. Bentley's Exerpta.

Fairfax's. Book of Arms.

Fernes. Blazon of Gentry. London 1586.

Foster. Pedigrees of the County Families of Yorkshire, 3 vols. 4to. London 1874.

Fuller. History of the Worthies of England, 2 vols. London 1814.

Gage, J. History of Hengrave, Suffolk. London 1822.

Gentleman's Magazine.

Gough. Sepulchral Monuments, 4 vols. 1792–9.

Grazebrook. The Heraldry of Smith, London 8 vo. 1870.

Guillim. A Display of Heraldry, 6th edit; fo: London 1724. This includes the arms of Baronets 1611 to 1720.

Hasted. History of the County of Kent. 4 vols. fo: Canterbury 1788–99.

Herald & Genealogist. 8 vols.

Hoare. History of Wiltshire, fo: London 1810.

Hunter. South Yorkshire. The History & Topography of the Deanery of Doncaster by the Rev. Joseph Hunter. 2 vols. fo: London 1828.

Hutchins. The History & Antiquities of the County of Dorset by John Hutchins, 3rd edit. by Shipp & Hodson, 1861.

James. History of Bradford. London 1841.

Lewis. Topographical Dictionary, 1st edit; 4 vols. London 1831.

Lyon Register.

Lysons. Magna Britannia, 4to. London 1806–22.

Morant's. History of the County of Essex. 2 vols. London 1768.

Syl. Morgan. The Sphere of Gentry by Sylvanus Morgan, fo: London 1661.

Moule The Heraldry of Fish. London 1842.

Nash. Collections for the History of Worcestershire. London 1781–99.

Nicholas. The History & Antiquities of Glamorganshire and its Families by Thomas Nicholas. London, Longmans 1874.

Nichols. The History & Antiquities of the County of Leicester, 4 vols. 1795–1815.

Nisbet. System of Heraldry.

Nobility Roll. Printed in Notes & Queries, 5th Series. p. 103. 25 Edw. II.

Noble. History of the College of Arms.

North Country Grants. Surtees Soc. vol. xli.

Ogborne. History of Essex. London 1814.

Ormerod. History of the County of Chester, 3 vol. fo: London 1819.

Parentalia.

Plot's. Oxfordshire. Oxford 1677.

Randle Holme. The Academy of Armory, 1 vol. fo: Chester 1688.

Rudder's Gloucester. Cirencester 1780.

Robson. The British Herald, 3 vols. 4to Sunderland 1830.

Scrope & Grosvenor's Controversy.

Shaw. The History & Antiquities of the County of Essex, 2 vols. fo: London 1768.

Shaw's. History of Staffordshire. Hanley 1829.

Stow. List of Nobility from Ed. VI–end of Queen Eliz. I. London 1638.

Surtees. The History & Antiquities of the County of Durham, 4 vols. fo: 1816–40.

Sussex Arch. Collections.

Tanner. Dugdale's Monasticon.

Taylor. Index Monasticus of the Abbeys in East Anglia, fo: London 1821.

Thoresby. Ducatus Leodiensis, fo: London 1715 & Whitaker's edit. 1816.

Tonge. Tonge's Visitation of the Northern Counties, 1530.

Topographer & Genealogist. 3 Vols. London 1846–58. Edited by J. G. Nichols.

Turner's. History of Grantham. London 1806.

Vincent. Grants.

Visitation of London. The Visitation of London by S. George 1633–35. Harl. Soc.

Visitation 1663. The Visitation of Derbyshire by W. Dugdale, Norroy 1662–3.

Walpole's. Anecdotes of Painting. j. 112.

Whitaker. The History of Craven. London, 1805

Whitaker's. Leeds ij. Leeds 1816.

Willement's. Heraldic Notes Canterbury Cathedral. London 1827.

Wright. Helyn's Helps to History.

Yorke. The Union of Honour with the Arms of the Gentry of Lincolnshire. fo: London, 1640.

A. Acre Roll. Dated A.D. 1192, (but? later). Ashmolean MS. 1120; Harleian MS. 6137.

A.A. A selection of Arms authorised by the laws of Heraldry by Sir Bernard Burke, London, Harrison 1863.

B. Roll. Circa A.D. 1240–45. Printed by Nicolas, 8vo., London 1829, from MS. L. 14, in the College of Arms.

C. Roll. Circa A.D. 1256–66. Printed in Leland's Collectanea, 8vo., Oxford 1707, ii, 610; Harl. MS. 6589.

C.C. Visitation of the county of Leicester by Wm. Camden, Clarenceux in 1619. Edited by John Fetherston. Harl. Soc. 1870.

C.L. Visitation of London by Robert Cooke, Clarenceux in 1563. Harl. Soc. London 1869.

C.R. Visitation of the county of Rutland by Wm. Camden 1618–19. Edited by C. J. Armytage. Harl. Soc. 1870.

C.W. Camden's Visitation of Warwickshire in 1619. Harl. Soc. 1877.

D. Roll. Circa A.D. 1286. Harl. MS. 6137.

E. Roll. Circa A.D. 1277–87. Harl. MSS. 6137 and 6589.

F. Roll. Circa A. D. 1262–92. Harl. MS. 6137.

G. Roll. Circa A. D. 1296. Harl. MS. 6137.

H. Falkirk Roll. A.D. 1298. Harl. MS. 6589.

I. Roll. Circa A.D. 1299. Harl. MSS. 6137 and 6589.

J. Roll. Circa A.D. 1300. Harl. MSS. 6137 and 6589.

K. Caerlaveroc Poem. A.D. 1301. Printed in Grose's Antiquarian Repertory, 4to., London 1779, ii, 107–281, from Cotton MS. Caligula A, 18; and by Nicolas, 4to., London 1828, from the same MS. and from another in the College of Arms: Harl. MSS. 6137 and 6589.

L. Dunstable Roll, A.D. 1308. Harl MSS. 6137 and 6589.

L.N. Le Neve's Pedigrees of the Knights made by Charles II, James II, William III and Queen Anne. Edited by G. W. Marshall. The dates quoted are the dates when knighted. Harl. Soc. 1873.

M. Roll. Circa A.D. 1300–12. Harl. MS. 6589.

N. Roll. Circa. A.D. 1308–14. Printed by Mores, 4to., Oxford 1749, from Queen's College (Oxford) MS. 158, and from Bodleian MS., Dodsworth 145–5086; in Grose's Antiquarian Repertory, 4to., London 1780, iii, 86, from Borret's MS; in Palgrave's Parliamentary Writs, fol., London 1827, i, 410; and by Nicolas, 8vo., London 1828, both from Cott. MS. Caligula A, 18: Ashmol. MS., Wood F, 33; Harl. MSS 4033, 5803, 6137 and 6589; Lansdowne MS. 855.

O. Boroughbridge Roll. A.D. 1322. Printed in Palgrave's Parliamentary Writs, fol. London 1830, ii, Appendix 196, from Wynn's MS. Ashmol. MS. 831.

P. Roll. After A.D. 1338. Printed in Nichols's Collectanea Topographica, 8vo., London 1834, ii, 320 from Grimaldi's MS.

Q. Calais Bannerets, A.D. 1345–48. Printed by Mores, 4to., Oxford 1749, from West's MS.; Ashmol. MS. 1120; Cotton MS. Tiberius E. 9; Harl. MSS. 6589 and 6595.

R. Calais Knights. A.D. 1348. Harl. MS. 6589.

S. Roll. Circa A.D. 1392–97. Printed by Willement, 4to., London 1834, from Newling's MS.

T. Rouen Roll. A.D. 1418 Ashmol. MS. 1120; Harl. MS. 6237.

U. Parliament Roll. A.D. 1512. Cole MS. 30: another, A.D. 1515, printed by Willement, fol., London 1829.

V. Glover's Ordinary. Cotton MS. Tiberius D. 10; Harl. MSS. 1392 and 1459.

V.C. The Visitation of the county of Cornwall in 1620. Harl. Soc. 1874.

V.D. The Visitation of the county of Devon in 1620. Edited by F. D. Colby. Harl... Soc. 1872.

V.E. The Visitations of the county of Essex by Hawley, 1552, Hervey 1528, Cooke, 1570, Raven 1612 and Owen & Lilly 1634, 2 vols. Harl. Soc. 1878.

V.H. The Visitation of Huntingdon by Wm. Camden and Nicholas Charles in 1613, Camden Society, London 1849.

V.L. Dugdale's Visitation of the County Palatine of Lancaster in 1664–5, Chetham Society 1872.

V.N. The Visitation of the county of Nottingham in 1569 & 1614. Edited by G. W. Marshall. Harl. Soc. 1871.

V.O. The Visitation of the county of Oxford, taken in the year 1566, by Hervey, 1574 by Ric. Lee and 1634 by Philpott. Edited by W. H. Turner, Harl. Soc. 1871.

V.S. The Visitation of the county of Somerset in 1623, Harl. Soc. 1876.

W. Withie's additions to Glover's Ordinary, in Harl. MS. 1459.

X. Jenyn's Collection, Harl. MS. 6589.

Y. Jenyn's Ordinary, partly printed by Nicolas. London, 1829.

Z. Sandford, Genealogical History, fol. London, 1707; the numerals which follow this letter refer to the pages in that book.

V*. Coats incorrectly given in the printed Glovers Ordinary which have been copied into books of reference and probably used as actual coats.

It should be noted that since the publication of Sir Anthony Wagner's *Catalogue of English Medieval Rolls Of Arms* (Harl. Soc. 1948) many of the rolls of arms have been re-named.

These references are to sources known to have been used by Burke and Morant but clearly there were a large number of others, such as church monuments. Some score of other sources cited in Morant's notes are insufficiently identified and the editions of some of those above are not distinguished.

It cannot be stressed strongly enough that the appearance of a blazon in this or any other armorial is no proof of an entitlement to armorial bearings. Such rights, if they exist, must be established by genealogical evidence to the satisfaction of the appropriate office of Arms.

Should there be any queries arising in this respect the Editor, will be happy to attempt to give guidance on further research to those who care to write to him at The Institute of Heraldic and Genealogical Studies, Northgate, Canterbury, Kent, England, CT1 1BA.